MODERN HUMANITIES RESEARCH ASSOCIATION
CRITICAL TEXTS
VOLUME 74

THE SHADOW OF NIGHT
&
OVID'S BANQUET OF SENSE

MHRA CRITICAL TEXTS

The MHRA Critical Text series aims to provide affordable critical editions of lesser-known literary texts that are out of copyright or are not currently in print (or are difficult to obtain). The texts are taken from the following languages: English, French, German, Italian, Portuguese, Russian, and Spanish. Titles are selected by members of the distinguished Editorial Board and edited by leading academics. The aim is to produce scholarly editions rather than teaching texts, but the potential for crossover to undergraduate reading lists is recognized.

Editorial Board

Chair: Dr Jessica Goodman (University of Oxford)

English: Professor Stefano Evangelista (University of Oxford)
French: Dr Jessica Goodman (University of Oxford)
Germanic: Professor Ritchie Robertson (University of Oxford)
Hispanic: Professor Ben Bollig (University of Oxford)
Italian: Professor Jane Everson (Royal Holloway, University of London)
Portuguese: Professor Cláudia Pazos Alonso (University of Oxford)
Slavonic: Professor David Gillespie (University of Bath)

texts.mhra.org.uk

THE SHADOW OF NIGHT
&
OVID'S BANQUET OF SENSE

BY

GEORGE CHAPMAN

EDITED BY

ZENÓN LUIS-MARTÍNEZ

MODERN HUMANITIES RESEARCH ASSOCIATION
Critical Texts 74
2026

Published by
The Modern Humanities Research Association
Salisbury House
Station Road
Cambridge CB1 2LA
United Kingdom

© Modern Humanities Research Association, 2026

Zenón Luis-Martínez has asserted his right under the Copyright, Designs and Patents Act 1988 to be identified as the author of this work. Parts of this work may be reproduced as permitted under legal provisions for fair dealing (or fair use) for the purposes of research, private study, criticism, or review, or when a relevant collective licensing agreement is in place. All other reproduction requires the written permission of the copyright holder who may be contacted at rights@mhra.org.uk.

First published 2026

ISBN 978-1-83954-613-6 (hardback)
ISBN 978-1-781889-80-0 (paperback)
ISBN 978-1-781889-81-7 (ebook)

Typeset in Minion 3 by Allset Journals & Books, Scarborough, UK

CONTENTS

Acknowledgements	viii
Abbreviations	xi
Introduction	1
1. Chapman's Early Poems in Context	6
2. Poetics: The Judicial Eye	17
3. Genre	34
3.1. *The Shadow of Night*	34
3.2. *Ovid's Banquet of Sense*	43
4. 'Sweet philosophic strains': Poetry and Philosophy	61
4.1. Philosophy and Myth: 'Hymnus in Noctem'	64
4.2. Sense and Intellect: *Ovid's Banquet of Sense*	72
5. Divine Shadows and Heroic Frenzies: The Brunian Mind	85
5.1. Diana in the Forest, the Moon in Heaven: *The Shadow of Night*	91
5.2. The Young Actaeon: *Ovid's Banquet of Sense*	99
6. Coda: Circles Never Closed	108
The Texts and the Present Edition	112
The Shadow of Night	119
To my dear and most worthy friend Master Matthew Roydon	123
Hymnus in Noctem	125
Hymnus in Cynthiam	143
Ovid's Banquet of Sense, A Coronet for His Mistress Philosophy and His Amorous Zodiac	169
To the truly learned, and my worthy friend, Master Matthew Roydon	175
Commendatory Sonnets	177
Ovid's Banquet of Sense	181
A Coronet for His Mistress Philosophy	231
The Amorous Zodiac	238
Commentary	248

Textual Notes	404
Appendix: A Note on Chapman's Prosody	411
Bibliography	415
Visual Sources: Paintings and Emblems	431

Figures

FIG. 1. Title page of the 1594 quarto of *The Shadow of Night* (Q*SN*)	121
FIG. 2. Title page of the 1595 quarto of *Ovid's Banquet of Sense* (Q*OB*)	171
FIG. 3. Final page of Q*OB*, containing printer Richard Smith's device	172
FIG. 4. Title page of the 1639 octavo of *Ovid's Banquet of Sens* (O*OB*), bound with William Marshall's engraved bust of Ovid and epigram	173

for Inés, for Débora

some kind of happiness is measured out in miles

ACKNOWLEDGEMENTS

THIS BOOK was completed under the auspices of the research project *Toward a New Aesthetics of Elizabethan Poetry: Critical Reassessments and New Editions of Neglected Works* (ENARGIA), funded by the State Agency for Research, Government of Spain, FFI2017-82269-P.

Work on this edition began in late 2017. Like many other of my scholarly projects, it was born in the conviction that I would never be able to finish it. As I write these lines, that conviction still persists, but fortunately it is becoming less certain. I proposed this book to the MHRA Critical Texts Series in the midst of the Covid-19 pandemic in 2020. The publisher's enthusiastic acceptance made my existence busier though happier in the post-pandemic world. My gratitude to the two MHRA publishing managers with whom I have worked, Gerard Lowe and Simon Davies, and to the scholars involved in the final decision to include the edition in the series, is immense, particularly for their confidence in a project that in its present state almost trebles the initial estimations of its length.

Project fundings permitted crucial periods of study leave in pre-Brexit and pre-Covid UK research centres, universities and libraries. I am grateful to James Loxley for facilitating my stay and work at Edinburgh University Library and the National Libraries of Scotland in the summers of 2018 and 2019, and to Susan Wiseman for providing support for my London visits in those same summers through the London Renaissance Seminar's fellowships. These visits made it possible to arrange consultation of manuscripts and rare books at the British Library, Senate House (University of London), the Victoria and Albert Museum, Winchester College, Cambridge University Library, Emmanuel College (Cambridge), the Bodleian Library and Wadham College (Oxford), and Sheffield University Library. I am grateful to the librarians and curators of all these institutions, but in particular to Sandra Bailey (Wadham) and Richard Foster (Winchester) for their hospitality and willingness to share their knowledge about early modern books. My favourite Cambridge pub, the Flying Pig, supplied the last pre-pandemic pint-and-burger menu in Britain. My next destination was to be the United States, but Covid-19 taught us not only an unknown reality but also new ways of doing research. When the world reopened fully, I found myself with less funds and time for my planned tour. For information, catalogues, images and/or permissions, I am grateful to the staff of the Huntington Library, Princeton University Library, and very especially the Harry Ransom Center, University of Texas, the generosity and photographing skills of whose Curator of Early Books and Manuscripts, Aaron Pratt, made work on the text of *The Shadow of Night* less umbrous and nocturnal.

Fellow researchers of the ENARGIA project, especially Sonia Hernández-Santano, María Vera-Reyes and Ana Ramírez-Camacho, have been supportive and helpful. Pablo Zambrano and Dominique Bonnet were kind enough to open, at the right moment, the doors of the Comparative Literatures and Cultures Research Group to me. Latin and Greek seem easier languages in the hands of Fernando Navarro, Miguel Ángel Márquez and Regla Fernández. Ongoing conversations about poetic difficulty and invention with Sarah Knight, Cassie Gorman and Rocío G. Sumillera have enlightened the arguments about Chapman's poetics that preside over this book and related publications these last few years. I have had the chance to speak about Chapman to several academic audiences. Fernando Galván, Montserrat Martínez, Jesús López-Peláez, Rosario Arias and Pablo Zambrano assessed an earlier version of this book as members of the board of examiners of my professorship promotion. The conferences of the Spanish and Portuguese Society for English Renaissance Studies (SEDERI) are as inimitable as the colleagues and friends with whom I have shared work and/or responsibilities on its board: Juan Antonio Prieto-Pablos, Clara Calvo, Jesús López-Peláez, Marta Cerezo, Cinta Zunino and Ana Sáez are topmost in an enumeration that should be longer. Few academic events compare to the Jágónak Shakespeare Conference at the University of Szeged, Hungary; its leading organizer, Attila Kiss, is a walking emblem of all that is good about scholarly life. Emma-Annette Wilson has always found the best arguments to convince me that, besides Chapman, I should keep Abraham Fraunce and Ramist logic in my thoughts. Ángel-Luis Pujante made the lamp of Shakespeare's memory shine over Chapman's 'spirit' and 'his compeers by night'. Morning coffees with Juan Gabriel Vázquez keep on reminding me that there is English beyond literature. Luis Gómez Canseco did much more than solve questions about how to proceed with an emendation or a variant; his scholarship and friendship remain permanent sources of inspiration. Email exchanges with Clark Hulse opened unimaginable lines of enquiry into Chapman's visual imagery. Manuel Gómez Lara discovered to me, more than three decades ago, numberless allegorical explanations of the myth of Actaeon and Diana in his lessons on Christopher Marlowe's *Edward II* — even the myth itself, at a time when Ovid was still a dim presence in my readings. The importance of that myth for these pages is conspicuous even before the book opens: the painting by Lucas Cranach the Elder (or a member of his workshop) on its cover remains for me the most fascinating of all Renaissance figurations of the primal splash. Matthias Weniger, Curator of the Bayerisches Nationalmuseum, and Gunnar Heydenreich, main researcher of the Cranach Digital Archive Project (CDA), kindly supplied beautiful images and granted permissions for their use (only one, alas, is credited on the back cover).

I take pride in the friendship of two exceptional road companions in this eight-year-long pilgrimage to Diana's fountain. Jefferey Simons has been a supportive reader of my earlier work on Chapman and, most importantly, a herald of rationality and good sense. Jonathan Sell will remain this edition's most insightful and generous critic: his eye, hand and mind are felt in not a few of its corners.

Outside academia, or not always quite so, and on the British side, Araceli Sánchez proved the kindest of strangers by lending us her Edinburgh apartment in the summers of 2018 and 2019. María José Carrillo, Keith Williamson and Carla Williamson made us want to return to the capital city of Scotland. Jonathan and Jules Huxley painted London summers with unexpected shapes and colours. On the Spanish side, Pablo Zambrano remains in office as best of virtual neighbours. Francisca Blanco, Roberto Vázquez Gay, Carlos Vacas and Paloma Jiménez have listened when I spoke too enthusiastically about this book. My mother, Teresa Martínez, is my best reminder that something rich and strange crystallizes against the sea-change of these years.

These pages bear witness to human endurance of sledge hammers, radial cutters, pneumatic drills and all the evil engines invented by the modern construction industry; if I have survived their siege, it is only thanks to my noise-cancelling earphones' capacity to turn the sounds of pandemonium into the lute of John Dowland, the organ of Johann Sebastian Bach, the piano of Isaac Albéniz, the orchestral harmonies of Jean Sibelius and the voice of Chris Isaak.

This book is dedicated to the dwellers of the neighbouring dens. My wife, Débora Betrisey, gifted anthropologist, shrewd analyst and sage confidant, keeps instructing me on how to cope with *the curse of having been born in a pre-Freudian country* (my emphasis, my translation); some inexplicable faith in me leads her to think that I am not (yet) an entirely lost case. Our daughter, Inés Luis Betrisey, Beatles fan, skilled accordionist and staunch believer in the Olympian deities, has supplied clever looks, sceptic frowns and instant reference to my queries about those details of Greek myths that so often slip from my memory. Her waning interest in my deadlines bears proof that her teens are bringing to her life new worries and pleasures.

ABBREVIATIONS

This list contains abbreviations used for frequently cited sources. On first appearance, and occasionally for convenience, full titles of works and poems are used.

Chapman's Works

'Banquet'	'Ovid's Banquet of Sense'
Bartlett	*The Poems of George Chapman*, ed. by Phyllis Brooks Bartlett (Modern Language Association of America, 1941)
Comedies	*The Plays of George Chapman: The Comedies. A Critical Edition*, ed. by Allan Holaday (University of Illinois Press, 1970)
'Contention'	'The Contention of Phillis and Flora'
'Coronet'	'A Coronet for His Mistress Philosophy'
'Cynthiam'	'Hymnus in Cynthiam'
Hudston	*George Chapman: Plays and Poems*, ed. by Jonathan Hudston (Penguin, 1998)
Nicoll	Chapman, George, *Homer: The Iliad, The Odyssey and The Lesser Homerica*, ed. by Allardyce Nicoll, 2 vols (Routledge and Kegan Paul, 1957)
'Noctem'	'Hymnus in Noctem'
OBS	*Ovid's Banquet of Sense, A Coronet for His Mistress Philosophy and His Amorous Zodiac*
'*OBS*: Argument'	'The Argument' (of 'Banquet')
'*OBS*: Davies 1'	'John Davies, of the Middle Temple'
'*OBS*: Davies 2'	'Another, by John Davies'
'*OBS*: Stapleton'	'Richard Stapleton to the Author'
'*OBS*: To Roydon'	'To the truly learned, and my worthy friend, Master Matthew Roydon' (Preface to *OBS*)
'*OBS*: Williams 1'	'Thomas Williams, of the Inner Temple'
'*OBS*: Williams 2'	'Another, by Thomas Williams'
O<small>OB</small>	*Ovid's Banquet of Sence. With a Coronet for His Mistresse Philosophy; and His amorous Zodiack* (London: R. Horseman, 1639), octavo edition
Q<small>OB</small>	*Ouids Banquet of Sence. A Coronet for his Mistresse Philosophie, and his amorous Zodiacke. With a translation of a Latine coppie, written by a Fryer, Anno Dom. 1400* (London: Richard Smith, 1595), quarto edition

Q_{SN}	Σκία νυκτός. *The Shadow of Night: Containing Two Poeticall Hymnes. Deuised by G. C. Gent.* (London: William Ponsonby, 1594), quarto edition
Shepherd	*The Works of George Chapman: Poems and Minor Translations* [ed. by Richard Herne Shepherd], intro. by Algernon Charles Swinburne (Chatto and Windus, 1875)
SN	*The Shadow of Night*
'SN: To Roydon'	'To my dear and most worthy friend Master Matthew Roydon' (Preface to *SN*)
Tragedies	*The Plays of George Chapman: The Tragedies, with Sir Gyles Goosecappe. A Critical Edition*, ed. by John Holaday (Boydell & Brewer, 1987)
'Zodiac'	'The Amorous Zodiac'

Other Works

Braden	*Sixteenth-Century Poetry: An Annotated Anthology*, ed. by Gordon Braden (Blackwell, 2005)
Conti	Conti, Natale, *Mythologiae, sive Explicationum fabularum, Libri decem* (Frankfurt: Andreas Wechel, 1581)
Liddell	Liddell, Henry George, and Robert Scott, *A Greek-English Lexicon*, rev. by Sir Henry Stuart Jones and Roderick McKenzie (Clarendon Press, 1940), online version, <https://www.perseus.tufts.edu/hopper/searchresults?q=Liddell>
Mulryan	Conti, Natale, *Mythologiae*, ed. and trans. by John Mulryan and Steven Brown, 2 vols (Arizona Center for Medieval and Renaissance Studies, 2006)
ODNB	*Oxford Dictionary of National Biography* online, <https://www.oxforddnb.com>
OED	*Oxford English Dictionary* online, <https://www.oed.com>
OLD	*Oxford Latin Dictionary* (Oxford University Press, 1968)
ZA	*Le zodiac amoreux* (original French poem by Giles Durant)

INTRODUCTION

The dialect of Chapman's poems is undoubtedly portentous in its general barbarism; and that study of purer writers, which might in another case have been trusted to correct and chasten the turgid and fiery vigour of a barbarian imagination, seems too often to have encrusted the mind with such arrogance and the style with such pedantry as to make certain of these poems, full of earnest thought, of passionate energy, of tumid and fitful eloquence, the most indigestible food ever served up to the guest of a man of genius by the master of the feast.

Algernon Charles Swinburne[1]

Σκία νυκτός, *The Shadow of Night, Containing Two Poetical Hymns* (1594, henceforth *SN*) was the first work published by English poet, dramatist and translator George Chapman (1559–1634). As the full title makes clear, the book comprises two poems: 'Hymnus in Noctem' and 'Hymnus in Cynthiam' (henceforth 'Noctem', 'Cynthiam').[2] Written in iambic pentameter couplets, and observing the Homeric tradition, these poems are supplications to the ancient goddesses Night and Cynthia (or the Moon), requesting that they bring their restorative powers to a decaying world. A year after this debut volume, Chapman published *Ovid's Banquet of Sense, A Coronet for His Mistress Philosophy and His Amorous Zodiac* (1595, henceforth *OBS*), featuring the three poems mentioned in the title: the long amatory elegy 'Ovid's Banquet of Sense' ('Banquet'), written in nine-line pentameter stanzas, recounts Roman poet Ovid's encounter with his mistress Corinna through a philosophical celebration of the five senses; 'A Coronet for His Mistress Philosophy' ('Coronet'), a ten-item corona of sonnets that is the first of its kind in English, makes a personified Philosophy the object of the lover's praise; and 'The Amorous Zodiac' ('Zodiac'), an unacknowledged translation of a French poem, *Le zodiac amoreux* (1587, *ZA*) by Giles Durant, Sieur de la Bergerie, transforms the contemplation of the mistress's body into a journey through the twelve constellations of the zodiac. To these three poems a fourth was appended, the pastoral poem 'The Contention of Phillis and Flora' ('Contention'), announced on the title page as 'a translation of a Latin copy, written by a Friar, *Anno Domini* 1400'.[3] This final poem, later reissued in an individual edition in 1598 that attributed its authorship to R. S. (most likely

---

1 Algernon Charles Swinburne, *George Chapman: A Critical Essay* (Chatto & Windus, 1875), p. 8.
2 Σκία νυκτός. *The Shadow of Night: Containing Two Poeticall Hymnes. Deuised by G. C. Gent.* (London: William Ponsonby, 1594). The abbreviation Q$_{SN}$ refers to this volume.
3 *Ouids Banquet of Sence. A Coronet for his Mistresse Philosophie, and his amorous Zodiacke. With a translation of a Latine coppie, written by a Fryer, Anno Dom. 1400* (London: Richard Smith, 1595). The abbreviation Q$_{OB}$ refers to this volume.

Richard Stapleton), was not included in the posthumous octavo edition of *OBS* (1639).[4]

While the title page of *SN* (Figure 1) attributed its authorship to 'G. C. Gent.', the first edition of *OBS* contained no similar announcement. However, each volume was prefaced by an epistle signed by the author and dedicated to his friend the poet Matthew Roydon ('*SN*: To Roydon'; '*OBS*: To Roydon'). *OBS* included other preliminary paratexts:

> 1) Five commendatory sonnets to the author, written by members of the Inns of Court: the first signed by Richard Stapleton ('*OBS*: Stapleton'), the next two by Thomas Williams ('*OBS*: Williams 1' and '*OBS*: Williams 2'), and the final two by John Davies ('*OBS*: Davies 1' and '*OBS*: Davies 2').
>
> 2) A brief prose argument of 'Banquet' ('*OBS*: Argument').

All these paratexts — except for '*OBS*: Argument' — were removed from the 1639 reissue, with the effect of erasing all traces of Chapman's authorship. Both *SN* and *OBS* also contained end and/or marginal glosses clarifying several passages in the light of their Greek and Latin sources. The poems and paratexts included in Chapman's first two volumes, with the exception of Stapleton's 'Contention', are the object of the present edition.

Any scholarly approach to Chapman's poetry must deal with the stigma of obscurity that has dogged his work. In a pioneering essay, Victorian poet and critic Algernon Charles Swinburne described Chapman's poems as 'indigestible' (see epigraph above). Swinburne's insightful appreciation of Chapman, inexhaustible in its critical insight and captivating in its mixture of admiration and repudiation of the poet's 'mind' and 'style', is representative of a critical bias that persists to our day.[5] 'Indigestible' is an epithet that

---

4 See *Phillis and Flora. The sweete and ciuill contention of two amorous Ladyes. Translated out of Latine: By R. S. Esquire* (London: Richard Jones, 1598); also, *Ovid's Banquet of Sence. With a Coronet for His Mistresse Philosophy; and His Amorous Zodiack* (London: R. Horseman, 1639). This latter volume is abbreviated throughout as O*OB*. 'Contention' has been excluded from this edition, as it is most certainly not Chapman's (Bartlett, p. 435).

5 Roy Battenhouse, 'Chapman's *The Shadow of Night*: An Interpretation', *Studies in Philology*, 38.4 (1941), pp. 584–608, affirms that *SN* 'is perplexingly metaphysical' (p. 584). Franck L. Schoell, *Études sur l'humanisme continental en Angleterre á la fin de la Renaissance* (Honoré Champion, 1926), considers Chapman's thought 'amorphous' (p. 32). T. S. Eliot, 'The Metaphysical Poets' (1921), in *The Complete Prose of T. S. Eliot: The Critical Edition. The Perfect Critic, 1919–1926* (Johns Hopkins University Press, 2014), pp. 375–85, attributes Chapman's metaphysical difficulty to 'a direct sensuous apprehension of thought' (p. 379). S. K. Heninger, Jr, *A Handbook of Renaissance Meteorology, with Particular Reference to Elizabethan and Jacobean Literature* (Duke University Press, 1960), describes Chapman as 'the most complex author of his age', and argues that his 'failure to create poetry with permanent vitality is difficult to reconcile with his exceptional talent and intellect' (p. 183). Millar MacLure, *George Chapman: A Critical Study* (University of Toronto Press, 1966), ascribes Chapman's 'appalling eclecticism' to his imprecise Neoplatonism (p. 32). Charles K. Cannon, 'Chapman on the Unity of Style and Meaning', *Journal of English and Germanic Philology*, 68.2 (1969), pp. 245–64, describes Chapman's

Chapman would not have found unfamiliar. The adjective 'indigest' appears twice in 'Noctem' to describe 'the formless matter of this world' in its primordial condition of 'Chaos' (30–31; also 59–60) — a condition that often has positive meanings in Chapman's poetic imaginary. Yet the word and its derivates can also be pejorative labels of a poetic style that Chapman actively combated. As he argues in the preface to *OBS*:

> Obscurity, in affection of words and indigested conceits, is pedantical and childish; but where it shroudeth itself in the heart of his subject, uttered with fitness of figure and expressive epithets, with that darkness will I still labour to be shadowed. ('*OBS*: To Roydon', lines 30–33).

This differentiation between two kinds of obscurity, one disabling and the other illuminating, is essential for Chapman's poetics. The poet was convinced that a certain darkness was the surest vehicle to revealing the true force of his inventions. Yet he more than once admitted that his verse fell short of that aim. In his dedicatory verse epistle post-facing one of his early translations of Homer, *Achilles Shield* (1598), he praises his friend the scientist Thomas Harriot as the ideal mind to untie the knots of his not always felicitous lines:

> O had your perfect eye Organs to pierce
> Into that Chaos whence this stifled verse
> By violence breakes: where Gloweworme like doth shine
> In nights of sorrow, this hid soule of mine:
> And how her genuine formes struggle for birth,
> Vnder the clawes of this fowle Panther earth;
> Then under those formes you should discerne
> My loue to you, in my desire to learne.[6]

Against the prevailing critical portrait of Chapman's authorial persona as an angry, contemptuous man of letters, this tortured recognition of his own shortcomings is a remarkable posture — and one which not many readers have highlighted.[7] These lines reveal as much about the painful 'struggle' to free the 'hid soule' and the 'genuine formes' of true poetry from the materiality of the poet's 'stifled verse' as about the part played by skilled readers in the accomplishment of this process. Elsewhere I have written about the centrality to Chapman's aesthetics of what he calls 'the true habit of poesy', a disposition

---

'symphonic' poetic thought as 'verbal texture composed of loosely woven strands of imagery, paradox, and invective' (p. 255). Raymond B. Waddington, *The Mind's Empire: Myth and Form in George Chapman's Narrative Poetry* (Johns Hopkins University Press, 1974), stresses Chapman's taste for 'riddle, enigma, parable, fable, myth, irony, [and] ambiguity' (p. 4). And William P. Weaver, 'The Banquet of the Common Sense: George Chapman's Anti-Epyllion', *Studies in Philology*, 111.4 (2014), pp. 757–85, doi:10.1353/sip.2014.0025, understands Chapman's readers as 'acolytes of a poetic mystery' (p. 761).

6 *Achilles Shield* (1598): 'To M. Harriots', lines 41–48, in Bartlett, p. 382.

7 For Margaret Bottrall, Chapman was a poet 'only partially in control of his faculties' who 'felt the conversion into words of a dimly apprehended idea' to be 'a very difficult and hazardous process' ('George Chapman's Defence of Difficulty', *The Criterion*, 16 (1937), pp. 638–54 (p. 642)).

which he describes in terms of a 'light-bearing intellect', and which, at least partly, he conceives of as the product of natural gift and inspiration. This disposition brings together several qualities: the 'labouring wits' of poets and readers in their struggles with linguistic difficulty, the cultivation of philosophical complexity, the avoidance of the straightforward path, and an overall commitment to learning.[8] When Chapman affirms in one of his prefaces that 'to him that is more than a reader I write', one may be tempted to detect arrogance on the part of a poet who judges his readership by the extent of his own privileged intellect.[9]

However, a different picture could emerge from the outlining in his paratexts of exceptionally judicious super-readers fashioned in the image and likeness of his most learned friends. The Harriot of *Achilles Shield* is said to be able to 'discerne' behind the text's shadows the poet's 'desire to learne'. The Roydon of *SN* and *OBS*, in his long acquaintance with 'the true habit of poesy', is praised for possessing the 'actual means to sound the philosophical conceits that [the poet's] new pen so seriously courteth' ('*OBS*: To Roydon', lines 44–45). Chapman frequently depicts the poetic process as a collaboration in which the reader plays an essential part in supplying the 'clearness of representation' that is 'required in absolute poems' (lines 13–14). Rather than to merely confirm a self-sufficient authorial image, the function of Chapman's habited reader is to perfect the poet's work.

It is the present editor's conviction that the two volumes of poetry presented here are digestible and enjoyable food. But enjoyment and digestion require the palate and the stomach's familiarization with their basic ingredients, their cooking methods, their seasonings and spices. This edition is conceived of as an aid to their pleasurable consumption, and thus as an attempt to reconstruct Chapman's meanings through his own idea of the habited reader. Modernized spelling, editorial punctuation, abundant lexical and explanatory notes, and a comprehensive introduction and commentary aim to combine rigorous closeness to the original texts with guidance through their long and often winding roads, illumination of their dark corners, and vindication of their frequent moments of brilliance. The task of editing Chapman may at some points be imagined to resemble that of Prince Henry's at the end of Shakespeare's *King John*: 'To set a form upon that indigest | Which he hath left so shapeless and so rude'.[10] However, and despite some crude moments,

---

8 Zenón Luis-Martínez, 'George Chapman's "Habit of Poesie"', in *Poetic Theory and Practice in Early Modern Verse: Unwritten Arts*, ed. by Zenón Luis-Martínez (Edinburgh University Press, 2023), pp. 258–85. See also Gilles Bertheau, 'Can a Poet be "Master of [his] owne Meaning"? George Chapman and the Paradoxes of Authorship', in *Self-Commentary in Early Modern European Literature, 1400–1700*, ed. by Francesco Venturi (Brill, 2019), pp. 284–315, doi:10.1163/9789004396593_012.
9 *Seaven Bookes of the Iliades* (1598): 'To the Reader', in Nicoll, I, p. 507.
10 William Shakespeare, *The Life and Death of King John*, ed. by A. R. Braunmuller (Oxford University Press, 1989), v. 7. 26–27.

Chapman's poems are far from shapeless. Moreover, the tools of twenty-first-century scholarship and the admirable work of former readers have assisted the present attempts to untangle the strings of these poems' diction and thought. In an age of professionalized literary studies, the readerly ideal that Chapman advocates is of necessity communal. This edition reveals a number of previously unnoticed sources and analogues for Chapman's poems, but also intends to bring together in a comprehensive though comprehensible manner those sources and analogues excavated by the work of its predecessors. It likewise proposes fresh arguments for a general interpretation of the poems and new readings of certain passages, but the roots of those arguments and readings often lie in the work of previous scholars.

This introduction begins by presenting the poems in relation to Chapman's life and their immediate literary context. It then proceeds with three sections on Chapman's practical poetics by focusing on his difficult style (2), his handling of genres (3), and his engagement with myth and philosophy in the shaping of major motifs and themes (4). A more speculative section examines the possible influence of Giordano Bruno upon Chapman's poetic and philosophical Platonism (5). A coda recaps on Chapman's poetic thought by focusing on his use of mottos and epigraphs (6). The introduction engages with prior interpretations and proposes alternative readings that do not aspire to be definitive. It also privileges the view of Chapman's two early volumes as parts of a common project and praxis of poetry over any attempt to establish interpretations of the poems individually. In the presentation of the texts themselves, lexical and explanatory notes are given as footnotes, while the commentary provides sources and analogues, and orients further readings of specific passages. A final note on Chapman's prosody and metre shows that the poet's preoccupation with this aspect of his verse prefigures his later developments and achievements in this field.

This edition cannot aim to rescue Chapman's early poems from their inevitable place among 'the most difficult poems in the language'.[11] But it aspires to rid difficulty — of execution, of language, of ideas, of interpretation — of its bad press. George Steiner's definition of poetic difficulty as 'an interference-effect between underlying clarity and obstructed formulation' is an important starting point for the present endeavour.[12] Steiner's taxonomy of four kinds of poetic difficulty, 'contingent', 'modal', 'tactical', and 'ontological', also applies here with different degrees of pertinence. Contingent difficulty — the kind that needs to be looked up — concerns the 'homework of

---

11 Frank Kermode, 'The Banquet of Sense', *Bulletin of the John Rylands Library*, 44.1 (1961), pp. 68–99 (p. 68).
12 George Steiner, 'On Difficulty', *The Journal of Aesthetics and Art Criticism*, 36.3 (1978), pp. 263–76, doi:10.2307/430437. For an approach to Renaissance poetic difficulty that considers Steiner's model, see Sarah Knight, 'The Worthy Knots of Fulke Greville', in *Poetic Theory and Practice*, ed. by Luis-Martínez, pp. 239–57 (esp. pp. 243–44). On Chapman's difficulty, see Bottrall, 'Chapman's Defence'.

elucidation'[13] that justifies the profusion of footnotes and the length of the present Commentary, the span of which ranges from language to alchemy, astrology, botany, mythology, philosophy and psychology. Chapman's modal difficulties — those which, according to Steiner, affect a poet's 'idiom and orders of apprehension' that 'are no longer natural to us'[14] — are less prominent when readers operate along those coordinates of form and genre that shape a tradition invoked more or less explicitly in his poems. Tactical difficulty, or the often-calculated distance 'between [a poet's] intention and his performative means',[15] leads to critical decisions as to whether a poem such as 'Banquet' needs to be read ironically or allegorically. Finally, Chapman seldom seeks to break the ontological contract with his readers: even when it is not fully achieved, clarity remains an aim of his poetry, and obstruction is mostly conceived of as a form of mediation rather than as mere interference. There is ultimately another form of difficulty which falls outside Steiner's taxonomy, and which one might call 'translational':[16] the concern with transferring to the artistic medium the complexities of the world. Chapman's conceits borrowed from the field of the visual arts express this concern — the question is dealt with extensively in the second section of this introduction. None of these forms of difficulty necessarily render the poems in this volume arcane or reader-hostile. Rather, their vindication as a living poetic corpus in the context of sixteenth-century English literature must be made in light of their defence of difficulty as one of their inherent elements, which can offer attractive opportunities for furthering their teaching, research and general reading.

1. *Chapman's Early Poems in Context*

George Chapman (1559–1634) was, in the words of Havelock Ellis, 'always naturally in conflict with the environment'.[17] Belligerence often erupts from the lines of *SN* and *OBS*. Chapman lived long and wrote much, and the many ways in which that pugnaciousness connects his writing to his life in its different phases cannot be traced in full in this introduction. Scholarship in the last century has illuminated some little-known angles of Chapman's life;[18]

---

13 Steiner, 'On Difficulty', p. 267.
14 Ibid., p. 270.
15 Ibid., p. 270.
16 'One might call' is a way of deferring to this footnote my gratitude to Jonathan Sell for baptizing my notion of this facet of Chapman's poetics. Serve this case as witness to many other of his insightful suggestions.
17 Havelock Ellis, *Chapman, with Illustrative Passages* (Nonesuch Press, 1934), p. 2.
18 For comprehensive accounts of Chapman's life, see Jean Jacquot, *George Chapman (1559–1634): sa vie, sa poésie, son théâtre, sa pensée* (Les Belles Lettres, 1951), pp. 3–58; and Charlotte Spivack, *George Chapman* (Twayne, 1967), whose first chapter (pp. 13–29) is significantly titled 'George Chapman, Second Son'. See also Ellis, *Chapman*, esp. pp. 7–50. Two illuminating accounts of Chapman's early years are Jean Robertson, 'The Early Life of George Chapman', *Modern Language Review*, 40.3 (1945), pp. 157–65, doi:10.2307/

and a full biography now in process promises to fill more gaps, particularly those that link Chapman's trajectory to the continent and his work to continental influences.[19] For the present purposes, a number of known facts and two hardly verifiable myths supply the context for the two volumes that are the object of this edition. The man that in his mid-thirties entered 'a booke intituled *Scianuctos, or the shadowe of nighte*' in the Stationers' Register on 31 December 1593 was born in Hitchin, Hertfordshire, the second son of Thomas Chapman, yeoman, and Joan Chapman, daughter of John Nodes — who served in Henry VIII's household — and second cousin of historian Edward Grimestone. The relatively comfortable position of his family was no guarantee of stability for a second son: while the elder son Thomas inherited the family house, George was left with one hundred pounds and two silver spoons. His attendance at Oxford University in 1574 where, as seventeenth-century antiquarian Anthony à Wood suggested, he must have excelled in classical languages over logic or philosophy, remains conjectural.[20] Documents and letters unearthed at the beginning of the last century permit certain steps to be traced in Chapman's trajectory before his first volume was given to the press.[21] The hypothesis that he could have accepted a teaching post in his native Hitchin after a short stay at Oxford has been mainly disregarded.[22] An inscribed dedication to Ralph Sadler of a presentation copy of *The Crowne of All Homers Workes* (1623), in which the poet proclaims to 'celebrate and eternize | The Noble Name and House where his youthe | was initiate', seems to place him in the service of the dedicatee's grandfather, Privy Councillor Sir Ralph Sadler, possibly since 1578 and until this gentleman's death in 1587. The date of 1578, suggested by Jean Robertson, would make Chapman an employee by the time the queen halted at Sadler's house in Standon, Hertfordshire, in her progress in July that year.[23]

Service to Sadler would find Chapman between his native Hertfordshire and London during those years. Marc Eccles's examination of the Chancery suit presented by Chapman on 17 April 1608 concerns a claim made by one John Wolfall of a debt of forty-nine pounds that the poet contracted with his

---

3716838; and Mark Eccles, 'Chapman's Early Years', *Studies in Philology*, 43.2 (1946), pp. 176–93. More recently, see Mark Thornton Burnett, 'George Chapman (1559/1560–1634)', *ODNB* (2004), doi:10.1093/ref:odnb/5118.

19 On this upcoming biography by Jessica Wolfe, see the note by Alyssa LaFaro, 'Curiosity Ignited', *UNC Research Stories* (21 April 2021), <https://endeavors.unc.edu/curiosity-ignited> [accessed 21 March 2025]. This note advances Wolfe's hypothesis that 'Chapman was employed in France by the English ambassador in the 1580s'.

20 Anthony à Wood, *Athenae Oxonienses*, 4 vols (Rivington, 1813, 1st edn 1691), II, col. 575.

21 Bertram Dobell, 'Newly Discovered Documents of the Elizabethan and Jacobean Periods: I. Letters and Documents by George Chapman', *The Athenaeum*, 383.3 (1901), pp. 369–70.

22 Robertson, 'Early Life', p. 160.

23 Ibid., p. 161.

father, a broker of London of the same name, in 1585. This suit not only corroborates Chapman's frequent financial problems; it also hints at other important events of his early life. Wolfall Jr's reply to this suit states that Chapman had been sued earlier for that debt — a circumstance that the poet denied — but that it had been forborne because of 'the absence of the saide Complainant by yonde the seas', and also because of Wolfall Sr's 'charitable disposition' to the debtor, 'whoe att the first beinge a man of verry good parts and expectacion, hath sethence verry vnadvisedly spent the most parte of his tyme and his estate in ffrutlesse and vayne Poetry'.[24] The respectable man become poor because of his extravagant dedication to the Muses reveals, beyond Wolfall's prejudice, the enduring obsession with the theme of 'riches' in Chapman's work, an issue whose centrality to his poetics has been noted recently.[25] Financial need may be in part behind Chapman's travel 'by yonde the seas'. In expectation of what future biographical work may reveal, France remains a candidate for a possible diplomatic employment and for acquaintance with the history and letters of that country in the late 1580s, as the third poem of *OBS*, 'Zodiac', attests. However, Willem Schrickx has questioned the French hypothesis and proposed instead, in the light of a Middelburg State Archives document containing a list of hospital admissions, that the 'Joris tshapmen onder capteine Robert Sidtne' that entered hospital on 20 October 1586 is in fact our poet.[26] He could have prolonged his life as a soldier in the Low Countries until 1591 or 1592, and thus his account of Sir Francis Vere's victorious skirmish against the Duke of Parma over the river Waal would make of the remarkable 'simile [...] from the honourable deeds of our noble countrymen' in 'Cynthiam' at least partly an eyewitness report.[27] Regardless of his whereabouts in Europe or the date of his return, Chapman was in London by December 1593, where he entered *SN* in the Stationers' Register on the last day of the year.[28]

The prefatory epistle to *SN* is indicative of some of Chapman's literary acquaintances and associates at the time of its publication. Both this epistle and the one prefacing *OBS* the ensuing year reveal as their dedicatee another

---

24 Quotes from Wolfall Jr's reply (27 April 1608) are from the transcriptions in Eccles, 'Chapman's Early Years', p. 184.
25 On the social and economic implications and pressures of Chapman's poetics, see John Huntington, *Ambition, Rank and Poetry in 1590s England* (University of Illinois Press, 2001), particularly in his reading of 'Coronet' (pp. 102–05) and 'Banquet' (pp. 106–46).
26 Willem Schrickx, 'George Chapman in Middelburg in 1586', *Notes and Queries*, 238 (1993), p. 165. Robert Sidney was later a dedicatee of one of Chapman's sonnets in his *Iliads* (1611); see Bartlett, p. 399.
27 See Commentary: 'Cynthiam', 326–49, and Gloss 19.
28 'Ultimo decembris. master Ponsonbye | Entred for his copie vnder the handes of the Bishop of LONDON and the wardens. a booke intituled | *Scianuctos, or the shadowe of nighte*' (*A Transcript of the Registers of the Company Stationers of London, 1554–1640*, ed. by Edward Arber, 4 vols (London, 1875), II, p. 303).

poet who happens also to count among Wolfall's debtors. That man is Matthew Roydon, known as the author of an 'Elegie, or Friends passion for his Astrophill', a poem commemorating Sir Philip Sidney's death.[29] Roydon was also connected to Henry Percy, Ninth Earl of Northumberland (1564–1632), and two other noblemen, Ferdinando Stanley (1559?–1594), Fifth Earl of Derby and Lord Strange, and George Carey (1547–1603), Second Earl of Hunsdon, if we attend to Chapman's affirmation in that first epistle that it was Roydon that 'reported [them] unto' him ('*SN*: To Roydon', lines 25–30). Of these, the first was the catalyst of an intellectual coterie of free-thinking intellectuals with an interest in mathematics and astronomy, but reportedly also in occult philosophy and alchemy. In addition to Roydon and Chapman, this group would count Sir Walter Raleigh, Christopher Marlowe, William Warner and Thomas Harriot among its members. Chapman's cultic worship of Night, the primordial Hesiodic goddess Νύξ, in the opening hymn of *SN* has proclaimed that poem the central manifesto of this group, for which Shakespeare's King of Navarre's apparently satiric exclamation in *Love's Labour's Lost* provided an enduring nickname: 'O paradox! Black is the badge of hell, | The hue of dungeons and *the school of night*'.[30]

Proposed by earlier scholars and formalized by Arthur Quiller-Couch and John Dover Wilson in their 1923 edition of *Love's Labour's Lost*, the hypothesis of a School of Night was developed by Muriel Bradbrook and Frances Yates in simultaneously published studies of 1936.[31] The formal existence of such a school and its primary dedication to studies of magic and occult philosophy seem improbable legends, dubious evidence for which was derived mainly from oblique references in Elizabethan literary quarrels. However, the activities of a more heterogeneous group of intellectuals with a serious interest in humanist knowledge and new philosophical thought, gathered under the auspices of the Earl of Northumberland and inspired by the scientific audaciousness of Harriot, make up a more likely narrative in the context of the London intellectual coteries of the late 1580s. Hilary Gatti's crucial work on the 'Brunian setting' of the activities of Northumberland and Harriot has served at least in part to free the interests of some of these men from the burden of a militant occultism, the picture of which has frequently bordered on caricature. Gatti's reassessment of the philosophical and scientific influence of Giordano Bruno (1548–1600) in England has brought to light the part

---

29 Eccles, 'Chapman's Early Life', p. 187. Roydon's poem was first printed in the anthology *The Phoenix Nest* (1593). See B. J. Sokol, 'Roydon, Matthew (fl. 1583–1622), Poet', *ODNB* (2004), doi:10.1093/ref:odnb/24238.
30 William Shakespeare, *Love's Labour's Lost*, ed. by H. R. Woudhuysen (Bloomsbury, 1998), IV. 3. 250–51, emphasis added.
31 William Shakespeare, *Love's Labour's Lost: The New Shakespeare*, ed. by Arthur Quiller-Couch and John Dover Wilson (Cambridge University Press, 1923; 2nd edn 1962); M. C. Bradbrook, *The School of Night: A Study in the Literary Relations of Sir Walter Ralegh* (Cambridge University Press, 1936); Frances A. Yates, *A Study of 'Love's Labour's Lost'* (Cambridge University Press, 1936).

played by his dialogues in Italian written during Bruno's London years (1583–1586), but also by his later scientific works in Latin written during his central European period (1586–1591), in the shaping of late Elizabethan literature — particularly what Gatti calls the Marlovian and Shakespearean 'drama of knowledge' (*Doctor Faustus, Hamlet*).[32] Gatti leaves Chapman outside a Brunian picture which his work certainly helps to delineate and colour — this issue is dealt with in section 5 of this introduction. The satire of which Chapman's first two volumes of poetry were a target, and the literary diatribe in which they were forced to engage, even if relatively well known, may familiarize us with the earthly matter around which the fledgling writer built some of his more heavenly poetic thoughts.

SN was registered for publication on the last day of 1593; that year has been assumed to be the date of its composition. However, Charles Nicholl has argued in his biography of Thomas Nashe that *SN* must have circulated in a more or less finished version by the summer of 1592. This would make Nashe's critique of Spenser's omission of 'Amyntas' — a name for Ferdinando Stanley, Lord Strange — from the 'honorable catalogue of our English Heroes' in *The Faerie Queene* the first known reference to Chapman's controversial poem:

> Perusing yesternight, with idle eyes,
> The fairy Singers stately tuned verse,
> And viewing after Chap-mens wonted guise,
> What strange contents the title did rehearse [...][33]

For Nicholl, Nashe's sonnet begins with an idle perusal of Spenser's poem in the accustomed manner of 'Chap-mens', or Chapman's, that is, a reading of *The Faerie Queene* in search for 'strange contents', a pun on Lord Strange's surname and occultist inclinations, as well as on Chapman's own esoteric verses. Nicholl sees further evidence for an early date for *SN* in Chapman's own words in his continuation of Marlowe's *Hero and Leander* (1598). The account of Marlowe's 'late desires' that Chapman 'to light surrender | [His] soules darke ofspring' is interpreted as the former having encouraged the latter to give to the press a manuscript of the poem.[34]

The early date, in Nicholl's argument, would make *SN* the third piece, with Nashe's *Pierce Pennilesse* (1592) and Marlowe's *Doctor Faustus* (1592), in a group of works addressing Lord Strange's occultist inclinations — Marlowe remaining in a more ambiguous middle point between Nashe's dissuasive attempts through overt mockery of alchemists, astrologers and

---

32 Hilary Gatti, *The Renaissance Drama of Knowledge: Giordano Bruno in England* (Routledge, 1989).
33 Thomas Nashe, *Pierce Pennilesse His Svpplication to the Divell*, in *The Works of Thomas Nashe*, ed. by Ronald B. McKerrow, 5 vols (Sidgwick & Jackson, 1910), I, p. 244, lines 15–18.
34 George Chapman, *Hero and Leander*, III. 195–97, in Bartlett, p. 138.

mathematicians, and Chapman's staunch defence of the nocturnal habits of the pursuers of esoteric knowledge.[35] Chapman's calling the false scholars' abuse of knowledge — 'to think Skill so mightily pierced with their loves' — 'a supererogation in wit' in the volume's prefatory epistle ('*SN*: To Roydon', lines 15–16) seems to contain a direct response to Nashe via Gabriel Harvey's *Pierce's Supererogation, or A New Praise of the Old Ass* (1593). Our poet must have thus taken Harvey's side in his dispute with Nashe by defending the former's views on the superiority of the scholar over the man of the world. Nashe's next pamphlet, *The Terrors of the Night* (1594), could also be read from its very title in a satirical key against Chapman's first poem. Its author's affirmation that 'Well haue the Poets tearmd night the nurse of cares, the mother of despaire, the daughter of hell' does not mention *SN*, but seems to echo the poem by attributing to night those qualities that Chapman strenuously strives to disclaim.[36] Charlotte Spivack goes further (though her evidence may be less convincing than Nicholl's) when she argues that Nashe could have seen Chapman's next poetry volume, *OBS*, in pre-print manuscripts by 1594. This possibility would make the 'miraculous waking visions' experienced by 'a Gentleman of good worship and credit', which Nashe acknowledges to be the 'accidentall occasion' on which his pamphlet was 'speedily botcht vp and compyled', a parody of Ovid's experience of his beloved by her temptation of his five senses. In Nashe's pamphlet, the gentleman's delirious vision also consists of five tableaux of temptation, including a company of drunken sailors, a group of money-bearing devils, a 'troupe of naked Virgins', 'a graue assembly of sober attyred Matrones' and, finally, 'a naked slender foote offring to steale betwixt the sheets in to him'.[37]

Spivack's conclusions testify to scholarly interest in possible topical allusions in and to Chapman's early work. Waddington sees 'an unmistakable allusion' to the Ovidian epigraph on the title page of Shakespeare's *Venus and Adonis* (1593) — '*Vilia miretur vulgus; mihi flavus Apollo | Pocula Castalia plena ministret aqua*' ('Let the rabble marvel at vile things; may fair Apollo serve for me bowls full of the Castalian waters') — in Chapman's critique of those 'flesh-counfounded souls | That cannot bear the full Castalian bowls' ('Cynthiam', 163–64).[38] For Waddington, Chapman's lines turn Ovid's words against Shakespeare's own intentions by placing his rival on the side of those sensual poets that appeal to vulgar tastes; yet the allusion 'would indicate

---

35 Charles Nicholl, *A Cup of News: The Life of Thomas Nashe* (Routledge & Kegan Paul, 1984), pp. 108–12.
36 Thomas Nashe, *The Terrors of the Night, or A Discourse of Apparitions*, in *Works of Thomas Nashe*, ed. by McKerrow, I, p. 346, lines 1–2.
37 Spivack, *George Chapman*, p. 15. See Nashe, *Terrors of the Night*, in *Works of Thomas Nashe*, ed. by McKerrow, I, pp. 376–82.
38 See William Shakespeare, *Venus and Adonis* (London: Richard Field, 1593), title page; and Ovid, *Amores*, I. 15. 35–36, in *Heroides and Amores*, ed. and trans. by Grant Showernam (Heinemann, 1914), p. 378; my translation.

more than a purely personal rivalry' by differentiating 'kinds of patrons' (i.e. 'Ralegh-versus-Southampton is more important than Chapman-versus-Shakespeare') and 'kinds of poetry' (i.e. philosophical versus erotic) — and, one could add, kinds of readers.[39] Of these, the Chapman-versus-Shakespeare issue drew most of the focus in the work of earlier critics. The part of Shakespeare's *Love's Labour's Lost* in the poets' wars involving Chapman was avidly defended by a host of editors and scholars until the end of the twentieth century. The suggestion that the nocturnal coterie was the target of Shakespeare's satiric portraits of the braggart soldier Armado, the schoolmaster Holofernes and the curate Nathaniel enabled larger political readings of a literary fray between those writers like Shakespeare under the patronage of Henry Wriothesley, Earl of Southampton, and Robert Devereux, Earl of Essex, and those like Chapman, who has traditionally been seen behind Shakespeare's Holofernes and who by that time was seeking the approval of Sir Walter Raleigh and the Earl of Northumberland. This theory relies on the also widely accepted date of composition for Shakespeare's comedy as late as 1594, and usually comes hand in hand with another doubtful myth: Chapman's identity as the 'rival poet' of Shakespeare's *Sonnets*. This was first suggested by Walter Minto in 1874, who saw in 'the proud full sail of his great verse, | Bound for the prize of all too precious you' a clear reference to Chapman's courting of Southampton's patronage through the inflated style of *SN* and the elaborate alexandrines of his early Homeric translations.[40]

The School of Night and the rival poet are weak as historical realities, and have proved more fruitful for literary fiction than for criticism. Their fundamental problem lies in the desire to 'personalize' contrasting philosophies of poetry and disparate literary interests.[41] The poetic rivalries fostered by these accounts are more suggestive than plausible, and stronger evidence could tell the story in quite different terms. One of the most recent editors of *Love's Labour's Lost*, H. R. Woudhuysen, has warned us about the unproductive consequences of such theories when analysing the Shakespearean text: 'The shifting sands of Elizabethan court intrigue and literary rivalry provide an attractive foundation on which to build theories about the play and about

---

39 Waddington, *The Mind's Empire*, pp. 93–94.
40 William Shakespeare, *Sonnets*, ed. by Katherine Duncan-Jones (Thomas Nelson, 1997), 86. 1–2, p. 283; and William Minto, *Characteristics of the English Poets from Chaucer to Shirley* (William Blackwood, 1874), pp. 289–92.
41 See Arthur Acheson, *Shakespeare and the Rival Poet* (John Lane, 1903); *Shakespeare's Lost Years in London* (Bernard Quaritch, 1920); and *Shakespeare's Sonnet Story, 1592–1598* (Bernard Quaritch, 1922) as instances of these critical practices. As early as 1941, Ernest H. Strathmann exposed their weaknesses: see his 'The Textual Evidence for "The School of Night"', *Modern Language Notes*, 56.3 (1941), pp. 176–86 (esp. p. 186). For fictional re-elaborations, see Lindsay Anne Reid, 'The Spectre of the School of Night: Former Scholarly Fictions and the Stuff of Academic Fiction', *Early Modern Literary Studies*, 23 (2014), Special Issue 'Christopher Marlowe: Identities, Traditions, Afterlives'), <https://extra.shu.ac.uk/emls/journal/indexphp/emls/article/view/182.html> [accessed 21 January 2025].

Shakespeare's early career, but they distract attention from the play's far more bracing engagement with its own art and ideas'.[42] The effect may not be different when the argument is applied to Chapman's early career, where genuine interest seems far from the contexts and works associated with these diatribes. On account of the debts shown in his early comedies, *The Blind Beggar of Alexandria* (1596) and *An Humorous Day's Mirth* (1597), Woudhuysen considers Chapman the 'earliest known admirer' of *Love's Labour's Lost*.[43] Katherine Duncan-Jones suggests that, if Chapman can be among the possible candidates for the title of 'rival poet' of Shakespeare's *Sonnets*, the reason would be both poets' later connections with William Herbert, Earl of Pembroke, by the time of their publication in 1609, rather than the liaisons with Southampton in the early and mid-1590s.[44] Moreover, Chapman's 'Coronet' sonnets show stronger connections with the English Petrarchan cycles such as Sidney's *Astrophil and Stella* and those under Sidney's posthumous influence in the 1590s (by Michael Drayton, Barnabe Barnes, or John Davies), than with those by Shakespeare.[45]

Another effect that the School of Night theory has had on Chapman's early poems is the tendency to regard them primarily as obscure philosophical poems, more concerned with alchemy, magic, astrology and other forms of occult knowledge than with their own status as poetic artefacts.[46] Yet Chapman's alleged membership of Northumberland's coterie lacks evidence beyond the names mentioned in the first of the Roydon epistles. Although his affinities with, or desires to approach, these men certainly testify to his philosophical or scientific interests, Chapman conceived of himself chiefly as a poet. This is made even more conspicuous in *OBS*. In the volume's prefatory epistle, the dedicatee Roydon continues to supply the connection with the Northumberland group, a connection which nevertheless seems to have been insufficient by that time to gain for Chapman a more overt recognition from a group of noble patrons of the sciences and arts. New endorsement of his work comes now in the form of five commendatory poems by three members of the London Inns of Court. The first of these is Richard Stapleton, the same man that Chapman identifies as 'my most ancient, learned and right noble friend M. Richard Stapilton, first most desertfull

---

42 'Introduction', in *Love's Labour's Lost*, ed. by Woudhuysen, p. 72.
43 Ibid., p. 75.
44 'Introduction', in *Shakespeare's Sonnets*, ed. by Duncan-Jones, p. 65.
45 Zenón Luis-Martínez, '"Friendlesse Verse": The Poetics of Chapman's "A Coronet for His Mistresse Philosophie" (1595)', *Studies in Philology*, 118.3 (2021), pp. 565–604, doi:10.1353/sip.2021.0018.
46 See MacLure, *George Chapman*, pp. 33–45, which reads *SN* in light of orphic theogony; and Waddington, *The Mind's Empire*, not only in his allegorical reading of *SN* (pp. 45–112) but remarkably in his suggestion that 'Banquet' can be interpreted as an allegory of certain alchemical practices (pp. 137–41). See also Commentary: 'Banquet', 47–48; and Frances A. Yates, 'Agrippa and Elizabethan Melancholy: George Chapman's *Shadow of Night*', in *The Occult Philosophy in the Elizabethan Age* (Routledge, 1979), pp. 157–71.

mover in the frame of our Homer' in the 'Preface to the Reader' of his 1611 *Iliads*.[47] Stapleton was most probably the author of the translation of 'Contention' appended to the volume, if we pay attention to the 1598 edition of the poem, on whose title page it is said to be translated by 'R. S. Esquire'.[48] He may be the same 'R. S. of the Inner Temple, Gentleman' that compiled the poetry anthology *The Phoenix Nest* (1593), as Hyder Rollins believed, although this has not been proved.[49] 'I. D. of the Middle Temple' is certainly the poet Sir John Davies, whose collection of epigrams had been published by then with Marlowe's partial translations of *Amores* in the volume *Epigrammes and Elegies*.[50] The third author involved in the composition of these commendatory sonnets, 'Tho[mas] Williams of the Inner Temple', resists clear identification.[51]

On the whole, the five commendatory sonnets map a scope of literary interests that transcends those of the Northumberland circle. Chapman's verse may still be depicted as one of 'Sweet philosophic strains' ('*OBS*: Stapleton', 8), 'too mystical and deep' for common wits ('*OBS*: Davies 1', 4). Yet Davies's praise of the author as Cupid's 'second master' ('*OBS*: Davies 2', 14), and thus as Ovid's rightful heir, vindicates for him a special position with respect to one of the most fashionable trends of English poetry in the 1590s. Despite the 'spright-filed darkness' of his style ('*OBS*: Williams 1', 7) and the 'deeper mysteries' of his content ('*OBS*: Davies 1', 14), or perhaps because of that style and content, Chapman is celebrated by Davies as the leading Ovidian poet of his generation, a fact that imagines him presiding over a Pleiad that would include Lodge, Marlowe and Shakespeare as subalterns to the inheritor of Ovid's true genius.[52] Davies's praise questions Waddington's assertion that in this poem 'Chapman satirizes the fad and ridicules the image of the erotic Ovid by making him the protagonist of a seduction poem'.[53] Far from this view, Davies's endorsement of Chapman's position constitutes the best proof that his poem should be read as 'a surprising

---

47 In Nicoll, I, p. 18.
48 *Phillis and Flora*, title page.
49 See 'Introduction', in *The Phoenix Nest (1593)*, ed. by Hyder Edward Rollins (Harvard University Press, 1931), pp. xxiv–xxxi.
50 The date of this publication is uncertain, although Fredson Bowers's claim for an imprint as early as 1593 is plausible. See 'The Early Editions of Marlowe's "Ovid's Elegies"', *Studies in Bibliography*, 25 (1972), pp. 149–72 (p. 150, n. 5). Krueger includes Davies's two dedicatory sonnets to Chapman among Davies's occasional poems. See *The Poems of John Davies*, ed. by Robert Krueger (Oxford University Press, 1975), pp. 201–02, and the commentary on p. 406.
51 On Williams, Bartlett notes: 'There are only two Thomas Williamses recorded as entered in the Inner Temple in the record of 1547–1660: 1) T. W., of Sowforde, near Ivybridge, Devon, second son of Thomas William M. P. Born 1542, died 1620. 2) T. W. of Wollaston, Salop, Eldest son of Reginald Williams, Sheriff of Montgomeryshire, 1574' (p. 430).
52 On this issue, see Introduction, pp. 43–52.
53 Waddington, *The Mind's Empire*, p. 156.

testimony to the continuing relevance of a responsible and considered engagement with Ovid'.[54] This issue is assessed more deeply later in this introduction. Here it serves to affirm that, despite his differences with his contemporaries, Chapman's attention to, and active engagement with, the poetry of his time should qualify other attempts to understand his poetry as mainly cryptic or esoteric.

With the exception of 'De Guiana', the prefatory poem to Lawrence Kemys's *A Relation of the Second Voyage to Guiana* (1596), no new works by Chapman were printed between *OBS* and 1598. This latter year proved for him a sort of *annus mirabilis*. *Hero and Leander* saw the light in two different editions, one containing only Marlowe's supposedly unfinished poem and the other including Chapman's continuation and arrangement into six 'sestyads'. None of Chapman's earlier poetry was reprinted before his death in 1634, but the 'complete' *Hero and Leander* was reissued six times after its first printing (1600, 1606, 1613, 1617, 1622 and 1629). Besides this, 1598 also saw the publication of the first two instalments of what would be a two-decade-long project of Homeric translations. *Seven Bookes of the Iliades of Homere, Prince of Poets* (1598) was dedicated to the Earl of Essex, and contained Books 1, 2, 7, 8, 9, 10 and 11. The also Essex-dedicated *Achilles Shield* (1598) makes an independent poem of the long ekphrastic description of Vulcan's shield for the Greek hero that occupies part of Book XVIII. The volume was post-faced by the above-quoted poem to Thomas Harriot. Chapman's intensive commitment to writing after 1595 was completed by his early comedies for the Lord Admiral's Men, a turn to the theatrical medium glimpsed at in the concluding sonnet of 'Coronet'.

By 1600 Chapman was already a highly appreciated poet and a well-known dramatist. A third comedy, *All Fools*, was performed in 1599, and Robert Allott's verse compilation *Englands Parnassus* (1600) included him with Spenser, Drayton, Daniel, Lodge and Shakespeare among its most often-quoted poets. Eighty-four passages are attributed to Chapman in this anthology, eleven of which are from *SN* and twenty-seven from *OBS*. Allott resorts to the poems in these volumes to exemplify subjects such as 'ambition', 'art', 'beauty', 'content', 'gifts', 'gentry', 'lechery', 'love', 'man', 'mind', 'opinion', 'pleasure', 'virtue', 'use' and 'wit', divinities such as Cynthia, stylistic features such as 'descriptions of beauty and personage', 'poetical comparisons' for 'beauty', 'dalliance' and 'liberty', and 'epithets' for 'trees and herbs' and 'hounds'.[55] The list is revealing of Chapman's aptness for illustrating common topics and figures of sixteenth-century poetry, and should persuade us to view his verse in a key which somehow counters the abstruse style and arcane

---

54 Daniel H. Moss, '"The Second Master of Love": George Chapman and the Shadow of Ovid', *Modern Philology*, 111.3 (2014), pp. 457–84 (p. 459), doi:10.2307/20466786.
55 Robert Allott, *Englands Parnassus* (1600), ed. by Charles Crawford (Clarendon Press, 1913). If the eight quotations from 'Contention' are removed, the total would be seventy-six.

subjects with which it has been often associated. Two years earlier, Francis Meres had mentioned Chapman alongside Sidney, Spenser, Daniel, Drayton, Shakespeare and Marlowe as one of those poets by whose works 'the English tongue is mightily enriched, and gorgeouslie invested in rare ornaments and resplendent abiliments'.[56] His dedication to 'fruitless and vain poetry' may not have alleviated his financial difficulties, but it attracted attention among Elizabethan poetry readers and playgoers.

The circumstances in which Chapman flourished as a poet in the first half of the 1590s and of his consolidation in the second half of that decade offer a rich portrait not only of the individual author of SN and OBS but more generally of the poet's profession. While the contrasting examples of Nashe's satire and Davies's extolment present a figure that navigates between, at one end, petulant detachment from current literary trends through pursuit of secret knowledge and, at the other, willing though critical engagement with the poetry of his time, anthologists and commentators place him naturally beside his best peers. Despite Chapman's self-image as an aggressive polemicist at home on the side of the learned few, he would have felt comfortable in the roles assigned to him by Meres and Allott. The financial problems of these years, which continued in later decades, directly connect with his active seeking of social recognition through patronage. The unclear position in which the first Roydon preface puts him with respect to the three noblemen to whom it alludes, and his later courting the favour of Essex and Sir Thomas Walsingham (to whose wife, Audrey Walsingham, he dedicated the continuation of *Hero and Leander*), are significant moves when read against those moments in his poems and prefaces that show overt resentment to money-mongering, protection-seeking poets and scorn for nobility of blood. Chapman's turn to the theatre must inevitably respond to more material factors than those adduced in the tenth sonnet of 'Coronet'. Yet the constant refuge in learning as supplier of 'comfort' and 'riches' that are not of a material kind ('Coronet', 9. 9) testifies to some resistance to acknowledging his social aspirations and financial needs in his works. Other patrons and other failures would come in later decades that do not fall within the scope of this introduction.[57] Ovid's prospects about his beloved Corinna (or Julia, Emperor Augustus's daughter) in the last stanzas of 'Banquet' voice Chapman's anxieties in this sense:

> To me (dear sovereign) thou art patroness,
> And I, with that thy graces have infused,
> Will make all fat and foggy brains confess
> Riches may from a poor verse be deduced;
>   And that gold's love shall leave them grovelling here,

---

56 Francis Meres, *Palladis Tamia, or Wit's Treasurie* (London: Cuthbert Burby, 1598), p. 280.
57 Introductory accounts to his later years can be consulted in Spivack, *George Chapman*, pp. 19–26; and Jacquot, *George Chapman*, pp. 33–58.

> When thy perfections shall to heav'n be Mused,
>   Decked in bright verse, where angels shall appear,
> The praise of virtue, love, and beauty singing,
> Honour to noblesse, shame to avarice bringing. ('Banquet', 115)

It is ultimately up to readers to decide whether the 'riches' sought here are merely intellectual and aesthetic, as in the previous example from 'Coronet', or whether they also hint at economic and social, not to say sexual interests. Years after this poem, Henry Percy, Earl of Northumberland's *Advice to his Son* (1609) warns his heir about the ways of some patronage-seeking scholars:

> Scholars may in some sort be ranked with these former, not in that you shall find them so flitting or generally so ambitious, or that amongst them you shall not find some very honest, very constant, very worthy men that no fortunes can beat from you, if they have but to suffice nature in a competent fashion. Yet are there again of them of many kinds, of many professions, that will desire to make you the bridge to go over to their conclusions.[58]

That someone who could have been a Northumberland man may project a similar self-image as an honest, unambitious man of letters is unsurprising; but it is difficult to determine whether the image invoked by Percy matches Chapman's life ethos. His philosophical inclinations and his cultivation of poetic obscurity were always to him indices of his intellectual uprightness and his distance from what he considered the corruptible ways and the facile poetics of the court. Using the social theories of Pierre Bourdieu, John Huntington has argued that this dialectics between aesthetic and social habitus determines Chapman's engagement with the literary field of the English 1590s.[59] As the 'poor verse' of Chapman's Ovid becomes the 'friendless verse' of the lyric voice of 'Coronet' (9. 13), readers are made aware that aloofness and resentment help to trace the not always straightforward paths that connect the difficult poet with the needy individual.

2. Poetics: The Judicial Eye

Many Elizabethan theorists of poetry were also practising poets: George Gascoigne's *Certaine Notes of Instruction Concerning the Making of Verse or Rhyme in English* (1575), Thomas Lodge's *A Defence of Poetry* (1579), Edmund Spenser's 'lost' treatise *The English Poet* (if we attend to E. K.'s words in *The Shepheardes Calender*),[60] Philip Sidney's *Defence of Poesy* (c. 1580), Thomas

---

58 Henry Percy, Ninth Earl of Northumberland, *Advice to His Son* (1609), ed. by G. B. Harrison (Ernest Benn, 1930), p. 116.
59 Huntington, *Ambition*, esp. pp. 89–105.
60 Spenser is supposed to have discussed ἐνθουσιασμός, or 'celestiall inspiration [...] in his booke called the English Poete', if we attend to E. K.'s 'Argument' to the 'October' eclogue of *The Shepheardes Calender* (1579); see *The Yale Edition of the Shorter Poems of Edmund Spenser*, ed. by William A. Oram and others (Yale University Press, 1989), p. 170.

Campion's *Observations in the Art of English Poesy* (1602), and Samuel Daniel's *Defence of Rhyme* (1603) are instances of works endorsed by the authority of practice. Even more systematic treatises like George Puttenham's *The Art of English Poesy* (1589) or William Scott's *The Model of Poesy* (1599) can be taken as instances of theory produced, if not by acknowledged masters, at least by connoisseurs and occasional practitioners of the art. Like these contemporaries, Chapman was also a poet deeply interested in poetics, but, unlike them, he never wrote a full defence or tract disclosing his ideas and opinions about poetry. Scholars have stressed his theoretical concerns, however, expounded in copious paratexts in prose and verse. Waddington has argued that 'Chapman's only critical remarks are scattered in the prefaces, dedications, epistles, and commendations', but their 'high degree of consistency in theory and attitude permits us to read these serial proclamations as a coherent statement of a poetics'.[61] More recently, Gilles Bertheau has taken up Waddington's argument to analyse Chapman's paratexts as forms of a 'self-commentary' that defend an idea of poetry as 'divinity', that 'manifests itself in deliberately hermetic language', but also in a hostile notion of the reader as 'an obstacle to the accomplishment of his authorship'.[62] Bertheau interestingly updates arguments that, since the late nineteenth century, have attended to the aesthetic dimension of Chapman's work, particularly to the problem of obscurity or difficulty. In these accounts, Chapman emerges as a fundamentally Platonic voice who traces the origin of poetic inspiration in divine fury, who uses mythic form and visual language to justify a moral point or an elitist idea of difficulty, or who makes obscurity a weapon and shield of his social concerns and position in the literary field of his time.[63]

Among recent scholarship, the work of Gerald Snare stands out for its attempt to contest the dominant view of Chapman's opinions as a systematic body, and of his poetics as primarily obscure or hermetic. For Snare, the common scholarly procedure of gathering critical remarks from a poet's work in order to derive 'some notion of a poet's belief, a belief conceived to

---

61 Waddington, *The Mind's Empire*, p. 5.
62 Bertheau, 'Paradoxes of Authorship', pp. 285–86.
63 On Chapman's Platonic poetics, see Leslie A. Rutledge, *George Chapman's Theory of the Soul and of Poetry* (unpublished doctoral thesis, Harvard University, 1938). See also Jacquot, *George Chapman*, which identifies Platonic themes in the poems such as the conflict between body and soul (pp. 199–231), and doctrines of poetic inspiration as an anticipation of Romantic ideas (pp. 233–54); similarly, Spivack sees in Chapman's early views a prefiguring of Shelley's *Defence of Poetry* (1821) and relates Platonic inspiration to philosophical and moral didacticism (*George Chapman*, pp. 30–44). On myth and allegory as informing principles of Chapman's poetics, see Waddington, *The Mind's Empire*, esp. pp. 14–17. On Chapman's use of visual metaphors to justify his theories of reading, see Waddington, *The Mind's Empire*, esp. pp. 141–51; and Jessica Wolfe, *Humanism, Machinery, and Renaissance Literature* (Cambridge University Press, 2004), pp. 161–202, for Chapman's special interest in developments in Renaissance optics as a basis for his theories of reading. On the social dimension of Chapman's profession of a poetics of obscurity, see Huntington, *Ambition*, pp. 66–146.

generate his practice', has been particularly damaging to Chapman studies.⁶⁴ Snare insists that, if we focus primarily on the awareness in Chapman's poems of their own status as 'constructed artifice', then a 'practical poetics' that is far from 'obscure, theoretically arcane, or predominantly moral' emerges from their lines.⁶⁵ Snare's conclusions may often be strained in their attempt to counter some of the arguments of that tradition which he intends to debunk. But his emphasis on practice endorses a necessary reconsideration of Chapman's early poems as self-conscious meditations on the origins, functions and conditions of existence of the art of poetry. When we consider Chapman's poetic practice alongside his critical ideas, and not as mere examples of pre-established theoretical principles that sometimes respond to the exigencies and motivations of particular works, then a different picture of the poet's art arises. This picture is often, as sketched in the opening pages of this introduction, that of an artist struggling, and sometimes failing, to find suitable verbal expression for his inner conceptions, yet nevertheless one who relies on laborious dedication to his task and on a more positive appreciation of the reader than his sometimes dismissive theoretical remarks display.⁶⁶

The picture of Chapman as a defender of theories of divine *furor* and of the role of the 'vatic poet' — i.e. the 'inspired prophet/priest who simultaneously protects his sacred trust from the many and imparts it to the few'⁶⁷ — needs to be modified with an insistence on 'labour', 'habit' and 'skill' as qualities that connect the roles of poet and reader,⁶⁸ particularly through a number of formulae and metaphors borrowed from the Renaissance visual arts. Chapman's reliance on visual tropes transcends those commonplace similes of poetry as a 'speaking picture', as standardized in the Horatian *ut pictura poesis* topos. Beyond these conventional standpoints, he believed that poets and readers must share an artistic *eye*. This argument is nowhere more clearly put than in his well-known definition of *enargia*, his own version of the classical and Renaissance rhetorical principles of *enargeia* and *energeia* — whose original spelling has been preserved here in the attempt to stress its peculiarities:

---

64 Gerald Snare, *The Mystification of George Chapman* (Duke University Press, 1989), p. 140.
65 Ibid., pp. 46–48.
66 Swinburne lucidly described Chapman's awareness of his artistic flaws as the foundation of his poetic practice: 'he appears from first to last to have erected his natural defects into an artificial system, and cultivated his incapacities as other men cultivate their faculties' (*George Chapman*, p. 8). Bottrall, 'George Chapman's Defence of Difficulty', understands Chapman's idea of difficulty mainly as a search for adequate poetic expression; she also explains his idea of 'good readers' as 'not born but made' (p. 654). On Chapman's inner struggles as an artist, see also MacLure, *George Chapman*, p. 9. On the notion of 'habit' as a key term for Chapman's theory of the reader, see Luis-Martínez, 'Habit of Poesie'.
67 Waddington, *The Mind's Empire*, p. 10.
68 Luis-Martínez, 'Habit of Poesie'.

That *enargia*, or clearness of representation, required in absolute poems, is not the perspicuous delivery of a low invention, but high and hearty invention expressed in most significant and unaffected phrase: it serves not a skilful painter's turn to draw the figure of a face only to make known who it represents, but he must limn, give lustre, shadow and heightening; which, though ignorants will esteem spiced and too curious, yet such as have the judicial perspective will see it hath motion, spirit and life. ('*OBS*: To Roydon', lines 13–20)

For Chapman, *enargia* is not simply the rhetorical quality known as *enargeia*, aiming at perspicuity through linguistic ornament, i.e. making visible for an audience those objects that are not present to their eyes — ἐνάργεια derives from Greek ἐναργής, visible, or manifest to the mind's eye. Rather, linguistic expression must convey the extraordinary capacity of poetic invention to transcend its own verbal medium. The comparison with painting is not meant as a mere reminder of the visual dimension of *enargeia*. True that 'lustre, shadow and heightening' have their basis in Greek ἄργος (shining, glistening). But *enargia* must also engage *energeia* — ἐνέργεια derives from Greek ἔργον, i.e. work, labour — in its Aristotelian sense of actuality, that is, the capacity to *animate* what is inanimate.[69] Thus, the poet's labour must go beyond the mere capacity of making recognizable the figure that their invention aims to represent by drawing attention to the very medium that will acquaint the reader with that invention's worthiness as poetic artifice, which is measured by the qualities of 'motion, spirit and life'. Ἔργον and ἄργος fuse in Chapman's idiosyncratic keyword: poets must show their cards, or make their labour visible, in order to represent not only the poetic object in motion but also the energy, or soul, that animates it; in doing so, its 'lustre' will disclose its inner *light* — an omnipresent word that in Chapman's poetry often points to the truth revealed by poetic expression.

In their attempt to translate Chapman's visual analogy into poetic terms, scholars have stressed the meanings of 'perspective' in the field of optics.

---

69 On *energeia*, or actuality, see Aristotle, *The Art of Rhetoric*, ed. and trans. by John Henry Freese (Heinemann, 1926), III. 11. 1–4, 1411b–1412a, pp. 404–07. Julius Caesar Scaliger, *Poetices libri septem* (Geneva: Jean Crispin, 1561), p. 116, col. 2, renders the term as 'efficacia' and 'vis orationis', while Sidney translates it as 'forcibleness' in the *Defence of Poesy*; see *Miscellaneous Prose of Sir Philip Sidney*, ed. by Katherine Duncan-Jones and Jan van Dorsten (Oxford University Press, 1973), p. 117. *Enargeia* — translated as *evidentia* — was raised to the status of a rhetorical category by Quintilian, *Institutio Oratoria*, ed. and trans. by H. E. Butter, 4 vols (Harvard University Press, 1920–1922), IV. 2. 63; VI. 2. 32; II, pp. 84–85, 434–37. Chapman could have merged Puttenham's two definitions:'That first quality the Greeks called *enargeia*, of this word *argos*, because it giveth a glorious luster and light. This latter they called *energeia* of *ergon*, because it wrought with a strong and virtuous [i.e. forceful] operation' (George Puttenham, *The Art of English Poesy*, ed. by Frank Whigham and Wayne A. Rebhorn (Cornell University Press, 2007), p. 227). On the theory and history of these two concepts, see Heinrich F. Plett, *Enargeia in Classical Antiquity and the Early Modern Age: The Aesthetics of Evidence* (Brill, 2012), esp. pp. 7–28, and 85–124.

Waddington reminds us of the term's frequent connotations of trickery, concluding that *enargia* constantly warns readers against the deceits of careless interpretation: a 'judicial perspective' thus counsels 'viewing experience [...] intelligently and with a moral responsibility'.[70] More recently, Jessica Wolfe has invoked Chapman's association with Harriot to suggest that the latter's work as developer of the telescope could have influenced the poet's notion that readers must rectify or clarify optically the obscurity of his text.[71] But Chapman's vocabulary of the visual arts is often intended more literally than metaphorically. The closest equivalent to the phrase 'judicial perspective' in the field of the visual arts is the commonly used term among sixteenth-century painters *giudizio dell'occhio* ('the eye's judgement'). As David Summers reminds us in his influential study of Michelangelo's aesthetics, this notion defines a trait 'possessed by the artist who departs from normative measure with complete mastery in response to the exigencies of practice'.[72] As an extension of the painter's *discrezione* ('discretion'), meaning the ability to transfer theoretical notions to daily practice, the eye's judgement places the skilled practitioner at odds with normative theory, often exposing its limitations. The painter's practical skills must transcend theory in the search for solutions for particular technical shortcomings — e.g. when a mechanical application of quantitative measures and proportions does not solve a compositional problem. The *giudizio dell'occhio* is a crucial aid to the gifted visual artist in the execution of compositional difficulty. Summers reminds us that *difficultà* is the most frequent and most important term of praise in late Renaissance painting and sculpture. In nature, its higher manifestation is the perfection of the human body in movement. In art, 'mastery of the living human body and the conquest of supreme *difficultà* were one and the same'.[73] Translated into Chapman's own terms, artistic *difficultà* is literally a matter of commanding the mysteries of 'motion, spirit and life'.

Yet the mastery of artistic difficulty was to little purpose without the existence of a knowledgeable audience of *giudiziosi* ('judicial beholders') and *intendenti* (Chapman calls his reader 'Understander' in the second preface to this work) — a minority whose training in the aesthetic appreciation of technical artifice prepared them for tasting the higher rewards of allegorical decoding and spiritual understanding of an artist's difficult inventions. For Summers, these terms, expressed in the writings of sixteenth-century theorists of painting, such as Giorgio Vasari's *Vite de piu eccellenti pittori, scultori e architettori* (1550), Vincenzo Danti's *Delle perfette proporzioni* (1567), Francisco

---

70 Waddington, *The Mind's Empire*, p. 151; see also pp. 117–19.
71 Wolfe, *Humanism*, pp. 163–88, discusses Chapman's concern with the eye's limitations and analyses the metaphor of optical technology as an aid to the reader's perception of poetic difficulty.
72 David Summers, *Michelangelo and the Language of Art* (Princeton University Press, 1981), p. 4.
73 Ibid., p. 184.

de Hollanda's *Da pintura antiga* (1548) or Giovanni Paolo Lomazzo's *Trattato dell'arte de la pittura* (1584), had their precedents in Giovanni Boccaccio's theories of poetic allegory and in the Renaissance art of the emblem.[74] The sixteenth century completed this interpenetration of the vocabularies of poetry and the visual arts. Titian captured the nude human figure in processes of motion and narrative change in his Ovidian mythological paintings. His series of six mythological tableaux commissioned by Philip II of Spain between 1553 and 1562 came to be known as *poesie*: in Titian, *poesia* refers to the easel painting as artefact as well as to the specific mythological content behind the composition.[75] To return to Chapman's analogy, the painter's technical vocabulary of ornamental colouring ('limn', 'heightening') and light ('lustre', 'shadow') that seeks the viewer's contemplation of the living body in motion correlates with the poet's expectations of the reader's appreciation of artifice as a path towards deeper understanding. Chapman's resort to mythological narratives and Ovidian subjects as contexts and materials for his 'high and hearty invention' must also be seen as an important component of his elaborate visual aesthetics.

Poetic conceits with a basis in the visual arts are a trademark of Chapman's poetry of the 1590s. These have often been read as confirmations of his notion of *enargia*: scholars have sought in these conceits hidden philosophical referents or, alternatively, as in Snare's opinion, confirmation of their quality as *artefacts* whose interest lies 'in bringing off a very complex invention'.[76] Yet the language of art supporting Chapman's visual conceits should dissuade us from regarding these two tendencies as inimical or incompatible. That the poet modified his terms, from the exclusive focus on poetry's commitment to 'the deep search of knowledge' in the preface to *SN* ('*SN*: To Roydon', line 1), to a more practical interest in the visual aesthetics of difficulty in the preface to *OBS*, clearly indicates a necessary extension of his scope, motivated by what he must have perceived as an insufficiency in the earlier proposal. In the latter volume, there is a concern with striking the difficult balance between two dimensions of his art that one may call — at the risk of oversimplifying — aesthetic and philosophical. His silent quotation of Plutarch's *Life of Homer* in his definition of '*schema*, varying in some rare fiction from popular custom' ('*OBS*: To Roydon', lines 6–7), as well as his insistence that poetic

---

74 Summers, *Michelangelo*, p. 182. Boccaccio argued that the function of poetic allegory is to 'protect' ('tegere') truth 'from the gaze of the irreverent' ('ab oculis torpentium auferre'). See *Genealogie deorum gentilium*, ed. by Vincenzo Romano, 2 vols (Laterza, 1951), XIV. 12, II, p. 715. For the translation, see *Boccaccio on Poetry*, ed. and trans. by Charles G. Osgood (The Liberal Art Press, 1956), p. 59. On the import of Boccaccio's theories in Chapman's poetry, see Luis-Martínez, 'Habit of Poesie', pp. 270–73.

75 Miguel Falomir, 'Titian and the *Poesie*: Experimentation and Freedom in Mythological Painting', in *Mythological Passions*, ed. by Miguel Falomir and Alejandro Vergara (Museo del Prado, 2021), pp. 15–39.

76 Snare, *Mystification*, p. 49.

obscurity must combat empty eloquence, stress the aesthetic dimension;[77] the endeavour to 'consecrate my strange poems to these searching spirits whom learning hath made noble, and nobility sacred' inclines towards philosophy ('*OBS*: To Roydon', lines 4–5). We should not try to find discord where the poet intended integration.[78]

Achilles Shield (1598), in its combination of Homeric translation, critical prose and programmatic verse, constitutes Chapman's most potent aesthetic statement of the 1590s. As a meditation on readers, poetic creation, and the relations between representation and its object, this peculiar work contains several clues to the poetic thinking of the earlier poems. The dedicatory preface to Essex opens with an account of the encoding and decoding of ekphrasis, on which the essential terms discussed in this section converge:

> Spondanus, one of the most desertfull Commentars of Homer, cals all sorts of all men learned to be judicial beholders of this more than Artificiall and no lesse than Divine Rapture, than which nothing can be imagined more full of soule and humaine extraction: for what is here prefigurde by our miraculous Artist but the universall world, which being so spatious and almost unmeasurable, one circlet of a Shield represents and imbraceth?[79]

In the god Vulcan but also in Homer, the two 'miraculous Artist[s]' of the shield, rapture and artifice are compatible sides of the creative process. Whereas Plato, in *Ion*, opposed τέχνη, or art, to ἐνθουσιασμός, or inspiration, Chapman does not need to conceive of them as inimical terms.[80] The 'universall world' that becomes the absolute object of artistic invention is described as 'spatious and almost unmeasurable', thus defying all rules of quantitative proportion. For that reason, its containment in 'one circlet of a shield', the result of poetic *enargia*, is made possible by the work of the artist's judicial eye. As Lomazzo reminds us of Michelangelo's frequent sayings:

> neither all the skill in geometry and Arithmeticke, nor the examples of the Perpectiues could any white profite a man without the eie, that is, without *the practice of the eie* [*l'essercitazione dell'occhio*]; whereby he *learneth how to behold things so* [*saper veder*], that he may bee *able to expresse them by hande* [*far fare alla mano*].[81]

---

77 On Chapman's use of Plutarch, see Commentary: '*OBS*: To Roydon', lines 6–8.
78 Elsewhere I have called the integration of these two dimensions 'didactic aestheticism'. See Luis-Martínez, 'Friendlesse Verse', and 'Habit of Poesie', esp. pp. 269–78.
79 *Achilles Shield* (1598): 'To the Most Honored Earle, Earle Marshall', in Nicoll, I, p. 543.
80 On this opposition and its pertinence to epic and lyric poetry, see Plato, *Ion*, 533E–534A, in *The Statesman, Philebus, Ion*, ed. and trans. by Harold N. Fowler (Harvard University Press, 1975), pp. 420–21.
81 Giovanni Paolo Lomazzo, *A Tracte Containing the Artes of Curious Paintinge Carvinge & Buildinge*, trans. by R. H. (Oxford: Richard Haydock, 1598), v. 7, p. 198. Italian original: *Trattato dell'arte della pittura, scoltura, et architettura* (Milano: Paolo Gottardo Pontio, 1584), v. 7, p. 262. Emphasis added.

Finally, learning is the quality of the *giudiziosi* and the *intendenti*, whose eye must make full sense of the complex nature behind the difficult invention. Chapman's interpretation of Homer's invention is therefore one in which minute attention to the shield's visual details matters as much as overall form and what the translator calls the 'ground of his invention'. Thus, 'all things described here by our divinest Poet' should be conceived of 'as if they consisted not of hard and solid mettals but of *a truely living and moving soul*'. The transformation of stasis into motion, of metal into soul, of 'the Orbiguitie of the Shield' into the 'roundnesse of the world', sums up the function and purpose of poetry. The artefacts designed by Vulcan — 'those Tripods of Vulcan and that Daedalian Venus αὐτοκινητέος [self-moving]' — epitomize the animating quality to which Chapman's verse aspires.[82]

We should follow Chapman's guide to his practical poetics when attempting to interpret his early poems. The process must necessarily begin with attention to how language pursues the representation of 'motion, spirit and life'. Only after this stage will our appreciation of form and structure and a more integral apprehension of sense ensue — even if, ideally, the trained poetic habit would perform some of these operations simultaneously. The remainder of this section thus concerns the first step, while the others are tackled in the subsequent two sections. The Commentary further attends to how this dimension of Chapman's art is materialized in other passages.

The description of Niobe's fountain at the beginning of 'Banquet' (stanzas 3–8) serves as a first instance, mainly because the frequent insistence on the function of this passage as a visual metaphor for the formal design and the overall meaning of the poem has often taken for granted its more immediate effects. In 1984, Janet Levarie Smarr construed the two pyramids crowned by a circular Sun and Moon of transparent glass that project light on Chapman's statue of Niobe as a symbol for the geometrical structure of the three poems of *OBS*: thus, in 'Banquet', Chapman would have arranged numerologically Ovid's ascent from the baser senses of smell and hearing to the highest sense, sight, the pyramid's apex, later to descend to touch and taste. The two circles that crown the pyramid — 'On whose sharp brows Sol and Titanides | In purple and transparent glass were hewed' ('Banquet', 6. 3–4) — would represent the circular crown of sonnets of 'Coronet' and the also circular movement of 'Zodiac', thus rounding off the volume's carefully planned proportional structure.[83] On a different note, the anamorphic statue of Niobe has been taken as a trope for the contrast between right and deceptive interpretation of the whole poem, thus insisting on

---

82 'To the Most Honored Earle, Earle Marshall', in Nicoll, I, p. 543, emphasis added. For a similar account, see Wolfe, *Humanism*, pp. 170–78, which discusses the relationship between Chapman's treatment of light and darkness in his poems with the painter's technique of *chiaroscuro*.
83 Janet Levarie Smarr, 'The Pyramid and the Circle: "Ovid's Banquet of Sense"', *Philological Quarterly*, 63.3 (1984), pp. 369–86.

Chapman's endorsement of a correct moral reading that would ultimately condemn Ovid's yielding to sensual pleasure:[84]

> So cunningly to optic reason wrought
>   That, afar off, it shewed a woman's face,
> Heavy and weeping; but, more nearly viewed,
> Nor weeping, heavy, nor a woman shewed. ('Banquet', 3. 6-9)

These lines are an instance of ekphrastic description of a statue made in accordance with the technique of anamorphosis: while from an appropriate distance the beholder will see a woman crying, the view from a shorter distance will reveal little else than a mass of stone whose most outstanding feature is the loss of all the statue's qualities as an imitation of a living human body's 'motion, spirit and life'.[85] Chapman's source, Natale Conti's *Mythologiae* (in its 1581 edition), specifies that the original statue was carved 'in the shape of a jagged precipice' ('praeruptam crepidinem').[86] In 'Banquet', Emperor Augustus has had the statue brought to his garden, where he orders the completion of the statuary by the addition of Niobe's fourteen dead children with breasts pierced by arrows, with 'looks so deadly sad, so lively done' that they become vivid images of a 'death' that 'lived' when lying 'apposed' to 'violent Niobe' ('Banquet', 5. 7-9). Moreover, we discover that the purpose of carving a sun and moon in transparent purple glass on top of the adjoining pyramids is to colour the dead children's bodies intermittently, making their breasts 'seem with blood imbrued' as they are murdered by Apollo and Diana ('Banquet', 6. 6).[87]

Chapman's pride in the difficulty of his writing is made self-evident. The problem with reading this complex sculptural set concerns the poet's demands on the reader's decoding abilities at this particular point. Are we being asked to meditate on the moral difference between looking from 'afar off' or viewing

---

84 Waddington, *The Mind's Empire*, pp. 129-32, and pp. 141-51. Waddington's conclusion admits no ambiguity of perspective: 'Although *Ovid's Banquet* is constructed to permit two different perspectives on the action and interpretations of meaning, I do not believe there can be any possibility that Chapman considered the perspectives equally valid' (p. 143). For a reading of Niobe's epistemological status as 'stone' or 'statue' in Marlowe's *Dido, Queen of Carthage*, which suggests the possibility that Chapman may have been inspired by his earlier associate, see Jonathan P. A. Sell, 'A Tragedy of Oversight: Visual Praxis in Christopher Marlowe's *Dido, Queen of Carthage*', *Medieval & Renaissance Drama in England*, 29 (2016), pp. 130-53 (pp. 131-34).
85 The anamorphic image, when observed from a conventional viewpoint, presents a misshapen figure that reveals its regular form only when the viewpoint shifts to an unusual angle. Hans Holbein the Younger's *The Ambassadors* (1536) is the standard example in sixteenth-century painting. For discussions of anamorphosis in painting and poetry, see Ernest Gilman, *The Curious Perspective: Literary and Pictorial Wit in the Seventeenth Century* (Yale University Press, 1978), which discusses its literary treatments in the context of other optical devices.
86 See Commentary: 'Banquet', 3-5, for a more detailed account of the source.
87 For Niobe's story, see Ovid, *Metamorphoses*, VI. 165-312 (ed. and trans. by Frank Justus Miller, 2 vols (Harvard University Press, 1951), I, pp. 298-309).

'nearly', as Waddington suggests? Are we being forced to detect the hidden numerical figures that will display the proportional forms and reveal the altered Neoplatonic hierarchy of the senses of Chapman's pyramid-shaped poem and its adjoining circular pieces, as Smarr proposes? Or are we *simply* being encouraged to focus on the oxymoron of a death that lives in order to derive from its artifice the intricacy of Chapman's poetic statuary? *Simply*, not because of its lack of difficulty, but because this latter option is the only one that relies on the immediacy of the text. What matters at this level of reading is the anamorphic composite of Niobe's seemingly living and moving body metamorphosed into a dead mass of stone — a clear instance of what Clark Hulse calls the 'metamorphic image'[88] — as well as the elaborate colouring device that depends both on nature (sunlight) and art (carved glass): dead stone becomes living art as it is 'cunningly to *optic reason* wrought', that is, designed by the artist's *giudizio dell'occhio* and then apprehended by the viewer's 'judicial perspective'. If we further attend to the language of the Renaissance visual arts, in turning her body toward her children's corpses, 'violent Niobe' displays the winding, spiral movement known as *figura serpentinata*, in which she 'deplore[s]', or pours herself — in tears feigned by the fountain's water — to 'a stone sepulchre' ('Banquet', 4. 7).[89] Niobe's story ends in Ovidian metamorphosis, and Chapman's translational skills stress the metamorphic nature of art: it is art's *difficultà* that transforms life into death, moving flesh into flowing tears, flowing tears into dead and rigid stone, and dead and rigid stone back into seemingly living and supple flesh.

The metamorphic quality of art appeals to the physical and intellectual eye as it prepares the reader for the scene's climax: 'To these dead forms came living beauty's essence, | Able to make them startle with her presence' ('Banquet', 6. 8–9). Corinna's irruption into the scene accompanied by a group of attending maids displaces the previous group of stone figures from the centre of the reader's attention. To the previous focus on art's metamorphosis of death into life, we must now add a new transition from sorrow to pleasure. Corinna's female figure comes wrapped in the volatile swiftness of her semi-transparent 'loose robe' and the 'downward-burning flame | Of her rich hair' ('Banquet', 7. 3–4), which by dint of another metamorphic trope

---

88 This kind of poetic image 'gradually extinguishes all points of unlikeness' between objects, thus suggesting 'the ecstasy or terror of the flesh made free to move across the categories of substance' (Clark Hulse, *Metamorphic Verse: The Elizabethan Minor Epic* (Princeton University Press, 1981), p. 7).
89 On the *figura serpentinata*, see John Shearman, *Mannerism* (Penguin, 1967), pp. 81–91; and Summers, *Michelangelo*, pp. 15–16, 28, 60–61, 87, 94. The formulation is found in Lomazzo, *Trattato*, I. 1, pp. 22–23; English translation; *Tracte*, p. 17: 'It is reported that *Michael Angelo* vpon a time gaue this observation to the Painter *Marcus de Sciena* his scholler, *that he should alwaies make a figure Pyramidall, Serpentlike [serpentinata], and multiplied by one two and three*. In which precept (in mine opinion) the whole mysterie of the arte consisteth. For the grace and life that a picture can haue is that it expresse *Motion*: which the Painters call the *spirite* of a picture [*furia de la figura*]'.

resolves into the swift and proud image of Phaeton's burning chariot — a figure that introduces the keys to allegorical, moral readings.[90] The doffing of her robe has the effect of evacuating other centres of attention:

> Then cast she off her robe, and stood upright:
> As lightning breaks out of a labouring cloud,
> Or as the morning heav'n casts off the night,
> Or as that heav'n cast off itself and showed
>   Heav'n's upper light, to which the brightest day
> Is but a black and melancholy shroud,
>   Or as when Venus strived for sovereign sway
> Of charmful beauty in young Troy's desire,
> So stood Corinna, vanishing her tire. ('Banquet', 8)

'Vanishing' robes displaying nude female bodies are everywhere in sixteenth- and seventeenth-century mythological paintings — Titian's six *poesie* can be invoked again here. Yet Corinna's 'upright', frontal nude is also a fleeting presence in Chapman's composition: a triple simile disposed in ascending climax (8. 2–6) provokes another vanishing effect whereby the gaze is displaced from Corinna's body toward heavenly light.[91] In Renaissance paintings, we often see light in the form of cloud-rending lightning, or in the mere display of 'Heav'n's upper light' breaking through the day, or in the more complex allegorical fiction of Aurora's displacement of the night as she ascends to heaven. Giulio Romano's *Birth of Bacchus* (c. 1540), Titian's *St John the Evangelist on Patmos* (1553) or Guido Reni's *Aurora* (1612) may be invoked as visual referents for these three similes.[92] When tenor and vehicle are juxtaposed here, the effect is less that of typical comparison than the temporary disappearance of the tenor: Corina's 'vanishing' of her tire deprives us even of the clear image of her body and leaves us with sheer, dazzling light, as if our gaze were directed to the upper, heavenly part of a canvas. Yet a fourth simile (8. 7–8) restores Corinna to the centre in a new movement that involves another sort of 'vanishing'. She is now like Venus in her 'striv[ing]' for 'sway', as the goddess of love poses with Juno and Pallas in symmetry-breaking *contrapposto*, awaiting Paris's judgement. 'Sway' means here both advancing motion and triumphant authority, or rather it means motion in the act of striving for triumph. A hundred-year tradition ranging from

---

90 Both Niobe and Phaeton have been read by Chapman scholars as warning signals of Corinna's pride. See Louise Vinge, 'Chapman's *Ovids Banquet of Sence*: Its Sources and Theme', *Journal of the Warburg and Courtauld Institutes*, 38 (1975), pp. 234–57 (pp. 235–37), doi:10.2307/750955; and Darryl Gless, 'Chapman's Ironic Ovid', *English Literary Renaissance*, 9.1 (1979), pp. 21–41, doi:10.1111/j.1475-6757.1979.tb01396.x.
91 I am deeply grateful to Clark Hulse, whose email reply to a question of mine about this stanza inspired the present discussion.
92 Giulio Romano, *The Birth of Bacchus* (c. 1540, The Getty Museum, Los Angeles); Titian, *Saint John the Evangelist on Patmos* (c. 1553–1555, National Gallery of Art, Washington, DC); Guido Reni, *L'Aurora* (c. 1613/1614, Casino Dell'Aurora Pallavicini, Rome). See Visual Sources.

Cranach to Rubens could help us to see the goddesses' *contrapposto* exaggerated to achieve a *figura serpentinata*.[93] However, in Chapman's simile Juno and Minerva are made as invisible by Venus's arresting beauty as Niobe and her children or Corinna's own maids are by the entrance of Corinna. When stanzas 9 and 10 provide the background to this sight in the form of a neat catalogue of garden plants and flowers — the same that drew Allott's attention in *Englands Parnassus*[94] — readers cannot but take its orderly tediousness as a soothing respite to their exhausted visual imaginations.

Chapman's writing in these stanzas occupies an initial reading in more immediate tasks than the moral or allegorical interpretations that may take shape at later re-readings. The lines encourage attention to their display of pictorial *difficultà* through poetic *enargia*. At the beginning of 'Banquet', this exercise functions mainly at the basic level of description. By contrast, in the central section of 'Cynthiam' (208-399), the second part of SN, *enargia* is put at the service of a more ambitious (and perhaps less accomplished) experiment in narrative virtuosity. Here the goddess Cynthia awaits the night to ascend to heaven, and, in order to pass the day's tedious hours, she devotes her magic powers to devising an elaborate entertainment. Out of 'a dazzling meteor' she fashions the nymph Euthymia. Then she produces new figures in the shapes of hunters and Actaeon's seventeen hounds out of 'flowers', 'shadows', 'mists' and 'meteors'. After metamorphosing Euthymia into a panther, a hunting scene ensues with the spectral hunters and hounds in chase of the no less spectral nymph. But this time the poet has decided to supply at least part of the moral interpretation in parallel to the narrative:

> And marvel not a nymph so rich in grace
> To hounds' rude pursuits should be giv'n in chase,
> For she could turn herself to every shape
> Of swiftest beasts, and at her pleasure scape —
> Wealth fawns on fools, virtues are meat for vices,
> Wisdom conforms herself to all earth's guises,
> Good gifts are often giv'n to men past good,
> And noblesse stoops sometimes beneath his blood.
>
> ('Cynthiam', 224-31)

This and other similar remarks alert the reader to a need to read the poem allegorically. Yet narrative progressively gains ground over moral enunciation, and the new digressive material that the poem offers while recounting the nymph's chase is of another sort. Similes of a certain length are a frequent device in Chapman's verse — a technique that he must have learned directly from his readings and translations of Homer. Mythology is a frequent source of similes in Homer, as it is in Chapman. However, good similes must be

---

93 See Lucas Cranach the Elder, *The Judgement of Paris* (1528, The Metropolitan Museum of Art, New York); Peter Paul Rubens, *The Judgement of Paris* (c. 1638, Museo del Prado, Madrid). See Visual Sources.
94 Allott, *Englands Parnassus*, pp. 354-55.

based on contrast and, as the main narrative subject now is itself a mythological fantasy, the element of contrast is sought in an earthlier sort of reality. Thus, the hounds' entrance into a thorny thicket that rends their skin and flesh is compared to the daily life of a group of schoolboys turned nightmare as they are surprised in the midst of their leisure by a ravenous wild animal ('Cynthiam', 256-66). The purpose is hardly allegorical here, and poetic artifice aims to offer the reader both scenes simultaneously. Later, the hounds turn game when they are surprised by a group of spirits lying in ambush within a grove, and a new simile provides a detailed account of the skirmish by which Sir Francis Vere defeated the Duke of Parma on 24 July 1591, during the Spanish siege of the Fort of Knodensburgh, facing the Dutch town of Nijmegen ('Cynthiam', 328-49). This scene has drawn readers' attention to Chapman's use of historical sources and to the suggestions that it opens for biographical research — particularly if it is assumed that the poet could have been a participant and therefore an eyewitness to the event.[95] Yet, even beyond the political effects that the poet may have sought by such vindication of national military pride, the two scenes hardly relate to each other, and their primary appeal is again aesthetic contrast through their mere juxtaposition. Seeking its meaning elsewhere may contravene the explanation provided by the glossarist's voice in the original quarto edition: 'And these like similes, in my opinion, drawn from the honourable deeds of our noble countrymen, clad in comely habit of poesy, would become a poem as well as further-fetched grounds, if such as be poets nowadays would use them' ('Cynthiam', Gloss 19). 'Habit' means clothing now, which makes the statement an overt vindication of the varied possibilities of poetic ornament and artifice. Chapman's narrative invites his judicial reader to carry out swift imaginative transitions from mythological fantasy to allegory, daily life and epic history, and then back again to its own mythic universe. For comparison's sake, one may recall the effect of Icarus falling in the waters near a sixteenth-century-looking fisherman, shepherd and ploughman, and amidst several three-masted warships, in Brueghel's *Landscape with the Fall of Icarus* (1555; see Visual Sources). Beyond the allegorical interpretations that they may elicit, the display of artistic difficulty in both the painting and the poem is materialized in their questioning of the homogeneity and hierarchy of the genre conventions of their respective arts.[96]

---

95 For Chapman's sources, see Commentary: 'Cynthiam', 326-49. For a critical commentary on this simile as political allegory, see Waddington, *The Mind's Empire*, pp. 73-78.
96 The theory of the hierarchy of genres in painting — from higher to lower, 1) history painting, 2) portraiture, 3) genre painting (depicting aspects of daily life), 4) landscape, 5) still life — was not formulated until the second half of the seventeenth century. See Emelyn Butterfield Rosen, 'The Hierarchy of Genres and the Hierarchy of Life-Forms', *Res: Anthropology and Aesthetics*, 73-74 (2020), pp. 76-93, doi:10.1086/711228. This theory emerged from the practice of specialization in the late medieval and Renaissance painters' workshops (E. H. Gombrich, *Norm and Form: Studies in the Art of the Renaissance*

However, Chapman's deliberate pursuit of that species of poetic difficulty that I have called 'translational', the conceptual basis of which lies in the Renaissance visual arts, should not conceal the obvious fact that the raw material of his poetry is the verbal medium. Words have ceased to be a primary concern of recent Chapman critics, who have preferred to excavate the roots of his obscurity in abstruse philosophical ideas. But the work of earlier scholars should remind us that the source of Chapman's difficulty lies in his style. J. M. Robertson called him 'the supreme neologist among the [Elizabethan] poets'.[97] Sister Maria del Rey Kelly's unpublished doctoral thesis on the diction of Chapman's poems remains an invaluable repository of his extraordinary verbal usages — and her work has a more potent influence upon this edition than frequent citation can recognize.[98] For Kelly, the poet's 'sometimes brilliant, almost always erratic coinages, his grammatically intricate compounds, and his private and particularized meanings attached to certain words' are the marks of 'the mode of diction ordinarily employed by Chapman in achieving his admittedly extraordinary effects'.[99] To this list we should add a deliberately winding syntax, the perplexing effects of which are aggravated by the often erratic punctuation of the original quartos; here, a deliberate obscuring and the material vicissitudes of print may join hands in increasing the quantity and quality of what Steiner terms 'contingent' poetic difficulty. Margaret Bottrall, whose work remains the most lucid account of Chapman's difficulty to date, depicts his struggles with poetic expression:

> Chapman felt the conversion into words of a dimly apprehended idea, or of a strongly felt emotion, to be a very difficult and hazardous process; involving the risk that his real meaning might be thwarted and obscured by the necessity of using a material medium, words, for its expression. In short, he knew that he could often see and feel things better than he could say them. A sense of imperfection is common to all poets, but not all are troubled by Chapman's fear of inarticulateness and unintelligibility.[100]

Yet Bottrall's convincing argument risks overstating the case of the poet's confessed sense of faltering expression. The question is less his fear of failure than his belief that the complexity of artistic vision demands a degree of accuracy of expression that can only be achieved in the act of straining one's diction.

Chapman's radical commitment to linguistic *difficultà* is nowhere felt more strongly than in his syntax. Kelly's affirmation that *SN* sets 'the basic diction

---

(Phaidon, 1978), p. 109). The mixing of genres is therefore conceived of as a display of mastery.
97 J. M. Robertson, *Shakespeare and Chapman* (T. Fisher Unwin, 1917), p. 54.
98 Sister Maria del Rey Kelly, *Poetic Diction in the Nondramatic Works of George Chapman* (unpublished doctoral dissertation, Fordham University, 1965).
99 Ibid., p. 7.
100 Bottrall, 'George Chapman's Defence of Difficulty', p. 642.

pattern that was to be Chapman's mode of expression up to his last published work' should make us seek our standard examples in that poem.[101] A passage from 'Noctem' serves as the theme of the principal instance discussed here: 'Chaos had soul without a body then, | Now bodies live without the souls of men — | Lumps being digested, monsters in our pride' (47–49). The starting point is the contrast between an original Chaos, whose 'soul' explains its secret order, with the chaos that Chapman sees in his own times, in which matter lacks an informing soul. This principle is illustrated with a long Homeric simile, the first of many in this poem and in Chapman's extensive oeuvre:

> And as a wealthy fount that hills did hide,
> Let forth by labour of industrious hands,
> Pours out her treasure through the fruitful strands,
> Seemly divided to a hundred streams,
> Whose beauties shed such profitable beams
> And make such Orphean music in their courses
> That cities follow their enchanting forces,
> Who, running far, at length each pours her heart
> Into the bosom of the gulfy desert,
> As much confounded there and indigest
> As in the chaos of the hills compressed,
> So all things now (extract out of the prime)
> Are turned to chaos, and confound the time. ('Noctem', 50–62)

The eleven-line comparative clause of the simile's vehicle contains a succession of embedded relative, participle and final clauses whose meandering progress imitates the 'hundred streams' that sustain its figurative force, curiously creating a linguistic counterpart to the pictorial *figura serpentinata*. Through these clauses, the poet narrates how a subterranean well emerges to the surface as the result of human art, which directs its course into multiple rivers; the wealth that these streams bring, embodied in the 'Orphean music in their courses', attracts human life and encourages the building of cities on their banks; but these streams end in the 'gulfy desert', where their courses blur and dissolve as if disappearing again into the shapeless subterranean spring in which they originated — two centuries in anticipation of Coleridge's *Kubla Khan* (1797). The concluding two-line tenor explains that, in a similar way, the brave new world that originated in primordial Chaos ('extract out of the prime') turns to a shapeless modern chaos that 'confound[s] the time'. Through powerful visual images, the poet compresses into a few lines a narrative of human creation whose civilizing powers ominously end in destruction — 'And 'mid this tumult Kubla heard from far | Ancestral voices prophesying war!'.[102] The pictorialism of Chapman's verbs proceeds by

---

101 Kelly, *Poetic Diction*, p. 11.
102 Samuel Taylor Coleridge, 'Kubla Khan', lines 29–30, in *Coleridge's Poetry and Prose*, ed. by Nicholas Halmi, Paul Magnuson and Raimonda Modiano (Norton, 2004), p. 182.

antithesis, thus 'compress[ing]' a chaos which human action 'let[s] forth'. Kelly, and Nicoll in his edition of *Chapman's Homer*, identifies 'gulfy' as the poet's neologism. Both Nicoll's definition as 'deep as an abyss' and *OED*'s 'full of eddies and whirlpools' are of relevance here. Kelly believes that it is the *OED* sense that prevails, and notes the oxymoron that ensues from the phrase 'gulfy desart'. Yet depth is also part of the adjective's paradoxical force: in Chapman's image, the desert absorbs the disappearing waters into its subterranean entrails, or 'bosom'.[103]

The overall effect of the simile is one in which words and syntax contribute a painting of a complex cosmological abstraction in identifiable geological terms. Chapman's similes often turn abstract concepts into sensory realities. These can be of a moral sort: thus, the former idea of chaos's loss of purity acquires overtones in his imagination of man's primeval innocence corrupted by his own passions. The simile explains now how man's 'ambition and self-desire' deform his moral sense just as a baby roe deer ('chevril') shrinks as it is roasted in the fire:

> All this world was named
> A world of him, for whom it first was framed,
> (Who, like a tender chevril, shrunk with fire
> Of base ambition and of self-desire,
> His arms into his shoulders crept for fear
> Bounty should use them and fierce rape forbear,
> His legs into his greedy belly run,
> The charge of hospitality to shun);
> In him the world is to a lump reversed,
> That shrunk from form, that was by form dispersed.
>
> ('Noctem', 93–102)

Once again, the twisted, elliptical syntax replicates the shrinking, shapeless body — an effect of the arms creeping into the shoulders and the legs bending onto the belly — as an attribute that is simultaneously predicated on the contracting animal's corpse and the moribund human soul. Phyllis Bartlett has argued that Chapman's abstractions are often given 'hands [and] feet':[104] this could be hardly more literal here. The neologism 'chevril' is a borrowing from French whose original Latin term, *capreolus*, clarifies its diminutive form. The word itself suggests the creature's frail and 'tender' nature in its succession of two fricatives which a fiery, crepitating 'r' disintegrates into the softer liquid 'l'.

Even some of Chapman's frequent Latinate coinages seem possessed of an unusual capacity to add unexpected nuances to concrete action. Thus, the 'Olympic sky' can 'embrace' the universe 'with tender circumvecture' ('Cynthiam', 199–200). The poet calls the distribution of light and darkness

---

[103] See Kelly, *Poetic Diction*, p. 30; and Nicoll, I, p. 713; see also footnote to 'Noctem', 58.
[104] Phyllis Brooks Bartlett, 'Stylistic Devices in Chapman's *Iliads*', *PMLA*, 57.3 (1942), pp. 661–75 (p. 663), doi:10.2307/458767.

along the universe their 'expansure' ('Noctem', 75). Translating and borrowing from French, the 'certain sphere' of a lady's neck materializes into a 'marble pillar and her lineature' ('Zodiac', 20. 3, 21. 2). The extraordinary suffix '-ure' seems to stamp a perfective aspect upon the action of occupying certain spaces. By contrast, other suffixes acquire equally unusual continuous senses:

> The virtue-tempered mind ever preserves
> Oils and *expulsatory* balm that serves
> To quench lust's fire in all things it anoints.
> ('Cynthiam', 132–34, emphasis added)

As in the previous instances, an abstraction is provided with surprising sensory qualities.

The list of effects could be endless, and the reader must be referred to Kelly and others, as well as to the Commentary in this edition, for further examples. For the present purposes, a final example from 'Banquet' illustrates how Chapman's verbal audacity can complicate one of the poem's textual cruxes:

> This said, he charged the arbour with his eye,
> Which pierced it through, and at her breasts reflected,
> Striking him to the heart with ecstasy,
> As do the sunbeams, gainst the earth *porrected*,
>   With their reverberate vigour mount in flames,
> And burn much more than when they were directed.
> ('Banquet', 49. 1–6, emphasis added)

'Porrected' is the present edition's emendation of Q$_{OB}$'s 'prorected', which all previous editors and commentators have accepted as Chapman's new coinage. Kelly devotes three pages to the discussion of this word, which in her opinion combines the Latin prefix *pro-* with the past-participle form of Latin *rego* (to lead) in order to form an adjective that means 'led straight along, drawn in a straight line'.[105] The meaning makes perfect sense, were there not already an English word, 'porrect', and its derivate adjective 'porrected', with that exact meaning: it derives from Latin *porrigo* (*OLD* defines it as 'to stretch out, straight out, extend', and also lists the past participle form *porrectus*). Its use, extant in English since the fourteenth century, is audacious enough as a poetic choice and reflects Chapman's keenness on Latinisms. The emendation is carried out on the basis that one should not make up a new word where there is one at hand. Yet Chapman's inventive capacities should not entirely rule out the option that to the present editor seems the result of a compositor's mistake when trying to make sense of an odd authorial choice. Ultimately, compositors, editors, critics and general readers must be taken as collaborative parties in the challenging trial-and-error game of interpreting Chapman's text 'judicially'.

---

105 Kelly, *Poetic Diction*, p. 107.

3. Genre

The extent to which the poet's judicial eye enables an individual poetic programme that is not bound to strict theoretical rules does not mean that there is not in Chapman's early poetry an attentive observance of traditions and principles with a basis in classical and Renaissance poetics. There are at least two interrelated fields which prove particularly productive in the shaping of these two collections: genre and metrical form. The more technical aspects of the latter are deferred to the Appendix. The former occupies the present section, as it remains an unexplored area of Chapman criticism. As Waddington aptly reminds us, Chapman's self-conception as a vatic poet makes his voice operate 'consciously in a public mode'. For this sort of poet, 'the question of genre occupies a position of fundamental importance', as it supplies 'a formal organizational principle for his matter' and elicits 'a generally appropriate level of response from his audience'.[106] Waddington considers genre an aspect of 'external form', supplying a recognizable vessel for the more transcendent 'inner form' of the poems: the latter is made of their less material — i.e. numerological, geometrical — structures, as well as of their dense mythological and philosophical content, allegorical and typological reinterpretations of which shape the poems' ultimate meaning.[107] Waddington's interest in mythic form leads in his study to a cursory and somewhat mechanical consideration of genre. He affirms that 'In his nondramatic verse — with a single and deliberate exception, *Ovids Banquet of Sence* — Chapman published nothing that did not have a distinct generic identity'.[108] The statement fares better without the exception, and the following pages will try to substantiate both the distinctiveness and the interconnectedness of the genre choices shaping *SN* and *OBS*. By making it an indispensable part of the poem's *difficultà*, Chapman's idea of genre as 'an instrument and not an end' guides the creative handling of poetic form as a crucial vehicle for his poetic vision.[109]

3.1. 'The Shadow of Night'

The full title of Chapman's debut volume, Σκία νυκτός, *The Shadow of Night, Containing Two Poetical Hymns*, reveals its unmistakeable generic identity. The bilingual title vindicates the Hellenic ancestry of the two-part poem. This tradition comprises a wide range of texts whose more representative specimens are the Homeric hymns (in the past attributed to Homer, although composed in the seventh and sixth centuries BC), the hymns of Callimachus (second century BC), the later Orphic hymns (second century AD) and the Neoplatonic hymns of Proclus (fifth century AD). But the few commentaries

---

106 Waddington, *The Mind's Empire*, pp. 10–12.
107 Ibid., pp. 14–16.
108 Ibid., p. 12.
109 The phrasing is from MacLure, *George Chapman*, p. 9.

on the poem's genre have often gone against some of its obvious identity signs. Thus, Roy Battenhouse reads 'Noctem', the first part, as a quasi-tragic ritual of purgative destruction, serving as a prelude to 'Cynthiam', the second part, in which the advent of the Moon goddess brings comedic renovation.[110] Battenhouse's argument rightly stresses the poem's unity, but tragedy and comedy remain alien to its nature. Waddington, who attends to the poem's use of the hymn, concludes that 'Chapman's poetic strategy is narrative rather than lyric', thus favouring philosophical interpretation of its mythic content over the 'intuitive apprehension of essences' that is often associated with the hymn's magical-religious spirit.[111]

However, the lyric and narrative modes are consubstantial to the hymn as genre, serving both structural and performative purposes. This convergence is apparent in the compositional principles of the hymn as they were systematized in early treatises of epideictic rhetoric, particularly in Menander Rhetor's Περὶ Ἐπιδεικτικῶν (third century AD), whose ideas Chapman could have known directly or through the summary by Julius Caesar Scaliger in Book III of *Poetices libri septem* (1560), or through Natale Conti's re-elaboration in the first book of his *Mythologiae* — the major source for *SN*.[112] Menander's generic classification is of relevance to Chapman's practice:

> Following our original division, let us first consider hymns to the gods. These hymns themselves are either (1–2) kletic (κλητικοί) or apopemptic (ἀποπεμπτικοί), or (3–4) scientific (φυσικοί) or mythical (μυθικοί), or (5–6) genealogical (γενεαλογικοί) or fictitious (πεπλασμένοι), or (7–8) precatory (εὐκτικοί) or deprecatory (ἀπευκτικοί), or else combinations (μικτοί) of two, three, or indeed all of these.[113]

The first pair differentiates between invocations of a god's presence or valedictions on their departure; the second distinguishes between accounts of the nature and qualities of gods and the allegorical explanations of their actions; the third discriminates between the use of narrative material from poetic theogonies (i.e. divine aetiologies) and the poetic invention of fictions that personify less well-known deities and daemons; finally, the fourth pair sets the contrast between positive and negative prayer (i.e. requesting the fulfilment or avoidance of some event). But the most important point is the recognition that these categories seldom occur in isolation, and that their combinations result in a variety of mixed kinds, including the possibility that many or all kinds will converge in a single rhetorical or poetic piece.

---

110 Battenhouse, 'Chapman's *The Shadow of Night*', pp. 607–08.
111 Waddington, *The Mind's Empire*, p. 107.
112 Book I of Treatise I of Περὶ Ἐπιδεικτικῶν (*Of Epideictic Speeches*) treats the rhetoric of the hymns to the gods: see *Menander Rhetor: A Commentary*, ed. and trans. by D. A. Russell and N. G. Wilson (Oxford University Press, 1981), I. 1. 331–44, pp. 2–29. For Scaliger's treatment, see *Poetices libri septem*, III. 92, p. 162, col. 2. Conti deals with the composition of hymns in I. 16: 'De hymnis antiquorum', pp. 57–60; Mulryan, pp. 47–49.
113 *Menander Rhetor*, I. 1. 333. 1–7, pp. 6–7.

SN exemplifies Menander's mixed kind. The 'kletic' component — i.e. a poetic voice requests the presence of the ancient goddesses Night and Cynthia to a place that can be identified as the poet's England — is predominant over the 'precatory' — i.e. supplicatory — quality. A formal principle in Menander that links the elements of invocation and prayer also applies to both hymns: 'if prayer follows the invocation, poets and prose-writers alike have still less opportunity for extensive treatment of the topic'.[114] This means that between the opening invocation and the closing prayer a variety of scientific (i.e. philosophical), mythological or genealogical (two categories that Menander treats as similar), and fictional material can fashion a narrative body that fleshes out the lyric/performative skeleton of the poem. Chapman's observance of these principles permits the consideration of SN as a two-part hymn, a diptych containing independent kletic sections to Night ('Noctem', 1–28) and Cynthia ('Cynthiam', 1–63) at the beginning of each part, as well as several precatory passages, although only one pure prayer to the latter goddess brings about the poem's closure — thus confirming Battenhouse's view of 'Noctem' as a prelude to 'Cynthiam':

> Then, in thy clear and icy pentacle,
> Now execute a magic miracle:
> Slip every sort of poisoned herbs and plants,
> And bring thy rabid mastiffs to these haunts;
> Look with thy fierce aspect, be terror-strong,
> Assume thy wondrous shape of half a furlong,
> Put on thy feet of serpents, vip'rous hairs,
> And act the fearfull'st part of thy affairs;
> Convert the violent courses of thy floods,
> Remove whole fields of corn and hugest woods,
> Cast hills into the sea and make the stars
> Drop out of heav'n and lose thy marinars.
>   So shall the wonders of thy power be seen,
>   And thou for ever live the planet's queen. ('Cynthiam', 515–28)

As Menander's framework permits a great deal of flexibility in the observance of rules, the poet's discretional judgement (*giudizio*) can emerge as an important quality of his art. S. K. Heninger has argued that Chapman's main defects as a poet are his 'inattention to form' and the lack of 'a well-ordered structure', which generally result in 'long and formless' compositions.[115] However, in the case of SN the amplification of the invocation–request pattern through philosophical and narrative elements suggests creative imitation of a variety of generic traditions at his disposal: the scientific or

---

114 *Menander Rhetor*, I. 1. 335.1–2, pp. 10–11; see William H. Race, 'Aspects of Rhetoric and Form in Greek Hymns', *Greek, Roman and Byzantine Studies*, 23.1 (1982), pp. 5–14. Race discusses the beginning in second person, or *du-Stil*, and the final request in the prayer as frequent elements of the classical hymnic form.
115 Heninger, *Handbook of Renaissance Meteorology*, pp. 183, 199.

philosophical element connects Chapman's writing with the Orphic and Proclean tradition; the narrative component, with the longer literary hymns of Callimachus and particularly of the pseudo-Homer — and it must be recalled that Chapman published his full translation of the Homeric hymns in 1623.

Viewed in this light, Battenhouse's conviction that *SN* has 'a logical plan and a consecutive argument' can be fully granted.[116] The sketch that follows does not aim to establish an integral or definitive structure for the poem, but rather to suggest its compositional guidelines. In 'Noctem', kletic invocation occupies the first two verse paragraphs (1–20, 21–28); it then introduces genealogical matter by means of Hesiodic theogony: in the beginning of times, Night preceded Chaos and was its soul or informing principle (29–49). This benign picture of primordial Chaos is drawn in order to set an antithesis with the present times, in which a new and negative chaos and a 'stepdame Night of mind' (63) have brought 'Ruin' (89) to the world (50–90). The epic similes and analogies of mythological content that ensue after these lines (91–200) create a contrast between the mythical past space and time inhabited by the deities and heroes invoked by the hymnic voice, and the historical space and time that this same voice inhabits in his own present. The central lines of this first poem (201–40) are essential for illustrating the contrast between that longed-for primordial order and the devastation of the present times through the cyclical succession of Night and Day as monarchs of heaven. The analogy serves to establish the struggle between two life attitudes, nocturnal and diurnal, and the rhetorical vehicle is again mythological matter: the story of Vulcan's making of a golden bed for the Sun that rests in the ocean, which Chapman derived from Conti's *Mythologiae*,[117] and the lines in the Orphic hymn 'To Night' (3. 10–11) — also via Conti — in which Night confines daylight to hell.[118] It is after this incursion into mythological matter that the second half of 'Noctem' (241–382) resumes invocations to Night (247, 268), Hercules (255), and the 'living spirits' (288) that comprise the hymn's audience. They draw our attention to what William H. Race has defined as the 'one dominant concern to all Greek hymns': χάρις, in the sense of courting a deity's favourable disposition.[119] Among the rhetorical strategies related to this concern, the use of epithets of praise to name the goddess is frequent in Chapman's text: 'most tender fortress of our woes' (247), 'Rich-tapered sanctuary of the blest' (298) are the most remarkable names given to Night. The primary message of this part is the desire that Night's favour may

---

116 Battenhouse, 'Chapman's *The Shadow of Night*', p. 584.
117 v. 17, 'De Sole', p. 537; Mulryan, p. 444. See Commentary: 'Noctem', 204, 378–83, and Introduction, pp. 67–72, for further discussion of Chapman's use of this myth.
118 'De Nocte', III. 12, p. 232, trans. by Mulryan, p. 192. See Commentary: 'Noctem', 215–17.
119 Race, 'Aspects of Rhetoric', pp. 8–10. On this particular sense of χάρις, see Liddell, A. II. 2.

materialize in the arrival of her eternal kingdom, and the permanent banishment of Day. This desire presides over the Moon's (i.e. Cynthia's) entrance (383–403), in which new epithets — 'glorious bride of brides' (386), 'great Hyperion's hornèd daughter' (394) — make mythological narrative and genealogical description converge in this transition to the poem's second hymn, 'Cynthiam'. Thus, *Night* becomes *night*: the goddess dissolves into nocturnal time and space to proclaim the reign of Cynthia as true 'Empress' and sole protagonist of the poem.[120]

'Cynthiam', though somewhat longer, is structurally neater than its predecessor. Its orthodox kletic opening (1–63) and precatory closure (515–28) envelop a longer central part, at the heart of which is the autonomous narrative of Cynthia's creation of the shape-shifting nymph Euthymia and her pursuit by hunting spirits leading Actaeon's hounds (208–399).[121] Chapman's narrative responds to Menander's description of the fictitious hymns, whose focus on obscure gods, daemons or spirits rather than the well-known gods of myths and genealogies is adduced as proof of poetic 'inventiveness' (ἐπίνοια).[122] Menander cites as examples certain deified abstractions such as Jealousy (Ζηλοτυπία), Envy (Φθόνος) and Strife (Ἔρις); Chapman's Euthymia — a derivation of the Senecan/Plutarchan virtue Tranquillity of Mind (Εὐθυμία) — is one such invention.[123] The historical similes mentioned above that adorn this long fiction succeed in setting the contrast between the remote past and the immediate present, the gods' mythical universes and the speaker and listeners' historical world. These antithetical spaces are emphasized in the two sections that precede and succeed Euthymia's narrative (64–207 and 400–514). Both sections exploit facets that relate to what Menander calls the scientific hymn: they assess historical knowledge about the lunar goddess (65–81, 418–55), describe her worship (170–207), and unfold mythic and philosophical meanings around Cynthia's triple identity as Diana, Luna and Hecate (144–69, 456–514).[124]

Viewing Chapman's two-part hymn in the light of these classical precedents clarifies its form, structure and principles of composition. N. Richardson has affirmed that 'It is easy to see the longer *Homeric Hymns* as miniature narrative

---

120 For a compelling discussion of Chapman's sensorial, atmospheric treatment of night (lower case intended), see Susan Wiseman, '"Did we lie downe, because 'twas night?": John Donne, George Chapman and the Senses of Night in the 1590s', in *The Senses of Early Modern England, 1558–1660*, ed. by Simon Smith, Jackie Watson and Amy Kenny (Manchester University Press, 2015), pp. 130–47 (pp. 139–43).
121 For further discussion of this crucial part of 'Cynthiam', see Introduction, pp. 92–99, as well as Commentary: 'Cynthiam', 208–399.
122 *Menander Rhetor*, I. 1. 342.20, pp. 24–25.
123 Ibid., I. 1. 342.7–9, pp. 22–25. For Chapman's reliance on Seneca and Plutarch, see Commentary: 'Cynthiam', 207–19.
124 For a more extensive treatment of this triple identity in the light of Conti's *Mythologiae* and other sources, as well as recent scholarly discussions, see Commentary: 'Cynthiam', 144–69, 456–514.

epics'.¹²⁵ Chapman's narrative content and his use of 'Our native robes (put on with skilful hands, | English heroics)' ('Cynthiam', 90–91) testify to his anglicization of these epic features and to his observance of the high style. This specification of the poem's metrical traits — heroic couplets in iambic pentameter — is important, as it signals the formal vehicle that accompanies other stylistic features of the epic poem such as epithets and similes. Recent critical focus on the narratological pattern of the Greek literary hymn is also of interest here. Regarding the hymns of Homer and Callimachus, scholars have differentiated two kinds: mimetic and non-mimetic. The mimetic hymns are poetic imitations of ritual scenes, even if they were not written for specific rites. Three of the six hymns by Callimachus — 'To Apollo' (2), 'On the Bath of Pallas' (5) and 'To Demeter' (6) — fall into this pattern, which involves several narrators that are participants in the ritual and bring about the gods' own voices. The long Homeric hymns and their imitations by Callimachus — 'To Zeus' (1), 'To Artemis' (3) and 'To Delos' (4) — are non-mimetic or diegetic. In them, a first-person narrator, who speaks on behalf of a collective, addresses the divinity in the *du-Stil* (thou-style, or second person), describes his/her qualities, and narrates his/her feats using the third person, or *er-Stil* (*sie-Stil* should be added here).¹²⁶ Chapman observes the pattern of the diegetic Homeric hymn in which one single first-person narrator addresses both the goddesses and listeners in the second person and recounts the narrative and descriptive parts in the third. Even if certain elements of worship evoke communal ritual performance (e.g. the altar in 'Noctem', 1–5; kneeling and singing in 'Cynthiam', 324, 401), the appeal to a collective listener responds to a calculated literary strategy. Thus, the mysteries of Night and Cynthia invoked by Chapman's hymnic voice become powerful correlates of the devotion to study and the pursuit of knowledge. Their mysteries are of a literary kind: behind the imagined initiates invoked by this vatic voice one should recognize Chapman's coterie of judicial readers.

Yet taking *The Shadow of Night* as a two-part literary hymn leaves a number of questions unanswered, particularly about the identity and functions of the two goddesses invoked, as well as about the relationship between them. And this final question brings back the problem of the relationship between the two parts of the poem. Millar MacLure understood 'Noctem' as 'contemplative, concerned with poetic wisdom and its enemies', and therefore 'with

---

125 N. Richardson, 'Constructing a Hymnic Narrative: Tradition and Innovation in the Longer *Homeric Hymns*', in *Hymnic Narrative and the Narratology of Greek Hymns*, ed. by Andrew Faulkner and Owen Hodkinson (Brill, 2015), pp. 19–30 (p. 19), doi:10.1163/9789004289512_003.

126 See M. Annette Harder, 'Insubstantial Voices: Some Observations on the Hymns of Callimachus', *The Classical Quarterly*, 42.2 (1992), pp. 384–94, doi:10.1017/S0009838800016013. The term 'diegetic' is used by S. A. Stephens, 'Callimachus and His Narrators', in *Hymnic Narrative and the Narratology of Greek Hymns*, ed. by Faulkner and Hodkinson, pp. 49–68, doi: 10.1163/9789004289512_005.

art'; by contrast, 'Cynthiam' 'turns to the life of action, to politics and morals', and its focus is 'nature'.[127] Waddington considers that MacLure's 'Spenserian scheme is too neat', as both poems, which 'abound with Orphean references to poetry, art and music', have a common concern with 'the supernatural'.[128] Waddington, who sees the poems mainly as Orphic hymns, argues that '*Noctem* should be considered as providing the context for the invocation in *Cynthiam*, which expresses the character of the Moon Goddess': thus the first hymn 'penetrates the darkness with which Cynthia, like all Orphic mysteries, is enveloped'.[129] For Waddington, these mysteries unfold in a complex network of references to lunar magic which, however, does not succeed in making the poem 'magically potent in any literal way'. For this reason, Waddington sees the hymn's magic symbols and invocatory rhetoric as elements that require 'philosophical interpretation' and thus as a 'metaphysical metaphor' for the moral and political themes explored primarily in 'Cynthiam'.[130]

But the philosophical element should not be viewed as something external to the hymn that allegoresis reveals. The problem with what, borrowing the phrase from Marco Piana and Matteo Soranzo, can be called a *reductio ad magiam* in Waddington's interpretation, is that the inherent philosophical aspect of the hymn as it was understood in Neoplatonic contexts is lost.[131] As Piana and Soranzo have argued, following the rediscovery of the hymn in quattrocento Italy, particularly by Marsilio Ficino, its composition and recitation were conceived of as parts of a philosophical, 'meditative practice, the function of which was to awaken and prepare the soul to experience an absolute, non-discursive form of knowledge'.[132] The philosophical hymns of Proclus, which had a considerable influence via Florentine Neoplatonism, supply a model for this meditative conception of the genre, which aims at predisposing the soul to a reversion (or epistrophe, from Greek ἐπιστροφή, return) from the material world to the life of the intellect (*Nous*, from Greek Νόος). In a recent reinterpretation of these hymns, R. M. van den Berg argues that Proclus understood hymn-singing as an essential part of the activity of the philosopher. Two notions explored by van den Berg emerge as essential to our present purpose. First, the idea of the hymnic poet as a searching philosopher — rather than religious hierophant or god-like

---

127 MacLure, *George Chapman*, p. 36.
128 Waddington, *The Mind's Empire*, p. 98.
129 Ibid., pp. 96, 98.
130 Ibid., pp. 107–08.
131 Marco Piana and Matteo Soranzo, 'The Way Philosophers Pray: Hymns as Experiential Knowledge in Early Modern Europe', *Mediterranea*, 5 (2020), pp. 51–89 (p. 57), doi:10.21071/mijtk.v5i.12087.
132 Ibid., p. 58. MacLure's undeveloped statement that *The Shadow of Night* 'belongs to a genre of didactic verse more widely practised by the continental humanists of the Renaissance than by English poets' advances my argument here (*George Chapman*, pp. 35–36).

magus.¹³³ If Proclus's own tripartite classification of poetry into divine, scientific and mimetic is to be considered, then the philosophical hymn, despite its aspiration to the divine, participates of the middle, scientific kind.¹³⁴ Second, the gods and goddesses addressed in these hymns are seldom superior deities; they are rather situated in lower levels of the transcendent realm so that they can perform the mediating function of inspiring and leading the soul in its reversion from the material world to the divine *Nous*. For van den Berg, these deities' function is twofold: on one hand, anagogic (from Greek ἀναγωγή, lifting, elevation), inducing divine madness in the human soul; on the other, leader deities that direct the soul towards divine intelligence in the apprehension of the Platonic triad of Truth, Beauty and Symmetry.¹³⁵

The structure and compositional principles observed by Chapman in *SN* are ultimately justified by the hymn's philosophical nature. For all their apparent violence and agitation, 'Noctem' and 'Cynthiam' aspire to be poetry of rational knowledge (ἐπιστήμη), intellect (νόος) and wisdom (φρόνησις).¹³⁶ As Proclus insists, this kind of poetry matches the middle life of the soul, that is, the contemplative life that, 'by establishing intellect and knowledge as first principles of its activity, unravels the multitude of *logoi*, and contemplates all of the variations among the forms' in the attempt to 'bring together as one thing that which thinks (τὸ νοοῦν) and the object of thought (τὸ νοούμενον)'.¹³⁷ In the attempt to establish this link between the intellect and the intelligible object (an aim that, as we will see, preoccupies Chapman), the poetry of knowledge 'brings each of the subjects that it treats into an interpretation (ἑρμηνεία) in metre and rhythm'.¹³⁸ This explains the importance in Chapman of the scientific (φυσικόν) component of the hymn, if we attend to Menander's classification: the hymns aspire to impart rational knowledge about the deities by researching, explaining and reinterpreting their genealogies, myths and properties — not only in verse but also through the addition of the prose glosses. Moreover, Night and Cynthia act as mediators between the material and the intellectual worlds. Their mediation

---

133 R. M. van den Berg, *Proclus' Hymns: Essays, Translation, Commentary* (Brill, 2001), pp. 20–23.
134 Ibid., pp. 136–38, on the hymn as scientific poetry. For Proclus's tripartite division of poetry, see Proclus, *Commentary on Plato's Republic*, ed. and trans. by Dick Baltzy, John F. Finamore and Graeme Miles (Cambridge University Press, 2018), VI. 2. 5–6, 177. 7–192. 2, pp. 289–302.
135 Van den Berg, *Proclus' Hymns*, pp. 61–65.
136 The terms correspond to Proclus's definition of philosophical poetry. See Proclus, *Commentary on Plato's Republic*, VI. 2. 6. 186.23–24, p. 298.
137 Ibid., VI. 2. 5. 177. 27–178. 1, p. 289.
138 Ibid., VI. 2. 5. 179. 7–9, p. 291. Chapman could have known Proclus's *Commentary* through the early sixteenth-century manuscript owned by Henry Wriothesley, Earl of Southampton, now at St John's College Library, Cambridge (MS F.15), which contains, among others, essays V and VI (see digitized copy at <https://cudl.lib.cam.ac.uk/view/MS-SJC-F-00015/1> [accessed 9 December 2024]. I thank Jonathan Sell for suggesting this possibility, which deserves further scrutiny.

is, however, of a different sort. As Chapman makes clear, Cynthia is 'the Night's fair soul' ('Cynthiam', 1) — an affirmation supported by a glossarial remark: 'He calls her the soul of the Night, since she is the purest part of her, according to common conceit' ('Cynthiam', Gloss 2). Cynthia is understood as a superior causative principle of Night, and consequently 'Noctem' has been interpreted as preparatory for 'Cynthiam'. MacLure's argument that 'Noctem' is concerned with art and 'Cynthiam' with nature is convincing: Night functions as an anagogic goddess, inducing the divine fury of the hymnodist-philosopher and predisposing him to accessing Cynthia, the leader-goddess of the divine intellect. Thus, 'Noctem' unfurls a hortatory, rapture-inducing rhetoric:

> let soft Sleep
> (Binding my senses) loose my working soul,
> That in her highest pitch she may control
> The court of Skill, compact of mystery,
> Wanting but franchisement and memory
> To reach all secrets. (10–15)

In contrast, 'Cynthiam' shifts to descriptive and narrative enquiry into the nature of the goddess, which culminates in the philosophizing mind's apprehension of the divine, embodied in Cynthia's amorous acceptance of Endymion for 'his studious intellect' (494).

Chapman's hymnic practice must then be understood as part of a tradition, the origins of which are unmistakeably classical but which had a strong impact in European Neoplatonic circles, which updated the meditative prayer for philosophical purposes. Piana and Soranzo have considered Spenser's *Fowre Hymns* (1596) an important member of a tradition transmitted to him by Ficino and by Pierre de Ronsard's *Hymnes* (1555).[139] Despite its differences with respect to Spenser's poems, *SN*, published two years earlier, needs to be regarded as another pioneering text in the canon of the English poetic hymn, one whose immediate influence was felt in the work of some of Chapman's contemporaries, such as Michael Drayton's *Endymion and Phoebe* (1595) or Thomas Edwards's *Cephalus and Procris* (1595).[140] Chapman's complex experiment in hymnic poetry is an audacious exercise in fashioning his idea of the art and his own skills as a poet, but also in creating an exploratory formal vehicle for what his preface defines as 'the deep search of knowledge'.

---

139 Piana and Soranzo, 'The Way Philosophers Pray', pp. 177–80.
140 See Odette de Mourgues, *Metaphysical, Baroque & Précieux Poetry* (Oxford University Press, 1953), pp. 44–45, for a passing but suggestive remark on Chapman's poetry as an epitome of the main tendencies of sixteenth-century French scientific poetry. And see MacLure, *George Chapman*, p. 36, n. 14, for a similarly passing mention of the influence of *The Shadow of Night* in the 1590s and early 1600s. Both issues need further research.

3.2. 'Ovid's Banquet of Sense'

The publication of *Ovid's Banquet of Sense, A Coronet for His Mistress Philosophy and His Amorous Zodiac* in 1595 meant a significant genre turn in Chapman's early career. The title suggests that the author must have conceived of his work for this volume as a poetic triptych. This tripartite structure partly questions the priority given by Chapman critics to 'Banquet' — an attitude that the volume itself supports by including a prose argument of this poem and by the special attention given to it in the five commendatory sonnets. One of the three titles, '*His* Amorous Zodiac', changes to '*The* Amorous Zodiac' in the running heads of the 1595 quarto. The change is significant: as mentioned above, this third poem is an unacknowledged translation of the French poem *Le zodiac amoreux* (1587), by Gilles Durant, Sieur de la Bergerie. The replacement seems to downplay the authorial claim implicit in 'his', even when the author's name was not printed on the title page (Figure 2). Another possibility is to understand 'his' on the title page as 'Ovid's', which may also explain the suppression of the author's name, which only appears in the signature of the prefatory epistle and in the first of John Davies's two commendatory sonnets. Davies's portrait of Chapman as a reincarnate and deeper Ovid insists on conflating the author's identity with that of his poet-protagonist.[141] This scenario is completed by the posthumous publication of a second edition of the work, with an identical title — this time without Stapleton's addition — in 1639. This octavo reissue was fully anonymized by the suppression of the prefatory epistle and the commendatory sonnets. The inner titles and running heads of the second and third poem become 'Ovid's Coronet for His Mistress Philosophy' and 'Ovid's Amorous Zodiac'. A few extant copies have survived as part of different *Sammelbände* including other seventeenth-century editions of translations of Ovid's works in octavo. I have elsewhere discussed the details of the bibliographic and literary circumstances surrounding this edition.[142] Here its existence is recalled simply as evidence that the early modern understanding of Chapman's work as a three-part Ovidian poem has important implications for determining the poet's genre choices.

The turn to Ovid emerges as the most remarkable change, particularly if certain aspects of *SN* — such as the abovementioned allusion to Shakespeare's

---

141 On the fiction of Ovid as 'author' of the volume, see Raymond Waddington, 'Visual Rhetoric: Chapman and the Extended Poem', *English Literary Renaissance*, 13.1 (1983), pp. 36–57, doi:10.1111/j.1475-6757.1983.tb00844.x. Waddington remarks that the volume 'lacks the apparatus necessary to make that fiction apparent' (p. 43). More recently, see Martin Wheeler, '"The obiect whereto all his actions tend: George Chapman's *Ouids Banquet of Sence* and the Thrill of the Chase', *Modern Language Review*, 101.2 (2006), pp. 325–46 (p. 344), doi:10.1353/mlr.2006.0050.
142 Zenón Luis-Martínez, 'Whose Banquet? Whose Coronet? Whose Zodiac? George Chapman and Seventeenth-Century Ovid *Sammelbände*', *Philological Quarterly*, 100.1 (2021), pp. 23–54.

Venus and Adonis — are considered anti-Ovidian attitudes. Ovid, the Ovidian corpus and the Ovidian tradition must be regarded as permanent sites of conflict in Chapman's early poems. Waddington sees in *SN* an attempt to wield a serious Ovidianism predicated on the allegorical interpretation of metamorphic myths and against the insubstantial fad of the erotic epyllion — an attitude that would find continuation in *OBS* if, as Waddington believes, we accept that the new poem must be read ironically.[143] In contrast, Daniel Moss detects straightforward anti-Ovidianism in the first book — a position that Chapman would moderate in the second by showing a more tolerant and constructive approach to the Roman poet.[144] Waddington can be granted the first and Moss the second part of their arguments: thus, the seed could be detected in *SN* that led Chapman to explore new facets of his already serious Ovidianism in *OBS*. Regarding the first poem, critics have not paid attention to the fact that the first sentence we read when we open the original quarto is a line by Ovid. The title-page epigraph is from a relatively rare Ovid, although one that was not unknown in Renaissance England: 'Versus mei habebunt aliquantum *Noctis*' ('My lines have something of [the] *Night*'). These words belong to the elegiac invective *Ibis*, one of the poems written during Ovid's exile in Tomis. In taking Ovid's words out of their original context, Chapman slightly but significantly alters Ovid's line: 'Utque mei versus aliquantum noctis habebunt, | Sic vitae series tota sit atra tuae' ('As my lines have something of the night, so let all your life's series be black').[145] Originally, these words were part of Ovid's curse on one of the unnamed Roman accusers that provoked his fall. Chapman transforms the causal clause into a statement and deifies Night through capitalization in order to make his line a staunch defence of the dark poetics consecrated to his goddess: 'No pen can anything eternal write | That is not steeped in humour of the Night' ('Noctem', 376-77). The appointment of the exiled Ovid as the presiding voice of Chapman's dark, allegorical poetry of shadows is therefore not far from John Davies's portrait of Chapman as a profound, serious Ovid in the conclusion of his commendatory sonnet: 'For Ovid's soul, now grown more old and wise, | Pours forth itself in deeper mysteries' (*OBS*: 'Davies 1', 13-14). The deeper mysteries of this *Ovidius redivivus* are those that the nocturnal poet of *SN* retrieved from the sombre elegiac tones and the dark hymnic invocations of *Ibis*, which could also have inspired Chapman's title:

---

143 Waddington, *The Mind's Empire*, pp. 113-14.
144 Moss, 'Second Master', p. 459.
145 Ovid, *Ibis*, lines 63-64, in *The Art of Love, and Other Poems*, ed. and trans. by J. H. Mozley (Heinemann, 1957), pp. 256-57. Thomas Underdowne's sixteenth-century translation of *Ibis* is revealing of the association of this poem with obscurity of style and content: 'And as my verses shalbe stufte, with some obscurytie: | So let the course of all thy life, be fyllde with myserie' (*Ouid his inuective against Ibis. Translated into English méeter* (London: Henry Bynneman, 1577), sig. B2ʳ).

Di maris et terrae, quique his meliora tenetis
Inter diversos cum Jove regna polos,
Huc, precor, huc vestra somnes advertite mentes,
Et sinite optatis pondus inesse meis:
Ipsaque tu tellus, ipsum cum fluctibus aequor,
Ipse meas aether accipe summe preces;
Sideraque et radiis circumdata solis imago,
Lunaque, quae numquam quo prius orbe micas,
Noxque tenebrarum specie reverenda tuarum.

(Gods of land and sea, and ye who hold with Jove a better realm than these between the sundered poles, hither, I pray, turn hither all of you your minds, and allow weight to my desires: and thou thyself, O Earth, and thyself, O Sea with thy waves, and thyself, O supreme Air, hear my petition; ye constellations, too, and the sun's ray-encircled image, and thou Moon that never shinest with the orb thou hadst before, *and Night, awful in the beauty of thy shadows.*)[146]

Despite these continuities, a distinct Ovid certainly emerges from *OBS*. Its first poem, 'Banquet', has 1062 lines distributed in 117 nine-line stanzas that follow a rhyme pattern of Chapman's own creation: *ababcbcdd* in iambic pentameter. The exception is stanza 12, in which the first four pentameter lines observe that *abab* pattern, while the rest of its fourteen tetrameter lines are arranged in sonnet form: *abba cddc effe hh*. The poem's stanzaic pattern seems to fall between the traditional Italian *ottava rima* of Renaissance epic — *abababcc* — and the also epic-oriented Spenserian nine-line stanza of *The Faerie Queene* (1590), *ababbcbdd*, yet without the latter's characteristic final alexandrine. The turn from the heroic verse of *SN* to the varied stanzaic forms of *OBS* — completed by the sonnet in 'Coronet' and the sixain in 'Zodiac' — betrays an interest in arranging the poems' narrative material in ways that resemble several of Chapman's fellow practitioners of the late sixteenth-century minor epic. *Ottava rima* in Spenser's *Muiopotmos* (1590), the sixain in Thomas Lodge's *Scilla's Metamorphosis* (1589), Shakespeare's *Venus and Adonis* (1593) and Thomas Heywood's *Oneone and Paris*, and rhyme royal in Shakespeare's *The Rape of Lucrece* (1594) and Thomas Edwards's *Narcissus* (1595) provide cases of this preference for stanzaic forms in shorter epics, while Marlowe's *Hero and Leander* (1593?), with Chapman's continuation (1598), or Edwards's own *Cephalus and Procris* (1595) employ the heroic couplet.

To a greater or lesser extent, all these poems bear proof of a fad for Ovidian subjects derived from the transformation narratives of *Metamorphoses* or the epistolary lamentations of *Heroides*. 'Banquet' has frequently been regarded as one such Ovidian short epic, or *epyllion*, even if for some scholars Chapman's approach to the genre is satiric or parodic.[147] His Ovidian matter

---

146 Ovid, *Ibis*, lines 67–75, emphasis added.
147 Elizabeth Story Donno includes 'Banquet' in her influential anthology *Elizabethan*

is undoubtedly a nod to these poems, particularly in his allusions to metamorphic myths such as those of Niobe and Actaeon, but his placing of the lover/poet Ovid in the centre of a 'historical' fiction signals the desire to distance his composition from his contemporaries' focus on erotic metamorphic narratives. The circumstances of Emperor Augustus's decree of Ovid's exile in Tomis from AD 8 until the end of his years were explained by Ovid himself in his late elegiac works *Tristia* and *De Ponto* as the result of 'carmen et error' ('a poem and a mistake').[148] While the 'poem' points directly to the lascivious content of *Ars amatoria* (a work mentioned in 'Banquet', 113. 5), the mystery of Ovid's 'mistake' was often a cause of debate, although tradition blamed his alleged affair with Julia (daughter, or granddaughter, of Augustus) as the ultimate motive of his banishment.[149] The narrative of 'Banquet' recreates Ovid's affair with Julia and prefigures the writing of *Ars amatoria*. It is hard not to see in the final stanza's announcement — 'Ovid well knew there was much more intended' (117. 8) — some sort of sinister wink at the Roman poet's fate as an exile.[150]

The poem's Ovidian ascription emerges primarily via biography and elegy. However, Chapman's associations with poets such as Marlowe and Davies in the early 1590s suggest an additional Ovidian link. In the early 1590s, a volume published under a false Middelburg imprint titled *Certaine of Ovids Elegies* (1593?) gathered a number of Marlowe's translations of Ovid's amatory elegies and *Amores*, preceded by a collection of satirical epigrams authored by Davies. To these, the full translated *Amores* were added in subsequent editions while Davies's epigrams were displaced to the end of the volume. Knowledge, translation and discussion of Ovid's amatory lyrics can therefore be assumed in those poetic circles in which Chapman was active during

---

Minor Epics (Columbia University Press, 1963), despite her caveat that 'Chapman provides no narrative beyond the simple fact of Ovid's appearing in a garden with Corynna' (p. 13). See also James Phares Myers, Jr, '"This Curious Frame": Chapman's *Ovid's Banquet of Sense*', *Studies in Philology*, 65.2 (1968), pp. 192–206 (p. 195); Weaver, 'Banquet', develops the argument that the poem takes seriously its aim as a satire of the erotic epyllion.

148 Ovid, *Tristia*, II. 207–12: 'perdiderint cum me duo crimina, carmen et error, | alterius facti culpa silenda mihi: | nam non sum tanti, renovem ut tua vulnera, Caesar, | quem nimio plus est indoluisse semel. | altera pars superest, qua turpi carmine factus | arguor obsceni doctor adulterii' ('Though two crimes, a poem and a blunder, have brought me ruin, of my fault in the one I must keep silent, for my worth is not such that I may reopen thy wounds, O Caesar; 'tis more than enough that thou shouldst have been pained once. The other remains: the charge that by an obscene poem I have taught foul adultery'). In *Tristia, Ex Ponto*, ed. and trans. by Arthur Leslie Wheeler (Harvard University Press, 1939), pp. 70–71.

149 Classic accounts of *Ars amatoria* and Julia's affair with Ovid as causes of his exile are John C. Thibault, *The Mystery of Ovid's Exile* (University of California Press, 1964), and G. P. Goold, 'The Cause of Ovid's Exile', *Illinois Classical Studies*, 8.1 (1983), pp. 94–107. See also Luis-Martínez, 'Whose Banquet?', pp. 36–39.

150 Moss, 'Second Master', p. 474; Raphael Lyne, 'Love and Exile after Ovid', in *The Cambridge Companion to Ovid*, ed. by Philip Hardie (Cambridge University Press, 2006), pp. 288–300 (p. 295); Huntington, *Ambition*, pp. 138–39.

these years. Critics like John Huntington and Daniel Moss have recently revived lines of argument that support the present hypothesis of the poem's kinship with Ovidian amatory and didactic elegy. Huntington is right when he argues that Ovid's *Amores*, I. 5, supplies a 'paradigmatic moment' that claims comparison with Chapman's poem; so is Moss's assertion that Chapman 'reimagines the *error* as the inspiration for the *carmen*', thus implying that *Ars amatoria* must bear some sort of relevance to Chapman's approach to Ovid in his new volume.[151]

The problem with extending these claims to a more consistent poetics of genre involves the question of *voice*. Ovid, the protagonist of Chapman's poem, is also a first-person voice in a number of stanzas in direct speech, for which the present text has added quotation marks. Daniel Moss reminds us that Ovid the poet/protagonist of Chapman's poem is artistically far removed from Ovid the Latin poet: he is one whose voice anachronistically conveys 'Petrarchan conceits, Neoplatonic commonplaces from Ficino, [and] snapshots from Spenser's Bower of Bliss' in his monologues and repartees with Corinna.[152] As Ovid is more than one Ovid, I will try to differentiate, when disambiguation makes it necessary and at the risk of tediousness, between the historical poet and Chapman's protagonist. Corinna's voice is also heard as the singer of the song/sonnet of stanza 12 and as the speaker of several replies to Ovid: these latter have also been printed in quotation marks in the present edition. There is a further first-person narrator that somehow blurs the boundaries between extradiegetic and intradiegetic positions. He relates to Chapman the author as the fictional Ovid relates to the historical poet Ovid. Moss's work is again of help here, particularly as he reminds us of the importance of Davies's two commendatory sonnets in bringing forth the notion of Chapman as a 'second master' of Cupid's art, reforming and reincarnating the original Ovid through the 'deeper mysteries' of his poetry.[153] It is precisely this authorial side that permits the identification of the narrative voice with Davies's idea of the reincarnated 'second master' of love. This first-person narrative voice is therefore another Ovidian voice, but in different ways from the other Ovids discussed above. This is precisely the voice that in the middle of the poems declares: 'Or else blame me as his [i.e. Ovid's] submitted debtor, | That never mistress had to make me better' ('Banquet', 57. 8–9). This mistress-less second master of love remains a debtor to the poetic teachings of Ovid the fictional character and the historical poet, and for that reason this Ovidian alter ego may surface in my account as the narrator, the elegist, the elegiac voice or the 'second master'. A final voice, which Gerald Snare has aptly called 'the glossarial interpreter', must also be

---

151 Huntington, *Ambition*, in particular Chapter 6, pp. 128–46, and, more specifically, his analysis of *Amores*, I. 5 (p. 131); and Moss, 'Second Master', p. 474.
152 Moss, 'Second Master', pp. 447–49, 474–75.
153 Ibid., pp. 457–59.

considered, here but also in *SN*: this voice takes responsibility for filling in the endnotes (*SN*) and marginal notes (*SN* and *OBS*) of these poems with obscure sources, learned Latin *sententiae*, and other sorts of general and particular explanations of certain difficult passages. The glossarial voice remains 'somewhat distant from the obsessions of poetic artifice and the voice invented to articulate them'.[154]

This complex play of voices determines Chapman's sophisticated approach to the elegy. As a genre, the elegy relies on a first-person voice. If the play of voices in 'Banquet' is understood in terms of one external narrator that imposes a judgemental control upon the amorous experience of the main character, then the kinship between the poem and the variety of forms of the Ovidian elegy — erotic, didactic, exilic — risks being misunderstood. If, on the contrary, we regard the poem as a tale of two masters of love, then its interdependent voices can better reveal the different facets that we associate with the genuine Ovidian amatory elegist — the lover of *Amores* and the *praeceptor amoris*, or 'love's master', of *Ars amatoria*.[155] One main difference between the two Ovidian voices in 'Banquet' is their different conception of their double role as lovers and as masters of love.

Chapman's immediate Ovidian context — one would dare say source — is *Amores*, I. 5, which instates 'Banquet' in the realm of the erotic elegy. The time of Ovid's elegy is a hot summer noon. In Marlowe's translation: 'In summers heate and mid-time of the day' ('Aestus erat, mediamque dies exegerat horam').[156] Chapman's first two stanzas amplify the description, but the 'heat' caused by the sun's 'right beams' ('Banquet', 1. 1–3) is proof that he has not altered the essence of Ovid's chosen hour and season for the erotic rendezvous. Both poems have the same protagonists, but Chapman inverts the plot: in *Amores*, Corinna comes to Ovid's lodgings, while in Chapman it is the protagonist that goes to Corinna's (actually her father's) garden. Ovid's Corinna arrives veiled in 'a long loose gown' ('tunica velata recincta', I. 5. 9); Chapman's Corinna, 'In a loose robe of tinsel, [...] | Nothing but it betwixt her nakedness | And envious light' ('Banquet', 7. 1–3). There is limited room for idealizing similes in *Amores*: 'Resembling fayre *Semiramis*

---

154 Snare, *Mystification*, p. 166.
155 Lyne, 'Love and Exile', pp. 289–90, differentiates two key poetic personae in Ovid's career: the lover and the exile. The first of these needs to be split into the amatory elegist of *Amores* and the didactic elegist — the *praeceptor amoris* — of *Ars amatoria* and *Remedia amoris*. See Richard Tarrant, 'Ovid and Ancient Literary History', in *Cambridge Companion to Ovid*, ed. by Hardie, pp. 13–33, for a portrait of Ovid as 'a poet who repeatedly dramatized the transformation of his *persona*: elegist into tragedian, lover-poet into *praeceptor amoris*, writer of light elegy into writer of epic and aetiological poetry, and, finally, all of the above into the poet of exile' (p. 27).
156 Ovid, *Amores*, I. 5. 1; Marlowe, *All Ovids Elegies*, I. 5. 1, in *The Complete Works of Christopher Marlowe*, ed. by Roma Gill and others, 5 vols (Oxford University Press, 1987), I, pp. 18–19. Further references to this poem by line numbers are given parenthetically in the text.

going to bed, | Or *Layis* of a thousand wooers sped' ('qualiter in thalamos famosa Semiramis isse | dicitur, et multis Lais amata viris', I. 5. 11-12). Chapman's copious similes and grand idealizations are the aesthetic *raison d'être* of the poem. In *Amores*, Ovid moves to rough assault:

> I snatcht her gowne: being thin, the harm was small,
> Yet striv'd she to be covered there withall.
> And striving thus as one that would be cast,
> Betray'd her selfe, and yeelded to the last.
>
> (Deripui tunicam — nec multum rara nocebat; | pugnabat tunica sed tamen illa tegi. | quae cum ita pugnaret, tamquam quae vincere nollet, | victa est non aegre proditione sua.) (I. 5. 13-16)

In 'Banquet', it is Corinna that delicately removes her robe, yet only to the eyes of the reader and those of the poem's vigilant 'second master' — see the analysis of stanza 8 in the previous section. Male physical assault and female resistance in *Amores* are transformed by Chapman into learned, witty repartee of metaphysical proportions between the protagonists. In *Amores*, Ovid's rude banquet of sense is circumscribed to a hurried surfeit of his sight and touch:

> Starke naked as she stood before mine eye,
> Not one wen in her body, could I spie.
> What armes and shoulders did I touch and see,
> How apt her breasts were to be prest by me.
> How smooth a belly vnder her wast saw I?
> How large a legge, and what a lustie thigh?
>
> (ut stetit ante oculos posito velamine nostros, | in toto nusquam corpore menda fuit. | quos umeros, quales vidi tetigique lacertos! | forma papillarum quam fuit apta premi! | quam castigato planus sub pectore venter! | quantum et quale latus! quam iuvenale femur!) (I. 5. 17-22)

Chapman's transformation of this scene into an orderly ritual of sensual enjoyment and philosophical praise via a peculiar rearrangement of the Neoplatonic hierarchy of the five senses is the philosophical *raison d'être* of his poem.

In *Amores*, interruption, or rhetorical aposiopesis, shows more than hides, and brings the brief encounter to a close:

> To leave the rest, all lik'd me passing well,
> I cling'd her naked body, downe she fell,
> Judge you the rest, being tirde she bad me kisse;
> *Jove* send me more such after-noones as this.
>
> (Singula quid referam? nil non laudabile vidi | et nudam pressi corpus ad usque meum. | Cetera quis nescit? lassi requievimus ambo. | proveniant medii sic mihi saepe dies!) (I. 5. 23-26)

Aposiopesis in Chapman is intent on showing the art of ending a poem through a new elegant painting simile — the half hand that the viewer perceives as whole — rather than on catching a glimpse of a postponed promised end for his own Ovid's banquet:

> But as when expert painters have displayed
> To quickest life a monarch's royal hand
> Holding a sceptre, there is yet bewrayed
> But half his fingers, when we understand
>   The rest not to be seen, and never blame
> The painter's art, in nicest censures scanned,
>   So in the compass of this curious frame
> Ovid well knew there was much more intended,
> With whose omission none must be offended. ('Banquet', 117)

Amores, I. 5, ends with the optimistic prospect of its frequent future repetition in ensuing summer afternoons; 'Banquet', with the ambiguous Latin tag '*Intentio, animi actio*': intention is the mind's action; or, less generally, the particular intention of this poem is to give the floor to the mind's own endeavours in the next poem, 'Coronet'. Not in vain, the new poem is an overt celebration of 'The majesty and riches of the mind' ('Coronet', 1. 13) rather than of sensual beauty.

Chapman has thus carefully expanded Ovid's twenty-six lines into the scaffolding of his 1062-line poem. An amatory elegy in skeleton, 'Banquet' becomes Chapman's particular version of the didactic elegy through the sinews and flesh of its own amplifications. The necessary referent for this genre is Ovid's *Ars amatoria*. The fictional Ovid's intention to write '*The Art of Love*' for the sake of touch — 'The object whereto all [Love's] actions tend' ('Banquet', 113. 3) — not only prefigures 'Banquet' as the primal scene for Ovid's exile and exilic poetry. It also puts Ovid's original poem and its philosophy of love as the referents against which the multi-layered art of love surfacing in Chapman's poem must be confronted. In the original *Ars amatoria*, Ovid's practical advice to male lovers on when, where and how to win their mistresses could offer endless matter for comparison with Chapman's particular case study of a furtive lover invading the gardens of the great. The original poem's ultimate aim is victory: 'Quisquis sapienter amabit | Vincet, et e nostra, quod petet, arte feret' ('Whoso loves wisely will be victorious, and by my art will gain his end');[157] and its principal means is eloquence:

> Disce bonas artes, moneo, Romana iuventus,
> Non tantum trepidos ut tueare reos;
> Quam populus iudexque gravis lectusque senatus,
> Tam dabit eloquio victa puella manus.
>
> (Learn noble arts, I counsel you, young men of Rome, not only that you may defend trembling clients: a woman, no less than populace, grave Judge or chosen senate, will surrender, defeated, to eloquence).[158]

---

157 *Ars amatoria*, II. 511–12.
158 Ibid., I. 459–62.

The love-inspired eloquence displayed by Chapman's fictional Ovid responds to a *furor poeticus* induced by *furor amatorius*, if we attend to Marsilio Ficino's Neoplatonic terms rather than to Ovid's more pragmatic ends.[159] Yet his reliance on practical means of eloquence does not, at least in appearance, make him different in attitude from his historical predecessor. Thus, in order to persuade himself of his own passion, and his mistress of its goodness, Chapman's protagonist can sometimes sound like a pre-Socratic atomist —

> And as gilt atoms in the sun appear,
> So greet these sounds the gristles of mine ear,
>
> Whose pores do open wide to their regreet,
> And my implanted air that air embraceth,
> Which they impress [...] (21. 8–22. 3)

— like a convinced Neoplatonist —

> For sacred beauty is the fruit of sight,
> The courtesy that speaks before the tongue,
> The feast of souls, the glory of the light,
> Envy of age, and everlasting young [...] (52. 1–4)

— or like an orthodox Aristotelian —

> This motion of my soul, my fantasy,
> Created by three senses put in act,
> Let justice nourish with thy sympathy,
> Putting my other senses into fact.
>   If now thou grant not, now change that offence:
> To suffer change doth perfect sense compact [...] (87. 1–6)

— all in one.[160] Whether these examples could take Dryden's dart at Donne for using 'nice speculations of philosophy' with mere pragmatic purposes or involve more serious explorations of the nature of desire is a question to which this introduction will return.[161]

Ovid's main counsel to women in *The Art of Love* to 'go into battle on equal terms' ('Ite in bella pares') with men can be assumed as Corinna's motto in Chapman's poem.[162] Corinna yields — and one may think too easily — to Ovid's reasons after having argued quite strongly against them. One may decide to see in her character little else than the puppet on the poet's strings. Yet the complaints in her sonnet against the foolishness of the love

---

159 See Marsilio Ficino, *Phaedrus*, 2. IV, in *Commentaries on Plato: Phaedrus and Ion*, ed. and trans. by Michael J. B. Allen (Harvard University Press, 2008), pp. 50–54. See also Commentary: 'Banquet', 15.
160 On the sources, analogues and meanings of these and similar passages, the reader can consult the Commentary in this edition.
161 Dryden's well-known phrase is from 'A Discourse Concerning the Original and Progress of Satire' (1593), in John Dryden, *Essays*, ed. by W. P. Ker, 2 vols (Oxford University Press, 1900), II, p. 19.
162 *Ars amatoria*, III. 3.

poet's books — 'Where wisdom sees in looks | Derision, laughing at his school' ('Banquet', 12, Song, 11–12) — reveal deeper layers of her character. The poem's protagonist ignores the message in Corinna's sonnet only to hear 'her sweet voice' ('Banquet', 17. 5). Similarly, the emblematic devices of Corinna's hairpins, containing important teachings about the philosophy of love and poetry, also escape her lover's physical and intellectual eye.[163] These teachings are hidden in those attributes of Corinna's that exceed the conspicuous sensual charms that the poem shamelessly exposes in almost pornographic ways. As the character Ovid fails to perceive those attributes, it is the task of the 'second master' to put them in front of the reader's own eye and understanding. Corinna is sometimes an outspoken defender and at other times an unwitting ensign of those attributes, glossed by the didactic voice of the second master. The narrator's teaching of the 'deeper mysteries' of his alternative art of love can be conveyed through overt philosophical exposition of Neoplatonic doctrine in rhetorically self-enclosed digressions (as in stanzas 51–55), through mythological allusion that invites allegoresis (Niobe in stanzas 2–6, Actaeon and Diana in 41), through elaborate similes that elicit moral reading (stanzas 44–46, stanza 117), or through cryptic emblematic devices and mottos (the volume's title page, its Latin epigraphs, or the overtly emblematic jewels described in stanzas 70 and 71) whose transcendent meanings are never fully disclosed. These constitute the didactic-elegiac contents of 'Banquet' and are clearly projected into the poetic universe of the next two poems.

The play of voices in 'Banquet' invites us then to return to the question of the volume's title, or of the absence of Chapman's name from the title page of the 1595 quarto and its disappearance entirely from the octavo of 1639. Whose mistress is Philosophy in 'A Coronet for His Mistress Philosophy'? And whose zodiac is 'His Amorous Zodiac'? Should we opt for a purely authorial solution — i.e. Chapman's — or should we follow the 1639 octavo and affirm that the answer is 'Ovid's'?[164] The first encourages a view of the volume as an amalgam of independent poems, while the second recommends

---

163 On the sources and meanings of these emblematic devices, see Commentary: 'Banquet', 69–71. See also Rhoda Ribner, 'The Compasse of This Curious Frame: Chapman's *Ovids Banquet of Sence* and the Emblematic Tradition', *Studies in the Renaissance*, 17 (1970), pp. 233–58 (p. 235), doi:10.2307/2857064; Huntington, *Ambition*, pp. 142–43; Wheeler, 'The obiect', pp. 335–36; and Luis-Martínez, 'Habit of Poesie', pp. 235–37. On the crucial part played by Corinna, 'an active and quite well-developed character', see Vinge, 'Chapman's *Ovids Banquet of Sence*', p. 237.

164 On the ten-item sequence of interlaced sonnets, certain scholars have concluded that there is continuity between 'Ovid', the protagonist of the first poem, and its first-person lyric voice. This reading usually supports views of 'Banquet' as a Neoplatonic poem of ascent to intellectual love. See Vinge, 'Chapman's *Ovids Banquet of Sence*', p. 234; John Huntington, 'Philosophical Seduction in Chapman, Davies, and Donne', *English Literary History*, 44.1 (1977), pp. 40–59 (pp. 51 and 58, n. 40), doi:10.2307/2872525; Wheeler, 'The obiect', p. 344. This interpretation is denied by Waddington, 'Visual Rhetoric', p. 43, who sees 'Coronet' as an attack on the kind of poetry satirized by 'Banquet'.

considering its parts as pieces of a fictional Ovidian triptych. The question has been considered particularly in relation to the first two poems in the volume, 'Banquet' and 'Coronet'. Formally, Chapman's corona of sonnets encourages the reader to look beyond the context of its original volume and find its kinship with the Elizabethan sonnet sequences of the 1590s.[165] The publication of the unauthorized first edition of Sidney's *Astrophil and Stella* (1591) was followed by Samuel Daniel's *Delia* (1592), Henry Constable's two editions of *Diana* (1592, 1594), Giles Fletcher's *Licia* (1593), Barnabe Barnes's *Pathenophil and Pathenophe* (1593), Thomas Lodge's *Phillis* (1593), Michael Drayton's *Idea* (1594), William Percy's *Coelia* (1594), and Edmund Spenser's *Amoretti* (1595).

The first difference between these collections and Chapman's is length: the shortest of these sequences, Percy's *Coelia*, doubles Chapman's 'Coronet' in number of sonnets. The second difference is Chapman's unusual choice of the corona, 'a short lyric cycle whose circularity relies on the repetition of the last line of one poem as the beginning of the next, with the last line of the final poem reprising the first of the opening one'.[166] Daniel's *Delia* and the apocryphal section of Constable's second *Diana* (1594) also used linking lines to connect a number of sonnets, while George Gascoigne had used the term 'sequence' to name some of his sonnets connected in this way in his *Posies* (1575). Sidney had completed a corona of ten dizains in his *Arcadia*; in a manuscript booklet his brother Robert broke off another corona of sonnets in the middle of its fifth sonnet; and Robert's daughter, Lady Mary Wroth, would finish a fourteen-sonnet corona in her *Pamphilia to Amphilanthus*. It is between the two Sidney generations that Chapman completed the first full corona of sonnets in English. Chapman's choice of ten sonnets for his collection may have numerological implications related to the form's circular structure. But the number could also have been inspired by the poet's knowledge in manuscript of his friend John Davies's two ten-sonnet sequences *Ten Sonnets to Philomel* and *Gullinge Sonnets*, both of which have been dated conjecturally to before 1595.[167] Davies's pastiche of conventional Petrarchism, particularly in the second of these collections, may be behind the third and most important difference between 'Coronet' and the published sonnet collections, i.e. its anti-Petrarchan tone. Like Davies, Chapman chose the formal vehicle of Petrarchan poetry to attack its conventions. Unlike Davies, he preferred serious invective over comic parody. The result was a profound critique not only of Petrarchan sensuality but also of its patrician culture and mimetic, courtly poetics.[168]

Yet the Petrarchan context of 'Coronet', far from isolating it from its

---

165 Luis Martínez, 'Friendlesse Verse', pp. 569–88.
166 Ibid., p. 566.
167 Ibid., pp. 572, 596.
168 Ibid. See also Huntington, *Ambition*, pp. 102–05.

neighbouring pieces in *OBS*, fosters new ways of approaching the idea of the poem's inner dialogue with its preceding poem. The extended titles of Daniel — *Delia* [...] *with the Complaint of Rosamond* (1592) — and Lodge — *Phillis* [...] *Where-unto is Added the Tragicall Complaint of Elstred* (1593) — reveal that their sonnet collections were followed by long narrative poems. Other works like Lodge's *Scillaes Metamorphosis* [...] *with Sundrie other Most Absolute Poems and Sonnets* (1589-90) show the inverse arrangement. Recent work on these collections has explored continuities of narrative/authorial/lyric voices across their parts.[169] Chapman likewise uses voice in order to assemble apparently disconnected sections and miscellaneous genres in *OBS*. The lyric persona of 'Coronet' seems formally coincident with the narrative voice of 'Banquet', the authorial 'second master' who declares himself Ovid's 'submitted debtor' but who nevertheless modulates his predecessor's passions and views. 'Coronet' thus completes the transmutation of the first into the second master of love through the 'deeper mysteries' of the latter's poetry.

The deepest of these mysteries is Philosophy, that is, the mistress of a lover 'that never mistress had' ('Banquet', 67). Mistress Philosophy is an abstraction that always remains in the antipodes of the flesh-and-blood Corinna. And yet, in an exercise of baroque *discordia concors*, the volume paradoxically forces the reader to see the former as an extension of the latter. Thus, the fictional Ovid's above-quoted desire that Corinna will become his 'patroness' and her 'perfections' a 'reward' much preferred to 'gold's riches' ('Banquet', 115) is matched by the similar announcement made by the lyric voice of the new poem about Mistress Philosophy:

> Herself shall be my comfort and my riches,
>   And all my thoughts I will on her convert;
> Honour, and Error, which the world bewitches,
>   Shall still crown fools, and tread upon desert. ('Coronet', 9. 9-12)

This coincidence between such antithetical mistresses seems to reconcile the two contending masters of love around a common social philosophy of poetry that attacks the 'servile feet' of flattering poets and the 'serving times' of self-abased courtiers ('Coronet', 10. 11-12). If these common terms manage to bring together the protagonist and narrator of the former poem, they also enable the rapprochement of Corinna and Mistress Philosophy as that poem's hidden intention both in its last stanza — 'Ovid well knew there was much more *intended*' ('Banquet', 117) — and in the closing epigraph — '*Intentio, animi actio*'. Both Latin *intentio* and English *intention* can mean purpose or

---

169 See Thomas P. Roche, *Petrarch and the English Sonnet Sequences* (AMS Press, 1989), pp. 343-44, 440-61; more recently, Heather Dubrow, '"Dressing old words new"? Re-evaluating the "Delian Structure"', in *A Companion to Shakespeare's Sonnets*, ed. by Michael Schoenfeldt (Blackwell, 2006), pp. 90-103; and Cinta Zunino-Garrido, 'Thomas Lodge's "Supple Muse": Imitation, Inspiration and Imagination in *Phillis*', in *Poetic Theory and Practice*, ed. by Luis-Martínez, pp. 216-37.

volition, but also intellection, or the application of the mind to the apprehension of concepts and intellectual categories.¹⁷⁰ All these senses lend weight to a reading of Philosophy — i.e. the apprehension of beauty as knowledge — as presenting in poetic form Ovid's sensory enjoyment of Corinna.

Ultimately, the Neoplatonic process that sublimates Corinna into Philosophy in 'Coronet' owes more to the poetics of genre that Chapman practised in *SN* than to 'Banquet' or the sonnet sequences. Chapman's Philosophy has nothing of the flesh-and-blood presence of a Stella, a Phillis or a Parthenophe, not even of a Draytonian Idea, whose Neoplatonic qualities in the 1590s he must have seen as a disguise of the love sonnet's hypocritical sensualism. She is rather a prefiguration of the Spenserian 'Heavenly Beautie' that culminates the *Fowre Hymnes* (1596). Chapman's epideictic rhetoric is certainly more akin to the hymn than to the serialized praise of the Elizabethan sonnet collections. Philosophy resembles those deified abstractions that Menander regarded as proper inventions for the 'fictitious hymn' to the gods. The formal circularity of the corona also contributes to the hymnic sense of descriptive and narrative content opening in invocation and closing with final prayer. The sequence begins with a call for the reformation of the Muses of sensual poetry followed by the praise of Philosophy's qualities (sonnets 1–4); it moves then to a narrative psychomachia that involves Philosophy's war with the world's vices and the conversion of the seven deadly sins to virtue (5–7); next, the poet seeks Philosophy's χάρις, or favourable disposition, through the interrogation of his own poetic worth and her appointment as his Muse and patroness (8–9); the sequence ends with invocation and prayer, whereby the poetic voice requests Philosophy's reinstatement of the reformed Muses: 'And let my love adorn with modest eyes | Muses that sing love's sensual emperies' ('Coronet', 10. 13–14).¹⁷¹ Philosophy's union with her poet/lover evokes Cynthia's union with Endymion at the end of 'Cynthiam' (490–94), and thus fulfils the aims of the hymn-like philosophical meditations revived by Florentine Neoplatonism. However, Chapman's referents are far from the pagan goddesses recreated by the Christian humanist filter of Renaissance mythographers and exploited in *SN*. Rather, Philosophy looks like a blend of the also Christianized Platonic narrative allegories that shape the maid Philology in Martianus Capella's *De nuptiis Philologiae et Mercurii* (*c.* AD 420), Dame Wisdom in Prudentius's *Psychomachia* (*c.* AD 395) and the lady Philosophy in Boethius's *De consolatione Philosophiae* (*c.* AD 525).¹⁷²

---

170 For an analysis of the senses of Latin *intentio* and English 'intention', see Commentary: 'Banquet', 116–17.

171 For a description of this structure in 'Coronet', see Luis-Martínez, 'Friendlesse Verse', p. 576; and for a proportional, numerological substantiation, pp. 595–604.

172 See Commentary: 'Coronet', 4 and 5. Also, Luis-Martínez, 'Friendlesse Verse', pp. 574–75, 581. On Chapman and Boethius, see Robert K. Presson, 'Wrestling with This World: A View of George Chapman', *PMLA*, 84.1 (1969), pp. 44–50 (p. 48), doi:10.2307/1261155.

Chapman's brief collection enlarges the scope of the Elizabethan sonnet cycle in ways unforeseen by its better-known practitioners. It also opens new perspectives on the ways in which a sonnet collection can fit into the elaborate dispositions rehearsed in late sixteenth-century poetry collections.

'The Amorous Zodiac' — or 'His Amorous Zodiac', or 'Ovid's Amorous Zodiac' — is the most problematic part of Chapman's triptych. First, the poem could be considered 'his' merely as an act of translation, to the extent that some scholars have preferred to pair it with the other translation in the original volume, Stapleton's 'Contention'. Different reasons have been adduced in order to deny Chapman's authorship, and consequently the poem has often been excluded from discussions of OBS.[173] However, QOB makes clear in its title that 'Zodiac' belongs in the triad of 'Banquet' and 'Coronet', and grants only 'Contention' the status of a translation. This is the strongest ground for admitting 'Zodiac' to Chapman's canon and for dismissing 'Contention'. OOB, which anonymized all the poems and excluded 'Contention', printed 'Zodiac' as the third part of its contents, clearly reinforcing its status as part of the 'original' material in the first edition. Furthermore, certain features of style in the translation are undoubtedly Chapmanesque.[174] That neither of the two editions recognizes the poem as *Le zodiac amoreux*, the original composition by Gilles Durant, seems the best proof for attributing to Chapman the responsibility for this plagiarized translation, as unrecognized borrowing in the form of versified translation is a common Chapmanesque practice. Chapman's omission of four of the original thirty-four stanzas of Durant's poem is the only substantial change to his source — a circumstance that Alastair Fowler has explained on numerological grounds.[175] On the other hand, the 1639 octavo's bizarre attribution of the poem to Ovid has the added advantage of extending the argument of the continuity of voices across the different poems in the volume. Chapman's erasure of all traces of the French source seems an attempt to accommodate his translation as the third part of

---

[173] Bartlett argues that 'there is no evidence that this translation is Chapman's' (p. 434). Kelly attempts to refute Chapman's authorship on grounds of style (*Poetic Diction*, p. 100). Waddington, even if he regards QOB as a carefully planned volume, believes that 'Zodiac' 'was included simply to flesh out the volume' ('Visual Rhetoric', p. 43). But Sydney Lee, first in 'Chapman's "Amorous Zodiack"', *Modern Philology*, 3.2 (1905), pp. 143–58, doi:10.1086/386671, and then in *The French Renaissance in England* (Charles Scribner's Sons, 1910), pp. 465–77, provided a parallel transcription of the French and English texts, and argued that Chapman 'led his readers to believe that the verses were his original composition' ('Chapman's "Amorous Zodiack"', p. 147), an argument that explains the idiosyncrasy of the volume's title.

[174] Despite her inclination to exclude the poem from her study as not by Chapman, Kelly provides evidence of characteristic Chapmanesque features, such as compounding (*Poetic Diction*, p. 100, n. 1).

[175] The reader can consult the parallel text in Lee, 'Chapman's "Amorous Zodiack"', pp. 8–16, or *French Renaissance*, pp. 469–77, for purposes of comparison, as well as the Commentary in the present edition.

a fully original triptych whose first-person speaker — made a third-person 'his' on the title page — can claim some kinship with the voices of the previous poems. Fowler even argues that, 'in view of the implied promise at the end of the immediately preceding "A Coronet for his Mistress Philosophy" to write another poem to the same mistress, there seems to be little reason to doubt Chapman's authorship'.[176]

Although Fowler's consideration of 'Zodiac' as the *lucidius* ('more lucid') variation on the preceding poem's subject remains conjectural, there are a number of ways in which the poem can be said to complete some of the unrealized intentions, omissions and interruptions of 'Banquet' in the light of the conclusions of 'Coronet'. The interruption of Ovid's pleasure in 'Banquet' contrasts with the treatment of erotic satisfaction in the Ovidian canon. Ovid's *Amores* I. 5 recreated lovemaking through the sight and touch of 'armes and shoulders', 'breasts', 'belly', 'legge' and 'thigh'; and *Ars amandi* disdained aposiopesis by overcoming shame: 'Ulteriora pudet docuisse' ('It causes shame to teach what comes next') is the prelude to the poem's unashamed account of coital positions.[177] Although Chapman's renewed Ovidian programme forbids such conclusions, his choice of Durant seems motivated by the possibilities offered by the poem's genre in the form of alternative endings. Fowler's precise description of the genre of Durant's original offers a useful starting point:

> The French poem is an elaborate panegyrical *blason* in the form of a mechanical *catalogue raisonée* itemizing a mistress' beauties from head to foot. Its sole point lies in a conceit, whereby the traditional medical melothesia distributing the body's 12 parts among the 12 governing signs is combined with an erotic *blason* of 12 physical charms. (Both schemes happened to start with the head and finish with the feet).[178]

For Fowler, the 'mechanical' quality of the French poem is manipulated by Chapman into an 'almost fanatical' numerical pattern of overlapping 'zodiacal, seasonal, diurnal and astronomical stanza arrays', which results in 'a *reductio ad absurdum* of mannerist love poetry'.[179] But the question is whether the combination of *melothesia* and *blason* is at the service of mere witty itemizing of the beloved's body and, particularly in Chapman's translation, of its own indulging in formal self-referentiality. With origins that have been traced to animist ideas in ancient Mesopotamia, the *melothesia*, or correspondence between the parts of the human body and the twelve astrological signs, has its classic formulation in Marcus Manilius's *Astronomica* (AD 10), and a later

---

176 Alistair Fowler, *Triumphal Forms: Structural Patterns in Elizabethan Poetry* (Cambridge University Press, 1970), p. 140, n. 3.
177 *Ars amandi*, III. 769–808.
178 Fowler, *Triumphal Forms*, pp. 140–41. For Fowler's full analysis of 'The Amorous Zodiac', see pp. 140–46.
179 See ibid., pp. 142, 146, and the Commentary for the details.

tradition in medieval and early Renaissance culture.[180] Two main meanings converge in these representations: on one hand, the conception of the human body as a microcosmos, or *mundus brevis*; on the other, the confluence of astrology and medicine, which understood human bodily processes and the healing of disease as the results of the influence of one astrological sign upon a certain area or part of the body.[181] In the sixteenth century, the new Copernican astronomy and the progress of anatomy meant the decline of medieval astrological medicine, but the microcosmos analogy remained a powerful trope in humanist philosophy.[182]

Early accounts and medieval manuscript illustrations of the astrological *homo signorum* ('the man of the signs') concern nude male bodies, so its adaptation to the itemized description of the female body in the context of the love lyric needs further attention. This context explains the changes in Durant/Chapman's conversion of the traditional body-sign equivalences in Manilius and later medical writers:[183]

Zodiacal sign	Medical zodiacal man	Poetic zodiacal mistress
Aries	head and face	head
Taurus	neck	brow
Gemini	arms and shoulders	eyes
Cancer	breast and lungs	nose
Leo	heart and liver	mouth
Virgo	belly and bowels	cheeks
Libra	buttocks, kidneys, anus	neck
Scorpio	genitals	breasts
Sagittarius	thighs	hands
Capricorn	knees	genitals
Aquarius	calves	thighs
Pisces	feet	calves and feet

180 For an account of the manuscript traditions of the zodiacal *melothesia*, with useful illustrations, see Harry Bober, 'The Zodiacal Miniature of the *Très Riches Heures* of the Duke of Berry: Its Sources and Meaning', *Journal of the Warburg and Courtauld Institutes*, 11.1 (1948), pp. 1–34, doi:10.2307/750460. For a useful overview of its classical and medieval traditions, see Charles Clark, 'The Zodiac Man in Medieval Medical Astrology', *Quidditas*, 3 (1982), pp. 13–38.
181 Clark, 'The Zodiac Man', p. 25, and ff.
182 Ibid., p. 38. For a classic account of the topic of the *mundus brevis* in Elizabethan England, see J. B. Bamborough, *The Little World of Man* (Longmans, Green & Co., 1951).
183 'Accipe diuisas hominis per sidera partes | singulaque in propriis parentia membra figuris, | in quis praecipuas toto de corpore uires | exercent. Aries caput est ante omnia princeps | sortitus censusque sui pulcherrima colla | Taurus, et in Geminis aequali bracchia sorte | scribuntur conexa umeris, pectusque locatum | sub Cancro est, laterum regnum scapulaeque Leonis, | Virginis in propriam descendunt ilia sortem, | Libra regit clunes, et Scorpios inguine gaudet, | Centauro femina accedunt, Capricornus utrisque | inperitat genibus, crurum fundentis Aquari | arbitrium est, Piscesque pedum sibi iura reposcunt' (Marcus Manilius, *Astronomicon*, ed. by Alfred Edward Housman, 2 vols (Georg Olms, 1972), II. 453–65, I, pp. 47–48).

The poet's departures from the traditional medical correspondences aim to adjust scientific discourse to the exigencies of lyric convention. Thomas Watson's seventh 'passion of loue' in his *Hekatompathia* (1582) provides a typical instance of the Petrarchan blazon in English Renaissance poetry:

> Harke you that list to heare what sainte I serue:
> Her yellowe *lockes* exceede the beaten goulde;
> Her sparkeling *eies* in heau'n a place deserue;
> Her *forehead* high and faire of comely moulde;
> Her wordes are musicke all of siluer sounde;
> Her wit so sharpe as like can scarce be found:
> Each *eybrowe* hangs like Iris in the skie;
> Her Eagles *nose* is straight of stately frame; blue
> On either *cheeke* a Rose and Lillie lies;
> Her breath is sweete perfume, or hollie flame;
> Her *lips* more red than any Corall stone;
> Her *necke* more white, than Swans that mone;
> Her *brest* transparent is, like Christall rocke;
> Her *fingers* long, fit for Apolloes Lute;
> Her slipper much as Momus dare not mocke;
> Her vertues all so great as make me mute:
> What *other partes* she hath I neede not say,
> Whose *face* alone is cause of my decaye.[184]

If we leave aside other qualities and attend to the bodily parts only, a comparison with the right-hand column of the table above reveals that Watson names virtually the same parts of the face found in Durant/Chapman, proceeds to the same upper parts of the body and interrupts his catalogue before naming the nether parts. Aposiopesis in the final couplet draws attention both to the 'face' as 'cause' of the lover's passion and to the irrelevance of the 'other partes'. The lyrical blazon certainly exerts its influence upon 'Zodiac': divided into six parts that are assigned to each of the six boreal signs, the face occupies the zodiac's northern hemisphere, while the rest of the bodily parts are distributed along the six austral constellations.

But the poetic *melothesia*, far from being a conventional game of correspondences, frees 'Zodiac' from the mechanical itemizing of the blazon, and from its attitudes of shame regarding the body. The satisfaction of sexual pleasure in the sign of Capricorn is called a 'gole' (25. 2) — which puns on 'goal' but whose primary meaning is a 'ditch' — that the lover passes in order to reach 'safer' places.[185] The lover acknowledges the difficulty of naming that bodily part 'with chastity', but embarrassment is overcome and genitality is naturalized alongside the other parts of the body. Joining anatomy and astronomy, the scientific nature of the conceit dignifies the lady's body and

---

184 Thomas Watson, *The ΕΚΑΤΟΜΠΑΘΙΑ, or the Passionate Centurie of Loue* (London: John Wolfe, 1582), sig. A4ʳ, emphasis added.
185 See note to 'Zodiac', 25. 2 and Commentary.

magnifies it to cosmic proportions. Watson's poem lacks verbs of movement. In Chapman's (even more than in Durant's original), these verbs make the first-person speaker the protagonist of a carefully planned epic journey: he announces that he will, Phoebus-like, 'roundly run, | To frame [...] an endless Zodiac' (3. 5–6); he will 'enter' (6. 3), 'move' (12. 3), 'haste' (19. 5), 'be passed' (22. 3), 'be displaced' (22. 6), 'dispatch' (26. 5) and 'descend' (28. 2), but also, Ulysses-like, will 'stay' (13. 5) and 'dwell' (12. 3) in those places whose enticements 'shall hold' his 'course' (18. 5). 'Zodiac' replaces the blazon's rhetoric of catalogue with a focus on 'course[s]' (4. 2, 13. 2, 18. 5), 'journeys' (26. 4), 'labour[s]' (19. 4) and 'race[s]' (23. 4). The solar 'ecliptic line' (23. 2) will take the speaker through multiple 'houses' (19. 3) of residence, which are depicted not only in stellar terms, but also orographically as vales, hills and mountains (21–22). While the blazon demands a distant, static gaze, the conceit of the zodiacal mistress permits the use of epic narrative as a vehicle for both erotic and intellectual enquiry.

Chapman's awareness of the genre conventions at work in Durant's poem helps answer the 'Zodiac' puzzle in *OBS*, particularly regarding its inclusion as the third panel of the volume's triptych. It may sound odd to assume that Chapman's first-person voice in this erotic poem coincides with the one that asks the Muses to 'abjure' all sensual 'joys' in 'Coronet' (1. 9). But it may be less odd to imagine Chapman's ventriloquizing of Durant's lyric voice as an effect of the reinstatement of the reformed sensual Muses at the end of 'Coronet'. If so, Chapman's taste for scientific, philosophical poetry resurfaces in 'Zodiac' to resume the narrative where 'Banquet' left it, but with the more 'modest eyes' with which the 'Muses that sing love's sensual emperies' can now 'adorn' Philosophy's beauties ('Coronet', 10. 13–14). As Fowler has argued, the poem's 'initial proposal is to shine in the mistress's beauties' through the mediation of the 'sun poet'.[186] 'Zodiac' reinstates erotic and didactic elegy into the collection, but its sensuality is infused with the 'philosophical conceits' that the volume's preface announces. Proclus's differentiation between, on one hand, a mimetic poetry that is concerned with the 'lesser powers' of the soul and tends to lower objects and, on the other, a rational, scientific poetry of intellect and knowledge, operates here through the zodiacal elevation of the erotic blazon.[187] Thus, 'Zodiac' reconciles the apparently antithetical nature of 'Banquet' and 'Coronet' by invoking the principle of *discordia concors*. The sun/poet's distribution of the lady's body along an ordered universe achieves her integration in the orderly system of his verse:

> But, gracious love, if jealous heav'n deny
> My life this truly-blest variety,
>   Yet will I thee through all the world disperse;
> If not in heav'n, amongst those braving fires,

---

186 Fowler, *Triumphal Forms*, p. 142.
187 See Introduction, p. 41, and notes 133–38 on Proclus.

> Yet here thy beauties (which the world admires)
> Bright as those flames shall glister in my verse. ('Zodiac', 30)

The poem's shining on the lady's beauty is reciprocated by her illumination of its lines. This integration is the work of a voice that has domesticated the erotic fury of the Ovid of 'Banquet':

> Now Ovid's Muse as in her tropic shined,
> And he (struck dead) was mere heav'n-borne become,
>   So his quick verse in equal height was shrined —
> Or else blame me as his submitted debtor,
> That never mistress had to make me better. ('Banquet', 57. 5–9)

Presented now as literally shining in a different tropic and transported to a different heaven, poetic inspiration in 'Zodiac' manages to find that mistress who makes the poet better by reconciling Corinna to Philosophy. The poet's Ovidian soul, 'now grown more old and wise', which 'Pours forth itself in deeper mysteries' (*OBS*: 'Davies 1', 13–14), emerges triumphantly from the complex game of genres and voices that is *OBS*. Waddington's exclusion of 'Zodiac' from Chapman's authorial part in the volume is subservient to his view of 'Banquet' as a satire of Ovidian sensuality. Its inclusion invites a reassessment of the collection as a triptych in which 'Banquet' still remains the central panel, but which promotes the side panels as crucial elements of its overall meanings. Genre is essential to this design: the incisive exploration of the Ovidian elegy through the intricate kaleidoscope of Renaissance literary forms makes of *OBS* Chapman's most accomplished experiment in poetic *difficultà*.

4. 'Sweet philosophic strains': Poetry and Philosophy

In the first of the commendatory sonnets included in *OBS*, Richard Stapleton imagines Chapman's Muse singing 'Sweet philosophic strains' ('*OBS*: Stapleton', 8).[188] The poet himself, in the prefatory letter to this same work, argues that his poetry is made of 'philosophical conceits' ('*OBS*: To Roydon', line 44). Three years later, addressing his friend Thomas Harriot in *Achilles Shield*, he uses narrative allegory to depict the interactions of poetry with philosophy, both of which he personifies:

> Yet where high *Poesies* natiue habite shines,
> From whose reflections flow eternall lines:
> Philosophy retirde to darkest caues
> She can discouer.[189]

Similarly, in the dedicatory verses to Prince Henry of his complete *Iliads* (1611), the poet couples 'Learning and her Lightner, Poesie'.[190] An image with

---

188 See Commentary: '*OBS*: Stapleton', 8.
189 *Achilles Shield* (1598): 'To M. Harriots', lines 137–40, in Bartlett, p. 384.
190 *Iliads* (1611): 'To the High Borne Prince of Men, Henrie', line 78, in Nicoll, I, p. 5.

clear Platonic reminiscences, Poesy's discovery of Philosophy by illuminating the latter's 'darkest caves' also evokes the well-known Renaissance emblematic topos of *Veritas filia Temporis* ('Truth is the daughter of Time'), originating in Aulus Gellius's *Noctes Atticae* (AD 177), the most frequent illustration of which is the young maid Truth rescued from a cave by aging Time, a representation of the god Chronos, sometimes confused or deliberately identified with Cronus, or Saturn — a common Renaissance embodiment of learning.[191] An emblematic illustration of this motif appears in *OBS*, as it was bookseller Richard Smith's device.[192] Often embodying temporal or Saturnian qualities, the not always successful endeavour of poetry to illuminate truth is a recurrent theme in Chapman's early work. In 'Cynthiam', the Moon goddess, who is 'All wisdom, beauty, majesty and dread', is asked to consume an enraptured Time with her fire's splendour: 'O let thy beauty scorch the wings of Time, | That, fluttering, he may fall before thine eyes | And beat himself to death before he rise' (18–20). In 'Banquet', Corinna will summon Time to eternize her qualities: 'She shall bid Time, and Time, so feasted never, | Shall grow in strength of her renown forever' (63. 8–9). In 'Coronet', poetry strives to give true expression to Mistress Philosophy's obscured beauty:

> And like the pansy, with a little veil,
>   She gives her inward work the greater grace,
>   Which my lines imitate, though much they fail —
> Her gifts so high, and *time's conceits so base*.
>
>   (8. 9–12, emphasis added)

These tropes, which are far from being merely ornamental, must be taken as guides to Chapman's ideas about the function of poetry. Criticism of *SN* and *OBS* has often attributed their obscurity of meaning to their philosophical nature, and has consequently tried to unveil the predominance of certain systems of thought, chiefly hermetic and Neoplatonic, as underlying structures of the poems.[193] However, such consistency is seldom a reality in a poet whose humanistic idea of knowledge aims to transcend dichotomies and to integrate multiplicity into a very personal idea of unity. The variety of sources

---

191 Aulus Gellius, *The Attic Nights*, ed. and trans. by John C. Rolfe, 3 vols (Heinemann, 1927), XII. 11. 3–7, II, p. 394–95. On the iconography of the motif, see Fritz Saxl, 'Veritas Filia Temporis', in *Philosophy and History: Essays Presented to Ernst Cassirer*, ed. by R. Klibansky and H. J. Paton (Oxford University Press, 1930), pp. 197–222. For its use as a printer's device, see Simona Cohen, *Transformations of Time and Temporality in Medieval and Renaissance Art* (Brill, 2014), pp. 253–64. For its English literary uses, see Soji Iwasaki, 'Veritas Filia Temporis and Shakespeare', *English Literary Renaissance*, 3.2 (1973), pp. 249–63, doi:10.1111/j.1475-6757.1973.tb00750.x. On Saturnian melancholy as emblem of knowledge and Chapman's *Shadow of Night*, see Yates, *Occult Philosophy*, pp. 157–71.
192 Chapman's desire to have his own device on the title page displaced Smith's to the last page of the volume (see Figures 2 and 3). On this issue, see Waddington, 'Visual Rhetoric', pp. 45–46, as well as the final section of the present Introduction.
193 On Chapman's hermeticism, see Yates, *Occult Philosophy*, pp. 157–71; Waddington, *The Mind's Empire*.

on which these poems draw testifies to the poet's willingness to accept arguments and ideas that would prove contradictory to one another in orthodox philosophical writing. But these arguments and ideas mix well when their aim is to provide the groundwork for poetic imagery. This is one way in which philosophy serves poetry: as a source for specific arguments, similes or metaphors. Yet this is seldom the end of the process: in the act of accommodating philosophical arguments into its lines, poetry infuses philosophy with its own light. Chapman would have rejected the Sidneian idea of philosophical poetry as merely 'the sweet food of sweetly uttered knowledge';[194] and he would have accepted Sidney's division of labour between the philosopher and the poet only upon certain conditions:

> the philosopher with his learned definition [...] replenisheth the memory with many infallible grounds of wisdom, which, notwithstanding, lie dark before the imaginative and judging power, if they be not illuminated or figured forth by the speaking picture of poesy.[195]

The main condition would be that the 'illumination' or 'figuring forth' be not ornamental but instrumental in the act of transmuting knowledge into truth. Poetry thus heralds the attainment of the Platonic equation of Beauty, Truth and Symmetry. Philosophy and poetry must be conceived of as reciprocally instrumental. On one hand, philosophical sources supply the abundant material with which *SN* edifies its visionary compound of mythological and magical knowledge; philosophical sources also provide the complex amalgam of theories of sensory and intellectual perception that informs *OBS*. Natale Conti's *Mythologiae* (1567, 1581), Marsilio Ficino's works and commentaries on Plato, and the Presocratic, Platonic, Aristotelian and peripatetic theories of the senses, collected from original sources or most likely from Renaissance handbooks, constitute an essential arsenal which the poet's transformative mind hardly leaves intact. On the other hand, there is the energy that animates and accompanies poetry's voyage to philosophy's truths — an energy that materializes in the Platonic/Brunian notion of frenzy, or *furor*. The two parts of the present section explore two important instances of Chapman's creative transformation of his 'philosophical' sources: the rewriting of the myth of Night that enables his equation of the nocturnal with the 'deep search of knowledge' in *SN*, and more particularly in 'Noctem'; and the problem of sensory perception and sensual enjoyment in relation to the intellect in *OBS*. The subsequent section reads the two volumes in the light of Giordano Bruno's notion of shadows as guiding signs to the frenzied lover's pursuit of intellectual beauty.

---

194 *Defence of Poesy*, in *Miscellaneous Prose*, p. 80.
195 Ibid., p. 86.

4.1. Philosophy and Myth: 'Hymnus in Noctem'

The two hymns contained in the original quarto of *SN* were printed with a number of learned glosses and some occasional marginal notes. This erudite apparatus includes citations from the hymns of Homer, Callimachus and Orpheus, from poetry of the Archaic period like Homer's *Iliad* and *Odyssey*, Hesiod's *Theogony*, and Pherecydes' *Histories*, from darker poems of the Hellenistic period such as Aratus's *Phaenomena* or Lycophron's *Alexandra*, from the geographical writings of Strabo and Pausanias, and from the philosophical works of Plato and Aristotle — all quoted in their original Greek or in Latin translation. In 1926, Franck Schoell noted that the near totality of these sources was in fact borrowed — or in some cases plagiarized — from the work of Italian mythographer Natale Conti (1520–82), whose *Mythologiae* (1567) Chapman used in its expanded Frankfurt edition of 1581. Chapman only mentions Conti's Latin name, 'Natalis Comes', in the seventh gloss of 'Noctem'. Schoell's study also revealed Chapman's use of other sources in his early poems such as Marsilio Ficino's works and commentaries on Plato.[196]

Schoell's work is seminal for the clarification of Chapman's sources and working methods. Yet his listing and reproduction of passages fashioned an image of the poet as a shameless plagiarist whose versifying of Conti's Latin produced formless, inarticulate poems lacking any aesthetic conception.[197] Leslie Rutledge's contention that 'however often Chapman pillaged his favorite ancient writers and Renaissance authorities for words and ornaments and for learned support of his precepts, he rarely takes over an idea unchanged' conveys a fairer portrait.[198] Rutledge's conviction of Chapman's philosophical integrity has drawn attention to the relationship between his sources and his commitment to the 'deep search of knowledge' of which he boasts in his first Roydon preface; the sentence inevitably hints at a connection with the 'deep-searching Northumberland', whose circle of speculative philosophers and scientists had allegedly cultivated the study of esoteric arts such as alchemy and magic. The groundbreaking work of scholars like Frances Yates and Raymond Waddington established a line of enquiry that leads from Chapman's debts to Conti to deeper interest in the Neoplatonic revival and translation of the Orphic hymns and of the Hermetic corpus (attributed to the legendary Hermes Trismegistus), and the writings on magic and alchemy of Henry Cornelius Agrippa (1486–1535), particularly his *De occulta philosophia*

---

196 Schoell, *Études*.
197 MacLure's complaint that *The Shadow of Night* 'gives voice to a set of obsessions rather than an imaginative vision, and with the complication of imperfection rather than profundity' is an effect of this image of the poet (*George Chapman*, p. 36).
198 Rutledge, *George Chapman's Theory of the Soul*, pp. iii–iv. Diametrically opposed, see Sears Jayne's portrait of Chapman as an amateur philosopher, whose 'borrowings from Ficino are simply stuck into his poems as cloves are stuck into a ham' ('Ficino and the Platonism of the English Renaissance', *Comparative Literature*, 4.3 (1952), pp. 214–38 (p. 218), doi:10.2307/1768535).

libri tres (1533). Yates sees both *SN* and *OBS* as products of 'the occult psychology in which the various planetary characteristics are combined or tempered with one another to form the complete personality' of 'Saturnian melancholy'.[199] With particular regard to *SN*, Waddington concludes that Chapman's poetics is based on 'the Platonic doctrine of reminiscence', through which 'the Orphic artist remembers the lost harmony of his own soul and recreates it in his own art', and which has an analogy in Giordano Bruno's transformation of 'Hermetic magic into an elaborate art of memory'.[200]

Waddington remains to date the staunchest defender of Chapman's Orphism.[201] The two specific mentions of the mythical poet Orpheus in *SN* ('Noctem', 55, 139–58) and the five citations from his extant work (via Conti) in the glosses ('Noctem', Gloss 8, 11; 'Cynthiam', Gloss 1, 3, 10) convince Waddington that the hymnodic voice of the poem perceives itself as the heir to an Orphic tradition. The Renaissance consideration of Orpheus as a primitive theologian (*priscus theologus*) and a descendant of Hermes Trismegistus, and the Neoplatonic revival of his figure through Ficino's Latin translation of the hymns and the association of the Orphic cults with Renaissance magic, would have been factors which, according to Waddington, brought Chapman near Orpheus. Even the obvious differences between 'Chapman's long, allegorical narratives' and 'the brief, mystical incantations attributed to Orpheus' must be diminished if the reader understands 'that Chapman imitates not the form but the spirit of the *Orphic Hymns*'.[202] This latter argument inevitably overstates Chapman's Orphic indebtedness. First, because both his moral reading of the Orpheus myth and the quotations of the poems attributed to the mythical Orpheus have their basis in Conti. Second, because Orpheus's role as ancient civilizer of men is shared in *SN* with other mythical figures: Prometheus, Hercules and Perseus — all via Conti as well. Particularly with Prometheus (more on the other two in the next section), Orpheus shares the title of educator of men into 'civil love of art and fortitude', if we attend to the long passage in 'Noctem' that compares their arts (131–70). Third, because, as argued in the previous section, the hymnic structure of *SN* owes more to the poetic theory learned in Menander and the poetic practice of Homer and Callimachus than to the brief Orphic hymn. As already mentioned in this introduction, for both the theory and practice of the hymn Conti's *Mythologiae* may have been an intermediary text, regardless of Chapman's probable acquaintance with the Greek originals.

Chapman's 'Orphic' voice and a number of other notions in *SN* need to be revised in the light of Conti's influence on the poem. In a note of 1952 that

---

199 Yates, *Occult Philosophy*, pp. 167–68.
200 Waddington, *The Mind's Empire*, p. 97.
201 Ibid., pp. 45–54
202 Ibid., p. 49.

revisited and amplified Schoell's list of Conti-inspired passages in Chapman's first poem, W. Schrickx concluded with an important siren call for Chapman scholars which has not yet been heeded:

> however manifold the interpretations of *The Shadow of Night* may be, there is still room left for an interpretation based on the mythological data supplied by Conti. And such an investigation would no doubt lay bare the workings of the poet's mind and show to what extremes he went in the application of his source-material. An enquiry undertaken from this angle would probably reveal that Chapman owes almost as much to Conti as to Neoplatonic or Hermetic philosophy.[203]

In fact, what this investigation may reveal is that Neoplatonic/Hermetic/Orphic influences are to a great extent debts to Conti. For Schrickx, Conti supplies 'the perceptible centre' which Swinburne missed in Chapman's poems — and, I would add, the key to the 'well-ordered structure' that Heninger also missed and that other critics have sought in hermetic philosophies.[204]

First published in 1567, Natale Conti's *Mythologiae* is, with Lilio Gregorio Giraldi's *De deis gentium varia et multiplex historia* (1548) and Vincenzo Cartari's *Le imagini degli dei degli Antichi* (1556), the most important mythographic work in the European sixteenth century.[205] Chapman seems to have known the three of them, but it is to Conti that he resorted for documentation and cribbing. Conti's ten-book treatise follows a systematic plan: the first book contains an exposition of the author's Platonized Christian philosophy of myth, based on the natural, moral and historical aspects of the legends of the ancient gods; the next eight books are a lengthy though ordered exposition of mythological material; the tenth book provides an epitome of book one and the allegorical meanings of the principal gods discussed in the central books. Conti summarizes his intention in the first chapter:

> We intend to gloss only those stories *that raise men to the heights of celestial knowledge* [*ad rerum coelestium cognitionem erigunt*], that *counsel proper behaviour* [*instituunt ad probitatem*] and discourage unlawful pleasures, that *reveal Nature's secrets* [*arcana naturae patefaciunt*], that ultimately teach us all we absolutely need to know to lead a decent human life, that enhance our understanding of all the great writers.[206]

---

203 Willem Schrickx, 'George Chapman's Borrowings from Natali Conti: Some Hitherto Unnoted Passages', *English Studies*, 32 (1951), pp. 107–12 (p. 112).
204 Ibid. See also Swinburne, *George Chapman*, p. 14; and Heninger, *Handbook of Renaissance Meteorology*, p. 199.
205 For an overview of these treatises in the context of their production, see Jean Seznec, *The Survival of the Pagan Gods: The Mythological Tradition and Its Place in Renaissance Humanism and Art*, trans. by Barbara F. Sessions (Princeton University Press, 1972), pp. 220–56. For the influence of these treatises on English Renaissance mythography and literature, see Anna-Maria Hartmann, *English Mythography in Its European Contexts, 1500–1650* (Oxford University Press, 2018), pp. 35–51.
206 Conti, 'Quod sit totius operis argumentum', I. 1, p. 3; Mulryan, p. 3; emphasis added.

There is nothing in this enunciation that Chapman would not have subscribed to: the purpose is to put the best ancient learning to the service of a profound enquiry into the secrets of Nature that will lead to moral edification and sublime elevation. As stated earlier, Chapman's reliance on Conti must have influenced his decision to use the poetic hymn and to observe its 'institutuum componendorum', or 'compositional structure', along the lines of Homer, Callimachus and Orpheus.[207] But he also felt free to alter Conti's interpretations of key myths to suit his own purposes. His method of creative transformation was not arbitrary, and he carefully studied his sources in search of reasons that could justify his changes.

Among Chapman's alterations of Conti, his reinvention of the myth of Night is the most significant for the conceptual design of *SN*, and it will be used for the purposes of detailed illustration in the following pages. As the protagonist of the first part of his poem, the Hesiodic goddess Night paves the way for Cynthia's absolute reign in the second part. Chapman follows Conti in considering Night the oldest goddess, whose primordial existence even preceded Chaos. But Conti's overall interpretation of the powers and meanings of Night is negative. Conti follows Cicero's *De natura deorum* in listing a number of plagues ('Love, Guile, Fear, Toil, Envy' etc.) which he identifies as Night's children. He also attributes all evils to 'Nox mentis', or Ignorance, while he explains the etymology of *Nox* from Latin *nocere*, to harm.[208] Chapman changes Conti by means of reinterpretation: true Night has been eclipsed by 'a stepdame Night of mind' ('Nox mentis') that 'broods beneath her hell-obscuring wings | Worlds of confusion' ('Noctem', 64–65). The effects of 'This horrid stepdame, Blindness of the Mind' are 'Disjunction' and 'Ruin' in the form of present moral chaos, and political and religious dissension ('Noctem', 63–90). The restoration of the authentic kingdom of 'sacred Night' has thus been impeded since the replacement of her full domination over the universe by the alternating rule of Night and Day: 'Why did thy absolute and endless sway | Licence heav'n's torch, the sceptre of the Day, | Distinguished intercession to thy throne | That long before all matchless ruled alone?' ('Noctem', 33–36). A new realm of Night ruled by lunar Cynthia must then be reinstated upon the condition of the permanent banishment of the Sun. The hymnic voice calls for this banishment by means of a common rhetorical strategy of the genre, the apopemptic speech (from Greek ἀποπέμπω, 'send off') whereby the Sun is dismissed:

---

207 Conti, 'De hymnis antiquorum', I. 16, pp. 56–57; Mulryan, p. 48.
208 See Conti, 'De Nocte', III. 2, p. 233; Mulryan p. 193. For Conti's text and its source in Cicero, *De natura deorum*, III. 44. 17, see Commentary: 'Noctem', 63–74. The etymology argument is a false one: neither the Latin nouns *noxa* and *noxia* nor the adjectives *noxialis* and *noxiosus*, which derive from *noceo*, have any connection with *nox* (*OLD*). The standard Contian account of Night as a source of evil in Elizabethan poetry, the status of which as a precedent for Chapman needs further investigation, is Edmund Spenser, *The Faerie Queene*, I. 5. 20–48; see ed. by A. C. Hamilton and others (Pearson, 2007), pp. 75–80.

> Hence, beasts and birds, to caves and bushes then,
> And welcome Night, ye noblest heirs of men;
> Hence, Phoebus, to thy glassy strumpet's bed,
> And never more let Themis' daughters spread
> Thy golden harness on thy rosy horse,
> But in close thickets run thy oblique course. ('Noctem', 378–83)

Yet this dismissal requires a careful re-accommodation of all the pieces of a legend which, again, Chapman derived from Conti. Phoebus is here not the Delphic Apollo, but the primordial Helios, or the Sun, son of the Titans Hyperion and Theia. He is asked to return to the bed that he shares with his 'strumpet', and thus to discontinue once and for all his daily ascent to the heavens. Our first guide to these lines' mythological content must be Chapman's own gloss, which identifies the three daughters of Themis and Jupiter, the Hours, as the Sun's diurnal assistants in preparing his horses and chariot. As is customary, the poet traces his ultimate source back to Orpheus, but without mentioning Conti as his intermediary. Conti's 'De Horis' quotes the beginning of Orpheus's hymn 'To the Hours', which identifies these deities' names and parentage: 'Hours, born from the seed of Jove and Themis, wealthy Eunomia (Good Governance), and Dice (Justice), and Eirene (Peace)'.[209] Not much, however, is said of the identity of Phoebus's 'glassy strumpet', mainly because the poet assumes that the reader may recall a former passage in the poem in which the arrival of Day is interpreted as disorder and chaos:

> And as when hosts of stars attend thy flight
> (Day of deep students, most contentful Night),
> The Morning (mounted on the Muses' stead)
> Ushers the sun from Vulcan's golden bed,
> And then, from forth their sundry roofs of rest,
> All sorts of men, to sorted tasks addressed,
> Spread this inferior element [...]
> So to the chaos of our first descent
> (All days of honour and of virtue spent)
> We basely make retreat, and are no less
> Than huge, impolished heaps of filthiness. ('Noctem', 201–24)

Two endnote glosses identify 'Morning' as Greek goddess Ἠώς, *Aurora* in Latin, Dawn in English. In Gloss 6, Chapman mentions an epic poem of Trojan matter, *Alexandra*, by Lycophron of Calchis (third century BC). Yet his quotation is actually a bowdlerized version of Conti's own translation of the Greek text. Chapman omits Conti's third line, which mentions Aurora's leaving her husband Tithonus alone in his bed. The line is added here:

---

209 Conti, 'De Horis', IV. 16, p. 418; my translation; see Orpheus, Ὡρῶν ('To the Hours'), 43. 1–3, in *Hymnes orphiques*, ed. by Marie-Christine Fayant (Les belles lettres, 2014), pp. 362–63.

> *Aurora montem Phagium advolaverat,*
> *Velocis altum nuper alis Pegasi.*
> *Cernam prope Tithonum in thoro reliquerat.*
>
> ('Dawn had been newly soaring over the steep mount Phegion on the swift wings of Pegasus. She had left Tithonus in his bed by Cerne.')[210]

The omission seems intentional. Tithonus, son of King Laomedon of Troy and the Naiad Strymo, was granted the gift of immortality to live eternally with his wife, Aurora, but she forgot to ask her father Jupiter to also give her husband the gift of eternal youth. Tithonus lived eternally in old age, and Aurora got tired of him, locked him away, and later metamorphosed him into a cicada. Homer's 'Hymn to Aphrodite', which Chapman himself translated later in his life, describes Tithonus's ageing and Aurora's growing dislike of him.[211]

The other gloss — the only moment in *SN* in which Chapman mentions his true source, Conti — informs us of the nature and origin of the Sun's bed, made by Vulcan, and from which Aurora, Chapman tells us, ushers him to his chariot:

> Some writers claimed that Vulcan made the Sun his own golden bed [*thorum*]. It was supposed to be so deep that once the Sun arrived at the shores of great Ocean, worn out from the daily effort of his trip, he could sail eastward in it, even while he was asleep. And the chariot would be ready and waiting for him when he arrived. Then he would jump into the chariot and sail for heaven.[212]

Conti's Latin term for bed, *thorus*, is synonymous with *thalamus*, i.e. marriage bed. The presence of Aurora ushering the Sun to his chariot and leading him in his ascension to heaven would complete the picture — a slightly later Italian Baroque fresco by Guido Reni, *L'Aurora* (1613–14), possibly sharing Conti as a literary source, could serve as a visual gloss.[213]

Besides the abovementioned excerpt from Conti alluding to Orpheus's hymn, Chapman's apostrophe to the Sun/Phoebus asking him not to return again seems inspired by two other passages from Conti that have not been noted earlier. The first of these is the continuation of the former description

---

210 Conti, 'De Aurora', VI. 2, p. 558; Mulryan, p. 461; see Commentary: 'Noctem', 201–24, and Gloss 6.
211 'To Aphrodite', 229–36, in *Hesiod, the Homeric Hymns and Homerica*, ed. and trans. by Hugh A. Evelyn-White (William Heinemann, 1920), pp. 422–23. Chapman's translation is given here: 'On his faire head and honorable Beard, | His first gray hayres to her light eyes apperd | She left his bed, yet gave him still for food | The god's Ambrosia, and attire as good — | Till even the hate of Age came on so fast | That not a lyneament of his was grac't | With powre of motion [...] | Her counsaile then thought best to strive no more, | But lay him in his bed and lock his Dore' (*Al the Hymnes of Homer* (1623): 'To Venus', lines 381–94, in Nicoll, II, p. 577).
212 Conti, 'De Sole', V. 17, p. 537; Mulryan, p. 444 ('Sun' has been capitalized). For Conti's Latin text, see Commentary: 'Noctem', 201–24.
213 Reni, *L'Aurora*. See Visual Sources.

of the Sun's bed. Here Conti quotes, in the original Greek and in Latin translation, a verse fragment from the ancient elegiac poet Mimnermus (fl. 630–600 BC), allegedly from the book of elegies dedicated to his slave/mistress Nanno:

> For the Sun's portion is labour every day, nor is there ever any rest either for him or his horses when rosy-fingered Dawn hath left the ocean and climbed the sky; for over the wave in *a delightful bed* [πολυήρατος εὐνή] forged of precious gold by the hand of Hephaestus, hollow and with wings, he is carried in pleasant sleep on the face of the waters from the Hesperian's country to the land of Aethiop, where his horses and swift chariot stand till early-begotten Dawn appear, and then the son of Hyperion mounts his car.[214]

A number of details in this text have surprised commentators. First, the presence of the 'delightful bed' where texts alluding to similar traditions usually have a 'cup' as the object that Vulcan built for the Sun. The Homeric formula πολυήρατος εὐνή described the marriage bed of Ulysses and Penelope at their reunion in Homer's *Odyssey* (the epithet was amplified by Chapman to 'sweet Haven' in his later translation); also in Hesiod's *Theogony*, the Titaness Phoebe comes to Coeus's 'delightful bed' to conceive their children, Leto and Asteria.[215] Second, as Emilio Suárez de la Torre has noted, this fragment belongs to a love elegy, mentioning together the Sun and Dawn: the Sun's nocturnal trip took place while Dawn slept with Tithonus, or at least until she transformed him into a cicada.[216] Despite Conti's silence in this matter, Chapman's explicit coupling of Aurora and the Sun shows awareness of the erotic meanings in these texts, to which he added moral condemnation through the epithet 'strumpet'.

Another relevant chapter for Chapman's lines is Conti's 'De Aurora'. That Chapman knew this passage is obvious from the 'roseos equos' which he transformed into his 'rosy horse' ('Noctem', 382), and which was inspired by the 'roseae quadrigae' driven by Dawn in Virgil's *Aeneid*.[217] More importantly for the present argument, Conti's chapter also explains, quoting Homer's

---

214 Mimnermus, Fragment 12. For the Greek text with English commentary, see Archibald Allen, *The Fragments of Mimnermus: Text and Commentary* (Franz Steiner, 1993), pp. 94–109; Conti, 'De Sole', v. 17, pp. 537–38; Mulryan, p. 444, emphasis added.

215 Allen, *Fragments of Mimnermus*, p. 103. Cartari, for instance, has 'a large drinking cup' ('un gran vaso de bere') in *Imagini degli dei degli Antichi* (see Commentary: 'Noctem', 255–67, for the text and full reference). On the use of the formula πολυήρατος εὐνή, see Homer, *Odyssey*, ed. and trans. by A. T. Murray, 2 vols (Harvard University Press, 1965), XXIII. 354, II, pp. 398–99; in Chapman's translation: 'And both arrived at this sweet Haven, our bed' (*Odysseys*, 510, in Nicoll, II, p. 403). See also Hesiod, *Theogony*, 404.

216 Emilio Suárez de la Torre, 'El viaje nocturno del Sol y la *Nanno* de Mimnermo', *Estudios clásicos*, 89 (1985), pp. 5–20 (pp. 16–17).

217 'De Aurora', VI. 2, pp. 557–56. See *Aeneid*, VI. 535, in *Virgil*, ed. and trans. by H. Rhuston Fairclough, 2 vols (William Heinemann, 1939), I, p. 542. See also Commentary: 'Noctem', 378–83.

hymn 'To Hermes', that Aurora rises from the Ocean 'like the Sun' ('tamquam Solem'). Conti's insistence on these affinities between Dawn and the Sun can be traced to his own physical explanations of the myth:

> Since in fact Dawn [*Aurora*] is the light that precedes the Sun's rising, they say that she's also carried along by the Sun's horses. The Sun was thought to be the master of the stars, and treasurer of the light and life of men, because it provides the light for all the other stars, and the vitality of all living things is tied to its course. [...] There's almost no limit to the wonderful things it does for us.[218]

Yet, far from having any beneficial effects on humanity, Chapman's Day, Sun and Dawn are made responsible for the 'huge, impolished heaps of filthiness' ('Noctem', 224) that prevent the nocturnal dedication to quiet study, the pursuit of truth and tranquil moral life. Conti's universe of mythological reference is drastically altered: while he advocates the complementary, harmonizing symbolism of the siblings Helios (Sun), Eos (Dawn) and Selene (Moon), children of Hyperion and Theia, Chapman builds up a narrative of irreconcilable opposites by transforming the πολυήρατος εὐνή of ancient epic and lyric into a mytheme suggesting adultery and incest. This new meaning supports his claim in favour of a definitive interruption of the sun/moon cycle in favour of an eternal kingdom of Night.

Chapman's mythographic reinterpretation of Night is certainly intricate, but that does not make it hermetic or esoteric. It demands readerly effort to navigate through the poet's half-acknowledged sources, particularly because he shows his cards only obliquely, and because, in order to make his pieces fit into a solid conceptual puzzle, he has sought the utmost consistency of detail. Making the puzzle poetically sound is the first step towards rendering it didactically and philosophically consistent. Chapman's renewed mythography rescues Night from the clutches of *Nox mentis*, the 'stepdame Night of mind' ('Noctem', 63) that endangers the poet/philosopher's dedication to learning, and from the diurnal forces that impede Cynthia's ascension and the establishment of her eternal reign in the second half of the poem. Rhetorically, these aims are pursued through magical invocations. Poetically, Chapman's method is painstaking search and meticulous interpretation of sources. With respect to his readers, Chapman prides himself on being more elusive than enlightening:

> For the rest of his own invention, figures, and similes, touching their aptness and novelty, he hath not laboured to justify them, because he

---

218 'Cum vero lux Aurora fit ante Solis ortum, iidem Solis equi dicuntur portare Auroram. Sol siderum dominus, et lucis, vitaeque mortalium quaestor habitus est, quoniam autor est luminis ceteris stellis, et pro illius cursu cuncta vigent animantia [...] ob infinita prope in omnes beneficia' (Conti, 'De Sole', v. 17, p. 543; Mulryan, pp. 448–49). Conti's source is Homer's hymn 'To Hermes', lines 184–85; see *Hesiod, the Homeric Hymns and Homerica*, pp. 376–77.

> hopes they will be proud enough to justify themselves, and prove sufficiently authentical to such as understand them. For the rest, God help them, I cannot (do as others) make Day seem a lighter woman than she is, by painting her. ('Noctem', final gloss)

Authenticity can hardly reveal knowledge by itself, but the glosses offer sufficient clues for engaging the reader in a similarly meticulous and painstaking endeavour. The hymnic voice's request that his initiates 'serve the Night, | To whom pale Day (with whoredom soakèd quite) | Is but a drudge' ('Noctem', 328–30) functions as the best metaphor for Chapman's demands on his labouring readers: they must embrace a poetry of light-revealing darkness that avoids the meretricious wisdom of false 'painting'.

4.2. Sense and Intellect: 'Ovid's Banquet of Sense'

In a characteristically intricate passage of 'Cynthiam', the hymnic voice rebukes those poets overridden by the pleasures of the flesh for their inability to grasp the true mysteries of their art:

> Presume not then, ye flesh-confounded souls
> That cannot bear the full Castalian bowls
> Which sever mounting spirits from the senses,
> To look in this deep fount for thy pretenses:
> The juice, more clear than day, yet shadows night,
> Where humour challengeth no drop of right;
> But judgement shall display to purest eyes,
> With ease, the bowels of these mysteries. ('Cynthiam', 162–69)

In contrast, the sublime pleasures offered by the depths of the Castalian fountain are only attainable by those who can 'sever' intellect from sense. Lacking 'no drop of right', the fountain's 'juice' will impart 'judgement' only to those 'purest eyes' whose guide is their intellectual faculty. Poetic inspiration enables access to philosophical knowledge and promises a banquet of the intellect. In 'Coronet', a similar hymnic voice opens the poem by condemning the 'Muses that sing love's sensual empery' for their failure to fix their aims on the rewards promised by a poetry of the mind.

By claiming the rapprochement of poetry and philosophy, the two hymns of SN and 'Coronet' endorse a similar poetics. However, the drastic severing from the senses proposed in the former is toned down by the reintegration of the sensual Muses at the end of 'Coronet' (10. 13–14). Behind the defence of a philosophical model of poetry lies the contention about the role that the sensory appreciation and the sensual enjoyment of beauty must play in the pursuit of the 'riches of the mind' ('Coronet', 1. 13). Even the poem that has traditionally been considered Chapman's staunchest denial of the senses ends with a note that recommends their reformation and readmission. We should ponder the extent to which the mysterious epigraph closing 'Coronet' — *'Lucidius olim'* — might be read as a commentary on this point, promising to clarify its implications in a future poem that never saw the light.

The sense/mind dilemma is central to 'Banquet', which, for its apparent ambiguities and undecidabilities, remains true to Frank Kermode's description of it as 'one of the most difficult poems in the language'.[219] Readers are divided into two camps around the idea of love that the poem's protagonist endorses. On one side, Janet Spens, Muriel Bradbrook, Hallett Smith, Louise Vinge, John Huntington and Martin Wheeler have read Ovid's sensual passion for Corinna as a vehicle for the attainment of intellectual beauty.[220] On the other side, and following Kermode, James Phares Myers, Daryll Gless, Raymond Waddington and William Weaver construe the poem in terms of Chapman's dismissal of his character's sensuality by means of 'ironic reversals' that invite readers to 'consider true love, in the main, by dramatizing its opposite'.[221] Their differences lie in their view of how Platonism operates in the poem: for the former, Chapman platonizes Ovid; for the latter, Chapman's Platonism condemns his protagonist. Few are the critics that contemplate a deliberate ambiguity or paradox as inherent to Chapman's argument;[222] when such a position is considered, doubts arise as to whether it is the effect of 'Chapman's own uncertainty' about his own paradoxes.[223]

Hardly any critical reading has managed to place the poem outside these Platonic coordinates, and very few critics have managed to avoid taking sides in the debate.[224] Platonism is a necessary key to ascertaining Chapman's

219 Kermode, 'Banquet of Sense', p. 68.
220 Janet Spens, 'Chapman's Ethical Thought', in *Essays and Studies by Members of the English Association: Vol XI.*, ed. by Oliver Elton (Oxford University Press, 1925), pp. 145–69. Spens argues that Chapman's poem is about 'the sublimation of the senses', and that Corinna/Julia is 'a name for what Shelley called Intellectual Beauty' (p. 159); Bradbrook, *School of Night*, p. 167; Hallett Smith, *Elizabethan Poetry: A Study of Conventions, Meaning, and Expression* (Harvard University Press, 1952), pp. 96–99; Vinge, 'Chapman's *Ovids Banquet of Sence*': 'Chapman's poem develops Renaissance Platonism by trying to give sensual love a place in its system, and striving to reconcile the dualistic concepts of divine and bestial love' (p. 257); Huntington, 'Philosophical Seduction', pp. 43–51, reaches a similar conclusion; Wheeler, 'The obiect', offers a thorough analysis of the poem to conclude that Chapman carries out 'an original reworking of Ficino and a morally legitimate conclusion to the spirit in which Ovid has pursued his other half' (p. 346).
221 Gless, 'Chapman's Ironic Ovid', p. 23. See also Kermode, 'The Banquet of Sense', in which the ironic reading was first proposed: 'It is therefore strange that Chapman should write in his fiction an apparent glorification of the sensual stimulation of the counter-Plato, Ovid. My own view is that this is ironical; that Chapman is here portraying the Ovid whom Apollo called "lasciui [...] praeceptor Amoris" (*Ars Amatoria*, II. 497)' (p. 84). Also: John Buxton, *Elizabethan Taste* (St Martin's Press, 1964), pp. 301–03; Myers 'This Curious Frame'; Waddington, *The Mind's Empire*, pp. 113–51, and 'Visual Rhetoric'; and Weaver, 'Banquet', which extends the scope of the poem's ironic stance to Chapman's attitude to the erotic epyllion.
222 This is notably Huntington's position: see 'Philosophical Seduction', pp. 43–51.
223 MacLure, *George Chapman*, p. 53.
224 Snare, *Mystification*, pp. 111–38, criticizes the ironic reading, but can be considered exceptional in refusing to read the poem along these coordinates.

meaning. There are, however, other levels of reading at which Platonism may not be so prominent. The concurrence of ideas that can be traced back to precedents such as Empedocles, Anaxagoras, Plato, Aristotle, Theophrastus, Lucretius, Aquinas and Ficino confers upon 'Banquet' a choral philosophical perspective that matches the presence of Homer, Hesiod, Callimachus, Orpheus, Virgil and Ovid on the literary side. Chapman's compilation of philosophical arguments concerning sense perception in 'Banquet' is not methodologically different from his gathering of mythological matter in SN. We can assume, with Schoell, that the poet had direct knowledge of Marsilio Ficino's works, traces of which are visible in the text of the poem.[225] We can also presuppose that he had read Plato's works in Ficino's translation, Aristotle's *De anima* (possibly in Latin translation too) and Lucretius's *De rerum natura*.[226] Chapman mentions Aristotle's disciple Theophrastus once in relation to a Latin *sententia* whose origins have not been traced.[227] He may have known Theophrastus's small treatise *On Odours* in Latin translation in a Paris edition of 1556.[228] It is more unlikely that he had read Theophrastus's *On the Senses* (*De sensu*) directly, as its circulation in Europe, of a later date than Chapman's poem, made Presocratic theories of sense perception widely known. His indirect acquaintance with Theophrastus's treatise must have been through Ficino's commentary on Priscian's own commentary of Theophrastus.[229] Chapman may also have accessed Presocratic ideas through Diogenes Laertius's *Lives of Eminent Philosophers*, which circulated in Latin translation in the second half of the sixteenth century.[230]

However, despite the direct use he may have made of these primary sources, Chapman mainly worked from manuals and epitomes. The most conspicuous instance is Joachim Curaeus's Περὶ αἰσθήσεως καὶ αἰσθητῶν, *Libellus*

---

225 Schoell, *Études*, pp. 1–21, offers an invaluable list of specific borrowings.
226 For a recent reading of 'Banquet' along Lucretian lines, see Cassandra Gorman, 'Atomies of Love: Material (Mis)interpretations of Cupid's Origin in Elizabethan Poetry', in *Poetic Theory and Practice*, ed. by Luis-Martínez, pp. 74–98 (pp. 84–88).
227 The abbreviated name 'Theophr.' occurs in the second marginal note to 'Banquet', 84. See Commentary on that stanza.
228 Theophrastus, *Libellus de odoribus* (Paris: Michel de Vascosan, 1556). On the late transmission of *De sensu*, see H. Baltussen, *Theophrastus against the Presocratics and Plato: Peripatetic Dialectic in 'De sensibus'* (Brill, 2000), pp. 12–15.
229 See Marsilio Ficino, 'Expositio in interpretationem Pisciani Lydi super Theophrastum', in *Opera*, II, 1801–35. For an English translation of Priscian, see *On Theophrastus on Sense-Perception with 'Simplicius': On Aristotle On the Soul 2.5–12*, ed. and trans. by Pamela Huby, Carlos Steel and J. O. Urmson, annot. by Peter Lautner (Bloomsbury, 2014). I thank Jonathan Sell for suggesting this line of enquiry. Although many of Chapman's ideas find analogies here, and deserve further scrutiny, I have not been able to trace verbal echoes.
230 See *Diogenis Laertii de vitis, dogmatis et apothegmatis Philosophorum* (Paris: Claude Baleu, 1585). On Chapman's uses of Diogenes Laertius in his later works, see Zenón Luis-Martínez, 'George Chapman's Musaean "Light": Origin, Primordiality and Priority from *The Divine Poem of Musaeus* (1616) to *Hero and Leander* (1598)', *Parergon*, 41.1 (2024), pp. 239–71 (pp. 251–53), doi:10.1353/pgn.2024.a935342.

Physicus (1572), known in later editions as *De sensu et sensilibus libri duo* (with editions in 1595 and 1596), which witnesses several cases of almost verbatim unacknowledged borrowing. Though less systematic, Chapman's perusal of Curaeus's manual is not different in method from his borrowing from Conti's *Mythologiae*. Chapman's debts to Curaeus, documented in the Commentary, are revealing when we try to clarify the poet's philosophical convictions or his (lack of) systematicity in following particular schools of thought. Curaeus's work is primarily a synthesis of Aristotelian theories of sense perception that function as tests for the views of former philosophers. However, Curaeus's Aristotelianism is less important for Chapman than the manual's potential for supplying philosophical explanations that he can later transform into successful poetic conceits. Chapman's poetic mind accommodates a high degree of eclecticism which ultimately needs to be gauged against a controlling Platonic stance. For the 'ironic' critics, this philosophical eclecticism would mainly serve Chapman's satiric representation of Ovid as an abuser of philosophical ideas for purposes of self-persuasion or seduction.[231] Against this, it can be argued that this pluralist treatment of philosophical sources fosters the more productive end of the 'deep search of knowledge', namely an exploratory attitude to the dilemmas of love and the contradictions of desire.

The key for ascertaining which version of Platonism — the ironic or the idealizing — prevails in 'Banquet' has been sought in the comparison of Chapman's narrative ordering of the senses with their hierarchical arrangement in literary and philosophical traditions. Ficino's treatment of the question in his *Commentary on Plato's Symposium* supplies a referent that Chapman knew and could have borne in mind. Ficino's hierarchy, in ascending order, is 1) touch, 2) taste, 3) smell, 4) hearing, 5) sight. The hierarchy is grounded on the distance between each sense and the supreme faculty of reason. Touch, taste and smell belong to the body and matter, while hearing and sight are grouped with reason as pertaining to the soul.[232] In Ficino's account of the connection between sensory perception and the higher intellective powers, 'Reason is assigned to supreme divinity, sight to fire, hearing to the air, smell to vapors, taste to water, and touch to the earth'.[233] But Chapman's ordering — 1) hearing, 2) smell, 3) sight, 4) taste, 5) touch — responds neither to an ascending nor a descending version of Ficino's hierarchy. In his study of the literary theme of the 'banquet of the senses',

---

231 Kermode, 'Banquet of Sense', p. 87.
232 'Ex his patere potest cuique, sex illarum animae virium, tres ad corpus et materiam potius: tactum scilicet et gustum, et odoratum; tres autem alias, rationem videlicet et visum et auditum ad spiritum pertinere' (Marsilio Ficino, *Commentary on Plato's Symposium*, ed. and trans. by Sears R. Jayne (University of Missouri Press, 1944), v. 2, p. 65; for the translation, p. 165).
233 'Ratio numini summo, visus igni, aeri auditus, vaporum odori olfactus, aquae gustus, tactus terrae tribuitur' (ibid., v. 2, p. 65; translation, p. 165).

Kermode points to several Renaissance instances in literature and art of a much more faithful adjustment of Ficino's hierarchy — though in descending order. One of Kermode's examples, extracted from Ben Jonson's comedy *The New Inn* (1631), comments directly on Chapman's poem and represents the Platonic and Ovidian traditions as antithetical — the 'philosophical feasts' against 'a banquet o' sense, like that of Ovid':

> A form to take the eye; a voice, mine ear;
> Pure aromatics to my scent; a soft,
> Smooth, dainty hand to touch; and for my taste
> Ambrosiac kisses to melt down the palate.[234]

For Kermode, Chapman's dual structure initiates Ovid's philosophical ascent to sight only to later represent his descent into debauchery through bestial enjoyment of the lower senses — a turn that explains the poem's moralizing stance.[235] Kermode believes that Chapman's concern with descent relates his conception of the banquet of the five senses to the classical topos of the *quinque lineae amoris* ('the five steps of love'), originally sketched by Donatus in his commentary on Terence's *Eunuchus*, and developed in numerous instances of medieval and early Renaissance poetry.[236] Donatus's formula intends to explain a lover's strategy to obtain his final aim. This aim justifies the design of his five *lineae*, or schemes in a plan of seduction: 1) the exchange of looks, 2) conversation, 3) fondling, 4) kissing and 5) full sexual intercourse.[237] And for John Buxton, the *quinque lineae amoris* function as a counterpoint to the Ficinian tradition, somehow short-circuiting it into irony.[238]

However, the pertinence of the *quinque lineae amoris* to Chapman's poem would be as oblique as Ficino's hierarchy. The five lines of love are only indirectly concerned with the five senses — in fact, their strongest similarity is the number five. Donatus and the tradition that followed him are not concerned with smell. Besides, the explicit inclusion of 'coitus' as the fifth line, no matter how clearly it discloses the final intentions of Chapman's protagonist in the opinion of the ironic critics, is never materialized in the poem. Moreover, these explanations assume a direct link between Chapman's

---

234 Ben Jonson, *The New Inn* (1631), ed. by Julie Sanders, III. 2. 123–28, in *The Cambridge Edition of the Works of Ben Jonson Online*, ed. by Martin Butler and others, <https://universitypublishingonline.org/cambridge/benjonson> [accessed 19 January 2023].
235 Kermode, 'Banquet of Sense', pp. 90–91; Myers, 'This Curious Frame', pp. 198–201.
236 Kermode, 'Banquet of Sense', p. 87.
237 Donatus's terms are the following: 'Quinque lineae perfectae sunt ad amorem: prima uisus, secunda alloquii, tertia tactus, quarta osculi, quinta coitus' ('Five schemes have been completed to achieve love: first looks, second conversation, third fondling, fourth kisses, fifth coition'). See *Commentum Terenti*, ed. by P. Wesner (Bibliotheca Teubneriana, 1902), I. 405, quoted in Lionel J. Friedman, 'Gradus Amoris', *Romance Philology*, 19.2 (1965), pp. 167–77 (p. 172).
238 Buxton, *Elizabethan Taste*, p. 302. Vinge, 'Chapman's Ovids Banquet of Sence', pp. 256–57, denies all pertinence of the *quinque lineae amoris* topos for Chapman's poem.

philosophical Platonism and his ironic censure of Ovid's words and actions. A different perspective is offered by Rhoda Ribner, who argues that Chapman's observance of a descending pattern in the second half of his poem 'is a result of dramatic necessity'. First, because 'A dramatic situation beginning with touch and progressing through taste, smell, and hearing to finish with sight is beyond the realm of plausibility if not physical possibility', while the conception of 'a straight descent' falls outside Chapman's interest.[239] Second, because 'dramatic necessity' — 'narrative' or 'poetic' would perhaps be more accurate labels — permits an 'element of control or retardation imposed upon sense perception; it is the ritual of art, as it were, imposed on nature'. This poetic scheme allows Chapman's Ovid 'to be analytic and inventive about his passion'[240] — instead of, as other critics see him, simply behaving as a sophistic abuser. Ribner's view of the protagonist's actions as mediated by the sophistications of art has the advantage of approaching differently the question of the five lines of love (or four, if final intercourse is suspended): sight leads first to elevated conversation; and the single kiss and touch are ritual actions whose aim seems more directed to the production of further discourse than to the aims expressed by Donatus — it is to the reader's relief that we are spared a similarly ritualized treatment of the fifth line.

If viewed from the perspective of poetic necessity, Chapman's design can be said to obey a less moralistic philosophical arrangement of the senses. In Aristotle's account of sensory perception in *De anima*, hearing, smell and sight are the three senses that require an external medium. The medium basically permits physical distance between object and sense organ. Hearing and smell share air as their medium, while in sight the transparent connects the object with the eye. For their part, in taste and touch the organ becomes the medium, as it requires direct contact with the object. Sight continues to occupy a central position as the closest sense to the intellect, and thus the most reliable.[241] Chapman re-elaborates the Aristotelian differentiation between the mediated (hearing, smell, sight) and unmediated senses (touch, taste) into an elegist/lover's narrative of his physical approach to his beloved — an approach that involves overcoming distances and obstacles and that takes him to Corinna's arbour. If one reduces this tale to a natural, animal-like conception of the senses, Ovid is guided, as a hound would be, through hearing and smell first toward seeing and then toward capturing his prey through taste and touch.

But Chapman's poetic mind certainly led him to explore less primitive literary possibilities in his ordering of the senses. Janet Levarie Smarr, in what remains the most ingenious structural analysis of the three poems in *OBS*, has argued that subtle numerological and geometrical arrangements

239 Ribner, 'Compasse of This Curious Frame', p. 243.
240 Ibid., pp. 243–44.
241 Aristotle, *De anima*, ed. and trans. by R. D. Hicks (Cambridge University Press, 1907), II. 7–11, 418b–423b, pp. 76–103.

sustain the volume's Neoplatonic stance. For Smarr, Fowler's abovementioned numerological explanation of the circular structure of 'Zodiac' is equally applicable to 'Coronet'. While the two shorter poems of the triptych are circular, the main poem is pyramidal: not only should the Niobe statuary at the beginning of the poem, including two pyramids crowned by two circles, be interpreted as a symbol of the collection's structure; the reference to the 'certain lines' that 'Move in the figure of a pyramis' linking Ovid's 'eye and object' in stanza 64 contains 'a pun which declares that the lines of Chapman's poem form a pyramid in which the poet is inscribing hieroglyphic verses'.[242] Smarr carefully interprets the elevation of the senses (hearing, smell and sight) and then their fall (sight, taste and touch) in terms of arithmetical and geometrical patterns that dispose hearing and smell chiastically with the descending senses of taste and touch. I represent the gist of Smarr's argument in a simple graphic and refer readers to her study for the details:

```
              59 Apex
              49–86 Sight (with digressions on Beauty)
      31 Smell         87 Taste
  16 Hearing               102 Touch
1 Base                         117 Base
```

Smarr's discussion has three advantages for the interpretation of the poem. The first is the invitation to detect in Chapman's predilection for proportional numerical forms serious pointers to his poetic thought. The second is the derivation of profound philosophical messages about the relationship between sensory perception and intellectual apprehension, between beauty and truth, between the realms of darkness, multiplicity and alterity and those of light and unity.[243] The third and most important is the suggestion that, if the philosophical content of the poem is disentangled from the humorous surface of its erotic narrative, then there is less need to see its intent as ironic or moralizing. For Smarr, the main problem with the ironic interpretations of 'Banquet' is that 'the philosophic elements have been treated as an ironic means to a moralizing end rather than as the chief end humorously parodied along the way by Ovid's love'.[244] If seen in this latter way, then we can see Ovid's resort to philosophy not as a seducer's abuse of learning but as a correlate to the poem's exploratory ideas of love. As Smarr concludes, 'the criticism of Ovid's fleshly love is not the deeper meaning of his poem but rather a humorous and superficial counterexample',[245] which welcomes independent reading as Ovidian erotic elegy while encouraging deeper enquiry into its mysteries in the same way as the hymnic structure of *SN* invites philosophical speculation.

242 Smarr, 'The Pyramid and the Circle', p. 370.
243 Ibid., p. 373.
244 Ibid., p. 376.
245 Ibid., p. 382.

Chapman's treatment of taste and touch, the senses on the descending slope of the pyramid, behave simultaneously as poetic motifs pointing to erotic satisfaction and as philosophical arguments that invite deeper speculation regarding the nature of beauty and pleasure. One instance is Corinna's granting of Ovid's request for a kiss on moral grounds — i.e. kissing will not involve a violation of chastity: 'Nor will I coyly lift Minerva's shield | Against Minerva; honour is not bruised | With such a tender pressure as a kiss' ('Banquet', 95.3–6). The kiss was an object of debate in sixteenth-century Italian treatises on love. Pietro Bembo's words in the fourth dialogue of Castiglione's *Il Corteggiano*, here in Thomas Hoby's English translation (1561), set a standard for Neoplatonic disputes on the matter:

> For sins a kisse is a knitting together both of body and soule, it is to be feared, least the sensuall lover will be more inclined to the part of the bodye, then of the soule: but the reasonable lover woteth well, that although the mouthe be a percell of the bodye, yet is it an issue for the wordes, that be the enterpreters of the soule, and for the inwarde breth, whiche is also called the soule: and therfore hath a delite to ioigne hys mouth with the womans beloved with a kysse: not to stirr him to anye unhonest desire, but bicause he feeleth that, that bonde is the openynge of an entry to the soules, whiche drawen with a coveting the one of the other, power them selves by tourn, the one into the others bodye, and be so mingled together, that ech of them hath two soules, and one alone so framed of them both ruleth (in a maner) two bodyes. Wherupon a kisse may be said to be rather a cooplinge together of the soule, then of the bodye, bicause it hath suche force in her, that it draweth her unto it, and (as it were) separateth her from the bodye. For this do all chast lovers covett a kisse, as a cooplinge of soules together. And therfore *Plato* the divine lover saith, that in *kissing, his soule came as farr as his lippes to depart out of the body*.[246]

A kiss occupies a liminal space between sensual and spiritual love, and Chapman's poem — like Castiglione and Plato — exploits such liminality. In her initial refusal to kiss Ovid, Corinna adduces 'virtual contact' as the vehicle to 'Pure love', which ensues 'not by application | Of lips or bodies, but of bodies' virtues' ('Banquet', 92. 7–9). Ovid's defence of the kiss explores a less spiritual side of the argument: 'virtual presence' offers to the senses the 'species' but not the 'substance' (93); however, just as words belong to the mouth and are formed by the compression of 'infinite' air, so a kiss relies on the 'tractability' — which puns on the lady's docility and the conduction of air through a tract — of Corinna's 'swelling' substance 'into a little place' (94).

---

246 Baldesare Castiglione, *The Courtyer*, trans. by Thomas Hoby (London: William Seres, 1561), Book IV, sig. Vv4ᵛ, emphasis added. The emphasized reference is to a poem attributed to Plato. See *Greek Anthology*, ed. and trans. by W. R Paton, 5 vols (Harvard University Press, 1956–1960), v. 78, I, pp. 76–77: 'τὴν ψυχήν, Ἀγάθωνα φιλῶν, ἐπὶ χείλεσιν ἔσχον | ἦλθε γὰρ ἡ τλήμων ὡς διαβησομένη' ('My soul was at my lips when I was kissing Agathon. | Poor soul! — she came hoping to cross over him).

In yielding to Ovid's request, Corinna 'spake in kissing' (97. 5), while in entering the lover's body, the kiss's 'perpetual-motion-making' effect is 'propagate[d] through all [Ovid's] faculties', thus passing from the senses to the soul (99. 6). Ovid's philosophy may be viewed as a sophister's means to an end, but his sensuality remains within the limits of what certain versions of Platonism considered acceptable.

Ovid's alleged descent into sensuality provides further examples of his — and the poem's — commitment to philosophical enquiry. The 'furious influence' (97. 9) that Corinna's kiss insufflates into Ovid's soul offers Chapman the possibility of assessing another key topic in the Renaissance philosophy of love: the insatiability of desire, which affects in equal degrees the pursuer of intellectual beauty and the seeker of sensual pleasure.[247] Ovid's sententious formulation of this topic resorts to the lexicon of banqueting: 'And thus, with feasting, love is famished more' (101. 1). But the argument leading to this conclusion contains the clearest example of transformation of the academic Latin of Curaeus's Περὶ αἰσθήσεως into elaborate English verse. Ovid's simile brings together, for the sake of comparison, the sonic effect of echo and his retention of only a minimal reminiscence of the pleasures that Corinna's kiss has awarded to his taste:

> But as when sounds do hollow bodies beat,
> Air gathered there, compressed and thickenèd,
> The selfsame way she came doth make retreat,
> And so effects the sound re-echoèd
>   Only in part, because she weaker is
> In that redition than when first she fled,
>   So I, alas, faint echo of this kiss,
> Only reiterate a slender part
> Of that high joy it worketh in my heart. ('Banquet', 100)

The marginal note to the first line, *Qua ratione fiat echo*, adapts the title of Curaeus, I. 41, '*Quid sit echo, et qua ratione fiat*' ('What echo is and the explanation of how it occurs'). The philosophical question — *quid sit* — cues on the definition found in Chapman's source — 'Echo, est reciprocatio soni, facta ex refractione aeris, in aliquo cavo opposito' ('Echo is the reciprocation of sound produced by the refraction of the air in some opposite cavity'). Chapman's first six lines translate the explanation — *ratio* — almost verbatim:

> Sed si corpus cavum est, aer in eo colligitur, condensatur et congeminatur, recurrit eodem, quo advenerat, tramite, et ita sonum reiterat. Quia autem in illa itione et reditione imbecillior fit, extremas tantum syllabas vocis, aut alterius soni, ad nostrum auditum defert.
>
> (But if the body is hollow, air is gathered, compressed and thickened in it, and goes all the same way again through which it came, and thus it

---

[247] The insatiability of love as an aspect of the insatiability of knowledge is a persistent motif of Giordano Bruno's *De gli eroici furori*, whose possible influence on Chapman is studied in the next section of this introduction.

reiterates the same sound. Because in going and returning it is made
weaker, as much as it delivers to our hearing the last syllables of a word
or of another sound).²⁴⁸

The poet's interest is not in testing the empirical truth of ancient acoustic
theory on this particular point, but its capacity to suggest synaesthetically
the benefits and the dangers of a kiss to the lover's soul.²⁴⁹ Besides, the
reasons for Chapman's choice of the aural trope to explain the effects of taste
may be found in Ficino's consideration of sound as one of the three sources
of human beauty — the other two are the soul and the body.²⁵⁰

This and similar stanzas emerge as proofs of Chapman's capacity to put
his virtuoso displays of artistic *difficultà* at the service of a serious, non-
ironic exploration of the limits of perception and the paradoxes of desire,
which are of both a moral and an epistemological sort. And this is why his
fictional Ovid complains that any philosophy of love is always in conflict
with its own vehicle of expression. The inevitable paradoxes to which the
lover is exposed have their reflection in language. The lover seeks to express
love's essence in philosophical language, the basis of which is formal logic.
But it ends up turning reason against itself:

> Love is a wanton famine, rich in food,
> But with a richer appetite controlled;
>   An argument in figure and in mood,
>   Yet hates all arguments — disputing still
> For sense, gainst reason, with a senseless will. (101. 5–9)

These are Ovid's words, not the narrator's. An ironic reading of the poem
could take these as proof of the character's own acknowledgement that he is
using sophistry as a method of seduction. They are taken here as a deeper,
and perhaps embarrassed, recognition that the poem's intrinsic difficulty is
ingrained in its subject, whose moral and epistemological challenges impel
its restless search for arguments and for the poetic expression of these argu-
ments. In this, the fictional Ovid and the second master of love share a
similar concern.

Ovid's philosophy of love in the poem thus admits its own contradictory
exposure to moral danger, materialized in the descending line that leads
from sight to taste, and then from taste to touch. The curious inversion of the
Midas legend that begins the account of the last of the senses presents Ovid's
insatiability as a desperate prospect: 'Without my touch are all things turned

---

248 Joachim Curaeus, Περὶ αἰσθήσεως καὶ αἰσσθητῶν; *Libellus physicus, continens doctrina de natura* (Wittenberg: Johann Schwertel, 1572), pp. 161–62. See also Commentary: 'Banquet', 100.
249 For another reading of the poem in the light of synaesthesia, see Sean Keilen, 'The Sense of a Poem: *Ovids Banquet of Sence* (1595)', in *Synaesthesia and the Ancient Senses*, ed. by Shane Butler and Alex Purves (Acumen, 2013), pp. 155–65.
250 On Ficino's triple beauty ('triplex pulchritudo'), see *Commentary on Plato's Symposium*, I. 4, pp. 40–41, 130.

to gold, | And till I touch I cannot joy my store' (101. 2–3). Touch would involve for certain Platonists an inexorable fall into the voluptuousness of bestial love.²⁵¹ But Chapman lends Ovid his Aristotle — and also his Lucretius — to construe touch under another prism: 'But give thy bounty true eternizement, | Making my senses' groundwork, which is feeling, | Effect the other endless excellent' (102. 4–6). The argument proceeds from Aristotle's *De anima*, which affirms that 'the primary sense in all animals is touch'.²⁵² Chapman again absorbs Aristotle's spirit through Curaeus's letter: 'tactus est fundamentum omnium aliorum sensum'.²⁵³ The reason behind the Aristotelian argument is not only the dependence of any sort of life on touch, but also the justification of man's pre-eminence over all animals on grounds of the superiority of this sense in him: for Aristotle, 'touch is the most exact of all man's senses' and the faculty to which 'he owes his superior intelligence'.²⁵⁴ Ovid's praise of 'sweet feeling' as 'the senses' emperor', as well as his conviction that the mind benefits as much from bodily sensations as the body does from the mind — 'Minds taint no more with bodies' touch, or tire, | Than bodies nourish with the mind's desire' (103. 8–9) — are not to be taken as sophistic abuses of philosophy but in the context of Chapman's explorations of received theories of sensory perception.

The protagonist's efforts to legitimize his intentions on philosophical grounds are similar to those in relation to kissing. Alchemical language, the presence of which throughout the poem has been noted by earlier critics, becomes now Ovid's main vehicle. Waddington has analysed the details of Chapman's alchemical lexicons to suggest that Chapman has his Ovid abuse the intricate notion of the alchemical wedding, or *chemica coniunctio*: the combination of opposite principles in the engendering of the philosopher's stone. In Waddington's reading, Ovid blatantly perverts this notion's symbolic use of sexual consummation to justify his debauchery.²⁵⁵ His categorical conclusions are quoted here as a characteristic instance of the poem's ironic readings:

---

251 See Ficino, *Commentary on Plato's Symposium*, VI. 8, pp., 86, 193. The importance of this question to the poem is dealt with in detail by Kermode, 'The Banquet of Sense', esp. p. 78.
252 Aristotle, *De anima*, II. 2, 413b4–5. See also Lucretius, *De rerum natura*, ed. and trans. by W. H. D. Rouse (William Heinemann, 1924), II. 434–39, pp. 114–15. The Lucretian theory that all the senses can be reduced to touch is grounded on the belief that sensation is caused by material emanations sent by the objects to the body in the form of atoms. On the priority given to the sense of touch in the ancient philosophy of the senses, see Rebecca Steiner Goldner, 'Aristotle and the Priority of Touch', in *Touch and the Ancient Senses*, ed. by Alex Purves (Routledge, 2018), pp. 50–63. In that same volume, and specifically on Lucretius, see David Sedley, 'The Duality of Touch', pp. 64–74 (pp. 67–74). See also Commentary: 'Banquet', 102–104.
253 Curaeus, Περὶ ἀισθήσεως, II. 41, p. 306.
254 Aristotle, *De anima*, II. 9, 421a20–25.
255 Waddington, *The Mind's Empire*, pp. 137–41.

Judged from all perspectives which Chapman builds into the poem counter to Ovid's own, the relationship is unnatural, the marriage demands annulment, and the experience can be interpreted as spiritual only by shutting out every viewpoint except that of Ovid's sophistic rhetoric.[256]

Yet Ovid's insistence on differentiating his use of 'nature's purities' from the 'corrupt effects' to which others put them can be read ironically only if an inconceivable degree of cynicism on Ovid's part is admitted (104. 5-7; see also Commentary: 'Banquet', 47-48 and 102-06). Besides, irony would bathetically deflate the virtuosity of some of Chapman's most dazzling poetic findings: thus, if the life-engendering qualities of Corinna's 'quick'ning side', in her capacity of transferring the primal female matter of quicksilver to the lover's male hand, are read ironically, then the prodigious metamorphic power of the image loses its force (104. 8).[257] Moreover, not 'all perspectives' in the poem conspire against Ovid's. It is the narrator that depicts Corinna as 'Worthily willing to have lawful grounds' to accept Ovid's reasons (105. 2); and it is also the narrator that, quite extraordinarily, devotes stanza 106 to carefully guiding our understanding of Ovid's speech about touch in stanzas 107 to 109. The narrator's gloss of Ovid's instructions to his own hand would seem redundant if meant ironically: 'To use with piety that sacred place, | And through his feeling's organ to disperse | Worth to his spirits, amply to supply | The poorness of his flesh's faculty' (106. 5-9). A narrator that improves rather than condemns Ovid's perspective while conducting a similar search for words and knowledge through intellectualizing erotic experience is a more plausible option. Besides, not all Platonic perspectives outside the poem would support the more orthodox Ficino on this point. Leone Ebreo's influential treatment of this question in his *Dialoghi d'amore* (1535) was particularly influenced by Aristotle's theories. In the opening dialogue, Filone instructs Sofia on the role of touch and taste as the two most important senses for the conservation of human life. For this reason, their participation in the act of generation is inevitable, and the insatiability of a love that springs in the heart ('il cordiale amore') fosters the continuous desire of the union of two bodies in one. To Sofia's argument that this is a way of admitting 'that the goal of desire resides in the most material of the senses, which is touch', Filone replies that 'when two spirits are united in spiritual love, their bodies desire to enjoy such union as is possible [...] since a corresponding physical union increases and perfect spiritual love'.[258] Filone and Sofia's repartee endorses the corporeal facet of the Platonic philosophy of love, which exceeds Ovid's own limits but whose philosophical bases are essentially those that Chapman's poem probes.

256 Ibid., p. 141.
257 See Commentary: 'Banquet', 104.
258 See Leone Ebreo, *Dialoghi d'amore*, ed. by Santino Caramella (Laterza, 1929), p. 50. English translation: *Dialogues of Love*, ed. and trans. by Rosella Pescatori and Damian Bacich (University of Toronto Press, 2009), pp. 63-64.

Chapman's narrative arrangement of the ascending and descending scale of the senses enables multiple enquiries into the philosophy of sense around, but also beyond, the Platonic question of love as a form of knowledge. It is the descending slope, on which this section has focused, that proves particularly fruitful in testing the moral limits and paradoxes of love. Despite obvious debts, Chapman's 'Banquet' does not bend easily to the exigencies of a Ficinian treatment of the senses or to the comic/satiric pattern of the *quinque lineae amoris*. The reason for this lies in the way in which an ampler, more plural look into the Renaissance philosophy of sense perception allies in the poem with its assemblage of amatory and didactic elegy. This is not to deny the importance of Platonism to 'Banquet' or to the collection of which it is part. In devising philosophical conceits as instruments of Ovid's defence of the spiritual benefits of the baser senses, Chapman is not necessarily depicting Ovid as a sophistic manipulator: in fact, he is not doing anything different from what the hymnic voice of 'Noctem' does when he alters the mythography of Night for the poem's own interests.[259] In its complex interplay of voices, 'Banquet' reads better as a non-condemnatory aestheticization of the Neoplatonic theory of the three kinds of love: *amor ferinus*, which favours the enjoyment of the senses, *amor humanus*, which privileges contemplation of beauty and conversation, and *amor divinus*, which sublimates human beauty into an image of the divine intellect. The correspondences of these three kinds of love with the earlier Platonic account of the three lives of the soul (*vita contemplativa*, which turns to divinity, *vita activa*, which turns to moral concerns, and *vita voluptuosa*, which turns to the body and the senses) and Proclus's ensuing classification of poetry into three kinds (divine, rational, mimetic) are of relevance here.[260] 'Banquet' is primarily about *amor humanus*, favouring contemplation and conversation, and for that reason the poem's most fitting generic pattern is the didactic elegy, which enables love's pleasures, difficulties and perils to be dramatized.

Yet Chapman never rests easily in the middle terms. The poem's explorations of sensuality and its sublimation often result in redefinitions of what these concepts mean, and the companion pieces in the collection are there to expand the scope of these meanings. Their presence permits further perspectives on the contradictions and the interrupted conclusion of 'Banquet'. The collection's ultimate aim is to endorse a philosophical and poetic practice in which love serves higher aims of intellectual enquiry. After all, erotic love has been since Plato an inevitable vehicle for speaking about intellectual pursuits. Chapman's use of plain erotic poetry as surface rather than as negative example enables a view of the poem's anamorphic division

---

259 Huntington ('Philosophical Seduction', pp. 50–51) reaches a similar conclusion about Chapman's manipulation of the meanings of day and night in *SN*.
260 On the different kinds of love and the corresponding lives of the soul, see Ficino, *Commentary on Plato's Symposium*, VI. 8, pp. 86, 193.

between literal (or 'nearly viewed') and allegorical (or distant) perspectives beyond moral, or hermeneutic, right and wrong. Idealization of Ovid's intentions or of Corinna's beauty is hardly its mode of expression, but the poem is equally far from satiric condemnation of its protagonists. Ambiguity and paradox seem much better lamps than irony to light the path to Corinna's fountain.

5. *Divine Shadows and Heroic Frenzies: The Brunian Mind*

Smarr's alternative to the rival interpretive models of irony and idealization concludes with a suggestion that enlarges the scope of Chapman's sources for *OBS*:

> The use of erotic to signify holy love is an age-old trick, but perhaps in this case Chapman was inspired to the joke by the example of Giordano Bruno whose *Eroici Furori*, modeled in turn on the *Song of Solomon*, put love poems to a philosophical and basically Neoplatonic use. As Bruno's preface corrects Petrarchan writing, so the dedicatory sonnets to Chapman's book refer to him as a corrected Ovid.[261]

The argument closes with a claim which, though plausible, has received scarce attention: 'Chapman was certainly likely to be aware of Bruno's work, which was well known to the circle of intellectuals, the so-called "School of Night", that Chapman aspired to join'.[262] The frequency with which Chapman has been left outside scholarly accounts of the 'Brunian setting' that influenced his closest intellectual acquaintances is as striking as the attraction that he must have felt to Bruno's speculative mind.[263] The sophisticated blend of poetry, myth, emblem and philosophy that made up Bruno's Italian dialogues must have appealed to a writer whose 'absolute' poems are the result of an equally intricate amalgam of elements.

The immediate referents for any account of the influence of the work of Giordano Bruno (1548–1600) in England are his six Italian dialogues published in London during his stay between April 1583 and the autumn of 1585 in the household of Michel de Castelnau, the French ambassador at the Elizabethan court. Bruno published these dialogues under false Paris and Venice imprints in the London workshop of Puritan printer John Charlewood: the first three,

---

261 Smarr, 'The Pyramid and the Circle', p. 380.
262 Ibid., p. 385, n. 39.
263 I borrow the phrase 'Brunian setting' from the title of the first chapter in Gatti, *Renaissance Drama of Knowledge*. Another account of Bruno's influence in England is found in the Introduction to Giordano Bruno, *Expulsión de la bestia triunfante*, ed. and trans. by Miguel A. Granada (Tecnos, 2022), pp. cxiv–cxxii. Granada mentions Marlowe and Shakespeare. A more thorough analysis is Barbara L. Lakin, 'The Magus and the Poet: Bruno and Chapman's *The Shadow of Night*', *The Sixteenth Century Journal*, 10.2 (1979), pp. 1–14, doi:10.2307/2539403. Huntington also hints towards a Brunian interpretation of the Actaeon myth in 'Banquet' in the light of the *Eroici furori* ('Philosophical Seduction', pp. 43–45) — an idea that this section develops.

La cena de le ceneri (*The Ash Wednesday Supper*, 1584), *De la causa, principio, e Uno* (*Cause, Principle and Unity*, 1584), and *Dell'infinito universo e mondi* (*On the Infinite Universe and Worlds*, 1584), discuss Bruno's theory of multiple universes, with a basis in Copernican cosmology, and its ontological consequences. The next two, *Spaccio della bestia trionfante* (*Expulsion of the Triumphant Beast*, 1584) and *Cabala del cavallo pegaseo* (*Kabbalah of the Horse Pegasus*, 1585) make his ideas of natural philosophy the foundation for his also revolutionary notions of ethical, political and religious conduct. The last and best known, *De gli eroici furori* (*On the Heroic Frenzies*, 1585), is an elaborate prosimetrum that develops Bruno's particular version of the Neoplatonic theories of love and knowledge into a dialogue commentary on a collection of Petrarchan poems and a series of emblematic devices. While the first three were dedicated to Castelnau, the last three contain dedicatory letters to Philip Sidney, whose attention and support for the continuation of his controversial stay in London Bruno failed to gain.[264]

Bruno's work in England is only a part of a vast production that also includes Latin works on the art of memory, treatises on magic, other cosmological tracts, as well as the early comedy in Italian *Candelaio* (*The Candlemaker*, 1582). His English reception is hard to ascertain, particularly due to the suspicions raised by the figure of an exiled, excommunicated Dominican friar whose heretical ideas about religious freedom were hardly assimilable in Protestant England, and whose extravagant scientific mind dared to challenge the Oxford University authorities. A mixture of scorn and respect for English courtly and intellectual life can be derived from Bruno's writings. A similar mixture of scorn and respect for the Nolan philosopher — although the balance inclines to the former — is also distilled from the extant accounts of Bruno's lectures, conversations and activity during his London years. The absence of Bruno's name in Chapman's writings would not be surprising even in the likely case that the Neapolitan philosopher had been an actual influence: to Chapman's frequent omission of his sources, one could add the inconvenience of invoking any allegiance to a figure who must have encountered hostility and indifference.[265]

The variety and idiosyncrasy of Bruno's production constitutes an added difficulty. In the English-speaking context, Frances A. Yates's seminal monograph established the prevalent picture of Bruno as a magus and hermetic

---

[264] On Bruno's failure to attract Sidney's sympathies, see Andrew D. Weiner, 'Expelling the Beast: Bruno's adventures in England', *Modern Philology*, 78.1 (1980), pp. 1–13, doi: 10.1086/391002; also, Diego Pirillo, *Filosofia ed eresia nell'Inghliterra del tardo cinquecento: Bruno, Sidney e i dissidenti religiosi italiani* (Edizioni di storia e letteratura, 2010), pp. 20–21.

[265] See Mordechai Feingold, 'Giordano Bruno in England, Revisited', *The Huntington Library Quarterly*, 67.3 (2004), pp. 329–46, doi:10.1525/hlq.2004.67.3.329. Feingold's study downplays the scope of this influence and sees in Bruno's own personal attitudes the cause of the hostility shown to him in Oxford and London.

philosopher.²⁶⁶ More recent work by scholars like Miguel Ángel Granada, Ingrid Rowland and Hilary Gatti has reassessed the import of Bruno's intellectual project as 'a slow and arduous process of progression towards ever fuller knowledge of the universal whole which linked him to all the true philosophers of both ancient and modern culture'.²⁶⁷ Against the Yatesian portrait, Gatti depicts Bruno's major contribution as a speculative enquiry into the ways in which the infinitude of the universe opens equally infinite possibilities for the human mind. Bruno's intellectual project defied philosophical and religious orthodoxies in his attempt to resolve multiplicity into oneness. This attempt explains his conception of the art of memory as an ordering of the multiplicity of chaos into a complex mnemonic system that aspires to absolute knowledge. It also underlies his challenge to religious authority through spiritual freedom. It similarly inspires his cosmology of multiple universes as mirrors of an infinite One. And it certainly determines his idea of knowledge as the lover's heroic pursuit of divine truth through the multiple vestiges of sensual beauty found in our world.²⁶⁸ Bruno's intellectual freedom opposed any restrictive system of thought. His hostility to formal academics matches his staunch belief in the independent spirit of the true philosopher. In *The Ash Wednesday Supper*, this latter idea is exemplified by Copernicus, who 'announce[s] the dawn that precedes the rising sun of the ancient and true philosophy, *buried for so many centuries in the dark caverns of a blind, malign, insolent, and envious ignorance*' ('*per tanti secoli sepolta nelle tenebrose caverne de la cieca, maligna, proterva, et invida ignoranza*').²⁶⁹ But it also reaches the reader through the arrogant self-portrait of a daring intellectual adventurer:

> Here, then, you see the man who has soared into the sky, entered the heavens, wandered among the stars, passed beyond the boundaries of the universe, effaced the imaginary barriers [...] and distorted vision of the commonly accepted philosophy.²⁷⁰

---

266 Frances Yates, *Giordano Bruno and the Hermetic Tradition* (Routledge, 2002, 1st edn 1964). Yates devotes four chapters (12–15, pp. 226–319) to Bruno's influence on English culture, but literature does not figure prominently in her book. This section seeks to throw light on her enticing affirmation that 'some of the most recondite productions of Elizabethan poetry use his imagery' (p. 319).
267 Gatti, *Renaissance Drama of Knowledge*, p. 28. For a recent intellectual biography, see Ingrid D. Rowland, *Giordano Bruno: Philosopher/Heretic* (University of Chicago Press, 2008). See also Miguel A. Granada, *Giordano Bruno: universo infinito, unión con Dios, perfección del hombre* (Herder, 2002), for a comprehensive account of Bruno's most important philosophical themes.
268 Gatti, *Renaissance Drama of Knowledge*, pp. 1–35.
269 Giordano Bruno, *The Ash Wednesday Supper*, ed. and trans by Hilary Gatti (University of Toronto Press, 2018), Dialogue I, pp. 30–31, emphasis added.
270 'Hor ecco quello ch'há varcato l'aria, penetrato il cielo, discorse le stelle, trapassati gli margini del mondo [...] et cieco veder di philosophi volgari' (Bruno, *Ash Wednesday Supper*, Dialogue I, pp. 34–35).

Gatti has traced the presence of Bruno's works in the library of the Earl of Northumberland and his direct influence on some of the latter's associates.[271] But she leaves Chapman outside a picture in which his work could claim a place on grounds of coincidences in artistic vision and attitudes to knowledge. One could detect these affinities by comparing Bruno's *Expulsion of the Triumphant Beast*, the first of the three dialogues dedicated to Sidney, with *The Shadow of Night*. Bruno's dialogue fictionalizes the Olympian gods' expulsion from the heaven of the traditional stellar constellations, most of which are regarded as representations of vice, and their replacement with a new zodiac of virtuous deities. As Miguel Á. Granada explains, this narrative becomes an allegory for the establishment of a new ethical, religious and political order whose rationale is an alliance with philosophy.[272] In *SN*, the replacement of a realm of Day with a kingdom of Night under the rule of Cynthia advocates an analogous revolution, the consequences of which also range from cosmic to worldly orders, and entails a similar conception of a philosophical utopia. The comparison could range from issues of aim and design to the use of common myths and allegories. In the Second Dialogue of *Expulsion*, Jupiter decides to remove the constellation Perseus from heaven and send him back to earth, furnished with Minerva's 'useful shining shield', to defeat the 'new Medusa' of superstition, false knowledge and religious dissension. The king of the gods designates Hercules' 'arm of Justice' and 'club of Judgment' ('braccio della Giustizia e bastone del Giudicio') as Perseus's necessary aids in this enterprise.[273]

In the dedicatory letter to Sidney, Bruno clarifies the moral allegory with which Perseus's heroic endeavour is identified: 'Where fierce Perseus shows us the Gorgonian trophy, ascend Labor, Solicitude, Study, Fervor, Vigilance, Commerce, Exercise, and Occupation, with the spurs of Zeal and Fear. Perseus possesses the talaria of Useful Concern and Contempt for Vulgar Wealth, with their ministers, Perseverance, Intelligence, Industry, Skill, Investigation, and Diligence'.[274] For his part, Chapman opens the prefatory epistle to *SN* with a declaration of the aspiring philosophical enterprise of his poem. He resorts to allegory in order to explain the programmatic aspiration of his work to higher forms of intellection:

> It is an exceeding rapture of delight in the deep search of knowledge (none knoweth better than thyself, sweet Matthew) that maketh men manfully endure the extremes incident to that Herculean labour: from flints must the Gorgonean fount be smitten. Men must be shod by

---

271 Gatti, *Renaissance Drama of Knowledge*, especially pp. 49–73. The second part of Gatti's study is devoted to Harriot, Marlowe and Shakespeare.
272 Granada, Introducción, in *Expulsión*, p. xxiv.
273 Giordano Bruno, *The Expulsion of the Triumphant Beast*, ed. and trans. by Arthur D. Imerti (Rutgers University Press, 1964), Dialogue II. 3, p. 188. For the Italian text, see *Opere italiane*, ed. by Giovanni Acquilecchia, 2 vols (UTET, 2004), II, pp. 306–07.
274 Bruno, *Expulsion*, Epistle, p. 82; *Opere italiane*, II, p. 189.

> Mercury, girt with Saturn's adamantine sword, take the shield from
> Pallas, the helm from Pluto, and have the eye of the Graeae (as Hesiodus
> arms Perseus against Medusa) before they can cut off the viperous head
> of benumbing ignorance, or subdue their monstrous affections to most
> beautiful judgement. (*SN*: 'To Roydon', lines 1–9)

Chapman's immediate source is Conti's *Mythologiae*.[275] Conti interprets Perseus's killing of Medusa as the defeat of 'immoral desires' ('illegitimas voluptates') by the intellectual faculties, while Medusa embodies 'sensuality, impulsiveness and arrogance' ('libidinem et temeritatem et arrogantiam'). For Chapman, these 'monstrous affections' are further identified with 'benumbing ignorance', and the intellectual enterprise to subdue them to 'most beautiful judgement' becomes a 'Herculean labour'. The poem later depicts the stellified Hercules' descent to earth as an act of moral renovation: 'Fall, Hercules, from heav'n in tempests hurled, | And cleanse this beastly stable of the world' ('Noctem', 255–56).[276] Besides, 'the deep search of knowledge' is inseparable from 'an exceeding rapture of delight' — the reward for the 'extremes' of painful endurance undergone in this enterprise. The Brunian conception of the intellectual endeavour as a heroic frenzy — the subject of the last of the London dialogues — becomes the key to Chapman's manifesto.

At the centre of Bruno's project is the elevation of a deified Truth to the position formerly occupied by the constellation Ursa Major 'in the most eminent seat' in heaven:

> for there the claws of Detraction do not reach, the lividness of Envy does
> not poison, the shadows of Error do not sink. There she [Truth] will
> dwell stable and firm; there she will not be shaken violently by waves
> and storms; there she will be the safe guide of those who go wandering
> through this tempestuous Sea of Errors; and thence she will show herself
> as a clear and polished mirror of contemplation.[277]

Chapman's Cynthia is appointed to occupy a similar seat in her 'rare Elysian palace' ('Cynthiam', 176) — a place that has also been granted by the Olympian king:

> Here as she sits, the thunder-loving Jove,
> In honours past all others, shows his love,
> Proclaiming her, in complete empery
> Of whatsoever the Olympic sky
> With tender circumvecture doth embrace,
> The chiefest planet that doth heav'n enchase. ('Cynthiam', 196–201)

---

275 See Commentary, '*SN*: To Roydon', lines 5–9.
276 The parallel with Bruno's *Expulsion* in relation to this point is suggested by Battenhouse, 'Chapman's *The Shadow of Night*', p. 594.
277 Bruno, *Expulsion*, Dialogue I. 3, p. 121; *Opere italiane*, II, p. 234.

Bruno's Truth 'loves the company of a few wise men, [...] hates the multitude, does not show herself before those who do not seek her for her own sake, and does not wish to be declared to those who do not humbly expose themselves to her, or to all those who fraudulently seek her; and therefore she dwells most high, whither all gaze, and few see'.[278] A similar Horatian spirit leads Chapman to declare: 'The profane multitude I hate, and only consecrate my strange poems to these searching spirits whom learning hath made noble, and nobility sacred' (*OBS*: 'To Roydon', lines 3–5). Or to imagine 'Skill' refusing to 'prostitutely show them [i.e. false scholars] her secrets, when she will scarcely be looked upon by others but with invocation, fasting, watching' (*SN*: 'To Roydon', lines 15–18).

Chapman's intellectual stance matches the Nolan philosopher's deep search for and zealous custody of knowledge from the noxious clutches of the ignorant many.[279] It also parallels Bruno's subordination of all orders of life to a philosophical dedication to the attainment of truth. But the analogous concepts, transferred images and assimilated arguments that hint at a Brunian legacy in Chapman's poems have received little scholarly attention. The exception is Barbara Lakin's study of *SN*, which argues that 'the similarities between Chapman's ideas, imagery, poetic stance, and use of myth in this poem and Bruno's treatment of the same elements deserve serious consideration'.[280] Lakin develops an earlier suggestion by Waddington, for whom the role of magic in Bruno's elaborate mnemonic systems matched Chapman's use of hermetic poetry to recreate an art of memory through which 'the Orphic artist remembers the lost harmony of soul and recreates it in his own art'.[281] Although Lakin and Waddington focus on the Yatesian image of Bruno as magus, their arguments usefully stress the role of names, images, symbols and myths as vestiges of higher ideas in Chapman's verse. Bruno's theory of shadows aids the conception of the obscure poem as a light-revealing scheme. In the context of the extensive use of myths in *SN* and *OBS*, Bruno's philosophical interpretation of the legend of Actaeon and Diana can claim to supply important keys to what, borrowing Sidney's expression, we could call

---

278 Bruno, *Expulsion*, Dialogue II. 1, p. 141. Italian text: 'ama la compagnia di pochi e sapienti, odia la moltitudine, non si dimostra a quelli che per se stessa non la cercano, e non vuol essere dechiarata a color che umilmente non se gli esponeno, né a tutti quei che con frode la inquireno: e però dimora altissima dove tutti remirano, e pochi veggono' (*Opere italiane*, II, p. 256).

279 With respect to this point, both writers show scorn for utilitarian conceptions of learning. As Bruno writes: 'Ut pauci sapientiam et rerum cognitionem adsequuntur, quia pauci serio eam quaerunt. Non enim sophiam appetit qui, ut ditescat, ut quaestum per illam faciat, elaborat; ut vulgi honores aucupetur et auram' ('Few are those who reach wisdom and the knowledge of things, because few pursue it seriously. He does not seek wisdom whose purpose is to get riches, to obtain some benefit through it, or to get public honours and fame') (*De Immenso*, VIII. 1, in *Opera latine conscripta publicis sumptibus edita*, ed. by F. Fiorentino, 3 vols (Morano, 1879), I, p. 288; my translation).

280 Lakin, 'The Magus and the Poet', p. 1.

281 Waddington, *The Mind's Empire*, p. 97.

the '*idea* or fore-conceit' of Chapman's poems.²⁸² Actaeon's contemplation of the naked hunting goddess supplies a structuring principle, but also a common poetics that heralds Chapman's verse as a love-enlightened voyage from darkness to light, from sense to intellect, and from ignorance to knowledge.

5.1. *Diana in the Forest, the Moon in Heaven: 'The Shadow of Night'*

Lakin's reading of *The Shadow of Night* considers Chapman's treatment of 'three of Bruno's most arresting notions': the transference of the figure of the magus to the 'poet/narrator'; the nostalgic attempt to restore hermeticism in a corrupt world; and the use of a memory system of Brunian inspiration to connect the magical images of the poem to an idea of Cynthia as 'divine mind'.²⁸³ Of these three lines of argument, the connections between the first and third prove particularly suggestive. The hymnic voice's conjuration of images from magic, myth or astronomy as shadows of a divine idea is meant to distil unity of 'soul' from the multiplicity of matter (see 'Noctem', 47–48). In her analysis, Lakin focuses on the six Italian dialogues, but neglects what is perhaps a key entrance into the poem: Bruno's first extant work, the mnemonic treatise *De umbris idearum* (*The Shadows of Ideas*, 1582). In this work, Bruno conceives of intellection as a Platonic ascent from the shadow of darkness to the shadow of light, from ignorance to knowledge. Shadows are the images or forms produced by the mind in the process of knowing; they are distant reflections or vestiges of ideas, which are also imperfect shadows of divinity. Bruno considers shadows intermediate entities between darkness and light:

> Shadow is not of darkness, but a footprint of darkness in light. Or a footprint of light in darkness. Or a share of light and darkness. Or a composite from light and darkness. Or a mixture from light and darkness. Or different from light and darkness and alien to both.²⁸⁴

As we cannot be in pure darkness or pure light, we come to know them only by means of shadows. Darkness signals the descending path of the senses, and light the ascending path of the intellect: thus, the mind directs its course towards knowledge by ascending from the shadow of darkness to the shadow of light. As Rowland summarizes it, 'those shadows of ideas [are] a medium between the darkness of ignorance and the light of wisdom'.²⁸⁵

---

282 For Sidney's well-known terms, see *Defence*, in *Miscellaneous Poetry and Prose*, p. 79, lines 7–8.
283 Lakin, 'The Magus and the Poet', pp. 2–3.
284 'Non est vmbra tenebrae: sed vel tenebrarum vestigium in lumine. Vel luminis vestigium in tenebris. Vel particeps lucis et tenebrae. Vel compositum ex luce et tenebris. Vel mixtum ex luce et tenebris. Vel neutrum a luce et tenebris, et ab utrisque seiunctum' (Giordano Bruno, *De umbris idearum* (Paris: Gilles Gorbin, 1582), sig. E2ᵛ, my translation).
285 Rowland, *Giordano Bruno*, p. 126.

Brunian shadows haunt Chapman's poem from its very inception. Its title, *The Shadow of Night*, remains mysterious, particularly as it camouflages the hymnic quality stated in the titles of its two poems under an obscure formulation. 'Night' refers readers to the goddess of the first hymn, but the word 'shadow' is confusingly polysemic in its various occurrences in the poem. Its first appearance after the title designates the hellish place inhabited by the 'horrid stepdame, Blindness of the Mind' ('Noctem', 71). Later, Night's benign 'shadows' are said to 'succour men dismayed' ('Noctem', 338). 'Shadows' are, with 'flowers', 'mists' and 'meteors' ('Cynthiam', 175), the subtle materials with which Cynthia shapes the nymph Euthymia, Actaeon's dogs and the hunters in the central scene of this second poem; and the juice of the Castalian fountain 'shadows night' ('Cynthiam', 166) in what seems the closest verbal formulation to the poem's title. Yet the most ingenious of all these occurrences is the pyramidal shadow projected by the building '*Pax Imperii*', with a base on the earth and an apex that reaches beyond 'the region of the Moon' ('Cynthiam', 189–94) — an image that Chapman borrowed from Conti.[286] Shadows are shapers, or perhaps only harbingers, of the poem's most secret truths. But it is the volume's Ovidian epigraph — 'Versus mei habebunt aliquantum *Noctis*' ('My lines have something of *Night*') — that more aptly glosses Chapman's title: in being a vestige, or a share (*aliquantum*), of Night's substance, the poem's verses are themselves shadows of Night.

The complex, interrelating images that make up the poem's philosophical allegory must be understood then as guides to Chapman's reformulation of the mythology of Night analysed above. Cynthia's entrance at the end of the first hymn unfolds the basic elements of this system:

> This train, with meteors, comets, lightenings,
> The dreadful presence of our Empress sings,
> Which grant for ever (O eternal Night)
> Till virtue flourish in the light of light. ('Noctem', 400–03)

The 'light of light' is the unknowable divinity, an essence that is beyond the human intellect. As the intellect's leader-goddess, Cynthia is the shadow of this light. Contrary to what Lakin affirms, Cynthia is not the shadow of Night but, as the first line of 'Cynthiam' affirms, its 'fair soul' or 'purest part'.[287] Night's capacity to 'grant' Cynthia's 'dreadful presence' justifies the former's anagogic (i.e. elevating) quality. Light, Cynthia, Night and the hymnic voice incarnating the human intellect (Lakin prefers to call this 'the magus') represent the rungs of the poem's descending ladder. But Cynthia is the highest point that the human mind can contemplate, as the end of the

---

286 See Commentary: 'Cynthiam', 176–95.
287 While I agree with Lakin when she affirms that Chapman's Cynthia represents the Brunian 'shadow of the divine mind', I find this contradictory with her affirmation that Cynthia is a 'shadow of Night' (Lakin, 'The Magus and the Poet', pp. 3–4).

second hymn makes clear: 'So shall the wonders of thy power be seen, | And thou for ever live the planet's queen' ('Cynthiam', 527–28).

The preparatory quality of 'Noctem' invites its superposition of images to be read as shadows to the revelation of Cynthia. The first of these are the depictions of a duplicated Chaos and a duplicated Night, whereby we are asked to differentiate between false avatars and authentic entities. The dominance exerted by the two false avatars at the beginning of the poem justifies its concern with epistrophe, or reversion to authenticity. Thus, the 'stepdame Night of Mind' is 'A Gorgon that with brass and snaky brows | (Most harlot-like) her naked secrets shows', subjugating the mind under the yoke of ignorance ('Noctem', 70–74). This 'harlot-like' Medusa is the 'Skill' that Chapman's preface imagines as 'so mightily pierced' with the 'loves' of the ignorant crowd 'that she should prostitutely show them her secrets' (*SN*: 'To Roydon', lines 15–17). In stark contrast with this false avatar, authentic Night, the 'Day of deep students' ('Noctem', 202), anticipates the kingdom of Cynthia, which symbolizes 'All wisdom, beauty, majesty and dread' ('Cynthiam', 8). Chapman's hymnic voice celebrates Cynthia's 'truly figuring [of] the forces of the mind' ('Cynthiam', 150–52). He also praises Cynthia's lunar identity, which eclipses the perfections of the Sun: 'Sing then withal her palace brightness bright, | The dazzle-sun perfections of her light | Circling her face with glories' ('Cynthiam', 156–58). This latter image has clear emblematic reminiscences. An *impresa* in Paolo Giovio's *Dialogo dell'imprese* (1574) shows a full moon adorned by an imperial crown with the Latin motto '*Quum plena est fit emula solis*' ('When it is full, it rivals the sun'), and the *subscriptio* 'To prove that she had so much splendor that she equalled herself to the Sun, making the night as clear as the day'.[288] Bruno's *Heroic Frenzies* also elaborates on a version of this *impresa*: his motto, '*Talis mihi semper et astro*' ('Ever thus for me and for the star') means that 'the Moon is always [...] full and glowing, filling the entire circumference of its circle'.[289] In its allegorical interpretation, 'the intellect engaged in action [...] always sees its object as firm, fixed and constant, always full, and always in the same splendor of beauty'.[290] Each version of the device points to one crucial feature of Chapman's Cynthia: Giovio stresses the Moon's emulation of the Sun, a feature which also appears in Bruno but which Chapman's mythographic re-elaboration alters; Bruno focuses on the Moon's full circular shape as symbolic of the object of the human intellect.

Chapman's hymnodist completes his praise of Cynthia by invoking her identity as the hunting goddess Diana:

---

288 'Per dimostrar, ch'egli haveva tanto splendore, che s'agguagliava al Sole, facendo la notte chiara come il giorno' (Paolo Giovio, *Dialogo dell'imprese* (Lyons: Guillaume Rouillé, 1574), p. 13; see Visual Sources.
289 'come si mostra qua piena e lucida nella circonferenza intiera del circolo' (Giordano Bruno, *On the Heroic Frenzies*, ed. by Eugenio Canone, trans. by Ingrid D. Rowland (University of Toronto Press, 2013), Part I, pp. 170–71).

>   sing the walks
> Where in her heav'nly magic mood she stalks;
> Her arbours, thickets and her wondrous game
> (A huntress, being never matched in fame). ('Cynthiam', 158–61)

Although there is sufficient material in Conti to support this portrait of Cynthia as hunter (*Diana venatrix*), Chapman's philosophical inspiration finds a powerful analogue in the Brunian allegory of the goddess as the species of intellectual beauty. Bruno describes one of the intellectual lovers of the *Heroic Frenzies* as 'captive to the vision he saw emerging from the forest, from the desert, from the woods, that is, from places far removed from the multitude, from company, from the crowd, places frequented only by a few'. In the midst of this forest, 'Diana, the splendour of intelligible species, is his *huntress*, because with her beauty and grace she first wounded him and then bound him'.[291] Bruno's Diana is the highest object of intellectual apprehension of which the human mind is capable. In Chapman's 'arbours', 'thickets' and 'wondrous game', but also in the 'hunters' and 'hounds' of Euthymia's chase, one must seek for similar philosophical allegories. Chapman's inclusion of Actaeon's seventeen dogs, whose names are taken from Conti, contributes to his shaping of the Diana myth along Brunian lines.[292]

Bruno devoted two sonnets with their extensive prose commentaries to the legend of Actaeon and Diana in the Fourth Dialogue of the First Part of the *Heroic Frenzies*. As Ingrid Rowland argues, his understanding of the myth was influenced by the writings of the sixteenth-century Augustinian cleric Giles of Viterbo (1472–1532), whose unprinted *Sententiae ad mentem Platonis* he would have read in manuscript during his Neapolitan period. Giles's metaphor of the Forest of Matter (*silva materiae*) derives from a mistranslation of Plato's ὕλη ('matter') as *silva*, which he found in medieval Latin versions of the *Timaeus*.[293] Yet the error yields a potent intellectual construction around the myth of Diana. Giles's Forest of Matter is a place where men try to hunt down divine knowledge, where the goddess Diana becomes the model of this intellectual search, and where the dogs track down the hidden footprints (*vestigia*) of divinity:

> The nature of intelligent creatures is split in two, for in part it pursues the tracks of divinity, but in part, clinging to heaven's palace, it has no

---

290 'l'intelleto in atto [...] sempre vede il suo ogetto fermo, fisso e constante, e sempre pieno e nel medesimo splendor di bellezza' (Bruno, *Heroic Frenzies*, Part I, pp. 172–73).
291 'cattivato a quella che vedde uscir da la foresta, dal deserto, da la selva; cioè da parti rimosse dalla moltitudine, dalla conversazione, dal volgo, le quali son lustrate da pochi. Diana splendor di specie intelligibili, è cacciatrice di sé, perché con la sua bellezza e grazia l'ha ferito prima, e se l'ha legato poi' (Bruno, *Heroic Frenzies*, Part II, pp. 270–71).
292 See Commentary: 'Cynthiam', 220–42. Lakin, 'The Magus and the Poet', pp. 9–10, reads the poem in the light of Bruno's Actaeon, yet the conclusions are different.
293 Rowland, *Giordano Bruno*, p. 47.

desire to hunt down sensible things. Thus, nature has prepared companions for our spirits, heavenly minds, and calls one Diana in the Forest, the other the Moon in Heaven. Indeed, Diana remains a virgin, because she is free from the forest and matter, although by her grace she is devoted to sacred hunting in those forests. It is said that heavenly minds have the same pure nature and intellectual power. For that reason, she is usually defined neither by number, nor species but by kind. These kinds of minds, which are called by the name of the moon, have an image that is more excellent than our own image, so that they love to improve ours earnestly and illuminate the shadows of our forests with the limpid rays of their light. On Mount Latmos the Moon is said to have loved Endymion, and to have kissed him at night when he was asleep. And this story is not without its point, but it means that we are loved and taught by those souls. Sleep means the contempt for human things, and the mount the sublime pursuit of divine matters.[294]

The opening lines of Bruno's first Actaeon sonnet design a careful allegorical programme along Giles's lines:

> Into the woods young Actaeon released
> His mastiffs and his hounds, when fateful force
> Set him upon the bold incautious course
> Of following the track of woodland beasts.[295]

For Bruno, Actaeon is 'the intellect intent on hunting divine wisdom, on grasping divine beauty'. The mastiffs and hounds are respectively the will and the intellect, the latter being swifter and the former being more persistent. The woods are 'wild and solitary places, visited and traversed by very few'. And the beasts are 'the intelligible outward images of ideal concepts: for the concepts themselves are hidden, pursued by only a few', and grasped only by those able to see the naked goddess.[296]

---

[294] 'Quas ob res natura intelligentium creatorum bifariam secatur. Partim enim vestigia in silvis sectatur rerum divinarum, partim ab hac nostra silva procul caeli regiam tenens, sensilium venationem non desiderat. Hinc animorum soboles, inde caelestium mentium expedita natura; altera Diana in silvis, altera Luna in caelo dici voluit. Diana quidem virgo habita, quod silva materiaque libera ex se sit, silvis tamen sanctae gratia venationis addicta; luna eadem dicitur, mentes enim caelestes naturam eandem simplicem et intelligendi potestatem habent. Ideo eadem non numero, non specie, sed genere dici solet. Id genus mentium, quod lunae nomine vocatum est, adeo imaginem habet nostra imagine praestantiorem, ut magnopere ament nostram excolere et limpidis radiis lucis suae nostrarum silvarum tenebras illustrare. In monte Latmo Endymionem adamasse dicta est, sopitumque nocte osculari consuevisse. Quae fabula ratione non caret, sed nos amari docerique ab illis significatum est. Sopor humanorum contemptum, mons sublimia indicat studia divinorum' (Giles of Viterbo, *The Commentary on the Sentences of Petrus Lombardus*, ed. by Daniel Nodes (Brill, 2010), III. 1–16, p. 177). I have used Ingrid D. Rowland's partial translation of this text (*Giordano Bruno*, p. 50) and completed it with my own.
[295] 'Alle selve i mastini e i veltri slaccia | il giovan Atteon, quand'il destino | gli drizz'il dubio et incauto camino, | di boscareccie fiere appo la traccia' (Bruno, *Heroic Frenzies*, Part I, pp. 104–07).
[296] 'Atteone significa l'intelletto intento alla caccia della divina sapienza, all'apprension

Chapman's digression on the 'goodly nymph' Euthymia elaborates on a number of Brunian meanings. Cynthia creates Euthymia as a shadow of her heavenly identity, a sort of earthly Diana whose capacity to 'turn herself to every shape | Of swiftest beasts' displays a number of simulacra of her intelligible species ('Cynthiam', 226–27). The dogs of the goddess's own creation are then deceived by their own will in their search for vain images. They enter an elaborate Forest of Matter, a noxious and impenetrable version of Bruno's 'wild and solitary places', where they are wounded with the thickets' thorns and struck by the vision of the tortured spirits of those who have dared to scorn Cynthia's worship. Mounted on higher intellectual powers — 'lions, boars and unicorns' — the hunters penetrate the forest but also fail in their chase of the godly *vestigia* — here the 'scent' of the panther into which Euthymia has transformed herself. Thus metamorphosed, Euthymia flees to a 'fruitful island',

> Full of all wealth, delight and empery,
> Ever with child of curious architect,
> Yet still delivered, paved with dames select,
> On whom rich feet in foulest boots might tread
> And never foul them, for kind Cupid spread
> Such perfect colours on their pleasing faces,
> That their reflects clad foulest weeds with graces. ('Cynthiam', 367–73)

Euthymia's shelter emerges as an ideal dream vision of Britain, but one in which nightmare is also possible. There, she is again transformed by Cynthia into a boar who, like its mythic Calydonian counterpart, wreaks further havoc in admonition of future neglect of worship of the island's goddess.

One may want to see an articulate programme here in which the most pressing events of Elizabethan political and religious life might contribute to clarifying the allegory. Chapman's contribution to the Elizabethan cult in 'Cynthiam' relied on a long-established tradition which scholars like Bradbrook, Battenhouse and Jacquot found ornamental or of subsidiary interest to the poem's meaning,[297] and which the work of Raymond Waddington has elevated to structural importance for the poem's design.[298] For Waddington, the mythic form of the poem, sustained by the triple identity of Cynthia as Luna, Hecate and Diana, finds in the latter its support for political allegory. Waddington traces the presence of a number of conventional topoi that establish the context for reading the poem as a piece of Elizabethan political propaganda: the identification of Elizabeth with Cynthia; the account of Sir

---

della beltà divina [...] "Alle selve", luoghi inculti e solitarii, visitati e perlustrati da pochissimi [...] i veltri e mastini appo la traccia di boscareccie fieri che sono le specie intelligibili de concetti ideali, che sono occolte, perseguitate da pochi' (Bruno, *Heroic Frenzies*, Part I, pp. 106–07).
297 Bradbrook, *The School of Night*, p. 127; Battenhouse, 'Chapman's *The Shadow of Night*', pp. 600–01; Jacquot, *George Chapman*, pp. 63–64.
298 Waddington, *The Mind's Empire*, pp. 71–92.

Francis Vere's defeat of Parma ('Cynthiam', 328–48); the possible reading of Cynthia's girding herself against 'Europe's Sun' (118) as a historical reminder of Elizabeth's refusal to marry the Duke of Alençon and a defence of her continued chastity; and the defeat of the Spanish Armada — 'And freest our ships when others suffer wrack' (508). For Waddington, these historical allegories set the context for the design of a triumphant image of Elizabethan imperialism around two central myths of Chapman's own invention. The first is Form's construction of Diana's magic, ethereal palace called '*Pax Imperii*', whose 'two superior pillars' transfer the imperial iconography associated with the *plus ultra* motto of Charles V to Elizabethan power (170–207). The second rewrites the myth of Actaeon and Diana in Cynthia's creation of Euthymia's chase by spirits in the form of dogs and hunters, which, in Waddington's argument, makes use of Renaissance interpretations of the Actaeon legend in political emblems to suggest Elizabeth's defence of her chastity and the punishment of her continental enemies.[299]

While the political messages in Waddington's reading are indubitably more than ornamental, understanding the Euthymia episode or the whole poem as primarily political and propagandistic may overstate its intentions. The Brunian imprint again emerges as a solid referent for Chapman's version of the cult of Elizabeth — and one that has passed unnoticed to commentators. In his London dialogues, and particularly in the *Expulsion*, Bruno imagined a commonwealth based on the love of true knowledge and free of scholastic constraints, which promoted a reformed social morality and a tolerant political authority.[300] Bruno's London dialogues often exemplify this ideal with the reign of Elizabeth I. In *Cause, Principle and Unity*, Elizabeth ('questa diva Elizabetta che regna in Inghilterra') is the paragon of all women governors of ancient history 'for corporeal beauty, knowledge of vernacular and learned tongues, grasp of the arts and sciences, vision in governing, grandeur of such great and long-lasting authority and other natural and civic virtues'.[301] In *Ash Wednesday Supper*, Elizabeth is said to exceed all male governors in 'judgement, wisdom and policy', for which 'she deserves to hold in her powerful hand the globe of a general and universal monarchy'.[302] And in *Heroic Frenzies*, the praise of the superiority of English women is epitomized by '*that one and only Diana (quell'unica Diana)*, whom I choose not to name'.[303] The dialogue ends with a procession of men whose blindness is

---

299 For a later reading of the poem in the light of Elizabethan chastity, see Philippa Berry, *Of Chastity and Power: Elizabethan Literature and the Unmarried Queen* (Routledge, 1989), pp. 139–43
300 Frank E. Manuel and Fritzie P. Manuel, *Utopian Thought in the Western World* (Harvard University Press, 1979), p. 229.
301 Bruno, *Cause, Principle and Unity*, Dialogue I, p. 33, in Giordano Bruno, *Cause, Principle and Unity and Essays on Magic*, ed. and trans. by Richard D. Blackwell and Robert de Lucca (Cambridge University Press, 2004). Italian text: *Opere italiane*, I, p. 643.
302 Bruno, *Ash Wednesday Supper*, Dialogue II, pp. 70–71.
303 Bruno, *Heroic Frenzies*, Argument, pp. 12–13, emphasis added.

cured as they enter 'under the temperate sky of the Britannic island'. Here are found 'Nymphs, who are the divine and blessed intelligences that assist and minister to that Prime Intelligence who resembles Diana', whose 'threefold virtue' ('triplicata virtute') has the power 'to open every seal, to unravel every knot, to disclose every secret and to unlock everything that is shut away'.[304]

Bruno's making of Elizabeth the centre of his utopian visions must have sprung from a mixture of true admiration, a desire to make Elizabethan England the mirror of his revolutionary ideas, and a more personal necessity to seek political benefactors at court. Like Bruno, Chapman's political concerns seem less the product of an active interest in politics than of a philosophical vision in which the political becomes an imaginary setting for a knowledge-seeking utopia. As Helen Hackett argues, 'the construction of the poet's own personal "Elizabeth" [...] is deployed in the service of his project of embracing complexities of meaning' which, for Chapman, matter more as a process of searching than as achieved signification.[305] Chapman's political vision emerges as a tentative shadow of his 'happy empire' of the mind. But it remains an imperfect, unfulfilled earthly shadow of Cynthia's heavenly power. For this reason, Cynthia dispels the nymph, the spirits, the forest and the island, forsakes her identity as earthly Diana and returns to her highest form as heavenly Luna:

> But Day's arm (tired to hold her torch to them)
> Now let it fall within the Ocean stream;
> The Goddess blew retreat, and with her blast
> Her morn's creation did like vapours waste:
> The winds made wing into the upper light,
> And blew abroad the sparkles of the night.
> Then (swift as thought) the bright Titanides,
> Guide and great sovereign of the marble seas,
> With milk-white heifers mounts into her sphere,
> And leaves us miserable creatures here. ('Cynthiam', 390-99)

There, as a guardian goddess to those who cultivate the perfection of their souls, Cynthia loves 'Endymion for his studious intellect' ('Cynthiam', 494). The final image of the union of the soul with a chaste and loving divinity symbolizes the reward for the human pursuit of intellectual beauty and the culmination of the Neoplatonic aspirations of Cynthia's devotees. But Endymion is a slight presence, a hint at a fulfilled aspiration of unity which Actaeon's dogs leave unaccomplished.

SN is then to be understood as a hymnic invocation of a succession of shadows that trace the intellectual voyage from darkness to light. The hymnodist adopts the identity of the magus in his attempt to guide this ascent

---

304 Bruno, *Heroic Frenzies*, Argument, pp. 28-29.
305 Helen Hackett, 'Dream Visions of Elizabeth I', in *Reading the Early Modern Dream: The Terrors of the Night*, ed. by Katharine Hodgkin, Michelle O'Callaghan and S. J. Wiseman (Routledge, 2008), pp. 45-62 (p. 47).

through the complex network of mythic and historical images conjured up in the poem. The huntress Diana, the highest object of intellectual apprehension, replicated first in the deceitful Euthymia and then in the imperial Elizabeth, signals the way to the sublime image of heavenly Cynthia as embodiment of intellectual beauty. The spectral hunters and hounds of Actaeon enact a frenzied search for those shadowy avatars, but their search ends in the transformation of dream into nightmare. Cynthia then dissolves their futile multiplicity, which can only be restored to unity in the image of Endymion as true intellectual lover. The absolute quality of this aspiration is downplayed by the closing epigraph: '*Omnis ut umbra*'. If 'all is like a shadow', the poem itself is an incomplete production of Brunian *umbrae* that place their pursuers on the path to its truths, but resists, or defers, the revelation of Truth.

5.2. *The Young Actaeon: 'Ovid's Banquet of Sense'*

Chapman's detailed naming of the seventeen dogs in *SN* is as remarkable as the exclusion of their owner, Actaeon, the hunter of divine beauty. His absence from the poem accounts for its sense of interrupted, unfinished intellectual search. In *OBS*, Actaeon reappears, now in an elusive marginal annotation that testifies to a certain philosophical continuity with the previous volume: 'Allusion to the transformation of Actaeon with the sight of Diana' ('Banquet', M8). The allusion that this gloss aims to clarify is found in the last line of a pivotal stanza in the narrative of 'Banquet', in which Corinna's song and odours have awakened Ovid's senses of hearing and smell, and with them the desire to see her:

> So vulture Love on his increasing liver
> And fruitful entrails eagerly did feed,
> And, with the gold'nest arrow in his quiver,
> Wounds him with longings, that like torrents bleed,
> To see the mine of knowledge that enriched
> His mind with poverty, and desperate need:
> A sight that with the thought of sight bewitched,
> A sight taught magic his deep mystery,
> Quicker in danger than Diana's eye. (41)

In invoking the myth of Actaeon in an amatory lyric context, Chapman has a vast tradition before him.[306] Besides the narrative in Ovid's *Metamorphoses*, the most important source for later treatments of the tale, the Roman poet had moralized the myth to explain the circumstances of his exile in *Tristia*.[307]

---

306 For a comprehensive history of the literary motif of Actaeon, see Bienvenido Morros Mestres, *El tema de Acteón en algunas literaturas europeas: de la antigüedad clásica hasta nuestros días* (Universidad de Alcalá/Centro de Estudios Cervantinos, 2010).
307 See Ovid, *Metamorphoses*, III. 138–252. Ovid's use of the myth in *Tristia*, II. 103–06, reflects on imprudence and mischance as causes of his political disgrace: 'cur aliquid

The dramatic situation invoking the 'historical' Ovid's affair with Julia thus acquires strong Actaeonian resonances. Chapman's recreation of this encounter between his Ovid and Julia's poetic alter ego, Corinna, reproduces the primal Actaeonian scene of male sight's encounter with female nudity.[308] Beyond these historical circumstances, Chapman resorts to well-known motifs of the tale and its later tradition. The 'arbour' that stands between his desire and its object is now, unlike the thorny thicket in 'Cynthiam', a classical *locus amoenus* in which desire's dangers lurk. In line with common elaborations of the myth in Petrarchan poetry, Ovid's later discovery in Corinna of 'th'extraction of all fairest dames' is pursued at the risk of his soul's 'freedom' ('Banquet', 49. 7, 50. 1). Actaeon enables a representation of the Petrarchan lover as eternally pursued and tortured by his thoughts and desires.[309]

But the terms of Chapman's Actaeon conceit transcend Petrarchan convention. The protagonist's sight aspires to discover a 'mine of knowledge' and to teach a 'deep mystery' — indeed one of the 'deeper mysteries' that, according to John Davies's first commendatory sonnet, 'pours forth' from 'Ovid's soul' ('*OBS*: Davies 1', 13–14). The brief allusion to Actaeon paradoxically invites readers to extract copious meaning from it — to regard it as one of those vestiges or shadows leading to more profound truths. But the allusion comes in anticipation of Ovid's actual sight of Corinna: it prefigures its effects externally instead of describing them as they happen. Chapman's interest focuses on 'Diana's eye' and its 'quick' response to Actaeon's 'sight' of her by means of 'transformation'. The 'deep mystery' underlying the tale refers not to Petrarchan suffering but to the nature of Actaeon's metamorphosis. Besides, it is the narrator's voice and not the protagonist's that invites readers to reconstruct the depth of the 'knowledge' and 'mystery' contained in the mythical scene. Far from being an effect of sophistry on the protagonist's part, philosophical allegory is encouraged by the first-person narrator, and then confirmed by the glossarist. Actaeon is thus an allegorical correlate of which the fictional Ovid remains totally unaware, so readers must explore

vidi? cur noxia lumina feci? | cur imprudenti cognita culpa mihi? | inscius Actaeon vidit sine veste Dianam: | praeda fuit canibus non minus ille suis' ('why did I see anything? Why did I make my eyes guilty? Why was I so thoughtless as to harbour the knowledge of a fault? Unwitting was Actaeon when he beheld Diana unclothed; none the less he became the prey of his own hounds') (*Tristia, Ex Ponto*, pp. 62–63).

308 See in this respect Luis-Martínez, 'Whose Banquet?', pp. 36–45.

309 See, among other instances, the description, in Samuel Daniel's *Delia* (1592), of the effects of Delia/Diana's throwing 'water-cold disdaine' upon the lover/Actaeon's face while his 'thoughts like hounds' chase him (*Delia*, v. 8–12, in Samuel Daniel, *Poems and A Defence of Rhyme*, ed. by Arthur Colby Sprague (Harvard University Press, 1930), p. 13). Similarly, Shakespeare depicts Orsino's imaginary transformation into a 'hart' and his 'desires' into 'fell and cruel hounds' (*Twelfth Night*, ed. by Keir Elam (Bloomsbury, 2008), I. 1. 18–22). For treatments of the Actaeon myth in Chapman's poem, see Huntington, 'Philosophical Seduction', pp. 43–45; Moss, 'Second Master', pp. 464–65; and Luis-Martínez, 'Whose Banquet', pp. 36–45.

its meanings behind Ovid's back. In the absence of further explanation, one must consider Chapman's Actaeon allusion as one of those conceits that 'prove sufficiently authentical to such as understand them' and whose interpretation is left to the reader's 'labour' alone ('Noctem', final gloss).

The 'mine of knowledge' that Ovid's sight of Corinna promises is ultimately not to Ovid's benefit but to the reader's. As discussed in the previous section, Ovid derives a great deal of philosophical meaning from his sensory perceptions. But he is also blind to a number of situations in the poem that are susceptible of serious philosophical enquiry. The clearest example of these intellectual shortcomings occurs in stanzas 70 and 71, in which Corinna dresses her heart-shaped hair with three 'jewels of device', each of which contains a symbolic *pictura* and a Latin 'motto', or 'posy'. The Commentary offers a detailed scrutiny of the meanings and sources of Chapman's own images and mottos in these stanzas. Here it suffices to point out that the three of them concern the search for intellectual beauty and the difficult poetic expression of its deep truths. Yet Chapman's main point goes beyond their ultimate meaning and focuses on how the different agents and voices in the poem participate in their construction. Corinna's action of adorning her hair with the jewels designates her as the sender of a message which Ovid's physical eye, too imbued in her sensual charms, fails to detect, and which he cannot consequently transform into intelligible species. The elegist's voice, the poem's second Ovid, narrates the scene and describes the devices without adding further symbolic elucidation. This latter function is reserved to the glossarist, who only hints at half explanations, teasing the reader about the 'many constructions' of the devices' 'application', and about the 'far higher intention[s]' of their 'conceit[s]' ('Banquet', M15 and M16). Ignorance of their secret meanings does not leave Ovid in the best of positions as an 'understander', so it is again up to the *giudiziosi* and *intendenti* to apply themselves to deeper search.

Discovering the meaning behind Actaeon's transformation is not the fictional Ovid's task but our own. In this, Chapman's perspective in the poem is also Brunian. Bruno's last English dialogue, *On the Heroic Frenzies*, consists mainly of a collection of love lyrics, or *furori* ('frenzies'), and of emblematic devices whose Petrarchan language is the object of detailed elucidation in the prose dialogues in the light of a personal version of the Neoplatonic philosophy of love, understood as an ascent from the perception of physical beauty toward the attainment of divine knowledge.[310] Bruno's rewriting of Petrarchan motifs into philosophical terms relies on a complex interplay of genres, in which the competing forms of lyric expression and didactic, philosophical prose prove complementary.[311] Lyric verse pinpoints

---

310 For a detailed account of Bruno's Neoplatonic theory of love in the context of the Italian dialogue, see John Charles Nelson, *Renaissance Theory of Love: The Context of Giordano Bruno's 'Eroici Furori'* (Columbia University Press, 1958).
311 See on this point Nuccio Ordine, *La soglia dell'ombra. Letteratura, filosofia e pittura*

its own way toward its philosophical interpretation in the dialogue, yet it would not be easily interpreted in the terms of the commentary did the poems stand by themselves. Bruno's lyric voices may advance intuitions of a theory that is only systematized by the dialogic voices, but as a general rule they remain blind to a philosophy that only emerges in the dialogue. Bruno's commentators filter the lyric experience in the form of extensive glosses and enlighten the reader's awareness of a complex path that must translate the paradoxical and insatiable nature of erotic experience into an equally endless search for the infinitude of truth.[312] Chapman's 'Banquet' demands a similar method of complementary reading. The parts in direct speech mark those paths along allegorical interpretation that the narrative and glossarial sections expand but do not fully disclose. Far from promoting an ironic narrative voice, this method fosters a consideration of the poem's interplay of voices as collaborative, complementary and didactic. In Chapman's poem, Ovid's lack of awareness of these voices' guidance of the reader's interpretation matches a similar ignorance of the task of their commentators on the part of Bruno's frenzied heroes.

At the heart of Bruno's work is the figure of the frenzied, or furious, hero. His frenzy is 'not a seizure in the snares of bestial passion [...] but a rational impulse that pursues the intellectual grasp of that goodness and beauty which is knowledge' ('Non è un raptamento [...] de ferine affezioni: ma un impeto razionale che siegue l'apprension intellettuale del buono e bello che conosce').[313] The lyric language of Bruno's frenzied heroes is the Petrarchan code that understands its object as a flesh-and-blood lady:

> In this eternal blaze
> I shudder, vex myself, ignite and burn.
> My lady's ice leaves nowhere else to turn;
> There neither love nor pity finds a place.
> Alas! She can't admire
> the chilly rigour of my ardent fire.[314]

The tension between the amatory poetry of Bruno's lyric pieces and their philosophical, heroic interpretation supports the differentiation between the two main kinds of frenzy unfolded in the dialogues. The first of these kinds displays 'an irrational impulse to senseless bestiality' ('impeto irrazionale, che tende al ferino insensato').[315] When this impulse is translated into its

---

in Giordano Bruno (Marsilio, 2003). I have consulted this work in Spanish translation: *El umbral de la sombra: literatura filosofía y pintura en Giordano Bruno*, trans. by Silvina Paula Vidal (Siruela, 2003), pp. 125–28.
312 Ordine, *El umbral de la sombra*, pp. 132–33.
313 Bruno, *Heroic Frenzies*, Part I, pp. 82–83.
314 'Io ne l'eterno foco | mi dibatto, mi struggo, scaldo, avvampo; | e al ghiaccio de mia diva per mio scampo; | né amor di me, né pietà trova loco: | lasso, per che non sente | quant'è il rigor de la mia fiamma ardente' (*Heroic Frenzies*, Part I, pp. 204–05).
315 Ibid., Part I, pp. 80–81.

common vehicle of poetic expression, it becomes what Bruno — and Chapman — identified as the malady of most love poetry of his time.[316] The second kind is the truly *heroic* frenzy, that is, '*a certain divine rapture [certa divina abstrazzione]* by which some individuals become superior, in fact, to ordinary people'.[317] This is the terrain in which Bruno's poems and dialogue sections move. Within this category, he distinguishes two subtypes: 'some, because they have come to harbour gods or divine spirits, say and do marvellous things without knowing the reasons why';[318] the others,

> practised or proficient in contemplation, and born with a lucid and intellectual spirit, are already driven by an inward stimulus and a natural fervour to a love of divinity, of justice, of truth, of glory, and these sharpen their senses in the flames of desire with the bellows of purpose, igniting the light of reason in the crucible of their cognitive faculty.[319]

Bruno's focus is on the efforts of the latter kind: their heroic condition is explained by their understanding of the human nature of a passion that nevertheless has the power, despite its paradoxes, to elevate them above their human condition. One of its more obvious paradoxes is its lyric mode of expression. But Bruno seems to solve this paradox with the kind of Chapmanesque resolution shown in the sonnets of 'Coronet'. In Bruno's lyric effusions, the sensual Muses of poetry are provided with Philosophy's 'eyes', which supply the apt perspective that aids their heroic interpretation.

Ovid features in 'Banquet' as a frenzied lover whose amatory rapture inspires his poetic fury. Like Bruno's 'giovan Atteon', Ovid is 'young in love' with Corinna's 'perfections' (13. 1-2) — Bruno sees youth as a sign that the lover's 'frenzy is unstable' ('è instabile il furore').[320] Ovid seeks his beloved 'like a fiery exhalation' (13. 5). The sound of his mistress's singing transports him to rapturous emotions that stimulate his poetic skills:

> Whereat his wit assumèd fiery wings,
> Soaring above the temper of his soul,
> And he the purifying rapture sings
> Of his ear's sense. (15. 1-4)

The language of Ovid's 'quick verse' (16. 4) — a phrase that expresses the swiftness of inspired fury — is equally descriptive of a sublime experience: Corinna's notes are 'led forth by furious trance' (16.6); her voice 'sweets, refines and ravisheth' the lover's soul (18. 5); and 'her tunes' have the power to 'invoke' 'all poets' furies' (16. 9). In the poem's specialized philosophical lexicon of sensory perception, the 'species' of Corinna's 'voice' travels through

---

316 On Bruno's attack on Petrarchism, in the very person of Petrarch, see his dedication to Sidney of the *Heroic Frenzies*: Argument, pp. 12-13.
317 Bruno, *Heroic Frenzies*, Part I, pp. 80-81, emphasis added.
318 Ibid., Part I, pp. 80-81.
319 Ibid., Part I, pp. 80-83.
320 Ibid., Part I, pp. 106-07.

the poet's 'sense' in order to raise his 'spirits' to 'their highest functions' (17. 5–6). The 'functions' invoked here are those of the intellect, by means of which the lover aspires to reach union with the object of his love. This aspiration to oneness finds its best expression in a philosophical simile that attempts to elevate the sensory experience of hearing to absolute intellectual apprehension:

> O that, as intellects themselves transit
> To each intelligible quality,*
>   My life might pass into my love's conceit,
> Thus to be formed in words, her tunes, and breath,
> And with her kisses sing itself to death.
>
> * The philosopher saith *Intellectus in ipsa intellegibilia transit*, upon which is grounded this invention: that in the same manner his life might pass into his mistress' conceit, intending his intellectual life, or soul, which by this analogy should be *intellectus*, and her conceit, *intelligibilis*.
> (24. 5–9, and M4)

'The philosopher' is often a tag that refers to Aristotle in Chapman's poems and other texts of the period, but the exact source of the gloss's Latin sentence remains untraced beyond its reminiscences of a passage in Aristotle's *De anima*, and the commentaries on this passage in Aquinas.[321] Aristotle's passage speaks about the active intellect's capacity to actualize knowledge in order to make it identical with the thing known. But this is hardly the meaning that the sentence has in Chapman, who Platonizes the Aristotelian formula in order to mean that it is the intellect that aspires to be made one with the knowledge it pursues; by extension, the lover aspires to be made one with the object of his love. This message is conveyed by the vehicle of Ovid's simile and its gloss. Ovid's tenor actually descends to a more concrete experience: the lover's life (or soul, or intellect) aspires to be made one with his 'love's conceit', which in the poem refers to the 'tunes' of Corinna's song as 'first conceivèd in her mental womb' (23. 3).[322] That Ovid's bizarre wish is the object of a Platonizing gloss that significantly whitewashes its meaning is revealing of the tendency toward taming Ovid that the poem's other voices display. These voices suggest that Ovid's lack of awareness of the philosophical import of his own verse aligns him with the unwittingly inspired heroes of Bruno's description, in need of the tutelage of those who are 'practised or proficient in contemplation'. Like Bruno's lyric lovers and enlightened fools, Ovid stands in need of external interpreters. But unlike the full explanation offered in *Heroic Frenzies*, the readers of Chapman's poem are teased with mere glimpses of promising shadows whose true sense is seldom or never revealed.

---

321 Aristotle, *De anima*, III. 5, 430a19–20. See Commentary: 'Banquet', 23–24, for a full account of these sources.
322 See Commentary: 'Banquet', 23–24.

It has never been noted by Chapman critics that this assimilation of the lover's intellect into the loved object — '*Intellectus in ipsa intellegibilia transit*' — corresponds exactly with the philosophical explanation that Bruno's speakers give of the Actaeon/Diana myth:

> TANSILLO: 'He saw her': he understood as much as was possible; 'and the hunter turned to prey': he set out to hunt and became the hunted, this young man who *hunts by the operation of the intellect, through which he converts the things he perceives into himself* [*per l'operazion de l'intelletto con cui converte le cose apprese in sé*]. [...] He hunts his prey, indeed, by the operation of his will, by whose action *he converts himself onto his own object* [*lui si converte nell'oggetto*].
>
> CICADA: I understand: because *love transforms and converts the lover into the thing beloved* [*lo amore transforma e converte nella cosa amata*].
>
> TANSILLO: [...] Thus, Actaeon, with those thoughts — those dogs — who sought outside himself for goodness, wisdom, beauty — the wild creatures — arrived into the presence of that prey, and was *enraptured* [*rapito*] outside himself by such beauty. *He became prey himself, and saw himself converted into what he sought* [*dovenne preda, veddesi convertito in quel che cercava*]. He realized then that he himself had turned into the longed-for prey of his own dogs, of his own thoughts, *because once he had contracted divinity into himself, he no longer needed to seek it outside himself* [*perché già avendola contratta in sé, non era necessario di cercare fuor di sé la divinità*].³²³

In the absence of more precise evidence of literal borrowings, this coincidence may open the case for Chapman's active use of Bruno as a direct source. However, Chapman's mention of the Actaeon myth comes only later in the poem, and there is no attempt to interpret the myth philosophically along lines to which he would have subscribed. One wonders why this is so. For Bruno, Actaeon's transformation into a stag designates the lover's final abandonment of his pursuit of worldly beauty in favour of the contemplation of divinity, and, in his opinion, 'there are few indeed who ever encounter the fountain of Diana':

> Rare indeed, I tell you, are the Actaeons whose destiny lets them contemplate the nude Diana, and become one of those who, captivated by the beautiful form of nature's body, and escorted by those twin lights of the twin splendour of divine goodness and beauty, are transformed into a stag, so that they are no longer hunters, but prey.³²⁴

Diana represents the furthest limit that the human mind can reach in its pursuit of beauty, goodness and truth: she is the 'shadow' ('ombra') of the 'absolute light' ('luce absoluta'). In accordance with Bruno's ontological metaphor of shadows, she is 'the light that is in the opacity of matter, that is,

---

323 *Heroic Frenzies*, Part I, pp. 108–11, emphasis added.
324 Ibid., Part II, pp. 284–85.

light that shines in darkness' ('la luce che è nella opacità della materia: cioè quella in quanto splende nelle tenebre').[325]

It remains to be decided whether the 'mine of knowledge' promised by the contemplation of Corinna involves any sort of approximation of the absolute light promised by Bruno's Diana. The brief allusion to the Actaeon myth in Chapman's poem is continued by long descriptions and dramatizations of Ovid's doubts as to pursuing the pleasures of sight or refraining from them. Bruno depicts Actaeon's doubts through the metaphor of the '*bold incautious course* [*il dubio et incauto camino*] of the uncertain and ambiguous reasoning and emotion that are depicted in the letter [Y] of Pythagoras'.[326] Chapman opts for the long simile of the meandering Thames: 'Forward, and back, and forward went he thus: | Like wanton Thamesis' (44. 1–2). In Chapman, the discrepancies between the two major Ovidian voices become more evident. The protagonist's resolution to see Corinna has one acknowledged purpose — 'My inward sight with outward seeing easing' (48. 3) — and one acknowledged consequence: sight will lead him 'To taste, and feel, and yet not there be stayed' (43. 7). Against these, in the 'digression' that occupies stanzas 51 to 55, the narrative voice insists on the deficiencies of sight as a guide in the pursuit of intellectual beauty. Yet division is the trait that characterizes the lover's soul. Bruno's long explanation of the Actaeon myth ends up acknowledging the plurality of situations that confront the soul torn between 'her' aspirations to higher truths and 'her' stubborn turn to lower objects: 'And because of her shared love for both matter and ideas, she feels torn apart and dismembered, until, in the end, she gives way to the stronger and more powerful drive'.[327] These drives, which will determine 'the soul's two progressions, upward and downward', depend on the soul's will for good (what Bruno calls 'appetito del bene') or fate's providence ('la providenza del fato').[328] In Chapman, while the poem's narrator can declare that 'sacred beauty' is a cause of the 'feast of souls' (52. 1–3), Ovid can also affirm that Cupid makes 'Nature (my fate) enforce me' (84. 8). The soul's will and the character's fate seem to lead in different directions. In Bruno, these differences are not perceived necessarily in terms of moral dichotomies. The conclusion to his allegorical interpretation of the Actaeon myth suggests the plurality of situations in which love can place the human soul:

> Now things happen differently to these individual souls; their habits and inclinations are affected by their different degrees of ascent or descent, so that they display different kinds and orders of frenzies, loves, and senses; not only on the ladder of nature [...] but also on the ladder of human affections, which has as many rungs as the ladder of nature, for man in all his powers displays all the species of being.[329]

---

325 Ibid., Part II, pp. 284–85.
326 Ibid., Part I, pp. 106–07, emphasis added.
327 Ibid., Part I, pp. 136–37.
328 Ibid., Part I, pp. 136–37.
329 Ibid., Part I, pp. 138–39.

There is one plain fact in 'Banquet': Chapman's Ovid *finds* the fountain of Corinna and *sees* her naked. And this fact unleashes in him a further desire to satisfy those senses that reverse his ascension on the Platonic ladder. If we try to test whether Ovid has behaved in the poem strictly as a Brunian Actaeon and whether seeing Diana has led him to pursue divine knowledge only within himself, then the result is failure. But Ovid is not Actaeon: he is a character in a poem whose action that poem has construed in analogy with the myth. The question should be whether the poem has guided readers to the possibility of understanding Ovid and Corinna as shadows of the philosophical Actaeon and Diana. The poem has done so in the same oblique ways as it has suggested their being shadows of the historical figures behind the doubtful affair that brought about Ovid's exile — a situation that would endorse a political rather than a philosophical interpretation of the tale. When Chapman's narrator describes Corinna's naked breasts being showered by the fountain and calls her a 'Roman Phoebe' (11. 3), how seriously or how ironically should we take this identification of the poem's character as the moon-goddess Diana? The historical identity of Corinna as Augustus's daughter Julia will lead us to conclude that she was anything but chaste and that the epithet is ironic — Kermode reminds us that she has been compared to Venus a little earlier in the poem (8. 7).[330] But a robust network of references depicts Ovid's contemplation of her beauty as a correlate of the intellect's union with the object of intellection. Ascent and descent, or idealization and irony, have been key concepts in the critical interpretation of Chapman's poem in either/or terms. The Brunian understanding of 'the ladder of human affections' as a manifestation of complex impulses should encourage us to see Ovid's banquet inclusively rather than disjunctively. The alternate 'degrees of ascent and descent' that direct the protagonist's inclinations are the effect of the poetic necessity dictated by Chapman's Ovidian artefact. Chapman's creative engagement with the variety of the Ovidian elegy matches the Brunian strategy of putting the conventions of secular amatory poetry at the service of higher intentions.[331]

John Huntington, the only Chapman critic that has tangentially hinted at the relevance of Bruno's philosophical Actaeon for an interpretation of 'Banquet', concludes that the poem permits readers 'to see both the moral dangers and the intellectual possibilities of Ovid's situation'.[332] The suggestion of Ovid's surrender to the temptations of the flesh at the end of the poem is as strong as the poem's attempt to read his sensory perceptions and sensual enjoyment as steps towards these higher purposes. The unfulfilled intentions at the end of the poem connect genre conventions with philosophical concerns

---

330 Compare here the ironic readings of Kermode, 'The Banquet of Sense', p. 89, or Gless, 'Chapman's Ironic Ovid', p. 34, with Moss, who argues that this is an example of Chapman's resignification of Ovid ('Second Master', pp. 481–82).
331 This is an instance of Moss's above-quoted idea of Chapman's 'responsible and considered engagement with Ovid' ('Second Master', p. 459).
332 Huntington, 'Philosophical Seduction', p. 45.

in the context of the tripartite structure of *OBS*. The outward lasciviousness of Ovid and Corinna that is built on the poem's surface constitutes one side of its undeniable and necessary paradox:[333] it declares the moral insufficiency of sensual enjoyment and the aesthetic inadequacy of the poetics of rapture practised by Chapman's character. The other side is their status as beautiful shadows signalling the always incomplete path to the infinitude of Philosophy's light: this side proclaims the necessity of the senses and the possibility of correcting Ovid's poetics through the interplay of renewed Ovidian voices. But the paradox demands integration in the spirit of *discordia concors* rather than ironic dislocation. If the Brunian shadows of Ovid and Corinna can signal the path to Actaeon and Diana, and if these can point further upward in the direction of Endymion and Cynthia, then they will be able to kindle the 'radiant and light-bearing intellect' that will lead readers 'through Corinna's garden without the help of a lantern' ('*OBS*: 'To Roydon', lines 46–48).

6. *Coda: Circles Never Closed*

In his description of Chapman's poetic mind, Millar MacLure invokes a passage from the later poem *Euthymiae Raptus*:

> but th'effect
> Proper to perfect Learning: to direct
> Reason in such an Art, as that it can
> Turne blood to soule, and make both, one calme man.[334]

In Chapman's idiom, a dedication to turning 'blood to soule' involves the struggle with poetic expression as the path toward its furnishing with philosophical meaning, described throughout this introduction. The insistence on the poet's strenuous exertions in the achievement of that goal is a constant motif in Chapman's writing. The achievement of 'one calme man' seems to have been in Chapman's poetry a goal always in process. As MacLure asserts, 'he was himself a divided man', and the attempts to construe his works in terms of homogeneity have risked misrepresentation. For MacLure, Chapman's poetic struggle involves a rebellion against what Keats called the Shakespearean 'negative capability': 'I am sure that Shakespeare was divided as many ways as an orange or as Montaigne, but he rested in the riddle, while Chapman (like Greville) was always irritably striving after reasons and conclusions [...] so that *the conflict keeps breaking through*'.[335]

---

[333] For a view of the poem as 'an extended exercise in paradox', see MacLure, *George Chapman*, pp. 53–59. MacLure, who accepts the validity of the two contending perspectives, is however more inclined towards the ironic reading.
[334] *Euthymiae Raptus, or The Tears of Peace*, lines 556–59, in Bartlett, *Poems*, p. 185.
[335] MacLure, *George Chapman*, p. 9, emphasis added. Keats's definition of the 'quality [...] which Shakespeare possessed so enormously' concerns the ability of 'being in uncertainties, Mysteries, doubts, without any irritable teacher after fact & reason' (*Keats's Poetry and Prose*, ed. by Jeffrey N. Cox (Norton, 2009), p. 109).

Understanding Chapman's poetry as *a poetry of conflict* means not only detecting disagreement and confrontation with his peers, but also a self-critical attitude that installs both form and meaning in a realm of provisionality striving for a not always achieved unity and consistency. The emblem of the letter C as a circle in progress drawn by a compass offers an accurate snapshot of poetic incompletion as it strives toward the perfection of the full circle:

> Contentment is our heav'n, and all our deeds
> Bend in that circle, seld or never closed,
> More than the letter in the word precedes;
> And to conduce that compass is reposed
>   More force and art in beauty joined with love
> Than thrones with wisdom. ('Banquet', 54. 1–6)

The source of these lines is an emblematic device of French printer Christopher Plantin, whose motto, '*Labore et Constantia*' ('With Labour and Constancy'), brings back the importance of continued laborious effort to Chapman's idea of the profession of poetry.[336] The Platonic joining of 'love' and 'beauty' is one important aim toward which the poet's struggle tends. But the aim seems to stand always beyond the poem. Chapman's addition of the motto '*Lucidius olim*' ('More lucidly at some future time') to the perfectly closed circle of his sonnet corona in *OBS* seems, if not an act of self-boycotting, at least of reinstatement of conflict at the heart of formal achievement and conceptual completion. Despite its circular closure, the poem attacks its own lack of lucidity — a term that foregrounds poetic *enargia*: further struggle with concepts and form is announced in order to reinstate 'soul' into 'blood'.

In the effort to complete the circle, Chapman's obsession with saturating his poems with meaning may often have proved as problematic for his aim as it is for his readers. This practice also operates at the level of the elaborate materiality of Chapman's printed books. Waddington has studied how the 'extended paraphernalia' of title pages, epigraphs, emblematic devices, as well as end and marginal glosses makes of Chapman's conception of the poetry volume 'an extended poem, as a means to establishing attitudes towards his material'.[337] The 1595 edition of *OBS* is presented by Waddington as a paradigmatic instance of authorial control of meaning through supervision of the production process. The displacement of the bookseller's device to the last page of the volume in favour of one of Chapman's own choice on the title page is the most remarkable feature of this practice.[338] The conceptual relevance of the device used by Chapman's bookseller, Richard Smith, has already surfaced in this introduction. It was an adaptation of the *Veritas filia Temporis* emblem, featuring an old and winged Time — here strangely

---

336 See Commentary: 'Banquet', 54, for sources and references, and Visual Sources.
337 Waddington, 'Visual Rhetoric', p. 40.
338 See Ronald B. McKerrow, *Printers' and Publishers' Devices in England and Scotland: 1485–1640* (The Bibliographical Society, 1949), p. 162; Waddington, 'Visual Rhetoric', pp. 45–46.

transformed into a satyr — rescuing Truth from its dark cave. Smith's motto — '*Tempore patet occulta Veritas*' ('Time reveals hidden Truth') — would have proved convenient to Chapman's purposes, in view of his uses of Time as a metaphor for the poet's labour (Figure 3). For this reason, its relegation in favour of another, showing a gnomon that stands in water and is refracted to appear crooked below the waterline, is the more significant. Its motto, '*Sibi conscia recti*' ('Conscious of its own rectitude'), is a truncated version of a Virgilian line (Figure 2).[339] Waddington has read this emblem as a call for a rectified interpretation of the poem — one that privileges the mind over the senses and that warns against the reader's tendency to sympathize with the sensual Ovid. Waddington, for whom 'the entire poem acts as the explanatory verse' of this latter emblem, traces the long philosophical tradition of this motif from Plato's *Republic* to Renaissance scepticism to conclude that Chapman's treatment of perspective and perception substantiates his conception of 'Banquet' as an ironic poem that condemns Ovid's point of view and, by extension, the sensuality of Ovidian poets and readers.[340] In Waddington's view, Chapman's choice of an epigraph from Persius's first satire — '*Quis leget haec? Nemo Hercule Nemo, | vel duo vel nemo*' ('Who will read this? Nobody, by Hercules, nobody: either two or nobody') — to accompany the emblem insists not only on his courting a select minority of readers but primarily on the condemnation of the decadent sensuality and erotic poetry unfurled in Persius's poem.[341]

To Waddington's superb analysis in his articles and monograph one must simply object the immense poetic effort spent on making Ovid's voice sound as poetically and philosophically able as the narrator's. But the critic's narrative is little altered if put at the service of allegory's sympathetic rectification of the poem's sensual surface, as an attempt to turn 'blood' into the transcendent unity of 'soule', to see the formless mass of stone as an integral and necessary part of Niobe's neat shape, or to straighten the stick's underwater obliqueness into its right line. MacLure, who makes the Virgilian motto and emblem the leitmotif of his arresting portrait of Chapman's poetic thought, understands Chapman's rectitude of mind as a commitment to 'a limited number of propositions' whose outward expression often miscarries as the effect of the poet's inward struggle with forms.[342] That the right mind is often obscured

---

339 'di tibi, si qua pios respectant numina, si quid | usquam iustitia est, et mens sibi conscia recti, | praemia digna ferant' ('May the gods, if any divine powers have regard for the good, if justice has any weight anywhere and if the mind has consciousness of its own rectitude, bring thee worthy rewards') (*Aeneid*, I. 603–05). These words are part of Aeneas's greeting to Dido.

340 Waddington, *The Mind's Empire*, p. 145.

341 Raymond B. Waddington, 'Chapman and Persius: The Epigraph to *Ovids Banquet of Sence*', *The Review of English Studies*, 74.1 (1968), pp. 158–62, doi:10.1093/res/XIX.74.158. For Persius's original, see *Juvenal and Persius*, ed. and trans. by G. G. Ramsay (William Heinemann, 1928), I. 2–3, p. 316.

342 MacLure, *George Chapman*, p. 228. See the final chapter, 'Conclusion: *Sibi conscia recti*', pp. 225–30.

by the intricacy of a style whose aim is to clarify it seems the fate of Chapman's poetry. That he subjected his meaning to constant deferral — '*Lucidius olim*' — speaks less about irresolution than about the seriousness of his project. *The Shadow of Night* and *Ovid's Banquet of Sense* compel their readers to navigate the waters of crooked refractions and to pry into the apparent shapelessness of unsculpted stones in the act of transmuting these raw materials into more potent shadows, and these shadows into firmer ideas: *omnis ut umbra*.

THE TEXTS AND THE PRESENT EDITION

Copy Texts and Collation

THIS EDITION of *The Shadow of Night* and *Ovid's Banquet of Sense* draws on the original quartos of 1594 and 1595 — Q*SN* and Q*OB* — as copy texts.

Q*SN* was entered in the Stationers' Register on 31 December 1593 (see Introduction, n. 28). Of the ten extant copies registered by the English Short Title Catlogue (ESTC), I have consulted six:

Q*SN*$_1$ British Library, C.39.d.62
Q*SN*$_2$ Huntington Library, Call Number 49637
Q*SN*$_3$ Oxford University, Malone Collection, Bodleian Mal.299(6)
Q*SN*$_4$ Winchester College Fellows Library Book No. 2259
Q*SN*$_5$ Victoria and Albert Museum, Dyce Collections, 2025 Dyce 25.C.5
Q*SN*$_6$ Carl H. Pforzheimer Library, Harry Ransom Center, The University of Texas at Austin, Pforz 160 PFZ

I inspected the four British copies (Q*SN*$_1$, Q*SN*$_3$, Q*SN*$_4$, Q*SN*$_5$) directly from the libraries. For Q*SN*$_2$ I used the EEBO reproduction. For Q*SN*$_6$ I relied on a high-resolution photographic reproduction kindly supplied by the Harry Ransom Center, University of Texas. All copies are virtually identical, and no significant variant readings between them have been noted.

All these copies are bound individually, with the exception of Q*SN*$_4$, which is preserved in a late seventeenth-century ten-item *Sammelband* named 'Miscellaneous Poems' (Winchester College Fellows Library Book No. 2259). This collection was compiled by the Oxford graduate and book collector Richard Triplett (1671–1720), and was donated to Winchester College by the Hampshire bibliophile Alexander Thistlethwayte (1718?–1771). The collection, which features poetry published between 1594 and 1637 ordered chronologically, comprises the following works: 1) George Chapman, *The Shadow of Night* (1594); 2) George Chapman, *Ouids Banquet of Sence* (1595); 3) William Basse, *Three Pastoral Elegies* (London: Valentine Simmes for J. Barnes, 1602); 4) Michael Drayton, *The Owle* (London: E. White and Nicholas Ling, 1604); 5) Giles Fletcher, *Christs victorie, and triumph in Heauen, and earth, ouer, and after death* (Cambridge: C. Legge, 1610); 6) Sir Thomas Overbury, *A Wife* (London: Lawrence Lisle, 1614); 7) Robert Anton, *Philosophers Satyrs* (London: Thomas Creede and Robert Alsop for Roger Jackson, 1616); 8) Samuel Daniel, *The Vision of the Twelve Goddesses*, extracted from *The Whole Workes of Samuel Daniel Esquire in Poetrie* (London: Nicholas Okes for Simon Waterson, 1623), pp. 403–20; 9) Aurelian Townshend, *Albion's Triumph*

(London: Robert Allot, 1632); 10) Shackerley Marmion, *Cupid & Psyche* (London: Nicholas and John Okes for H. Sheppard, 1637). On this *Sammelband*, see Carly Emma Watson, *The Legacy of an Eighteenth-Century Gentleman: Alexander Thistlethwayte's Books in Winchester College Fellows' Library* (unpublished PhD thesis, University of Birmingham, 2013), pp. 139–56.

Of the seven extant copies of Q*OB* registered by ESTC, I have consulted the following five:

Q*OB*$_1$ British Library, London, C.56.c.6
Q*OB*$_2$ Huntington Library, San Marino, Ca. Call Number 49638
Q*OB*$_3$ Oxford University, Malone Collection, Bodleian Mal.210(5)
Q*OB*$_4$ Winchester College Fellows Library Book No. 2259
Q*OB*$_5$ Victoria and Albert Museum, Dyce Collections, 2026 Dyce 25.C.6

I inspected the four British copies (Q*OB*$_1$, Q*OB*$_3$, Q*OB*$_4$, Q*OB*$_5$) directly from the libraries. For Q*OB*$_2$, I used the two electronic reproductions available online (*EEBO* and HathiTrust Digital Library). All copies are practically identical, so no copy variants have been considered in the textual notes.[1]

Three of these copies are bound individually (Q*OB*$_1$, Q*OB*$_3$ and Q*OB*$_5$). Q*OB*$_4$ is preserved in the abovementioned late seventeenth-century ten-item *Sammelband* at Winchester College.

The second edition of *OBS*, in octavo — O*OB* — was published in 1639, five years after Chapman's death. This latter edition is significant for its suppression of the paratexts and therefore of all mentions of Chapman's authorship. Its title page (Figure 4), running heads and inner titles support the fiction of Ovid's authorship. Several copies of this edition are preserved in *Sammelbände* with English translations of Ovid. Yet this octavo, which clearly derives from the earlier quarto, has no real interest from a textual point of view: it seldom clarifies cruxes or corrects errors from Q*OB*, and it occasionally adds new ones. For this reason, I have not listed the eight copies of O*OB* that I have inspected, but the reader can consult my recent study of the textual and literary history of this edition for further details.[2]

Neither Q*OB* nor O*OB* were entered in the Stationers' Register.

For the present text of *SN*, Q*SN* has been collated with Shepherd, Bartlett, and Hudston (the latter includes 'Preface to Roydon' and 'Noctem' only). Emendations in the Latin quotations in Chapman's glosses often note corrections by former editors, and consider Chapman's main source, Conti. Occasionally, these quotations have been expanded to complete a sentence; in those cases, the additional lines are printed in square brackets.

For the text of *OBS*, Q*OB* has been collated with O*OB*, Shepherd, Bartlett,

---

[1] Specifically on *OBS*, Bartlett notes that 'The copies are extraordinarily similar, printing rather crowded and somewhat careless' (p. 429).
[2] Luis-Martínez, 'Whose Banquet'. See also Introduction, p. 43, and Commentary: *OBS*, Title pages.

Hudston (which includes 'Preface to Roydon' and 'Banquet' only) and Braden (which provides a modern-spelling text of 'Banquet' only).

The Textual Notes register variant readings, emendations in this and in previous editions, as well as those cases of spelling regularization that involve significant choices — e.g. capitalizations, genitives, plural forms.

Spelling and Punctuation

The decision to modernize spelling and punctuation is one that presents both advantages and disadvantages. In their recent manual *A Handbook of Editing Early Modern Texts*, Claire Loffman and Harriet Phillips include a useful chapter that discusses these pros and cons before concluding that preferences for old or for modern spelling and punctuation are less a matter of personal choice than of editorial context and the necessities of particular texts.[3] The last complete edition of these two volumes of poetry is in Bartlett's old-spelling *The Poems of George Chapman*. The poems in these collections have also featured in later anthologies and editions, but always fragmentarily. Chapman's verse has been the object of two recent MHRA editions in the Tudor and Stuart Translations series, where editorial policy prescribes modern spelling and punctuation. These are the editions of the translations of the *Iliad* and *Odyssey*, by Robert S. Miola and Gordon Kendal respectively.[4] In the introduction to the latter, Kendal lucidly affirms that 'however passionate Chapman was about obscurity, he wanted to be understood, and the extra barrier of old spelling conventions was no part of his hermeneutical plan'.[5] The present edition fully subscribes to this statement, which can be extended to include punctuation. A similar editorial policy to that of the Tudor and Stuart Translations series has been observed in the conviction that intrinsic difficulties of Chapman's vocabulary and syntax are sometimes less so with the help of regularized spelling and punctuation.[6]

For spelling, the limits to modernization should be set where an orthographic change can alter an obvious phonic effect — e.g. when it affects metre or rhyme. In those cases, certain old spellings have been retained and explained in footnotes. Difficult cases like the rhyming pairs 'starres/Marinars' (Q*SN*, sigs B4^v–C1^r) and 'starrs/Mariners' (Q*SN*, sig. E2^v) have been regularized to 'stars/marinars', despite present-day 'mariners', in the belief that Chapman felt this option to be the most apt for purposes of rhyme. When originally contracted forms like 'transformd' or 'advanc't' do not affect pronunciation,

---

[3] See H. R. Woudhuysen and others, 'Text: Modernisation and Translation', in *A Handbook of Editing Early Modern Texts*, ed. by Claire Loffman and Harriet Phillips (Routledge, 2018), pp. 94–113.
[4] George Chapman, *Homer's Iliad*, ed. by Robert S. Miola (MHRA, 2017), and *Homer's Odyssey*, ed. by Gordon Kendal (MHRA, 2016).
[5] *Homer's Odyssey*, ed. by Kendal, p. 35.
[6] See the section by Neil Rhodes, 'Translations', in the above-cited chapter from *A Handbook of Editing Early Modern Texts*, pp. 109–13.

they have been regularized to 'transformed' and 'advanced'. Apostrophes that alert readers to elide a vowel have been often preserved; sometimes apostrophes have been added in order to regularize the quarto's method of marking an elision: e.g. 'sendst' becomes 'send'st', 'rendring' becomes 'rend'ring', 'ventrous' becomes 'ventr'ous', 'stolne' becomes 'stol'n', etc. Words that in Chapman are almost always monosyllabic by the loss of a weak vowel, like 'heaven', 'given' or 'even', have been spelt 'heav'n', 'giv'n' or 'ev'n', unless they were meant to be disyllabic for metrical purposes (e.g. at the end of a line). However, 'power', 'flower' and 'bower', which as a general rule are pronounced monosyllabically in Chapman, have been kept in their present-day form, as such pronunciation is still common in English. Similarly, 'every' and 'ivory', always meant as disyllabic, are kept in their present-day spelling. Unusual pronunciations due to elisions of weak vowels are explained in the notes. Grave accents have been added to alert the reader that the vowel of '-èd' should be pronounced for metrical reasons.

For spelling, OED has supplied the rule, and exceptions or departures are noted. When OED gives two spelling forms, the one used in the quartos is retained; the same procedure has been adopted when a spelling in the quartos is listed separately as an archaic form by OED.

The use of capitals in the original quartos poses a particularly challenging problem. Frequent uses of capitalized initials which do not affect the sense of a word have been reverted to lower-case: e.g. the abovementioned 'Marinars' have become 'marinars'. However, it is sometimes difficult to decide when Chapman means to allegorize, personify or deify a common noun: 'night' and 'morning', particularly in Qsn, must sometimes become 'Night' and 'Morning'; and 'loue' must frequently become 'Love' when the god of love is meant. These cases are often noted and explained. Ultimately, readers willing to consult these texts in original spelling can resort to Bartlett's authoritative edition, or to the original quartos, and for that reason signature marks have been retained in the margins.

The original punctuation of the quartos could be behind many obscurities and misunderstandings, particularly where a modern reader may perceive excessive, missing or misplaced commas. Semicolons and commas are often used interchangeably in these original editions, while colons also appear quite unsystematically, not always with the intention of marking rhetorical pauses. For these reasons, punctuation of the present text is editorial. As Neil Rhodes has argued, 'emending the punctuation in order to aid the sense is the most challenging task for the editor, but potentially the most valuable feature of the edited text for the reader'.[7] As these poems pose considerable difficulties in this respect, one only hopes to have been instrumental to the aim. I have consulted previous modernizations of these texts, like Shepherd's (published in 1875 and not always helpful) or the more recent and useful

---

7 Rhodes, 'Translations', in *A Handbook of Editing Early Modern Texts*, p. 112.

texts of Fowler's text for 'Zodiac', or Braden's for 'Banquet'.[8] Cases in which an editorial choice in this edition drastically alters the original or intends to clarify an obscure passage have been explained in footnotes and/or registered in the Textual Notes.

In *SN*, verse paragraph divisions are marked by slight indentation. I have followed Q*SN* in most cases, although I have merged two paragraphs in one or added a new division occasionally. These changes are indicated in the Textual Notes and the Commentary. In *OBS*, the original quarto only numbers stanzas in 'Zodiac', so the numbering is editorial in the case of 'Banquet' and 'Coronet'. Quotation marks have been added to direct speech in *OBS*.

When texts in English and in other languages (Latin, French, Italian) have been reproduced from early modern editions, these have been left unmodernized, although *i-j* and *u-v* have been regularized to modern usage, and diacritics and ampersands have been expanded.

Sources, Annotation, Appendix

Chapman used notes and glosses in the original quartos for different purposes. In *SN*, end glosses are the preferred option following the text of each of the two hymns, and their function is to provide learned sources or to clarify obscure passages. Endnote calls in Q*SN* are numerical, often appearing before the word or passage concerned. These have been regularized to the modern custom of placing the calls after the corresponding word or phrase. Occasionally, marginal glosses were used — twice in each hymn. These marginal notes are not different in hermeneutic nature from the end glosses and have been incorporated into the latter without altering the original numbering — i.e. the two marginal glosses of 'Noctem' become glosses 4a and 4b, as these occur between the calls for end glosses 4 and 5. All these have been printed as a first layer of footnotes in this edition. There are no end glosses in Q*OB*. Its use of marginal notes — only for 'Banquet' — responds to two functions: 1) structural markers, i.e. they signal who is speaking, insert structural divisions or supply factual details of the narrative in the fashion of dramatic stage directions; 2) hermeneutic notes providing learned references or clarifying difficult passages. While in the first case these have been left in the margins and printed in italics, in the second case the procedure is similar to the one used for *SN*: a numerical call in the text refers the reader to a first layer of footnotes, in which each note is marked as M preceding arabic numbers. Translations of Greek and Latin texts in the glosses are supplied in parentheses; all these translations are mine unless specified otherwise. If a term or phrase in the glosses needs further explanation, this has been supplied in square brackets.

In Chapman's poems, what I have called, following Steiner, 'contingent

---

8 Fowler, 'Triumphal Forms', pp. 208–14; Braden, pp. 430–61.

difficulties' (see Introduction, pp. 5–6) become endemic. This circumstance has the inevitable corollary of profuse editorial annotation, which is of two kinds. A second layer of footnotes mainly intends to clarify lexical and syntactic difficulties, and often involve paraphrases of one or more sentences, of longer passages or of full stanzas. Translations of foreign-language words and passages in Chapman's text have been included in footnotes too. Occasionally, footnotes have been used in order to clarify cultural or literary references when brevity allows. Readers wishing further elucidation of sources and meaning should consult the Commentary, which is meant to be comprehensive.

The annotation of sources and analogues becomes the most difficult task for an editor of Chapman. The poet's consultation and active use of Latin, Greek, French and possibly Italian sources in these volumes compel the editor to make decisions about how to present these materials. This edition's attention to Chapman's poetics and compositional habits relies on the conviction that the consultation of those sources in their original language is often necessary or advantageous for the reader. For this reason, the Introduction, Commentary and footnotes frequently quote these texts in both their original languages and English translation. Sometimes, long texts have been provided in English translation accompanied by relevant phrases or keywords in the original language, with the intention to signal specific sentences or phrases that may have caught Chapman's attention. The order in which original and translation are reproduced prioritizes convenience of presentation over consistency. For Conti's *Mythologiae*, Chapman's preferred source, Mulryan and Brown's translation of Conti's *Mythologiae* is consistently used, although I have needed to modify it or to provide my own translations on a small number of occasions (and have noted this accordingly). For Latin and Greek texts, I have relied on present-day editions and translations when available, often the bilingual texts in the Loeb, I Tatti or similar series. Translations from early modern editions are my own. All efforts have been made to trace the authorship of each and every translation in the Commentary and the final Bibliography. Similarly, all efforts have been made to acknowledge the work of previous scholars in the detection of Chapman's sources.

Chapman's talent for lexical innovation has been frequently noted. Sister Maria del Rey Kelly's unpublished thesis on Chapman's poetic diction in his nondramatic works continues to be an indispensable, unparalleled source of information and arguments that any Chapman scholar should consult. Different procedures of word formation, particularly the poet's idiosyncratic use of prefixes and suffixes and his abilities in compounding, are accounted for and catalogued by Kelly. Neologizing is another frequent practice: Nicoll's, and more recently Miola's and Kendal's, lists of neologisms in their editions of Chapman's Homer should be consulted too. I have sometimes found that words provided in those lists have precedents in the poems edited here. Similarly, I have found in these poems first uses of words attributed by *OED* to later works by Chapman or other authors. I have noted these in footnotes, but have not compiled a new list of neologisms, which may have ended up being confusing. I believe that a detailed study of Chapman's lexicon with the help of modern technologies is in order, but the task is beyond the present edition. That study should begin with consideration of the pioneering work of George G. Loane on Chapman's vocabulary and continue with Kelly's thesis.[9] For these reasons, and due to the numerous lexical annotations in this edition's footnotes, a final glossary would have been imprecise and redundant.

The Appendix on Chapman's metrical forms is not exhaustive but merely illustrative, and its main source is again Kelly. It intends to stress the poet's serious commitment to his task as a versifier, as well as the interest of these poems for the later development of metrical forms in his works.

The Bibliography is completed by a list of 'Visual Sources: Paintings and Emblems', ordered alphabetically, with reference to websites where relevant images can be accessed.

---

9 Besides Kelly, *Poetic Diction*, see George G. Loane, *A Thousand and One Notes on 'A New English Dictionary'* (Philipot & Co., 1920); 'A Thousand and Two Notes on *A New English Dictionary*', *Philological Society Transactions*, 30.1 (1930), pp. 38–199; 'A Third Thousand Notes on *N.E.D.*', *Notes and Queries*, 171 (1936), pp. 202–05; 'Chapman's Compounds in *N.E.D.*', *Notes and Queries*, 181 (1941), pp. 130–31; 'Chapman and Holofernes', *Notes and Queries*, 172 (1937), p. 7.

THE SHADOW OF NIGHT

Versus mei habebunt aliquantum Noctis] 'My lines have something of the Night'. Adapted from Ovid, *Ibis*, 63-64: 'Utque mei versus aliquantum noctis habebunt, | Sic vitae series tota sit atra tuae' ('As my lines have something of the night, so let your life's series be all black', in *The Art of Love, and Other Poems*, pp. 256-57). On this epigraph, see Introduction, pp. 44-45. Chapman deifies Ovid's 'noctis' through capitalization.

Antilo.] This obscure word remains unexplained. It may abbreviate Latin *antilogia*, or its English derivates 'antilogy' or 'antiloquy', both of which are defined by *OED* as 'a discourse that contradicts or argues against something'. The word could reinforce the polemical spirit of the poem.

Anchora spei] 'Hope's anchor'. This device belonged to printer Richard Field between 1588 and 1624 (see McKerrow, *Printers*, 64, pp. 59-60). On hope as the soul's anchor ('spem [...] anchoram animae'), see Hebrews 6. 18-19 (*Biblia Vulgata*, ed. by Alberto Colunga and Laurentio Torrado (Biblioteca de Autores Cristianos, 1994), p. 1160).

R[ichard] F[ield] for William Ponsonby] See Commentary: *SN*, Title page.

Σκία νυκτὸς.

THE SHADOVV
OF NIGHT: CONTAINING
TWO POETICALL HYMNES.

Deuised by *G. C. Gent.*

Versus mei habebunt aliquantum Noctis.
Antilo.

AT LONDON,
Printed by *R. F.* for *William Ponsonby.*
1594.

FIG. 1. Title page of the 1594 quarto of *The Shadow of Night* (Q*sn*). Carl H. Pforzheimer Library, Harry Ransom Center, The University of Texas at Austin, Pforz 160 PFZ.

To my dear and most worthy friend Master Matthew Roydon   A2ʳ

IT IS AN exceeding rapture of delight in the deep search of knowledge (none knoweth better than thyself, sweet Matthew) that maketh men manfully endure the extremes incident to that Herculean labour: from flints must the Gorgonean fount be smitten. Men must be shod by Mercury, girt with Saturn's adamantine sword, take the shield from Pallas,   5
the helm from Pluto, and have the eye of the Graeae (as Hesiodus arms Perseus against Medusa) before they can cut off the viperous head of benumbing ignorance, or subdue their monstrous affections to most beautiful judgement.

How then may a man stay his marvelling to see passion-driven men,   10
reading but to curtail a tedious hour, and altogether hidebound with affection to great men's fancies, take upon them as killing censors as if they were judgement's butchers, or as if the life of truth lay tottering in their verdicts.

Now what a supererogation in wit this is, to think Skill so mightily   15
pierced with their loves that she should prostitutely show them her secrets, when she will scarcely be looked upon by others but with invocation, fasting, watching, yea not without having drops of their souls like an heavenly familiar. Why then should our *Intonsi Catones*, with their profit-ravished gravity, esteem her true favours such questionless   20

---

11 *curtail*] shorten in duration (*OED*, v., 3).
11–12 *hidebound ... fancies*] made short-sighted by their servility to the caprices of great men. *OED* records this figurative sense for *hidebind* (v.) and *hidebound* (adj., 4. a: 'restricted in view or scope').
12 *take upon them as*] assume the role of.
12 *censors*] Q*sn* reads 'censures', which *OED*, *censor*, registers as an early modern spelling. Modernization renders its meaning unambiguous — i.e. adverse critics (n., 3. b).
13 *tottering*] swinging, as from the gallows (*OED*, *totter*, v., †1. b), as an effect of the censors' verdict.
15 *supererogation*] superfluous quantity or expenditure, excess. See Commentary: '*SN*: To Roydon', 15–16.
15 *Skill*] Art (here, of poetry). Shepherd's capitalization of Q*sn*'s 'skil' is adopted here, as the concept is clearly personified. On the importance of this notion in Chapman, see 'Noctem', 13, and Commentary.
18 *yea*] truly, certainly (*OED*, adv., †3. a).
19 *an heavenly familiar*] a heavenly spirit (*OED*, *familiar*, n., 3. a); 'heavenly' would be pronounced without aspirated 'h'.
19 *Intonsi Catones*] unshaven Catos. See Commentary: '*SN*: To Roydon', 19.
20 *profit-ravished gravity*] dignity sequestered by the prospect of economic benefit. However, the late sixteenth-century spelling 'profit' also stands for 'prophet' (*OED*). As 'ravishment' can refer to the prophet's, and the poet's, divine rapture, Chapman may mean, ironically, 'with the gravity of an enraptured prophet'.
20 *her*] Skill's.

vanities as, with what part soever thereof they seem to be something delighted, they queamishly commend it for a pretty toy. Good Lord, how serious and eternal are their idolatrous plats for riches! No marvel sure they here do so much good with them. And heaven no doubt will grovel on the earth (as they do) to embrace them. But I stay this spleen when I remember, my good Matthew, how joyfully oftentimes you reported unto me that most ingenious Derby, deep-searching Northumberland, and skill-embracing heir of Hunsdon had most profitably entertained learning in themselves, to the vital warmth of freezing science and to the admirable lustre of their true nobility, whose high-deserving virtues may cause me hereafter strike that fire out of darkness, which the brightest day shall envy for beauty. I should write more, but my hasting out of town taketh me from the paper; so, preferring thy allowance in this poor and strange trifle to the passport of a whole city of others, I rest as resolute as Seneca, satisfying myself if but a few, if one, or if none like it.

By the true admirer of thy virtues and perfectly vowed friend,

George Chapman.

21–22 *with what part ... delighted*] with whatever part of her (i.e. Skill) they may be delighted in some way; see *OED*, *something*, adv.: somewhat, in some way.
22 *queamishly*] fastidiously, as if affected with nausea. *OED* enters *queamish* separately from *squeamish*, and gives this example as the only use of its derivate adverb.
22 *it*] the part of Skill with which they are delighted.
23 *plats*] schemes or plots (*OED*, n., 4, 2nd edn); in this context, the 'idolatrous plats' of amateurish, ignorant poets are their plans to acquire benefit ('riches') by flattering great men in their poems.
25 *spleen*] ill humour originated in the spleen; indignation, anger.
29 *to the vital warmth of freezing science*] i.e. for the revitalization of decaying knowledge.
33 *allowance*] praise, commendation (*OED*, n., †7. a), but with an ironic hint at its usual sense of monetary compensation, which is what Chapman's rival poets seek from their patrons, and which the poet knows he will not obtain from his friend.
34 *passport*] a document granting recommendation or some other privilege (see *OED*, n., 6. †b, for mainly early modern uses).

HYMNUS IN NOCTEM

GREAT GODDESS, to whose throne in Cynthian fires[1]
This earthly altar endless fumes expires —
Therefore, in fumes of sighs and fires of grief
To fearful chances thou send'st bold relief —
Happy, thrice happy type, and nurse of Death,[2]   5
Who, breathless, feeds on nothing but our breath,
In whom must virtue and her issue live
Or die forever, now let humour give
Seas to mine eyes, that I may quickly weep
The shipwreck of the world; or let soft Sleep   10
(Binding my senses) loose my working soul,
That in her highest pitch she may control

GLOSS 1. He calls these 'Cynthian fires', of Cynthius, or the Sun, in whose beams the fumes and vapours of the earth are exhaled, the earth being as an altar, and those fumes as sacrificing smokes, because they seem pleasing to her in resembling her. That the earth is called an altar, Aratus in *Astronomicis* testifies in these verses:
ἀλλ' ἄρα καὶ περὶ κεῖνο Θυτήριον ἀρχαίη Νύξ, etc.
Nox antiqua suo curru convolvitur Aram
Hanc circum, quae signa dedit certissima nautis,
Commiserata virum metuendos undique casus.
(Ancient Night in her triumphal chariot circumvents this Altar, so that she gave most certain signs to sailors, commiserating the fearful mischances of men from all places.)
In which verses the substance of the first four verses is expressed.

GLOSS 2. Night is called the 'nurse', or mother, 'of Death' by Hesiodus in *Theogonia*, in these verses repeating her other issue:
Nox peperit Fatumque malum, Parcamque nigrantem
Et Mortem et Somnum, diuersaque Somnia: natos
Hos peperit, nulli dea Nox coniuncta marito.
(Night gave birth to noxious Fate and the gloomy Parca, and Death, and Sleep, and the many Dreams. The goddess Night bore these children without coupling with any husband.)

---

6 *Who, breathless ... breath*] This relative clause has 'Death' (not 'Great goddess', or Night) as its antecedent.

7–8 *In whom ... forever*] The antecedent for the relative clause is 'Great goddess'.

8 *humour*] the aqueous or watery humour filling the anterior chamber of the eye (*OED*, n., 1. c). See Helkiah Crooke, *Mikrokosmographia* (London: William Jaggard, 1615): 'The watery humour is called [...] *humor tenuis* the thin humour, and by some *Aqueus*, because it is fluide like water and also transparent' (p. 565; see also p. 570). The origin of tears is in this watery substance.

11 *loose*] let loose, release (*OED*, v., 1. a). QSN's 'lose' has been emended here. This emendation supports a reading of the line in terms of the release of the poet's soul, thus in antithetical relation to the binding of the senses.

The court of Skill, compact of mystery,
Wanting but franchisement and memory³
To reach all secrets; then in blissful trance   15
Raise her (dear Night) to that perseverance,
That, in my torture, she all earth's may sing,
And force to tremble in her trumpeting
Heav'n's crystal temples;⁴ in her powers implant
Skill of my griefs, and she can nothing want.   20
    Then like fierce bolts, well rammed with heat and cold
In Jove's artillery, my words unfold,
To break the labyrinth of every ear   A3ᵛ
And make each frighted soul come forth and hear;
Let them break hearts, as well as yielding air,   25
That all men's bosoms (pierced with no affairs
But gain of riches) may be lancèd wide,
And with the threats of virtue terrified.
    Sorrow's dear sovereign, and the queen of rest,
That, when unlightsome, vast and indigest   30

GLOSS 3. Plato saith *discere* is nothing else but *reminisci*.
[*discere*: learning. *reminisci*: recalling.]
GLOSS 4. The heavenly abodes are often called celestial temples by Homer *et aliis*.
[*et aliis*: and others.]

---

13 *Skill*] On the capitalization of this word, see Commentary: 'Noctem', 13.
13 *compact*] joined in league, associate (*OED*, †adj., 2). This use is earlier than *OED*'s first instance.
14 *franchisement*] the action of setting free; freedom, release. *OED* cites Chapman's *Iliads*: 'He could scarce enjoy | The benefite of franchisement' (v. 374–75).
15–17 *then ... sing*] 'then, dear Night, inspire in my soul a heavenly rapture that will lead her to that perseverance (i.e. in pursuing learning through memory), so that, in the torture of my heavenly rapture, she will sing about all the secrets of the earth.' 'She' and 'her' refer to the soul; 'earth's' modernizes Qsɴ's 'earths', assuming its genitive relation to 'secrets' — or even to 'torture'.
18–19 *And force ... temples*] 'and force my soul to cause heaven's crystal temples to tremble with the sound of her music.' For the verb's transitive use, see *OED*, *tremble*, v., 4, whose first instance is from Edmund Spenser, *Virgils Gnat* (1591): '*Scipion* | [...] To whom the ruin'd walls of *Carthage* vow'd | Trembling their forces' (lines 613–17, in *Shorter Poems*, p. 323).
21 *bolts*] stout arrows, but also thunderbolts, like those of 'Jove's artillery' (see Commentary: 'Noctem', 21–24).
23 *labyrinth*] The osseous labyrinth is the system of canals in the temporal bone and inner ear. Compare Crooke, *Mikrokosmographia*: 'This bone is exceeding hard for the security of the Organ of Hearing, and harder indeed then any bone of the body. [It] is called *Os labyrinthi*, the bone of the Labyrinth' (p. 583).
25 *them*] 'my words' (22).
27 *lancèd wide*] pierced deeply as with a lance, causing a wide opening.
30 *unlightsome*] unilluminated, dark. *OED* lists this as the second instance, the first one dating to 1570.
30 *indigest*] undigested, confused, shapeless (*OED*, † adj. and n.). See also Introduction, pp. 2–3.

The formless matter of this world did lie,
Filled'st every place with thy divinity,
Why did thy absolute and endless sway
Licence heav'n's torch, the sceptre of the Day,
Distinguished intercession to thy throne   35
That long before, all matchless, ruled alone?
Why lett'st thou order orderless disperse
The fighting parents of this universe?
When earth, the air and sea in fire remained,
When fire, the sea and earth the air contained,   40
When air, the earth and fire the sea enclosed,
When sea, fire, air in earth were indisposed,
Nothing, as now, remained so out of kind,
All things in gross were finer than refined;
Substance was sound within and had no being,   45
Now form gives being, all our essence seeming;
Chaos had soul without a body then,
Now bodies live without the souls of men —
Lumps being digested, monsters in our pride.
    And as a wealthy fount that hills did hide,   50
Let forth by labour of industrious hands,
Pours out her treasure through the fruitful strands,
Seemly divided to a hundred streams,
Whose beauties shed such profitable beams
And make such Orphean music in their courses   55 A4ʳ
That cities follow their enchanting forces,

---

33 *sway*] A pun on two meanings: on one hand, 'the motion or rotation of a revolving body' (*OED*, n., 1); on the other, 'overpowering, or controlling influence' (*OED*, n., 5).
37 *orderless*] disorderly, understood either adjectivally (qualifying 'order') or as an adverb of manner (qualifying 'disperse').
42 *indisposed*] not arranged or disposed, out of order, disorganized.
44 *in gross*] in bulk (*OED*, gross, n., P. 1. d); thus, in a shapeless or formless mass.
47 *Chaos*] The Hesiodic deity Chaos, one of the three 'fighting parents of this universe' (see 38, and Commentary: 'Noctem', 39–49ff.). It should be differentiated from non-capitalized 'chaos' (60, 62), a state of utmost confusion and disorder.
49 *Lumps ... in our pride*] i.e. although possessing harmony or order (see *OED*, digested, adj., 1), human bodies are mere lumps; our pride in our bodies makes us monstrous.
50–62 *And as a wealthy fount ... confound the time*] See Introduction, pp. 30–32, for an account of Chapman's intricate syntactic arrangement and the meaning of this first Homeric simile in the poem.
50 *fount*] fountain. On this chielfly poetic use, see *OED*, n.¹, whose first instance is also of 1594.
55 *Orphean music*] The running streams attract human life with their sound just as Orpheus's song attracted animals. On Orpheus, 'the sweetest Muses' son' (139), see Commentary: 'Noctem', 139–58.

Who, running far, at length each pours her heart
Into the bosom of the gulfy desart,
As much confounded there and indigest
As in the chaos of the hills compressed, 60
So all things now (extract out of the prime)
Are turned to chaos, and confound the time.
   A stepdame Night of mind about us clings,
Who broods beneath her hell-obscuring wings
Worlds of confusion, where, the soul defamed, 65
The body had been better never framed.
Beneath thy soft and peaceful covert then
(Most sacred mother both of gods and men)
Treasures unknown and more unprized did dwell;
But in the blind-born shadow of this hell, 70
This horrid stepdame, Blindness of the Mind,
Nought worth the sight, no sight, but worse than blind,
A Gorgon that with brass and snaky brows
(Most harlot-like) her naked secrets shows.
For in th'expansure and distinct attire 75
Of light and darkness, of the sea and fire,
Of air and earth and all, all these create,
First set and ruled in most harmonious state,
Disjunction shows, in all things now amiss,
By that first order, what confusion is: 80

---

57 *Who*] The antecedent is 'a hundred streams' (53).
58 *gulfy*] 'deep as an abyss' (Nicoll, I, p. 713); also 'full of eddies and whirlpools' (*OED*, adj.). On these two meanings, see Introduction, pp. 31–32.
58 *desart*] Q*SN*'s 'desart' has been preserved, as it forms a rhyming pair, though imperfect, with 'heart' (in Q*SN* also visually, with 'hart'). The stress falls on the first syllable, and the second, extrametrical syllable provides the imperfect rhyme. On this and other similar instances, see Appendix.
61 *extract*] Used participially, i.e. extracted (*OED*, adj., †2). This instance is earlier than those in *OED*.
63 *stepdame*] stepmother. On the implications of this word, see Introduction, pp. 67, 71, and Commentary: 'Noctem', 63–74.
64 *hell-obscuring*] i.e. that make hell dark. On this sort of compound in *SN*, see Kelly, *Poetic Diction*, pp. 50–53.
67 *covert*] authority, jurisdiction (*OED*, n., †6); also, protection.
69 *unprized*] beyond price, inestimable. *OED*, adj., †2, only lists a later instance (1600).
75–80 *For in th'expansure ... what confusion is*] 'For in the distribution and distinctive array of light and darkness, of the sea and fire, of air and earth and all the created elements, which were originally disposed in proper harmony, disjunction shows what confusion is when the present disorder of the elements is compared with that original order.'
75 *expansure*] *OED* only gives instances by Chapman, all later than this one, and glosses the neologism as 'expansion, process of expanding'. But its meaning here is rather 'distribution'. See Introduction, p. 33.
77 *create*] as in *OED*, †adj.: 'that is or has been created'.

Religious curb, that managed men in bounds
Of public welfare, loathing private grounds,
Now cast away by self-love's paramours,
All are transformed to Calydonian boars
That kill our bleeding vines, displow our fields,   85
Rend groves in pieces, all things nature yields
Supplanting, tumbling up in hills of dearth
The fruitful disposition of the earth —
Ruin creates men, all to slaughter bent,
Like envy, fed with others' famishment.   90
    And what makes men without the parts of men
Or, in their manhoods, less than childeren,
But manless natures? All this world was named
A world of him, for whom it first was framed
(Who, like a tender chevril, shrunk with fire   95
Of base ambition and of self-desire,
His arms into his shoulders crept for fear
Bounty should use them and fierce rape forbear,
His legs into his greedy belly run,
The charge of hospitality to shun);   100
In him the world is to a lump reversed,
That shrunk from form, that was by form dispersed,
And in nought more than thankless avarice,
Not rend'ring virtue her deservèd price.

81–88 *Religious curb... disposition of the earth*] This syntactically intricate passage explains 'what confusion is' (80). Its first three lines are an absolute participle clause. Paraphrase: 'Once religious restraint, which kept men within the bounds of public welfare and made them loathe private interest, has been scorned by practitioners of self-love, these men are transformed into Calydonian boars that tread on our vines (crushing the grapes as if they bled), destroy our ploughed fields and rend groves into pieces, tearing up by the roots all things given to us by nature and turning upside down the fruitful disposition of the earth.'
87 *Supplanting*] taking up or tearing by the roots (*OED*, *supplant*, v., †6).
92 *childeren*] *OED* registers this early modern variant spelling, which Chapman uses for metrical reasons, and is thus left unmodernized.
93 *manless*] unmanly, inhuman. This sense is not in *OED*.
95 *chevril*] a small roe or deer. Chapman's neologism; see Commentary: 'Noctem', 95–100.
97 *His*] man's (not the chevril's).
95, 102 *shrunk*, 97 *crept*, 99 *run*] All these verbs are in past forms.
101–02 *In him the world... by form dispersed*] 'The world, when observed in man (that is, when man is regarded as a little world or microcosmos), is inverted, and thus deformed as a lump that shrank from its original form, or that was scattered by form.' Each occurrence of 'form' means something different: 1) the primeval disposition of man and the world as originated from Chaos, which Chapman praises; 2) the present order of civilization, which has set in disarray the virtues that made up man's first nature.

Kind Amalthea was transferred by Jove 105
Into his sparkling pavement, for her love,
Though but a goat, and giving him her milk —
Baseness is flinty, gentry soft as silk.
In heav'ns she lives, and rules, a living sign
In human bodies; yet not so divine 110
That she can work her kindness in our hearts.
    The senseless Argive ship, for her deserts,
Bearing to Colchos, and for bringing back
The hardy Argonauts secure of wrack,
The fautor and the god, of gratitude, 115
Would not from number of the stars exclude.
A thousand such examples could I cite
To damn stone-peasants, that like Typhons fight
Against their Maker, and contend to be
Of kings the abject slaves of drudgery — 120
Proud of that thraldom, love the kindest least,
And hate, not to be hated of, the best.
    If then we frame man's figure by his mind,
And that at first his fashion was assigned
Erection in such god-like excellence 125
For his soul's sake, and her intelligence,
She, so degenerate and grown depressed,
Content to share affections with a beast,

105–07 *Amalthea ... a goat*] The nurse that secretly brought up the child Zeus/Jupiter in Mount Ida when Cronus/Saturn tried to devour him. In certain sources, Amalthea is identified as the goat that suckled him. On her identity, her stellification, and the moral meanings of the myth in Chapman's source, Conti's *Mythologiae*, see Commentary: 'Noctem', 105–11.
108 *flinty*] hard, impenetrable, like flint.
108 *gentry*] courtesy, honourableness (*OED*, n., †2).
109 *sign*] constellation.
112–16 *The senseless Argive ship ... the stars exclude*] The ship Argo bore Jason and the Argonauts from their native Iolcus, in Thessaly, to Colchis, on the east coast of the Black Sea in search of the Golden Fleece. On the ship's stellification and its moral meanings in Chapman's source, Conti's *Mythologiae*, see Commentary: 'Noctem', 112–16.
115 *fautor*] protector (*OED*, n., †2), here Zeus.
118 *stone-peasants*] base, ignorant people whose nature is rugged and hard like stone, or 'flinty' (see 108).
118 *Typhons*] rebellious giants. The many-headed giant Typhon, or Typhoeus, rebelled against Zeus and manged to take him prisoner. On Chapman's sources and moral meanings, see Commentary: 'Noctem', 118–20.
120 *Of kings ... drudgery*] the servile slaves of kings (i.e. humiliating themselves for self-interest).
125 *Erection*] advancement in dignity (*OED*, n., †2).
127 *depressed*] lowered, sunken (*OED*, adj., 2), as opposed to 'erection' (125).
128 *affections*] dispositions, properties, qualities (see *OED*, n., 12 and 13).

> The shape wherewith he should be now indued,
> Must bear no sign of man's similitude. 130
> Therefore Promethean poets,⁴ᵃ with the coals
> Of their most genial, more-than-human souls,
> In living verse created men like these,
> With shapes of Centaurs, Harpies, Lapithes,
> That they, in prime of erudition, 135
> When almost savage vulgar men were grown,
> Seeing themselves in those Pierian founts,
> Might mend their minds, ashamed of such accounts.
> So, when ye hear the sweetest Muse's son,⁴ᵇ
> With heav'nly rapture of his music, won 140
> Rocks, forests, floods and winds to leave their course
> In his attendance, it bewrays the force
> His wisdom had, to draw men grown so rude
> To civil love of art and fortitude,
> And not for teaching others insolence,⁵ 145
> Had he his date-exceeding excellence
> With sovereign poets but for use applied,
> And in his proper acts exemplified;
> And that, in calming the infernal kind,
> To wit, the perturbations of his mind, 150
> And bringing his Eurydice from hell
> (Which justice signifies), is provèd well.
> But if in right's observance any man
> Look back, with boldness less than Orphean,
> Soon falls he to the hell from whence he rose: 155
> The fiction then would temperature dispose

B1ᵛ

GLOSS 4a (marginal). He calls them 'Promethean poets' in this high conceit by a figurative comparison betwixt them that, as Prometheus with fire fetched from heaven made men, so poets with the fire of their souls are said to create those Harpies and Centaurs, and thereof he calls their souls 'genial'.

GLOSS 4b (marginal). Calliope is called 'the sweetest Muse', her name being, by signification, *Cantus suavitas, vel modulatio*.

[Calliope: in Greek, Καλλιόπη means 'sweet-voiced'. *Cantus suavitas, vel modulatio*: sweetness, or cadence, of song.]

GLOSS 5. 'Insolence' is here taken for rareness or unwontedness.

---

129 *indued*] invested, endowed (*OED*, endue/indue, v., †8).
132 *genial*] possessing the natural aptitudes of creativity (*OED*, adj.¹, 3); possessing the intellectual power of a genius (adj.¹, 6). Of this latter sense, *OED*'s earliest example is of 1825. Also, as Bartlett notes, in the original sense of Latin *genialis*, 'pertaining to generation, generative' (p. 424, n. 132), and thus life-giving, which reinforces the 'Promethean' nature of poets; see *OED*, adj.¹, 1. For this latter meaning, see 'Cynthiam', 21.
146 *date-exceeding*] ageless, eternal.
156 *temperature*] temperance, moderation (*OED*, n., †3).
156 *dispose*] dispense, supply (*OED*, v., †4).

In all the tender motives of the mind,
To make man worthy his hell-daunting kind.
The golden chain of Homer's high device
Ambition is, or cursèd avarice, 160
Which, all gods haling, being tied to Jove,
Him from his settled height could never move,
Intending this: that though that powerful chain,
Of most Herculean vigour to constrain
Men from true virtue or their pristine states, 165
Attempt a man that manless changes hates
And is ennobled with a deathless love
Of things eternal, dignified above,
Nothing shall stir him from adorning still
This shape with virtue and his power with will. 170
    But as rude painters that contend to show
Beasts, fowls, or fish, all artless to bestow
On every side his native counterfeit,
Above his head his name had need to set,
So men that will be men in more than face 175
(As in their foreheads) should in actions place
More perfect characters, to prove they be
No mockers of their first nobility,
Else may they eas'ly pass for beasts or fowls:
Souls praise our shapes, and not our shapes our souls. 180
    And as when Chloris paints th'enamelled meads,
A flock of shepherds to the bagpipe treads
Rude rural dances with their country loves,   *B2ʳ*
Some afar off, observing their removes,
Turns and returns, quick footing, sudden stands, 185
Reelings aside, odd actions with their hands,
Now back, now forwards, now locked arm in arm,
Not hearing music, think it is a charm

---

157 *tender motives of the mind*] those destabilizing impulses and passions that make the mind weak.
158 *To make ... hell-daunting kind*] to make man worthy of Orpheus, who challenged hell. *OED* glosses *daunt* as 'subdue', 'vanquish', which is not entirely coincident with Chapman's use here, as Orpheus was not victorious in 'bringing his Eurydice from hell' (151).
161 *haling*] hauling, dragging.
163 *Intending this*] with the following meaning.
172 *Beasts*] terrestrial animals (*OED*, 3. a).
180 *praise*] to cause someone or something to be praised; to reflect praise or honour on (*OED*, v.¹, †d).
181 *Chloris*] goddess of spring, gardens and flowers (Roman Flora). On the long simile that has Chloris as protagonist, see Commentary: 'Noctem', 181–200.

That, like loose frows at Bacchanalian feasts,
Makes them seem frantic in their barren jests, 190
And being clustered in a shapeless crowd
With much less admiration are allowed,
So our first excellence, so much abused,
And we (without the harmony was used
When Saturn's golden sceptre stroke the strings 195
Of civil government) make all our doings
Savour of rudeness and obscurity,
And in our forms show more deformity
Than if we still were wrapped and smotherèd
In that confusion, out of which we fled. 200
 And as when hosts of stars attend thy flight
(Day of deep students, most contentful Night),
The Morning (mounted on the Muses' stead)⁶
Ushers the sun from Vulcan's golden bed,⁷
And then, from forth their sundry roofs of rest, 205
All sorts of men, to sorted tasks addressed,
Spread this inferior element, and yield
Labour his due (the soldier to the field,
Statesmen to counsel, judges to their pleas,
Merchants to commerce, mariners to seas), 210
All beasts and birds the groves and forests range
To fill all corners of this round Exchange,

GLOSS 6. Lycophron, in *Alexandra*, affirms the Morning useth to ride upon Pegasus *in his versibus*:
 Aurora montem Phagium advolaverat
 Velocis altum nuper alis Pegasi.
 (Dawn had been newly soaring over the steep mount Phegion on the swift wings of Pegasus.)
 [*in his versibus*: in these lines.]
GLOSS 7. Vulcan is said, by Natalis Comes in his *Mythologiae*, to have made a 'golden bed' for the Sun, wherein he swum sleeping till the morning.

---

189 *frows*] frenzied women, Bacchantes. *OED*, *frow*, n., †3, cites an instance by Chapman of 1606: 'The Ladies of this land would teare him peece-meal | (As did the drunken Froes, the *Thratian Harper*)' (*Monsieur D'Olive*, II. 1. 180–81, in *Comedies*, p. 420).
194 *without the harmony was used*] without the harmony that was used. See Commentary: 'Noctem', 181–200.
195 *Saturn's golden sceptre*] On this icon as symbol of justice and good government, see Commentary: 'Noctem', 181–200.
202 *contentful*] causing content or satisfaction (*OED*, adj., †b).
203 *stead*] steed, horse; the original spelling has been kept for the sake of rhyme. On Pegasus as 'the Muses' stead', see Commentary: 'Noctem', 203 and Gloss 6.
206 *sorted*] assigned, ordained (*OED*, *sort*, v.¹, †1).
212 *this round Exchange*] the world conceived of as a place of worldly business and economic transactions, as an effect of diurnal activity and in contrast with nocturnal retirement and study.

Till thou (dear Night, O goddess of most worth)
Lett'st thy sweet seas of golden humour forth,
And, eagle-like, dost with thy starry wings 215
Beat in the fowls and beasts to Somnus' lodgings,
And haughty Day to the infernal deep,⁸
Proclaiming silence, study, ease, and sleep
(All things before thy forces put in rout,
Retiring where the morning fired them out), 220
So to the chaos of our first descent
(All days of honour and of virtue spent)
We basely make retreat, and are no less
Than huge, impolished heaps of filthiness.
Men's faces glitter, and their hearts are black, 225
But thou (great mistress of heav'n's gloomy rack)
Art black in face, and glitter'st in thy heart:
There is thy glory, riches, force, and art.
Opposèd Earth beats black and blue thy face,
And often doth thy heart itself deface, 230
For spite that to thy virtue-famèd train
All the choice worthies that did ever reign
In eldest age were still preferred by Jove,

GLOSS 8. *Quae lucem pellis sub terras*: Orpheus.
([Thou, Night,] who banishest light beneath the earth.)

---

214 *sweet seas of golden humour*] the constellations, metaphorically imagined as seas of golden tears (the stars); by metonymy, 'humour' means 'tears' (see note to line 8).
216 *Beat in*] force in by beating (*OED, beat*, phrasal verbs, 1).
216 *Somnus*] The god Sleep, one of the sons of Night. On his genealogy, dwelling and moral meanings, see Commentary: 'Noctem', 10–11, 201–40, 266–67.
221 *the chaos of our first descent*] moral disorder (chaos) after our fall (from original Chaos).
223 *make retreat*] The original spelling 'retrait', common for 'retreat' in the sixteenth century, has a separate entry in *OED*, now obsolete, meaning 'portrait'. Here it has been regularized to 'retreat' in consonance with a similar use in 'Banquet', 100. 3: 'The selfsame way she came doth make retreat' (original spelling: 'retreate').
224 *impolished*] unpolished, rude. See *OED*, †adj., whose earliest instance is dated to 1583.
226 *rack*] a mass of cloud or mist (*OED*, n.², 3).
225–28 *Men's faces ... force, and art*] i.e. Night's glory, riches, force and art reside in her heart, shining from inside through the brightness of the stars. This is the reason why, in opposition to men's false 'glitter', Night is black only 'in face'.
229–34 *Opposèd Earth ... to his love*] 'Unfriendly Earth beats your face black and blue and often disfigures your own heart, mistrustful that Jove could still promote those constellations that reigned in heaven in past ages to membership of your famous train of virtuous attendants, esteeming that that deserved honour is just the result of Jove's whimsical love to them.'
229 *Opposèd*] opposite, facing (*OED*, adj., 3. a); also hostile, unfriendly (2. a).
232–33 *choice worthies ... eldest age*] Hudston (p. 396, nn. 232–34) rightly observes that these worthies are the abovementioned 'kind Amalthea' (105) and 'the senseless Argive ship' (112), stellified by Jove in reward for their service to him (see Commentary: 'Noctem', 105–20).
233 *preferred*] promoted; by hyperbaton, the prepositional phrase ruled by this verb occurs two lines earlier, i.e. 'to thy virtue-faméd train' (231).

Esteeming that due honour to his love.
There shine they, not to seamen guides alone, 235
But sacred presidents to everyone,
There fixed for ever, where the Day is driven
Almost four hundred times a year from heaven.
In hell then let her sit, and never rise
Till Morn's leave, blushing at her cruelties. 240
    Meanwhile, accept, as followers of thy train
(Our better parts aspiring to thy reign)
Virtues obscured, and banishèd the Day
With all the glories of this spongy sway
Prisoned in flesh, and that poor flesh in bands 245
Of stone and steel, chief flowers of virtues' garlands.
    O then, most tender fortress of our woes, B3ʳ
That bleeding lie in virtues' overthrows,
Hating the whoredom of this painted light,
Raise thy chaste daughters, ministers of right, 250
The dreadful and the just Eumenides,
And let them wreak the wrongs of our disease,
Drowning the world in blood, and stain the skies
With their spilt souls, made drunk with tyrannies.
    Fall, Hercules, from heav'n in tempests hurled, 255
And cleanse this beastly stable of the world;
Or bend thy brazen bow against the Sun,

---

234 *due*] deserved, merited.
236 *presidents*] Two meanings seem to coexist here: 1) presiding guardians or patrons (*OED*, president, n., 1. b); and 2) models, exemplars to be followed (*OED*, precedent, n., †4. a, for which 'president' is a variant spelling). Although the second sense would counsel modernization to 'precedent', the original spelling 'presidents' favours polysemy.
237 *where*] i.e. whereas, used adverbially here, in adversative sense (*OED*, adv., 12. b).
241–46 *Meanwhile ... virtues' garlands*] 'In the meantime, accept as members of your retinue our obscured virtues (obscured because they belong to Night), while Day is banished with all the splendours of its weak dominion, imprisoned in flesh, and that flesh in chains of stone and steel, which are the chief adornments of the victorious garlands of our virtues.' On the obscurity of this passage and its interpretation, see Commentary: 'Noctem', 241–46.
247 *most tender fortress of our woes*] kindest fortress where our sorrows take shelter; this is an epithet for the goddess Night.
248 *That*] The relative pronoun's antecedent is 'woes', not 'fortress', as the plural form of the verb 'lie' makes clear.
248 *virtues' overthrows*] The genitive is used here objectively (i.e. the defeat of the virtues).
251 *Eumenides*] The three Eumenides, Furies (see 272) or Erinyes — Tisiphone, Alecto and Megaera — are underworld deities of revenge. See Commentary: 'Noctem', 247–54, 268–79.
254 *their spilt souls, made drunk with tyrannies*] i.e. the Eumenides' souls, stained with blood, and satiated in their thirst for avenging men's cruelties. See Commentary: 'Noctem', 247–54.

As in Tartessus, when thou hadst begun
Thy task of oxen; heat in more extremes
Than thou wouldst suffer with his envious beams;⁹ 260
Now make him leave the world to Night and dreams.
Never were virtue's labours so envied
As in this light: shoot, shoot, and stoop his pride.
Suffer no more his lustful rays to get
The Earth with issue; let him still be set 265
In Somnus' thickets, bound about the brows
With pitchy vapours and with ebon boughs.
   Rich-tapered sanctuary of the blest,¹⁰
Palace of ruth, made all of tears and rest,
To thy black shades and desolation 270
I consecrate my life and living moan,
Where Furies shall for ever fighting be,
And adders hiss the world for hating me,
Foxes shall bark, and night-ravens belch in groans,
And owls shall hollow my confusions; 275
There will I furnish up my funeral bed,
Strewed with the bones and relics of the dead;
Atlas shall let th'Olympic burthen fall
To cover my untombèd face withal. B3ᵛ
And when as well the matter of our kind 280
As the material substance of the mind

GLOSS 9. Here he alludes to the fiction of Hercules, that, in his labour at Tartessus fetching away the oxen, being (more than he liked) heat with the beams of the Sun, he bent his bow against him, etc. *Ut ait Pherecides in tertio libro Historiarum.*

[heat: heated. *Ut ait ... Historiarum*: As Pherecides says in his third book of the *Histories*.]
GLOSS 10. This *periphrasis* of the Night he useth, because in her 'the blest' (by whom he intends the virtuous), living obscurely, are relieved and quieted, according to those verses before of Aratus: *Commiserata virum metuendos undique casus.*

[before of Aratus: i.e. in Gloss 1.]

258 *Tartessus*] Ancient civilization in the south-west of the Iberian Peninsula (present-day Huelva, Cádiz and Seville) that flourished between the twelfth and fifth centuries BC. Tartessus is the land from which Hercules retrieved Geryon's cattle.
260, 261, 264, 265 *him, his*] the Sun, the Sun's.
262–63 *Never were ... in this light*] 'Virtue's Herculean tasks were never so much envied as they are when observed in daylight.'
268 *Rich-tapered*] richly lighted with tapers, or devotional candles, here the stars. The religious sense matches 'sanctuary' (268).
270, 275 *desolation, confusions*] The first is pentasyllabic, the second tetrasyllabic; in both cases, a stress on the last syllable enables the rhyme.
280–87 *And when ... my miseries*] On the interpretation of this passage, see Commentary: 'Noctem', 280–87.
281 *substance*] foundation, something that provides support (see *OED*, n., †3).

    Shall cease their revolutions, in abode
Of such impure and ugly period
As the old essence and insensive prime,
Then shall the ruins of the fourfold time,   285
Turned to that lump (as rapting torrents rise),
For ever murmur forth my miseries.
    Ye living spirits then, if any live,
Whom like extremes do like affections give,
Shun, shun this cruel light, and end your thrall   290
In these soft shades of sable funeral,
From whence with ghosts, whom vengeance holds from rest,
Dog-fiends and monsters, haunting the distressed,
As men whose parents tyranny hath slain,
Whose sisters rape and bondage do sustain.   295
But you that ne'er had birth, nor ever proved
How dear a blessing 'tis to be belov'd,
Whose friends' idolatrous desire of gold
To scorn and ruin have your freedom sold,
Whose virtues feel all this and show your eyes   300
Men made of Tartar and of villainies

---

282 *revolutions*] days, in cyclical repetition (as in *OED*, n., 4. †c); but the theological sense in *OED*, n., 6, could be also possible, even if the examples adduced are a century older than this: i.e. the complete series of lives or reincarnations of a human soul.
282 *abode*] announcement, prophecy (*OED*, †n.²). *OED*'s first instance is from 1598, and the second is from Chapman's *Iliads* (1611): 'the best of gods | High-thundering Juno's husband | stirres my spirit with true abodes' (XIII. 144-46).
283 *period*] an end, a point of completion of a length or course of time (*OED*, n., 11. b).
284 *insensive*] Not in *OED*. No opposite meaning to *OED*'s 'sensive' seems relevant. Hudston (p. 396, nn. 280-87) believes that Chapman's neologism matches *OED*'s 'insensible' (adj., 1. a), i.e. 'non-material'. *OED* has *incensive* (inflamed), for which 'insensive' would be a sixteenth-century spelling. Another meaning of *insensible* (adj., †2), i.e. unintelligible or incomprehensible, also suggests itself. The poem's description of Chaos as having 'soul without a body' (47) recommends Hudston's belief, even if the idea of the inflaming, creative powers of Chaos would also admit 'incensive' as a plausible reading.
286 *rapting*] sweeping, ravishing; *OED*, †adj., lists this as its first example.
287 *murmur forth*] scatter forth a complaint. The suggestion of muttered, inarticulate speech is in accordance with the idea of the unintelligibility of Chaos conveyed in this passage.
288-323 *Ye living ... he puts on*] For the interpretation see Commentary: 'Noctem', 288-323.
291 *sable*] mourning-black.
293 *Dog-fiends*] This compound is obscure. It may refer to familiar spirits, usually a witch's companions taking the form of animals.
296 *that ne'er had birth*] the unborn; or, those that were not born of noble descent (see *OED*, *birth*, n., 2. a).
301 *Tartar*] the classical Tartarus, or infernal regions.

Aspire th'extraction and the quintessence
Of all the joys in earth's circumference:
With ghosts, fiends, monsters, as men robbed and racked,
Murthered in life, from shades with shadows blacked, 305
Thunder your wrongs, your miseries and hells,
And with the dismal accents of your knells
Revive the dead, and make the living die
In ruth and terror of your tortury;
Still all the power of art into your groans, 310
Scorning your trivial and remissive moans,
Compact of fiction and hyperboles
(Like wanton mourners, cloyed with too much ease),
Should leave the glasses of the hearers' eyes
Unbroken, counting all but vanities; 315
But paint, or else create in serious truth
A body figured to your virtues' ruth,
That to the sense may show what damnèd sin
For your extremes this Chaos tumbles in.
But woe is wretched me, without a name: 320
Virtue feeds scorn, and noblest honour, shame;
Pride bathes in tears of poor submission,
And makes his soul the purple he puts on.
    Kneel then with me, fall worm-like on the ground,
And from th'infectious dunghill of this round, 325
From men's brass wits and golden foolery,
Weep, weep your souls into felicity;

B4ʳ

---

302 *Aspire*] inhale, breathe or suck in (*OED*, v., †1, transitive). This and other transitive uses are common in Chapman: see, for instance, 'Banquet', 33. 3, 62. 2.
302 *th'extraction and the quintessence*] the distillation of the fifth essence, i.e. the substance beyond the natural four elements of which heavenly bodies are made (*OED*, *quintessence*, n.). Here the alchemical metaphor refers to the enjoyment of sensual pleasures.
305 *from shades with shadows blacked*] blackened with Night's potent shadows and distanced from the 'shades' that have kept them in thraldom until this point (in view of the 'soft shades of sable funeral' in the previous lines).
309 *tortury*] torture, torment. The neologism seems motivated by rhyme.
314 *Should*] i.e. which should. The omitted relative pronoun has 'moans', and its apposed 'Compact of fiction and hyperboles' (311–12), as antecedents.
314 *glasses of the hearers' eyes*] the eyes as mirrors of the soul. For literary analogues, see Commentary: 'Noctem', 314.
318 *sense*] the ratiocinative capacity, the understanding (*OED*, n., 11).
318–19 *what damnèd sin ... this Chaos tumbles in*] i.e. what damned sin is destroyed by this Chaos. See *OED*, *tumble*, v., 4. c, meaning 'throw down and destroy', 'reduce to ruins'.
326 *men's brass wits and golden foolery*] i.e. men's poor or valueless intelligence and immense foolishness, or foolishness caused by the love of gold. These expressions intensify the poem's disparagement of Day's servants.

Come to this house of mourning, serve the Night,
To whom pale Day (with whoredom soakèd quite)
Is but a drudge, selling her beauty's use   330
To rapes, adult'ries, and to all abuse.
Her labours feast imperial Night with sports,
Where Loves are Christmased with all pleasures' sorts,
And whom her fugitive and far-shot rays
Disjoin, and drive into ten thousand ways;   335
Night's glorious mantle wraps in safe abodes,
And frees their necks from servile labours' loads;
Her trusty shadows succour men dismayed
Whom Day's deceitful malice hath betrayed;
From the silk vapours of her ivory port   340
Sweet Protean dreams she sends of every sort:
Some taking forms of princes, to persuade
Of men deject we are their equals made;   B4ᵛ
Some clad in habit of deceasèd friends,
For whom we mourned and now have wished amends;   345
And some (dear favour) lady-like attired,
With pride of Beauty's full meridian fired,
Who pity our contempts, revive our hearts —
For wisest ladies love the inward parts.
    If these be dreams, e'en so are all things else   350
That walk this round by heav'nly sentinels;
But from Night's port of horn she greets our eyes
With graver dreams inspired with prophecies,
Which oft presage to us succeeding chances,
We proving that, awake, they show in trances.   355

---

328 *house of mourning*] Night's abode, which has been called above a 'sanctuary' (268) and a 'palace' (269) accommodating the speaker's 'funeral bed'.
330 *drudge*] slave, here with sexual implications.
330 *her beauty's use*] the putting of her (i.e. Day's) beauty at the service of sexual pleasure. Compare 'thy love's use' (*Shakespeare's Sonnets*, 20. 14, p. 151).
333 *Loves*] Cupids, in plural (see Commentary: 'Noctem', 324–39).
333 *Christmased*] filled with Christmas-like mood, celebrated in Christmas-like fashion. *OED*, *Christmas*, v., †1, provides this only instance.
347 *Beauty's full meridian*] *OED* records this example of *meridian* (n., 4. b) as the originator of a figurative sense derived from the term's astronomical meaning. Just as the meridian passes through the celestial pole, and is crossed by the sun at noon at its zenith, so the 'full meridian' refers to Beauty's splendour and highest perfection. See a similar use in 'Banquet', when Corinna, by rising her arm, 'stretcheth a meridian from her blood' (69. 6). As the phrase refers to the idea of beauty rather than to its bodily realization, the original capitalization has been retained, although not Q*sn*'s 'Meridian'.
354 *succeeding chances*] future events.
355 *We proving that, awake, they show in trances*] i.e. when we are awake, we realize that prophetic dreams open the door to ('show in') moments of rapture and ecstasy.

If these seem likewise vain, or nothing are
Vain things, or nothing come to virtue's share —
For nothing more than dreams with us she finds.
Then, since all pleasures vanish like the winds,
And that most serious actions, not respecting   360
The second light, are worth but the neglecting;
Since day, or light, in any quality,
For earthly uses do but serve the eye,
And since the eye's most quick and dangerous use
Inflames the heart, and learns the soul abuse;   365
Since mournings are preferred to banquetings,
And they reach heav'n, bred under sorrow's wings;
Since Night brings terror to our frailties still,
And shameless Day doth marble us in ill —
All you possessed with indepressèd spirits,   370
Indued with nimble and aspiring wits,
Come consecrate with me to sacred Night
Your whole endeavours, and detest the light.
Sweet Peace's richest crown is made of stars,
Most certain guides of honoured marinars;   375   C1ʳ
No pen can anything eternal write
That is not steeped in humour of the Night.
 Hence, beasts and birds, to caves and bushes then,
And welcome Night, ye noblest heirs of men;
Hence, Phoebus, to thy glassy strumpet's bed,   380

---

360 *respecting*] as regards, with respect to (here in prepositional use).
361 *The second light*] i.e. Night.
364 *the eye's most quick and dangerous use*] the use of sight for sensual pleasure is called keen, or penetrating (*OED, quick*, adj.¹, 24) and, for that reason, injurious (*OED, dangerous*, adj., †5).
365 *learns*] teaches (*OED*, v., 4. c).
366 *mournings*] ceremonial manifestations of sorrow (*OED*, n.¹, 5. b). This use admits the plural form.
368 *Night brings terror to our frailties*] Night punishes our weaknesses or sins by bringing terrifying dreams or visions. Thomas Nashe's pamphlet *The Terrors of the Night*, also published in 1594, may have been inspired by this and other lines in 'Noctem' for its satire.
369 *marble*] harden, or turn to marble. *OED*, v., 1, gives this as its first instance. This sense seems to accord with the Medusa conceit in the prefatory letter — i.e. Day's 'ills' thus being the effects of 'benumbing ignorance', in opposition to Night's beneficial effects upon scholarly minds.
370 *indepressèd*] undepressed, not dejected (tetrasyllabic).
371 *Indued*] endowed (see 'Noctem', 129).
380 *glassy*] glass-like, vitreous. Although a quality of Oceanus, on whose surface the Sun's bed sails, it is applied here to the bed's owner, the 'strumpet' Aurora. See Introduction, pp. 67–69, and Commentary: 'Noctem', 378–83 and Gloss 11.

And never more let Themis' daughters[11] spread
Thy golden harness on thy rosy horse,
But in close thickets run thy oblique course.
   See, now ascends the glorious bride of brides,
Nuptials and triumphs glitt'ring by her sides;   385
Juno and Hymen do her train adorn,
Ten thousand torches round about them borne;
Dumb Silence, mounted on the Cyprian star,
With becks rebukes the winds before his car
Where she advanced; beats down with cloudy mace   390
The feeble light to black Saturnius' palace.
Behind her, with a brace of silver hinds,[12]
In ivory chariot, swifter than the winds,
Is great Hyperion's hornèd daughter[13] drawn
Enchantress-like, decked in disparent lawn,   395
Circled with charms and incantations

GLOSS 11. Themis' daughters are the three Hours, viz., Dice, Irene, and Eunomia, begotten by Jupiter. They are said to make ready the horse and chariot of the Sun every morning, *ut* Orpheus:
> Et Iovis et Themidis Horae de semine natae,
> [*Eunomia, atque Dice, atque Irene dives*]
> (Hours, born from the seed of Jove and Themis, [wealthy Eunomia (Good Governance), and Dice (Justice), and Irene (Peace)].)

[*ut* Orpheus: as Orpheus writes.]

GLOSS 12. Cynthia, or the Moon, is said to be drawn by two white hinds, *ut ait* Callimachus:
> Aurea nam domitrix Tityi sunt arma Diana
> Cuncta tibi, et zona, et iuga quae cervicibus aurea
> Cervarum imponis currum cum ducis ad aureum.
> (Diana, vanquisher of Tityus, all thy weapons are golden, and thy belt, and thou layest golden yokes on the necks of thy deer when thou ridest on thy golden car.)

[*ut ait* Callimachus: as Callimachus says.]

GLOSS 13. Hesiodus, in *Theogonia*, calls her the daughter of Hyperion and Theia, *in his versibus*:
> Thia parit Solem magnum, Lunamque nitentem,
> Auroram quae fert lucem mortalibus almam,
> Coelicolisque Deis cunctis; Hyperionis almi
> Semine concepit namque illos Thia decora.
> (Theia gave birth to the great Sun, and to the shining Moon, and to Dawn, who brings nourishing light to the mortals and to all the heaven-dwelling gods; for indeed fair Theia conceived them with Hyperion's fertile seed.)

So is she said to wear party-coloured garments; the rest intimates her magic authority.

[*in his versibus*: in these lines. party-coloured garments: multicoloured clothes, or, as in line 396, 'disparent'.]

---

389 *becks*] gestures, nods (*OED*, n.²).
391 *palace*] The stress falls on the first syllable, making a visual, imperfect rhyme with 'mace'.
394 *Hyperion's hornèd daughter*] The shape of the lunar crescent is represented as a pair of bull's horns. On Cynthia, or the Moon, as daughter of the Titan Hyperion, see Commentary: 'Noctem', 392–97, and Glosses 12 and 13.

That ride huge spirits and outrageous passions:
Music and mood she loves, but love she hates
(As curious ladies do their public cates).
This train, with meteors, comets, lightenings,   400
The dreadful presence of our Empress sings,
Which grant for ever (O eternal Night)
Till virtue flourish in the light of light.

Explicit Hymnus.

For the rest of his own invention, figures, and similes, touching their aptness and novelty, he hath not laboured to justify them, because he hopes they will be proud enough to justify themselves, and prove sufficiently authentical to such as understand them. For the rest, God help them, I cannot (do as others) make Day seem a lighter woman than she is, by painting her.

---

395 *disparent*] diverse, of various appearance. In Gloss 13, Chapman explains 'disparent lawn' as 'party-coloured garments'. This word is Chapman's neologism. See 'Banquet', ll. 5; and *Hero and Leander* (1598): 'A rich disparent Pentackle she weares, | Drawne full of circles and strange characters' (III. 123-24, in Bartlett, p. 137).
397 *ride*] drive off, dissuade.
398 *mood*] mind, courage (*OED*, n.¹, †1 and †2).
398 *love*] sensual love, as Cynthia is chaste.
399 *As curious ladies do their public cates*] As fastidious ladies do when they refuse to taste delicacies in public.
403 *the light of light*] the supreme light or truth, the unknowable divinity (see Introduction, pp. 92-93, and Commentary: 'Noctem', 384-91).
Explicit Hymnus] here the hymn ends.

HYMNUS IN CYNTHIAM

$C2^v$

Nature's bright eyesight,[1] and the Night's fair soul,[2]
That with thy triple forehead dost control
Earth, seas and hell,[3] and art in dignity
The greatest, and swift'st planet in the sky;
Peaceful and warlike, and the power of fate,[4]   5

GLOSS 1. He gives her that periphrasis, *viz.*, 'Nature's bright eyesight', because that, by her store of humours, issue is given to all birth; and thereof is she called Lucina, and Ilithyia, *quia praeest parturientibus cum invocaretur*, and gives them help, which Orpheus in a hymn of her praise expresseth, and calls her besides Prothyraea, *ut sequitur*:
    Κλῦθί μοι, ὦ πολύσεμνε θεά, etc.
    Audi me veneranda Dea, cui nomina multa,
    Praegnantium adiutrix, parientium dulce levamen,
    Sola puellarum servatrix, solaque prudens:
    Auxilium velox teneris Prothyraea puellis.
    (Hear me, reverend goddess, who hast many names: aid to pregnant women, sweet solace of those giving birth, sole attendant of young women, and only prudent one. Prothyraea, swift helper of tender girls.)
And a little after, he shows her plainly to be Diana, Ilithyia and Prothyraea in these verses:
    Solam animi requiem te clamant parturientes.
    Sola potes diros partus placare dolores.
    Diana, Ilithyia gravis, simul et Prothyraea.
    (Birthgiving women invoke thee alone for peace of mind. Only thou canst alleviate the dire labours of childbirth. [Thou art] Diana, grave Ilythyia, and also Prothyraea.)
[*quia praeest... invocaretur*: because she presides over women in labour, as I mentioned. *ut sequitur*: as follows.]

GLOSS 2. He calls her the soul of the Night, since she is the purest part of her, according to common conceit.

GLOSS 3. Orpheus, in these verses in *Argonauticis*, saith she is three-headed, as she is Hecate, Luna and Diana, *ut sequitur*:
    Cumque illis Hecate properans horrenda cucurrit,
    Cui trinum caput est, genuit quam Tartarus olim.
    (And hastening, horrid Hecate ran with them. She has a triple head, the woman whom Tartarus fathered long ago.)
The rest above will not be denied.
    [*ut sequitur*: as follows.]

GLOSS 4. That she is called 'the power of fate', read Hesiodus in *Theogonia*, when he gives her more than this commendation, in these verses:
    Iupiter ingentes illi largitur honores,
    Muneraque imperium terraeque marisque profundi:
    Cunctorumque simul, quae coelum amplectitur altum,
    Admittitque preces facilis Dea, prompta, benigna:
    Divitias praebet, quid ei concessa potestas,
    Imperat haec cunctis, qui sunt e semine nati:
    Et terrae et Coeli, cunctorum fata gubernat.
    (Jove granted her splendid honours, and the gift of commanding the earth and the depths of the sea, and also of everything which the high heavens encompass. And

In perfect circle of whose sacred state
The circles of our hopes are compassèd —
All wisdom, beauty, majesty and dread
Wrought in the speaking portrait of thy face —
Great Cynthia, rise out of thy Latmian palace,[5]   10
Wash thy bright body in th'Atlantic streams,[6]
Put on those robes that are most rich in beams,
And in thy all-ill-purging purity
(As if the shady Cytheron did fry
In sightful fury of a solemn fire)[7]   15
Ascend thy chariot, and make Earth admire
Thy old swift changes, made a young fixed prime;

the ready goddess easily accepts our prayers, prompt and benevolent. She provides riches, for that power is granted to her. She rules above all those that were born of seed; and she governs the fates of all, both in earth and heaven).

GLOSS 5. In Latmos she is supposed to sleep with Endymion, *ut Catullus*:
Ut Triviam furtim sub Latmia saxa relegans,
Dulcis amor gyro devocet aerio.
(How sweet love diverts Trivia from her ethereal circuit, banishing her furtively to the rocks of Latmus.)
[*ut Catullus*: as Catullus writes]

GLOSS 6. Homer, with a marvellous poetical sweetness, saith she washes her before she apparels herself in the Atlantic sea. And then shows her apparel, as in these verses: *In Oceano lavari*.
Rursus Atlanteis, in lymphis membra lavata,
Vestibus induta et nitidis, Dea Luna micantes,
Curru iunxit equos celeres, quibus ardua colla.
(Again, having washed her body in the Atlantic waters and dressed in her shining clothes, the divine Moon yoked the strong necks of her swift, gleaming horses to her chariot.)
[*In Oceano lavari*: To be washed in the Ocean.]

GLOSS 7. Cytheron, as Menander saith, was a most fair boy, and beloved of Tysiphone, who, since she could not obtain his love, she tears from her head a serpent, and threw it at him, which, stinging him to death, the Gods in pity turned him to a hill of that name, first called Asterius, full of woods, wherein all poets have affirmed wild beasts live, and use it often to express their haunts, or store of woods; whereupon he invokes Cynthia to rise in such brightness, as if it were all on fire.

6–7 *In perfect circle ... compassèd*] i.e. towards whose completion as a full moon all our hopes are directed.
6 *state*] *OED*, n., 3. b: 'a phase of the moon, *spec.* † that when the whole disc appears illuminated (full moon)'.
7 *compassèd*] completed in the form of a circle, as with a compass (see *OED*, v.¹, 6, 11). See also line 446. On the compass as a symbol of perfection, see 'Banquet', 54. 4, Commentary: 'Banquet', 54, and Introduction, p. 109.
15 *sightful*] sightly, pleasant to the eye (*OED*, †adj., 3). See Commentary: 'Cynthiam', 13–17.
17 *old swift changes ... young fixed prime*] the four phases of the moon, whose changes have been repeated since the beginning of time, are now fixed into a shining full moon; *OED* defines *prime*, n., †5, as a 'young crescent moon'. This is exactly the phase of the moon that the hymn invokes, as the convex shape of the crescent moon resembles the shape of the 'adamantine Harpey' with which Saturn castrated Uranus.

O let thy beauty scorch the wings of Time,
That, fluttering, he may fall before thine eyes
And beat himself to death before he rise.   20
And, as Heav'n's genial parts[8] were cut away
By Saturn's hands with adamantine Harpey,[9]
Only to show that, since it was composed
Of universal matter, it enclosed
No power to procreate another heaven,   25
So, since that adamantine power is given   C3ʳ
To thy chaste hands to cut off all desire
Of fleshly sports, and quench to Cupid's fire,
Let it approve no change shall take thee hence,
Nor thy throne bear another inference;   30
For if the envious forehead of the Earth
Lour on thy age and claim thee as her birth,
Tapers, nor torches, nor the forests burning,
Soul-winging music, nor tear-stilling mourning
(Used of old Romans and rude Macedons   35
In thy most sad and black discessions),
We know can nothing further thy recall
When Night's dark robes (whose objects blind us all)

GLOSS 8. This is expounded as followeth by Giraldus Lillius, the application most fitly made by this author.

GLOSS 9. 'Harpe' should be written thus, not with a 'y', yet here he useth it lest some, not knowing what it means, read it for a harp, having found this grossness in some scholars. It was the sword Perseus used to cut off Medusa's head.

---

21 *Heaven's genial parts*] Uranus's genitalia, or birth-giving parts. See note to 'Noctem', 132.

22, 26 *adamantine Harpey, adamantine power*] On the meaning and spelling of 'Harpey', see Gloss 9. In addition to the reasons considered in Chapman's gloss, the word's form may also be motivated by the need to rhyme with 'away'. In order to avoid a hypermetric line, 'adamantine' (*OED*, *adamantine*, adj., having the qualities of adamant, or a diamond, i.e. hardness and sharpness) could have three syllables, so the vowel between 'd' and 'm' may be elided. However, in line 26 the word keeps its four syllables, while 'power' is monosyllabic.

28 *quench*] the action of cooling a heated object or of extinguishing a fire; the 'adamantine power is given' as 'quench to Cupid's fire'. See *OED*, n., 1, with an example by Chapman: 'a harmfull fire [...] none came | To give it quench' (*Iliads*, XIX. 360–63).

30 *inference*] intrusion. This use is Chapman's neologism. But *infer* (*OED*, v., †6) can mean 'insert'.

34 *soul-winging*] that gives wings to the soul and allows it to fly (*OED*, *wing*, v., 4. b).

34 *tear-stilling*] tear-distilling, that causes tears to trickle down (*OED*, *still*, v.², †1. a).

36 *discessions*] separations. Bartlett (p. 425) glosses it as 'eclipses', a sense that can be understood metaphorically, i.e. the Moon becomes 'black' through separation from light. The word is pronounced tetrasyllabically.

37 *recall*] Chapman's word choice draws on Plutarch's 'revocantibus' (see Commentary: 'Cynthiam', 31–39).

Shall celebrate thy changes' funeral.
    But, as in that thrice-dreadful foughten field 40
Of ruthless Cannae, when sweet Rule did yield
Her beauties' strongest proofs and hugest love,
When men as many as the lamps above
Armed Earth in steel and made her like the skies,
That two Auroras did in one day rise, 45
Then with the terror of the trumpet's call
The battles joined as if the world did fall,
Continued long in life-disdaining fight —
Jove's thund'ring eagles, feathered like the night,
Hov'ring above them with indifferent wings — 50
Till Blood's stern daughter, cruel Tyche[10] slings
The chief of one side to the blushing ground,
And then his men (whom griefs and fears confound)
Turned all their cheerful hopes to grim despair,
Some casting off their souls into the air, 55
Some taken pris'ners, some extremely maimed,
And all (as men accursed) on Fate exclaimed,

GLOSS 10. Fortune is called Tyche, as witnesseth Pausanias in *Messeniacis*, who affirms her to be one of the daughters likewise of Oceanus, which was playing with Proserpine when Dis ravished her:
    Una omnes vario per prata comantia flore,
    Candida Leucippe, Phaenoque, Electraque, Ianthe,
    Melobosisque, Tyche, Ocyrhoe praesignis ocellis.
    (All together in the leafy meadows among a variety of flowers: fair Leucippe and Phaeno and Electra and Ianthe, and Melobosis, Tyche, Ocyrhoe, fair for her eyes.)
And Orpheus, in a hymn to Fortuna, saith she is the daughter of blood, *ut in his*:
    Sanguine prognatam, Vi et inexpugnabile numen.
    (Born of Blood, and her invincible divinity from Power.)
[*ut in his*: as in these.]

---

40 *foughten field*] battlefield.
43–45 *When men ... in one day rise*] 'When an army of armed and armoured men as numerous as the stars in heaven made earth shine like the skies, displaying two dawns, one in heaven and one on earth.'
47 *battles*] armies in battle array (*OED*, n., 8).
51 *Blood's stern daughter, cruel Tyche*] On Chapman's mistaken interpretation of Tyche, or Fortune, as Blood's daughter, see Commentary: 'Cynthiam', 51 and Gloss 10.
51 *slings*] *OED*, v., 1.: 'To strike, to bring or knock down, by means of a sling'. This meaning motivates the emendation of Q*ob*'s 'flings' with 'slings'. See Commentary: 'Cynthiam', 40–63.
52 *The chief of one side*] The consul and general Lucius Aemilius Paulus (see Commentary: 'Cynthiam', 40–63).
53 *confound*] defeated, overthrew. As *OED* attests, 'confound' was a frequent early modern past tense form.
57 *on Fate exclaimed*] invoked Fate. The meaning of 'exclaim on' (i.e. to apostrophize, as in *OED*, exclaim, v., 2. b) makes clear that 'Fate' is the personified god of destiny of Roman mythology (Pierre Grimal, *The Dictionary of Classical Mythology* (Blackwell, 1986), p. 162). I have capitalized it despite Q*sn*.

HYMNUS IN CYNTHIAM

    So (gracious Cynthia) in that sable day
When interposèd Earth takes thee away
(Our sacred chief and sovereign general),   60
As crimson a retreat and steep a fall
We fear to suffer from this peace and height,
Whose thankless sweet now cloys us with receipt.
    The Romans set sweet Music to her charms,[11]
To raise thy stoopings with her airy arms,   65
Used loud resoundings with auspicious brass,
Held torches up to heav'n, and flaming glass,
Made a whole forest but a burning eye,
T'admire thy mournful partings with the sky.
The Macedonians were so stricken dead,   70
With skilless horror of thy changes dread,
They wanted hearts to lift up sounds, or fires,
Or eyes to heav'n, but used their funeral tires,
Trembled and wept, assured some mischief's fury
Would follow that afflicting augury.   75
    Nor shall our wisdoms be more arrogant
(O sacred Cynthia) but believe thy want
Hath cause to make us now as much afraid;
Nor shall Democrates, who first is said
To read in nature's brows thy changes' cause,   80
Persuade our sorrows to a vain applause.
    Time's motion, being like the reeling suns,
Or as the sea reciprocally runs,
Hath brought us now to their opinions,
As in our garments ancient fashions   85
Are newly worn; and as sweet Poesy
Will not be clad in her supremacy

GLOSS 11. Plutarch writes thus of the Romans and Macedons in *Paulus Aemilius*.

---

62 *peace and height*] peaceful height (i.e. of Cynthia's heavenly throne).
63 *Whose thankless sweet now cloys us with receipt*] i.e. our receiving Cynthia's sweetness surfeits us, even if it remains unthanked (*OED, thankless*, adj., 3) by us.
64, 65 *her*] Music's.
66 *loud resoundings with auspicious brass*] See Commentary: 'Cynthiam', 64–75.
69 *mournful partings*] Compare 'black discessions' (25).
71 *skilless horror of thy changes dread*] i.e. terrified by their ignorance of the changes of the moon and their inability to interpret its portents.
73 *funeral tires*] mourning clothes.
76–81 *Nor shall ... vain applause*] 'Even if we know more than the Macedonians did, this knowledge will not make us arrogant, and we will still believe that your absence is a bad sign, which should make us afraid of its consequences. Not even Democritus's knowledge, who is reputed to be the first interpreter of your changes, can persuade us to change our sorrow for your temporary absence into useless contentment.'
79 *Democrates*] Democritus of Abdera; see Commentary: 'Cynthiam', 76–81.

With those strange garments (Rome's hexameters),
As she is English, but in right prefers
Our native robes (put on with skilful hands,   90   C4ʳ
English heroics) to those antique garlands,
Accounting it no meed but mockery,
When her steep brows already prop the sky,
To put on startups, and yet let it fall.
No otherwise (O queen celestial)   95
Can we believe Ephesia's state will be
But spoil with foreign grace and change with thee
The pureness of thy never-tainted life,¹²
Scorning the subject title of a wife,
Thy body not composèd in thy birth   100
Of such condensèd matter as the earth,
Thy shunning faithless men's society,
Betaking thee to hounds and archery,
To deserts and inaccessible hills,
Abhorring pleasure in earth's common ills   105
Commit most willing rapes on all our hearts,
And make us tremble, lest thy sovereign parts
(The whole preservers of our happiness)
Should yield to change, eclipse or heaviness.

GLOSS 12. These are commonly known to be the properties of Cynthia.

82–94 *Time's motion ... let it fall*] 'The cyclical movements of time have brought back to us the opinions of the ancients, just as the sun returns cyclically or the ocean ebbs and flows every day, and just as we revive ancient fashion in our contemporary clothing; yet not with poetry, which will not be clothed in the unfamiliar garments of Latin hexameters but will prefer skilfully composed English heroic verse, considering it no recompense but humiliation to use high-heeled shoes (i.e. an extra metrical foot) to raise her feet (i.e. verse) in order to support the sky with her high forehead, and yet to let it fall (i.e. as those shoes, or metrical patterns, do not suit her).'
83 *reciprocally*] in alternately backward and forward movement, i.e. ebbing and flowing; see *OED*, *reciprocal*, adj., 3. a, which supplies an adjectival use by Chapman: 'Eurynome, that to her father had | Reciprocall Oceanus' [Greek 'ἀψορρόου Ὠκεανοῖο', i.e. that flows back on itself] (*Iliads*, XIX. 354–55).
91 *English heroics*] iambic pentameter rhyming in couplets, which is the kind of verse Chapman uses here, in contrast with the 'hexameters' (88) of ancient epic.
92 *meed*] recompense.
94 *startups*] high-heeled shoes or props.
95–109 *No otherwise ... eclipse or heaviness*] 'By no means, O celestial queen, can we believe that your Ephesian temple (also, your status as a virgin) will be spoiled with foreign qualities, and will change in you the pureness of your unspotted chastity, which scorns the title of a wife (which would make a subject of you), because your body is not composed of earthly matter; and because you avoid the company of faithless men, committing yourself to the activity of hunting with your hounds and your archery in deserts and inaccessible hills, and abhorring that the pleasure that we find in common earthly evils should cause most violent harm in all our hearts, and make us tremble for fear that your sovereign parts (the whole preservers of your welfare) should yield to change, eclipse or dullness.' See Commentary: 'Cynthiam', 82–115.

    And as thy changes happen by the site 110
Near or far distance of thy father's[12a] light,
Who (set in absolute remotion) reaves
Thy face of light, and thee all darkened leaves,
So for thy absence, to the shade of death
Our souls fly mourning, wingèd with our breath. 115
Then set thy crystal and imperial throne
(Girt in thy chaste and never-loosing zone)[13]
Gainst Europe's Sun directly opposite,
And give him darkness, that doth threat thy light.
    O how accursed are they thy favour scorn:[14] 120
Diseases pine their flocks, tares spoil their corn;
Old men are blind of issue, and young wives   C4ᵛ
Bring forth abortive fruit, that never thrives.
    But then how blest are they thy favour graces:
Peace in their hearts, and youth reigns in their faces; 125

GLOSS 12a (marginal). Euripides, in *Phoenisses*, calls her the daughter, not sister, of the Sun: *O clarissimi filia | Solis Luna aurei circuli | Lumen, etc.* (O Moon, child of the Sun, light of the golden circuit.)

GLOSS 13. This zone is said to be the girdle of Cynthia. And thereof when maids lost their maidenheads, amongst the Athenians they used to put off their girdles. And after, custom made it a phrase, *zonam solvere*, to lose their maidenheads, *ut Apollonius, libro primo*:
    Prima soluta mihi est postremaque zona, quod ipsa
    Invidit multos natos Lucina misellae.
    (My virgin zone was loosed first and last, because the goddess Lucina grudged many children to poor me.)
    [*ut Apollonius, libro primo*: as Apollonius writes, in his first book.]

GLOSS 14. These are the verses of Callimachus translated to effect:
    O miseri, quibus ipsa gravem tu concipis iram.
    [*Nam morbus depascit oves, segetemque pruinae.*
    Orbanturque senes natis, et foemina abortum
    Mox pariunt.]
    (O miserable men, on whom thou wilt impart thy heavy wrath. [Thus disease consumes their sheep, and hoarfrost their corn. And old men are bereaved of offspring, and their wives prematurely deliver abortions.])

110–15 *And as thy changes ... with our breath*] 'And, as your changes are caused by the nearness or the remoteness of the Sun's light, who, when he is completely absent from you, deprives your face from light and leaves you in total darkness, so because of your absence we fly in mourning to the darkness of death, propelled by (the wings of) our sighs.' Editorial punctuation restores the chiastic structure 'site near' / 'far distance' by removing obstructing commas in the original.

112 *remotion*] departure (*OED*, n., 4).

112 *reaves*] deprives by force, despoils, bereaves (*OED*, reave, v., 2. a).

116–19 *Then set ... thy light*] 'Then, wrapped in your chaste and always firm girdle, set your throne right between Europe and the sun in order to cause an eclipse in that very star that threatens with depriving you of light.'

117 *zone*] girdle, from Greek ζώνη, Latin *zona* (*OED*, 3. a, chiefly poetic use). See Commentary: 'Cynthiam', 116–19.

121 *pine*] afflict with pain, torment.

121 *tares*] darnel, a weed injurious to corn (*OED*, 3. a, notes its use in Biblical translations to render Greek ζιζάνια, in Latin *zizania*).

Health strengths their bodies, to subdue the seas
And dare the Sun, like Theban Hercules,
To calm the furies and to quench the fire;
As at thy altars in thy Persic Empire
Thy holy women walked with naked soles,   130
Harmless and confident, on burning coals,¹⁵
The virtue-tempered mind ever preserves
Oils and expulsatory balm that serves
To quench lust's fire in all things it anoints,
And steels our feet to march on needles' points,   135
And 'mongst her arms hath armour to repel
The cannon and the fiery darts of hell.
She is the great enchantress that commands
Spirits of every region, seas and lands;
Round heav'n itself and all his sevenfold heights   140
Are bound to serve the strength of her conceits:
A perfect type of thy almighty state,
That hold'st the thread and rul'st the sword of Fate.
    Then you that exercise the virgin court
Of peaceful Thespiae, my Muse consort,   145

GLOSS 15. This Strabo testifieth, *libro duodecimo*.
[*libro duodecimo*: in the twelfth book].

129–37 *As at thy altars ... darts of hell*] 'As at Cynthia's Persian altars her votaresses confidently walked barefoot on burning coals without being harmed, so a mind fortified by virtue always keeps oils and balms that protect all the things that it anoints against the fire of lust, steeling our feet so that they can walk on needles' points; and the mind's arms are covered by an armour that repels the cannonballs and darts shot from (desire's) hell.'
133 *expulsatory*] repellent (this is the first chronological example in OED).
138–43 *She is ... sword of Fate*] 'Cynthia's virtue-tempered mind is the great enchantress that commands spirits of all maritime and terrestrial regions; round heaven and its seven circles are bound to serve her mind's strength of disposition: [heaven is] a perfect dome for your almighty state, which controls Fate's thread and sword.' Cynthia's 'mind' is referred to here in the third person ('she'), while Cynthia herself is addressed, in hymnic *du-Stil*, as 'thou'.
140 *sevenfold heights*] the seven spheres of heaven, the best-known literary representation of which is Dante's *Paradiso*.
141 *type*] pronounced /tiːp/; a dome (OED, † tipe | type, n.¹, 1). See 'Noctem', 5, and 'Cynthiam', 181.
144–55 *Then you ... mere divine*] 'Then, you that rule the virgin Thespian court (i.e. the nine Muses), guide my inspiration, making it drunk with the waters of your fount, and with it instil all your poetic frenzy, so that it may reach the peak of high Olympus, crowned with laurel, and sing the praises of mighty Cynthia, truly representing her sovereignty as Hecate and also, in figuring forth her power, the virtues of the mind — an argument that can enrapture and purify an earthly soul, thus transforming it into a divine one.'
144 *exercise*] rule (see OED, v., 5. f).
145 *Thespiae*] The Boeotian city at the foot of Mount Helicon near the fount Hippocrene, alluded to in the following line and in Gloss 16 (see also Commentary: 'Banquet', 15. 4); William Smith (ed.), *A Dictionary of Greek and Roman Biography and Mythology*, 3 vols (John Murray, 1880), III, p. 1100.

Making her drunken with Gorgonean dews,[16]
And therewith all your ecstasies infuse,
That she may reach the topless starry brows
Of steep Olympus, crowned with freshest boughs
Of Daphnean laurel, and the praises sing 150
Of mighty Cynthia, truly figuring
(As she is Hecate) her sovereign kind
And, in her force, the forces of the mind —
An argument to ravish and refine
An earthly soul, and make it mere divine; 155
Sing then withal her palace brightness bright,
The dazzle-sun perfections of her light
Circling her face with glories; sing the walks
Where in her heav'nly magic mood she stalks;
Her arbours, thickets and her wondrous game 160
(A huntress, being never matched in fame).
Presume not then, ye flesh-confounded souls
That cannot bear the full Castalian bowls
Which sever mounting spirits from the senses,
To look in this deep fount for thy pretenses: 165

GLOSS 16. Pegasus is called Gorgoneus, since poets feign that, when Perseus smote off Medusa's head, Pegasus flew from the wound, and therefore the Muses' fount, which he made with his hoof, is called Gorgon.

---

145 *Muse*] poetic inspiration, as induced by the Muses (see OED, 1. b). Though not capitalized in QsN, her deification is made clear in the next lines.
145 *consort*] escort, guide, accompany.
149 *steep Olympus*] the high mount in north-east Thessaly whose summit rose above the clouds and was the home of the gods.
150 *Daphnean laurel*] Daphne, the daughter of the Thessalian river Peneus, was loved by Apollo, and was transformed in her flight from the god into an evergreen laurel tree. On symbolic meanings, see Commentary: 'Cynthiam', 150.
156 *palace*] i.e. palace's.
157 *dazzle-sun*] sun-dazzling.
157–58 *perfections ... Circling ...*] On the circle as a symbol of perfection and the shape of the Moon, see Commentary: 'Cynthiam', 6–9.
162–69 *Presume not ... these mysteries*] 'Then you, whose souls have been conquered by earthly pleasures and who cannot tolerate the effects of the waters from the Castalian spring, which separate enraptured spirits from their senses, dare not look into this deep fountain in search of your aspirations: its waters, even if they are clearer than day, are able to darken night, whose moisture lacks no drop of goodness; only to the eyes of the purest souls will judgement easily show the heart of these mysteries.'
162 *flesh-confounded*] defeated by the pleasures of the flesh.
163 *Castalian bowls*] by metonymy, the waters of the well Castalia, into which the nymph of that name threw herself when pursued by Apollo. These waters were consecrated to Apollo and the Muses and were the source of artistic inspiration. See Commentary: 'Cynthiam', 144–69, and Introduction, pp. 11–12, 72.
165 *this deep fount*] Two fountains with equal art-inspiring properties, Hippocrene and the Castalian spring, have been mentioned in the previous lines, although the reference is clearly to the latter.

    The juice, more clear than day, yet shadows night,
Where humour challengeth no drop of right;
But judgement shall display to purest eyes,
With ease, the bowels of these mysteries.
    See then this planet of our lives descended   170
To rich Ortygia,¹⁷ gloriously attended
Not with her fifty ocean nymphs, nor yet
Her twenty foresters, but doth beget
By powerful charms' delight some servitors
Of flowers and shadows, mists and meteors.   175
Her rare Elysian palace she did build
With studied wishes, which sweet Hope did gild
With sunny foil that lasted but a day,
For Night must needs importune her away.
The shapes of every wholesome flower and tree   180
She gave those types of her felicity.
And Form herself she mightily conjured
Their priceless values might not be obscured
With disposition baser than divine,
But make that blissful court of hers to shine   185
With all accomplishment of architect,   *D1ᵛ*
That not the eye of Phoebus could detect.
Form then 'twixt two superior pillars framed
This tender building, *Pax Imperii* named,
Which cast a shadow like a pyramis,   190
Whose basis in the plain or back part is
Of that quaint work, the top so high extended
That it the region of the Moon transcended:
Without, within it, every corner filed

GLOSS 17. Ortygia is the country where she was brought up.

---

167 *humour*] moisture.
167 *challengeth*] is found at fault with, lacks (see *OED*, challenge, v., 2. a, here used passively).
178 *foil*] thin layer placed behind the glass of a mirror to produce a reflection (*OED*, n.¹, 5. a).
181 *types*] domes, in the same architectural sense as above ('Noctem', 5; 'Cynthiam', 142).
182–87 *And Form ... Phoebus could detect*] 'And Cynthia solemnly called up Form herself so that the priceless values of her palace's shapes might not be debased by any artistic design that is not of a divine character, and thus to make her heavenly abode shine in rarest architectural perfection that would remain enigmatic even to the eye of Apollo (the Sun).' On the personified abstractions 'Form' and 'Hope', see Commentary: 'Cynthiam', 176–95.
189 *this tender buiding*, Pax Imperii *named*] On the name and iconography of Cynthia's palace, see Commentary: 'Cynthiam', 176–95.
193 *transcended*] overtopped.

By beauteous Form, as her great mistress wild.   195
Here as she sits,[18] the thunder-loving Jove,
In honours past all others, shows his love,
Proclaiming her, in complete empery
Of whatsoever the Olympic sky
With tender circumvecture doth embrace,   200
The chiefest planet that doth heav'n enchase:
Dear Goddess, prompt, benign and bounteous,
That hears all prayers from the least of us,
Large riches gives, since she is largely given,
And all that spring from seed of earth and heaven   205
She doth command, and rules the fates of all —
Old Hesiod sings her thus celestial.
  And now, to take the pleasures of the day,
Because her night star soon will call away,
She frames of matter intimate before   210
(To wit, a bright and dazzling meteor)
A goodly nymph, whose beauty, beauty stains
Heaven's with her jewel; gives all the reins
Of wishèd pleasance; frames her golden wings,
But them she binds up close with purple strings,   215
Because she now will have her run alone

GLOSS 18. These are the verses of Hesiodus before.
  [before: in Gloss 4.]

194–95 *Without ... mistress wild*] 'Every corner of the palace, outside and inside, was polished to perfection by beauteous Form, in the image of her great mistress.'
200 *With tender circumvecture*] in delicate circuit; 'circumvecture' is Chapman's neologism, not recorded by *OED*, which enters *circumvect* and *circumvection* (from Lat. *circumvehere*, to carry about). See Introduction, pp. 32–33.
201 *enchase*] adorn, as a set jewel on a surface; thus, the Moon is a jewel that is set in heaven.
202 *prompt*] ready in mind, disposed (*OED*, adj., 2. †b).
210 *of matter intimate before*] of the abovementioned matter, i.e. in 173–75, where Cynthia fashions her own train of servants out of different natural elements. One of these elements is 'meteors', the substance out of which Euthymia is said to be made in the next line. The adjective 'intimate' is Chapman's neologism, a derivate of the verb, meaning 'indicate' (*OED, intimate*, v., 2). Yet Bartlett (p. 426, n. 210) glosses it as 'essential', on account of *OED*, adj., 1, which seems mistaken here.
212–13 *whose beauty, beauty stains | Heaven's with her jewel*] even if the comma after the first 'beauty' in QsN has been kept, the use of epizeuxis makes the sentence odd or agrammatical. The repetition could be understood as a mere duplication of the subject, and then 'Heavens' (plural) as an object of 'stains'. Another possibility, the one adopted here, is to read 'Heaven's' as a genitive singular, and therefore a modifier of the second, objective 'beauty' (i.e. 'whose beauty stains heaven's beauty with her jewel'). The 'jewel' is the 'dazzling meteor' whose substance has formed Euthymia. Quite exceptionally, in this line both 'Heaven' and 'jewel' are pronounced disyllabically.

And bid the base to all affection;
And Euthymia is her sacred name, D2ʳ
Since she the cares and toils of earth must tame.
Then straight the flowers, the shadows, and the mists 220
(Fit matter for most pliant humorists)
She hunters makes, and of that substance hounds
Whose mouths deaf heav'n, and furrow earth with wounds;
And marvel not a nymph so rich in grace
To hounds' rude pursuits should be giv'n in chase, 225
For she could turn herself to every shape
Of swiftest beasts, and at her pleasure scape —
Wealth fawns on fools, virtues are meat for vices,
Wisdom conforms herself to all earth's guises,
Good gifts are often giv'n to men past good, 230
And noblesse stoops sometimes beneath his blood.
The hounds that she created, vast and fleet,
Were grim Melampus, with th'Ethiop's feet,
White Leucon, all-eating Pamphagus,
Sharp-sighted Dorceus, wild Oribasus, 235
Storm-breathing Lelaps, and the savage Theron,
Wing-footed Pterelas, and hind-like Ladon,
Greedy Harpyia, and the painted Stycte,
Fierce Tigris, and the thicket-searcher Agre,
The black Melaneus, and the bristled Lachne, 240
Lean-lustful Cyprius, and big-chested Alce.
These and such other now the forest ranged,

---

217 *bid the base to all affection*] i.e. challenge, with the purpose of controlling, or defeating, the passions of the mind. Bartlett rightly traces the meaning of this expression to the game of 'prisoners' base', or 'prisoners' bars', 'a chasing game played by two sides occupying distinct areas, the object being to catch and take prisoner any player from the other side running from his or her home area' (*OED, prisoners' base*, n.). See for instance Spenser's 'October', 4–5: 'Whilome thou wont the shepheards laddes to leade, | In rymes, in ridles, and in bydding base' (Spenser, *The Shepheardes Calender*, 'October', 4–5, in *Shorter Poems*, p. 171). Euthymia's challenge of her pursuers to a catch becomes the controlling motif of the ensuing allegorical narrative (Bartlett, p. 426, n. 217).
218 *Euthymia*] Literally, Tranquillity of Mind. See Commentary: 'Cynthiam', 208–19.
221 *pliant*] supple, easily folded, but also in its moral sense, easily influenced, docile.
221 *humorists*] Bartlett finds the meaning of this word to be different from those in *OED*, and thus exclusive to Chapman: a 'humorist' would be someone 'made out of such natural objects' as mists or similarly moist substances, or humours (p. 427, 221 n). A moral explanation of Cynthia's making of the hunters can also apply, and thus this use would fit *OED*, n., †2: 'A person who is subject to fancies'.
223 *deaf*] deafen.
233–41 *Melampus ... Alce*] On the names of the seventeen hounds, see Commentary: 'Cynthiam', 220–42. The pronunciation of these names is conditioned by prosody. Notice, for instance, that while 'Leucon' should make three syllables, 'Dorceus' in the next line should be disyllabic.

And Euthymia, to a panther changed,
Holds them sweet chase; their mouths they freely spend
As if the earth in sunder they would rend; 245
Which change of music liked the Goddess so
That she before her foremost nymph would go,
And not a huntsman there was eag'rer seen
In that sport's love (yet all were wondrous keen)
Than was their swift and windy-footed queen. 250
But now this spotted game did thicket take,
Where not a hound could hung'red passage make:
Such proof the covert was, all armed in thorn,
With which in their attempts the dogs were torn,
And fell to howling in their happiness — 255
As when a flock of schoolboys, whom their mistress
(Held closely to their books) gets leave to sport,
And then, like toil-freed dear, in headlong sort,
With shouts and shrieks they hurry from the school
(Some strow the woods, some swim the silver pool, 260
All as they list to several pastimes fall
To feed their famished wantonness withal),
When straight, within the woods some wolf or bear
The heedless limbs of one doth piecemeal tear,
Affrighteth other, sends some bleeding back, 265
And some in greedy whirlpits suffer wrack —

242–50 *These and such other ... windy-footed queen*] 'By metamorphosing herself into a panther, Euthymia leads the hounds' chase, whose own mouths they employed freely as if they would rend the earth into pieces with their loud barks. This change of sound pleases Cynthia so much that she starts to run before the nymph occupying first position (i.e. Euthymia), and there was not a huntsman seen there that loved this sport as much (and all of them were extremely keen on it) as their swift and windy-footed queen (i.e. Cynthia) did.'
244 *Holds them sweet chase*] leads the hunting dogs in their chase (as in *OED*, hold, v., 7. e).
245 *in sunder*] into separate parts, into pieces (see *OED*, in sunder, adv., 2).
246 *liked*] pleased (*OED*, like, v., 1. a, archaic).
252 *hung'red passage*] crossing (of the dangerous thicket) impelled by hunger.
255 *happiness*] excitement, as the effect of their pursuit of the panther.
258 *dear*] darlings (used nominally, and in plural sense).
258 *in headlong sort*] i.e. in an impetuous, precipitate way.
260 *strow*] This sixteenth-century variant spelling of 'stroll' has been retained from Qsn, as its pronunciation would be different from the present-day English form.
262 *famished wantonness*] repressed unruliness, as a consequence of school discipline.
263 *straight*] (Qsn's 'strait', here modernized) immediately, without delay (*OED*, adv., 3). The comma clarifies this temporal sense, as it separates the word from 'within'.
266 *some in greedy whirlpits suffer wrack*] some fall and drown in a river's voracious whirlpool.

So did the bristled covert check with wounds
The lick'rous haste of these game-greedy hounds.
   In this vast thicket (whose description's task
The pens of furies and of fiends would ask,   270
So more than human-thoughted horrible)
The souls of such as lived implausible
In happy empire of this goddess' glories,
And scorned to crown her fanes with sacrifice,
Did ceaseless walk, expiring fearful groans,   275
Curses and threats for their confusions.
Her darts and arrows some of them had slain;
Others her dogs ate, painting her disdain,
After she had transformed them into beasts;
Others her monsters carried to their nests,   280
Rent them in pieces, and their spirits sent
To this blind shade, to wail their banishment.   D3^r
The huntsmen hearing (since they could not hear)
Their hounds at fault, in eager chase drew near,
Mounted on lions, unicorns and boars,   285
And saw their hounds lie licking off their sores,
Some yearning at the shroud, as if they chid
Her stinging tongues, that did their chase forbid —
By which they knew the game was that way gone.
Then each man forced the beast he rode upon   290
T'assault the thicket, whose repulsive thorns
So galled the lions, boars and unicorns,
Dragons and wolves, that half their courages
Were spent in roars and sounds of heaviness;
Yet being the princeliest and hardiest beasts   295
That gave chief fame to those Ortygian forests,

---

268 *lick'rous*] The adjective combines two senses in *OED*, *lickerous*, adj.: 'having a keen relish or desire for something pleasant' (adj., 2. b) and 'lecherous' (adj., 3). Q*sn*'s original 'licorous' is considered by *OED* a variant spelling.
271 *more than human-thoughted horrible*] worse than the horrors that can be conceived of by a human mind.
272 *implausible*] not worthy of applause, abominable.
274 *fanes*] temples. Although Chapman consistently spells this word with initial 'ph-', it has been regularized to 'f-' in line with its etymology, i.e. Latin *fanum*.
275 *expiring*] exhaling.
283 *they*] Cataphoric, i.e. 'their hounds' (284).
287 *yearning*] baying, yelping (used of hunting dogs at the sight of game; see *OED*, 5. †a).
287 *shroud*] shelter, retreat (*OED*, n., †3); also, a shade or cover (n., †5); see 'blind shade' (282).
292 *galled*] wounded, as by friction (*OED*, *gall*, v., 1. a).
296 *Ortygian forests*] See Commentary: 'Cynthiam', 170–75.

And all their riders furious of their sport,
A fresh assault they gave, in desperate sort,
And with their falchions made their ways in wounds:
The thicket opened, and let in the hounds.   300
But from her bosom cast prodigious cries,
Wrapped in her Stygian fumes of miseries,
Which yet the breaths of those courageous steads
Did still drink up, and cleared their vent'rous heads —
As when the fiery coursers of the Sun   305
Up to the palace of the Morning run,
And from their nostrils blow the spiteful day,
So yet those foggy vapours made them way.
But preasing further, saw such cursèd sights,
Such Etnas filled with strange tormented sprites,   310
That now the vap'rous object of the eye
Out-pierced the intellect in faculty.
Baseness was nobler than nobility,
For ruth (first shaken from the brain of love,   D3ᵛ
And love the soul of virtue) now did move   315
Not in their souls (spheres mean enough for such)
But in their eyes; and thence did conscience touch
Their hearts with pity, where her proper throne

---

299 *falchions*] 'broad, curved swords, with the edge on the convex side' (*OED*, n., 1. a).
301–25 *But from her bosom ... through their hearts*] See Commentary: 'Cynthiam', 301–25, for a full paraphrase.
301 *her*] the thicket's (here and in the next line).
301 *cast*] emerged, came out (used intransitively or reflexively); or, emitted (*OED*, v., † 8; used transitively, in which case 'the thicket' is the subject).
302 *Stygian*] pertaining to the river Styx, bordering the infernal regions; hellish.
303 *Which*] The antecedent is 'cries, | Wrapped in [...] fumes'; this relative pronoun is the direct object of 'did ... drink up', but the subject of 'cleared'.
303 *steads*] steeds (see note to 'Noctem', 203).
304 *vent'rous*] adventurous, daring (*OED*, venturous, adj., 1. a).
306 *Up*] rise, move upward (*OED*'s instances for these verbal senses are of later dates, mainly from the seventeenth and eighteenth centuries; see *up*, v., 7).
309 *preasing*] pressing. *OED* only records 'prease' as a historical spelling of 'press', but the form has been kept for its possibly differentiated pronunciation from the standard form.
310 *Such Etnas filled with strange tormented sprites*] The suffering spirits or creatures mentioned in the lines above are figuratively called 'Etnas', as their 'sprites', or passions, manifest themselves violently, like the eruptions of Mount Etna, the Sicilian volcano. *OED* records this lexicalized use (n., 1), although its earliest instance is from 1619. Compare Dryden, *Annus Mirabilis* (1666), 84. 333–35: 'Sometimes from fighting squadrons of each fleet [...] | Two grappling Etnas on the Ocean meet' (John Dryden, *Selected Poems*, ed. by Paul Hammond and David Hopkins (Routledge, 2014), p. 75). See also *OED*, *sprite*, n., 1. †b, for its sense here when used in plural form.
311 *vap'rous*] vaporous (Q$_{SN}$'s 'vaprous').
312 *Out-pierced*] pierced deeper than (Chapman's neologism, not in *OED*).

Is in the mind, and there should first have shone —
Eyes should guide bodies, and our souls our eyes, 320
But now the world consists on contraries.
So sense brought terror, where the mind's presight
Had safed that fear and done but pity right;
But servile fear now forged a wood of darts
Within their eyes, and cast them through their hearts. 325
Then turned they bridle; then, half slain with fear,
Each did the other backwards overbear —
As when th'Italian Duke a troop of horse
Sent out in haste against some English force
From stately-sited, sconce-torn Nimigan, 330
Under whose walls the Waal[19] most Cynthian
Stretcheth her silver limbs loaded with wealth,
Hearing our horse were marching down by stealth;
(Who looking for them) war's quick artisan,
Fame-thriving Vere, that in those countries wan 335
More fame than guerdon, ambuscados laid
Of certain foot, and made full well apaid

GLOSS 19. The Waal is a most excellent river in the Low Countries, parting with another river called the Maze, near a town in Holland called Gurckham, and runs up to Gelderland under the walls of Nijmegen. And these like similes, in my opinion, drawn from the honourable deeds of our noble countrymen, clad in comely habit of poesy, would become a poem as well as further-fetched grounds, if such as be poets nowadays would use them.

---

322 *presight*] foresight (Chapman's neologism, not in *OED*).
323 *safed*] past participle of *safe*. *OED*'s sense 'to make safe' is not relevant here. It rather seems to mean 'to keep at bay', a sense that accords with the metaphor in 324–25, which depicts 'fear' shooting arrows into the huntsmen's hearts.
326 *turned they bridle*] rode back, retreated (*OED*, *turn*, v., 50).
328 *th'Italian Duke*] Alessandro Farnese (1545–1592), third Duke of Parma, and general of the Spanish Army, serving in the Netherlands between 1587 and 1592 (see Commentary: 'Cynthiam', 326–49).
330 *stately-sited, sconce-torn Nimigan*] splendidly located Nijmegen, rent asunder from the sconce, or fort, by the river Waal (which actually divides Nijmegen from Knodensburgh). Bartlett mistakenly interprets the latter compound as describing a fort that had been torn (p. 427, n. 330). I have kept the original 'Nimigan', spelled differently from Q$_{SN}$'s 'Nimigen' in Gloss 19 (where I have modernized to 'Nijmegen'), as it was intended so for the sake of rhyme.
334 *Who*] 'Fame-thriving Vere' (cataphoric).
334 *quick*] deft, skilled (*OED*, adj., 20).
335–36 *Fame-thriving Vere … | More fame than guerdon*] Sir Francis Vere (1569–1609) gained his military reputation in the Netherlands War beginning in 1585, and later in the sack of Cádiz under the Earl of Essex in 1596. Chapman's complaint echoes Queen Elizabeth's refusal to grant a title to one of her best generals (Bartlett, pp. 427–28, nn. 335–36); see also Clement H. Markham, *The Fighting Veres* (Houghton, Mifflin & Co., 1888, pp. 362–63). See Commentary: 'Cynthiam', 326–49.
336–37 *ambuscados laid | Of certain foot*] laid ambushes on a secure position.

The hopeful enemy, in sending those,
The long-expected subjects of their blows,
To move their charge; which straight they give amain,   340
When, we retiring to our strength again,
The foe pursues, assurèd of our lives,
And us within our ambuscado drives,
Who straight with thunder of the drums and shot,
Tempest their wraths on them that wist it not;   345
Then (turning headlong) some escaped us so,
Some left to ransom, some to overthrow —
In such confusion did this troop retire,
And thought them cursèd in that game's desire.
Out flew the hounds, that there could nothing find   350
Of the sly panther, that did beard the wind,
Running into it full, to clog the chase
And tire her followers with too much solace.
And but the superficies of the shade
Did only sprinkle with the scent she made —   355
As when the sunbeams on high billows fall
And make their shadows dance upon a wall
That is the subject of his fair reflectings;[19a]
Or else, as when a man in summer evenings,
Something before sunset, when shadows be   360
Racked with his stooping, to the high'st degree,
His shadow climbs the trees, and scales a hill,
While he goes on the beaten passage still —
So sleightly touched the panther with her scent
This irksome covert, and away she went   365

GLOSS 19a (marginal). *Simile ad eandem explicat.* (This simile is explained by itself.)

337–38 *made full well apaid | The hopeful enemy*] made the enemy fully rewarded in their expectations (ironic).
340 *amain*] with all their strength, in great numbers.
342 *assurèd of our lives*] i.e. convinced that they would obtain our lives as trophy of war.
344 *Who*] The antecedent is 'us', the English troops, now regaining the role as subject of the action (the main verb being 'Tempest').
345 *Tempest their wraths on them that wist it not*] i.e. turned their own wraths violently on those that did not expect this attack. 'Wist' is the past form of *OED, wit*, v., 2. a.
348 *this troop*] the riding huntsmen created by Cynthia, and in pursuit of Euthymia. Their narrative is resumed after the martial digression in the form of a Homeric simile.
351 *beard*] confront, defy (*OED*, v., 3).
352 *clog*] obstruct (*OED*, v., 3. b).
353 *solace*] delight, caused by the panther's scent. It should be pronounced [sə'leɪs].
361 *Racked*] stretched, increased in length. *OED*, v.¹, 1. a, cites this line.
364 *sleightly*] subtly.
365 *irksome*] disgusting, here with olfactory connotations.

Down to a fruitful island sited by,
Full of all wealth, delight and empery,
Ever with child of curious architect,
Yet still delivered, paved with dames select,
On whom rich feet in foulest boots might tread   370
And never foul them, for kind Cupid spread
Such perfect colours on their pleasing faces,
That their reflects clad foulest weeds with graces:
Beauty strikes fancy blind, pied show deceives us,
Sweet banquets tempt our healths when temper leaves us; 375
Inchastity is ever prostitute,
Whose trees we loathe when we have plucked their fruit.
    Hither this panther fled, now turned a boar $D4^v$
More huge than that th'Aetolians plagued so sore,
And led the chase through noblest mansions,   380
Gardens and groves, exempt from paragons,
In all things ruinous, and slaughter some,
As was that scourge to the Aetolian kingdom;
After, as if a whirlwind drave them on,

---

366 *fruitful island*] fertile grove (see *OED, island*, n., 2. a), in opposition to the 'irksome covert' (365). 'Island' and 'covert' are almost synonymous; the phrase is here allusive to the isle of Britain (see Introduction, pp. 96–97).

368–69 *Ever with child of curious architect | Yet still delivered*] full of, as if pregnant with, intricate architectural devices. On the use of 'architect' as 'architecture' (not in *OED*), see Bartlett (p. 428, n. 368). Bartlett also notes the presence of this same construction in 'Banquet': 'Pleasure herself lies big with issue panting, | Ever delivered, yet with child still growing, | Full of all blessings, yet all bliss bestowing' (109. 7–9). Both instances stress the paradoxical simultaneity of what is still in process and completed, a favourite theme in Chapman that is expressed by other conceits, such as the incomplete circle (see 'Banquet', 54 and Commentary; also Introduction, p. 109).

373 *reflects*] reflections; this is the first chronological instance provided by *OED*, n.

374 *pied*] dappled, patched in different colours, and, figuratively, inconstant (*OED*, adj.¹, gives this example for the latter meaning). For other instances of this word in Chapman, see the metamorphosis of the nymph Adolesche into 'the pied-plum'd Psittacus' (*Hero and Leander*, v. 421, in Bartlett, p. 161).

376 *Inchastity*] unchastity. For Chapman's other uses of this prefix, see, for instance, 'impolished' ('Noctem', 224).

379 *th'Aetolians plagued so sore* / 383 *scourge to the Aetolian kingdom*] On the Calydonian Boar as the scourge of the Aetolians, see Commentary: 'Noctem', 84.

384–89 *After, as if … is rent*] 'The hounds ran after the boar, as if a whirlwind drove them on, in full cry and together, as if they all were one single beast, and frightened the earth with the sound of their barks, making it tremble, as when winds are trapped inside it and fight to come out, with whose fierce shaking and shivering all the world is torn open.'

384 *drave*] drove (archaic past tense).

384 *on*] The historical spelling 'one' for the preposition *on* has been modernized to avoid confusion, even if the eye-rhyme with 'one' in the next line is lost.

>   Full cry, and close, as if they all were one, 385
> The hounds pursue, and fright the earth with sound,
> Making her tremble, as when winds are bound
> In her cold bosom, fighting for event,
> With whose fierce ague all the world is rent.
>   But Day's arm (tired to hold her torch to them) 390
> Now let it fall within the Ocean stream;
> The Goddess blew retreat, and with her blast
> Her morn's creation did like vapours waste:
> The winds made wing into the upper light,
> And blew abroad the sparkles of the night. 395
> Then (swift as thought) the bright Titanides,
> Guide and great sovereign of the marble seas,
> With milk-white heifers mounts into her sphere,
> And leaves us miserable creatures here.
>   Thus nights fair days, thus griefs do joys supplant, 400
> Thus glories grav'n in steel and adamant,
> Never supposed to waste, but grow by wasting
> (Like snow in rivers fall'n), consume by lasting.
> O then, thou great elixir of all treasures,[20]
> From whom we multiply our world of pleasures, 405
> Descend again, ah never leave the earth,
> But as thy plenteous humours gave us birth,[21]

GLOSS 20. The philosopher's stone, or *philosophica medicina*, is called 'the great elixir', to which he here alludes.
  [philosopher's stone: the ultimate, much-sought alchemical substance, able to transform base metals into pure gold. See Lyndy Abraham, *A Dictionary of Alchemical Imagery* (Cambridge University Press, 1998), pp. 145-48.]
GLOSS 21. This of our birth is explained before.
  [before: i.e. in Gloss 1.]

---

385 *Full cry*] When applied to hunting dogs, the expression means in full pursuit and noise (*OED*, *cry*, n., 12. b).
386 *fright*] frighten.
388 *event*] discharge or release of wind. *OED* records verbal, but not nominal, uses of this sense: see †v., 1.
389 *ague*] a fit of shaking and shivering, used metonymically here as an effect of the earth's disease, caused by the cold winds inside it.
390 *her torch*] i.e. the sun ('it' in the next line).
391 *the Ocean stream*] the outer or open sea, in opposition to inland seas such as the Mediterranean.
394 *made wing*] made their way by flying (*OED*, *wing*, n., P2. b).
395 *blew abroad the sparkles of the night*] spread the night's scintillations with their blows.
397 *marble seas*] Virgil frequently calls the sea's surface 'marmo': 'quam multi Libyco volvuntur marmore fluctus' (*Aeneid*, VII. 718), which English translator Thomas Phaer freely rendered: 'As thick as winter waves in Marble seas ar turnd and tost' (*Nyne First Bookes of the Eneidos* (London: Rowland Hall, 1562), sig. V4ᵛ). *OED* (adj., 3) stresses its figurative/poetic quality, combining tactile and visual connotations (i.e. smoothness and brightness), both of which are applicable here.

So let them drown the world in night, and death
Before this air leave breaking with thy breath.
Come, Goddess, come: the double-fathered son[22]   410
Shall dare no more amongst thy train to run,
Nor with polluted hands to touch thy veil;
His death was darted from the scorpion's tail,
For which her form to endless memory
With other lamps doth lend the heav'ns an eye;   415
And he that showed such great presumption
Is hidden now beneath a little stone.
If proud Alpheus[23] offer force again,
Because he could not once thy love obtain,
Thou and thy nymphs shall stop his mouth with mire,   420
And mock the fondling for his mad aspire.
   Thy glorious temple (great Lucifera[24]),

GLOSS 22. The 'double-fathered son' is Orion, so called since he was the son of Jove and Apollo, born of their seed enclosed in a bull's hide, which abhorreth not from philosophy (according to poets' intentions) that one son should have two fathers, for in the generation of elements it is true, since *omnia sint in omnibus*. He, offering violence, was stung of a scorpion to death, for which the scorpion's figure was made a sign in heaven, as Nicander in *Theriacis* affirms:

> Grandine signatum Titanis at inde puella
> Scorpion immisit, qui cuspide surgat acuta,
> Boeoto ut meditata necem fuit Orioni,
> Impuris ausus manibus quia prendere peplum
> Ille Deae est. talum percussit Scorpius illi,
> Sub parvo lapide occultus vestigia propter.

(And thence the Titan's daughter sent forth the aforesaid scorpion with its sharp sting, when she planned the murder of Boeotian Orion, beacause he dared to lay his impure hands on the goddess's robes. Then the scorpion, which lay hidden beneath a little stone, strung him in the ankle.)

[*omnia sint in omnibus*: all the elements are present in the [generation of] all the elements.]

GLOSS 23. Alpheus, taken with the love of Cynthia, not answered with many repulses, pursued her to her company of virgins, who, mocking him, cast mire in his face and drave him away. Some affirm him to be a flood, some the son of Parthenia, some the wagoner of Pelops, etc.

[cast mire in his face: On Chapman's misunderstanding, or manipulation, of the legend, see Commentary: 'Cynthiam', 418–21 and Gloss 23.]

GLOSS 24. Lucifera is her title, and Ignifera, given by Euripides in *Iphigenia in Tauris*.

[Lucifera, Ignifera: light-bearing, fire-bearing (Greek φωσφόρος).]

404–09 *O then ... with thy breath*] 'O then, you philosophical stone that are able to transform all substances, from whom we receive all sorts of benefits, descend again and never leave the earth; but, just as your moisture is the origin of our lives, so let these moist humours cause the drowning of this world into night, and with your breath leave death breaking before this air.' On Cynthia as the alchemical 'great elixir' or philosopher's stone, see Commentary: 'Cynthiam', 404–09.

413–17 *the scorpion's tail ... a little stone*] On the myth of Diana and Orion, and Chapman's misinterpretation of his sources, see Commentary: 'Cynthiam', 410–17 and Gloss 22.

415 *lamps*] stars.

421 *fondling*] given to fondling, i.e. to lust; foolish (*OED*, adj., and n., †1).

421 *aspire*] aspiration.

That was the study of all Asia,
Two hundred twenty summers to erect,
Built by Chersiphrone thy architect,   425
In which two hundred twenty columns stood,
Built by two hundred twenty kings of blood,
Of curious beauty and admirèd height,
Pictures and statues of as praiseful sleight,
Convenient for so chaste a Goddess' fane   430
(Burnt by Herostratus), shall now again
Be re-exstruct, and this Ephesia be,
Thy country's happy name come here with thee:
As it was there, so shall it now be framed,
And thy fair virgin-chamber ever named.   435
And as in reconstruction of it there,
There ladies did no more their jewels wear,
But frankly contribute them all to raise
A work of such a chaste religious praise,
So will our ladies, for in them it lies   440
To spare so much as would that work suffice:
Our dames well set their jewels in their minds;   E1ᵛ
Insight illustrates, outward bravery blinds;
The mind hath in herself a deity,
And in the stretching circle of her eye   445
All things are compassed, all things present still;
Will, framed to power, doth make us what we will.
But keep your jewels, make ye braver yet,
Elysian ladies, and (in riches set
Upon your foreheads) let us see your hearts;   450

---

423 *study*] object that is worthy of examination (*OED*, n., 9. b), model; or, perhaps here, wonder.
425 *Chersiphrone*] The architect Chersiphron of Cnossus began the construction of the Temple of Diana in 560 BC. See Commentary: 'Cynthiam', 422–55 and Gloss 24.
427 *kings of blood*] kings by lineage.
428 *curious*] artful, the result of skilful artistry, beautifully wrought (*OED*, adj., †7. a).
429 *Pictures and statues of as praiseful sleight*] i.e. paintings and sculptures made with the same commendable skill as the building itself. See *OED*, *praiseful*, adj., †1, and *sleight*, n.¹, 1.
430 *fane*] temple (see note to 274).
431 *Herostratus*] An Ephesian madman, who burnt down the Temple in 356 BC on the same night as Alexander the Great was born. See Commentary: 'Cynthiam', 422–55 and Gloss 24.
432 *re-exstruct*] rebuilt (*OED*, † *exstruct*, v., 'build or pile up', of which this is the only instance).
432 *and this Ephesia be*] and this will be the new temple of Ephesus.
443–47 *Insight... what we will*] 'Insight illuminates, outward ostentation blinds; the inner mind has a divine quality, and, in the stretching circle of the mind's eye, all things are contained and remain eternally present; our will, framed within the power of the mind, makes us reach whatever we aim at.'
443 *bravery*] ostentation (*OED*, 3. a).

> Build Cynthia's temple in your virtuous parts,
> Let every jewel be a virtue's glass.
> And no Herostratus shall ever race
> Those holy monuments, but pillars stand
> Where every Grace and Muse shall hang her garland.   455
>   The mind, in that we like, rules every limb,
> Gives hands to bodies, makes them make them trim;
> Why then, in that the body doth dislike,
> Should not his sword as great a veny strike?²⁵
> The bit and spur that monarch ruleth still,   460
> To further good things and to curb the ill:
> He is the Ganymede the bird of Jove
> Rapt to his sovereign's bosom for his love;
> His beauty was it, not the body's pride,
> That made him great Aquarius stellified;   465
> And that mind most is beautiful and high,
> And nearest comes to a divinity,
> That furthest is from spot of earth's delight —
> Pleasures that lose their substance with their sight.
> Such one Saturnius ravisheth to love,   470
> And fills the cup of all content to Jove.
>   If wisdom be the mind's true beauty then,
> And that such beauty shines in virtuous men,
> If those sweet Ganymedes shall only find   E2ʳ

GLOSS 25. The beauty of the mind being signified in Ganymede, he here by prosopopoeia gives a man's shape unto it.
   [prosopopoeia: The rhetorical figure of personification, by which we 'attribute any human quality [...] to dumb creatures or other insensible things' (Puttenham, *The Art of English Poesy*, p. 324).]

---

453 *race*] pluck off, tear, destroy (*OED*, †v.¹, 2).
456-59 *The mind ... a veny strike?*] 'The mind, in all that is pleasant in us, rules every limb; it gives hands to bodies and makes those hands make the body trim; why then should not the mind's sword remove all in which we are displeasing?' 'Like' and 'dislike' are used intransitively here (*OED, like*, v.¹, 1. c; the sense 'to be displeasing' is not recorded by *OED, dislike*, v.).
459 *veny*] a thrust in fencing, a blow (*OED*, n.; an altered form of *venue*).
462-65 *Ganymede ... Aquarius stellified*] Ganymede was abducted by Jupiter so that he could become his cupbearer in Olympus; he was later transformed into the constellation Aquarius. On Chapman's use of Conti's *Mythologiae* for moral meanings, see Commentary: 'Cynthiam', 456-71 and Gloss 25.
463 *Rapt*] ravished, transported; past form of *rap* (*OED*, †v.⁴).
474 The absence of a line containing a rhyme with 'find' suggests a missing line by compositorial eye-skip. Yet the sense is not necessarily interrupted. Thus, the 'sweet Ganymedes' 'find [...] Love of Olympius'. If the myth of Zeus and Ganymede is interpreted spiritually, as the ascent of the soul toward divine, intellectual beauty (see Commentary: 'Cynthiam', 456-71 and Gloss 25), then it stands in contrast with 'those wizards wise' who seek nothing but material rewards by means of their knowledge. This is a recurrent theme in Chapman's poetry.

> Love of Olympius, are those wizards wise 475
> That nought but gold and his dejections prize?
> This beauty hath a fire upon her brow,
> That dims the sun of base desires in you;
> And as the cloudy bosom of the tree,
> Whose branches will not let the summer see 480
> His solemn shadows, but do entertain
> Eternal winter, so thy sacred train,
> Thrice mighty Cynthia, should be frozen dead
> To all the lawless flames of Cupid's godhead.
> To this end let thy beams' divinities 485
> For ever shine upon their sparkling eyes,
> And be as quench to those pestiferent fires
> That, through their eyes, empoison their desires.
> Thou never yet wouldst stoop to base assault;
> Therefore, those poets did most highly fault 490
> That feigned thee fifty children by Endymion,²⁶
> And they that write thou hadst but three alone:
> Thou never any hadst, but didst affect
> Endymion for his studious intellect.
> Thy soul-chaste kisses were for virtue's sake; 495
> And since his eyes were evermore awake
> To search for knowledge of thy excellence
> And all astrology, no negligence
> Or female softness fed his learned trance,
> Nor was thy veil once touched with dalliance. 500
> Wise poets feign thy godhead properly
> The thresholds of men's doors did fortify,

GLOSS 26. Pausanias, in *Eliacis*, affirms it; others, that she had but three, *viz.* Paeon, which Homer calls the Gods' physician, Epeus, and Aetolus, etc. Cicero saith she had none, but only for his love to the study of astrology gave him chaste kisses.

475 *Olympius*] Zeus/Jupiter, ruler of Olympus.
476 *dejections*] leftovers, excrements (*OED*, n., 6).
487 *quench*] a substance used to extinguish the 'pestiferent fires' mentioned in the same line; this nominal use suggests a sense not in *OED*, n.
487 *pestiferent*] pestiferous, causing a contagious disease (Chapman's neologism is not recorded in *OED*).
488 *empoison*] infect.
498–500 *negligence... softness... dalliance*] Chapman's rebuttal of earlier writers' charges against Endymion adapts in these three nouns the adjectives 'segnem' and 'voluptarium' (i.e. 'lazy' and 'sensual') in his source. See Commentary: 'Cynthiam', 489–500.
499 *learned trance*] self-absorption through dedication to learning (*OED*, *trance*, n., 3. b).
501–02 *Wise poets ... did fortify*] 'Wise poets duly tell in their fictions that your divinity fortified the thresholds of men's doors.' QSN's comma at the end of line 501 has been suppressed. On Cynthia's role as guardian (or 'president' in 505), see Commentary: 'Cynthiam', 501–04, 505–14.

And therefore built they thankful altars there,
Serving thy power, in most religious fear.
Dear president for us to imitate, 505
Whose doors thou guard'st against imperious Fate,
Keeping our peaceful households safe from sack,
And freest our ships when others suffer wrack,
Thy virgin-chamber[27] then, that sacred is,
No more let hold an idle Salmacis, 510
Nor let more sleights Cydippe injury,
Nor let black Jove, possessed in Sicily,
Ravish more maids, but maids subdue his might
With well-steeled lances of thy watchful sight.
   Then, in thy clear and icy pentacle,[28] 515
Now execute a magic miracle:
Slip every sort of poisoned herbs and plants,
And bring thy rabid mastiffs to these haunts;
Look with thy fierce aspect, be terror-strong,
Assume thy wondrous shape of half a furlong, 520
Put on thy feet of serpents, vip'rous hairs,
And act the fearfull'st part of thy affairs;
Convert the violent courses of thy floods,
Remove whole fields of corn and hugest woods,
Cast hills into the sea and make the stars 525

GLOSS 27. Her temple in Ephesus was called her 'virgin-chamber'.
GLOSS 28. All these are proper to her, as she is Hecate.
Explicit Commentarius.
   [*Explicit Commentarius*: Here the Commentary ends.]

---

505 *president*] The two meanings explained in the note to 'Noctem', 236, also apply here, and for that reason the spelling has not been modernized to 'precedent'.
506 *Whose doors*] our doors (the antecedent is 'us' in the previous line).
510–11 *Salmacis, Cydippe*] The naiad Salmacis seduced Hermaphroditus when she saw him bathing in her pool. Cydippe had to marry Accontius after he fell in love, inscribed an apple with the words 'I swear by the sanctuary of Diana that I will marry Accontius', and threw it in front of her. See Commentary: 'Cynthiam', 505–14.
511 *sleights*] tricks, deceits.
511 *injury*] wrong (*OED*, v., 1, obsolete).
512 *black Jove*] Pluto, as Bartlett aptly notes (p. 428, n. 512). See also Commentary: 'Cynthiam', 505–14.
515 *pentacle*] five-pointed star; see Commentary: 'Cynthiam', 515–28.
518 *haunts*] resorts, habitations, but also feeding places for deer or game — the latter explains the mention of 'rabid mastiffs' (see *OED*, n., 3).
520 *half a furlong*] traditionally, a furlong was the equivalent of a Roman *stadium*, one-eighth of a mile, so 'half a furlong' suggests gigantic stature (approximately a hundred metres).
521 *vip'rous*] viperous (pronounced disyllabically).

Drop out of heav'n and lose thy marinars.
So shall the wonders of thy power be seen,
And thou for ever live the planet's queen.

Explicit Hymnus.
Omnis ut umbra.

---

526 *lose*] destroy, bring to perdition (*OED*, v.¹, †2. a).
526 *marinars*] Q*SN* has 'mariners' here; however, and in line with 'Noctem', 375, which has 'marinars' to also rhyme with 'stars', what looks like Chapman's most probable choice has been adopted here.
Explicit Hymnus. Omnis ut umbra.] 'Here the hymn is ended. All is like a shadow.' On the meanings of 'shadow' and this particular *sententia*, see Introduction, pp. 91–99, and Commentary.

OVID'S BANQUET OF SENSE

A CORONET FOR HIS
MISTRESS PHILOSOPHY

&

HIS AMOROUS ZODIAC

a translation of a Latine coppie, written by a Fryer, Anno Dom. 1400] 'The Amorous Contention of Phillis and Flora' (QOB, sigs G2^r–I2^r) translates 'with some literalness a mediaeval Latin poem that was at one times wrongly attributed to Walter Mapes. [...] The Latin poem probably dates from the twelfth century; it is far earlier than 1400' (Lee, *The French Renaissance in England*, p. 467, n. 1). QOB also prints an excerpt from the Latin original, 'Certamen inter Phillidem et Floram' (sigs I2^r–I3^v).

Quis leget haec? Nemo Hercule Nemo, vel duo vel nemo: Persius] 'Who will read this? Nobody, by Hercules, nobody, either two or nobody'. For the original, see Persius, Satire I. 2–3, in *Juvenal and Persius*, p. 316. See also Introduction, p. 110, and Waddington, 'Chapman and Persius'.

Sibi conscia recti] 'Conscious of its own rectitude'. On the relevance of this Virgilian motto (*Aeneid*, I. 604) for the interpretation of the poem and more generally for Chapman's poetics, see Introduction, p. 110, and n. 339. See also MacLure, *George Chapman*, pp. 225–30, and Waddington, *The Mind's Empire*, pp. 143–48.

I[ames] R[oberts] for Richard Smith] See Commentary: OBS, Title pages.

Ouids Banquet of
SENCE.

A Coronet for his Miſtreſſe Phi-
loſophie, and his amorous
Zodiacke.

VVith a tranſlation of a Latine coppie, written
by a Fryer, Anno Dom. 1400.

Quis leget hæc? Nemo Hercule Nemo,
vel duo vel nemo : Perſius.

AT LONDON,
Printed by I. R. for Richard Smith.
Anno Dom. 1595.

FIG. 2. Title page of the 1595 quarto of *Ovid's Banquet of Sense* (QOB). Henry E. Huntington Library, San Marino, California, Call Number 49638.

Certamen inter &c.

Quis amicos copulit nostros loro pari?
Lex, Natura prohibent illos copulari
Meum semper præmium dare tuo dari
Meus nouit ludere, tuus epulari
Haurit flora sanguinem vulta verecundo
Et apparet pulchrior in risu secundo
Et tandem eloquio reserat facundo
Quæ corde conceperat artibus facundo
Satis inquit libere Phyllis es loquuta
Multum es eloquio velox et acuta
Sed non efficaciter verum prosequuta
Vt per te præualeat lilio cicuta
Dixisti de Clerico qui indulgit sibi
Seruum somni nominas & potus & cibi
Sic solet ab inuido probitas describi
Ecce parem pattere respondebo tibi
Tot et tanta fateor, &c.

FINIS.

FIG. 3. Final page (sig. I3ᵛ) of QOB, containing printer Richard Smith's device. Henry E. Huntington Library, San Marino, California, Call Number 49638.

Tempore patet occulta Veritas] 'Time reveals hidden Truth'. On the displacement of printer Richard Smith's motto to the last page of QOB, and the relation of this motto to Chapman's philosophical poetics and the emblem tradition, see Introduction, pp. 62 and 109–10. See also Waddington, 'Visual Rhetoric'.

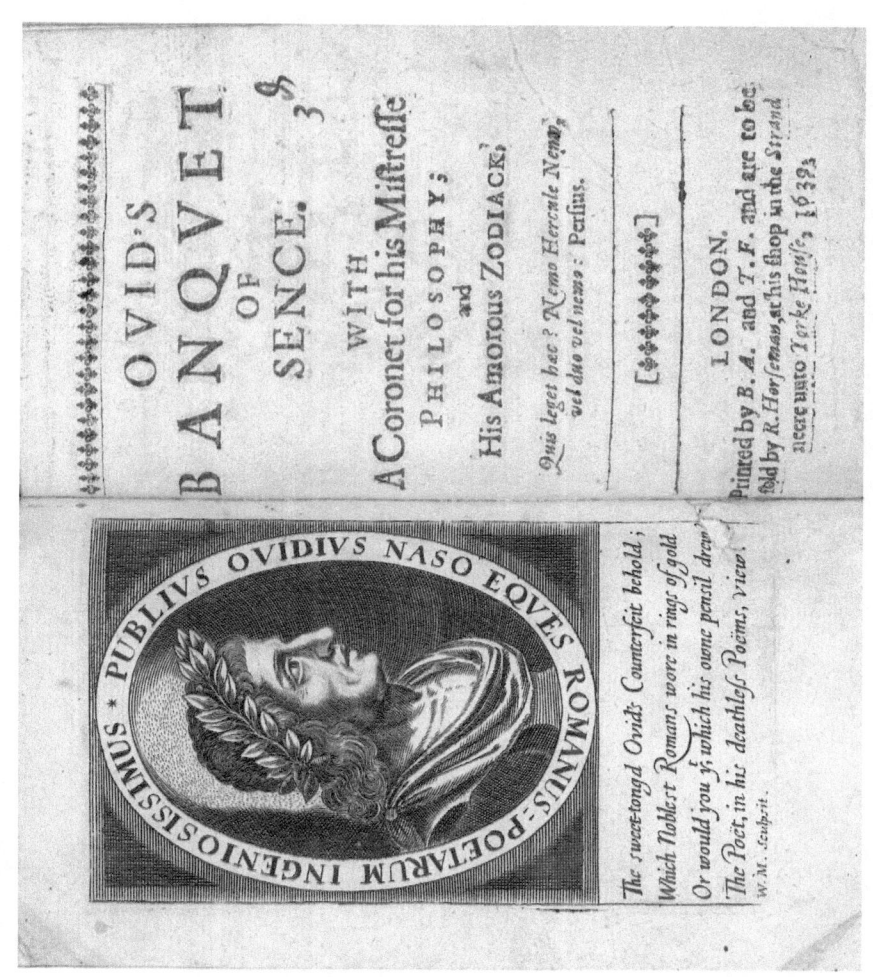

Fig. 4. Title page of the 1639 octavo of *Ovid's Banquet of Sense* (O0B), bound with William Marshall's engraved bust of Ovid and epigram. Henry E. Huntington Library, San Marino, California, Call number 98520.

Quis leget...] See p. 170.
B[ernard] A[lsop] and T[homas] F[awcett] ... R[ichard] Horseman] On the printers and bookseller of the 1639 octavo, the making of the octavo, and the attached engraving of Ovid (which is not part of the volume proper), see Commentary: *OBS*, Title pages.

To the truly learned, and my worthy friend, A2ʳ
Master Matthew Roydon

SUCH IS the wilful poverty of judgements, sweet Matthew, wandering, like passportless men, in contempt of the divine discipline of poesy, that a man may well fear to frequent their walks. The profane multitude I hate, and only consecrate my strange poems to these searching spirits whom learning hath made noble, and nobility sacred, endeavouring   5
that material oration, which you call schema, varying in some rare fiction from popular custom, even for the pure sakes of ornament and utility —
this of Euripides exceeding sweetly relishing with me: *Lentem coquens ne quicquam olentis addito.*

But that poesy should be as pervial as oratory, and plainness her special   10
ornament, were the plain way to barbarism — and to make the ass run proud of his ears, to take away strength from lions, and give camels horns.

That *enargia*, or clearness of representation, required in absolute poems, is not the perspicuous delivery of a low invention, but high and hearty invention expressed in most significant and unaffected phrase: it   15
serves not a skilful painter's turn to draw the figure of a face only to make known who it represents, but he must limn, give lustre, shadow

---

1 *wilful poverty of judgements*] obstinate ignorance of those who believe they have good judgement. See *OED*, *judgement*, n., 1. †c: 'a person capable of good judgement; a competent critic'; here, in obviously ironic sense.
1 *wandering*] moving without a fixed course, but also, figuratively, falling into error (*OED*, *wander*, v.¹, 3. b).
2 *passportless*] without an authorization to travel; *OED*, adj., lists this as its first historical example.
3 *their walks*] the errant opinions of these 'judgements', in consonance with the simile of the 'passportless men'.
3–4 *The profane multitude I hate*] On Chapman's use of Horace, *Odes*, III. 1. 1, in context, see Commentary: '*OBS*: To Roydon'.
8 *exceeding*] exceedingly.
8–9 *Lentem coquens ne quicquam olentis addito*] 'When cooking lentils, add no unguent'. See Commentary: '*OBS*: To Roydon', for Chapman's sources and his critique of excessive adornment in style.
10 *pervial*] transparent, clear. *OED*, adj., records instances by Chapman only.
11–12 *and to make ... give camels horns*] On the meanings and sources of these proverbs, see Commentary: '*OBS*: To Roydon'.
13 *That*] Understood as demonstrative here, and thus the comma after it in Q*OB* has been suppressed.
13–20 *enargia ... spirit and life*] Chapman's idea of '*enargia*', or perspicuity, which he glosses as 'clearness of representation', draws on the classical rhetorical notions of *enargeia* and *energeia*. On this notion in relation to Renaissance theories of vividness and difficulty in painting, see Introduction, pp. 20–29.
15–17 *it serves not ... whom it represents*] 'drawing the figure of a face just to make known whom it represents is not sufficient for a skilful painter's aim.' See *OED*, *turn*, n., P.1.b.i: 'to serve a person's turn'.

and heightening; which, though ignorants will esteem spiced and too curious, yet such as have the judicial perspective will see it hath motion, spirit and life.

There is no confection made to last, but it is admitted more cost and skill than presently-to-be-used simples; and, in my opinion, that which, being with a little endeavour searched, adds a kind of majesty to poesy is better than that which every cobbler may sing to his patch.

Obscurity, in affection of words and indigested conceits, is pedantical and childish; but where it shroudeth itself in the heart of his subject, uttered with fitness of figure and expressive epithets, with that darkness will I still labour to be shadowed: rich minerals are digged out of the bowels of the earth, not found in the superficies and dust of it; charms made of unlearned characters are not consecrate by the Muses, which are divine artists, but by Evippe's daughters, that challenged them with mere nature, whose breasts I doubt not had been well worthy commendation if their comparison had not turned them into pies.

Thus (not affecting glory for mine own sleight labours, but desirous others should be more worthily glorious, nor professing sacred poesy in any degree), I thought good to submit to your apt judgement, acquainted long since with the true habit of poesy, and now since your labouring wits endeavour heaven-high thoughts of nature, you have actual means to sound the philosophical conceits that my new pen so

---

21–22 *There is no confection ... presently-to-be-used simples*] 'No medical preparation is made to last, unless it is put in it more cost and more art than ready-made simple ingredients.' As Loughlin and others note, Chapman's pharmaceutical conceit differentiates between artful and artless poetry (*The Broadview Anthology of Sixteenth-Century Poetry and Prose*, ed. by Marie H. Loughlin, Sandra Bell, and Patricia Brace (Broadview, 2012), p. 1165, n. 1). See *OED*, *confection*, n., †5. b: 'a medicinal preparation compounded of various drugs'; and *simple*, n. 17.a: 'of a medicinal preparation; consisting of or containing a single active ingredient'. Hyphenation of 'presently-to-be-used' is editorial.

22–24 *and, in my opinion ... to his patch*] 'and, in my opinion, that which, being pursued with effort, adds some splendour to poetry is better than that which any shoe-mender may sing while patching a pair of shoes.' This reading depends on editorial repunctuation of this sentence, particularly the suppression of a semicolon after 'poesy'.

30 *affection*] affectation, unnecessary artificiality.

33 *digged*] dug.

34–35 *charms made of unlearned characters*] singing made of intuitively known notes, thus not by art; see *OED*, *charm*, n.², †2. a, applied to birds specifically, as the 'pies' at the end of this paragraph.

35 *consecrate*] On its use as past participle, i.e. consecrated, see *OED*, adj., 1. a.

36–38 *Evippe's daughters ... pies*] On the transformation of Evippe's daughters after their contention with the Muses, see Commentary: '*OBS*: To Roydon'.

37 *breasts*] singing voices (*OED*, 5. †c).

38 *comparison*] rivalry, contention (*OED*, n., †7), i.e. in comparing themselves to the Muses.

39 *sleight*] subtle, skilful; with a pun on 'slight' (i.e. trifling), of which 'sleight' is also a historical spelling.

44 *my new pen*] by metonymy, my new poem (*OED*, *pen*, n.³, 1. b).

seriously courteth. I know that empty and dark spirits will complain of 45
palpable night; but those that beforehand have a radiant and light-
bearing intellect will say they can pass through Corinna's garden without
the help of a lantern.

Your own most worthily and sincerely affected,

George Chapman.

Richard Stapleton to the Author A3ʳ

Phoebus hath giv'n thee both his bow and Muse:
    With one thou slay'st the artisans of thunder,
    And to thy loose dost such a sound infuse
    That gathered storms therewith are blown in sunder;
The other decks her with her golden wings, 5
    Spread beyond measure in thy ample verse,
    Where she (as in her bowers of laurel) sings
    Sweet philosophic strains that fiends might pierce.
The soul of brightness in thy darkness shines
    Most new and clear, unstained with foreign graces; 10
    And when aspiring sprites shall reach thy lines,
    They will not hear our treble-termèd basses.
With boldness then thy able poems use —
Phoebus hath giv'n thee both his bow and Muse.

---

46 *palpable night*] a darkness so intense that seems almost tangible (see *OED*, *palpable*, adj., 2, specifically applied to night and darkness).
Stapleton
2 *artisans of thunder*] bombastic poets.
3 *loose*] See *OED*, n., 1: '*Archery*. The act of discharging an arrow'. See also Commentary: '*OBS*: Stapleton'.
4 *in sunder*] into separate parts, into pieces (see *OED*, *in sunder*, adv., 2). See also 'Cynthiam', 245.
5 *her*] herself.
6 *ample*] copious, in the rhetorical sense (*OED*, adj., 3); also, far-reaching (adj., 1, and 2. b).
8 *strains*] verse sequences or passages (*OED*, n.², 13. a and 13. b).
8 *fiends*] enemies, rivals (*OED*, n., in the etymological sense of OE *féond*, i.e. hating one).
10 *foreign*] not one's own (*OED*, adj., †3. a), and thus superfluous, unnecessary.
11 *when aspiring sprites shall reach thy lines*] i.e. when ambitious minds shall soar high in order to read and understand your poetry. 'Aspiring' refers both to intellectual ambition and to upward movement (see *OED*, adj., 1, 2. a, and 2. b), the latter suggesting the sublime quality of Chapman's poetry; 'sprites' is the modern-spelling form of Q*OB*'s 'sprightes'. See *OED*, *sprite*, n., 1. †a: meaning mind, or soul.
12 *our treble-termèd basses*] i.e. our humble commendatory poems. The metaphor imagines these five commendatory sonnets as 'basses', or bass voices that accompany Chapman's verses, which act as the main solo voice. These accompanying voices will not be noticed by those 'aspiring' minds, captivated by Chapman's poem only. This explains the obscure compound 'treble-termèd', that is, the voices that are suffocated, or terminated, by Chapman's 'treble' voice. See *OED*, *term*, v., 1: to terminate.

Thomas Williams, of the Inner Temple

Issue of Semele, that will embrace
    With fleshly arms the three-winged withe of thunder:
    Let her sad ruin such proud thoughts abase,
    And view aloof this verse in silent wonder;
If nearer your unhallowed eyes will pierce,   5
    Then (with the satyr) kiss this sacred fire
    To scorch your lips, that, dearly taught thereby,
    Your only souls fit objects may aspire.
But you, high spirits, in this cloud of gold
    Enjoy (like Jove) this bright Saturnian Muse: 10
    Your eyes can well the dazzling beams behold
    This Pythian light'ner freshly doth effuse
To daunt the baseness of that bastard train
Whose twice-born judgements formless still remain.

Another [by Thomas Williams]   A3ᵛ

Ungrateful farmers of the Muses' land
    That (wanting thrift and judgement to employ it)
    Let it manureless and unfencèd stand
    Till barbarous cattle enter and destroy it:
Now the true heir is happily found out   5
    Who (framing it t'enrich posterities)

Williams 1
1 *that*] The antecedent is 'Semele', not her 'Issue', or offspring. On the use of this myth, see Commentary: '*OBS*: Williams 1'.
2 *withe*] *OED*, n., 1. a: 'A band, tie, or shackle consisting of a tough flexible twig or branch, or of several twisted together'. This refers to Jupiter's 'three-winged' thunderbolt. On the emendation of Q₀ʙ's 'wife', see Commentary: '*OBS*: Williams 1'.
3 *abase*] humble, humiliate.
4 *aloof*] from afar (*OED*, adv., 2. a), in contrast with 'nearer' in the next line.
4 *in silent wonder*] awestruck by the sublime character of Chapman's poetry.
7–8 *that, dearly ... may aspire*] i.e. if the satyr and the reader are carefully instructed, the former on the use of fire and the latter on the right way of reading these poems, then their peerless souls will soar to the beneficial effects of the fire and the poems. See *OED*, *dearly*, adv., †3. b: carefully; *only*, adj., 3. a: unique; and *aspire*, v., †8: soar to, reach, attain (transitive).
12 *This Pythian light'ner*] i.e. the poem. See Commentary, '*OBS*: Williams 1'.
12 *effuse*] shed, pour forth (light) — *OED*, v., 2.
13 *bastard train*] here a metaphor for bad readers, in opposition to the 'high spirits' of line 9; 'bastard' relates to Bacchus, indirectly alluded to in the next line, who was Jupiter's illegitimate 'issue of Semele'. See Commentary: '*OBS*: Williams 1'.
Williams 2
2 *thrift and judgement*] labour (see *OED*, *thrift*, n., †1. b) and discernment, two key qualities in Chapman's poetics.
6 *t'enrich posterities*] to secure future harvests, and, metaphorically, to grant the long-lasting survival of the poem.

Walls it with spright-filed darkness round about,
  Graffs, plants and sows, and makes it Paradise;
To which without the Parcae's golden bough
  None can aspire, but stick in error's hell —   10
A garland to engird a monarch's brow.
  Then take some pains to joy so rich a jewel:
Most prize is grasped in labour's hardest hand,
And idle souls can nothing rich command.

John Davies, of the Middle Temple

Only that eye which for true love doth weep,
  Only that heart which tender Love doth pierce,
  May read and understand this sacred verse,
  For other wits too mystical and deep.
Between these hallowed leaves Cupid doth keep   5
  The golden lesson of his second artist,
  For love till now hath still a master missed
  Since Ovid's eyes were closed with iron sleep.
But now his waking soul in Chapman lives,
  Which shows so well the passions of his soul,   10
  And yet this Muse more cause of wonder gives,
  And doth more prophet-like love's art enrol:
For Ovid's soul, now grown more old and wise,
Pours forth itself in deeper mysteries.

---

7 *Walls it with spright-filed darkness round about*] i.e. encloses the Muse's land with darkness, as if with an arrow fence. On this obscure line, see Commentary: '*OBS*: Williams 2'.
8 *Graffs*] grafts; *OED* lists a separate entry for *graff*, an archaic form of *graft*, v.: 'to insert a scion of a tree into a different stock'.
9 *Parcae's golden bough*] On the modernization/emendation of Q*OB*'s 'bow' to 'bough', and on this obscure allusion, see Commentary: '*OBS*: Williams 2'.
10 *aspire*] soar to, reach, attain (transitive, as in *OED*, v., †8).
12 *joy*] enjoy (*OED*, v., 4. a, archaic).
14 *command*] have at their disposal (*OED*, v., 11).
Davies 1
1–2 *true love ... tender Love*] Although neither is capitalized in Q*OB*, the second 'Love' clearly names Cupid, who 'doth pierce' the 'heart' with his darts.
4 *mystical and deep*] Both adjectives insist on the allegorical, obscure and philosophical qualities of Chapman's poetry.
8 *iron sleep*] death (*OED*, iron, adj., 7).
11 *this Muse*] metonymically, inspiration, the inspired poem, or the poet (*OED*, n., 1, records all these figurative senses).
12 *And doth more prophet-like love's art enrol*] Chapman's Muse has written a more profound *Art of Love* than Ovid's. See *OED*, enrol, v., 1: write, record, register (see also the multiple writing senses of the verb, *OED*, I).

Another [by John Davies]

Since Ovid (Love's first gentle master) died,
   He hath a most notorious truant been,
   And hath not once in thrice five ages seen
   That same sweet Muse that was his first sweet guide.
But since Apollo, who was gratified   5
   Once with a kiss, hunting on Cynthus green,
   By Love's fair mother, tender Beauty's Queen,
   This favour unto her hath not envied —
That into whom she will she may infuse,
   For the instruction of her tender son,   10
   The gentle Ovid's easy, supple Muse,
   Which unto thee (sweet Chapman) she hath done —
She makes (in thee) the spirit of Ovid move,
And calls thee second master of her Love.

Futurum invisibile.

Davies 2
2 *He*] Cupid, or Love, as he is called in line 1.
3 *thrice five ages*] three times five centuries, or one thousand and five hundred years, approximately the time span between Ovid's death in 17 AD and Chapman's publication of *OBS* (1595).
7 *Love's fair mother, tender Beauty's Queen*] Venus is both mother of Cupid and Beauty's Queen, a title conferred on her after Paris appointed her the fairest of the Olympian goddesses, surpassing Juno and Minerva.
8 *This favour unto her hath not envied*] i.e. Apollo has not refused to grant this favour unto Venus; see *OED*, envy, v., †3. a: 'refuse to give (a thing) *to* (a person)'. The favour is described in the next quatrain.
9 *infuse*] pour in, instil: 'Ovid's easy, supple Muse' is poured into the vessel of Chapman's body. Compare 'Ovid's soul […] | Pours forth itself' in the last couplet of the previous sonnet.
Futurum invisibile] 'The future is inscrutable'. See Commentary: '*OBS*: Davies 2'.

OVID'S BANQUET OF SENSE

The Argument

OVID, newly enamoured of Julia (daughter to Octavius Augustus Caesar, after by him called Corinna), secretly conveyed himself into a garden of the Emperor's court, in an arbour whereof Corinna was bathing, playing upon her lute and singing; which Ovid overhearing, was exceedingly pleased with the sweetness of her voice, and to himself uttered the comfort he conceived in his sense of hearing. *AUDITUS*

Then, the odours she used in her bath breathing a rich savour, he expresseth the joy he felt in his sense of smelling. *OLFACTUS*

Thus, growing more deeply enamoured, in great contentation with himself, he ventures to see her in the pride of her nakedness; which doing by stealth, he discovered the comfort he conceived in seeing, and the glory of her beauty. *VISUS*

Not yet satisfied, he useth all his art to make known his being there without her offence, or (being necessarily offended) to appease her; which done, he entreats a kiss to serve for satisfaction of his taste, which he obtains. *GUSTUS*

Then proceeds he to entreaty for the fifth sense, and there is interrupted. *TACTUS*

1–4 *Ovid ... Julia ... Octavius Augustus Caesar ... Corinna ... Emperor's court*] See Commentary: '*OBS*: Argument', on Chapman's design of a 'historical' setting for the poem.
7 *comfort*] pleasure (*OED*, v., †3); also, relief (*OED*, v., †4 and 5) from the pangs of desire.
10–12 *in great contentation with himself ... by stealth*] i.e. experiencing self-satisfaction, without revealing his presence to her. Ovid's experience of Corinna's beauty through the senses of hearing, smell and sight occurs without Corinna's awareness of his presence.
11–12 *in the pride of her nakedness*] in the full splendour of her naked body's beauty (see *OED*, pride, n., †7. a).
18 *entreaty for the fifth sense*] negotiation aiming at Corinna agreeing to satisfy Ovid's sense of touch.

1   THE EARTH from heav'nly light conceivèd heat,   *Narratio*
       Which mixèd all her moist parts with her dry,
   When with right beams the sun her bosom beat
   And with fit food her plants did nutrify;
       They (which to earth as to their mother cling   5
   In forkèd roots), now sprinkled plenteously
       With her warm breath, did hasten to the spring,
   Gather their proper forces, and extrude
   All power but that with which they stood indued.

2   Then did Cyrrhus[1] fill his eyes with fire, $B1^v$
   Whose ardour curled the foreheads of the trees
   And made his green-love burn in his desire,
   When Youth and Ease (collectors of Love's fees)
       Enticed Corinna to a silver spring   5
   Enchasing a round bower, which with it sees[2]
       (As with a diamant doth an amelled ring);
   Into which eye most pitifully stood
   Niobe, shedding tears that were her blood.

M1. Cyrrhus is a surname of the Sun, from a town called Cyrrha, where he was honoured.
M2. By prosopopoeia, he makes the fountain the eye of the round arbour, as a diamant seems to be the eye of a ring; and therefore says the arbour sees with the fountain.
   [prosopopoeia: personification; see 'Cynthiam', Gloss 25.]

1 'In being impregnated by the sunlight, the earth conceived heat, which mixed her moist and dry parts when the noon's direct sunrays beat on her womb, thus nourishing her plants with necessary food. The plants (which adhered to earth with their forked roots as a child embraces its mother), now irrigated all over by the earth's heated breath, ran to the spring, where they gathered force from the water's moisture, thrusting forth all their vital energy except that with which they were supplied in order to stand firm on the earth.'
1. 4 *nutrify*] nourish.
1. 8–9 *extrude | All power*] expel all vital energy; i.e. shoot or sprout (*OED, extrude*, v., 1. a: thrust forth).
1. 9 *indued*] supplied (*OED, indue*, v., †8. c).
2 'Then the sun filled his eyes with fire, whose burning passion curled the trees with blooms and made them burn with his love for their leaves, when Corinna was impelled by youth and freedom to a silver spring adorning a round bower with which the bower can see, as if the spring were the bower's eye (and as a diamond is encrusted in an enamelled ring), inside which [a statue of] Niobe stood most pitifully, shedding tears as if these were her own blood.'
2. 4 *Youth and Ease (collectors of Love's fees)*] 'Youth', 'Ease' and 'Love' have been capitalized, despite QOB's use of lower case, as the latter designates Cupid, a king for whom the other two personified agents act as tax collectors from those who serve their master. Thus, as Corinna's own qualities, they 'entice' her to the spring; they will later collect 'Love's fees' from the enamoured Ovid.
2. 6 *Enchasing*] setting, as a jewel, in gold or metal (*OED, enchase*, v.², 1).
2. 7 *diamant*] diamond. The obsolete spelling suggests a different pronunciation from that of its present-day form.
2. 7 *amelled*] covered with enamel (*OED*, † *amelled*, adj., gives this example).
2. 9. *Niobe*] Niobe mocked Latona for having only two children, Apollo and Diana, who killed Niobe's seven sons and seven daughters. She was later metamorphosed into a

3   Stone Niobe, whose statue to this fountain
    In great Augustus Caesar's grace was brought
    From Sipylus, the steep Mygdonian mountain
    (That statue 'tis), still weeps for former thought
        Into this spring, Corinna's bathing place: 5
    So cunningly to optic reason wrought
        That, afar off, it shewed a woman's face,
    Heavy and weeping; but, more nearly viewed,
    Nor weeping, heavy, nor a woman shewed.

4   In summer only wrought her ecstasy;
    And, that her story might be still observed,
    Octavius caused, in curious imagery,
    Her fourteen children should at large be carved,
        Their fourteen breasts with fourteen arrows gored,   5
    And set by her that, for her seed so starved,
        To a stone sepulchre herself deplored;
    In ivory were they cut, and on each breast
    In golden elements their names impressed.

5   Her sons were Sipylus, Agenor, Phaedimus,
    Ismenus, Argus, and Damasicthen,
    The seventh, called like his grandsire, Tantalus;
    Her daughters were the fair Astiochen,
        Chloris, Naera, and Pelopie,   5
    Phaeta, proud Phthia, and Eugigen:
        All these, apposed to violent Niobe,

---

stone, from which tears kept flowing, and transported to Mount Sipylus by a wind. On Niobe and her fouteen children, listed in stanza 5, see Commentary: 'Banquet', 2. 8–9 and stanzas 3–5. On the myth's importance to Chapman's poetics, see Introduction, pp. 24–28.

3. 4 *(That statue 'tis)*] The parenthetical value of this clause justifies the editorial addition of brackets and the suppression of Q*OB*'s colon after 'mountain'. Even if the parenthetical clause aims to clarify that the 'stone Niobe' in the garden is the statue and not the authentic, metamorphosed Niobe, yet the sentence creates some vacillation about its real identity. This ambivalence adds more confusion to the double image of the anamorphic statue (see Commentary: 'Banquet', 6–9).

3. 6 *to optic reason*] The phrase translates Conti's 'optica ratione' (ablative). See Commentary: 'Banquet', 3.

3. 7, 9 *shewed*] showed. The archaic spelling is preferred for reasons of repetition and rhyme.

4. 2 *observed*] commemorated through private worship or public ritual, treated with worship (*OED*, v., †4).

4. 6 *for her seed so starved*] consumed by grief for the death of her offspring.

4. 7 *To a stone sepulchre herself deplored*] shed water upon a tomb of stone; metamorphosed herself into a tomb of stone by too much weeping (see *OED*, deplore, v.).

4. 8 *ivory*] as elsewhere, pronounced disyllabically: ['aɪvri].

4. 9 *In golden elements ... impressed*] stamped in golden letters (*OED*, element, n., 14. a).

5. 7 *apposed*] placed beside.

5. 7 *violent*] extreme in (her) passion.

  Had looks so deadly sad, so lively done
  As if death lived in their confusion.

6 Behind their mother, two pyramides
  Of freckled marble through the arbour viewed,
  On whose sharp brows Sol and Titanides
  In purple and transparent glass were hewed,
   Through which the sunbeams, on the statues staying, 5
  Made their pale bosoms seem with blood imbrued,
   Those two stern planets' rigours still bewraying;
  To these dead forms came living beauty's essence,
  Able to make them startle with her presence.

7 In a loose robe of tinsel forth she came,
  Nothing but it betwixt her nakedness
  And envious light. The downward-burning flame
  Of her rich hair did threaten new access
   Of vent'rous Phaëton to scorch the fields. 5
  And thus to bathing came our poet's goddess,
   Her handmaids bearing all things pleasure yields
  To such a service: odours most delighted,
  And purest linen which her looks had whited.

---

5. 9 *confusion*] ruin, overthrow, perdition (*OED*, n., 1. a); pronounced tetrasyllabically.
6 'Behind the statue of Niobe, two pyramids of speckled marble kept their watch through the arbour, on whose pointed tops two figures of the Sun and the Moon, carved on transparent glass, had been placed (in the manner of eyes), through which the sunbeams entered and, stopping on the statues of Niobe's children, made their pale bosoms look as if they were drenched with blood, displaying the cruelty of those two stern planets (since the Sun and the Moon represent the children's murderers, Apollo and Diana); the quintessence of living beauty (Corinna) came near these dead forms, and her presence was able to make them shudder in surprise.'
6. 1 *pyramides*] A common early modern form of *pyramid* in the singular and plural (here obviously the latter), retained for reasons of rhyme.
6. 3 *Sol and Titanides*] the sun and moon, representing Apollo and Diana, children of the Titaness Leto, or Latona. 'Titanides' specifies this bond of kinship for Diana only.
6. 4 *hewed*] sculpted, carved.
6. 6 *imbrued*] drenched, soaked.
6. 9 *startle*] 'undergo a sudden involuntary movement of the body' (*OED*, v., 3), as a result of an external stimulus — here, Corinna's beauty.
7. 1 *tinsel*] thin gauze embroidered with golden thread, baudekin (*OED*, n.³, †2. a).
7. 3 *downward-burning flame*] Through oxymoron, as flames always expand upwards, the poet signifies the extraordinary beauty of Corinna's red hair (described as 'glowing' in 69. 8).
7. 5 *vent'rous*] adventurous; also, imprudent: both are qualities of Phaeton (see Commentary: 'Banquet', 6).
7. 8 *delighted*] delightful. *OED*, adj., †2, registers this use as the first in the language.
7. 9 *purest linen which her looks had whited*] the light emanating from Corinna's eyes had whitened the fresh towels and robes carried by the handmaids.

8   Then cast she off her robe, and stood upright:
    As lightning breaks out of a labouring cloud,
    Or as the morning heav'n casts off the night,
    Or as that heav'n cast off itself and showed
        Heav'n's upper light, to which the brightest day   5
    Is but a black and melancholy shroud,
        Or as when Venus strived for sovereign sway
    Of charmful beauty in young Troy's desire,
    So stood Corinna, vanishing her tire.

9   A soft enflowered bank embraced the fount,
    Of Chloris' ensigns an abstracted field,
    Where grew melanthy, great in bees' account,
    Amaracus, that precious balm doth yield,
        Enamelled pansies, used at nuptials still,   5
    Diana's arrow, Cupid's crimson shield,
        Ope-morn, nightshade, and Venus' navill,
    Solemn violets, hanging head as shamed,
    And verdant calamint, for odour famed.

10 Sacred nepenthe, purgative of care,
    And sovereign rumex, that doth rancour kill,
    Sya and hyacinth, that furies wear,
    White and red jasmines, merry, meliphill,
        Fair crown imperial, emperor of flowers,   5
    Immortal amaranth, white aphrodill,
        And cup-like twillpants, strewed in Bacchus' bowers:

---

8. 2 *labouring*] obscuring; see *OED*, adj., 2. c, often in reference to the sun and the moon when causing an eclipse.
8. 7–8 *as when Venus … young Troy's desire*] Venus competed with Juno and Miverva to be appointed the fairest of goddesses by Paris. Paris's judgement and choice of Venus led to the Trojan War. On the importance of this stanza, see Introduction, pp. 26–28, and Commentary: 'Banquet', 7–8).
8. 7 *sway*] sweeping motion (*OED*, n., 2); also, controlling influence, dominion (*OED*, n., 5).
8. 8 *charmful*] with an ability to enchant or bewitch (*OED*, adj., where the first example is from 1656).
8. 9 *vanishing her tire*] causing her robe to disappear (see *OED*, *vanish*, v., 4, transitive use; and *tire*, n.¹, 2); but also (if in its unusual intransitive sense), while her robe vanished.
9. 2 *Of Chloris' ensigns an abstracted field*] a heraldic surface (i.e. of a shield or escutcheon) that comprises all Chloris's badges, or emblems (of plants and flowers, as Chloris is the goddess of gardens). See *OED*, *abstracted*, adj., †4: 'epitomized'; and *field*, n., 17. a. On Chloris, and on the catalogue of plants and flowers in this and the next stanza, see Commentary: 'Banquet', 9–10.
10. 2 *rancour*] rancidity or putrefaction (*OED*, n., †2), also with a suggestion of reeking odour.
10. 7 *strewed*] strewn, scattered.

These cling about this nature's naked gem,
To taste her sweets, as bees do swarm on them.

11 And now she used the fount where Niobe,
Tombed in herself, poured her lost soul in tears
Upon the bosom of this Roman Phoebe;
Who, bathed and odoured, her bright limbs she rears,
    And drying her on that disparent round,   5
Her lute she takes t'enamour heav'nly ears
    And try if, with her voice's vital sound,
She could warm life, through those cold statues spread
And cheer the dame that wept when she was dead.

12 And thus she sung, all naked as she sat,
Laying the happy lute upon her thigh,
Not thinking any near to wonder at
The bliss of her sweet breast's divinity:

THE SONG OF CORINNA
'Tis better to contemn than love,   5
And to be fair than wise,
For souls are ruled by eyes,
And Jove's bird seized by Cypris' dove.
It is our grace and sport to see
Our beauty's sorcery,   10
That makes (like destiny)

---

11 'And then she used the fount where Niobe, buried in her own stone statue, poured her confused soul in the form of tears upon Corinna, a new Diana, who, once bathed and perfumed, withdrew her bright limbs and, drying herself upon the variously adorned arbour, took her lute in order to enamour the ears of heaven and to try if, with the life-giving sound of her voice, she could sprinkle warm life on those cold statues (of Niobe's children), and cheer the still-weeping dead lady (Niobe).'

11. 4 *rears*] lifts (*OED*, v., 7. a).

11. 5 *her*] herself.

11. 5 *disparent*] exhibiting various shapes and colours. Chapman's neologism has no further life beyond his works. See 'Cynthiam', 396.

11. 5 *round*] in reference to the circular shape of the arbour.

12. 2 *happy lute*] 'happy' because of its melody, but also because of its enjoyment of the privilege of touching Corinna's naked thigh.

12. 4 *The bliss of her sweet breast's divinity*] If interpreted visually, the line refers to Corinna's naked breasts; if interpreted aurally, the 'bliss' concerns her voice, as in '*OBS*: To Roydon', line 37, where 'breasts' means singing voices. To maintain the ambiguity, QOB's 'brests' has been interpreted as genitive singular.

12. 8 *Jove's bird seized by Cypris' dove*] Jove's bird is the eagle, while the dove belongs to the Cyprus-born Venus. This is an image of the world upside down, as the stronger bird, who carried Ganymede to heaven (a myth that embodies the ascent of the soul in 'Cynthiam', 456–61), is led by the weaker, lustful dove.

12. 10 *Our beauty's sorcery*] our deceitful, bewitching beauty. This is the antecedent of the two relative clauses introduced by 'That' (11, 13).

Men follow us the more we flee;
That sets wise glosses on the fool,
And turns her cheeks to books,
Where wisdom sees in looks   15
Derision, laughing at his school,
   Who (loving) proves profaneness holy,
   Nature our fate, our wisdom folly.

13   While this was singing, Ovid, young in love   B3ʳ
     With her perfections, never proving yet
     How merciful a mistress she would prove,
     Boldly embraced the power he could not let,
        And, like a fiery exhalation,   5
     Followed the sun he wished might never set,
        Trusting herein his constellation
     Ruled by love's beams, which Julia's eyes erected,
     Whose beauty was the star his life directed.

14   And having drenched his ankles in those seas,
     He needs would swim, and cared not if he drowned:
     Love's feet are in his eyes, for if he please
     The depth of beauty's gulfy flood to sound,
        He goes upon his eyes, and up to them   5
     At the first step he is. No shader ground
        Could Ovid find, but in love's holy stream

---

12. 13–18 *That sets ... wisdom folly*] 'Beauty's sorcery leads poets to make fools of their ladies by adorning them with witty poetic glosses, thus transforming a lady's cheeks into full books of praise, while on the contrary (true) wisdom sees that the lady's looks are actually of derision, laughing at the school of love poets, who (by loving) prove a number of contraries: 1) that the lady's profaneness, or vulgarity, becomes holy in the lover/poet's eyes; 2) that the lady's nature (her beauty, her being 'fair', as expressed in the second line of the song), dooms her to being an object of foolish poetic idealization; and yet 3) that in the very fact of being made a fool of by the poet's idealization lies the source of her wisdom, which leads her to scorn him.'
13. 2 *never proving yet*] having not yet experienced (see *OED, prove*, v., 2).
13. 4 *Boldly embraced ... let*] daringly accepted the power of the passion that he was unable to restrain (see *OED, let*, v.², †2. a).
13. 5–9 *like a fiery exhalation ... his life directed*] The astronomical/astrological metaphor conceives of Ovid's love as a 'constellation', or loving disposition of the mind (*OED, constellation*, n., †1. b) influenced by a star or sun, i.e. the beauty of Corinna/Julia's eyes, which directs it upwards ('erected', with an inevitable sexual pun) like an incandescent body or meteor (*OED, exhalation*, n., 3).
14. 6 *shader*] safer? Hudston (p. 406, 14. 6, note), Braden, and Loughlin and others gloss this word as 'shadier', while Shepherd actually emends to 'shadier'. However, this leaves a comparative term missing; besides, the meaning of 'shadier' is uncertain. 'Shader' could derive from the verb *shade* (*OED*, v., 2. †d), in which case it would mean 'protecting' or 'sheltering': thus, Ovid's eyes (in which 'Love's feet' are found) are covered by the sea waters but cannot reach the bottom.

Was past his eyes; and now did wet his ears,
For his high sovereign's silver voice he hears.

15 Whereat his wit assumèd fiery wings,   *Auditus*
Soaring above the temper of his soul,
And he the purifying rapture sings
Of his ear's sense, takes full the Thespian bowl
   And it carouseth to his mistress' health,   5
Whose sprightful verdure did dull flesh control;
   And his conceit he crowneth with the wealth
Of all the Muses in his pleasèd senses,
When with the ear's delight he thus commences:

16 'Now, Muses, come, repair your broken wings
(Plucked and profaned by rustic Ignorance)
With feathers of these notes my mistress sings,
And let quick verse her drooping head advance
   From dungeons of contempt to smite the stars;   5
In Julia's tunes, led forth by furious trance,
   A thousand Muses come to bid you wars;
Dive to your spring, and hide you from the stroke:
All poets' furies will her tunes invoke.

17 'Never was any sense so set on fire   *B3ᵛ*
With an immortal ardour as mine ear's:
Her fingers to the strings doth speech inspire

---

14. 9 *silver*] soft-toned, sweet, melodious (*OED*, adj., 6. a).
15. 6 *Whose sprightful verdure did dull flesh control*] Corinna's lively youth aroused even the most insensitive flesh.
15. 7–9 *And his conceit ... he thus commences*] 'And he adorns his thoughts (about the pleasures of his senses) with the wealth of all the Muses when he thus begins by singing the delights of the sense of hearing.' This sentence anticipates Ovid's verses on the five senses: 'crown' contains the idea of the laureated poet, but also a sense of completion of the full banquet of the senses (*OED*, crown, v., 3 and 7).
16. 3 *With feathers of these notes my mistress sings*] with feathers of these notes *which* my mistress sings.
16. 4–5 *And let quick verse ... smite the stars*] 'Let the swift verse of Corinna's song make her reclining head ascend from the dungeons of contempt to the heavens, where it will smite the stars.' See *OED*, quick, adj., †12, i.e. lively, in reference to speech; here it also means inspired, passionate, as caused by 'furious trance' (16. 6).
16. 7 *A thousand Muses*] On the meaning of this multiplication of the Muses, see Commentary: 'Banquet', 16.
16. 7 *bid you wars*] offer battle to the Muses, challenge them to war (*OED*, bid, v., 2. a).
16. 8 *spring*] either Aganippe or Hippocrene, the two springs at Mount Helicon that are sacred to the Muses.
17 'Never was any sense thus set on fire with an immortal ardour as is my sense of hearing (my ear's sense): Corinna's fingers inspire melody ("speech") and harmony ("numbered laughter") to the lute's strings, which provide the instrumental accompaniment to her sweet voice, whose (i.e. her voice's) perceptible forms ("species") raise my bodily spirits

And numbered laughter, that the descant bears
    To her sweet voice, whose species through my sense   5
My spirits to their highest function rears;
    To which, impressed with ceaseless confluence,
It useth them as proper to her power,
Marries my soul, and makes itself her dower.

18 'Methinks her tunes fly gilt, like Attic bees
To my ears' hives, with honey tried to air.
My brain is but the comb, the wax, the lees;
My soul the drone, that lives by their affair.
    O so it sweets, refines and ravisheth!   5
And with what sport they sting in their repair!
    Rise then in swarms and sting me thus to death,
Or turn me into swound; possess me whole,
Soul to my life, and essence to my soul.'

---

through my sense organ up to the mind (the spirits' "highest function"), to which it (i.e. her voice's "species"), impregnated with the uninterrupted convergence (of her voice and the instrument's sound), uses them ("my spirits") as the proper vehicle for transmitting her voice's power, thus marrying my soul and making it ("her species") her voice's dowry.'

17. 4 *numbered laughter*] metaphorically, the melody and rhythm of Corinna's song; 'numbered' must be understood in the musical and prosodic senses of *OED*, *number*, n., †14.

17. 4 *descant*] This noun had several musical senses in the sixteenth century. Here it means the instrumental accompaniment that the lute 'bears' to Corinna's singing.

17. 5, 6 *species, spirits, highest function*] The sensible 'species' is the emanation from a material object that is perceived by the senses, which carry these impressions through the bodily fluids, or 'spirits', to the intellect, here called the 'highest function'. See Commentary: 'Banquet', 17.

17. 9 *dower*] dowry.

18 'It seems to me that her tunes, gilt with honey that is distilled into air, fly like Attic bees to my ears' hive: my brain is the honeycomb, the wax and the dregs (i.e. the material centre of sense perception); my soul is the drone, which receives the highest benefit from the bees' affair. O how the bees' affair (the song) sweetens, refines and ravishes the drone (my soul)! And with what pleasure the bees (the tunes) sting as they gather together! Rise then in swarms, O tunes, and sting me thus to death, or turn me into sound; possess my whole self, since you are my vital principle.'

18. 2 *tried*] extracted, in two senses here: for its primary meaning, see *OED*, *try*, v., 4: 'to extract (wax) from a honey-comb'; yet the alchemical sense of refining or distilling matter into a purer substance fits here too (*OED*, v., †3).

18. 5 *sweets*] sweetens (*OED*, v., 1. a); also, delights (*OED*, v., 2).

18. 6 *repair*] gathering, assembling, coming together (*OED*, n., †1. a).

18. 8 *swound*] swoon or fainting-fit; also, sound. The spelling allows for the combination of both senses: the buzzing sound of bees into which Ovid aspires to be metamorphosed in his ecstasy, and the fainting-fit that is the result of that ecstasy. The spelling 'swound', which *OED* registers as an archaic variant of 'swoon', was also a possible spelling of 'sound' in the late sixteenth century, as also testified by *OED*.

19   'Say, gentle air, O does it not thee good
     Thus to be smit with her correcting voice?
     Why dance ye not, ye daughters of the wood?
     Wither forever, if not now rejoice.
        Rise, stones, and build a city with her notes;   5
     And notes, infuse with your most Cynthian noise
        To all the trees, sweet flowers, and crystal floats
     That crown and make this cheerful garden quick,
     Virtue, that every touch may make such music.

20   'O that, as man is called a little world,
     The world might shrink into a little man,
     To hear the notes about this garden hurled,
     That skill, dispersed in tunes so Orphean,
        Might not be lost in smiting stocks and trees   5
     That have no ears, but, grown as it began,
        Spread their renowns as far as Phoebus sees
     Through earth's dull veins, that she like heav'n might move
     In ceaseless music, and be filled with love.

21   'In precious incense of her holy breath,   B4ʳ
     My love doth offer hecatombs of notes
     To all the gods, who now despise the death
     Of oxen, heifers, wethers, swine and goats.
        A sonnet, in her breathing sacrificed,   5

---

19. 2 *smit*] smitten.
19. 2 *correcting*] applied to Corinna's voice, having a fine-tuning or harmonizing effect.
19. 3 *daughters of the wood*] dryads, or wood nymphs.
19. 6–9 *And notes ... such music*] 'And notes, infuse virtue to all the trees, sweet flowers and crystal waters which crown and give life to this cheerful garden with your most Cynthian noise, so that every touch of them may produce such music.'
19. 6 *Cynthian*] pertaining to the goddess Cynthia, or the Moon; thus, chaste, and in line with the 'virtue' (19. 9) that the notes are asked to 'infuse' into the garden plants.
19. 7 *crystal floats*] gem-like flowers topping, or floating on the thick garden vegetation (*OED, float*, n., 6. a: 'a mass of weeds, ice, etc., floating on the surface of water').
19. 8 *quick*] animate, alive, yet also pregnant.
20 'O that, as man is called a little world, the world might shrink into a little man, so that it could hear the notes (of Corinna's song) cast around this garden, so that her art ("skill"), scattered in melodies that are worthy of those of Orpheus, might not be lost as they clash against tree trunks that have no ears, but, having grown since it (i.e. her art) originated in Corinna's song, it could spread their rumours as fast as the sun can pierce into the entrails of the earth, so that she (the earth, which is not a heavenly sphere) might be able to produce music while in motion like the celestial spheres, and thus be filled with heavenly harmony.'
20. 4 *tunes so Orphean*] Orpheus's song attracted the natural elements. On 'Orphean music' ('Noctem', 56), and Orpheus, 'the sweetest Muses' son' ('Noctem', 139), see Commentary: 'Noctem', 139–58.
21. 2 *hecatombs*] sacrifices of many animals; etymologically, of a hundred oxen: ἑκατόν hundred + βοῦς ox (*OED*, n.).
21. 4. *wethers*] castrated rams.

Delights them more than all beasts' bellowing throats,
    As much with heav'n as with my hearing prized.
And as gilt atoms in the sun appear,
So greet these sounds the gristles of mine ear,

22   'Whose pores do open wide to their regreet,
    And my implanted air that air embraceth,
Which they impress. I feel their nimble feet
Tread my ear's labyrinth; their sport amazeth —
    They keep such measure, play themselves and dance.   5
And now my soul in Cupid's furnace blazeth,
    Wrought into fury with their dalliance.
And as the fire the parchèd stubble burns,
So fades my flesh, and into spirit turns.

23   'Sweet tunes, brave issue, that from Julia come,
    Shook from her brain, armed like the Queen of Ire:
For, first conceivèd in her mental womb
And nourished with her soul's discursive fire,[3]
    They grew into the power of her thought;   5
She gave them downy plumes from her attire,
    And them to strong imagination brought;

M3. In this allusion to the birth of Pallas, he shows the conceit of her sonnet both for matter and note, and by metaphor he expresseth how she delivered her words and tunes, which was by commission of the order philosophers set down in apprehension of our knowledge and effection of our senses: for first, they affirm, the species of every object propagates itself by our spirits to our common sense; that delivers it to the imaginative part; that, to the cogitative; the cogitative, to the passive intellect; the passive intellect, to that which is called *dianoia*, or *discursus*; and that delivers it up to the mind, which order he observes for utterance.
    [*dianoia*, or *discursus*: logical reasoning, or rational thought, here opposed to the passive intellect. See Commentary: 'Banquet', 23-24 and M3 and M4.]

---

21. 9-22. 1 *gristles ... pores*] The 'gristles' are the ear's cartilage, while the 'pores' open to the passing of sound through the ducts or channels of the ear. See Commentary: 'Banquet', 21-22.
22. 1 *regreet*] greeting in return for a previous one (i.e. the ear's conducts or pores open in order to return the sounds' previous greeting). See *OED*, †n.
22. 2 *implanted air*] i.e. the air that is inside the ear (see Commentary: 'Banquet', 21-22).
22. 4 *ear's labyrinth*] the system of canals contained in the temporal bone and inner ear. See 'Noctem', 23, and note.
22. 6 *Cupid's furnace*] the heart (see Commentary: 'Banquet', 21-22).
23. 2 *Queen of Ire*] Pallas Athena, or Roman Minerva, goddess of knowledge. The title may refer to her status as goddess of war; or, contrarily, her capacity to control anger, as with Achilles (*Iliad*, 1. 207-08). In Chapman's translation: 'I come from heaven to see | Thy anger settled'.
23. 3 *her mental womb*] In its capacity to 'conceive' her song, Corinna's mind is identified with Jupiter's head, which acted as a womb in its delivery of Minerva.
23. 6 *downy plumes*] soft feathers, possibly the words that are the 'attire' of Corinna's thoughts. In fact, 'words' are one of the three components materializing Corinna's 'conceit', as explained below in 24. 8. See *OED*, *downy*, adj.¹, 3, from *down*, n.².

That, to her voice, wherein most movingly
She (blessing them with kisses) lets them fly;

24 'Who fly rejoicing, but (like noblest minds)
In giving others life themselves do die,
Not able to endure earth's rude unkinds,
Bred in my sovereign's parts too tenderly;
    O that, as intellects themselves transit
To each intelligible quality,[4]
    My life might pass into my love's conceit,
Thus to be formed in words, her tunes, and breath,
And with her kisses sing itself to death.

25 'This life were wholly sweet, this only bliss;
Thus would I live to die; thus sense were feasted;
My life that in my flesh a chaos is
Should to a golden world be thus digested;
    Thus should I rule her face's monarchy,
Whose looks in several empires are invested,
    Crowned now with smiles, and then with modesty;
Thus in her tunes' division I should reign;
For her conceit does all, in every vein.

M4. The philosopher saith *Intellectus in ipsa intellegibilia transit*, upon which is grounded this invention: that in the same manner his life might pass into his mistress' conceit, intending his intellectual life, or soul, which by this analogy should be *intellectus*, and her conceit, *intelligibilis*.
  [*Intellectus in ipsa intellegibilia transit*: 'The intellect passes into the very intelligibles.' See Commentary: 'Banquet', 23–24 and M3, M4.]

---

24. 3 *earth's rude unkinds*] the unrefined, unkind inhabitants of earth; see *OED*, *rude*, adj., 4; and *unkind*, n., 2 (here used in plural form).
24. 7 *my love's conceit*] i.e. Corinna's song as 'first conceived in her mental womb' (23. 3). See Commentary: 'Banquet', 23–24.
25. 2 *thus sense were feasted*] thus should the mind be celebrated, as in a banquet.
25. 4 *a golden world*] here, the intellectual life of the mind.
25. 4 *digested*] disposed or ordered methodically (*OED*, v., 2); also, assimilated through digestion, in relation to the 'flesh' (25. 3).
25. 5–7 *Thus should I rule ... with modesty*] 'Thus I would rule in the kingdom of her face, whose looks, crowned with her modest smile, are proclaimed monarchs of several empires.'
25. 8 *her tunes' division*] the melody dividing the longer notes of her tunes into elaborate phrasings of shorter notes (*OED*, *division*, n., †7); also, the division of sound into atoms suggested by the simile in 21. 8–9.
25. 9 *her conceit*] See note to 24. 7.
25. 9 *in every vein*] literally, since her 'notes' are later said to 'sit with fiery wings' in Corinna's 'blood' (26. 6); but also, figuratively, in every musical mood or style (*OED*, *vein*, n., 11).

26   'My life then turned to that, t'each note and word
     Should I consort her look, which sweeter sings
     Where songs of solid harmony accord,
     Ruled with Love's rule, and pricked with all his stings;
         Thus should I be her notes before they be,⁵   5
     While in her blood they sit with fiery wings,
         Not vapoured in her voice's stillery:
     Nought are these notes her breast so sweetly frames
     But motions, fled out of her spirits' flames.

27   'For as when steel and flint, together smit,
     With violent action spit forth sparks of fire,
     And make the tender tinder burn with it,
     So my love's soul doth lighten her desire
         Upon her spirits in her notes' pretence,⁶   5
     And they convey them (for distinct attire)
         To use the wardrobe of the common sense,
     From whence in veils of her rich breath they fly,
     And feast the ear with this felicity.

M5. This hath reference to the order of her utterance, expressed before.
   [before: i.e. in stanza 24 and M4.]
M6. So is this likewise referred to the order above said, for the more perspicuity.
   [perspicuity: clarity, transparency; the term translates *enargia*, the rhetorical ideal invoked by Chapman in '*OBS*: To Roydon', lines 13–20.]

---

26. 1 *My life then turned to that*] i.e. my intellectual life having thus been transferred to her conceit (absolute participle clause).
26. 2 *consort*] combine in musical harmony (*OED*, v., †7).
26. 2 *sweeter*] more sweetly (used adverbially).
26. 3 *solid harmony*] Verging on oxymoron if read literally (unless we conceive of sounds as carried by material 'atoms'), the phrase suggests continuity and vigour (as with senses 9 and 13 of *OED*, solid, adj.).
26. 4 *Ruled with Love's rule, and pricked with all his stings*] Cupid's rule, or authority, and the 'stings' of his arrows are expressed through musical imagery here. In music, to 'rule' is to mark paper with the straight lines, or rules, of the stave (*OED*, v., 10. a), while to 'prick' is to set down or to mark out musical notation on a score (*OED*, v., 20. a). In the logic of the stanza, Corinna's 'look', in harmony with 'each note and word', sounds more sweetly if the song is inspired by Cupid; similarly, musical notation must be transformed from its look on the score into actual sound.
26. 7 *stillery*] still, or distillery (*OED* registers this form as Chapman's neologism).
26. 9 *spirits'*] Qob's spelling 'spirits' has been modernized to a genitive plural form (Shepherd and Braden make it genitive singular, i.e. 'spirit's'). The word is not taken here to mean the soul, but the material, rarefied substances carried through the blood from the vital organs. Thus, Corinna's spirits sit 'in her blood' and are carried 'with fiery wings' (26. 6).
27. 5 *pretence*] intention, design (*OED*, n., †6).
27. 6 *they convey them*] the spirits convey the notes (or rather, the notes' 'pretence', before their material realization).
27. 7 *common sense*] Aristotle's κοινὴ αἴσθησις (Latin *sensus communis*) is the first of the four inner senses in the process of perception; it receives and unifies external sensations (see Commentary: 'Banquet', 27, for sources and Chapman's 'wardrobe' metaphor).

28   'Methinks they raise me from the heavy ground
       And move me swimming in the yielding air,
       As Zephyr's flowery blasts do toss a sound;
       Upon their wings will I to heav'n repair
         And sing them so, gods shall descend and hear.   5
       Ladies must be adored that are but fair,
         But apt besides with art to tempt the ear
       In notes of nature is a goddess' part,
       Though oft men nature's notes please more than art.

29   'But here are art and nature both confined —
       Art casting nature in so deep a trance
       That both seem dead because they be divined.
       Buried is heav'n in earthly ignorance:
         Why break not men then strumpet Folly's bounds   5
       To learn at this pure virgin utterance?
         No, none but Ovid's ears can sound these sounds,
       Where sing the hearts of love and poesy,
       Which make my Muse so strong, she works too high.'

30   Now in his glowing ears her tunes did sleep;
       And as a silver bell, with violent blow
       Of steel or iron, when his sounds most deep

---

28. 1–3 *Methinks ... a sound*] 'It seems to me that, just as the west wind's blasts on the flowers produce sounds, Corinna's notes raise me from the heavy ground and send me swimming to the acquiescent air.'
28. 2 *yielding*] acquiescent, soft, giving way to physical pressure.
28. 3 *Zephyr*] the west wind when deified in Greek mythology; Zephyrus was one of the four Ἄνεμοι, or wind-gods; he was husband of Chloris, goddess of flowers and spring (see 9. 2, and 'Noctem', 181, with their respective commentaries).
28. 3 *flowery blasts*] i.e. blows on the flowers.
28. 4 *repair*] return (*OED*, v.¹, 1. a).
29 'But in Corinna's notes and self both art and nature are imprisoned, art causing such a deep state of unconsciousness in nature (because of its strong powers) that both seem dead as the effect of having been made divine (and thus unavailable to men's understanding). For that reason, heaven (i.e. divine art and nature) is dead and buried in men's ignorance (i.e. unavailable to most men's knowledge). Why then cannot men break the prison of strumpet Ignorance (in whom art and nature are confined) in order to obtain knowledge from Corinna's pure and chaste utterance? Only the ears of Ovid among all men are able to comprehend the sounds of her song, where (i.e. in Corinna's song, but also in Ovid's ears) the essence of love and poetry sings, and which (the sounds) give Ovid's Muse her incomparable strength to soar to heavenly heights with her poetry.'
29. 5 *strumpet Folly*] a personified allegory of 'earthly ignorance' as a prostitute, which strengthens the opposition with Corinna's 'virgin utterance' and, more generally, with the aspiration to knowledge personified by Mistress Philosophy in the ensuing crown of sonnets (see 'Coronet' and its commentary).
30. 2 *as a silver bell*] For a reading of the simile and its possible antecedent, see Commentary: 'Banquet', 30.

    Do from his sides and air's soft bosom flow,
        A great while after murmurs at the stroke,   5
    Letting the hearer's ears his hardness know,
        So chid the air to be no longer broke,
        And left the accents panting in his ear,
    Which in this banquet his first service were.

31   Herewith, as Ovid something nearer drew,   *Olfactus*
    Her odours, odoured with her breath and breast,
    Into the sensor of his savour flew,
        As if the Phoenix, hasting to her rest,
           Had gathered all th'Arabian spicery   5
    T'embalm her body in her tomb, her nest,
        And there lay burning gainst Apollo's eye,
    Whose fiery air, straight piercing Ovid's brain,
    Inflamed his Muse with a more odorous vein.

32   And thus he sung: 'Come, sovereign odours, come $C1^v$
    Restore my spirits, now in love consuming;
    Wax hotter, air, make them more savoursome,
    My fainting life with fresh-breathed soul perfuming.
        The flames of my disease are violent,   5
    And many perish on late helps presuming,

---

30. 7 *chid*] scolded, complained through murmuring, in consonance with 30. 5. See *OED*, chide, v., 1. †b.
30. 7 *broke*] broken, as by the sound of Corinna's voice.
30. 8 *accents*] tunes (*OED*, n., 4. a).
30. 9 *first service*] Corinna's song is the first course served at the banquet of the senses (see *OED*, service, n., 29. a).
31. 2 *Her odours, odoured with her breath and breast*] Corinna's artificial perfumes are perfumed with the natural odours of her breath and breast, so, in terms of smell, nature prevails over art by improving it.
31. 3 *the sensor of his savour*] i.e. the nose, which is the external organ of smell. *OED* registers a specifically Chapmanesque meaning of 'sensor' as nose, of which this is the first instance (n., †1).
31. 4–7 *As if the Phoenix ... Apollo's eye*] The Phoenix is the mythological bird that, after sacrificing itself in a perfumed funeral pyre every 500 years, was born again from its own decomposed body. 'Apollo's eye' is the sun. For Chapman's sources, see Commentary: 'Banquet', 31.
31. 9 *Inflamed his Muse with a more odorous vein*] i.e. inspired in Ovid a discourse about odours (see *OED*, vein, n., 11. b). The speech is 'more odorous' than the previous one, whose subject was sound and hearing.
32. 1–2 *come | Restore*] come in order to restore.
32. 3 *savoursome*] of a pleasant smell (*OED*, adj., records this word as Chapman's neologism).
32. 5–7 *The flames ... stand content*] 'The flames of my love sickness are violent, and many of them die while they expect a later remedy, with whose hard fate (i.e. their death) I must nevertheless content myself.'

With which hard fate must I yet stand content:
As odours put in fire most richly smell,
So men must burn in love that will excel.

33 'And as the air is rarefied with heat,
But thick and gross with summer-killing cold,
So men in love aspire perfection's seat,
When others, slaves to base desire are sold;
    And if that men near Ganges lived by scent   5
Of flowers and trees, more I a thousandfold
    May live by these pure fumes that do present
My mistress' quick'ning and consuming breath,
Where her wish flies with power of life and death.

34 'Methinks, as in these liberal fumes I burn,
My mistress' lips be near with kiss-entices,
And that which way soever I can turn
She turns withal, and breathes on me her spices,
    As if, too pure for search of human eye,   5
She flew in air disburthening Indian prizes,
    And made each earthly fume to sacrifice.
With her choice breath fell Cupid blows his fire,
And after, burns himself in her desire.

35 'Gentle and noble are their tempers framed
That can be quickened with perfumes and sounds,
And they are cripple-minded, gout-wit lamed,

---

33. 2 *gross*] dense, and so synonymous with 'thick' (see *OED*, adj., 8. †a).
33. 3 *aspire*] soar to, ascend to; also, breathe desire towards, have an ardent desire of (*OED*, v., 4 and 5, though used transitively).
33. 4 *others, slaves, to base desire are sold*] others are sold as slaves to base desires. The original comma after 'slaves' marks the hyperbaton.
33. 5 *men near Ganges*] the tribe of the Astomi, according to Pliny the Elder (see Commentary: 'Banquet', 33).
33. 8 *quick'ning and consuming*] life-giving (*OED, quickening*, adj., 1) and eroding, as if by effect of fire (*OED, consume*, v., 2. a), and thus life-depriving.
34. 1 *liberal*] abundant (*OED*, adj., 1. b).
34. 2 *kiss-entices*] enticements, invitations to kiss. *OED* does not record any nominal uses of 'entice'.
34. 4 *withal*] to the same place.
34. 6 *disburthening*] discharging (*OED*, v., 2. a). The pronunciation is trisyllabic: /dɪsˈbəːðnɪŋ/.
34. 6 *Indian prizes*] rewards from India (i.e. spices, with a hint of the legend of the Astomi referred to in the previous stanza; see Commentary: 'Banquet', 33).
34. 8 *fell*] cruel (*OED*, adj.¹, 4).
34. 9 *in her desire*] i.e. in Cupid's desire for her.
35. 3 *gout-wit lamed*] synonymous with the former 'cripple-minded'; i.e. affected by a gout-like disease of the wit.

That lie like fire-fit blocks, dead without wounds,
 Stirred up with nought but hell-descending gain — 5
The soul of fools that all their souls confounds,
 The art of peasants and our noblesse's stain,
The bane of virtue and the bliss of sin,
Which none but fools and peasants glory in.

36 'Sweet sounds and odours are the heav'ns on earth C2ʳ
Where virtues live of virtuous men deceased,
Which in such like receive their second birth,
By smell and hearing endlessly increased.⁷
 They were mere flesh were not with them delighted, 5
And every such is perished like a beast,
 As all they shall that are so foggy-sprighted.
Odours feed love, and love clear heav'n discovers:
Lovers, wear sweets then; sweetest minds, be lovers.

37 'Odour in heat and dryness is concite;
Love, then, a fire, is much thereto affected;
And as ill smells do kill his appetite,
With thankful savours it is still protected.
 Love lives in spirits, and our spirits be 5
Nourished with odours, therefore love refected;

M7. By this allusion, drawn from the effects of sounds and odours, he imitates the eternity of virtue, saying the virtues of good men live in them, because they stir up pure inclinations to the like, as if infused in perfumes and sounds. Besides, he infers that such as are neither delighted with sounds (intending by sounds all utterance of knowledge, as well as musical affections) nor with odours (which properly dry the brain and delight the instruments of the soul, making them the more capable of her faculties), such, saith he, perish without memory.

---

35. 4 *fire-fit blocks*] logs that are fit for burning (*OED*, † *fire-fit*, adj.).
35. 5 *hell-descending gain*] riches that cause avarice, condemning greedy men to hell; 'gain' is the antecedent for a series of ensuing attributive phrases (35. 6–9).
35. 7 *noblesse*] nobility of rank, and of mind. Qᴏʙ prints 'Nobles', a possible sixteenth-century spelling of 'noblesse', according to *OED*; 'peasants' may then be pronounced monosyllabically.
36. 3 *in such like*] in such sounds and odours.
36. 7 *foggy-sprighted*] foggy-spirited, i.e. of a dull, muddled disposition of mind.
36. 9 *sweetest*] most gracious.
36. 9 *sweets*] perfumes (*OED*, n., 6 and 7).
37. 1 *concite*] excited, stirred up (*OED*, † *concite*, v.), used here as a past participle.
37. 2 *Love, then, a fire, is much thereto affected*] Braden's punctuation is followed here. Paraphrase: 'In being a fire, love is then much naturally disposed to odours, which are stirred up in hot and dry environments.'
37. 5–6 *Love lives ... love refected*] These two lines are disposed in syllogistic form: 1) Love lives in our bodily spirits; 2) our bodily spirits are nourished with odours; 3) therefore, love is nourished with odours. See Commentary: 'Banquet', 37.
37. 6 *refected*] fed, refreshed with food and drink.

And air, less corpulent in quality
  Than odours are, doth nourish vital spirits;
  Therefore may they be proved of equal merits.

38 'O sovereign odours, not of force to give
  Food to a thing that lives nor let it die,
  But to add life to that did never live,
  Nor to add life, but immortality,
      Since they partake her heat that, like the fire 5
  Stol'n from the wheels of Phoebus' waggonry,
      To lumps of earth can manly life inspire;
  Else be these fumes the lives of sweetest dames
  That (dead) attend on her for novel frames.

39 'Rejoice, blest clime, thy air is so refined
  That while she lives no hungry pestilence
  Can feed her poisoned stomach with thy kind,
  But as the unicorn's pregredience
      To venomed pools doth purge them with his horn, 5
  And after him the desert's residence
      May safely drink, so in the wholesome morn,
  After her walk, who there attends her eye
  Is sure that day to taste no malady.'

---

37. 9 *they*] i.e. air and odours (see Commentary: 'Banquet', 37).
38. 1 *not of force*] not of necessity, not by compulsion (*OED*, n., †19, *(of) force*).
38. 5–7 *Since they ... life inspire*] 'Because those things such as odours take part of the heat of immortality which, like the fire emanating from the wheels of Phoebus's chariot, can infuse human life to [inanimate] lumps of earth.' See Commentary: 'Banquet', 38.
38. 6 *waggonry*] chariot. *OED*, which lists this as its only instance, glosses the word as 'chariots collectively'. There is no reason to assume the collective sense here, as the suffix seems mainly motivated by metre and rhyme.
38. 7 *manly*] human (*OED*, adj., †1).
38. 7 *inspire*] infuse, breathe into.
38. 8–9 *Else be ... novel frames*] 'Or else, these odours are the souls of most gracious ladies who, after having died, attend on Corinna in search of new bodies ("frames") where they can be reincarnated.' See Commentary: 'Banquet', 38.
39. 1 *blest clime*] blessed region, whose climate is privileged by Corinna's odours. This explains Ovid's apostrophe.
39. 3 *her*] i.e. hungry pestilence's.
39. 3 *thy*] i.e. blest clime's.
39. 4 *unicorn's pregredience*] the unicorn's precedence, arrival in advance or ahead of others. See *OED*, *pregredience*, n., of which this is the only instance. On this ability of the unicorn's, see Commentary: 'Banquet', 38–39.
39. 8 *her eye*] On the shift of focus from smell to sight, see Commentary: 'Banquet', 38–39.

40   Thus was his course of odours sweet and sleight,
     Because he longed to give his sight assay;
     And as in fervour of the summer's height
     The sun is so ambitious in his sway
          He will not let the night an hour be placed,
     So in this Cupid's night (oft seen in day,
          Now spread with tender clouds these odours cast)
     Her sight (his sun) so wrought in his desires,
     His savour vanished in his visual fires.

41   So vulture Love on his increasing liver
     And fruitful entrails eagerly did feed,
     And, with the gold'nest arrow in his quiver,
     Wounds him with longings, that like torrents bleed,
          To see the mine of knowledge that enriched
     His mind with poverty, and desperate need:
          A sight that with the thought of sight bewitched,
     A sight taught magic his deep mystery,
     Quicker in danger than Diana's eye.[8]

M8. Allusion to the transformation of Actaeon with the sight of Diana.

---

40. 1 *sleight*] Braden (40. 1, note) modernizes the original 'sleight' to 'slight', which in this context means 'trifling', 'fleeting' (*OED*, adj., 5. b). While this meaning is undeniable, this edition keeps 'sleight', as the meaning 'subtle', 'artful', is also part of the perfumes' powers. 'Sleight' is a frequent early modern spelling of 'slight', so both senses are preserved if the original spelling is retained.

40. 2 *give his sight assay*] give his sight a try; also, give his sight the opportunity to assault Corinna (see *OED*, assay, n., †15), thus exploiting the conceit of the beloved as a besieged fortress.

40. 3 *fervour of the summer's height*] the intense light and heat (*OED*, fervour, n., 1. a) of the summer solstice.

40. 6 *Cupid's night (oft seen in day ...)*] the night as the realm of desire, which so often happens during the day.

40. 8-9 *Her sight ... visual fires*] 'Ovid's sun, that is, his wish to see Corinna so quickly, made its way into his desires that his sense of smell vanished in his strong yearning to see her (i.e. his "visual fires").'

40. 8 *wrought in*] made its way into (see *OED*, work in, v., 2, although here it is used transitively).

41. 1 *vulture Love*] 'Love' has been capitalized here, as the 'arrow' and 'quiver' of line 3 identify him as Cupid. Yet this deified Cupid is also imagined as a vulture feeding on Ovid's Prometheus-like liver (for which see Commentary: 'Banquet', 41).

41. 7 *A sight ... bewitched*] 'A sight that bewitched with the mere thought (or imagination) of sight, that is, before physically piercing Ovid's sense of sight.'

41. 8-9 *A sight ... Diana's eye*] 'A sight that contained the very explanation of its magic powers, readier (i.e. the sight, its powers) in its power to harm than Diana's eye when she discovered that Actaeon was looking at her.' See Commentary: 'Banquet', 41.

41. 9 *danger*] power to harm (*OED*, n., 1 and 2).

42 'Stay therefore, Ovid, venter not a sight
    May prove thy rudeness more than show thee loving,
    And make thy mistress think thou think'st her light —
    Which thought with lightest dames is nothing moving.
        The slender hope of favour thou hast yet   5
    Should make thee fear, such gross conclusions proving;
        Besides, the thicket Flora's hands hath set
    To hide thy theft is thin and hollow-hearted,
    Not meet to have so high a charge imparted;

43 'And, should it keep thy secrets, thine own eye
    Would fill thy thoughts so full of lightenings
    That thou must pass through more extremity,
    Or stand content to burn beneath their wings:
        Her honour gainst thy love in wager laid,   5
    Thou would'st be pricked with other senses' stings,
        To taste, and feel, and yet not there be stayed.'
    These casts he cast, and more — his wits more quick —
    Than can be cast by wit's arithmetic.

44 Forward, and back, and forward went he thus:⁹   C3ʳ
    Like wanton Thamesis, that hastes to greet

M9. A simile expressing the manner of his mind's contention in the desire of her sight and fear of her displeasure.

---

42. 1 *venter*] venture (left unmodernized to cohere with 46. 5).
42. 1–2 *venter not ... thy rudeness*] i.e. venture not a look (that) may demonstrate your rudeness.
42. 4 *Which thought ... nothing moving*] 'Thinking that an unchaste woman is not chaste could hardly affect her reputation (as it does when a woman's chastity is put to question).'
42. 7 *Flora*] Roman goddess of flowers, called Chloris earlier in this poem (9. 2), and in 'Noctem', 181. On the origins of the Latin name, see Commentary: 'Noctem', 181–200.
42. 8 *thy theft*] i.e. Ovid's surreptitious spying of Corinna.
42. 8 *hollow-hearted*] with no trees and vegetation in the middle (the area where Niobe's fountain is).
42. 9 *Not meet ... a charge imparted*] 'Not apt or ready to have to receive a share of the attack ("charge") launched by Ovid's eye, and thus likely to reveal Ovid's secret spying on Corinna.' See 49. 1: 'he *charged* the arbour with his eye' (emphasis added).
43. 1–7 *And, should ... not there be stayed*] 'Yet, even if the thicket kept your secrets, your own eye would fill your thoughts with such violent rays of light issued from them that you would be exposed to more suffering, or remain content to burn under the wings of those rays: Corinna's honour then being pawned against your love (as an effect of your growing desires), you would be stung with the passions caused by the other senses, so you would desire to taste and touch her, and even want much more than that.'
43. 2 *lightenings*] lightnings (expanded to a three-syllable word for metrical reasons).
43. 5 *in wager*] at stake, laid down in a bet or pawned in a pledge (*OED*, n., 2. a).
43. 8–9. *These casts ... wit's arithmetic*] 'He calculated all these operations, and more than those that can be calculated by the arithmetic of a mathematician (as Ovid's wits were quicker than his).'
44. 2 *Thamesis*] Latin name for the river Thames.

The brackish court of old Oceanus,
And, as by London's bosom she doth fleet,
   Casts herself proudly through the bridges' twists,   5
Where (as she takes again her crystal feet)
   She curls her silver hair like amorists,
Smooths her bright cheeks, adorns her brows with ships,
And empress-like along the coast she trips,

45   Till, coming near the sea, she hears him roar,
Tumbling his churlish billows in her face;
Then, more dismayed than insolent before,
Charged to rough battle for his smooth embrace,
   She croucheth close within her winding banks,   5
And creeps retreat into her peaceful palace;
   Yet straight high-flowing in her female pranks,
Again she will be wanton, and again,
By no means stayed, nor able to contain —

46   So Ovid, with his strong affections striving,
Masked in a friendly thicket near her bower,

---

44. 3 *The brackish court of old Oceanus*] the half-salty waters of the courtyard-like entrance to the ocean (see *OED*, *brackish*, adj., 1; *court*, n.¹, 1). 'Old Oceanus' is the 'ocean sea' or 'Great Outer Sea', as opposed to inland seas (*OED*, *ocean*, n., 1). Yet the epithet and initial capital point to the Titan Oceanus, son of Uranus and Gaia, and husband of Tethys, with whom he begot many rivers and river nymphs (Smith, *Dictionary*, III, p. 2). Thus his representation here as an arrogant, 'churlish' male.
44. 4 *fleet*] flow (*OED*, v.¹, †7. a), here initiating the rapid movement suggested by the next line.
44. 5 *bridges' twists*] the girders or beams that form the span of a bridge (see *OED*, *twist*, n.¹, 3. †b, for eighteenth- and nineteenth-century examples in which a 'twist' is identified as a 'girder').
44. 7 *amorists*] lovers, with a suggestion of promiscuity (thus, 'wanton'). *OED*, *amorist*, gives another instance from QOB (from 'Contention', not included in this volume).
45. 2 *Tumbling his churlish billows in her face*] QOB, and all editions after it, print 'her' instead of 'his' as the first possessive in the line. The emendation is for the sake of sense: the female river hears the male ocean roar as he throws ('tumbling') '*his* churlish billows in her face': 'churlish' (*OED*, adj.: rude, ungracious, brutal) relates to 'churl', a term that designates a male, while 'billows' preferably refers to the waves (*OED*, n., 1 and 2). Thus, the Ocean's throwing of his swelling waters over the river's 'face', besides the violent sexual connotations, contributes to the river's 'dismayed [...] retreat' (45. 3–6) before her new seduction attempt (45. 7–9).
45. 4 *Charged to rough battle for his smooth embrace*] forced to a harsh fight for trying to obtain a gentle embrace.
45. 6 *And creeps retreat into her peaceful palace*] i.e. and withdraws creeping into her peaceful palace. The Thames's 'palace' features in opposition to Oceanus's 'court'.
45. 7 *female pranks*] prance or dance (see *OED*, †n.³), fitting the river's female nature, with suggestions of sensuous promiscuity in accordance with the rest of the simile, and in contrast with the ocean's violent 'tumbling'.
46. 1–7 *So Ovid ... her beauty's ocean*] In the logic of the simile, Ovid is like the female

Rubbing his temples, fainting and reviving,
Fitting his garments, praying to the hour,
   Backwards and forwards went, and durst not venter   5
To tempt the tempest of his mistress' lour,
   Or let his eyes her beauty's ocean enter.
At last, with prayer he pierceth Juno's ear,
Great goddess of audacity and fear:

47   'Great goddess of audacity and fear,
Queen of Olympus, Saturn's eldest seed,
That dost the sceptre over Samos bear
And ruls't all nuptial rites with power and meed,
   Since thou in nature art the mean to mix   5
Still sulphur humours, and canst therefore speed
   Such as in Cyprian sports their pleasures fix,
Venus herself and Mars by thee embracing,
Assist my hopes, me and my purpose gracing:

48   'Make Love within me not too kind, but pleasing,   C3^v
Exiling aspen fear out of his forces,
My inward sight with outward seeing easing;

Thames, while Corinna's beauty plays the male Oceanus (48. 7). This gender inversion depicts Ovid's excess as weak and unmanly. His actions (46. 3–4) replicate those of a lady's toilette, just as those attributed to the female Thames (44. 6–8).

46. 5 *venter*] venture (left unmodernized for the sake of rhyme).

46. 6 *lour*] gloomy look, frown. *OED*, n.¹, gives 'lour' as alternative spelling of 'lower'.

46. 8–9 *with prayer ... audacity and fear*] See Commentary: 'Banquet', 47–48, on the next two stanzas as a hymn to Venus.

47. 3 *Samos*] a city on a Greek island of the same name, birthplace of Juno, with a temple consecrated to the goddess (see Commentary: 'Banquet', 47).

47. 4 *rul'st all nuptial rites*] On Juno, Jupiter's sister and wife, as goddess of marriage, see Commentary: 'Banquet', 47.

47. 4 *meed*] excellence.

47. 5 *mean*] agent, mediator; translating Latin 'media' in Chapman's source (see Commentary: 'Banquet', 47–48).

47. 6 *sulphur humours*] substances derived from sulphur, one of the three alchemical bases; the phrase translates 'sulphureis humoribus' in Chapman's source (see Commentary: 'Banquet', 47–48).

47. 7 *Cyprian sports*] Venus's pleasures, i.e. sexual intercourse (see Commentary: 'Banquet', 47–48, also on the myth of Venus and Mars in the next line).

48. 1 *Love*] The next line suggests that Cupid is meant here, so 'Love' is capitalized despite Q*OB*'s 'loue'.

48. 1 *not too kind, but pleasing*] The moderation of enthusiasm in love is a theme of the stanza, in accordance with the Ovidian *ars amatoria* (see Commentary: 'Banquet', 47–48).

48. 2 *aspen fear*] the asp (*populus tremula*) is a tree whose trembling leaves are associated with fear, and thus its related adjective (*OED*, aspen, adj.). Compare 'Possess'd with aspen feare' (Chapman, *Seaven Bookes of the Iliads*, VIII. 401; in Nicoll, I, p. 178; see 1598 variant reading, p. 596).

48. 2 *his forces*] Cupid's army.

  And if he please further to stretch his courses,
   Arm me with courage to make good his charges. 5
  Too much desire to please pleasure divorces;
   Attempts, and not entreats, get ladies' largesse;
  Wit is with boldness prompt, with terror daunted,
  And grace is sooner got of dames than granted.'

49 This said, he charged the arbour with his eye,   *Visus*
  Which pierced it through, and at her breasts reflected,
  Striking him to the heart with ecstasy,
  As do the sunbeams, gainst the earth porrected,
   With their reverberate vigour mount in flames, 5
  And burn much more than when they were directed.
   He saw th'extraction of all fairest dames:
  The Fair of Beauty, as whole countries come
  And show their riches in a little room.

50 Here Ovid sold his freedom for a look,
  And with that look was ten times more enthralled:
  He blushed, looked pale, and like a fever shook;
  And as a burning vapour, being exhaled,
   Promised by Phoebus' eye to be a star, 5
  Heav'n's walls denying to be further scaled,
   The force dissolves that drew it up so far,

---

48. 3 *My inward sight with outward seeing easing*] i.e. alleviating Ovid's pangs of desire by replacing the phantasms of Corinna produced by Ovid's imagination with the actual sight of her.

48. 5 *make good his charges*] repair (the damaging effects of) Cupid's assault (see *OED*, make good, P. 1. c).

48. 7 *largesse*] Q*ob*'s 'larges' is registered by *OED* as an early modern form of 'largesse', n., and has been modernized accordingly.

48. 9 *grace is sooner got of dames than granted*] ladies decide to favour their lovers before making it known to them.

49. 4 *porrected*] stretched out, extended forward, as in a straight line (*OED*, porrect, v. and adj.). Q*ob*'s 'prorected', which former scholars have explained as a neologism of Chapman's (see, for instance, Kelly, *Poetic Diction*, pp. 105–08), has been emended to this rare but attested English word. See Introduction, p. 33.

49. 5 *With their reverberate vigour*] with increased strength that is the effect of rebounding or reflection. *OED*, reverberate, adj., 2, lists this as the word's earliest instance.

49. 7 *extraction*] in alchemy, the process of distillation of the essence of a substance, or the result of that process; see Commentary: 'Banquet', 49–50 and M10.

49. 8–9 *The Fair of Beauty ... in a little room*] The idea behind the Fair of Beauty (not capitalized in Q*ob*) is the *Wunderkammer*, or curiosity cabinet, exhibiting wonders from several parts of the world and conceived as natural history collections. See Commentary: 'Banquet', 49–50 and M10.

50. 2 *enthralled*] held in thraldom, or slavery (see 'lost his freedom' in the previous line).

50. 4–8 *And as a burning vapour ... and falls*] On the meaning and sources of the simile, as explained by Chapman's own gloss, see Commentary: 'Banquet', 49–50 and M10.

    And then it lightens gainst his death and falls,[10]
    So Ovid's power this powerful sight appals.

51 This Beauty's Fair is an enchantment made
    By nature's witchcraft, tempting men to buy,
    With endless shows, what endlessly will fade,
    Yet promise chapmen all eternity;
        But, like to goods ill got, a fate it hath   5
    Brings men enriched therewith to beggary —
        Unless th'enricher be as rich in faith,
    Enamoured (like good self-love) with her own
    Seen in another: then 'tis heav'n alone.

52 For sacred beauty is the fruit of sight, $C4^r$
    The courtesy that speaks before the tongue,
    The feast of souls, the glory of the light,
    Envy of age, and everlasting young,
        Pity's commander, Cupid's richest throne,   5
    Music entrancèd, never dully sung,

M10. This simile expresseth the cause and substance of those exhalations which vulgarly are called falling stars: so, Homer and Virgil call them *stellas cadentes*, Homer comparing the descent of Pallas among the Trojans to a falling star.
    [exhalations: incandescent bodies or meteors (see 13. 5). *stellas cadentes*: 'falling stars'; here in the accusative case, as in Chapman's direct source (see Commentary: 'Banquet', 49–50 and M10).]

50. 9 *So Ovid's pow'r this pow'rful sight appals*] i.e. so this powerful sight weakens Ovid's own energies (see *OED*, appal, v., †6; literally, makes pale).
51 'This Fair of Beauty is a charm devised by nature's witchcraft, which uses endless shows to tempt men to buy charms that are destined to perpetual decline, even if they promise eternity to those who trade in them; but, like those riches obtained through illegitimate means, this false beauty condemns to poverty those men enriched with it — unless the giver of riches (i.e. the beautiful beloved) be as rich in her affection ("faith") to her lover as he is to her, being in love with her own beautiful image reflected in the other (this being an instance of the good kind of self-love): in that case, beauty is a very heaven.'
51. 4 *chapmen*] merchants, traders, with an obvious play on the poet's surname.
51. 8 *good self-love*] On self-love, see Commentary: 'Banquet', 51.
52 'For that reason, sacred beauty is the object enjoyed by sight, the courtesy that is spoken even before the tongue speaks, the souls' enjoyment, the splendour of the light, the envy of old age (because it is eternally young), the reason why lovers ask to be pitied, Cupid's richest treasure, ecstatic music that is never sung clumsily, the epitome and example of all harmony, and (so that I may give dull speeches their due) all the figures of rhetoric gathered without the need of words.'
52. 1 *fruit*] enjoyment or profit (see *OED*, n., 7. c, and Commentary: 'Banquet', 52).
52. 2 *courtesy*] graceful manners, but also the expression of these manners by means of action or gesture (*OED*, n., 1 and †8).
52. 3 *glory*] splendour, effulgence (*OED*, n., 6).
52. 6 *dully*] Q$_{OB}$'s 'duely' has been interpreted as 'duly' in previous modernizations (Shepherd, Braden). The emendation to 'dully' is for the sake of sense, and in line with 'dull' (52. 8).

    The sum and court of all proportion;
    And, that I may dull speeches best afford,
    All rhetoric's flowers in less than a word

53 Then in the truest wisdom can be thought —
    Spite of the public axiom worldlings hold
    That nothing wisdom is that getteth nought —
    This all-things-nothing, since it is no gold,
        Beauty-enchasing love, love-gracing beauty,   5
    To such as constant sympathies enfold,
        To perfect riches doth a sounder duty
    Than all endeavours, for by all consent
    All wealth and wisdom rests in true Content.

54 Contentment is our heav'n, and all our deeds
    Bend in that circle, seld or never closed,
    More than the letter in the word precedes;
    And to conduce that compass is reposed
        More force and art in beauty joined with love   5

---

52. 7 *court*] metonymically, model, as the court is supposed to be, and thus in line with 'sum', or epitome, in the same line.
52. 8 *afford*] give their due (a sense that is not registered by *OED*).
52. 9 *rhetoric's flowers*] the figures or ornaments of rhetoric; the metaphor was common in the period, and explains titles like Henry Peacham's treatise *The Garden of Eloquence* (1579). 'Flowers' is pronounced disyllabically.
53 'Then (it) can be thought in the truest wisdom — in spite of the opinion held by common people that wisdom is to no purpose if it does not render any material benefit — [that] this trifle (since it does not render any gold) called beauty-enhancing love, or love-gracing beauty, is more beneficial for the acquisition of perfect riches than any other efforts to those that embrace constant affections, since by all consent all wealth and wisdom are found in true contentment.'
53. 2 *public axiom*] commonly held principle.
53. 2 *worldlings*] people devoted to worldly interests.
53. 4 *this all-things-nothing*] this trifle, i.e. love joined with beauty.
53. 5 *Beauty-enchasing love, love-gracing beauty*] love that is set in beauty as a jewel is set in gold, and beauty that adds splendour to love (see Commentary: 'Banquet', 53). Hyphenations are editorial.
53. 6 *enfold*] embrace.
53. 9 *Content*] See Commentary: 'Banquet', 53, 54.
54 'Contentment is our heaven, and all our deeds are placed on the curve of its circumference, seldom or never closed, any more than the letter C that begins the word "Contentment". And, in order to drive that compass, more labour and skill are placed in joining beauty with love (in the drawing of the circumference) than in joining thrones with wisdom: joys made of the former (i.e. beauty joined with love) are more effective weapons to combat any grief which we may encounter than all the virtue-scorning wretchedness of the latter (i.e. thrones joined with wisdom), or all the moral sentences engraved with Stoic seriousness.'
54. 2 *seld*] seldom.
54. 4 *reposed*] placed, conferred upon, applied (*OED*, v., 4 and 6).

> Than thrones with wisdom: joys of them composed
>   Are arms more proof gainst any grief we prove
> Than all their virtue-scorning misery,
> Or judgements grav'n in Stoic gravity.
>
> 55 But as weak colour always is allowed
> The proper object of a human eye,
> Though light be with a far more force endowed
> In stirring up the visual faculty,
>   This colour being but of virtuous light   5
> A feeble image, and the cause doth lie
>   In th'imperfection of a human sight,
> So this for love and beauty: love's cold fire
> May serve for my praise, though it merit higher.
>
> 56 With this digression, we will now return   C4ᵛ
> To Ovid's prospect in his fancy's storm:
> He thought he saw the arbour's bosom burn,
> Blazed with a fire wrought in a lady's form,
>   Where silver passed the leaf, and nature's vant   5
> Did such a precious miracle perform,
>   She lay, and seemed a flood of diamant

---

54. 7 *prove*] experience (*OED*, v., 2).
54. 9 *judgements*] opinions, sentences (*OED*, n., 2).
55 'But as weak colour is always considered to be the proper matter of human sight, even though light may be said with much more reason to be endowed with the capacity of exciting our faculty of vision — colour being just a poor image seen in powerful light, and the cause of our reliance on colour being the imperfection of the human organ of sight — so it goes for love and beauty: love's cold fire may be a fit object of my praise, although it must deserve a higher praise (i.e. as pure love, which is the enjoyment of incorporeal beauty).'
55. 1, 5 *weak colour, virtuous light*] the weakness of colour as a quality (not a particular weak colour) must be understood in opposition to 'virtuous (i.e. vigorous) light'.
55. 1 *allowed*] admitted to be.
55. 3-4 *endowed | In*] endowed with capacity of.
55. 5-7 *This colour ... human sight*] On the relationship between colour and light, see Commentary: 'Banquet', 55.
56. 2 *prospect*] vision (see Commentary: 'Banquet', 56-57 and M11).
56. 3 *bosom*] surface or ground, but also the interior part (*OED*, n., 2 and 5).
56. 5 *silver passed the leaf*] On the emendation of Qob's 'least', re-punctuation of the sentence and conjectural interpretations of the passage, see Commentary: 'Banquet', 56-57 and M11.
56. 5 *vant*] vaunt (left unmodernized for its rhyme with 'diamant'), which may mean boast (*OED, vaunt*, n.¹), or, by extension here, audacious action.
56. 7 *flood*] river.
56. 7 *diamant*] diamond, left unmodernized for the sake of rhyme.

Bounded in flesh, as still as Vesper's hair
When not an aspen leaf is stirred with air.

57 She lay at length, like an immortal soul
At endless rest in blest Elysium;[11]
And then did true felicity enrol
So fair a lady, figure of her kingdom.
  Now Ovid's Muse as in her tropic shined,   5
And he (struck dead) was mere heav'n-borne become,
  So his quick verse in equal height was shrined —
Or else blame me as his submitted debtor,
That never mistress had to make me better.

58 Now as she lay, attired in nakedness,
His eye did carve him on that feast of feasts:
'Sweet fields of life, which Death's foot dare not press,[12]
Flowered with th'unbroken waves of my love's breasts,
  Unbroke by depth of those her beauty's floods,   5
See where, with bent of gold curled into nests,
  In her head's grove the spring-bird laureate broods:

M11. The amplification of this simile is taken from the blissful state of souls in Elysium, as Virgil feigns, and expresseth a regenerate beauty in all life and perfection, not intimating any rest of death. But in place of that eternal spring, he pointeth to that life of life, this beauty-clad naked lady.

M12. He calls her body (as it were divided with her breasts) the fields of Paradise, and her arms and legs the famous rivers in it.

---

56. 8 *Bounded*] bound, wrapped (past participle of *bind*). See 'Prisoned in flesh' ('Noctem', 245).

56. 8 *Vesper*] Hesper, or Hesperus, the evening star, here suggesting a deified or anthropomorphic evening.

57. 2 *Elysium*] the Elysian Fields, or resting place of the souls of heroes and virtuous people after death (see M11 and Commentary: 'Banquet', 56–57 and M11).

57. 3 *enrol*] wrap up, enfold (*OED*, v., 7. b).

57. 6 *heav'n-borne become*] transported into heaven, as the effect of seeing Corinna.

57. 8–9 *submitted debtor ... never mistress had*] obliged by his debt to Ovid, his poetic master, from whom he has 'borrowed' his mistress (see Commentary: 'Banquet', 56–57 and M11).

58. 2 *His eye did carve him on that feast of feasts*] His eye assigned him a large portion on this most pleasant of banquets (see *OED*, carve, v., 9).

58. 3 *Sweet fields of life*] the Judeo-Christian Paradise, which gives continuance to the Virgilian Elysium of the former stanza (see Commentary: 'Banquet', 58–62, and M12, M13).

58. 6 *bent*] slope (*OED*, n., 6).

58. 7 *In her head's grove the spring-bird laureate broods*] 'The spring bird hatches her eggs in the nest built on her head, crowned as if with laurel by her curls of hair'; or 'the spring bird, whose song crowns her with the laurel, hatches her eggs in her abundant hair'. In the absence of a better solution, this edition accepts the emendation of meaningless 'Lameate' with 'laureate', first suggested by Bartlett (p. 432, 58. 7, note), although not incorporated into her text.

        Her body doth present those fields of peace
        Where souls are feasted with the soul of ease.

59   'To prove which paradise that nurseth these,
     See, see the golden rivers that renown it:
     Rich Gihon, Tigris, Pishon, Euphrates.
     Two from her bright Pelopian shoulders crown it,
        And two out of her snowy hills do glide,   5
     That with a deluge of delights do drown it;
        The highest two their precious streams divide
     To ten pure floods that do the body duty,
     Bounding themselves in length, but not in beauty.

60   'These wind their courses through the painted bowers,[13] $D1^r$
     And raise such sounds in their inflection
     As ceaseless start from earth fresh sorts of flowers,
     And bound that book of life with every section.
        In these the Muses dare not swim for drowning,   5
     Their sweetness poisons with such blest infection,
        And leaves the only lookers on them swooning;
     These forms so decks, and colour makes so shine,
     That gods for them would cease to be divine.

61   'Thus, though my love be no Elysium
     That cannot move from her prefixèd place,
     Yet have her feet no power from thence to come,
     For where she is is all Elysian grace.
        And as those happy men are sure of bliss   5
     That can perform so excellent a race

M13. He intends the office of her fingers in attiring her, touching this of their courses, in their inflection following, their playing upon an instrument.

---

59. 1 *To prove which paradise that nurseth these*] i.e. to experience that paradise which nurses these souls (with pleasure).
59. 3 *Rich Gihon, Tigris, Pishon, Euphrates*] The four rivers of the Garden of Eden (on these and the ensuing lines, see Commentary: 'Banquet', 58–62, and M12, M13).
59. 8 *ten pure floods*] the ten fingers branching from Corinna's arms.
59. 9 *Bounding themselves in length, but not in beauty*] i.e. limited in their length, but unlimited in their beauty.
60. 2 *inflection*] bending movement, as of the fingers when playing upon the strings of an instrument.
60. 5 *In these*] In the southern rivers, Tigris and Euphrates, i.e. Corinna's legs (see Commentary: 'Banquet', 58–62, and M12, M13).
60. 8 *These forms so decks, and colour makes so shine*] The subject of this sentence is 'their sweetness' (60. 6), so: 'Their sweetness so adorns their forms and makes their colour shine so.'
61. 2 *That cannot move from her prefixèd place*] Understood as a non-defining relative clause; 'her' refers simultaneously to the two terms of the analogy, Elysium and Corinna (see Commentary: 'Banquet', 58–62, and M12, M13).

>   As that Olympiad where her favour is,
>   So she can meet them, blessing them the rather,
>   And give her sweets, as well as let men gather.
>
> 62 'Ah, how should I be so most happy then
>   T'aspire that place, or make it come to me?
>   To gather, or be giv'n, the flower of women?
>   Elysium must with virtue gotten be,
>   With labours of the soul and continence,   5
>   And these can yield no joy with such as she:
>   She is a sweet Elysium for the sense,
>   And nature doth not sensual gifts infuse
>   But that with sense she still intends their use.
>
> 63 'The sense is giv'n us to excite the mind,
>   And that can never be by sense excited
>   But first the sense must her contentment find.
>   We therefore must procure the sense delighted,
>   That so the soul may use her faculty;   5
>   Mine eye then to this feast hath her invited,
>   That she might serve the sovereign of mine eye;
>   She shall bid Time, and Time, so feasted never,
>   Shall grow in strength of her renown forever.
>
> 64 'Betwixt mine eye and object, certain lines $D1^v$
>   Move in the figure of a pyramis,
>   Whose chapter in mine eye's gray apple shines,
>   The base within my sacred object is;
>   On this will I inscribe in golden verse   5
>   The marvels reigning in my sovereign's bliss,

---

61. 7 *Olympiad*] here, the Olympic games (see Commentary: 'Banquet', 58–62, and M12, M13).
61. 8 *the rather*] all the more.
62. 2 *aspire*] attain, or reach by means of soaring up to (*OED*, v., †8, transitive).
62. 3 *flower of women*] quintessence, choicest example of womanhood, but also suggestive of sexual favour or loss of virginity (the innuendo is reinforced in the subsequent lines); see Commentary: 'Banquet', 58–62, and M12, M13.
62. 8–9 *And nature ... their use*] 'And nature does not instil sensual gifts (into us) unless she intends them to be enjoyed by our senses' (Commentary: 'Banquet', 58–62, and M12, M13).
63. 8 *bid Time*] command, enjoin Time. I have kept Q*OB*'s capitalizations of Time, as it must be understood emblematically (see Commentary: 'Banquet', 63–68).
64. 1 *lines*] light rays, but also lines of verse (see Commentary: 'Banquet', 63–68).
64. 2 *pyramis*] pyramid, in reference to the Euclidean theory of vision (see Commentary: 'Banquet', 63–68).
64. 3 *chapter*] chapiter, i.e. the cusp or apex of the pyramid (*OED*, n., †9).
64. 3 *apple*] pupil (*OED*, n., 6. a).
64. 6 *bliss*] glory (*OED*, n., †3).

The arcs of sight, and how her arrows pierce:
This in the region of the air shall stand
In Fame's brass court, and all her trumps command.

65 'Rich Beauty, that each lover labours for,
Tempting as heaps of new-coined-glowing gold
(Racked of some miserable treasurer),
Draw his desires, and them in chains enfold,
    Urging him still to tell it, and conceal it.   5
But Beauty's treasure never can be told:
    None can peculiar joy, yet all must steal it.
O Beauty, this same bloody siege of thine
Starves me that yield, and feeds me till I pine.

66 'And as a taper burning in the dark
(As if it threatened every watchful eye
That, viewing, burns it) makes that eye his mark,
And hurls gilt darts at it continually,
    Or as it envied any eye but it   5
Should see in darkness, so my mistress' beauty
    From forth her secret stand my heart doth hit,
And like the dart of Cephalus doth kill
Her perfect lover, though she mean no ill.

67 'Thus, as the innocence of one betrayed
Carries an Argus with it, though unknown,
And Fate to wreak the treachery bewrayed —

---

64. 7 *arcs of sight*] Corinna's eyes, whose curved shape resembles bows (and hence their shooting of the 'arrows' that 'pierce' Ovid's eyes).
64. 9 *Fame's brass court ... trumps*] Fame's ensemble of brass instruments, or trumpets, whose music proclaims Corinna's beauty.
65. 1–5 *Rich Beauty ... conceal it*] 'Rich Beauty, which each lover pursues with labour, tempting as heaps of glowing, freshly coined gold extorted by some miserable usurer, attract each lover's desires and wrap up these heaps of gold in chains, urging him (the lover, as if he were a usurer) to count it and keep it concealed.'
65. 2 *new-coined-glowing*] shining, as the effect of having been recently coined.
65. 7 *None can peculiar joy, but all must steal it*] 'Nobody can make joy one's own, even if all must steal it'; on Chapman's use of enallage, or the use of a word in an unusual grammatical category — here the adjective 'peculiar' as a verb — see Kelly, *Poetic Diction*, p. 127.
65. 8–9 *O Beauty ... till I pine*] 'O Beauty, this bloody siege to which you subject me makes me starve as I surrender, and feeds me until it makes me starve again' (see Commentary: 'Banquet', 63–68).
66. 5 *but*] lest.
66. 7 *stand*] place or position from which the hunter shoots the game (*OED*, n.¹, 16).
66. 8 *dart of Cephalus*] Cephalus shot dead his wife, Procris, while she was hidden behind a bush, thinking that she was an animal (see Commentary: 'Banquet', 63–68).
67. 2 *Argus*] On the Ovidian myth of hundred-eyed Argus watching over Io, see Commentary: 'Banquet', 63–68.
67. 3 *bewrayed*] revealed (*OED*, v., †4).

Such vengeance hath my mistress' beauty shown
　　　　On me, the traitor to her modesty —
　　So, unassailed, I quite am overthrown,
　　　　And, in my triumph, bound in slavery.
　　O Beauty, still thy empire swims in blood,
　　And, in thy peace, War stores himself with food.

68　'O Beauty, how attractive is thy power!
　　For as the life's heat clings about the heart,
　　So all men's hungry eyes do haunt thy bower.
　　Reigning in Greece, Troy swum to thee in art;
　　　　Removed to Troy, Greece followed thee in fears;
　　Thou drew'st each sireless sword, each childless dart,
　　　　And pulled'st the tow'rs of Troy about thine ears.
　　Shall I then muse that thus thou drawest me?
　　No, but admire I stand thus far from thee.'

69　Herewith she rose like the Autumnal Star,
　　Fresh burnished in the lofty ocean flood,
　　That darts his glorious influence more far
　　Than any lamp of bright Olympus' brood.
　　　　She lifts her light'ning arms above her head,
　　And stretcheth a meridian from her blood,
　　　　That slept awake in her Elysian bed;
　　Then knit she up, lest, loose, her glowing hair
　　Should scorch the centre and incense the air.

---

68. 4 *in art*] with skill and stealth in Paris's kidnapping of Helen; on Helen as the personification of beauty, see Commentary: 'Banquet', 63–68.
68. 5 *in fears*] in the horrors of war.
68. 6 *each sireless sword, each childless dart*] i.e. each sword and dart left without their dead owner, in reference to losing one's father or children in battle.
68. 7 *pulled'st the tow'rs of Troy about thine ears*] made the towers of Troy fall down around you, or at your mercy.
68. 9 *admire I stand thus far from thee*] i.e. admire my own ability to stand far from you while I contemplate your beauty (see Commentary: 'Banquet', 69–71, and M14, M15, M16).
69. 1 *Autumnal Star*] Sirius, or *Canis Maior*. The phrase translates Homer's 'ἀστέρ ὀπωρινός' (*Iliad*, v. 5: Nicoll, I, pp. 194–95). In Chapman's 1611 translation: 'rich Autumnus golden lampe' (v. 6). The term 'autumnal' actually refers to the late summer (the late days of July and early days of August).
69. 4 *Olympus' brood*] the heavens.
69. 6 *stretcheth a meridian from her blood*] in lifting her arm, she extends a circle from her bosom (i.e. the site of the heart, from which her blood circulates).
69. 8–9 *Then knit ... the air*] 'Then she tied up her glowing hair, lest she should ignite her own head and set the air on fire.' See *OED*, incense, v.², †1. a. Chapman's peculiar syntax here makes the phrase 'her glowing hair' function simultaneously as the direct object of 'knit up' in the main clause and the subject of 'scorch' in the subordinate clause.

70 Thus when her fair, heart-binding hands had tied
    Those liberal tresses, her high frontier part
    She shrunk in curls and curiously plied
    Into the figure of a swelling heart,
        And then with jewels of device it graced.   5
    One was a sun graven at his even's depart,
        And under that a man's huge shadow placed,[14]
    Wherein was writ, in sable charactery,
    Decrescente nobilitate, crescunt obscuri.

71 Another was an eye in sapphire set,
    And close upon it a fresh laurel spray;
    The skilful posy was *Medio caret*,[15]
    To show not eyes but means must truth display.
        The third was an Apollo with his team   5
    About a dial and a world in way;[16]
        The motto was *Teipsum et orbem*,

M14. At the sun going down, shadows grow longest, whereupon this emblem is devised.
M15. Sight is one of the three senses that hath his medium extrinsically, which now (supposed wanting) lets the sight by the close apposition of the laurel, the application whereof hath many constructions.
    [lets: prevents.]
M16. The Sun hath as much time to compass a dial as the world, and therefore the world is placed in the dial, expressing the conceit of the imprese morally, which hath a far higher intention.
    [imprese: device, emblem.]

70. 1 *heart-binding hands*] The phrase is obscure: perhaps, hands that enfold the lover's heart because of their beauty; or hands that fold themselves into the shape of a heart; or, redundantly, folding the hair into the shape of a heart, as described in the next lines (70. 2-4).
70. 2 *liberal*] abundant (*OED*, adj., 1. a, 1. b).
70. 2 *her high frontier part*] the hair falling freely before her forehead. This phrase is the object of 'shrunk' and 'plied' in the next line.
70. 3 *curiously*] artfully, elaborately (*OED*, *curious*, adj., 3. a).
70. 5 *jewels of device*] jewels containing emblematic devices (for a description, see Commentary: 'Banquet', 69-71, and M14, M15, M16).
70. 6 *even*] evening (*OED*, *even*, n.¹).
70. 8 *sable charactery*] in black letters (heraldic).
70. 9 *Decrescente nobilitate, crescunt obscuri*] 'Nobility going down, obscure men grow' (see Commentary: 'Banquet', 69-71, and M14, M15, M16). While the other two Latin mottos fit well into the metre and rhyme patterns of the next stanza, this line is extrametrical if considered from the point of view of English syllabic standards.
71. 3 *posy*] an emblematic motto or inscription.
71. 3 *Medio caret*] 'It lacks its own medium.' For the meaning of this motto, explained in the next line, and of Chapman's gloss (M15), see Commentary: 'Banquet', 69-71, and M14, M15, M16.
71. 5 *team*] a group of horses harnessed together to pull a chariot (*OED*, n., 4. c).
71. 7 *Teipsum et orbem*] 'Yourself and the world.' For the meanings of the motto and of Chapman's gloss (M16), see Commentary: 'Banquet', 69-71, and M14, M15, M16.

Grav'n in the dial. These, exceeding rare,
And other like accomplements she ware.

72 'Not Tigris, Nilus, nor swift Euphrates,'
Quoth Ovid now, 'can more subdue my flame;
I must through hell adventure to displease,
To taste and touch: one kiss may work the same.
    If more will come, more than much more I will; 5
Each natural agent doth his action frame
    To render that he works on like him still:
The fire, on water working, doth induce
Like quality unto his own in use.

73 'But heav'n in her a sparkling temper blew
(As love in me), and so will soon be wrought;
Good wits will bite at baits most strange and new,
And words well placed move things were never thought.
    What goddess is it Ovid's wits shall dare 5
And he disgrace them with attempting nought?
    My words shall carry spirits to ensnare:
The subtlest hearts affecting suits importune;
Best loves are lost for wit when men blame Fortune.'

---

71. 8 *exceeding rare*] exceedingly unusual and obscure in meaning.
71. 9 *accomplements*] Braden glosses this noun as 'ornaments'; *OED* explains it as synonymous with 'accomplishment', which more aptly stresses the extraordinary craftsmanship of the jewels.
71. 9 *ware*] wore.
72. 1 *Tigris, Nilus ... Euphrates*] used here as instances of abundant rivers.
72. 3 *displease*] be displeasing, cause displeasure (by importuning Corinna). On this intransitive use, see *OED*, v., 1. a.
72. 4 *one kiss may work the same*] i.e. one kiss may be equally pleasant to the senses of taste and touch.
72. 6–9 *Each natural agent ... in use*] On the sources and meanings of this Neoplatonic argument, see Commentary: 'Banquet', 72–73.
73 'But heaven blew in her its own sparkling temper (as love did with me), so she will be soon worked upon (i.e. predisposed to accepting my advances): people of sharp wits will be easily seduced by the bait of rare and extraordinary words, and rhetorically apt speech has the capacity to move emotions that one never thought could be easily moved. What goddess is it that Ovid's wits shall dare to seduce if he puts his wits to discredit by not using them? My words will carry spirits (i.e. wit, compared here to the substance carried by blood) in order to entrap Corinna: arresting suits can influence the most delicate hearts; the opportunity to use wit in the best love affairs is missed when men choose to complain about their misfortune instead of taking action.'
73. 6 *And*] if.
73. 6 *disgrace*] discredit (here in the subjunctive mood). See *OED*, v., †5. a.

74	With this, as she was looking in her glass,	*Narratio*
	She saw therein a man's face looking on her,	*Ovid standing*
	Whereat she started from the frighted grass	*behind her, his*
	As if some monstrous serpent had been shown her,	*face was seen*
	Rising as when (the sun in Leo's sign)	*in the glass.* 5
	Auriga, with the heav'nly Goat upon her,	
	Shows her horned forehead with her Kids divine,	
	Whose rise kills vines, heav'n's face with storms disguising —	
	No man is safe at sea, the Haedi rising.	

75 So straight wrapped she her body in a cloud,
    And threatened tempests for her high disgrace;
    Shame from a bower of roses did unshroud
    And spread her crimson wings upon her face;
        When running out, poor Ovid, humbly kneeling   5
    Full in the arbour's mouth, did stay her race
        And said: 'Fair nymph, great goddess, have some feeling
    Of Ovid's pains; but hear, and your dishonour,
    Vainly surmised, shall vanish with my horror.'

76 'Traitor to ladies' modesties,' said she,   *D3ʳ*
    'What savage boldness hardened thee to this?
    Or what base reck'ning of my modesty?
    What should I think thy fact's proud reason is?'
        'Love (sacred madam), love exhaling me   5
    (Wrapped in his sulphur) to this cloud of his,
        Made my affections his artillery,
    Shot me at you, his proper citadel,
    And, loosing all my forces, here I fell.'

---

74. 4–9 *As if ... the Haedi rising*] On the simile's meaning, astronomical references, and sources, see Commentary: 'Banquet', 74–75.
75. 2 *disgrace*] dishonour, as the result of having been seen naked.
75. 3 *unshroud*] unveil (not in *OED*).
75. 8–9 *and your dishonour ... my horror*] 'and your dishonour, contrived by me in vain, shall disappear at the same time as will the horror that my sight causes in you.'
75. 9 *surmised*] planned, contrived (*OED*, v., †2).
76. 3 *reck'ning*] reckoning.
76. 4 *What should I ... reason is*] i.e. what should I think is the proud reason of your action?
76. 5–9 *Love ... here I fell*] 'Love, sacred madam, evaporating me (wrapped in his gunpowder) into his cloud, made my desires his ammunition, and shot me at you, the citadel that was the object of his assault, and, as the result of his releasing all my energies, I fell here.'
76. 6 *sulphur*] sulphurous vapours; also, in line with the military lexicon of the stanza, gunpowder (for similar uses, see *OED*, n., 4. †a).
76. 9 *loosing all my forces*] discharging all my artillery. Q*ob*'s 'loosing' makes a modern-spelling editor decide between 'losing' (with 'I' as subject, as Braden reads it) and the

77 'This gloss is common, as thy rudeness strange
    Not to forbear these private times,' quoth she,
    'Whose fixèd rites none should presume to change,
    Not where there is adjudged inchastity;
        Our nakedness should be as much concealed   5
    As our accomplishments desire the eye:
        It is a secret not to be revealed,
    But, as virginity and nuptials, clothed,
    And to our honour all to be betrothed.

78 'It is a want where our abundance lies,
    Giv'n a sole dower t'enrich chaste Hymen's bed,
    A perfect image of our purities,
    And glass by which our actions should be dressed,
        That tells us honour is as soon defiled —   5
    And should be kept as pure and incompressed —
        But sight attainteth it: for Thought, Sight's child,
    Begetteth sin, and Nature bids defame
    When light and lawless eyes bewray our shame.'

79 'Dear mistress,' answered Ovid, 'to direct
    Our actions by the straitest rule that is,
    We must in matters moral quite reject
    Vulgar Opinion, ever led amiss,
        And let authentic Reason be our guide,   5
    The wife of Truth, and Wisdom's governiss.

---

option chosen here — for whose lexical substantiation, see *OED*, *loose*, v., 4. a: 'to shoot or let fly (an arrow)'.

77. 1 *gloss*] explanation; also, a verse stanza, such as the lines of Ovid's reply are.

77. 2 *forbear*] abstain, refrain from.

77. 4 *Not where there is adjudged inchastity*] i.e. not where unchaste behaviour can be pronounced as a sentence.

77. 5–6 *Our nakedness ... the eye*] 'Our nakedness should be concealed from the eye as much as our beauties invite that eye to behold them.' For that reason, nakedness 'is a want where our abundance lies' (78. 1). See *OED*, *accomplishment*, n., 3. †b; and *desire*, v., †8.

78. 2 *dower*] dowry.

78. 2 *Hymen*] the ancient god of marriage.

78. 8–9 *Nature bids defame ... our shame*] 'Our natural desires invite dishonour when light and unlawful eyes expose female nakedness.' QOB's 'bides' has been emended to 'bids' for sense's sake.

78. 9 *bewray*] reveal, expose.

78. 9 *our shame*] our naked bodies (see *OED*, *shame*, n., 7).

79. 2 *straitest*] most rigorous, scrupulous, i.e. guided by the principles of 'authentic Reason' (*OED*, *strait*, adj., 5 and 6).

79. 4–6 *Opinion, Reason, Truth, Wisdom*] QOB's capitalizations have been kept, as these abstract notions are personified here. On the nature of these personifications, see Commentary: 'Banquet', 79.

79. 6 *governiss*] governess. QOB's 'governisse' is not registered by *OED* as a historical

The nature of all actions must be weighed,
And as they then appear, breed love or loathing:
Use makes things-nothing huge, and huge things nothing.

80 'As in your sight, how can sight, simply being
    A sense receiving essence to his flame
    Sent from his object, give it harm by seeing,
    Whose action in the seer hath his frame?[17]
        All excellence of shape is made for sight;
    Else, to be like a beast were no defame;
        Hid beauties lose their ends, and wrong their right;
    And can kind love (where no harm's kind can be)
    Disgrace with seeing that is giv'n to see?

81 "Tis I (alas) and my heart-burning eye
    Do all the harm, and feel the harm we do:
    I am no basilisk, yet harmless I
    Poison with sight, and mine own bosom too;
        So am I to myself a sorceress,
    Bewitched with my conceits in her I woo;
        But you, unwronged and all dishonourless,
    No ill dares touch; affliction, sorcery
    One kiss of yours can quickly remedy.

82 'I could not times observe, as others might
    Of cold affects and wat'ry tempers framed,

M17. *Actio cernendi in homine vel animali, vidente collocanda est* (Aristoteles).
(The action of seeing should be placed in the seeing human or animal (Aristotle).)

---

spelling of 'governess', so it must be assumed that this is Chapman's own choice for reasons of rhyme.
79. 9 *things-nothing*] trifles; hyphenation, not in QOB, has been added here for reasons of consistency with 53. 4.
80 *and Gloss*] On the meanings and sources of this stanza, see Commentary: 'Banquet', 80 and M17.
80. 1–4 *As in your sight ... his frame?*] 'As for my seeing you, how can sight, which is just a sense that receives in the eye's fiery substance an essence sent from the object of vision, do any harm by seeing, whose action has its physical site in the seer?'
80. 8 *where no harm's kind can be*] where there cannot be any sort of harm.
81. 2 *we*] i.e. 'I [...] and my heart-burning eye'.
81. 3 *basilisk*] also called a cockatrice, this mythical serpent had the power to kill by skin, breath or eye contact.
81. 6 *Bewitched with my conceits in her I woo*] i.e. bewitched by my own thoughts of my beloved.
80. 7 *unwronged and all dishonourless*] free from any wrong and from all dishonour.
82. 1–6 *I could ... in me inflamed*] 'I could not, as others (framed of cold affects and watery tempers) might, respect your private times; on the contrary, I was convinced that the wonder of your appearance was so far from being defamed by my sight that your love shall shine in the temple of memory for ever as the effect of my sight, inflamed by my fiery tempers (i.e. my "heart-burning eye").'

Yet well assured the wonder of your sight
Was so far off from seeing you defamed
   That ever in the fane of memory 5
Your love shall shine by it, in me inflamed.
   Then let your power be clad in lenity;
Do not (as others would) of custom storm,
But prove your wit as pregnant as your form.

83 'Nor is my love so sudden, since my heart
Was long Love's Vulcan, with his pants' unrest
Hamm'ring the shafts bred this delightsome smart;
And as when Jove at once from east and west
   Cast off two eagles, to discern the sight 5
Of this world's centre, both his birds joined breast
   In Cynthian Delphos, since Earth's navel hight,
So casting off my ceaseless thoughts to see
My heart's true centre, all do meet in thee.

84 'Cupid, that acts in you, suffers in me   D4ʳ
To make himself one triumph-place of twain:
Into your tunes and odours turnèd he,
And through my senses flew into my brain,
   Where rules the Prince of Sense, whose throne he takes,[18] 5
And of my motions' engines framed a chain
   To lead me where he list; and here he makes

M18. *In cerebro est principium sentiendi, et inde nervi, qui instrumenta sunt motus voluntarii oriuntur.*
(In the brain is the first organ of sensation, and from it are born the nerves, which are instruments of voluntary motion.)

---

82. 5 *fane*] temple.
82. 9 *pregnant*] abundant, in reference both to the readiness of Corinna's 'wit' and to the exuberance of her beauty, or 'form' (*OED*, adj., 2 and 4).
83. 2 *Love's Vulcan*] Cupid's own goldsmith, or forger of his love shafts; Q<small>OB</small>'s 'loues' has been capitalized and interpreted as a genitive singular.
83. 2–3 *with his ... delightsome smart*] i.e. panting in agitation as he (Vulcan) hammers the shafts with which Cupid inflicts his pleasant injuries.
83. 4–9 *And as when Jove ... meet in thee*] On the meaning and sources of this simile, see Commentary: 'Banquet', 83–84 and M18, M19.
83. 7 *Cynthian*] of mount Cynthus, in the island of Delos, which was the birthplace of both Diana and Apollo, and thus used as epithet for both: See Gloss 1 to 'Noctem'. Here it modifies 'Delphos', so the allusion is to Apollo.
84. 2 *one triumph-place of twain*] one triumphal monument that brings together the two separated lovers ('twain') together.
84. 5 *Prince of Sense*] brain; 'Prince' translates here Latin '*principium*' in M18.
84. 6 *motions' engines*] i.e. nerves (see '*nervi*' in M18, and Commentary: 'Banquet', 83–84, M18 and M19).
84. 7 *list*] may wish (in the subjunctive mood).

Nature (my fate)¹⁹ enforce me, and resigns
The reins of all to you, in whom he shines.

85 'For yielding love then, do not hate impart,
Nor let mine eye, your careful harbinger
That hath purveyed your chamber in my heart,
Be blamed for seeing who it lodgèd there:
   The freer service merits greater meed;   5
Princes are served with unexpected cheer,
   And must have things in store before they need;
Thus should fair dames be wise and confident,
   Not blushing to be noted excellent.'

86 Now, as when Heav'n is muffled with the vapours
His long-since just-divorcèd wife, the Earth,
In envy breathes to mask his spurry tapers
From the unrich abundance of her birth,
   When straight the western issue of the Air   5
Beats with his flowery wings those brats of dearth
   And gives Olympus leave to show his fair,

M19. *Natura est uniuscuiusque Fatum, ut Theophrastus.*
(Nature is the fate for each and every one, as Theophrastus writes.)

---

84. 8 *resigns*] yields the control of (see Commentary: 'Banquet', 83–84, M18 and M19, for the interpretation of the allegory).
85. 2 *harbinger*] an official that acts as purveyor of lodgings, i.e. for a monarch or a royal train (*OED*, n., †1); the eye makes Corinna queen (thus the reference to 'Princes' in 85. 6) in the chamber of Ovid's heart.
85. 3 *purveyed*] made ready, furnished.
85. 5 *The freer service merits greater meed*] By seeing Corinna, the service as a disinterested royal harbinger performed by Ovid's eye deserves a higher recompense.
85. 6 *unexpected*] i.e. by princes, so they must keep goods in store to reward their servants.
85. 8 *wise and confident ... noted excellent*] i.e. prudent and self-reliant, not blushing shyly as a hypocritical sign of superiority.
86. 1, 5, 8 *Now, as when ... When ... So*] On the syntax, style, meaning and sources of Chapman's simile, see Commentary: 'Banquet', 86.
86. 1, 2 *Heav'n, Earth*] QOB's capitals have been preserved, as these refer to Uranus and Gaia, the married Titan-gods of heaven and earth.
86. 2 *long-since just-divorcèd wife*] married for a long time, though recently divorced wife; hyphenation is editorial.
86. 3 *spurry tapers*] the stars, represented here as rowel-shaped burning tapers, thus having spur-like projections. See *OED*, spurry, adj., †1, where the only instance is: 'His crested helmet ... like a star [...] cast a spurry ray' (Chapman, *Iliads*, XIX. 366–67).
86. 4 *unrich abundance of her birth*] i.e. the ungenerous abundance produced by her soil. The phrasing is obscure: the oxymoron presents the earth as simultaneously fertile and stingy; 'birth' suggests produce, crops, as in *OED*, n.¹, †9.
86. 5 *western issue of the Air*] Zephyrus, the west wind, also a god.
86. 6 *brats of dearth*] the abovementioned offspring of Earth, i.e. the mists that veil the shining stars.
86. 7 *fair*] beauty (for this nominal use, see *OED*, n.¹, †1); perhaps also a fair or exhibition (*OED*, n., 2), a meaning that is also present in this poem (e.g. 49. 8, 51. 1).

So fled th'offended shadows of her cheer,
And showed her pleasèd count'nance full as clear.

Which, for his fourth course,
made our poet court her, etc.

87 'This motion of my soul, my fantasy,   *Gustus*   D4ᵛ
    Created by three senses put in act,
    Let justice nourish with thy sympathy,
    Putting my other senses into fact.
      If now thou grant not, now change that offence: 5
    To suffer change doth perfect sense compact;[20]
      Change then, and suffer for the use of sense.
    We live not for ourselves: the ear and eye
    And every sense must serve society.

88 'To furnish then this banquet, where the taste
    Is never used, and yet the cheer divine,
    The nearest mean, dear mistress, that thou hast
    To bless me with, it is a kiss of thine;
      Which grace shall borrow organs of my touch   5
    T'advance it to that inward taste of mine,[21]
      Which makes all sense, and shall delight as much.

M20. *Alterationem pati est sentire.*
(To experience sensation is to suffer change.)
M21. He intends the common sense, which is *centrum sensibus et speciebus*, and calls it last because it doth *sapere in effectione sensum.*
    [*centrum sensibus et speciebus*: the centre for all senses and emanations. *sapere in effectione sensum*: it reaches knowledge by its accomplishment of sensations.]

---

86. 9 *full as clear*] as full as it was clear, i.e. both in its fullness and brightness, once the shadows of anger were vanished.
fourth course] taste, the fourth sense in Ovid's banquet.
87. 1–4 *This motion ... into fact*] 'Corinna, let your justice nourish this impulse in my imagination, created by the three senses stimulated so far, with your favour, by setting to motion the other two senses (i.e. taste and touch).'
87. 1 *fantasy*] imagination; on the role of this faculty of the soul in the process of perception, see Commentary: 'Banquet', 87–88 and M20, M21.
87. 3 *sympathy*] favour (*OED*, n., 3. d).
87. 6 *To suffer change doth perfect sense compact*] This line is an elaborate poetic translation of the Latin tag in M20: *Alterationem pati est sentire* ('To undergo change is to experience sensation').
87. 8 *We live not for ourselves*] On the Ciceronian source and Ovid's use, see Commentary: 'Banquet', 87–88 and M20, M21.
88. 1 *furnish*] complete.
88. 2 *cheer*] food and drink enjoyed in a banquet (*OED*, n., 6).
88. 5 *borrow organs of my touch*] On the Aristotelian equation of taste and touch, see Commentary: 87–88 and M20, M21.
88. 6 *advance*] push forward (for this transitive use, see *OED*, v., 6. a).
88. 6 *inward taste*] On Chapman's gloss (M21) of this phrase as the Aristotelian 'common sense', see Commentary: 87–88 and M20, M21.

Then with a kiss (dear life) adorn thy feast,
And let (as banquets should) the last be best.'

89 'I see unbidden guests are boldest still,   *Corinna*
And well you show how weak in soul you are
That let rude sense subdue your reason's skill
And feed so spoilfully on sacred fare;
    In temper of such needless feasts as this   5
We show more bounty still the more we spare,
    Chiefly where birth and state so different is.
Air too much rarefied breaks forth in fire,
And favours too far urged do end in ire.'

90 'The difference of our births (imperial dame)   *Ovid*
Is herein noted with too trivial eyes;
For your rare wits, that should your choices frame
To state of parts that most doth royalize,
    Not to commend mine own but that in yours   5
Beyond your birth, are peril's sovereignties,
    Which (urged) your words had strook with sharper powers:
'Tis for mere look-like ladies, and for men
To boast of birth that still be childeren,

91 'Running to father straight to help their needs.   E1^r
True dignities and rites of reverence
Are sown in minds, and reaped in lively deeds,
And only policy makes difference
    'Twixt states, since virtue wants due imperance.   5

---

88. 9 *the last*] taste, and also touch, whose organs taste will borrow.
89. 4 *spoilfully*] by indulging in pillage and destruction (see *OED*, † *spoilful*, adj., with examples from Spenser and Chapman).
89. 5 *temper*] moderation (*OED*, n., 3).
89. 8 *rarefied*] refined, thinned. On the sources and meaning of this line, see Commentary: 'Banquet', 89.
90. 3-7 *your rare wits ... with sharper powers*] On the interpretation of this obscure passage, see Commentary: 'Banquet', 90–91.
90. 3 *choices*] i.e. of arguments and words.
90. 4 *state of parts*] listing or enumeration of qualities (*OED*, state, n., 34. b).
90. 4 *royalize*] excel, rule as a monarch (*OED*, v., †2, intransitive use).
90. 7 *strook*] struck, in this case meaning 'impressed', 'stamped' (*OED*, strike, v., 28); also 'pierced' (v., 31). The historical form of the past participle has been preserved for reasons of phonetic difference.
90. 8–91. 1 '*Tis for mere look-like ladies ... their needs*] i.e. to boast of noble birth is for would-be ladies and for men that are mere children, running straight to their fathers to help their needs.
91. 2 *dignities*] titles of nobility (*OED*, n., 3).
91. 2 *rites of reverence*] signs/gestures of respect paid to those of noble rank.
91. 4–5 *only policy ... due imperance*] only government makes the difference between social ranks, since virtue is not an innate quality of those that hold political authority.

Virtue makes honour, as the soul doth sense,
   And merit far exceeds inheritance;
The Graces fill Love's cup, his feasts adorning,
Who seeks your service now, the Graces' scorning.'

92 'Pure love', said she, 'the purest grace pursues,
And there is contact, not by application
Of lips or bodies, but of bodies' virtues,
As in our elemental nation
   Stars by their powers, which are their heat and light, 5
Do heav'nly works; and that which hath probation
   By virtual contact hath the noblest plight,
Both for the lasting and affinity
It hath with natural divinity.'

93 Ovid replied: 'In this thy virtual presence
(Most fair Corinna) thou canst not effuse
The true and solid parts of thy pure essence,
But dost thy superficial beams produce
   Of thy rich substance, which, because they flow 5
Rather from form than from the matter's use,
   Resemblance only of thy body show,
Whereof they are thy wondrous species,
And 'tis thy substance must my longings ease.

94 'Speak then, sweet air, that giv'st our speech event,
And teach my mistress tractability,
That art to motion most obedient;

---

91. 9 *the Graces' scorning*] scorning the Graces' service, because Love prefers being Corinna's servant to being served by the cup-filling Graces. The genitive interprets Q*OB*'s 'Graces'.
92. 1 *grace*] the beloved's favour.
92. 4 *elemental nation*] the heavens.
92. 6 *probation*] demonstrative evidence (*OED*, 4. b).
92. 7 *virtual contact*] pertaining to virtue; also, by contact in essence or potentiality, but not in material actuality (see *OED*, *virtual*, adj., †1 and 4. a).
92. 7 *plight*] pledge, assurance.
92. 9 *natural divinity*] the divine quality of natural elements, here the stars.
93. 1 *virtual presence*] emanation that is perceived by the senses (particularly by sight).
93. 2 *effuse*] issue, pour fourth (see note to '*OBS*: Williams, 1', 11).
93. 4 *superficial beams*] effusions or emanations producing the 'resemblance' of Corinna's body.
93. 6 *form ... matter*] On the theory of perception that sustains this stanza, see Commentary: 'Banquet', 93–94.
93. 8 *species*] See 17. 5, and Commentary: 'Banquet', 17.
94. 1 *event*] discharge, release; *OED* registers this sense in verbal uses (†v.¹). Compare: 'A loose and rorid vapour that is fit | T'euent his searching beames' (*Hero and Leander*, III. 241–42, in Bartlett, p. 139).
94. 2 *tractability*] docility. On Chapman's wordplay, see Commentary: 'Banquet', 93–94.

And though thy nature swelling be and high,
    And occupiest so infinite a space,
Yet yield'st to words, and art conduced thereby
    Past nature, pressed into a little place.
Dear sovereign, then, make air thy rule in this,
And me thy worthy servant with a kiss.'

95 'Ovid,' said she, 'I am well pleased to yield:
Bounty by virtue cannot be abused,
Nor will I coyly lift Minerva's shield
Against Minerva; honour is not bruised
    With such a tender pressure as a kiss,
Nor yielding soon to words, though seldom used;
    Niceness in civil favours folly is;
Long suits make never good a bad detection,
Nor yielding soon makes bad a good affection.

96 'To some, I know (and know it for a fault),
Order and reverence are repulsed in scaling;
When pride and rudeness enter with assault,
Consents to fall are worse to get than falling;
    Willing resistance takes away the will,
And too much weakness 'tis to come with calling;
    Force in these frays is better man than skill;
Yet I like skill, and, Ovid, if a kiss
May do thee so much pleasure, here it is.'

97 Her moving towards him made Ovid's eye
Believe the firmament was coming down
To take him quick to immortality,
And that th'ambrosian kiss set on the crown.
    She spake in kissing, and her breath infused

---

94. 6 *yield'st to words*] On the theory of voice invoked here, see Commentary: 'Banquet', 93–94.
94. 7 *Past nature*] beyond or against what is natural to it, i.e. expanding and soaring high.
95. 3 *Minerva's shield*] The shield of Minerva (or Pallas), goddess of wisdom, was used by Perseus to reflect Medusa's petrifying look (see 'SN: To Roydon', and Commentary).
95. 6 *Nor yielding ... seldom used*] i.e. honour is not bruised with yielding soon to words, even if this attitude is infrequent.
95. 7 *Niceness*] coyness; also, fastidiousness (*OED*, n., †3, and 6. a).
95. 7 *civil*] courteous (*OED*, adj., 7. a).
95. 8 *detection*] choice (Hudston, p. 413). This sense is not in *OED*.
95. 9 *affection*] passion (*OED*, n.¹, 1. †b).
96. 2 *scaling*] attacking (see 'assault', 96. 3), or ascending with a scaling ladder (*OED*, v.³, 1), here with a hint of social transgression.
97. 4 *ambrosian*] resembling ambrosia, the nectar of the Olympian gods; thus, fragrant and sweet-tasting, but also celestial.
97. 4 *set on the crown*] put the crown on him; crowned him to make him immortal, like gods.

Restoring syrup to his taste, in swoon;
    And he imagined Hebe's hands had bruised
A banquet of the gods into his sense,
Which filled him with this furious influence:

98 'The motion of the heav'ns that did beget
The golden age, and by whose harmony
Heav'n is preserved, in me on work is set:
All instruments of deepest melody,
    Set sweet in my desires to my love's liking,   5
With this sweet kiss in me their tunes apply,
    As if the best musicians' hands were striking.
This kiss in me hath endless music closed,
Like Phoebus' lute on Nisus' towers imposed.

99 'And as, a pebble cast into a spring,
We see a sort of trembling circles rise,
One forming other in their issuing
Till over all the fount they circulize,
    So this perpetual-motion-making kiss   5
Is propagate through all my faculties,
    And makes my breast an endless fount of bliss,
Of which, if Gods could drink, their matchless fare
Would make them much more blessèd than they are.

100 'But as when sounds do hollow bodies beat,[22]
Air gathered there, compressed and thickenèd,
The selfsame way she came doth make retreat,
And so effects the sound re-echoèd

M22. *Qua ratione fiat echo.*
(The explanation of how echo occurs.)

---

97. 7 *Hebe*] goddess of youth (she is called Iuventas in Roman mythology), daughter of Juno and Jupiter, to whom she served as cupbearer (see Commentary: 'Banquet', 97).
97. 7 *bruised*] beaten, damaged, or squeezed (*OED*, v., 3–5).
97. 9 *this furious influence*] i.e. the ensuing speech (stanzas 98–104), which is an effect of amatory and poetic fury.
98. 1 *motion of the heav'ns*] the concentric movement of the heavenly spheres, producing celestial music (see also 'Banquet', 20 and its commentary).
98. 2 *golden age*] the primitive age of plenty and harmony, which Ovid describes in *Metamorphoses*, I (see Commentary: 'Banquet', 98).
98. 9 *Nisus' towers*] Nisus was the king of Megara, in whose towers still resonated the notes of Apollo's lyre, which the god laid there (see Commentary: 'Banquet', 98).
98. 9 *imposed*] laid, placed (*OED*, v., 1. a).
99. 4 *circulize*] expand in concentric circles (see Commentary: 'Banquet', 99).
99. 6 *propagate*] reproduced and multiplied, but also extended in size (see Commentary: 'Banquet', 99).
99. 6 *all my faculties*] i.e. the inner senses (see Commentary: 'Banquet', 27, 87–88, 99).
100 On the sources, phrasing and meaning of this simile, see Commentary: 'Banquet', 100 and M22

>   Only in part, because she weaker is 5
> In that redition than when first she fled,
>   So I, alas, faint echo of this kiss,
> Only reiterate a slender part
> Of that high joy it worketh in my heart,

101 'And thus, with feasting, love is famished more.
   Without my touch are all things turned to gold,
      And till I touch I cannot joy my store:
   To purchase others, I my self have sold.
      Love is a wanton famine, rich in food, 5
   But with a richer appetite controlled;
      An argument in figure and in mood,
   Yet hates all arguments — disputing still
   For sense, gainst reason, with a senseless will.

102 'Then, sacred madam, since my other senses   *Tactus*
   Have in your graces tasted such content,
      Let wealth, not to be spent, fear no expenses,
   But give thy bounty true eternizement,
      Making my senses' groundwork, which is feeling, 5
   Effect the other endless excellent,
      Their substance with flint-soft'ning softness steeling:

---

100. 6 *redition*] the action of returning. On Chapman's use through translation, see Commentary: 'Banquet', 100 and M22.
100. 8 *reiterate*] walk over again: *OED*, v., †3, only provides a later example, so this would be Chapman's neologism.
101. 1–3 *And thus ... my store*] See Commentary: 'Banquet', 101, on the indebtedness of these lines to the myths of Narcissus and Midas.
101. 4 *my self*] Q*ob*'s 'my self' has been maintained here, as 'self' is used nominally.
101. 5 *wanton*] abundant, rich, extravagant (*OED*, adj., 5), and thus an oxymoron in combination with 'famine'.
101. 6 *appetite*] craving for food; and, more generally, desire.
101. 6 *controlled*] overruled, overpowered (*OED*, v., †5).
101. 7 *An argument in figure and in mood*] a proof of logical invention disposed correctly in a syllogism (on the use of logical terms in this stanza, see Commentary: 'Banquet', 101).
101. 9 *For sense, gainst reason, with a senseless will*] i.e. in favour of sexual pleasure, and thus against reason, with a sensual inclination that does not attend to reason. 'Sense' suggests here one thing (passion; *OED*, *sense*, n., 15) and its opposite (reason; *OED*, n., 17).
102. 4 *eternizement*] immortal fame. *OED* registers this use only, so it must be assumed to be Chapman's neologism.
102. 5 *groundwork*] basis, foundation.
102. 5 *feeling*] the sense of touch; see Commentary: 'Banquet', 102–04 on the role of touch in theories of sensation.
102. 6 *Effect the other endless excellent*] i.e. render the other senses long-lasting in their excellence (see *OED*, 'effect', v., 1. †a). This reading relies on the editorial deletion of Q*ob*'s comma after 'other'.
102. 7 *substance*] qualities as material objects.
102. 7 *flint-soft'ning softness steeling*] On this paradox and its meaning, see Commentary: 'Banquet', 102–04.

> Then let me feel, for know, sweet Beauty's Queen,
> Dames may be felt, as well as heard or seen.

103 'For if we be allowed to serve the ear
    With pleasing tunes, and to delight the eye
    With gracious shows, the taste with dainty cheer,
    The smell with odours, is't immodesty
        To serve the senses' emperor, sweet feeling,
    With those delights that fit his empery?
        Shall subjects free themselves, and bind their king?
    Minds taint no more with bodies' touch, or tire,
    Than bodies nourish with the mind's desire.

104 'The mind then clear, the body may be used,
    Which perfectly your touch can sp'ritualize,
    As by the great elixir is transfused
    Copper to gold; then grant that deed of price.
        Such as transform into corrupt effects
    What they receive from nature's purities
        Should not wrong them that hold her due respects:
    To touch your quick'ning side then give me leave;
    Th'abuse of things must not the use bereave.'

105 Herewith, ev'n glad his arguments to hear,
    Worthily willing to have lawful grounds

---

102. 8 *Beauty's Queen*] Corinna is identified as Venus, chosen by Paris as the most beautiful of all goddesses.
103. 3 *dainty cheer*] delicacies served at a banquet (see *OED*, dainty, adj. 3; and *cheer*, n., 6).
103. 5 *the senses' emperor*] On Ovid's views on the pre-eminence of touch, see Commentary: 'Banquet', 102–04.
103. 8–9 *Minds taint ... mind's desire*] 'Just as bodies can be nourished moderately with the mind's passions (and are not consumed by them), minds will not wear out or become corrupted with the use of touch.'
103. 8 *taint*] lose vigour (*OED*, v., †8. b); also, become corrupted (v., 9. b).
103. 8 *tire*] become weak (*OED*, v.¹, 2); this verb is synonymous with 'taint', with which it is coordinated syntactically.
103. 9 *nourish*] receive nourishment, are fed (*OED*, v., †8).
104. 2 *your touch*] your being touched (with Corinna as object).
104. 2 *sp'ritualize*] convert or reduce to a rarefied or volatile substance, as in alchemical processes (*OED*, spiritualize, v., †1); it has inevitable religious undertones. Here, the pronunciation is trisyllabic.
104. 3 *great elixir*] red elixir, or philosopher's stone (on the stanza's alchemical imagery, see Commentary: 'Banquet', 102–04).
104. 4 *price*] worth, honour, praise (*OED*, price, n., †1); Q*OB*'s 'prise' is a historical spelling, here modernized.
104. 8 *quick'ning*] inspiring, life-giving, life-restoring, with a strong spiritual, religious sense; *OED*, quicken, v.¹, 2.
104. 8 *side*] synecdochically, and euphemistically, breast.
104. 9 *bereave*] prevent, deprive.

To make the wondrous power of heav'n appear,
In nothing more than her perfections found,
 Close to her navel she her mantle wrests,   5
Slacking it upwards, and the folds unwound,
 Showing Latona's twins, her plenteous breasts,
The Sun and Cynthia in their triumph-robes
Of lady-skin, more rich than both their globes,

106 Whereto she bad blest Ovid put his hand.
He, well acknowledging it much too base
For such an action, did a little stand,
Ennobling it with titles full of grace,
 And conjures it with charge of rev'rend verse   5
To use with piety that sacred place,
 And through his feeling's organ to disperse
Worth to his spirits, amply to supply
The poorness of his flesh's faculty.

107 And thus he said: 'King of the king of senses,   E3ʳ
Engine of all the engines under heaven,
To health and life defence of all defences,
Bounty by which our nourishment is given,
 Beauty's beautifier, kind acquaintance-maker,   5
Proportion's oddness that makes all things even,
 Wealth of the labourer, wrong's revengement-taker,
Pattern of concord, lord of exercise,
And figure of that power the world did guise —

---

105. 5–6 *she her mantle ... the folds unwound*] 'She holds her mantle with a twisting movement, loosening it by a lifting turn, and so undoes the folds (to finally withdraw it from her breasts).' See *OED*, *wrest*, v., 1, and *slack*, v., 6. a.
105. 7–8 *Latona's twins ... The Sun and Cynthia*] Apollo and Diana. See Commentary: 'Banquet', 105–06.
105. 9 *globes*] celestial spheres of the sun and the moon (*OED*, n., 1. †b).
106. 5 *charge*] admonition, mandate (*OED*, n., 15).
106. 5 *rev'rend*] solemn, reverence-inspiring (*OED*, *reverend*, adj., 3).
106. 7 *disperse*] distribute (*OED*, v., 4. a); 'dispense' (i.e. administer, in its religious sense) offers an alternative reading, although rhyme discourages emendation.
106. 8 *supply*] compensate by providing what is missing (*OED*, v.¹, †2. b).
107. 2 *Engine of all the engines*] most powerful of mechanisms on earth.
107. 3 *To health ... defences*] supreme weapon or tool for the defence of health and life.
107. 5 *Beauty's beautifier*] shaper of beauty, as in the work of the painter or sculptor. 'Beautifier' should be trisyllabic to avoid an extrametrical line.
107. 6 *Proportion's oddness that makes all things even*] i.e. the five fingers of one hand become ten when multiplied by two, thus transforming an odd number into an even one. See Commentary: 'Banquet', 107–09.
107. 7 *labourer*] Pronounced disyllabically, /ˈleɪbrə/, to avoid an extrametrical line.
107. 9 *guise*] shape (*OED*, v., 1. †c).

108 'Dear hand, most duly honourèd in this,
And therefore worthy to be well employed,
Yet know, that all that honour nothing is
Compared with that which now must be enjoyed;
   So think in all the pleasures these have shown 5
(Likened to this) thou wert but mere annoyed,
   That all hands' merits in thyself alone
With this one touch have more than recompense,
And therefore feel, with fear and reverence.

109 'See Cupid's Alps, which now thou must go over,
Where snow that thaws the sun doth ever lie;
Where thou may'st plain and feelingly discover
The worlds forepast that flowed with milk and honey;
   Where (like an empress seeing nothing wanting 5
That may her glorious childbed beautify)
   Pleasure herself lies big with issue panting,
Ever delivered, yet with child still growing,
Full of all blessings, yet all bliss bestowing.'

110 This said, he laid his hand upon her side,
Which made her start like sparkles from a fire,
Or like Saturnia from th'ambrosian pride
Of her morn's slumber, frighted with admire
   When Jove laid young Alcides to her breast: 5
So startled she, not with a coy retire,
   But with the tender temper she was blest,

---

108. 1 *in this*] in all the qualities and actions explained in the previous stanza.
108. 4 *that*] the action of touching Corinna.
108. 5–6 *So think ... mere annoyed*] 'So think that in all the pleasures that all these previous actions and qualities have shown to you (i.e. my hand) you found mere annoy rather than actual pleasure.'
109. 2 *snow that thaws the sun*] There is no inversion of word order here (i.e. the snow thaws the sun).
109. 3 *plain*] plainly.
109. 4 *worlds forepast*] bygone worlds.
109. 5–9 *Where ... all bliss bestowing*] See Commentary: 'Banquet', 107–09, on the meanings and function of this simile.
110. 1 *side*] breast (see 104. 8, and note).
110. 3, 5 *Saturnia, Alcides*] On Saturn's daughter, i.e. Juno, and Hercules, see Commentary: 'Banquet', 110.
110. 3 *ambrosian*] celestial (see 97. 4, and note).
110. 6 *startled*] recoiled, rose with a start (*OED*, v., 3. c).
110. 6 *retire*] retreat, withdrawal (*OED*, n.¹, 2).
110. 8 *undulled*] not dulled or rendered blunt by use.

   Proving her sharp, undulled with handling yet,
  Which keener edge on Ovid's longings set.

111 And feeling still, he sighed out this effect: *E3ᵛ*
  'Alas, why lent not heav'n the soul a tongue,
  Nor language, nor peculiar dialect,
  To make her high conceits as highly sung,
   But that a fleshly engine must unfold   5
  A sp'ritual notion? Birth from princes sprung
   Peasants must nurse; free virtue wait on gold;
  And a professed though flattering enemy
  Must plead my honour and my liberty.

112 'O Nature, how dost thou defame in this
  Our human honours, yoking men with beasts
  And noblest minds with slaves? Thus beauty's bliss,
  Love and all virtues that quick spirit feasts
   Surfeit on flesh; and thou that banquet'st minds,   5
  Most bounteous mistress, of thy dull-tongued guests
   Reap'st not due thanks; thus rude frailty binds
  What thou giv'st wings; thus joys I feel in thee
  Hang on my lips, and will not uttered be.

113 'Sweet touch, the engine that Love's bow doth bend,
  The sense wherewith he feels him deified,
  The object whereto all his actions tend,
  In all his blindness his most pleasing guide,

---

110. 9 *Which keener edge*] Whose keener edge, i.e. the sharp edge of Corinna, her breasts (nipples?), but with an inevitable pun on Ovid's own 'edge' (i.e. erection).
111. 1 *sighed out*] spoke out, uttered in sighs (see Commentary: 'Banquet', 111).
111. 1 *effect*] impression, i.e. produced by the sense of touch (*OED*, n., 9. a).
111. 3 *peculiar dialect*] a language pertaining to the soul only (*OED, peculiar*, adj., 2. c).
111. 4 *her high conceits*] her excellent qualities, or ornaments (see *OED, conceit*, n., 9. a); also, the 'sp'ritual notion' born from her conceptions (see 'Birth' in this stanza, and also 109. 7–9).
111. 5 *a fleshly engine*] the tongue as producer of speech (in opposition to the language of the soul that Ovid reclaims).
111. 7 *wait*] must wait.
111. 8 *a professed though flattering enemy*] the body, or the flesh (or Nature).
112. 1 *defame*] denigrate, disparage.
112. 1 *in this*] i.e. in not giving me a language of the soul.
112. 2 *yoking*] levelling (*OED*, v., 6. a); also, fastening with a yoke.
112. 4 *that quick spirit feasts*] that our living soul entertains (i.e. hosts).
112. 5 *banquet'st*] entertain (second person singular, disyllabic); see *OED*, v., 1. a.
112. 6 *Most bounteous mistress*] Nature.
113. 1 *the engine*] the hand.
113. 2 *him*] himself.

For thy sake will I write the *Art of Love*, 5
Since thou dost blow his fire and feed his pride,
    Since in thy sphere his health and life doth move;
For thee I hate who hate society,
And such as self-love makes his slavery.

114 'In these dog days how this contagion smothers
The purest bloods with virtue's diet fined,
Nothing their own, unless they be some others
Spite of themselves, are in themselves confined
    And live so poor they are of all despised. 5
Their gifts, held down with scorn, should be divined,
    And they like mummers mask, unknown, unprized:
A thousand marvels mourn in some such breast
Would make a kind and worthy patron blest.

115 'To me (dear sovereign) thou art patroness, E4ʳ
And I, with that thy graces have infused,
Will make all fat and foggy brains confess
Riches may from a poor verse be deduced;
    And that gold's love shall leave them grovelling here, 5
When thy perfections shall to heav'n be Mused,
    Decked in bright verse, where angels shall appear,
The praise of virtue, love, and beauty singing,
Honour to noblesse, shame to avarice bringing.'

---

113. 5 *For thy sake*] For the sake of touch (see Commentary: 'Banquet', 113).
113. 5 *Art of Love*] *Ars amandi*, or *Ars amatoria*, Ovid's didactic elegy of that title (see Commentary: 'Banquet', 113; and Introduction, pp. 50–52).
113. 7 *in thy sphere*] in your orbit, encircling you.
113. 8 *who hate society*] Compare 87. 9: 'And every sense must serve society'; see Commentary, 87.
113. 9 *self-love*] Compare 'good self-love' (51. 8); see Commentary: 'Banquet', 51 and 113.
114 'In these evil times, how this disease of vanity infects the bloods of those pure men that are refined with virtue's diet, [this disease being] in no way their own unless they be some others (i.e. they are no longer themselves); in spite of themselves, they are imprisoned in themselves and live so poorly that they are despised by all. Their talents, reviled with scorn, should be made divine, and they mask like mummers, unknown, unvalued: a thousand wonders that are kept mourning in those men's breasts would be a blessing for a kind and worthy patron.'
114. 1 *dog days*] Latin *caniculares*, associated with the rising of the Dog Star (or Sirius); these are the hottest days of the late summer, and a time of ill omens. Also figuratively, ill times (*OED*, n. 1 and 2); on 'Banquet' as a summer poem, see Introduction, p. 48.
114. 1 *this contagion*] self-love.
114. 3 *Nothing*] in no way (*OED*, adv., B. 1).
114. 7 *mummers*] mimes, actors in the holiday performances known as mummers' plays.
114. 7 *unprized*] not prized or valued.
115. 4 *deduced*] drawn, obtained (*OED*, v., 3. a).
115. 6 *Mused*] sung in verse as inspired by the Muses (Chapman's neologism).

116 Here Ovid, interrupted with the view
   Of other dames, who then the garden painted,
   Shrouded himself, and did as death eschew
   All note by which his love's fame might be tainted;
       And as when mighty Macedon had won   5
   The monarchy of earth, yet when he fainted,
       Grieved that no greater action could be done,
   And that there were no more worlds to subdue,
   So love's defects love's conqueror did rue.

117 But as when expert painters have displayed
   To quickest life a monarch's royal hand
   Holding a sceptre, there is yet bewrayed
   But half his fingers, when we understand
       The rest not to be seen, and never blame   5
   The painter's art, in nicest censures scanned,
       So in the compass of this curious frame
   Ovid well knew there was much more intended,
   With whose omission none must be offended.

   Intentio, animi actio.

   Explicit convivium.

---

116. 2 *painted*] decorated with their presence (as if they were part of a painting); see Commentary: 'Banquet', 116–17.

116. 5 *mighty Macedon*] On this reference to Alexander the Great, see Commentary: 'Banquet', 116–17.

116. 6 *fainted*] lost courage (*OED*, v., 1); this, together with 'grieved' in the next line, seems an attempt to translate Latin 'flevit' (wept, lamented) in Xylander's Plutarch (see Commentary: 'Banquet', 116–17).

116. 9 *love's defects*] those actions that prevent love's completion, and thus the consequences of interruption (116. 1); 'defects' must be understood etymologically as 'lack of action', i.e. from Latin *de* + *facio*.

117. 3 *bewrayed*] revealed, exposed.

117. 5–6 *and never blame ... censures scanned*] i.e. after scrutinizing the work with most meticulous observation, they find no fault with the painter's art.

117. 7 *in the compass of this curious frame*] i.e. in the space into which this intricate design is circumscribed (see Commentary: 'Banquet', 116–17).

Intentio, animi actio. Explicit convivium] 'Intention, an act of the mind. Here ends the banquet.'

A CORONET FOR HIS
MISTRESS PHILOSOPHY

1   Muses that sing love's sensual empery,
        And lovers kindling your enragèd fires
        At Cupid's bonfires burning in the eye,
        Blown with the empty breath of vain desires,
    You that prefer the painted cabinet   5
        Before the wealthy jewels it doth store ye,
        That all your joys in dying figures set,
        And stain the living substance of your glory,
    Abjure those joys, abhor their memory,
        And let my love the honoured subject be   10
        Of love and honour's complete history;
        Your eyes were never yet let in to see
    The majesty and riches of the mind,
    But dwell in darkness, for your god is blind.

2   But dwell in darkness, for your god is blind:
        Humour pours down such torrents on his eyes,
        Which (as from mountains) fall on his base kind,
        And eat your entrails out with ecstasies.
    Colour (whose hands for faintness are not felt)   5

Coronet] The diminutive suggests a small crown (*OED*, n., 1. a), here in reference to the brevity of the sonnet sequence, which follows the pattern of a corona (see Commentary: 'Coronet', 1).
1. 1 *Muses*] On the meaning of the word in the sequence, see Commentary: 'Coronet', 1.
1. 1 *empery*] dominion, sovereignty.
1. 2 *enragèd*] inflamed, ardent (*OED*, adj., †2).
1. 7 *dying figures*] mortal bodies (*OED*, *figure*, n., 4 and 5), in opposition to the immortal soul, or 'living substance' (1. 8); also, with a possible pun on 'dyeing' (see Commentary: 'Coronet', 1).
1. 8 *stain*] alter the natural colour of, defile (*OED*, v., 4 and 5).
1. 10–11 *And let my love ... complete history*] 'And let my beloved be the honoured subject of a comprehensive treatise on love and honour.' See *OED*, *history*, n., 6, for a similar sense.
1. 14 *your god is blind*] On Cupid's blindness and his representation as blindfolded, see Commentary: 'Coronet', 1.
2. 2 *Humour*] the watery, or aqueous humour, a liquid and transparent substance filling the anterior chamber of the eye (*OED*, n., 1. c); see 'Noctem', 8, and note.
2. 3 *Which*] The antecedent is 'torrents'.
2. 3 *his base kind*] Cupid's low descent or kindred (*OED*, n., †10).
2. 5–9 *Colour ... with a pant*] See Commentary: 'Coronet', 2, for a conjectural interpretation of this quatrain, which is characteristic of Chapman's obscure style.
2. 5 *faintness*] dimness (*OED*, n., 4).

      Can bind your waxen thoughts in adamant,
      And with her painted fires your hearts doth melt,
      Which beat your souls in pieces with a pant.
  But my love is the cordial of souls,
      Teaching by passion what perfection is,   10
      In whose fixed beauties shine the sacred scrolls
      And long-lost records of your human bliss.
  Spirit to flesh, and soul to spirit giving,
  Love flows not from my liver, but her living.

3   Love flows not from my liver, but her living,   F1^r
      From whence all stings to perfect love are darted,
      All power and thought of prideful lust depriving,
      Her life so pure and she so spotless-hearted;
  In whom sits beauty with so firm a brow   5
      That age, nor care, nor torment can contract it:
      Heav'n's glories shining there do stuff allow,
      And virtue's constant graces do compact it.
  Her mind (the beam of God) draws in the fires
      Of her chaste eyes from all earth's tempting fuel,   10
      Which upward lifts the looks of her desires
      And makes each precious thought in her a jewel.
  And as huge fires compressed more proudly flame,
  So her close beauties further blaze her fame.

4   So her close beauties further blaze her fame
      When, from the world into herself reflected,
      She lets her (shameless) glory in her shame,

---

2. 7 *her*] i.e. colour's.
2. 9 *my love*] my beloved.
2. 9 *cordial*] a medicinal drink for invigorating the heart (from Latin *cor*, heart), metaphorically applied to the beloved's effect on the lover's soul (*OED*, n., 1. a).
2. 11–12 *the sacred scrolls | And long-lost records*] i.e. texts preserved in long-lost ancient manuscript scrolls, like the Sacred Scriptures.
2. 13–14 *Spirit to flesh ... but her living*] 'Love emanates not from my liver, the bodily site of the passions, but from her living presence, thus supplying life to the flesh, and an incorporeal soul to the spirit-animated flesh.' See Commentary: 'Coronet', 2.
3. 3 *prideful*] arrogant, full of pride.
3. 4 *spotless-hearted*] having a heart without any moral blemish. Hyphenation is editorial.
3. 6 *contract*] lessen, diminish (*OED*, v., 9. a); also, confine (9. c).
3. 7 *allow*] provide, supply (*OED*, v., 8).
3. 8 *compact*] knit together.
3. 10 *fuel*] in figurative sense, a combustible to inflame the passions (*OED*, n., 1. c). Compare Drayton (1594): 'My blandishments were fewell to his fyer' (*Peirs Gaveston*, 279, in *The Works of Michael Drayton*, I, p. 166).
3. 11 *Which*] The antecedent is 'Her mind', the subject of 'lifts' and 'makes'.
3. 14 *blaze*] proclaim, divulge (*OED*, v.², 2. a); emblazon in verse (v.², †6); also, with a pun on *blaze*, v.1, i.e. cause (her fame) to shine (like fire).

Content for heav'n to be of earth rejected.
She, thus depressed, knocks at Olympus' gate, 5
    And in th'untainted temple of her heart
    Doth the divorceless nuptials celebrate
    'Twixt God and her, where Love's profanèd dart
Feeds the chaste flames of Hymen's firmament,
    Wherein she sacrificeth, for her part, 10
    The robes, looks, deeds, desires and whole descent
    Of female natures, built in shops or art:
Virtue is both the merit and reward
Of her removed and soul-infused regard.

5   Of her removed and soul-infused regard, *F1*^v
    With whose firm species (as with golden lances)
    She points her life's field (for all wars prepared),
    And bears one chanceless mind in all mischances.
Th'inversèd world that goes upon her head 5
    And with her wanton heels doth kick the sky
    My love disdains, though she be honourèd,
    And without envy sees her empery,

---

4. 3–4 *She lets ... of earth rejected*] i.e. she admits her unblemished glory into her modest self, pleased that her heavenly virtues are banned from earth.
4. 5 *depressed*] overcome, put down (by earth's rejection).
4. 6 *untainted*] unblemished, pure.
4. 7 *divorceless*] not liable to divorce; this word is Chapman's neologism (see *OED*, adj.; and Kelly, *Poetic Diction*, p. 160).
4. 8 *Love's profanèd dart*] Cupid's arrow, tainted with lust, i.e. the 'stings' that are 'darted' against 'perfect love' (3. 2). See Commentary: 'Coronet', 4.
4. 9 *Hymen's firmament*] Hymen's temple or dwelling-place, as he is the divinity of marriage.
4. 10–12 *Wherein she ... shops or art*] i.e. in Hymen's temple Philosophy sacrifices all the artificial instruments of female seduction (gestures, actions, clothing).
4. 13 *merit and reward*] cause and effect, i.e. virtue is what makes Philosophy deserve reward, as well as the reward derived from her virtuous countenance.
4. 14 *removed and soul-infused*] distant and demure (see *OED*, *removed*, adj.), as well as instilled with soul.
4. 14 *regard*] appearance (particularly of the face), countenance (*OED*, n., †6); also, gaze (n. 7. a).
5. 1 *regard*] The second sense glossed above, i.e. gaze, is prominent now.
5. 2 *species*] the spiritual emanation issued from her gaze.
5. 3 *points*] equips (*OED*, †v.², 2).
5. 4 *chanceless*] independent of chance, and thus opposite of 'chanceful' (see *OED*, 1. a; and Kelly, *Poetic Diction*, p. 160).
5. 5–12 *Th'inversèd world ... renown or grace*] 'My beloved disdains the world upside-down which walks upon her head and kicks the sky with her wanton heels, even if she (the world) is reverenced, and she (my beloved) contemplates without envy this world's authority (and) loathes all her (the world's) trifles and lustful thoughts, thus deploying in the army of her (my beloved's) face all the forces of virtue, in order to dismay those immodest eyes that stand against good reputation and virtue.'

Loathes all her toys and thoughts cupidinine,
   Arranging in the army of her face   10
   All virtue's forces, to dismay loose eyen
   That hold no quarter with renown or grace:
War to all frailty, peace of all things pure
Her look doth promise and her life assure.

6   Her look doth promise and her life assure
       A right line, forcing a rebateless point,
       In her high deeds, through every thing obscure
       To full perfection. Not the weak disjoint
    Of female humours, nor the Protean rages   5
       Of pied-faced fashion, that doth shrink and swell,
       Working poor men like waxen images,
       And makes them apish strangers where they dwell,
    Can alter her; titles of primacy,
       Courtship of antic gestures, brainless jests,   10
       Blood without soul of false nobility,
       Nor any folly that the world infests
    Can alter her, who with her constant guises
    To living virtues turns the deadly vices.

7   To living virtues turns the deadly vices: F2ʳ
       For covetous she is, of all good parts;
       Incontinent, for still she shows entices

---

5. 9 *cupidinine*] lustful, full of cupidity (not in *OED*, which records *cupidinous*). As Kelly remarks, Chapman's coinage seems motivated by the rhyme with 'eyen' (*Poetic Diction*, pp. 157–58).
5. 13–14 *War ... her life assure*] i.e. her look promises war to all frailty, and her life assures peace to all pure things.
6. 2 *rebateless*] without any diminution or lessening (see *OED*, *rebate*, v.¹, and † *rabate*, n.); sharp, as of a weapon (Kelly, *Poetic Diction*, pp. 158–59). On the implications of this term in the context of the sonnet and the sequence, see Commentary: 'Coronet', 6.
6. 3 *every thing obscure*] every obscure thing.
6. 4 *disjoint*] the condition of being out of joint, imbalance (i.e. of 'humours').
6. 5 *rages*] follies (*OED*, n., 4. †a).
6. 6 *pied-faced*] mottle-faced, with painted face, as a sign of inconstancy (*OED*, *pied*, adj.¹, 1 and 2).
6. 7 *Working*] shaping, moulding (as into 'waxen images'); see *OED*, v., 26.
6. 8 *apish*] fantastically foolish; imitative, like apes.
6. 10 *Courtship*] the state befitting a courtier, courtly office (*OED*, n., †2 and †3).
6. 10 *antic gestures, brainless jests*] bizarre carriage, foolish pranks.
6. 11 *Blood without soul of false nobility*] false nobility due to blood, instead of true nobility of soul. On this theme, see Commentary: 'Coronet', 6, 'Cynthiam', 220–42, and 'Banquet', 90–91.
6. 13 *guises*] manners; also, clothes (*OED*, n., †3 and 4).
7. 1 (and 6. 14) *deadly vices*] the seven deadly sins, on whose transformation into 'living virtues' see Commentary: 'Coronet', 7.
7. 3 *Incontinent*] unchaste (*OED*, adj., 1).

>   To consort with them sucking out their hearts;
> Proud, for she scorns prostrate humility;   5
>   And gluttonous in store of abstinence,
>   Drunk with extractions stilled in fervency
>   From contemplation and true continence;
> Burning in wrath, against impatience;
>   And sloth itself, for she will never rise   10
>   From that all-seeing trance (the band of sense)
>   Wherein in view of all souls' skills she lies:
> No constancy to that her mind doth move,
> Nor riches, to the virtues of my love.

> 8   Nor riches to the virtues of my love
>   Nor empire to her mighty government,
>   Which, fair analysed in her beauties' grove,
>   Shows laws for care, and canons for content.
> And as a purple tincture giv'n to glass   5
>   By clear transmission of the sun doth taint
>   Opposèd subjects, so my mistress' face
>   Doth reverence in her viewers' brows depaint;
> And like the pansy, with a little veil,
>   She gives her inward work the greater grace,   10
>   Which my lines imitate, though much they fail —
>   Her gifts so high, and time's conceits so base:

---

7. 5 *prostrate humility*] servile self-abasement (as of courtiers).
7. 6 *in store of abstinence*] in continued self-restraint from food and drink (literally, in abundance of abstinence).
7. 7–8 *extractions ... true continence*] thoughts distilled in the ardour of philosophical contemplation and self-restraint (see *OED*, extraction, n., 3. a; 'still', v., 3. a; and *fervency*, n. 1 and 2; see also Commentary: 'Coronet', 7).
7. 11–12 *that all-seeing trance ... she lies*] 'that divine rapture in which she lies in contemplation (or to be the object of contemplation) of all the arts and knowledges of which the soul is capable.'
7. 11 *the band of sense*] the chain fettering or restraining the senses (see *OED*, band, n., 1. a).
7. 13–14 *No constancy ... my love*] 'No perseverance moves my beloved's mind to that trance of contemplation, nor riches move her mind to the pursuit of virtue.'
8. 2 *Nor empire to her mighty government*] 'Nor thirst for worldly power (moves her mind to) her supreme rule.' The previous sonnet supplies the missing syntactic parts.
8. 3 *Which*] The antecedent is 'her mighty government'.
8. 4 *canons*] rules or laws formulated as the effect of logical analysis, as 8. 3 suggests.
8. 5–7 *as a purple tincture ... Opposèd subjects*] See 'Banquet', 6, and Commentary.
8. 8 *depaint*] depict.
8. 9 *pansy*] heartsease, or *viola tricolor*, a flower whose centre has a darker purple blotch. On the importance of this conceit, see Commentary: 'Coronet', 8.
8. 12 *time's conceits*] time-bound poetic expressions, unable to capture the excellence and timelessness of Philosophy's beauty.

Her virtues then above my verse must raise her,
For words want art, and art wants words to praise her.

9   For words want art, and art wants words to praise her;   F2ᵛ
        Yet shall my active and industrious pen
        Wind his sharp forehead through those parts that seise her,
        And register her worth past rarest women.
    Herself shall be my Muse, that well will know   5
        Her proper inspirations, and assuage
        (With her dear love) the wrongs my fortunes show,
        Which to my youth bind heartless grief in age.
    Herself shall be my comfort and my riches,
        And all my thoughts I will on her convert;   10
        Honour, and Error, which the world bewitches,
        Shall still crown fools, and tread upon desert.
    And never shall my friendless verse envy
        Muses that Fame's loose feathers beautify.

10 Muses that Fame's loose feathers beautify,
        And such as scorn to tread the theatre,
        As ignorant the seed of memory
        Have most inspired, and shown their glories there:
    To noblest wits and men of highest doom   5
        That for the kingly laurel bent affair,

---

8. 14 *words want art, and art wants words*] On the theme of the insufficiency of the poet's art, see Introduction.

9. 3 *seise*] endow, invest, put in possession of (in a specialized legal sense). The spelling in Q*OB*'s 'saise' has been regularized to the also archaic form 'seise'.

9. 3 *Wind*] cause to move in a sinuous, curved course; here the pen winds its own point, or 'forehead', in the act of writing (*OED*, v., 6).

9. 6 *inspirations*] those qualities in the Muse that inspire the poet.

9. 10 *convert*] direct, turn toward (*OED*, v., †2).

9. 11 *which*] The antecedent is 'Error' only, which explains the comma after 'Honour' and the third-person-singular form of 'bewitches'.

9. 13 *friendless verse*] unfriendly; also, without friends, or without a conventional friend, or mistress, unlike other sonnet sequences; see Commentary: 'Coronet', 9, on the import of this phrase to Chapman's poetics.

9. 14 *Muses that Fame's loose feathers beautify*] i.e. Muses that beautify the loose feathers of Fame. 'Muses' is the subject of the action and 'Fame's loose feathers' is the object. On the Virgilian monster *Fama*, depicted with wings and feathers, see Commentary: 'Coronet', 9.

10. 3 *ignorant*] predicated of those poets that 'scorn to tread the theatre': thus, followed by a nominal clause, i.e. 'ignorant (that) the seed of memory [...]' (see *OED*, adj., 1. c).

10. 3 *the seed of memory*] ancient dramatists, or plays ('seed' is used as a mass noun, and is thus the grammatical subject of 'Have [...] inspired, and shown', and the antecedent of 'their').

10. 4 *most inspired*] been an inspiration to (i.e. most theatregoers).

10. 6 *bent affair*] aimed (their) business or endeavour; for 'affair', compare Chapman, *Seaven Bookes* (1598), and *Iliades* (1611): 'fierce Mars flew through the aire | And gathered

    The theatres of Athens and of Rome
    Have been the crowns, and not the base impair.
Far then be this foul, cloudy-browed contempt
    From like-plumed birds; and let your sacred rhymes   10
    From Honour's court their servile feet exempt
    That live by soothing moods and serving times;
And let my love adorn with modest eyes
Muses that sing love's sensual emperies.

    Lucidius olim.

---

darknesse from the fight, and, with his best affaire, | Obeyed the pleasure of the Sunne' (v. 502–04). On this latter instance, see Nicoll's glossary (1, p. 690), and *OED*, n., †4. d.
10. 8 *impair*] damage, impairment. Compare, among numerous instances in Chapman's work, Achilles' words on the Trojans in *Iliads* (1611): 'Phthia, whose bosome flowes | With corne and people, never felt empaire of her increase | By their invasion' (1. 156–58).
10. 10 *like-plumed birds*] poets who, like Fame (9. 14), also have 'loose feathers'.
10. 10 *let*] The addressee changes now from 'Muses' to Philosophy.
10. 11 *servile feet*] metrical feet, metonymically referring to the verses written by servile poets.
10. 11 *exempt*] exclude.
10. 12 *soothing*] flattering, blandishing (*OED*, adj., †1).
10. 12 *serving*] servile, a sense not recorded by *OED*.
10. 13–14 *And let ... sensual emperies*] On the inherent ambiguity of this final sentence, particularly in relation to Q*OB*'s punctuation, its interpretation and its aptness as the corona's close, see Commentary: 'Coronet', 10.
Lucidius olim] 'More lucidly at some future time'. On the importance of this motto for the interpretation of *OBS*, see Commentary: 'Coronet', and Introduction, pp. 57, and 72–73.

THE AMOROUS ZODIAC   F3ʳ

1   I NEVER see the Sun but suddenly
    My soul is moved with spite and jealousy
        Of his high bliss, in his sweet course discerned;
    And am displeased to see so many signs
    As the bright sky unworthily divines   5
        Enjoy an honour they have never earned:

2   To think heav'n decks with such a beauteous show
    A Harp, a Ship, a Serpent and a Crow,
        And such a crew of creatures of no prices,
    But to excite in us th'unshamefast flames
    With which (long since) Jove wronged so many dames,   5
        Reviving in his rule their names and vices.

3   Dear mistress, whom the gods bred here below
    T'express their wondrous power and let us know
        That before thee they nought did perfect make,
    Why may not I (as in those signs the Sun)
    Shine in thy beauties, and as roundly run,   5
        To frame (like him) an endless Zodiac?

4   With thee I'll furnish both the year and sky,
    Running in thee my course of destiny;

---

1. 2 *spite*] indignation, envious malice (*OED*, n., 2); translates 'dépit' (ZA, 1. 2).
1. 4 *signs*] constellations (*OED*, n., 6. b).
1. 5 *divines*] divinizes, worships (*OED*, v., †6. a).
2. 2 *A Harp, a Ship, a Serpent and a Crow*] translates 'Un serpent, un corbeau, un Nef, une lyre' (ZA, 2. 2). See Commentary: 'Zodiac', 1–5, on the identity and symbolic meanings of these constellations.
2. 3 *of no prices*] of no value; translates 'qui ne servent' (ZA, 2. 3).
2. 4 *excite*] awaken, induce; translates 'ramentevoir' (ZA, 2. 4), i.e. remind.
2. 4 *unshamefast*] immodest; translates 'impudiques' (ZA, 2. 4).
2. 6 *in his rule*] in his territory or realm; translates 'au Ciel' (ZA, 2. 6), i.e. in the sky.
3. 1 *Dear mistress*] ZA apostrophizes the mistress by her name, 'Charlote'.
3. 6 *Zodiac?*] The question mark, not in QoB, is added in observance of the interrogative sense of the sentence, and of its presence in ZA.
4. 1 *With thee I'll furnish both the year and sky*] 'With you (i.e. with your body) I will complete the whole course of the astronomical year and sky.' 'I'll furnish' translates 'fournirois', which in French has the sense 'accomplish, complete' (*Centre National de Ressources Textuelles et Lexicales*, *fournir*, v., I. A), current in Middle and Early Modern English, though obsolete now.
4. 2 *Running ... my course*] ZA reads 'l'acheverois [...] ma course'; 'achever' insists on the

And thou shalt be the rest of all my moving.
But of thy numberless and perfect graces
(To give my moons their full in twelve months' spaces)　　　　5
 I choose but twelve in guerdon of my loving.

5 Keeping ev'n way through every excellence,
I'll make in all an equal residence
Of a new Zodiac, a new Phoebus guising,
When (without altering the course of nature)
I'll make the seasons good, and every creature　　　　5
 Shall henceforth reckon day from my first rising.

6 To open then the springtime's golden gate, $F3^v$
And flower my race with ardour temperate,
I'll enter by thy head, and have for house
In my first month this heaven-Ram-curled tress,
Of which Love all his charm-chains doth address:　　　　5
 A sign fit for a spring so beauteous.

---

idea of completion (*Centre National de Ressources Textuelles et Lexicales*, *achever*, v., I. A. 2), as the previous verb 'fournir'.
4. 3 *rest of all my moving*] This phrase translates French 'séjour' — 'stay', but also 'room' (*Centre National de Ressources Textuelles et Lexicales*, *séjour*, n., A. 1. C) — as 'rest', suggesting that the lady will be the place of rest during his travelling along her body.
4. 6 *in guerdon of my loving*] in reward of my love; this phrase has no equivalent in *ZA*.
5. 1–2 *Keeping ev'n way ... in all an equal residence*] 'Spending the same time and allotting the same space in each part, i.e. devoting the same number of stanzas to the praise of each part of the lady's body.' This rule has exceptions: see 12. 6, and Commentary: 'Zodiac', 10–12.
5. 3 *a new Zodiac, a new Phoebus guising*] i.e. the Zodiac (of the lady's body), which will fashion the lover/poet as a new Phoebus, or sun.
5. 5 *make the seasons good*] replace the traditional seasons with the new ones of the lady's body — 'rendroy les Saisons' (*ZA*, 5. 5).
5. 6 *reckon day from my first rising*] i.e. each rising of the new Phoebus will be counted as a new day — 'Se reigleroit le jour a mon premier resueil' (*ZA*, 5. 6).
6. 2 flow'r] open, expand, as if in blossoming — 'commencer' (*ZA*, 6. 2).
6. 2 *ardour temperate*] restrained heat or passion (proper of the springtime, in which the heat is not yet excessive); this oxymoron renders literally 'ardeur temperée' (*ZA*, 6. 2).
6. 4 *my first month*] March, the beginning of the solar year.
6. 4 *heaven-Ram-curled tress*] The original 'Tresse bessonne' (*ZA*, 6. 4) means 'interwoven locks'; 'heaven-Ram' is Chapman's addition, which equates the sign of Aries with the lady's curly hair. 'Heaven' is disyllabic here.
6. 5 *of which Love all his charm-chains doth address*] with which (i.e. the hair) Love adorns all his bewitching chains; the original French is 'Tresse dont Cupidon tous ses liens façonne' (*ZA*, 6. 5), i.e. 'locks where Cupid fashions his chains'. As in the previous line, 'charm-chains' is another Chapmanesque compound with an amplifying function. 'Address' means 'prepare, make ready' (*OED*, *address* v., †12); compare Chapman's *Iliads* (1598, 1611): 'And Hebe, she proceeds | T'address her chariot' (v. 730).

7   Lodged in that fleece of hair, yellow and curled,
    I'll take high pleasure to enlight the world,
       And fetter me in gold, thy crisps' implies:
    Earth at this spring, spongy and languorsome
    (With envy of our joys in love become),   5
       Shall swarm with flowers, and air with painted flies.

8   Thy smooth embowed brow, where all grace I see,
    My second month, and second house, shall be;
       Which brow with her clear beauties shall delight
    The Earth (yet sad), and overture confer
    To herbs, buds, flowers, and verdure-gracing Ver,   5
       Rend'ring her more than summer exquisite.

9   All this fresh April, this sweet month of Venus,
    I will admire this brow so bounteous:
       This brow, brave court for Love and Virtue builded,
    This brow where Chastity holds garrison,

---

7. 1 *fleece*] literal translation of French 'toison' (ZA, 7. 1).
7. 2 *enlight*] enlighten, illumine.
7. 3 *And fetter me in gold, thy crisps' implies*] 'M'empestrant parmy l'or de tes beaux crepillons' (ZA, 7. 3) — i.e. 'wrapping myself around the gold of your beautiful curls'; see *OED, crisp,* n., †4, whose later examples, meaning 'curl of hair', suggest that the word must be Chapman's neologism. Fowler's reading, which makes QOB's 'crisps' a genitive plural and 'implies' a noun, is adopted here; the latter is explained as a 'latinizing coinage' of *implexus,* meaning 'entwinings, tangles' (*Triumphal Forms,* p. 209, n. 2). *OED* records *imply,* v., †1, meaning 'enfold', a similar verbal sense.
7. 4–5 *Earth at this spring, spongy and languorsome | (With envy of our joys in love become)*] QOB begins the parenthesis after 'Earth', but the original punctuation and the sense counsels otherwise: i.e. earth has fallen in love because of her envy of the lovers' joys.
7. 4 *spongy and languorsome*] 'morne & langoureuse' (ZA, 7. 4) (i.e. 'afflicted and languorous'). 'Spongy' can suggest morbid softness; see *OED,* adj., 1, and compare: 'With all the glories of this spongy sway' ('Noctem', 244); and Fulke Greville, *Alaham*: 'the spungie hearts of men | Their hollowes gladly fill with womens loue' (II. 3. 83–84, in *Poems and Dramas,* II, p. 168); 'languorsome' is not recorded in *OED,* and can be regarded as a neologism. Both adjectives conform to Chapman's habits of word formation.
7. 6 *painted flies*] butterflies (French 'papillons', ZA, 7. 6).
8. 1 *embowed*] convex, bow-shaped (*OED,* adj., 1. a).
8. 2 *second month*] April, in the sign of Taurus.
8. 4 *yet sad*] On the Earth's sadness see the previous stanza.
8. 4 *overture confer*] The meaning is unclear; in ZA, 'feroit overture'; the suggestion is that the lady's brow announces the budding, or opening, of the spring vegetation.
8. 5 *verdure-gracing Ver*] the spring, which beautifies the greenery. The epithet is an addition to ZA's 'verdure' (8. 5). QOB does not hyphenate 'verdure-gracing'. When capitalized, the Latin term *Ver* is a personification of spring (*OED,* † *ver,* n.¹).
8. 6 *more than summer exquisite*] more exquisite than summer.
9. 1 *April, this sweet month of Venus*] On the consecration of April to the worship of Venus, called in ZA, 9. 1, 'la Cyprygne', or Cyprian, see Commentary: 'Zodiac', 9–10.
9. 3 *builded*] built.
9. 3–4 *Love, Virtue, Chastity*] 'Amour', 'Vertu' and 'Chasteté' are capitalised in ZA (9. 3–4), with a personifying intention; QOB only capitalizes 'Chastity'.

This brow that (blushless) none can look upon, 5
   This brow with every grace and honour gilded.

10 Resigning that, to perfect this my year
I'll come to see thine eyes, that now I fear:
   Thine eyes that, sparkling like two twin-born fires
(Whose looks benign and shining sweets do grace
May's youthful month with a more pleasing face), 5
   Justly the Twins' sign, hold in my desires,

11 Scorched with the beams these sister-flames eject; F4ʳ
The living sparks thereof Earth shall effect,
   The shock of our joined-fires the summer starting.
The season by degrees shall change again;
The days their longest durance shall retain, 5
   The stars their amplest light and ardour darting.

12 But now I fear that, throned in such a sign,
Playing with objects pleasant and divine,
   I should be moved to dwell there thirty days.
O no, I could not in so little space
With joy admire enough their plenteous grace, 5
   But ever live in sunshine of their rays.

13 Yet this should be in vain: my forcèd will
My course designed (begun) shall follow still.
   So forth I must when forth this month is wore,
And of the neighbour sign be born anew,

---

9. 6 *gilded*] translates French 'revestu', i.e. covered (ZA, 9. 6).
10. 3–6 *Thine eyes that ... | Justly the Twins' sign, hold in my desires*]: 'Tes yeux [...] | Ont à bon droit le lieu du Signe des Gemeaux' ('Your eyes [...] are in their own right the domain of the sign of Gemini': ZA, 10. 3–6). Chapman's changes stress the function of the eyes as both the originators and the fetters of desire.
10. 6 *the Twins' sign*] the sign/constellation of Gemini, beginning on 21 May.
11. 1–3 *Scorched with the beams ... the summer starting*] Chapman makes the past-participle clause occupying 11. 1 depend on 'desires' (10. 6). For Chapman's syntactic rearrangement, compare with ZA: 'Me brulant aux rayons de ces Flames iumelles. | La Terre en sentiroit les viues etincelles, | Le choc de nos deux feux feroit naistre l'Este' ('Burning me with the rays of their twin flames, the earth would feel its living sparks; the clash of our two fires will cause the summer's birth'). Qob's hyphenation of 'sister-flames' and 'joined-fires' has been retained. Although the second is odd, its aim seems to be to reinforce visually the idea of joining.
12. 6 *But ever live in sunshine of their rays*] In the French original, 'Je croy que je voudrois y demeurer' ('I think I would stay here'). On the meaning of this delay in the sign of Gemini, and on the extra stanza given to this sign, see Commentary: 'Zodiac', 10–12.
13. 3–4 *this month is wore | And of the neighbour sign be born anew*] i.e. this month (May) is worn out, and the new month (June) will be born out of the neighbour sign (Cancer). Qob's 'Signes' have been emended to 'sign' (singular) to accord with the original: 'Et au signe d'apres, soudain venir renaistre' (ZA, 13. 4).

Which sign perhaps may stay me with the view, 5
  More to conceive, and so desire the more:

14 It is thy nose (stern to thy Bark of love),
   Or which pine-like doth crown a flowery grove,
      Which Nature strived to fashion with her best,
   That she might never turn to show more skill,
   And that the envious fool (used to speak ill) 5
      Might feel pretended fault choked in his breast.

15 The violent season in a sign so bright,
   Still more and more become more proud of light,
      Should still incense me in the following sign:
   A sign whose sight desires a gracious kiss,
   And the red confines of thy tongue it is, 5
      Where, hotter than before, mine eyes would shine.

16 So glow those corals, nought but fire respiring, F4ᵛ
   With smiles, or words, or sighs her thoughts attiring;
      Or be it she a kiss divinely frameth,
   Or that her tongue shoots forward and retires,
   Doubling, like fervent Sirius, summer's fires 5
      In Leo's month, which all the world inflameth.

17 And now, to bid the boreal signs adieu,
   I come to give thy virgin-cheeks the view

---

13. 5–6 *Which sign ... the more*] Chapman either alters or mistranslates the original: 'Signe, dont la beauté m'empescheroit peut-estre | De plus penser en eux & de les regretter' ('A sign where its beauty may prevent me from thinking further about them (Charlote's eyes) and from lamenting their absence'). Instead of drawing attention to the eyes and the former sign, these lines focus on the lover's new aim.
14. 1 *thy nose (stern to thy Bark of love)*] The parenthetical addition, absent in ZA, is the only indication that the nose is situated by the sign of Cancer. On the 'Bark' as *Argo Navis*, or the Ship, see Commentary: 'Zodiac', 13–14.
14. 2 *Or which*] or that which.
15. 1 *The violent season in a sign so bright*] The summer as the sun reaches the sign of Cancer.
15. 3 *the following sign*] Leo, starting on 21 July.
15. 5 *the red confines of thy tongue*] the lips.
15. 6 *Where, hotter than before, mine eyes would shine*] In the original: 'Où ie me feroy voir plus chauld qu'auparavant' ('Where I would make myself look hotter than before').
16. 4 *shoots*] Emendation of Qob's 'shoaks'; translates 's'elance' (ZA, 16. 4).
16. 5–6 *Doubling, like fervent Sirius, summer's fires | In Leo's month*] The Dog-Star ('Canicule' in the original, from Latin *canicula*), or Sirius, rises in the hottest days of the summer. See 'Banquet', 114. 1, and Commentary.
17. 1 *boreal signs*] the six Northern signs of the Zodiac: Aries, Taurus, Gemini, Cancer, Leo and Virgo.
17. 2 *virgin-cheeks*] not only because the cheek's blush is this a sign of chastity, but because of their identification with the sign of Virgo; hyphenation is from Qob.

>   To temper all my fire and tame my heat,
>   Which soon will feel itself extinct and dead
>   In those fair courts with modesty dispread,   5
>   With holy, humble, and chaste thoughts replete.

18   The purple tinct thy marble cheeks retain,
      The marble tinct thy purple cheeks doth stain,
        The lilies duly equalled with thine eyes,
      The tinct that dyes the morn with deeper red,
      Shall hold my course a month, if (as I dread)   5
        My fires to issue want not faculties.

19   To balance now thy more obscurèd graces,
      Gainst them the circle of thy head enchases
        (Twice three months used, to run through twice three houses),
      To render in this heav'n my labour lasting,
      I haste to see the rest, and with one hasting   5
        The dripping time shall fill the earth carouses.

20   Then by the neck my autumn I'll commence:
      Thy neck, that merits place of excellence
        Such as this is, where, with a certain sphere
      In balancing the darkness with the light,
      It so might weigh, with scales of equal weight,   5
        Thy beauties seen with those do not appear.

---

17. 5 *with modesty dispread*] 'couvert de modestie' (ZA, 17. 5); 'dispread' means 'spread out'; however, the sense implied here is 'clothed with modesty', as in the original French.
18. 3 *lilies*] the cheeks, because of the whiteness of their 'marble tinct'.
18. 5–6 *Shall hold ... want not faculties*] Chapman alters or mistranslates the original: 'me retiendroient un moys: & si je crains encore | Que mes feux au sortir n'en fussent désolez' ('they will hold me one month, if I believe that my fires, as they depart, will not leave me grieving': ZA, 18. 5–6).
19. 1–3 *To balance now ... three houses)*] 'To balance now your more hidden charms against those which are enchased in the circle of your head (having already used six months, and still with six new signs to run).' In the original, the use of brackets is different: they affect the first two lines, thus suggesting a different syntactic arrangement, although the sense is not altered substantially.
19. 4 *this heav'n*] the lady's body.
19. 6 *The dripping time shall fill the earth carouses*] The rainy season (i.e. the autumn) shall fill the earth with cupfuls. See *OED*, carouse, n., †2: cupful.
20. 3 *with a certain sphere*] drawing a circular line (i.e. the curved shape of the neck); translates 'ou d'un certain compas' (ZA, 20. 3).
20. 4–5 *balancing ... with scales of equal weight*] A reference to the sign of Libra, identified as the neck (see Commentary: 'Zodiac', 19–20).

21 Now past my month, t'admire for built most pure
    This marble pillar and her lineature,
        I come t'inhabit thy most gracious teats,
        Teats that feed Love upon the white Riphees,
        Teats where he hangs his glory and his trophies   5
    When victor from the gods' war he retreats.

22 Hid in the vale 'twixt these two hills confined,
    This vale, the nest of Loves and Joys divined,
        Shall I enjoy mine ease, and fair be passed
        Beneath these parching Alps; and this sweet cold
        Is first this month heav'n doth to us unfold,   5
    But there shall I still grieve to be displaced.

23 To sort from this most brave and pompous sign
    (Leaving a little my ecliptic line,

---

21. 1 *past my month*] This is the only indirect reference to October, and thus to the sign of Scorpio, embodied in the lady's breasts.
21. 1 *built*] construction style or structure; *OED*, †n., 1, gives as its first use a later instance by Chapman: 'a saile | Of forreigne built' (*Odysseys*, XI. 145-46).
21. 2 *This marble pillar and her lineature*] i.e. the lady's neck and the bodily contour it delineates; 'lineature' is the French original term, whose borrowing presumably makes up the word's first use in English (*OED* gives seventeenth-century instances only).
21. 3 *teats*] 'Tetons' in ZA suggests that the translation 'teats' should be understood as the full breasts rather than as nipples, its usual English sense.
21. 4 *Teats that feed Love*] Chapman alters the less decorous original by transforming Cupid into the object rather than the subject of the action: 'Tetons qu'Amour poistrist' ('breasts that Cupid kneads': ZA, 21. 4). 'Amour' is capitalized in ZA, and serves as basis for the present capitalization of QOB's 'loue', which becomes 'he' (i.e. Cupid) in the next line.
21. 4 *the white Riphees*] Not capitalized in QOB, ZA's 'neiges Riphées' ('snowy Ripheans') refer to a legendary mountain range in Scythia (see Commentary: 'Zodiac', 21-22).
21. 5, 6 *he*] Love.
22. 2 *the nest of Loves and Joys divined*] i.e. the nest of divine Cupids and the three Graces. Although QOB does not capitalize, the original poem reads 'Nid des Amours & des Graces divines' (ZA, 22. 2). The adjectival participle 'divined' seems to suggest the need to capitalize both 'Loves' (i.e. Cupids) and 'Joys' (i.e. the Graces). On the idea of multiple Cupids, see Commentary: 'Noctem', 322-49.
22. 4 *Beneath these parching Alps*] Chapman's oxymoron alters ZA, 22. 4, which reads: 'Sous l'abry de ces mons' ('under cover of this hill'). The burning Alps contrast with the snowy, 'white Riphees' of the previous stanza — although both name the lady's breasts. Compare 'Banquet', 109. 1: 'Cupid's Alps'.
22. 4-5 *and this sweet cold ... to us unfold*] i.e. this sweet cold of October is the first that heaven announces to us.
22. 6 *there*] i.e. to the next cold seasons, where the lover 'grieve[s] to be displaced'.
23. 1 *sort*] sally out, leave hastily; this directly translates French 'sortir'; *OED*, †v.², gives later examples, so this may be regarded as Chapman's neologism.
23. 1 *this most brave and pompous sign*] Scorpio; ZA, 23. 1, refers here to 'ce lieu' ('this place', i.e. the breasts) as 'brave & magnifique'; 'pompous' does not have negative connotations here (see *OED*, adj., 2: 'magnificent, splendid').
23. 2 *ecliptic line*] 'the circle of the celestial sphere which is the apparent orbit of the sun' (*OED*, ecliptic, adj., A. †b).

    Less superstitious than the other Sun),
    The rest of my autumnal race I'll end
       To see thy hand (whence I the Crown attend),   5
       Since in thy past parts I have slightly run:

24 Thy hand, a lily gendered of a rose,
    That wakes the Morning, hid in night's repose,
       And from Apollo's bed the veil doth twine;
    That eachwhere doth th'Idalian minion guide,
    That bends his bow, that ties and leaves untied   5
       The silver ribbands of his little ensign.

25 In fine (still drawing to th'Antarctic Pole),
    The Tropic sign I'll run at for my gole,
       Which I can scarce express with chastity:
    I know in heaven 'tis called Capricorn —
    And, with the sudden thought, my case takes horn: 5
       So (heav'n-like) Capricorn the name shall be.

---

23. 4 *end*] complete ('parachever' in *ZA*, 23. 4).
23. 5 *Crown*] Neither Q*OB*'s 'crown' nor the original French 'couronne' are capitalized; however, it refers to the constellation *Corona Australis* (in substitution for Sagittarius) and should be treated as a proper noun (see Commentary: 'Zodiac', 23–24).
23. 6 *Since in thy past parts I have slightly run*] Chapman's translation departs from the original: 'Que j'ay peu meriter en chantant ton bel oeil' ('since I have deserved little in singing your beautiful eye': *ZA*, 23. 6). The sense is similar: Durant's lover acknowledges having spent too long in singing the eyes (an extra stanza), while Chapman's admits vaguely to 'have slightly run', that is, to have observed negligently the rule of 'Keeping even way through every excellence' (*ZA*, 5. 1).
24. 1 *gendered*] engendered, conceived (*ZA*, 24. 1: 'engendra').
24. 2–3 *Morning, Apollo's bed*] Q*OB* does not capitalize 'morning', but French 'l'Aube' and the reference to Apollo's bed make clear that this is the goddess Dawn, or Aurora, which suggests a link with Chapman's treatment of this myth in 'Noctem', 378–83. 'Apollo' translates French 'Phoebus', i.e. the sun, and the 'veil' is actually the bed's curtain ('rideau': *ZA*, 24. 3). See Commentary: 'Zodiac', 23–24.
24. 3 *twine*] separate, part (*OED*, v.²). This translates 'entr'rovure', from French 'entrouvrir' (to open halfway).
24. 4 *eachwhere*] everywhere, on all sides.
24. 4 *th'Idalian minion ... little ensign*] Ganymede, Jove's cupbearer, who was kidnapped by the god on Mount Ida. However, the 'bow' and 'ensign', which suggests an odd conflation with Cupid here, is the effect of mistranslation. See Commentary: 'Zodiac', 23–24.
25. 1 *In fine*] finally; the phrase translates directly *ZA*'s 'En fin'; see *OED*, 'fine', n., 3.
25. 2 *gole*] channel, ditch (*OED*, †n²). Lee considers it a misprint for 'goal' (i.e. aim), but the word suggests a figurative use for the female pudenda. The original text is of no help here ('l'autre Signe Tropique').
25. 4 *heaven*] Pronounced disyllabically.
25. 4 *Capricorn*] The sign starting on 21 December, here identified with the female genitals.
25. 5 *with the sudden thought, my case takes horn*] Literal translation of *ZA*'s 'en y pensant soudain mon cas prit corne'. The sense in French suggests an indecent pun, which explains why that part of the body cannot be named 'with chastity'. In English, 'case' suggests the vagina (*OED*, n., †8), which the poetic voice makes his 'gole', or 'goal', and which 'takes' a 'horn', or erect penis (*OED*, n., 5. c). In French, 'corne' also has that sense (*Centre National de Ressources Textuelles et Lexicales*, *corne*¹, n., C. 2).

26 This (wondrous fit) the wintry solstice seizeth,
    Where darkness greater grows and day decreaseth,
        Where rather I would be in night than day;
    But when I see my journeys do increase,
    I'll straight dispatch me thence, and go in peace   5
        To my next house, where I may safer stay.

27 This house alongst thy naked thighs is found,
    Naked of spot, made fleshy, firm and round,
        To entertain love's friends with feeling sport;
    These, Cupid's secret mysteries enfold,
    And pillars are that Venus' fane uphold,   5
        Of her dear joys the glory and support.

28 Sliding on thy smooth thighs to this month's end,
    To thy well-fashioned calves I will descend
        That soon the last house I may apprehend:
    Thy slender feet, fine slender feet that shame
    Thetis' sheen feet, which poets so much fame;   5
        And here my latest season I will end.

---

26. 1 *wondrous fit*] extraordinary state of hardship, danger, or excitement (*OED, fit*, n., 2, †2a), in this case caused by the snares of desire. ZA, 26. 1, speaks rather of a 'lieu fort', i.e. a formidable, or unassailable, place.
26. 4 *journeys*] days, labours of a day, or the daily courses of the sun (*OED*, n., †1. a, 5, and 2. d); these senses are similar to ZA's 'journée' (26. 4).
26. 6 *safer*] in opposition to the sense of peril suggested by 'fit' (ZA, 26. 1).
27. 1 *This house ... is found*] The next sign is Aquarius, beginning on 21 January, and identified with the lady's 'naked thighs'.
27. 2 *Naked of spot*] unblemished; in French, 'Nües de toute tache' (ZA, 27. 2).
27. 3 *love's friends*] in French, 'aux Amans' (ZA, 27. 3).
27. 4 *pillars are that Venus' fane uphold*] the thighs are the entrance columns that uphold the female pudenda, or temple of Venus.
28. 3 *That*] so that.
28. 3–4 *last house ... Thy slender feet*] The lady's feet are identified with Pisces, the last of the signs of the Zodiac, beginning on 20 February.
28. 5 *sheen*] beautiful (*OED*, adj., 1); this translates ZA's 'beaux' (28. 5); 'bright', or 'shining' (*OED*, adj., 2. a), reflect Chapman's translation better, which renders Durant's 'dont l'ont fait tant de conte' as 'which poets so much fame'. Poetic praise of the feet of Thetis, Achilles' mother, comes through Homeric epithet throughout the *Iliad*: 'Θέτις ἀργυρόπεζα', 'silver-footed Thetis'. Homer's meaning is 'nimble', although with a suggestion of radiance and beauty.
28. 6 *latest season*] the winter, which puts an end to the zodiacal year.

L'Envoi:

29 Dear Mistress, if poor wishes heav'n would hear,
    I would not choose the empire of the water,
        The empire of the air, nor of the earth,
    But endlessly my course of life confining
    In this fair Zodiac, forever shining,   5
        And with thy beauties make me endless mirth.

30 But, gracious love, if jealous heav'n deny
    My life this truly-blest variety,
        Yet will I thee through all the world disperse;
    If not in heav'n, amongst those braving fires,
    Yet here thy beauties (which the world admires)   5
        Bright as those flames shall glister in my verse.

Finis

L'Envoi] Originally in French, i.e. 'the envoy', which is the concluding part of a poetical composition, in which the poetic voice 'sends' (French *envoyer*) his words in the manner of a dedication or apostrophe (*OED*, envoy, n.¹). In *ZA*, this last part (which contains three of the four stanzas left untranslated by Chapman) is not marked by Durant explicitly as an envoy. See Gilles Durant, Sieur de la Bergerie, *Les oeuvres poetiques du Sieur de la Bergerie, avec les imitations tirees du Latin de Jean Bonnefons* (Paris: Abel l'Angelier, 1594), p. 24. On the omissions and the general meaning of this envoy, see Commentary: 'Zodiac', 29–30, *L'Envoi*.
29. 1 *Dear Mistress*] in the original, the endearing term 'Mignonne' (*ZA*, 30. 1), i.e. my love, my precious one.
29. 4 *But endlessly my course of life confining*] The absence of a main verb in this sentence is an effect of translation. Compare *ZA*: 'Ie voudroy seulement, sans cesse, me conduire [...]' ('I would only wish to conduct myself, endlessly': 30. 4).
30. 1 *gracious love*] in the original, 'Charlote' (*ZA*, 34. 1).
30. 2 *this truly-blest variety*] i.e. the lady's body parts, comprising a new heavenly Zodiac.
30. 6 *glister*] sparkle, glitter.

COMMENTARY

1. *The Shadow of Night*

Title page

Richard Field for William Ponsonby] Richard Field (1579–1624) was born in Stratford-upon-Avon, where he must have been an early acquaintance of Shakespeare's. He was the printer of *Venus and Adonis* (1593, 1594, 1595 and 1596) and *The Rape of Lucrece* (1594). William Ponsonby (1571–1603), reputedly the most important Elizabethan bookseller, is known for having published Sidney's *Arcadia* (1590, 1593) and the works of Edmund Spenser. See H. G. Aldis and others, *A Dictionary of Printers and Booksellers in England, Scotland and Ireland, and of Foreign Printers of English Books, 1557–1640* (Blades, East & Blades, 1910), pp. 102–03, 217–18.

To my dear and most worthy friend Master Matthew Roydon

1 *Matthew Roydon*] or Mathew Royden (*fl.* 1580–1622), as Chapman and other contemporaries spell it, is the dedicatee of this volume and of *Ovid's Banquet of Sense*. A poet of some prominence, among his early extant compositions are the commendatory poem opening Thomas Watson's *Hekatompathia*, and another to George Peckham's *A True Report of the Late Discoveries of the New-founde Landes* (1583). He knew Sidney, Spenser and Lodge, and his funeral poem in honour of the former, 'Elegie, or Friends passion for his Astrophill', was first printed in *The Phoenix Nest* (sigs B1^r–B4^v). His association with Marlowe and Chapman as part of the alleged group of intellectuals known as the School of Night remains conjectural (Bradbrook, *School of Night*, pp. 23, 27). In his preface to Robert Greene's *Arcadia* (1587), Thomas Nashe said that Roydon 'shewed himselfe singular in the immortall Epitaph of his beloved *Astrophell*, besides many other most absolute Comike inventions' (sig. B3^r). In *Palladis Tamia*, Francis Meres hyperbolically listed him with other English poets that could compare to the great Italian poets of the Renaissance (sig. Oo2^v). Later in his life, Robert Armin lamented Roydon's being 'a Poeticall light, which shines not in the world as it is wisht' (*The Italian Taylor and His Boy* (London, 1609), sig. A3^r). Chapman's choice of Roydon is motivated by his learning, as well as for allegedly having drawn his attention to the group of noblemen mentioned in the epistle.

4–9 from flints must the Gorgonean fount ... beautiful judgement] The legend of Perseus and Medusa is used as an analogy for the poet/philosopher's heroic search for knowledge and defeat of ignorance. Schoell (*Études*, p. 179) traced Chapman's source to Conti, *Mythologiae* ('De Medusa', VII. 11, pp. 748–49; Mulryan, p. 635). Conti recounts how Perseus was sent to kill Medusa. He first stole 'the one eye and the one tooth' ('unicum occulum [...] et unicum dentem') shared by the Graeae, and 'refused to return them until they brought him to the Nymphs'. Later, these 'gave him the winged sandals, the wallet of knapsack, Pluto's helmet, Mercury's invincible sword and Pallas's mirror' ('calceis volucribus Nympharum, pera sive sacculo, galeaque Plutonis, et adamantina falce Mercurii, et speculo Palladis'), with which he fought the Gorgons. Schoell also points to Conti's interpretation of Perseus's feat as an example of intellectual insight: 'Thus the ancients also said that Perseus conquered these monsters and escaped unscathed, but only because he had Pallas's help, the Graeae's eye, Pluto's helmet, and Mercury's sword. For the first thing we need if we want to complete any kind of laborious task is wisdom. We also need insight, a subtle awareness, and a sharp native intelligence...' ('Dictus est idcirco etiam Perseus, non sine Palladis auxilio ac oculo Graearum, Plutonisque galea, et ense Mercurii illas superasse, et incolumis evasisse, quoniam in omnibus rebus arduis ac difficilibus opus est sapientia primum, et animi perspicientia, et subtilitate, atque adeo acumine ingenii...': 'De Gorgonibus', VII. 12, p. 755; Mulryan, p. 640).

QSN's reading 'the eyes of Graea' has been emended here to 'the eye of the Graeae' for the sake of sense, as Chapman's source is unmistakeable about the only eye shared by the Graeae, or grey sisters, daughters of the sea deities Phorcys and Ceto, and sisters of Medusa and the Gorgons. Hesiod mentions only two Graeae (*Theogony*, 273). Conti identifies three, following Euripides' *Prometheus* and other sources ('De Gorgonibus', VII. 12, p. 755). Chapman's mention of 'Hesiodus' alludes to Hesiod's description of Perseus's 'winged sandals' ('πτερόεντα πέδιλα') and 'black-sheathed sword' ('μελάνδετον ἄορ': *Shield of Heracles*, 220–21). Chapman could also have found this description in Conti ('De Medusa', VII. 11, p. 749).

15–16 *supererogation ... pierced*] A retort to Thomas Nashe via Gabriel Harvey's *Pierce's Supererogation, or A New Praise of the Old Ass* (1593). Our poet took Harvey's side in his dispute with Nashe by defending the former's views on the superiority of the scholar over the man of the world. Nashe first used the word 'supererogation' in his pamphlet *Strange Newes* (1592), a treatise against Harvey in defence of Robert Greene: 'I would do workes of supererrogation in answering the Doctor' (*Works of Thomas Nashe*, I, p. 259). Nashe meant the word in its original theological sense, 'the performance of good works beyond what God commands or requires' (*OED*, n., 1). Harvey replied with the abovementioned work, whose title also refers to Nashe's *Pierce Pennilesse* (1592). See Nicholl, *A Cup of News*, pp. 106–12, 172–79.

19 *Intonsi Catones*] Horace, *Odes*, II. 15, 10–12: 'non ita Romuli | praescriptum et intonsi Catonis | auspiciis veterumque norma' ('Such things were not permitted by the authority of Romulus and shaggy Cato and the standard of the men of old', *Odes and Epodes*, ed. and trans. by Niall Rudd (Harvard

University Press, 2004), pp. 126–27). The reference in Horace is to Marcus Porcius Cato (234–149 BC), known as Cato the Elder, or Cato the Censor, an example of old moral austerity and integrity, despite, or because of, his unshaven appearance. Chapman's target here is obscure, and several conjectures have him aim at Nashe and Greene (see Hudston, p. 391, n. 19). The allusion to Cato also explains 'killing censors' ('*SN*: To Roydon', line 12).

27 *most ingenious Derby*] Ferdinando Stanley (1559?–94), Fifth Earl of Derby and Lord Strange. He was an amateur poet and alchemist, patron of letters and principal sponsor of the theatre company known as Lord Strange's Men. For Bartlett, Derby's death in 16 April 1594 is a *terminus ad quem* for the publication of *The Shadow of Night* (p. 422, n. 30). Derby was the model for Spenser's Amyntas in *Colin Clouts Come Home Again* (1595). Hudston notes that Nashe's dedication to Amyntas of his *Pierce Pennilesse* also refers to him, as well as the obscene poem about frequenting prostitutes 'The Choise of Valentines', and notes that Chapman's 'prostitutely' may have been a jibe against Nashe (p. 391, n. 27). On Derby's activity as a poet, see Steven May, 'Spenser's "Amyntas": Three Poems by Ferdinando Stanley, Lord Strange, Fifth Earl of Derby', *Modern Philology*, 70.1 (1972), pp. 49–52, doi:10.1086/390376.

27 *deep-searching Northumberland*] Henry Percy (1564–1632), Ninth Earl of Northumberland. Known as the 'wizard earl', Percy was a speculative, 'deep-searching' philosopher and scientist, and one of the catalysts of the intellectual coterie gathering Harriot, Roydon, Raleigh, Marlowe, Chapman and others. Percy's interests in sciences and the occult are synthesized in the dedicatory poem by George Peele, *The Honour of the Garter* (London: John Busby, 1593): 'Renowmed Lord [...] | By whose directions undeceiueable, | (leaving our Schoolmens vulgar trodden pathes) | And following the auncient reverend steps | Of *Trimegistus* and *Pythagoras*, | Through uncouth waies and unaccessible, | Doost passe into the spacious pleasant fieldes | Of divine science and Phylosophie, | From whence beholding the deformities | Of common errors and worlds vanitie, | Doost heere enioy that sacred sweet content | That baser soules not knowing, not affect' ('Ad Maecaenatem Prologus', sig. A4ʳ). The terms of Peele's praise address a conception of deep learning against conventional scholarship that shows many affinities with Chapman's ideas. Even in his later life of imprisonment in the Tower (1606–17), Percy kept his coterie of scientists and continued to cultivate learning. On his scientific pursuits and his library, see Robert Hugh Kargon, *Atomism in England from Hariot to Newton* (Oxford University Press, 1966), pp. 5–16; Hilary Gatti, 'Giordano Bruno: The Texts in the Library of the Ninth Earl of Northumberland', *Journal of the Warburg and Courtauld Institutes*, 46.1 (1983), pp. 63–77, doi:10.2307/751114; and *Renaissance Drama of Knowledge*, pp. 35–48.

28 *skill-embracing heir of Hunsdon*] George Carey (1547–1603), Second Earl of Hunsdon, was briefly Lord Chamberlain of England between 1596 and 1597, and patron of Shakespeare's theatre company, the Lord Chamberlain's Men, succeeding his father, Henry Carey (1526–96), who was first cousin to Queen Elizabeth I — thus his status as 'heir' in 1594. 'Skill-embracing' metonymically refers to his welcoming of literary talent as a patron of the arts, even if his intellectual inclinations are more difficult to ascertain than those of the other two noblemen mentioned in the epistle. Nashe dedicated *The Terrors of the Night* to Carey's daughter Elizabeth. The work, which was printed, like *The Shadow of Night*, in 1594, is described by Hudston as 'a rationalist counter-pull' to Chapman's occultist inclinations (p. 391, n. 31).

31–32 *strike that fire out of darkness, which the brightest day shall envy for beauty*] This is the first of many references in Chapman's work to the idea of obscurity as a vehicle to knowledge. This theme justifies the inversion of the traditional meanings of night and day, as well as the re-elaboration of the myth of Night in this work (see Introduction, pp. 64–72).

32–33 *my hasting out of town*] No evidence has been found of an actual trip of Chapman's to which this may refer. However, the phrase looks like a rhetorical formula that puts an end to the epistle.

34 *poor and strange trifle*] Chapman's own poem. While the phrase conforms to the modesty topos conventional in dedications, 'poor' and 'strange' are polysemous adjectives here. 'Poor' certainly stresses the insignificant value of his work, but also poverty as a feature of the true poet who scorns fame and material riches, and disdains the company of great men for mere self-interest. Chapman discusses poverty as a feature of the poet several times in his work, although his most overt declaration in this respect is in his *Iliads*: 'We have example sacred enough that true Poesie's humility, poverty and contempt are badges of divinity, not vanity' ('Preface to the Reader', in Nicoll, I, p. 15). 'Strange' marks his work as obscure, but also underscores its extraordinary character while it subtly recommends itself to one of the above-mentioned noblemen, 'most ingenious Derby', or Lord Strange.

34–35 *as resolute as Seneca ... none like it*] 'si non tangent pauca, ne plura quidem' ('If a few do not move him, neither will more': Seneca, *De Constantia*, XV. 2, in *Moral Essays*, ed. and trans. by John W. Bashore, 3 vols (William Heinemann, 1928), I, pp. 92–93). The original context for Seneca's words is his defence of constancy against the opinions of the crowd. Chapman's boast of constancy is actually about artistic self-assurance.

Hymnus in Noctem

1–20, 21–28

'Noctem' opens with two verse paragraphs in which the hymnodist invokes the goddess Night. The identity of this goddess corresponds with Hesiod's

Night (Νύξ), a daughter of primal Chaos: 'ἐκ Χάεος δ' Ἔρεβός τε μέλαινά τε Νὺξ ἐγένοντο' ('From Chaos came forth Erebus and black Night': *Theogony*, 123). The speaker addresses the goddess with four main requests: 1) that she give him tears to weep the present world's decay and corruption; 2) that she induce Sleep to free his soul so that his memory can help his art to reach nature's secrets; 3) that she elevate his soul to the trance that will allow him to sing his grief and nature's secrets; 4) that she affect his hearers with the 'threats of virtue'. The invocation responds to the so-called 'kletic' component of the ancient hymn (see Introduction, pp. 35–38), and its theme is the artistic process. Platonic theories of divine inspiration as expressed in Plato's *Ion*, and in Marsilio Ficino's commentaries on Plato (see Introduction, p. 51, and n. 159), are relevant to Chapman's ideas about poetic 'trance' and inspiration. Yet the attention paid to 'Skill' (as explained below) brings into the poem an important counterpart to ideas of poetic frenzy, or *furor poeticus*. On the function of Night as anagogic, or inspiring goddess, see Introduction, pp. 92–93.

1–4 *Great goddess ... bold relief* and Gloss 1] Chapman bases these lines on a reference to Aratus, *Phaenomena*, or *Astronomica*, 408–10, extracted from his main source: Conti, 'De Nocte', III. 12, p. 231. Chapman's Gloss only gives Aratus's first Greek line, followed by Conti's inexact Latin translation. As Hudston notes, (pp. 391–92, nn. 1–4), Conti's Latin is a free translation (loosely based on Cicero's *Carmina Aratea*, lines 432–34), which adds details like Night's wrapping of the constellation of the Altar as she rides her chariot. None of this is found in Aratus, which Conti reproduces: 'ἀλλ' ἄρα καὶ περὶ κεῖνο Θυτήριον ἀρχαίη Νύξ, | ἀνθρώπων κλαίουσα πόνον, χειμῶνος ἔθηκεν | εἰναλίου μέγα σῆμα' ('But that Altar even beyond aught else hath ancient Night, weeping the woe of men, set to be a mighty sign of storm at sea': *Callimachus, Lycophron, Aratus*, ed. and trans. by G. R. Mair (Heinemann, 1921), p. 413). Conti is the source of Chapman's confusion, which takes the altar to be the earth, wrapped around by Night. However, the Altar is originally meant as the altar upon which Zeus and the Olympian gods swore allegiance before their wars against Cronus and the Titans, later stellified. Neither Aratus nor Conti are of much relevance to Chapman's theme here, whose only interest is in the conceit of the earth as an altar and the 'fearful chances', or prospects, that Night can dispel with her sacrificial 'fumes of sighs' and 'fires of grief'. This conceit sets to work the ritual poetics of this hymn, an idea for which Chapman may have found inspiration from his readings of Conti, particularly 'De propiis ritibus' (I. 15, pp. 54–56), and 'De hymnis antiquorum' (I. 16, pp. 57–60). See Introduction, p. 35.

5 *nurse of Death* and Gloss 2] Night as a mother of Death is derived from Conti, 'De Nocte' (III. 12, p. 233), which quotes and freely translates Hesiod, *Theogony*, 211–13 (see *Hesiod, the Homeric Hymns and Homerica*, trans. by

Evelyn-White, pp. 94–95, for the original Greek and translation). Conti's chapter 'De Morte' (III. 13, pp. 234–36) also insists on Death's descendance from Night.

10–11 *Sleep ... working soul*] Although Q*sn* does not capitalize it, 'Sleep' is here the Hesiodic god Ὕπνος, Latin *Somnus*, one of the children of Night mentioned in the quotation from Hesiod/Conti of Gloss 2. Sleep is Death's stepbrother, as he is the child of Night and Erebus, the latter being a child of primordial Chaos and a personification of Darkness. See also Conti's chapter 'De Somno' (III. 14, pp. 236–40). Chapman's description of Sleep's beneficial effects, capturing the bodily senses and freeing the soul, recalls Alcyone's invocation as she enters Sleep's house in Ovid, *Metamorphoses*, XI. 623–25, a passage quoted by Conti, 'De Somno' (III. 14, p. 237; Mulryan p. 196): 'Somne, quies rerum, placidissime, Somne, deorum, | pax animi, quem cura fugit, qui corpora duris | fessa ministeriis mulces reparasque labori' ('O Sleep, thou rest of all things, Sleep, mildest of the gods, balm of the soul, who puttest care to flight, soothest our bodies worn with hard ministries, and preparest them for toil again!': *Metamorphoses*, trans. by F. J. Miller, II, pp. 164–65).

13 *The court of Skill*] According to Bradbrook, 'Skill was [Chapman's] name for any specialized study: [in *SN*] he speaks of the Court of Skill, that is, the School of Night' (*School of Night*, p. 130). Bradbrook's equation remains as conjectural as the existence of such a group (see Introduction, pp. 9–12). Yet she is right in granting the term a certain pre-eminence in Chapman's poetics. The word means specialized knowledge and training, particularly in science and the arts, yet its sense has to be extended to the poet's capability to disclose philosophical knowledge (see Introduction, p. 19). Skill's inhabiting and ruling a 'court' justifies its personified/deified use here, and thus the capitalization of Q*sn*'s 'skill'. But the small initial of 'court' is preserved, as the place does not seem to acquire the entity of, for instance, Spenserian allegorical sites (e.g. the House of Pride).

14–15 *memory ... secrets* and Gloss 3] Chapman's Gloss 3 —'Plato saith *discere* is nothing else but *reminisci*' — refers to Socrates' words: 'our learning [μάθησις] is nothing else than recollection [ἀνάμνησις]' (Plato, *Phaedo*, 72E, in *Euthyphro, Apology, Crito, Phaedo, Phraedrus*, ed. and trans. by Harold North Fowler (Harvard University Press, 1914), pp. 252–53). *Phaedo* (73–76, pp. 252–69) further develops a theory of knowledge as an effect of anamnesis, which enables the comprehension of the ideas. This is the basis of Chapman's belief that memory leads to the attainment of secret knowledge.

19 *Heav'n's crystal temples* and Gloss 4] Chapman's gloss attributes to this image the quality of a commonplace in Homer and several other authors. In his *Iliads*, he speaks of the 'Christall walls of heaven' (VIII. 384) to

render Homer's 'ἐνώπια παμφανόωντα' (i.e. radiant entrance wall, *Iliad*, VIII. 435, ed. and trans. by A. T. Murray, 2 vols (William Heinemann, 1928), I, p. 360). Chapman may have derived the idea loosely from Conti's description of Heaven as 'nothing but the ether that takes its shape from the fires ignited at the summit of the universe' ('nisi hunc aethera qui constat ex altissimis illis ignibus': 'De Coelo', II. 3, p. 131; Mulryan, p. 110). Conti attributes this description to Orpheus, 'Οὐρανοῦ' ('Of Heaven', *Hymnes Orphiques*, 4. 1, pp. 44–45).

21–24 *like fierce bolts ... come forth and hear*] Swinburne, and later Hudston, detect equivalent uses in Chapman's later works. See *Bussy D'Ambois*: 'the bullets that (to wreake the skie) | the Cyclops ramme in Joves artillery' (IV. 2. 16–17, in *Tragedies*, Q1, p. 136). Also *Caesar and Pompey*: 'those dreadfull bolts, | the Cyclops Ram in Joves Artillery' (II. 5. 3–4, *Tragedies*, p. 566). Chapman's actual source for these lines is again Conti, 'De Cyclopes' (IX. 8, pp. 989–90; Mulryan, p. 850). Conti describes the Cyclopes' forging of Jupiter's 'thunder, lightning and thunderbolt' ('tonitrua, et fulgura, et fulmina') whose intention was 'to strike fear into the hearts of everyone' ('quibus omnes mortales perterrefaceret'). The use of 'heat and cold' as the materials with which they 'rammed' Jupiter's thunderbolt comes from Virgil's *Aeneid*: 'tris imbris torti radios, tris nubis aquosae | addiderant, rutili tris ignis et alitis Austri. | fulgores nunc terrificos sonitumque metumque | miscebant operi flammisque sequacibus iras' ('Three rays of twisted hail had they added to it, three of watery cloud. Three of ruddy flame and the winged southern wind; now they were blending it with the sound of frightful flashes, sound, and fear, and wrath with pursuing flames': VIII. 428–32). This passage is quoted by Conti. In Chapman, the simile confers epic dignity upon the hymnodist's inspired words. The anatomical reference to the ears' 'labyrinth' is also integrated into the epic, martial image: thus, the poet's words are bolts that break first the maze-like, defensive bulwark of the ears of ignorant, insensible men, and then pierce their hardened hearts.

29–49

Addressing Night in the *du-Stil*, the hymnodist begins the account of her primordial hegemony during the stage of primitive Chaos (Night's father), and laments her decision to share her rule with Day. The consequences of their 'distinguished intercession', or turn-taking, in heaven was the replacement of old Chaos, in which the four elements were mixed into one single substance, with a new order in which corruption and deformity lurk under the apparent harmony of form. Two major sources preside over the composition of this verse paragraph. On one hand, Hesiod's *Theogony* supplies the background for Night's descent from Chaos. On the other, Guillaume Salluste Du Bartas's *La Sepmaine, ou Création du monde* (1578).

This work was translated by Josuah Sylvester: *Bartas His Deuine Weekes & Workes* (London: H. Lownes, 1608). Fragments of the translation had been published since 1592. Chapman may have known Sylvester's translation, or could have relied on the French original.

> 31 *the formless matter of this world*] Compare: 'That first World (yet) was a most forme-lesse *Forme*' (Josuah Sylvester, *The Divine Weeks and Works of Guillaume de Salluste, Sieur Du Bartas*, ed. by Susan Snyder, 2 vols (Oxford University Press, 1979), I, Day 1, Week 1, 105, p. 118).

> 38 *fighting parents of this universe*] If we attend to Hesiod's account, the three primordial forces of the universe were Chaos, Earth and Eros (*Theogony*, 115–20). The presentation of primordial forces in strife refers to the state of the four elements during the rule of Chaos. Compare: 'A Gulph of Gulphes, a Bodily compact, | An ugly medly, where all difference lackt: | Where th'Elements lay jumbled all together, | Where hot and colde were jarring each with either' (Sylvester, *The Divine Weeks*, I, Day 1, Week 1, 107–11, p. 118). Chapman's main difference from Bartas/Sylvester's account is that he sees the hegemony of Chaos as a positive, productive period.

> 39–42 *When earth ... were indisposed*] Compare: 'and while this brawle did laste, | The Earth in Heau'n, the Heau'n in earth was plaste: | Earth, Aire, and Fire, were with the Water mixt, | Water, earth, Aire, within the Fire were fixt, | Fire, water, earth, did in the Aire abide, | Aire, Fire, and Water, in the Earth did hide' (Sylvester, *The Divine Weeks*, I, Day 1, Week 1, 114–19, p. 118).

> 43–49 *Nothing ... our pride*] Chapman moves in the opposite direction from Du Bartas/Sylvester's account. Cf. 'For yet th'immortall, mighty thunder-darter, | The Lord high-Marshall, unto each his quarter | Had not assigned: the Celestiall Arkes | Were yet not spangled with their fierie sparkes,| As yet no flowers with odours Earth revived, | No scaly shoales yet in the waters dived, | Nor any Birds with warbling harmonie | Were borne as yet through the transparant Skie' (Sylvester, *The Divine Weeks*, I, Day 1, Week 1, 120–27, p. 118). While, for Du Bartas, Chaos involves lack of forms and, consequently, absence of universal harmony, Chapman's Chaos consists of a primordial soul that has not been contaminated by bodily shapes.

50–62

This verse paragraph is the first of Chapman's characteristic 'as/so' Homeric similes. The simile uses the vehicle of a subterranean well bursting into 'a hundred streams' to explain how the world springing from primordial Chaos has turned to a greater chaos in the present time. For a more detailed commentary on this simile's form and meaning, see Introduction, pp. 30–32.

63–90

In the present state of chaos, a false avatar of Night reigns. The rule of this 'stepdame Night of mind', whose appearance recalls the Gorgon Medusa, is defined in opposition to authentic Night's 'soft and peaceful covert': it is thus characterized by 'disjunction' and 'confusion' of its parts, in opposition to the 'expansure and distinct attire' of the primordial elements. The inhabitants of this new order, maddened by self-love, cause the ruin of the present world by their refusal to observe true religion, just as Diana's boar wreaked havoc on the countryside of Calydon after the Calydonians refused to offer her the first fruits of their harvest.

63–74 *A stepdame Night... her naked secrets show*] For Bartlett, the 'striking figure' of the 'stepdame Night of mind' contained in this passage 'is the nearest thing one can point to as the theme of the poem' (p. 423, nn. 63–74). Schoell (*Études*, pp. 179–80) notes its indebtedness to Conti, 'De Nocte' (III. 2, p. 233; Mulryan, p. 193). Conti's passage opens the chapter's allegorical remarks about the myths concerning Night: 'Ex illa nuper commemoratae pestes natae esse dicuntur, quoniam inscitia et malitia mortalium, quae Nox est mentis, omnium prope calamitatum quae humanum genus invadunt, parens est et altrix, cum aequitas [...] has ex hominum conspectu[m] possit propellere. Haec enim omnia inscitiam consequuntur' ('The plagues just listed are called her children, because, in man, ignorance and ill will (i.e. the Night of the mind) create and nurture almost every misfortune which descends on humankind, while decent behaviour [...] can drive them out of our sight. Ignorance is the source of these things'). The 'plagues' alluded to by Conti refer to a passage from Cicero, in which the children of Night and Erebus are listed: 'Amor, Dolus, Metus, Labor, Invidentia, Fatum, Senectus, Mors, Tenebrae, Miseria, Querella, Gratia, Fraus, Pertinacia, Parcae, Hesperides, Somnia' ('Love, Guile, Fear, Toil, Envy, Fate, Old Age, Death, Darkness, Misery, Lamentation, Favour, Fraud, Obstinacy, the Parcae, the Daughters of Hesperus, the Dreams': *De Natura Deorum*, III. 17. 44, ed. and trans. by H. Rackham (Harvard University Press, 1967), pp. 328–29). Despite his reliance on this source, Chapman's content and method depart from Conti. For Conti, 'Nox mentis', or Ignorance, explains allegorically Night's mothering of all the mentioned calamities. For Chapman, the 'stepdame Night of mind' is an evil avatar of the authentic, benign goddess that presides over his poem. As a replica of true Night, she has 'hell-obscuring wings'. Like the inauthentic Skill imagined by 'passion-driven men' as 'prostitutely show[ing] them her secrets' (*SN*: 'To Roydon', lines 10, 15–16), this 'horrid stepdame [...] (Most harlot-like) her naked secret shows'. As a representation of 'Blindness of the Mind', she is a 'Gorgon' with 'snaky brows', just like the Preface's 'Medusa', who inhabits the 'Gorgonean fount' and whose 'viperous head of benumbing ignorance' must be 'cut off' (*SN*: 'To

Roydon', lines 4, 7–8). These differences between the authentic goddess and her false incarnation prove the inventiveness and originality of Chapman's mythographic recreation of Night (see Introduction, p. 67).

84 *Calydonian boars*] The Boar of Calydon is the wild beast that goddess Artemis/Diana sent from Mount Oeta to the Calydonian fields ruled by Oenus, king of Aetolia, in punishment for offering sacrifices to a number of Olympian gods in thanksgiving for the good harvests, but not to her. Chapman could have found the story in a large number of sources ranging from Homer, *Iliad*, IX. 536–52, to Ovid, *Metamorphoses*, VIII. 272–328. But his allegorical use of this legend is a new borrowing from Conti, who sees in calamities such as 'sterile fields' ('sterilitas agrorum') or 'huge monsters' ('immanitas monstruorum') 'the result of religious neglect or dishonest behavior' ('vel propter neglectam religionem, vel propter hominum improbitatem': 'De apro Calydonio', VII. 3, p. 720; Mulryan, p. 608).

91–111

The hymnodist laments man's loss of his original condition and, consequently, of his privileged position in nature. His present deformity, caused by the effects of 'ambition', 'self-desire' and avarice, is compared to the shrinking of the body of a small roe or kid ('chevril') when it is roasted in the fire. Man's corruption is contrasted with the kindness of the goat Amalthea, who was stellified by Jupiter.

95–100 *Who, like a tender chevril... hospitality to shun*] These lines suggest that the shrinking body, the arms creeping onto the shoulders and the legs bending onto the belly, are man's and not the chevril's, thus presenting metaphorically man's succumbing to the passions as a violent sacrifice. The word 'chevril', meaning a small roe deer, is Chapman's neologism, and derives from Middle and Early Modern French *chevrol*, or *chevreuil* — Latin *capreolus* (*Dictionnaire de l'Académie française*, chevreuil, n.). Its similarity to *chévre*, a goat, and its proximity to the story of Amalthea in the poem, may also suggest a kid — Hudston suggests that 'chevril' means 'the skin from a kid-goat' (p. 393, n. 84). Man's ambition and avarice contrast with the example of Amalthea (105–11).

105–11 *Kind Amalthea... in our hearts*] Schoell notes Chapman's reliance on Conti: 'Plaeclarum est eius quod dicebam argumentum, quia capram etiam, quod de Iove benemerita sit, cum illi lac praebuerit [...] inter sidera collocarunt. [...] Cur inter sidera Caprae signum relatum fuerit, iam explicavimus superius [...] Enimvero quod haec non capra, sed mulier fuit' ('The proof of what I was just talking about is made obvious by the goat's example. Jupiter was certainly in her debt, because she had fed him with her milk. And so the goat was [...] placed among the stars. [...] We have already explained why the Goat was placed as a sign among the stars. [...]

In fact this creature was actually a woman, not a goat': 'De Capra celesti', VI. 11, pp. 609–10; Mulryan, pp. 509–10). The reasons to which Conti refers concern examples of kindness ('beneficentia') argued at the end of his previous chapter, 'De Argonavi' (VI. 10, p. 609). Kindness is certainly Chapman's moral explanation for Jove's gratitude to the goat, whose animal nature lives stellified, thus being a 'living sign', a constellation but also a model, for men. The reason for Amalthea's kindness, as Conti explains, is that she was originally not a goat, but an Arcadian nymph. Chapman remarks that her animal kindness is superior to human nature, even if she ultimately fails to 'work her kindness in our hearts'. The gentle nature of the goat also contrasts with the monstrosity of the Calydonian Boar, and with the frailty of the 'tender chevril' in the previous lines.

112–22

A new instance of kindness rewarded by Jove comes from the ship Argo, on which Jason and the Argonauts sailed from Iolcus to Colchis in search of the Golden Fleece. While this and other models prove the good nature of animals and inanimate objects, men remain examples of rebellion against the gods and of base servitude to other men for mere self-interest.

112–16 *The senseless Argive ship … the starts exclude*] Schoell notes the indebtedness of this passage to the concluding remarks in Conti's 'De Argonavi': 'Hanc navim fuisse inter sidera collocatam fabulati sunt, cum fuisset Palladis consilio fabricata, quia cum nullam beneficentiam sine remuneratione Deus esse patiatur: tum illa praecipue grata est Deo, quae a sapientia et consilio proficiscitur. […] Cum vellent igitur homines antiqui ad beneficentiam adhortari; rem divinam, et quae proxime ad Deorum immortalium naturam accedat, liberalitatem et munificentiam esse dixerunt, quippe cum ad exemplum liberalitatis et animalia complura, et res sensu carentes, quia de Diis putarentur fuisse benemeritae, inter siderum numerum fuerint relatae, et proxime ad Deos ascitae' ('The ancients fabled that this ship was placed among the stars, because Pallas had advised that it be built; for God does not allow any kindness to go without reward. And any project that begins wisely and with careful planning is certainly pleasing to God. […] Since the ancients wanted to encourage men to be kind, they said that generosity and philanthropy were immortal virtues, and put us in touch with the natures of immortal gods. The ancients also put a lot of animals and insentient things among the stars as examples of generosity, because they were to have earned the thanks of the gods, and were almost accepted as gods themselves': VI. 10, p. 609; Mulryan, p. 509). The major moral point here is consonant with the example of Amalthea: the goat's animal kindness, and the generosity shown by a ship that is 'senseless' ('res sensu carentis'), are virtues of which those 'self-love paramours' that present-day men have become are incapable.

118–20 *to damn stone-peasants ... slaves of drudgery*] Hudston's explanation of the compound 'stone-peasants' in the context of the affirmation that 'Baseness is flinty' (108) is plausible (p. 393). The 'thousand such examples' (116) from myth could be mirrors for those flint-hearted, ignorant men who scorn religion and miserably serve the great in pursuit of mere self-interest. Chapman's analogy between these men and 'Typhons' may have been inspired by Conti, 'De Typhone' (VI. 22, 653–62). Typhon, or Typhoeus, was a deformed giant, with many serpent heads springing from his shoulders, born after Heaven and Earth granted Juno the desire to bear a child without sexual intercourse. Typhon rebelled against Jupiter and took him prisoner, but the god was freed by Mercury, who wounded Typhon with a thunderbolt. For Conti, Typhon represents ambition, which makes men forget 'religion or humanity or justice' (p. 662; Mulryan, p. 553). Chapman's meaning is in consonance with Conti's moral interpretation.

123–70

The hymnodist argues that man's excellence should be measured by the soul's dedication to intellectual activity and not by its surrender to bodily affections. For that reason, poets, whose verses resemble Promethean fire in their creative capacity, fashioned legends about savage creatures in order to prove to men how far they had deviated from their true nature. Similarly, just as Orpheus was able to alter the paths of nature and command the natural elements, so poets will be able to teach men the love of art and virtue. Men should also imitate Orpheus in bringing Eurydice from hell — an action that signifies the taming of the passions — but without looking back. Finally, men should remain unalterable in their moral principles, just as Jupiter/Zeus resisted the attempt of the other gods to remove him from heaven with a golden chain.

123–30 *If then we frame ... of man's similitude*] Chapman brings Ficinian Neoplatonism to his argument. The measure of man's true form is his mind, first framed in the image of God's mind; for that reason, the mind pursues its own 'erection' (i.e. ascension) to 'god-like excellence', achieved by means of the mind's 'intelligence', or understanding, of the immortality of the rational soul, which is the nexus between human matter and the angelic and divine world. But the understanding of this nexus involves the recognition of the disparity between the soul and the body, which justifies the conclusion that 'she' (the soul) 'Must bear no sign of man's similitude'. For Ficino's own summary of this argument, see Marsilio Ficino, *Platonic Theology*, ed. by Michael J. B. Allen, 6 vols (Harvard University Press, 2001–2006), I. 1, I, pp. 14–17.

131–38 *Therefore Promethean poets ... such accounts* and Gloss 4a] This passage is the consequence of the former argument. The poets' inspired creations of fantastic, monstrous beings will serve as moral mirrors of their own vulgarity and savagery, and will thus mend their own minds (and their readers'). Chapman's marginal note explains Prometheus's stealing of heavenly fire as an allegory of poetic inspiration. The Centaurs were savage beings who originally inhabited the mountains of Thessaly, part human and part horse. The Harpies were ugly winged women sent by the gods as punishment for men's crimes. The Lapithes defeated the Centaurs in the mountains of Thessaly for control of Perithous's kingdom. The 'Pierian founts' refer to the spring in Macedonia that was sacred to the Muses, and thus a place of artistic inspiration. The name is derived from King Pierus, father to the Pierides, the nine girls that challenged the Muses to a contest of song. On the Pierides, see Commentary: '*OBS: To Roydon*', lines 36–38.

139–58 *So, when ye hear... his hell-daunting kind* and Gloss 4b] As Schoell explains, this passage is proof of Chapman's helter-skelter insertions of certain classical quotations found in Conti's *Mythologiae*. The source here is a number of scattered passages from 'De Orpheo' (VII. 14, pp. 765–72; Mulryan, pp. 648–54): 'Fuit Orpheus [...] Apollinis et Calliopes unius Musarum filius. [...] Hunc tanta canendi peritia exceluisse inquiunt, ut fluvii ad eius cantum firmarentur, aves advolarent, ferae properarent, sylvae, et saxa, et venti, et omnium vel sensu carentium genera accurrerent. [...] Hic idem cum in rudes adhuc mortales incidisset [...] tantum dicendo, et orationis suavitate valuit, ut ad mansuetius viate genus homines traduxerit, illos in unum locum convocarit, civitates condere docuerit, legibusque civitatum obtemperare. [...] Eurydicen in lucem adducere conatus est, quae, ut nomen ipsum significat, nihil aliud est quam iustitia et aequitas. Fuit rursus ad inferos illa retracta ob nimium Orphei amorem, quia neque iustitiae quidem opus est nimis esse cupidum, cum perturbationes animi placentur ratione: atque si quis paulo fuerit in hac re negligentior aut magis cupidus, tanquam ab aliqua vi externa repellitur, et eodem relabitur. [...] Ut igitur moderationem animi affectibus adhibeamus [...] ab antiquis de Orpheo memoriae prodita fuerunt' ('Orpheus was the son of Apollo and Calliope, one of the Muses. [...] He had such superb skill in playing music that rivers would stop flowing when he began to sing; the birds above would fly toward him; ferocious beasts would gallop in the direction of his song; and woods, stones, winds, and every insensible thing would rush to hear him. [...] Orpheus found himself living with boorish, lawless men who had no notion of how to behave. [...] But these men responded so well to his smooth speech and convincing talk that he was able to turn around their whole way of life, in a gentler, more sophisticated direction. He convinced them to consolidate, to form states of their own, to obey the laws of the new governments. [...] He tried to bring Eurydice into the world of light. For her own name tells us that Eurydice can only refer to justice and decent treatment. She was sucked back into the underworld because Orpheus cared too much for her; this means that we don't have to go crazy looking for justice, because reason keeps our emotions under control. And if we become either too neglectful or too eager about seeking justice, we'll run into a blank wall and be bounced right back to where we started from. [...] Thus the ancients made up these stories about Orpheus to help us control our mental state'). Conti's moral explanations are significant to the poem. However, Chapman's massive borrowings from Conti usually involve significant changes. The main difference here lies in his conception of Orphean poetry as originated in 'heavenly rapture', while Conti's focus is on 'peritia' ('skill').

159–70 *The golden chain of Homer's... his power with will*] Schoell identifies the source of this passage in Conti, 'De Iunone' (II. 4, pp. 138, 142; Mulryan, pp. 116, 119–20): 'Istud ipsum significavit aurea Homeri cathena, ex qua pendebant Dii omnes Iovem de coelo detrahere conantes, quorum tamen conatus fuit irritus. [...] Quod attinet ad auream cathenam [...] ego modo avaritiam, modo ambitionem esse auream cathenam crediderim; quae etsi potentissima est, multosque a vera Dei religione ad falsa dogmata retraxit [...] tamen virum bonum suo loco dimovere non poterit, neque veritatem ullo tempore labefactare, quae adversus omnes iniurias inconcussa persistit. Qui enim vir bonus vere existit, ille neque avaritia neque ambitione ulla loco dimovetur' ('The golden chain that Homer referred to was the same one all the gods hung on to in an attempt to oust Jupiter from Heaven, but they accomplished nothing by it. [...] As for the golden chain [...] it seems to me that it refers to someone's greed or ambition. For it's clear that it's a very strong chain, strong enough to drag many men away from God's true religion and in the direction of false belief. [...] All the same, the chain can never dislodge a good man from his position, or shake him loose from the truth, or ever destroy truth, which is impervious to damage. For the man who has really led a decent life can never be tempted to abandon his moral stance for the sake of ambition or greed').

Conti cites two passages from the *Iliad*. The first is xv. 18–24, in which Zeus reminds Hera of his having punished her by suspending two anvils on her feet and by tying her with a golden chain; the second, and of more relevance here, is VIII. 18–28, in which the same golden chain is used by the gods in their vain attempt to drag Zeus from heaven. In Chapman's later translation: 'let downe our golden chaine, | And at it let all Deities their utmost strengths constraine | To draw me to the earth from heaven; you never shall prevaile, | Though with your most contention ye dare my state assaile. | But when my will shall be disposed to draw you all to me, | Even with the earth itself and seas ye shall enforced be. [...] | So much I am supreme to Gods, to men supreme as much' (VIII. 16–24). For Hudston, lines 163–70 'are some of the most difficult (and worst) ever written by Chapman', but it is his gloss that complicates the lines' syntax by making 'manless' qualify 'man' rather than 'changes', and by making the 'powerful chain' instead of 'man' the subject of 'is ennobled' (pp. 394–95, nn. 159–70). Otherwise, the passage reads transparently (it is rather one of Chapman's neatest), and can be paraphrased thus: 'the man that hates inhuman changes is unmoveable in his religious and moral principles and immune to ambition, just as Zeus was against the attempt of the other gods to drag him from heaven with the golden chain. For that reason, nothing will prevent him from adorning his own bodily shape with moral virtues, and his own power with moral determination'.

171–80

This new Homeric simile, ending in a one-line aphoristic conclusion, develops the last argument of the previous verse paragraph: the moral need to adorn man's outer shape with inner virtues. The artlessness of 'rude painters', who need to add phylacteries above the heads of animal figures to identify them, surprisingly becomes the positive vehicle of the simile. Just like those painters, men that are men in anything else than their external shapes or faces should write their essence with the letters ('characters') of their actions in order to prove that they are no mere 'mockers' of their essential humanity, and thus mere animals. The last line affirms that it is our souls that, like those phylacteries, must confirm our human shapes, and not vice versa. The 'rude painters' in these lines contrast with the 'expert painters' in the last stanza of 'Banquet' (117. 1).

181–200

No sources for the vehicle of this new Homeric simile have been traced by earlier critics. The motif is pastoral. Chloris was the wife of Zephyrus, and the goddess of flowers, so she is identical with Roman Flora, as Ovid recalls: 'Chloris eram, quae Flora vocor: corrupta Latino | nominis est nostri littera Graeca sono' ('I who now am called Flora was formerly Chloris: a Greek letter of my name is corrupted in the Latin speech': *Fasti*, ed. and trans. by Sir James George Frazer (Heinemann, 1959), v. 195–96, pp. 274–75). Chapman's scene is slightly reminiscent of Ovid's description of the rural celebrations of Chloris 'with merry games' ('ludis iocosis': v. 183, pp. 274–75): 'ebrius incinctis philyra conviva capillis | saltat et imprudens utitur arte meri; | ebrius ad durum formosae limen amicae | cantat, habent unctae mollia serti comae. | nulla coronata peraguntur seria fronte. […] | Bacchus amat flores. […] | scaena levis decet hanc: non est, mihi credite, non est | illa coturnatas inter habenda deas' ('The drunken guest dances with his hairs bound by linden wreaths, and imprudently revels in the art with wine; drunken he sings at the hard threshold of his fair mistress, soft garlands crown his perfumed locks. No serious business affects a crowned brow. Bacchus loves flowers. […] A light scene becomes Chloris: she is not, believe me, she is not to be regarded as one of those buskined goddesses': v. 337-48, p. 284, my translation).

Chapman may have been inspired by the reference to Bacchus and the wanton and drunken dance to compose an original, elaborate scene of ritual dancing that serves as vehicle to a complex argument. His most original element here is the insertion of an observer of the dance who, failing to see clearly and to hear the bagpipe music due to the far distance, mistakes the different rhythmical moves and turns for the chaotic, frenzied and lascivious actions of a 'shapeless crowd' of Bacchantes, thus crediting the scene with 'much less admiration' than it deserves. Just as the observer misinterprets these rituals, we abuse 'our first excellence' due to the distance between those primitive times and ours. The times invoked are two different moments of mythical history, here conflated: the oldest of these is 'that confusion, out of which we fled', which means primeval Chaos, which Chapman ardently defends in this poem; the later moment is the Golden Age, ruled by Saturn's 'golden sceptre', the characterization of which as a time of 'civil government' seems directly inspired by Conti's commentary on Virgil's defence of the natural goodness of Roman consuetudinary laws as a result of Saturn's legacy (*Aeneid*, VII. 202-04), in opposition to 'the man who acts morally only because he's afraid of being punished, or is forced to live his life in compliance with soundly written laws, and not because it is the right thing to do' ('is [...] quidem qui ob metum poenarum solum, aut ad scriptarum legum integritatem vitam suam accommodare cogitur, at non sponte facit quae recta sunt': Conti, 'De Saturno', II. 2, p. 117; Mulryan, p. 99). Written laws appear here as an instance of the useless sophistication of our times, against which Chapman opposes the more superior simplicity of an idealized mythic prehistory. As a whole, this simile brings forth for the first time a motif that will recur later in 'Banquet': erroneous perception as an effect of perspective. In contrast with '*OBS*: Williams 1', 5-9, and 'Banquet', 3. 6-9, distant observation here means the opposite of right perception.

201-40

This long verse paragraph has two well-differentiated parts. The first (201-24) is an elaborate Homeric simile that compares man's moral descent into the new chaos of corrupted civilization to human and animal activity during the day, the effects of which are only restored by the new arrival of the night; the image of Night's forcing of all animal life into the cave of Sleep ('Somnus' lodgings') and Day into 'the infernal deep' thus entails the triumph of human intellect. The second part (225-40) is an instance of Chapman's creative mythography: Night's blackness is explained as the result of Earth's mistreatment of her face for fear that Jove will favour the 'worthies', or constellations, that shine on it while Day is driven away from heaven. For that reason, Night's dark colour, an effect of the violence done on her, is a sign of dignified superiority.

203 *Muses' stead* and Gloss 6] Pegasus, the steed of the Muses. 'Stead' has not been modernized in order to preserve the rhyme. Gloss 6 cites the cryptic poem *Alexandra*, by Lycophron of Calchis (third century BC), an account of Cassandra's various prophecies about the Trojan War reported by the slave Alexandra. Schoell (*Études*, pp. 182–83) identifies Chapman's borrowing as coming from his usual source, Conti ('De Aurora', VI. 2, p. 558), in which Lycophron's description of Dawn's rising is quoted. Chapman manipulated Conti's quotation by expunging the last line in the Greek text (see *Alexandra*, 16–19, in *Callimachus, Lycophron, Aratus*, ed. and trans. by A. W. Mair and G. R. Mair (Heinemann, 1921), pp. 494–95) and in the Latin translation. On this manipulation, which is central to the rewriting of the meanings of Night in the poem, see Introduction, pp. 68–69, in which Conti's missing line is added.

204 *Ushers the sun from Vulcan's golden bed* and Gloss 7] This is the only instance in the glosses in which Chapman acknowledges having borrowed from Conti ('De Sole', v. 17, p. 537; Mulryan, p. 444): 'Verum dixerunt nonnulli Vulcanum throrum fabricasse Soli ita profundum ex auro, ut in eo per noctem, cum ad Oceanum defessus diurno labore itineris pervenisset, vel dormiens navigare posset ad orientem. Ibi currus illi experrecto astabat, quem ascendens coelum conscenderet, quod faciebat quotidie' ('Some writers claimed that Vulcan made the Sun his own golden bed. It was supposed to be so deep that once the Sun arrived at the shores of great Ocean, worn out from the daily effort of his trip, he could sail eastward in it, even while he was asleep. And the chariot would be ready and waiting for him when he arrived. Then he would jump into the chariot and sail for heaven'). On Chapman's re-elaboration of this myth, see Commentary: 'Noctem', 378–83 and Gloss 11; also Introduction, pp. 69–71.

215–17 *And, eagle-like ... infernal deep* and Gloss 8] Conti ('De Nocte', III. 12, p. 232; Mulryan, p. 192): 'Et Orpheus ad inferos lucem mittere, ac rursus ipsam ad illos accedere scribit in eo carmine: "Quae lucem pellis sub terras, rursus et ipsa | Tartara nigra petis."' ('In this verse Orpheus has her bearing light to the underworld and also arriving there herself: *You the one who drives light beneath the earth, and seek yourself once again, black Tartarus*'). See Orpheus, 'Νυκτός', in *Hymnes Orphiques*, pp. 35–36; trans. by Mulryan, p. 192. Hudston sees in Chapman's (slight) amplification of the lines in the Orphic hymn a basis for his hymnic poesis in *The Shadow of Night* (p. 395, nn. 215–17). Hudston bases his discussion on Snare, *Mystification*, pp. 152–53. In the present case, the amplification concerns Night's driving of beasts and birds into 'Somnus' lodgings'. Chapman relies on Ovid's detailed description of the 'ignavi domus et penetralia Somni' ('home and chamber of sluggish Sleep') in *Meta-*

morphoses, XI. 592–615, which is also quoted in Conti ('De Somno', III. 14, p. 237; Mulryan, p. 196).

237, 240 *Day, Morn*] Despite being preceded by an indefinite article, 'Day' is a feminine personification here, so the initial capital of Q*sn* has been kept. In Hesiod, Day (Ἡμέρη) was, like Aether, born from Night and Erebus (*Theogony*, 123-24). 'Morn', or 'Morning', is Aurora (Ἡώς), daughter of Hyperion and Theia (Conti, 'De Aurora', VI. 2, pp. 557–60). Chapman could have been inspired by the opening lines of the Orphic hymn 'To Dawn': 'Κλῦθι, θεά, θνετοῖς φαεσίμβροτον Ἦμαρ ἄγουσα, | Ἡὼς λαμπροφαής, ἐρυθαινομένη κατὰ κόσμον' ('Hear me, O Goddess, who bring to mortals the light of day, | shining Dawn, who blush over the universe': *Hymnes Orphiques*, "Ἡους", 78. 1-2, p. 613, my translation).

241–46

This brief verse paragraph has been considered one of the most obscure passages of the poem. The confusing syntax and erratic punctuation contribute to the general obfuscation of sense. It has been interpreted in imagistic fashion, not always satisfactorily. Huntington, who titles one of the chapters of his monograph 'Virtues Obscured', considers that this phrase is deliberately ambiguous, meaning the obscuring of virtue by our excessive reliance on the soul and the flesh, but also claiming positive meanings for obscurity as a virtue: the passage would then constitute 'an objection to the unjust world which obscures virtue, and a praise of a hermetic virtue that transcends the "glories" of the day' (*Ambition*, p. 100). Hudston confusingly reads 'virtues' garlands' as ironic, as they are 'not meant to be the usual straightforward symbols of distinction and victory', but a sign of the defeat of the virtues (and thus their 'overthrows' in the next verse paragraph), which also explains their being obscured (p. 196, n. 246). However, the passage does not need to be read ambiguously or ironically. Q*sn*'s punctuation has been altered here: original commas after 'train', 'day', 'sway' and 'stone' have been removed, in order to suggest that 'With all the glories' is a prepositional phrase referring to those that accompany 'Day' — which has been capitalized — to her banishment during the reign of Night. 'Prisoned in flesh' is a passive participle clause whose subject is 'glories', while the 'chief flowers' refer appositionally to 'bands | Of stone and steel'. The opening adverb 'Meanwhile' marks a transition from the descriptive/narrative mode of the first part to a new kletic invocation of Night. This transition reinforces the performative here-and-now of the invocation. Thus, the passage announces the arrival of night, as well as the replacement of the rule of Day with the rule of Night. If read thus, then, the banished Day is the moment when all the glories of its weak rule ('spongy sway'), imprisoned in the flesh, are fettered in stone and steel. These chains are then the victorious flowers worn by the 'virtues', which are 'obscured' because they belong to Night's darkness. This victory is of course temporary, since Day will return from her banishment once summoned again by Dawn. This interpretation solves the apparent contradiction of finding victoriously obscure virtues in this passage, as well as the reference to 'virtues' overthrows' in the next, since virtue is defeated only during the rule of Day.

247–54

The invocation of Night is continued from the previous verse paragraph. The opening epithet regards her as a loving shelter for her followers' sorrows, who lament Day's defeat of the virtues during her rule. In order to avenge the wrongs caused by the 'painted', or false, 'light' of Day, the hymnodist asks Night to send the Eumenides to perform bloody deeds against Day's vice-drunken partisans. The Eumenides, or Erinnyes, or Furies, were personifications of curses pronounced against criminals. Of the many interpretations of the parentage of the three Eumenides (Tisiphone, Alecto and Megaera) discussed by Conti ('De Eumenidibus', III. 10, p. 218), Chapman chooses that in Lycophron's *Alexandra*: 'Νυκτὸς κόραι', or Night's maiden daughters (437–38, in *Callimachus, Lycophron, Aratus*, pp. 530–31). Conti cites Lycophron's poem by the title *Cassandra*: 'Eumenidas fuisse Noctis filias testatur Lycophoron in Cassandra' ('In his *Cassandra*, Lycophoron claims that the Eumenides are the daughters of Night'). The Furies' conventional role as 'ministers of right' is in consonance with Conti's term 'ministrae': 'quae Iovis coelestis et inferni mandata afficiendis meritis calamitatibus hominibus exequerentur, et quae ministrae essent praedictorum iudicum in excutiendis cuisque sceleribus' ('These deities responded to Jupiter's commands in both heaven and the underworld, by giving men the bad luck they deserved, and helping the judges to force the truth out of them': 'De Eumenidibus', III. 10, p. 218; Mulryan, p. 182). Although Conti does not explicitly call these goddesses 'chaste', Chapman's epithet seems inspired by Conti's moral explanation of the Eumenides' actions as punishments of 'inappropriate and bestial' ('indecorum tanquam belluam') behaviour in pursuing 'vulgar delights' ('impuris voluptatibus': 'De Eumenidibus', III. 10, p. 226; Mulryan, p. 188).

255–67

The addressee of the invocation in this verse paragraph is now Hercules, who is asked to fall from heaven, where he was stellified by Jupiter after his death, in the form of a violent tempest. Chapman may have been inspired by Giordano Bruno's *Spaccio della bestia trionfante* (see *Expulsion*, Dialogue II. 3, p. 188, and Introduction, p. 88, note 273), in which Jupiter decides to send the constellation Hercules to earth. Yet the various aspects of the mythology of Hercules which are brought together here have their main source in Conti's *Mythologiae*.

> 255–63 *Fall, Hercules ... stoop his pride* and Gloss 9] Chapman's hymnodist requests from Hercules that he revive his seventh task: cleaning out

the dung from Augeas's stables. Besides the obvious moral connotation in the act of cleansing 'the beastly stable of the world', Chapman may have been attracted to Conti's allusion to historical accounts of Augeas as 'the son of the Sun' ('Solis filius'), which partly explains why 'his land lay fallow, useless, and covered with dung' ('maxima pars agri simo obducta otiosa et inculta iaceret': 'De Hercule', VII. 1, p. 710; Mulryan, pp. 598–99). The other story alluded to in these lines, and explained in Gloss 9, relates to Hercules' tenth task: the retrieving of Geryon's cattle from Tartessus. As Schoell (*Études*, pp. 181, 183) notes, Chapman's source is again Conti: 'Fabulantur Herculem post ductos ad Tartessum boves poculum suum Soli reddidisse: nam dicitur Hercules cum ad boves contenderet, Solis radiis nimium calefactus arcum vel in ipsum solem intendisse, quare sol eius vires, et animi magnitudinem admiratus, aureum poculum illi donavit, in quo Oceanum ad boves capiendos traiecit, ut ait Pherecydes in tertio libro historiarum' ('The story goes that after Hercules led the cattle to Tartessus, Hercules gave his cup back to the Sun. For when Hercules was out laboring away with those cattle, he's supposed to have gotten so hot from the Sun's rays that he actually drew his bow against the planet. The Sun was so impressed by Hercules' great power and courageous spirit that he gave the hero a golden cup. Then Hercules sailed across the Ocean in that cup so that he could bring back the cattle. Pherecydes confirms the story in the third book of his *Histories*': 'De Hercule', VII. 1, p. 690; Mulryan, p. 580).

As usual, Chapman omits Conti and only acknowledges Conti's source, Pherecydes of Syros (sixth century BC). Chapman abridges Conti in order to omit the Sun's favouring of Hercules by presenting him with a golden cup that served him as a barge to cross the ocean. Further details are provided in Vincenzo Cartari, *Le imagini de i dei de gli Antichi* (Venice: Giordano Ziletti, 1571), p. 345: 'il Sole donò un gran vaso da bere ad Hercole, col quale egli passò il mare' ('the Sun presented a large drinking cup to Hercules, with which he crossed the sea'). Chapman's avoidance of Conti may in this case be motivated by the latter's moral epitome of the legend of Hercules 'ad Solis naturam' ('as an explanation of the Sun's nature': 'De Hercule', VII. 1, p. 713; Mulryan, p. 602). Any attempt to conceive of Hercules as a heroic sun figure is against the agenda of Chapman's poem, whose intention is to denigrate the Sun as Day's agent.

264–65 *his lustful rays to get* | *The Earth with issue*] The inspiration for these lines is again Conti ('De Tellure', v. 20, pp. 549–50; Mulryan, p. 454): 'Quid sit Tellus omnibus patet: at cur finxerint antiqui illam Titanis aut Coeli fuisse uxorem, illis patebit, qui in illam Solem assidue agere considerarint, illamque tanquam foeminam, Solis ipsius calore ad generationem excitari, et tanquam semina ex omnibus elementis vim condensatam in se recipere' ('We are all clear about what earth is. But if we think about the Sun's continuous influence on earth, we'll also be able to understand why the ancients made her the wife of Titan or Heaven. For the heat of the Sun prods the Earth into productivity just as if she were a woman, and the Earth absorbs the condensed force of the elements like so many seeds'). To Conti's explanation Chapman adds his characteristically derogatory view of the Sun.

266–67 *In Somnus' thickets ... and with ebon boughs*] These lines are reminiscent of Ovid's description of the house of Sleep (*Metamorphoses*, XI. 592–615), which in turn relies on Lucian's description of the city of Sleep (*True Story*, II. 32–33, in *Lucian*, ed. and trans. by A. M. Harmon, 8 vols (Heinemann, 1913), I, pp. 336–39). Both sources are cited by Conti ('De Somno', III. 14, pp. 237, 238). Yet Ovid seems the immediate source for Chapman, whose 'thickets' evoke the 'innumerae[que] herbae, quarum de lacte soporem | Nox legit et spargit per opacas umida terras' ('countless herbs, from whose juices dewy night distils sleep and spreads its influence over the darkened lands': *Metamorphoses*, XI. 606–07); whose 'pitchy vapours' may be those of 'Lethes, per quem cum murmure labens | invitat somnos crepitantibus unda lapillis' ('Lethe, whose waves, gently murmuring over the gravelly bed, invite to slumber': XI. 603–04); and whose 'ebon boughs' resemble the materials of which Sleep's bed is made: 'at medio torus est ebeno sublimis in antro, | plumeus, atricolor, pullo velamine tectus, | quo cubat ipse deus membris languore solutis' ('But in the cavern's central space there is a high couch of ebony, downy-soft, black-hued, spread with a dusky coverlet. There lies the god himself, his limbs relaxed in languorous repose': XI. 610–12).

268–87

The hymnodist promises to consecrate his life to Night through a vision of self-immolation that announces the end of the life of the body.

268–79 *Rich-tapered sanctuary ... face withal* and Gloss 10] The epithet 'Rich-tapered sanctuary' is explained in Gloss 10 by reference to the 'altar' of line 1, and of Gloss 1, via the lines in Aratus's *Astronomica* quoted by Conti ('De Nocte', III. 12, 231), a spatial conceit that is amplified here by a second epithet that calls Night a 'Palace of ruth'. The place to which the poetic voice means to 'consecrate' his life is presided over by the 'Furies' (the 'Eumenides' of the previous lines), Night's own daughters, and by a violent, vociferous fauna of 'adders', 'foxes', 'night-ravens' and 'owls' — the latter two usually understood as the same species. Like Ovid's bed in the house of Sleep (see note above), Night's palace will become the venue for the erection of a gruesomely ornamented 'funeral bed' in which the poetic voice's 'untombed face' (by synecdoche, his body) will be interred by the massive 'burden' of the celestial vault. The hyperbolic image of the body's engulfment by the heavens on Night's altar is characteristic of

Chapman's sublime imagery. The burial is imagined as the effect of the fall of the heavens from Atlas's shoulders. In Hesiod's *Theogony*, the rebellious Atlas, son of the Titan Iapetus and the Oceanid Clymene, was condemned by Zeus to bear the heavens (Chapman's 'Olympic burden') upon his shoulders (*Theogony*, 517–20).

> 280–87 *And when ... my miseries*] These lines are characteristically obscure. Hudston (pp. 396–97, nn. 280–87) provides a full gloss that contains enlightening details, yet is on the whole unsatisfactory. The passage needs to be read as a consequence of the previous lines, in which the poetic voice envisions his self-immolation in Night's sanctuary as the effect of the fall of the heavens from Atlas's shoulders upon his own body. This image presides over the full cessation of the life of the body (the support or 'material substance' of the human 'mind'), which will take place in advance ('abode') of the ending ('period') of the present time in human history, brought about by the return of primordial Chaos ('the old essence and insensive prime'). Then the ruins or spoils left after the destruction caused by the 'rapting torrents' of Chaos ('the fourfold time') will turn into a 'lump' — one of Chapman's favourite terms denoting shapelessness — and will voice the speaker's complaints. These lines echo the thoughts, conveyed in lines 47–49, of an originally bodiless Chaos, whose return is prophesied here.

288–323

The interpretation of what is arguably the obscurest verse paragraph of 'Noctem' is complicated by the absence of sources. Its violent imagery, if at times conventional, springs from the poet's own invention. On the whole, the passage is an invocation addressed to all sorts of suffering men, dead and living, and to all sorts of supernatural agents of revenge, to join the forces of Night and voice their lamentations. The passage also explores, in metapoetic fashion, the limits of language and the artist's search for authenticity of expression.

> 288–95 *Ye living spirits ... do sustain*] The 'living spirits' to whom the first invocation is addressed seem to be the improbable survivors ('if any live') of the destruction perpetrated by the return of primitive Chaos in the previous lines. These men, who are afflicted with the same 'extremes' and 'affections' as the speaker is, are asked to abjure daylight in the company of other suffering men (those whose parents have been murdered by tyrannous acts and whose sisters endure the consequences of rape and bondage, and who therefore feel upon themselves the duty of revenge), and of the ministers of punishment ('ghosts', 'dog-fiends' and 'monsters'). This company of men and spirits will thus escape from the 'soft' (i.e. light, idle) shades in which they are captive in order to embrace authentic Night.

296–309 *But you ... your tortury*] The apostrophe begun in the previous lines is extended now to include a similar category of suffering men: unborn spirits, or, more plausibly, those who never enjoyed the rewards of high rank due to lineage ('birth') nor the benefits of being loved; those who were betrayed by their friends' greed; and, most particularly, those who, despite their virtuous life, see how it is evil men that suck in ('aspire') all the substance ('th'extraction and the quintessence') of earthly joys and pleasures. The speaker's request to these men is that they join the abovementioned 'dog-fiends' and 'monsters' in lamentations whose force will violently turn the world upside down (i.e. 'Revive the dead, and make the living die').

310–19 *Still all ... tumbles in*] The speaker asks all the abovementioned mourners to transform their lamentations into art. This passage is a typically Chapmanesque allegory of his ideas about the art of poetry. 'Still' is the keyword here. Distillation symbolizes the extraction of the essence, or authenticity, of artistic expression, against the 'vanities' of other poetic forms, whose 'compact of fiction and hyperboles' may 'cloy' the sense but leave true hearers indifferent and their eyes' 'glasses' 'unbroken' — i.e. without tears. This alchemical distillation of the quintessence of art may lead the abovementioned mourners — and, by extension, poets — to 'paint, or else create in serious truth | A body figured' in the image and likeness of the substance that this 'body' intends to represent. This is the only way in which art will be able to convey the image of the sins that the newly arrived Chaos will destroy and reduce to ruins. The use of partial synonyms in rhyming position, 'groans' and 'moans', reinforces the opposition between these two views of art: the authenticity distilled from the 'groans' contrasts with the 'remissive', waning 'moans'. The idea of poetic expression as accurate painting defended here matches the notion of *enargia*, and its appeal to the 'sense', discussed in '*OBS*: To Roydon', lines 13–20, and in Introduction, pp. 19–24.

314 *the glasses of the hearers' eyes | Unbroken*] Bartlett (p. 425, n. 314) notes this phrase's indebtedness to the popular Neoplatonic conceit of the eyes as mirrors of the soul. She adduces analogues in Donne's 'The Canonization', in which 'the whole world's soul' is said to be 'contract[ed]' into the beloved's eyes/glasses (40–44, in John Donne, *The Complete Poems*, ed. by Robin Robins (Longman, 2010), p. 155); and Shakespeare's *Richard II*, in which the King sees his uncle Gaunt's 'grieved heart' reflected 'in the glasses of [his] eyes' (*King Richard II*, ed. by Charles Forker (Thomson, 2002), I. 3. 208–09). For all the importance of this conceit, the idea here is that of a mirror left unbroken by the absence of tears. Another moment in *Richard II*, the Queen's conceit of 'Sorrow's eyes, glazed with blinding tears' (II. 2. 16), seems more to the point.

320–23 *But woe ... he puts on*] The verse paragraph ends with an image of the world upside down, as the result of the destruction brought about by avenging Chaos. 'Without a name' may refer to the 'nameless' (unfamed) poet that voices the hymn; yet it may also allude to his lacking the capacity of naming, in opposition to the ideal of distilled, authentic poetic expression in the previous lines. That loss of the ability to name seems behind the triumph of 'scorn' and 'shame', which prey on 'virtue' and 'honour', and of 'pride', which 'bathes in tears of poor submission', and dresses in its opponent's robes.

324–49

The poetic voice closes his petition to those mourners apostrophized in the former verse paragraph by asking them to join him in the worship of Night in her own 'house of mourning'. In comparison to Night's majesty, Day is identified as a sexual slave that prostitutes her beauties and consents to all forms of abuse (324–31). The rest of this verse paragraph presents, in quasi-dramatic fashion, a contention between Day and Night that ends in the latter's triumph (332–49).

332–49 *Her labours ... inward parts*] Cast in the role of a 'drudge' (330), Day feasts Night with celebrations in which 'Loves' (i.e. Cupids) revel in all forms of bodily pleasure. Day's light beams act like Cupid's arrows, i.e. with 'fugitive and far-shot rays' that decompose ('Disjoin') these Loves (the antecedent of 'whom') into innumerable particles ('and drive into ten thousand ways'). On multiplying Cupids and atoms as originating forces of desire in Elizabethan and later poetry, see Gorman, 'Atomies of Love'. Against Day's disintegrating action, Night spreads her mantle to offer a protective environment in which these Cupids are freed from the sensual thraldom imposed by Day. Night's 'trusty shadows' oppose the mollifying 'soft shades' (291) that characterize Day's 'deceitful malice'. The 'sanctuary' of Night is accessed through 'her ivory port', from which several kinds of dreams are sent to the sleepers. Chapman could have relied on Penelope's speech to Ulysses in Homer (*Odyssey*, XIX. 560–67), or on the description of Hades in Virgil (*Aeneid*, VI. 892–96). In both texts, the 'ivory port' is the gate of false dreams, while the 'port of horn' (352) gives access to true dreams. Yet the main source here is Conti ('De Somno', III. 14, p. 238), who provides a detailed commentary on Lucian (*True Story*, II. 32–34), which Chapman seems to have consulted directly too. In Lucian and Conti, the ivory gate leads into the city of Sleep, while here it is a direct entrance to the 'sanctuary' ('templum') of Night. Conti's commentary is not specific about the contents of these dreams.

However, of the three kinds of dreams mentioned by Chapman, the first two have their source in a passage by Lucian not quoted by Conti. Those dreams, 'taking forms of princes' in order to persuade all men of their being equal in degree, recall those in Lucian that 'promised to make us kings' ('ὑπισχνούμενοι βασιλέας τε ποιήσειν'). And those 'clad in habit of deceasèd friends' are reminiscent of those in Lucian that 'gave us a sight of friends and family' ('τὰς πατρίδας καὶ τοὺς οἰκείους ἐπεδείκνυον', II. 34). The third kind of dreams, in 'lady-like' shapes, reverse the conventional 'contempt' shown by Petrarchan mistresses for 'pity', unusually showing sympathy for the 'inward parts' that grace those men devoted to intellectual activity. The adjective 'Protean' as applied to dreams seems inspired by Conti's 'nulli eadem est forma' ('[they] do not all have the same shape': 'De Somno, III. 14, p. 238; Mulryan, p. 197). But Chapman could also have consulted Conti's 'De Proteo' (VIII. 8, pp. 849–50; Mulryan, p. 725), which recounts the plan of Idothea, Proteus's daughter, to have her father prophesy Menelaus's future: 'quo tempore sub meridiem Proteus in siccum exiens inter phocas dormire consuevit, atque illum dormientem comprehendere, tamdiuque retinere in varias formas se mutantem, quamdiu in pristinam formam redierit. Nam tunc futura demum illis praedicet omnia' ('For since Proteus used to come ashore around noon to have an afternoon nap with the seals, Idothea told Menelaus to grab Proteus while he was sleeping, and then hold on to him as he went through his various changes, until he went back to his original shape. And that's when he would tell them exactly what was going to happen in the future').

350–77

This verse paragraph can be conceived of as a conclusion to the speaker's reasons for trying to gain men for Night's cause. It first discusses the quality of two kinds of dreams: those coming through Night's 'ivory port' (explained in the previous lines), and those from her 'port of horn', inspiring more serious, prophetic dreams. Men are asked to rely on dreams, despite their vain appearance. Besides, since all that Night can offer is to be trusted above anything that comes from Day, men should consecrate their 'endeavours' and their 'aspiring wits' to the intellectual and moral rewards promised by Night.

> 350–55 *If these ... in trances*] The classical distinction between the false dreams passing through the 'ivory port' and the true dreams sent through the 'port of horn' (see references to Homer and Virgil in the previous note) is treated slightly differently here. The first kind refers to ideal situations, and their lighter content seems to be embodied by the 'silk vapours' (line 340) of the ivory gate. The second kind concerns the 'graver dreams inspired with prophecies' belonging to the gate of horn. All may show a 'vain' appearance, but the speaker encourages his listeners to embrace them.
>
> 356–58 *If these ... she finds*] These lines are written in quasi-syllogistic fashion, although Chapman would not pass the logician's test. The lines

can be glossed as follows: as virtue finds nothing in us but dreams, then if all dreams were vain, they would have no share in virtue. The conclusion would seem to affirm that there are also virtuous dreams, and that not all dreams should be considered vain.

359–73 *Then, since ... detest the light*] These lines, like the preceding ones, are fashioned in the form of logical reasoning. Four premises introduced by the causal connective 'since' lead to a final concluding effect: a request for those 'possessed with indepressèd spirits' and 'Indued with nimble and aspiring wits' to consecrate themselves to the cult of Night and to abhor daylight. The first of the premises (359–61) adduces the vanity of all pleasures, but also of those 'serious actions' that do not observe Night's habits; the second (362–65) establishes daylight's subservience to the eyes, and therefore to sensual passions, which are inimical to the soul; the third (366–67) defends heaven's preference for sorrow over cheer; the fourth (368–69) compares Night and Day in terms of their moral effects upon their followers.

373–74 *Sweet Peace's richest crown ... honoured marinars*] Peace (Greek Εἰρήνη, Latin *Pax*), daughter of Zeus and Themis, is one of the three Hours (Latin *Horae*), again alluded to in line 381 in relation to their servitude to Phoebus, or the Sun. Chapman may be relying here on Conti's comments on Ovid (*Fasti*, I. 125), in which the Hours watch over heaven's gates, and on Homer (*Iliad*, v. 749–51), where this role as gatekeepers of heaven also relates to their power to 'attend heaven's gates' ('portas coeli servare'), call back the clouds ('nubes inducere') and 'calm the heavens' ('serenum facere coelum': 'De Horae', IV. 16, p. 419; Mulryan, p. 341). Peace's controlling powers of the forces of nature and her role as guide to 'honoured marinars' makes her an ally to Night, in contrast with the role allotted to the Hours in the next verse paragraph.

376–77 *No pen ... humour of the Night*] This statement is one of the central arguments of the poem, i.e. the relevance of Night as a symbol of Chapman's poetics of difficulty or obscurity. The pen whose point is 'steeped' in 'humour of the Night', or melancholy, emblematizes a poetics that flees sensuality in favour of the Saturnian cultivation of the search for truth, which the poem associates with nocturnal study. On the connections between this poem and Renaissance Saturnian melancholy, see Yates, *Occult Philosophy*, pp. 157–71.

378–83 and Gloss 11

The hymnodist first summons diurnal creatures to withdraw, and then nocturnal men to welcome the arrival of Night. Then he commands Phoebus, or the Sun, not to rise again and to constrain his 'oblique course' to 'close thickets', thus allowing for Night's eternal reign over the world. What Phoebus is asked exactly is to lie on Morning's, or Aurora's ('thy glassy strumpet's'), bed upon the sea, or Oceanus, and to impede the Hours' attiring of his horses and chariot, on which he usually returns to heaven with the rise of dawn. Chapman's elaborate mythography here is the result of the combination of different passages from Conti, which in turn refer to different classical sources. Schoell (*Études*, p. 184), and all editors and commentators after him, have pointed at Gloss 11's attribution to Orpheus ("Ωρων', 43. 1–3, in *Hymnes Orphiques*, pp. 362–63) of the Hours' ('Themis' daughters') making ready the horse and chariot of the Sun, as quoted and commented on by Conti ('De Horis', IV. 16, p. 418). But Chapman's apostrophe to Phoebus actually relies on two other passages from Conti. In the first of these ('De Sole', V. 17, pp. 537–38; Mulryan, p. 444), Conti quotes, in Greek and in Latin translation, a verse fragment by the elegiac poet Mimnermus (fl. 630–600 BC). I quote the text from Allen's edition and Mulryan's English translation: Ἥλιος μὲν γὰρ ἔλαχεν πόνον ἤματα πάντα, | οὐδέ ποτ' ἄμπαυσις γίνεται οὐδεμία | ἵπποισίν τε καὶ αὐτῶι, ἐπὴν ῥοδοδάκτυλος Ἠώς | Ὠκεανὸν προλιποῦσ' οὐρανὸν εἰσαναβῆι· | τόν μὲν γὰρ διὰ κῦμα φέρει πολυήρατος εὐνή | κοιλή Ἡφαίστου χερσὶν ἐληλαμένη | χρυσοῦ τιμήεντος, ὑπόπτερος, ἄκρον ἐφ' Ἑσπερίδων | γαῖαν ἐς Αἰθιόπων, ἵνα δὴ θόον ἄρμα καὶ ἵπποι | ἑστᾶσ', ὄφρ' Ἠὼς ἠριγένεια πόληι· | ἔνθ' ἐπέβη ἑτέρων ὀχέων Ὑπερίονος υἱός ('For the sun's portion is labour every day, nor is there ever any rest either for him or his horses when rosy-fingered Dawn hath left the ocean and climbed the sky; for over the wave in a delightful bed forged of precious gold by the hand of Hephaestus, hollow and with wings, he is carried in pleasant sleep on the face of the waters from the Hesperian's country to the land of Aethiop, where his horses and swift chariot stand till early-begotten Dawn appear, and then the son of Hyperion mounts his car', Mimnermus, Fragment 12, in Allen, *Fragments of Mimnermus*, p. 94).

Conti comments as follows: 'Fuerunt etiam qui putarint ubi ad orientem Sol pervenisset, currum illi ab Horis paratum, at non sua sponte assistere, cum illae sub iugum equos Solis veniente Aurora adducerent' ('Some writers thought that when the Sun reached the eastern portion of the sky, the Hours prepared his chariot for departure; it didn't get ready by itself, for as soon as dawn broke the Hours yoked the Sun's horses to that chariot'). Chapman draws on this text for the presence of the Hours, but alters the motif of Vulcanus's golden cup of the Sun (see Commentary: 'Noctem', 255–63), which is now a bed shared adulterously with Aurora.

The other relevant passage from Conti ('De Aurora', VI. 2, 557–60; Mulryan, pp. 461–63) supplies the 'rosy horse[s]' ('roseos equos') from the *roseae quadrigae* driven by Dawn in Virgil (*Aeneid*, VI. 535). Most importantly, this chapter also quotes Homer's hymn 'To Hermes' (184–85, in *Hesiod, the Homeric Hymns and Homerica*, pp. 376–77) to prove that Aurora also rises from the Ocean, 'like the Sun' ('tamquam Solem'). Conti's insistence on this liaison, which he sees as beneficial for men, is rewritten by Chapman in pejorative terms. For a detailed analysis of these sources and on the importance of this passage for Chapman's rewriting of the mythology of Night, see Introduction, pp. 70-71.

384-403

The first hymn ends climactically with Night's ascension to heaven in nuptial procession, accompanied by a train formed by Juno, Hymen, Silence (mounting on Venus), and Cynthia, or the Moon — whose presence acts as a prelude to the ensuing hymn, 'Cynthiam'. This train sings in worship of Night's rule, whose prospects of eternity are conceived of by the lyric voice as a fulfilment of the wished-for advent of virtue to the world.

384-91 *See, now ... Saturnius' palace*] Night's triumphal appearance as the 'bride of brides' may refer to Conti's Hesiodic insistence on the consideration of Night as the first of all goddesses and mother of all deities ('De Nocte', III. 12, p. 231). The nuptial procession justifies the company of both Juno and Hymen, both goddesses of marriage. More mysterious, and arguably more relevant to the general purposes of the hymn, is the presence of 'Dumb Silence' (388-91) among Night's train. Silence is certainly the Egyptian deity Horus, or Greek Harpocrates. Originally a sun divinity in Egyptian mythology, the child Horus became associated with secrecy and silence for his having been born with a finger on his mouth — a conventional feature of his iconography. This made Horus an essential figure to the Hermetic tradition, which associated silence with the pursuit of truth through secret studies (*A Dictionary of Greek and Roman Biography and Mythology*, ed. by William Smith, 3 vols (John Murray, 1880), II, p. 528). The 'becks' with which he 'rebukes the winds' evoke this iconic gesture of commanding silence. Silence's riding on 'the Cyprian star' nods to Orpheus, again via Conti ('De Nocte', III. 12, p. 231), who makes explicit the identification of Night as Venus: 'Νύκτα θεῶν γενέτειραν ἀείσομαι ἠδέ καὶ ἀνδρῶν. | Νύξ γένεσις πάντων, ἥν καὶ Κύπριν καλέσωμεν' ('We sing of you, Night, nourishing parent of men and gods, the parent of all things, whom we call the Cyprian', 'Νυκτός'/'To Night', 3. 1-2, in *Hymnes Orphiques*, pp. 35-36; trans. by Mulryan). The second action performed by Silence is more difficult to interpret: the extinction with 'cloudy mace' of the 'feeble light' leading to Jupiter's Olympian palace seems to insist on the association of this deity with mystery and obscurity.

392-97 *Behind her ... outrageous passions* and Glosses 12 and 13] The last member of Night's train is Cynthia, or the Moon. Her being horned ('cornuta') is mentioned by Conti ('De Luna', III. 17, p. 256; Mulryan, p. 211), with a reference to Orpheus, ''Εις Σελήνην' ('To the Moon'), 9. 2, in which she is called 'ταυρόκερως', bull-horned (*Hymnes Orphiques*, pp. 90-91). As Gloss 12 explains, the source for the 'brace of silver hinds' leading Cynthia's chariot is Callimachus ('To Artemis', III. 110–12, in *Callimachus, Lycophron, Aratus*, pp. 68–71), as Schoell (*Études*, p. 184) reminds us, via Conti's fairly faithful translation of Callimachus's Greek ('De Diana', III. 18, p. 269). Similarly, Gloss 13 proves Hyperion's fathering of Cynthia by reference to Hesiod (see *Theogony*, 371–74), again omitting the debt to Conti's slightly altered translation of Hesiod's Greek ('De Aurora', VI. 2, p. 557). The Moon's entrance 'decked in disparent lawn', confirmed by Gloss 13's explanation of her 'party-coloured garments', draws on Conti ('De Luna', III. 17, p. 255; Mulryan, p. 210), who attributes to 'hymnographus Homerus' a description of her appearance as 'sometimes bright, and sometimes hazy, depending on the brightness of her clothing' ('nunc lucida, nunc obscura sit pro vestium splendore'). Yet Homer only mentions 'her far-gleaming raiment' ('εἵματα τηλαυγέα': 'To Selene', 8, in *Hesiod, the Homeric Hymns and Homerica*, pp. 460–61). Conti adds that 'the Moon dressed in garments of different colours [...] was a device to explain the complicated phases of the Moon' ('Quod vestes indueret variorum colorum, id excogitatum fuit ad explicandas multiplices mutationes', p. 262; Mulryan, p. 216). Her skills as a sorcerer, or 'magic authority', is also a subject in Conti. Her chastity and 'moods' are conventional.

400–03 *This train ... of light*] The hymn ends in ritualized worship of Night ('our Empress') in the form of a public song by the members of her train, and the expectation that her virtuous reign may be finally manifested in the eternal, divine light ('the light of light').

Hymnus in Cynthiam

1–40

1–4 and 5–63 make up an inconsistent division of verse paragraphs in Q*SN*. These have been rearranged by assembling 1–4 with 5–40 into one first paragraph and giving 41–63 (the first long Homeric simile in this hymn) independent status as a second paragraph. Thus, the first 40 lines of the poem comprise the kletic element of the hymn. The hymnodist asks Cynthia to ascend to heaven, there to be admired by Earth in the splendour of her changing phases. In heaven, Cynthia will triumph over Time by establishing her eternal kingdom, where she will shine like Perseus's 'adamantine Harpey', or 'harpe', whose convex, protruding edge resembles the moon in her crescent phase, or 'prime'. This sword-like moon, also resembling Saturn's sickle, with which he castrated Uranus, or heaven, will 'cut off all desire', thus appointing chastity as the most important virtue of Cynthia's rule. The eternal, chaste empire of Cynthia will avoid all intrusions of Earth in the form of 'envious' eclipses, against which no human rituals have any power.

1–4 and Glosses 1, 2 and 3] A series of periphrastic vocatives precedes the apostrophe to Cynthia (10) at the opening of this second hymn. The first,

'Nature's bright eyesight', is explained in Gloss 1. As Schoell (*Études*, p. 193) has noted, the source for the gloss is Conti: 'Cum igitur obstetricis munere fungeretur, dicta est a Graecis Εἰλείθυια, a Latinis Lucina, quia nascentia omnia in lucem evocaret' ('Since she acted in the role of midwife, she is called Eileithyia by the Greeks, and Lucina by the Romans, for she conjures all births to light': 'De Diana', III. 18, p. 268, my translation). It is the Latin phrase 'in lucem' that seems to have inspired Chapman's periphrasis. The attribution of a 'store of humours' to the Moon in Gloss 1 also draws literally on Conti: 'Haec eadem confert parturientibus, quia ob humoris copiam facilius partus oriuntur' ('She is especially devoted to labouring women, because births are given more easily with the help of her abundance of humours': 'De Diana', III. 18, p. 273, my translation). Gloss 1's added causal clause in Latin, '*quia praest parturientibus cum invocaretur*' ('because she presides over labouring women, as I mentioned') is also reminiscent of Conti: 'Praefecta fuit praeterea parturientibus' ('She was also the patroness of women in labor': 'De Diana', III. 18, p. 267; Mulryan, p. 221). Ilithyia, or Eleithyia ('she that comes in need'), was, according to Hesiod (*Theogony*, 921–22), daughter of Zeus and Hera. Even if initially a different goddess from Artemis/Diana, they became virtually identical (Smith, *Dictionary*, II, p. 6). Prothyraea (from πρόθυρον, 'front gate') is an epiclesis, or surname, of the same goddess. As Schoell also notes, the rest of the text of Gloss 1 and the lines from Orpheus, 'To Prothyraea' (2. 1–4, 10–12), are taken from Conti ('De Lucina', IV. 1, p. 291). The gloss faultily transcribes part of the first Greek line and Conti's Latin translation. For the Greek text, see 'Προθυραίας', 2. 1–2 (*Hymnes Orphiques*, p. 28).

The second periphrasis, 'Night's fair soul', is explained in Gloss 2 by recourse to 'common conceit', whereby the Moon is acknowledged to be Night's 'purest part'. The phrase is important thematically, as it completes the transition from the first to the second hymn, understanding the advent of Night as a prelude to the Moon's dominance. Schoell (*Études*, p. 193) notes the source of Gloss 3 to be Conti ('De Hecate', III. 15, p. 240), which translates Orpheus (*Argonautica*, 975–77, in *Orphica*, ed. by Jenö Ábel (G. Freytag, 1885), p. 38). The Moon's 'triple forehead' is explained by Gloss 3 as corresponding to a triple identity that from the heavens can control 'hell' (Hecate), the 'seas' (Luna) and 'earth' (Diana). Conti also contributes to Chapman's explanation: 'Cum eadem Luna sit, et Hecate, et Diana, tamen non omnes hae vires, quae per has intelliguntur, uno nomine dicuntur, etsi ab uno fonte manant' ('Although the Moon, Hecate, and Diana are all the same, and the powers associated with these terms all flow from the same source, they are still distinguished by different names'). Equally, calling the Moon 'in dignity | The greatest, and swift'st planet' derives from this same passage in Conti: 'haec velocissimus sit planeta, cuius multiplex est potentia in rebus inferioribus' ('it is the swiftest planet, whose influence is manifold over inferior things': 'De Diana', IV. 18, p. 264, my translation).

5 *Peaceful and warlike, and the power of fate* and Gloss 4] The paradoxical nature of the epithets 'peaceful' and 'warlike' defines Diana in Conti ('De Diana', III. 18, pp. 264-73). On one hand, she is associated with the love of harmony, music, chastity and childbirth. On the other, she is the goddess-huntress. These features also define the poem's lyrical progression from the account of violent episodes of battles and hunting to Cynthia's harmonious and peaceful triumph in the last part. Gloss 4 justifies calling the Moon 'the power of fate' by reference to a passage from Hesiod, *Theogony* (411–22), cited silently from Conti's Latin translation of lines 412–14 and 419–22 ('De Hecate', III. 15, pp. 243–244; Mulryan, p. 201), in which Hecate's 'vires et officia' ('powers and responsibilities'), offered to her by Zeus/Jupiter, are detailed. Chapman's attribution of 'the power of fate' to Cynthia/Hecate is based on Conti's interpretation of Hesiod's description of Hecate's gift (line 413): 'μοῖραν ἔχειν γαίης τε καὶ ἀτρυγέτοιο θαλάσσης' ('to have a share of the earth and the unfruitful sea'). Hesiod's 'μοῖρα' means 'share', or 'lot', yet the word by extension may also mean 'one's lot in life', 'fate'. Conti's lexicon of power in his translation (nouns like 'imperium' or 'potestas' and verbal forms like 'imperat' or 'gubernat') exaggerates Hesiod's point, and is the basis for Chapman's imperial view of Cynthia. The phrase 'the power of fate' is actually borrowed from another passage in Conti, cited in the previous note ('De Diana', IV. 18, p. 264; Mulryan, p. 217): there Hecate is said to represent 'fatorum vis a Deo proficiscens' ('the power of fates whose source is God').

6–9 *In perfect circle ... portrait of thy face*] The worshippers' hope is to contemplate the full circle that Cynthia will form when becoming a full moon. The magic associations linking the circle to the Moon connect these lines with 'Noctem', 399, in which Cynthia is said to enter 'Circled with charms and incantations'. Cornelius Agrippa comments on the circle's embodiment of perfect unity and infinity as the basis for the magic properties and uses of this geometrical figure: 'Hinc circularis figura omnium amplissima et perfectissima, ligationibus et exorcismis aptissima censetur: unde qui malos daemones adiurant, circulo sese communire solent' ('hence a circular figure being the largest and perfectest of all is judged to be most fit for bindings and conjurations; whence they who adjure evil spirits are wont to environ themselves about with a circle': *De Occulta Philosophia Libri Tres*, ed. by V. Perrone Compagni (Brill, 1992), II. 23, p. 319; English translation: *Three Books of Occult Philosophy*, ed. by Donald Tyson, trans. by James Freake (Llewellyn, 1993), p. 330).

Elsewhere Chapman uses the compass as an instrument that aspires to, though does not always achieve, the completion of the perfect circle: see 'Banquet', 54, in which the letter C is invoked as a 'circle, seld or never closed', driven by the 'compass' of 'our deeds'. This explains the hymn's idea of human 'hopes', which always seek yet ultimately fall short of the circle's perfection, here embodied by the still unrealized 'state' of the full moon. The Moon's 'face' as a 'speaking portrait' of 'wisdom, beauty, majesty and dread', and as a reflecting mirror of secret thoughts and hopes, may refer to a magic trick ('praestigium') referred to by Agrippa (*De Occulta Philosophia*, I. 6, p. 98; trans. by Freake, p. 18): 'pictis certo artificio imaginibus scriptisve literis, quis nocte serena plenae Lunae radiis opponat, quarum simulacris in aëre multiplicatis sursumque raptis et una cum Lunae radiis reflexis, alius quispiam rei conscius per longam distantiam videt, legit et agnoscit in ipso disco seu circulo Lunae' ('If anyone shall take images artificially painted, or written letters, and in a clear night set them against the beams of the full Moon, whose resemblances being multiplied in the Air, and caught upward, and reflected back together with the beams of the Moon, any other man that is privy to the thing, at a long distance sees, reads, and knows them in the very compass, and circle of the Moon'). Conti mentions this passage from Agrippa ('De Luna', III. 17, p. 257). On Cynthia's circle, see Waddington, *The Mind's Empire*, p. 102.

10–12 *Great Cynthia ... rich in beams* and Glosses 5, 6] The hymn invokes for the first time the goddess by the name of Cynthia, the Greek name given to Artemis (Diana), which derives from mount Cynthus, in the island of Delos, her birthplace. By rising from her bed, washing in the Ocean, dressing and ascending to heaven in her chariot, Cynthia (the Moon) is asked to perform the opposite voyage to that of her brother Phoebus (the Sun) in 'Noctem', 380–84. Schoell (*Études*, p. 193) identifies Conti ('De Luna', III. 17, p. 261) as the source from which Catullus's poem 'De coma Berenices' (66. 5) is extracted. These lines explain the lunar eclipse in terms of the Moon's secret visit to her lover Endymion in a cave of Mount Latmus, on the coast of Caria, in modern Turkey (see Catullus, *C. Valerii Catvlli Carmina*, ed. by Ana Pérez Vega and Antonio Ramírez de Verger (Fundación El Monte, 2005), p. 587, nn. 5–6). The epithet 'Trivia' commonly identifies Diana. Catullus's lines and Conti's commentary portray Diana as sexually active in her loves with Endymion: 'Multae fuerunt fabulae de Luna fictae, quod dormientem Endymionem in Latmo Cariae monte adamarit, et cum eo concubuerit' ('The ancients spun many tales about the Moon falling in love with Endymion while he slept on the Carian mountain of Latmus, and then having sex with him'). The end of the poem (490–95) unsurprisingly contradicts this notion of the Moon's unchastity. Schoell also notes the indebtedness of Gloss 6's quotation and commentary on the Homeric hymn 'To Selene' (7–9, in *Hesiod, the Homeric Hymns and Homerica*, pp. 460–61) to Conti ('De Luna', III. 17, p. 255; Mulryan, p. 210). Chapman's words in the gloss, 'In Oceano lavari', draw literally on Conti's account. The 'robes' that are 'rich in beams' translate Conti's 'vestibus [...] nitidis' in the Homeric hymn (the above-mentioned 'εἵματα τηλαυγέα', line 8; see Commentary: 'Noctem', 393–97). On Hecate as 'Trivia', see also Conti, 'De Hecate', III. 14, p. 242.

13–17 *And in thy ... fixed prime* and Gloss 7] These lines complete the hymnodist's petition that all-purifying Cynthia ascend to heaven by riding the chariot alluded to in Gloss 6, there to be admired by Earth. Cynthia's 'old swift changes' are said now to be paradoxically 'fixed' into the 'young [...] prime' of the crescent moon. The parenthetical simile recounting the mythological tale of the love of one of the three Erinyes, Tisiphone, for the handsome youth Cytheron is mistakenly attributed to 'Menander' in Gloss 7 through Chapman's inattentive reading of Conti ('De Eumenidibus', III. 10, p. 220; Mulryan, p. 184). The poet was misled by the absence of punctuation in the 1581 edition (which I add in square brackets): 'Fabulati sunt antiqui neque has quidem severissimas Deas Cupidinis vim potuisse devitare, quando scriptum reliquit Maenander in rebus fabulosis[.] Tisiphonem in amorem cuiusdam pueri formosi Cytheronis nomine incidisse, cuius desiderium cum ferre non posset, verba de congressu ad illum preferenda curavit. At is formidandum aspectum veritus, neque responso quidem dignam fecit, quo illa unum e suis draconibus e capillis convulsum in eum coniecit, quem serpens intra nodos constringens interemit, ubi Deorum misericordia mons ab illo dictus fuit, qui prius Asterius dicebatur' ('According to ancient myth, these very cruel goddesses were still no match for Cupid's strength. Menander's mythological tales bear this out. For example, Tisiphone fell in love with a handsome boy named Cytheron; she could not control her passion for Cytheron and had someone send him a message to arrange a clandestine meeting. But Tisiphone was so ugly that she frightened Cytheron, and he didn't bother to respond to her request. So she tore one of the serpents from her head and sent it after him. The serpent killed Cytheron by knotting itself around his neck and choking him to death. Mount Asterius, where the murder took place, was then renamed Cytheron, as an expression of the gods' pity for the boy's situation').

Mulryan's translation repunctuates the passage in order to separate the reference to Menander from the recounting of the myth. Mulryan also argues that Conti's actual source is the Pseudo Plutarch, *De Fluviorum et Montium Nominibus*, which Conti himself translated. The tale of Cytheron and Tisiphone is told in the second chapter of this work (*De terminis rhetoricis* [...] *Plutarchi item opusculum de montibus* (Basel, 1560), sig. aa5^v). Conti transferred a great deal of his earlier translation to the *Mythologiae* without citing himself. Although Chapman makes use of the *Mythologiae*, his addition of one detail seems to point to his knowledge of the Pseudo Plutarch's *Fluviorum* in Conti's translation: this is the mention in the gloss of 'wild beasts' living on Mount Asterius, as this work affirms that Cytheron's murder took place 'ubi Asterius in editioribus montis partibus gregem pasceret' ('where Asterius on the highest parts of the mount feeds the beasts'; my translation). It is not clear why Chapman chose this simile as an analogy of the Moon's rising over the earth to appear in its prime. The gloss justifies it poorly by arguing that Cynthia's brightness when rising over the earth looks as if Mount Cytheron were in flames. However, fire is not a significant part of this tale. What the simile seems to convey is that Earth is inflamed by the Moon's presence, just as 'shady' Mount Cytheron would have 'fr[ied]' if, instead of being presented with Tisiphone's dreadful sight (Conti's 'formidandum aspectum'), he had beheld the Moon's 'solemn fire'. 'Sightful fury' does not then refer to Cytheron's passion as excited by the sense of sight, but to the pleasant-looking, sightly vigour of Cynthia's light, in stark contrast with the visibly ugly 'fury' Tisiphone.

18–20 *O let... he rise*] Time is the primeval deity Chronos, often confused with Cronus, or Saturn. It was represented as a monster with wings in the ancient Orphic theogonies. See W. K. C. Guthrie, *Orpheus and Greek Religion: A Study of the Orphic Movement* (Methuen, 1966), pp. 85–92. Time's death as his wings are burnt by Cynthia's light rewrites the myth of Icarus, whose wings were melted by the sun (Ovid, *Metamorphoses*, VIII, 195–235). Time's scorched wings embody Cynthia's freeing herself from the fetters of time, as the hymn aims to proclaim the eternal character of her 'sacred state'.

21–30 *And, as Heav'n's... another inference* and Glosses 8, 9] The argument of the simile is intricate. Just as Saturn's castration of his father Uranus (or Heaven) with a sword of adamant shows that, since Uranus was made of ether, he could not procreate a new heaven, so Cynthia's sickle-like shape when in her crescent phase can cut off all sexual desire; for that reason, she, unlike Uranus, will not be removed from her kingdom, and her rule will admit no daily interruptions by the Sun. As Schoell notes (*Études*, p. 27, n. 2), Gloss 8 confuses Giglio Gregorio Giraldi's *De Deis Gentium Libri* (Lyon, 1565) with Chapman's usual source, Conti's *Mythologiae*. Conti explains the meanings of Saturn's castration of Uranus in several passages of Book II ('De Iove', II. 1, p. 108; 'De Saturno', II. 2, p. 122; 'De Coelo', II. 3, p. 132; Mulryan, pp. 90, 104, 111). The latter of these texts provides the closest 'application' made in the poem, as Gloss 8 calls it: 'Exectus fuit igitur Coelus, ut ego quidem sentio, quia unus sit aether, unumque coelum. [...] Nam cum unus sit mundus, at non plures, cum neque esse possint, merito dicunt Coelum exectum a filio, quia sibi simile quidpiam tempus non finet procreari' ('As far as I'm concerned, Heaven was castrated because there's only one ether, and one heaven. [...] And since there's only one world, and not many (which is impossible), the ancients spoke accurately when they said that Heaven was castrated by his son, for Time will not allow anything to be born that resembles itself'). Conti ('De Iove', II. 1, pp. 87–88) also refers to Jupiter's castration of his father Saturn as recounted by some ancient sources (Lycophron, *Cassandra*, 761–62, in *Callimachus, Lycophron, Aratus*, pp. 556–57). As Schoell also notes, Conti's own explanation of this legend provides a direct source for Chapman's verse: 'Huic *partes genitales abscidit* Iupiter, quia *nullo tempore alius mundus generabitur*, cum *hic constet ex universa materia*' ('Jupiter cut off his father's genitals because another world can never be created in some other time period, since the first one has absorbed the totality of matter': 'De Iove', II. 1, p. 109; Mulryan, p. 91, emphasis added).

Gloss 9] As Schoell notes (*Études*, p. 193), Chapman may have found the Latin term *harpe* (from Greek ἅρπη, i.e. sickle, scimitar, but also 'falchion', used later in the poem) in Conti ('De Typhoeo', VI. 22, p. 654; Mulryan, p. 548): 'At ille Iovem deinde captum detinuit, cui harpe illa, quam illi ademit, nanuum pedumque nervos secuit' ('then he [Typhoeus] took Jupiter's own sickle away from him and used it to slice off the tendons of his hands and feet'). However, his direct source is most plausibly Ovid, who accounts for Perseus's killing of Lyabas with the same hooked sword with which he had cut off Medusa's head: 'vertit in hunc harpen spectatam caede Medusae | Acrisioniades adigitque in pectus' ('Acrisius' grandson quickly turned on him that hook which had been fleshed in Medusa's death, and drove it into his breast': *Metamorphoses*, v. 69–70).

31–39 *For if the envious … thy changes' funeral*] The opening causal connective, 'For', marks the relation between the previous lines and this passage, which describes 'another inference' into Cynthia's changing reign. The passage can be paraphrased as follows: 'If Earth's centre ("envious forehead") frowns ("lour") on the Moon's hegemony ("age") by aligning with it, thus causing a lunar eclipse, and claims her (the Moon) as her (the Earth's) daughter, none of the rituals used by the ancient Romans and Macedonians to bring back her light (such as tapers, torches, music or mourning) can actually help to claim her return, while Night, in her dark robes, officiates a funeral rite for the temporary loss of her light'. Schoell (*Études*, pp. 185–86) notes that these lines draw on Conti ('De Luna', III. 17, p. 258; Mulryan, p. 213), but only quotes half of Conti's relevant passage. It is given in full here, with Conti's quotation of Plutarch in italics: 'Ubi fuerint oppositi isti planetae, ita, ut alterius centrum centro alterius ac centro terrae per rectam lineam opponatur, tunc Luna incidens in umbram tota occultatur, ac deficit repente illius lumen, cum nequeat tanquam speculum lumen ab eo accipere. [...] Quantus esset antiquorum timor, quantaque trepidatio cum Luna deficeret, declaravit Plutarchus ita in Paulo Aemilio: [Greek text omitted] *Repente vero Luna cum plena esset et sublimis, facta est obscura: lumineque deficiente multiplicibus mutatis coloribus evanuit. Romanis (sicut est apud eos consuetudo) aris tinnitu lumen revocantibus, ignesque multos, et faces, et taedas in caelum protendentibus nihil simile fecerunt Macedones: sed timor et trepidatio multa a universum habuit exercitum*' ('When those planets are set against one another in such a way that the center of the one is the opposite the center of the other, and the center of the Earth is in direct line, then the Moon lapses into the shadow, and is completely hidden; suddenly its light is lost, for it can no longer function as a mirror, receiving light by virtue of its position. [...] Plutarch, in his *Life of Aemilius Paulus*, describes how fearful and terrified the ancients became when the Moon is in a decline: *On a sudden the moon, which was full and high in the heavens, grew dark, lost its light, took all sorts of colours in succession, and finally disappeared. The Romans, according to their custom, tried to call her light back by the clashing of bronze utensils and by holding up many blazing fire-brands and torches toward the heavens; the Macedonians, however, did nothing of this sort, but amazement and terror possessed their camp*': Plutarch, *Life of Aemilius Paulus*, 17. 3–4, in *Plutarch's Lives*, ed. and trans. by Bernadotte Perrin, 11 vols (Heinemann, 1918), VI, pp. 400–03).

Chapman's 'forehead of the Earth' translates Plutarch's 'centro terrae', yet poeticizes it by deifying the planet and calling her 'envious'. Thus, Earth jealously claims to be Cynthia's mother by interposing herself between the Sun and the Moon. The Moon's (and the Sun's) actual mother is Theia (Hesiod, *Theogony*, 371–74), traditionally considered the mother of all light. Yet Conti also echoes other versions of this genealogy that make the Moon the Sun's daughter (rather than his sister and Hyperion's daughter): 'Cum [Luna] lumen a Sole accipiat, Solis filia dicta est' ('Since the Moon gets her light from the Sun, she was called the daughter of the Sun': 'De Luna', III. 17, p. 262; Mulryan, p. 216). In either case, parenting the Moon involves feeding her with light and granting her a role as a reflecting mirror. Earth's envious usurpation of that role deprives the Moon of her natural light, and causes Night to wear dark, mourning robes. Night's clothing, and the blindfolding garments that adorn her, are taken from Conti: 'Finxerunt hanc Deam antiqui nigris vestibus indutam, nigroque capitis velamine, quam etiam sequerentur astra, at non solum praecederent' ('The ancients thought of this goddess dressed in black garments with a black veil upon her head. There were stars behind her as well as in front': 'De Nocte', III. 12, p. 232; Mulryan, p. 192).

40–63

This far-fetched Homeric simile recreates the death of General Lucius Aemilius Paulus at the Battle of Cannae (216 BC) at the hands of Hannibal's Carthaginian army during the Second Punic War, and the devastating effects of that death upon the crumbling Roman army, as a vehicle for the Moon's darkening during a lunar eclipse and its equally dismal consequences. If we attend to the tenor's logic, 'interposèd Earth' is like the Carthaginian army, Cynthia ('our sacred chief and sovereign general') resembles the fallen Paulus, and her followers ('we') stand for the Roman army. Chapman could have read about this episode in Polybius (*The Histories*, ed. and trans. by W. R. Paton, 6 vols (Harvard University Press, 1969), III. 116; II, pp. 284–89), but most likely in Livy's *Ab Urbe Condita*, which mentions the 'sling' ('funda') that causes Paulus's death wound (*History of Rome*, ed. and trans. by B. O. Foster, 14 vols (Harvard University Press, 1929), XXII. 49. 1; V, pp. 358–59). This latter text motivates this edition's preference for 'slings' (51) over 'flings' as the correct reading of Q*SN*.

51 *Blood's stern daughter, cruel Tyche* and Gloss 10] Schoell (*Études*, 193) notes the indebtedness of Gloss 10 to Conti: 'Homerus in hymno quodam in Cererem illam fuisse Oceani filiam innuit, et testatur Pausanias in Messeniacis, quippe cum illam etiam cum reliquis filiabus Oceani cum Proserpina colludentibus connumeravit, quam Tychen Graeci appellant, quorum carminum haec est sententia: [Latin lines quoted by Chapman] Orpheus in hymno quem scripsit in Fortunam, illam natam fuisse e sanguine ait in his: [Greek and Latin lines quoted by Chapman]' ('Homer, in the hymns that he wrote to Ceres, suggested that Fortune was Ocean's daughter; and Pausanias, in his description of Messenia, reached the same conclusion, for he counted her along with the other daughters of Ocean who were playing with Proserpine. The Greeks called her Tyche, as we can see from these verses. [...] Orpheus, in his hymn to Fortune, says that he gave birth through blood, as we can see from these verses [...]': 'De Fortuna', IV. 9, p. 339; Mulryan, p. 278). This Gloss again testifies to Chapman's somewhat careless handling of Conti, as he misattributes to Pausanias three lines translating Proserpine's words in the Homeric hymn 'To Demeter': 'All we were playing in a lovely meadow, Leucippe and Phaeno and Electra and Ianthe, Melita also and Iache with Rhodea and Callirhoe and Melobosis and Tyche and Ocyrhoe, fair as a flower' (417–20, in *Hesiod, the Homeric Hymns and Homerica*, pp. 318–19). While Tyche's cruelty is a trait that may derive from the Orphic hymn quoted by Conti, both Conti and Chapman misinterpret the hymn by extracting one single line out of context and making 'Blood' (which Chapman personifies) Tyche's (or Fortune's) parent: 'sanguine prognatam'. However, the actual meaning of this phrase in Orpheus depends on the previous line: 'born of Eubouleus's blood' ('Εὐβουλῆος αἵματος | ἐκγεγαῶσαν': Orpheus, 'Τύχη', 72. 3–4, in *Hymnes Orphiques*, p. 579). Eubouleus is a demigod often regarded as the son of Demeter/Ceres, or associated with her myths (Grimal, *Dictionary*, p. 154).

64–75

As Schoell notes (*Études*, p. 186), these lines draw, like lines 31–39, on Conti ('De Luna', III. 17, p. 258), who in turn draws on Plutarch, *Life of Aemilius Paulus*, 17. 3. This passage by Plutarch compares the knowledge of, and attitude to, eclipses of the Roman and Macedonian armies during the Battle of Pydna (168 BC) in the Third Macedonian War. The Roman consul and general Lucius Aemilius Paulus Macedonicus (229–160 BC, son of the Paulus Aemilius that was killed at Cannae, for whom see Commentary: 'Cynthiam', 40–63) was acquainted with the portentous nature of lunar eclipses, which allowed him to read the auguries of victory. See Commentary: 'Cynthiam', 31–39, for relevant source texts.

76–81

The hymnodist acknowledges that not even scientific lore about the temporary nature of Cynthia's invisibility during eclipses will prevent her worshippers from mourning her absence. As Schoell points out (*Études*, p. 187), Chapman's source is Conti's mention of 'Democrates' ('De Luna', III. 17. 256; Mulryan, p. 211): 'ad Democratis usque tempora vulgo Solis Lunaeque defectus abolitiones appelaverint' ('right up to the time of Democritus, the popular phrase for an eclipse of the Sun or the Moon was a "destruction"'). 'Democrates' is a corruption of Democritus of Abdera (*c*. 460–*c*. 370 BC), the so-called 'laughing philosopher', known for his contributions to atomism. Other contemporary texts witness this spelling: 'And for those things that *Heraclitus* wept bitterlie, *Democrates* laughed joyfully' (Humfrey Gifford, *A Posie for Gilliflowers* (London, 1580), sig. D4^v).

82–115

The difficulty of this verse paragraph mostly lies in its syntax. Tentative paraphrases of its most intricate passages have been provided in the explanatory footnotes. Its structure has been slightly rearranged. Thus, lines 116–19, which in QSN make up an independent verse paragraph, have been attached to 83–115, as they provide a conclusion to the earlier arguments. The paragraph's thematic inconsistency is less so if understood as organized around the idea of Cynthia's absence as the result of lunar changes and eclipses. Thus, it begins with a reference to the influence upon the present times of the opinions of the ancients about these subjects. Whereas, according to the hymnodist, the content of those opinions are to be respected, the forms in which they have usually come to the present time must be replaced with those of English poetry. The Englishness of the poem's verse (i.e. the use of heroic couplets) serves to introduce another English subject: the identification of Cynthia with Elizabeth I. Thus, 'Ephesia's state' is the English court, but also Elizabeth's virginity (by reference to Diana Ephesia), which will not tolerate being eclipsed by the presence of a foreign suitor to the queen. Diana's chaste virtue, exemplified by her shunning the company of men and her devotion to hunting, becomes symbolic of the virtues of the queen and of the English nation, which should not fear any change in the behaviour of its leader. After this digression about English and England, the speaker returns to the scientific explanation of lunar eclipses and the feelings of mourning that these eclipses cause in Cynthia's followers. The paragraph concludes with the petition that Cynthia may turn her English light against the sun of Europe in order to oppose his threats. These lines have been interpreted as a comment on Elizabeth's rejection of one of her suitors, François Hercule Valois, Duke of Alençon. See in this respect Waddington's detailed analysis (*The Mind's Empire*, esp. pp. 72–78).

96 *Ephesia's state*] 'Ephesia' is a common epithet of Diana. Conti reminds us that Diana's main temple was in Ephesus: 'celeberrimum omnium templorum et augustissimum' ('the most renowned and revered of all her temples': 'De Diana', III. 18, p. 271; Mulryan, p. 223). The temple, and the story of its building and destruction, reappears later in the poem (423–35). For this reason, 'state' could also mean throne or altar here, although Diana's identification with Elizabeth points to her chastity, and to England, as referents. On the theme of chastity in *SN*, see Berry, *Of Chastity and Power*, pp. 138–45.

98–106 *The pureness ... all our parts* and Gloss 12] The gloss indicator in the text follows 'never-tainted life' (98), but it actually refers to the string of juxtaposed present-participle explanatory phrases and clauses that list the 'commonly known [...] properties of Cynthia'. All these properties are explained by Conti, from whose text there are clear borrowings in the form of direct translation: 'Cum vero corpus Lunae non sit ex aliqua materia densa ut terra est' ('De Luna', III. 17, p. 260) becomes 'Thy body not composèd in thy birth | Of such condensèd matter as the earth' (100–01).

111 *thy father's light* and Gloss 12a] The Latin translation from Antigone's words in Euripides, *Phoenician Maidens* (175–79), asserting that the Moon is the Sun's daughter, is taken from Conti ('De Luna', III. 17, p. 254). See *Euripides*, ed. and trans. by Arthur S. Way, 4 vols (Heinemann, 1912), III, pp. 358–59.

116–19 *Then set ... thy light* and Gloss 13] As Schoell notes (*Études*, p. 193), the source for the explanation of 'the girdle of Cynthia' is Conti: 'Deinde cum ita uterus excrevisset gravidis puellis, ut sueta zona uti amplius non possent, eam zonam mos fuit in templo Dianae λυσίζωνα cognomento zonam solventis scilicet, quod fuit apud Athenienses, deponere. Quare postea dictum est zonam solvere, pro eo quod est gravida fieri, quod patet ex carminibus Apollonii lib. primi: [followed by Greek text and Latin translation, the latter reproduced in Chapman's Gloss]' ('When the wombs of pregnant girls had grown so large that they could not get into their girdles any more, the Athenians used to put those girdles in the temple of Diana λυσίζωνα, an epithet meaning "girdle loosener". Thus the phrase "to loosen the girdle" replaced the phrase "to become pregnant", as these verses from the first book of Apollonius make clear': 'De Diana', III. 18, p. 268; Mulryan, p. 221; for the original Greek text reproduced in Conti, see Apollonius Rhodius, *Argonautica*, ed. and trans. by R. C. Seaton (Heinemann, 1912), I. 288-89, pp. 22-23). These lines are implicitly a compliment and a petition to Elizabeth I.

120-23 and 124-43

The brief verse paragraph of four lines seems to stand by itself in contrast with the longer subsequent one, as the first deals with the curses and the second with the blessings resulting respectively from Cynthia's scorn and favour. In the latter, those favoured by Cynthia are first compared to Hercules, who dared challenge the heat of the Sun (here embodying lust), and to Diana's own priestesses, who could walk on burning coals without any injury to their bare feet. Deixis may be confusing in this passage. Cynthia is consistently addressed in the second person — i.e. 'thou', 'thy'. The third-person 'She' (138) is here understood as referring to Cynthia's mind, which transmits her 'virtue-tempered' qualities to her worshippers, acting as soothing 'balm' and as 'steel' that protects her followers' 'feet'. Cynthia's mind is accordingly the 'type', or dome, that crowns her 'almighty state'.

120-23 *O how accursed ... never thrives* and Gloss 14] Schoell (*Études*, p. 193) notes that Gloss 14 (and consequently, these lines) draws on Conti ('De Diana', III. 18, p. 269; Mulryan, p. 222): 'Illam facultatem idcirco Dianae trinuit Callimachus, ut gravissimis afficiat calamitatibus quos libuerit, ut est in his: [followed by Greek text and Latin translation, only the first line of which is reproduced in Chapman's original Gloss]' ('Callimachus therefore claimed that Diana had the skill to inflict very dark catastrophes on anyone she wanted, as these verses testify'). For the Greek text quoted in Conti, see Callimachus, 'To Artemis', III. 124-27, in *Callimachus, Lycophron, Aratus*, pp. 70-71. The missing text of Conti's Latin translation of Callimachus has been added to the gloss in square brackets, as Chapman's four lines are a direct translation of it.

124-28 *But then ... quench the fire*] In the logic of Chapman's hymn, Cynthia's followers are identified as Herculean heroes for their capacity to 'dare the Sun'. On Hercules' bending the Sun's bow to avert its heat, see 'Noctem', 257-59, Gloss 9. On Chapman's reliance on Conti for this myth, see Commentary: 'Noctem', 255-67. As explained in that note, Conti's account of Hercules as a Sun figure is quite contrary to Chapman's interests.

129-37 *As at thy altars ... dart of hell* and Gloss 15] As Gloss 15 points out, the simile's vehicle relies on Strabo: 'ὧν ἐν τοῖς Κασταβάλοις ἐστὶ τὸ τῆς

Περασίας Ἀρτέμιδος ἱερόν, ὅπου φασὶ τὰς ἱερείας γυμνοῖς τοῖς ποσὶ δι' ἀνθρακιᾶς βαδίζειν ἀπαθεῖς' ('At Castabala is the temple of the Perasian Artemis, where the priestesses, it is said, walk with naked feet over hot embers without pain': Strabo, *Geography*, ed. and trans. by Horace Leonard Jones, 8 vols (Heinemann, 1928), XII. 2. 7, IV, pp. 358–59). Yet, as Schoell notes, Chapman's source is Conti ('De Diana', III. 18, p. 270: 'Et Strabo libro duodecimo Castabalim fanum fuisse Dianae Persicae scribit, ubi sacrae mulieres illaesis pedibus super prunas ambularent'.

144–69

The hymnodist asks the Nine Muses to inspire him so that he can sing Cynthia's perfections. He also scorns those poets whose incapacity to dissociate the senses from purely intellectual aspirations make them unfit for Cynthia's mysteries. This passage testifies to the importance of the theory of poetic inspiration, which constitutes a crucial facet of Chapman's poetics. Inspired poetry allows its practitioners to elevate their spirits above the base pleasures of the senses. In this passage, and particularly in 163–69, readers have seen a critique of Ovidian poets and poems, and more particularly Shakespeare's *Venus and Adonis* (1593) and the epigraph of its title page: 'Vilia miretur vulgus; mihi flavus Apollo | Pocula Castalia plena ministret aqua' ('Let base conceipted witts admire vilde things, | Faire Phoebus lead me to the Muses springs') (Ovid, *Amores*, I. 15. 35–36; English translation: *All Ovids Elegies*, I. 15. 35–36). On the importance of Platonic theories of poetic frenzy and divine inspiration as expressed in Plato's *Ion*, and in Marsilio Ficino's commentaries on Plato, see Introduction, p. 23, and n. 80. Yet poetic inspiration does not by itself explain Chapman's poetic credo here: while, on one hand, poetry is conceived of in terms of mysteries that are revealed through sacred ritual (just as hidden truths can be read by priests in sacrificed animals' 'bowels'), such revelation is only accessible to those studious spirits who have properly cultivated their 'judgement'. The 'apt judgement' and the 'judicial perspective' of readers and poets emerge as crucial concepts of Chapman's poetics, particularly in '*OBS*: To Roydon'.

> 146 *Gorgonean dews* and Gloss 16] The birth of Pegasus from the severed head of the Gorgon Medusa is recounted by Hesiod: 'And when Perseus cut off her head, there sprang forth great Chrysaor and *the horse Pegasus* [Πήγασος ἵππος] who is so called because he was born *near the springs* [περὶ πηγὰς] of Ocean; and that other, because he held a golden *blade* [ἄορ] in his hands' (*Theogony*, 280–83, emphasis added). Yet Chapman may also have drawn on Conti ('De Medusa', VII. 11, p. 749; Mulryan, p. 635): 'Ex capite Medusae defecto Pegasus alatus equo repente prosiliit' ('And then the winged horse Pegasus suddenly sprang out of Medusa's severed head'). 'The Muses' fount' is Hippocrene (Greek Ἵππου κρήνη, i.e. the Horse's spring), whose waters brought poetic inspiration and around which the Muses gathered to sing and dance.

150 *Daphnean laurel*] Lexically, the phrase is redundant, as δάφνη means laurel in Greek. On the symbolism of the laurel: 'The crowning of the poet, the artist or the conqueror with laurel leaves meant to represent not the external and visible consecration of an act, but the recognition that that act, by its very existence, presupposes a series of inner victories over the negative and dissipative influence of base forces' (Juan Eduardo Cirlot, *A Dictionary of Symbols*, trans. by Jack Sage (Philosophical Books, 1971, 2nd edn), p. 181).

152–55 *As she is Hecate ... mere divine*] On the identifications of the Moon and Hecate, which Chapman takes from Conti, see Commentary: 'Cynthiam', 5, 10–12. In the magic 'force' of the goddess-sorceress Hecate, the 'ravish[ed]' poet finds the source for 'figuring' the 'arguments' of her praise, which ultimately works the 'refine[ment]' of his 'soul' and that of his listeners. On the soul's divine transformation through understanding of its own immortality, see Commentary: 'Noctem', 123–30, particularly its reference to Ficino's *Platonic Theology*. On Hecate's magical force as symbolic of Chapman's inspired poetics, see Waddington's fine analysis in *The Mind's Empire*, pp. 91–108.

160 *huntress*] Conti ('De Diana', III. 18, p. 273) closes his long list of epithets of Diana with 'Venatrix' (i.e. huntress).

170–207

Three different scenes make up the complex tableau of this verse paragraph. In the first (170–75), the listeners are alerted by the hymnodist to Cynthia's descent from heaven to the place of her birth, Ortygia, with a train of servitors fashioned by her magic arts. The second scene (176–95), narrated in the past tense, recounts the erection of an also magic 'Elysian palace', the pillars of which project a pyramidal shadow that overtops the lunar regions; this palace is built by Hope and Form at Cynthia's command. The third scene (196–207) resumes the present tense of the first scene and shows Cynthia sitting in her palace, exhibiting her authority, benignity and bounty while she is proclaimed by Jupiter to be the main planet in the sky.

170–75 *See then ... and meteors* and Gloss 17] In this brief passage, Cynthia's activity displays her triple identity as Luna, Diana and Hecate. As Luna, she descends from heaven to Ortygia, which, according to Gloss 17, 'is the country where she [Diana] was brought up'. Ortygia is often identified as 'the ancient name of Delos, an island off Syracuse' (Smith, *Dictionary*, III, p. 63). The phrasal verb 'brought up' seems to refer to Diana's birth rather than simply to her upbringing. Chapman derives the place name from several references in Conti ('De Diana', III. 18, p. 265; Mulryan, p. 219): the Pseudo Homer ('To Apollo', 16, in *Hesiod, the Homeric Hymns and Homerica*, pp. 324–25) says that Leto gave birth '[to Diana] in Ortygia and [to Apollo] in rocky Delos' ('τὴν μὲν ἐν Ὀρτυγίῃ, τὸν δὲ κραναῇ ἐνὶ Δήλῳ'). In Conti's Latin translation: 'Edita in Ortygia haec, in Delo est ortus Apollo'. But Conti also quotes Tacitus, who in *Annales* voices the Ephesians' claim that Apollo and Diana were not born at Delos. Rather: 'apud se Cenchrium amnem, lucum Ortygiam, ubi Latonam partu gravidam et oleae, quae tum maneat, adnisam edidisse ea numina' ('In Ephesus there was a river Cenchrius, with a grove Ortygia; where Latona, heavy-wombed and supporting herself by an olive-tree which remained to that day, gave birth to the twins': III. 61, in *Tacitus*, ed. and trans. by Clifford H. More and John Jackson, 4 vols (Harvard University Press, 1962), pp. 618–19). Here Ortygia is identified as a 'lucus' (grove), which in Conti is corrupted to 'lacus' (lake), but Chapman later speaks about 'Ortygian forests' (286). Tacitus derives his description from Strabo, who locates Ortygia in Ephesus, and is described as 'a magnificent grove of all kinds of trees' (Ὀρτυγία, διαπρεπὲς ἄλσος παντοδαπῆς ὕλης': *Geography*, XIV. 1. 20).

Yet, despite Cynthia's identity as Diana, Chapman insists that she is not accompanied by the escort given to her by Jupiter, which the poet derives from Conti ('De Diana', III. 18, p. 266; Mulryan, p. 219), with some differences in the numbers: 'Arcus praeterea et sagittas et puellas socias sexaginta Oceaninas, et alias viginti, quae illi arcus cothurnosque et canes curarent Jupiter postulanti tribuit' ('Jupiter also surrendered to her demands and gave her, in addition to a bow and arrows, some sixty Oceanids for companions (and twenty more besides to look after her bows, arrows, hunting boots, and dogs)'). Rather, Cynthia acts here in her role as Hecate, that is, as a sorceress, by creating her own servants out of different natural elements ('flowers', 'shadows', 'mists' and 'meteors'). Chapman's positive view of Hecate nevertheless departs from Conti, whose account associates her with evil sorcery bringing misfortune ('De Hecate', III. 15, p. 247).

176–95 *Her rare ... great mistress wild*] This heavily allegorical passage needs to be read as a unit, as it deals with the building of Cynthia's palace. While two motifs in these lines are derived from Conti, the rest of the passage seems, if not necessarily original, at least designed to suit Chapman's plan. Two personified abstractions, Hope and Form, presumably members of that train of magic 'servitors' to the goddess, assume unequal creative roles in the making of the palace. While Hope supplies a number of fleeting ornaments such as its 'sunny foil' and the 'shapes of every flower and tree' on its 'types', or domes, the role of Form is to prevent its beauties from being 'obscured' by a 'disposition baser than divine'. Thus, Form provides the palace's enduring architecture as the effect of a design whose 'accomplishment' must remain inscrutable even to 'the eye of Phoebus'.

The idea of the Elysian essence of the palace may have been inspired by Conti ('De campis Elysiis', III. 19, p. 274; Mulryan, p. 226): 'Alii [campos Elysios tradiderunt] circa lunarem globum, ubi purior est aer' ('Some accounts placed the Elysian fields around the lunar sphere where the air is purer'). Yet, as Schoell notes (*Études*, p. 188), the palace's architecture is adapted from another passage by Conti ('De Luna', III. 17, p. 258; Mulryan, pp. 212–13): 'Anaxagoras [...] declaravit, quod terra inter duos praestantiores planetas interposita, umbram tanquam pyramidem facit, cuius basis sit in planitie, dorsoque ipsius terrae, conus vero vel ita extendatur ut lunae regionem pertranseat' ('Anaxagoras [...] explained that the earth, because it situated itself between more imposing planets, creates a pyramidical shadow, whose base is on a flat plain at the very back of the earth itself. Its cone extends just far enough to cross into the Moon's quarter'). This edition's attempt to trace any relation of this idea to the cosmology of Anaxagoras has been unsuccessful. Chapman's adaptation replaces cosmological with architectural elements: the earth thus becomes the central 'tender building', while the two interposing larger planets are now the 'two superior pillars' that flank the palace. This disposition between two columns alludes to Charles V's iconography of the imperial eagle standing between two pillars, representing *Pax Imperii*. The pyramidal shadow ascending from the round though flat, drum-shaped 'basis' of the earth along the larger planets is reproduced in the palace's projection of an also mounting, pyramidal or cone-like, shadow on the pillars that 'transcend[s]' the lunar region.

Smarr reads these lines in relation to the pyramid images in 'Banquet' (6 and 64); she also explores emblematic analogues — particularly in Achille Bocchi's *Symbolicae Quaestiones* (Bologna: Societas Typographiae Bononiensis, 1574), II. 48, 'Resurgit ex Virtute Vera Gloria', sigs $N4^v$–$O1^r$; and IV. 97, 'Qua te fieri nullo impetu mentem bonam', sigs $Cc3^v$–$Cc4^r$ (see Visual Sources). Smarr concludes that their Neoplatonic quality suggests 'an unfolding of forms from the mind' ('Pyramid', pp. 378–79). Frances A. Yates interprets the passage as a political emblem of a '"Pax Imperii" symbolised by the Moon' (*Astraea: The Imperial Theme in the Sixteenth Century* (Routledge, 1975), pp. 76–77). Waddington emphasizes the 'expansionist motif' and the heavenly sanction in Chapman's symbolic portrait of Elizabethan imperialism (*The Mind's Empire*, pp. 82–83). Philosophical and political meanings actually merge in Chapman's idealized proposal of an imperial Cynthia/Elizabeth that aspires to empyreal expansion by embracing poetry and learning.

196–207 *Here as... thus celestial* and Gloss 18] The description of Cynthia's palace is crowned by her presence, sitting in her throne as a controlling goddess. Hesiod's lines alluded to in the poem and Gloss 18 are from *Theogony*, 411–22, taken silently from Conti ('De Hecate', III. 15, pp. 243–44), and partially reproduced in Gloss 4. See also Commentary: 'Cynthiam', 5 and Gloss 4.

208–68

This verse paragraph opens the longest part of the poem (208–399), which narrates in epic fashion Cynthia's self-designed diurnal entertainment (i.e. 'to take the pleasures of the day') while she awaits the coming of the night ('Because her night star soon will call away'). This narrative interlude recounts Cynthia's magic creation of the nymph Euthymia and her subsequent metamorphoses into wild animals that instigate a cynegetic scene with hunters and dogs, made out in similar magic fashion. These chase Euthymia, first in the shape of a panther, into a dangerous thicket, whose thorny vegetation rends the dogs' skins as they try to cross it.

208–19 *And now ... must tame*] Cynthia's identity as the sorceress Hecate is patent in her capacity to frame visions out of natural 'matter'. Her main creation is the nymph Euthymia. Q$_{SN}$'s spelling 'Euthimya' has been emended here. Former editors and critics have preferred the original spelling, perhaps in an attempt to differentiate this character from the 'Euthymia' of Chapman's long philosophical poem *Euthymiae Raptus, or The Teares of Peace* (1614). In both cases, the word's origin is clearly Greek εὐθυμία (cheerfulness, tranquillity), and there is no necessity to differentiate them. Euthymia represents 'tranquillity of mind', acting as a curb to pleasure (i.e. 'gives all the reins | Of wishèd pleasance', 'bid the base to all affection') and as consolation for 'the cares and toils of earth'. Chapman's inspiration was the Stoicism of Seneca's *De tranquilliate animi* and Plutarch's Περὶ εὐθυμίας (which he read, as Schoell has demonstrated, in Xylander's translation of 1570). In this poem, Euthymia's most conspicuous physical trait is her 'golden wings', which are nevertheless tied with 'purple strings' so that she remains on earth. In allegorical terms, the nymph is kept away from riches and fancies — another feature of Senecan and Plutarchan tranquillity (see, for instance, Plutarch, 'On Tranquillity of Mind', in *Moralia*, ed. and trans. by W. C. Hembold, 15 vols (Harvard University Press, 1932), 477A, VI, pp. 236–37).

220–42 *Then straight ... the forest ranged*] Cynthia first transforms different natural elements into hunters, and then makes the wild hounds of the same matter. The narrative's indebtedness to the myth of Actaeon and Diana is confirmed by the names of Actaeon's seventeen dogs, for which Chapman draws on Conti ('De Actaeone', VI. 24, p. 672; Mulryan, p. 562), as Schoell (*Études*, pp. 189–90) and others after him have noted: 'Nomina vero canum, a quibus Actaeon fuit laniatus, nihil aliud quam vel colores corporum, vel sagacitatem significant, quae convenit canibus. Haec autem sunt: Melampus, nigros habens pedes; Ichnobates, per vestigia sequens; Pamphagus, omnia comedens; Dorceus, perspicax; Oribasus, montivagus;

Nebrophonos, hinnulos occidens; Laelaps, procella; Theron, ferus; Pterelas, alatus; Agre, inquirens; Hylaeus, sylvestris; Nape, saltus pererrans; Poemenis, pastorum canis; Harpyia, rapax; Ladon, hinnulo similis; Dromas, cursor; Canache, fremens; Sticte, picta; Tigris, fera; Alce, robusta; Leucon, albus; Asbolus, fuliginosus; Lacon, reboans; Aello, procellosus; Thous, celer; Cyprius, libidinosus; Lycisca, lupina; Harpalos, rapax; Melaneus, niger; Lachne, hirsuta; Labros, rapidus; Agriodos, agrestibus viis aptus; Hylactor, latrator. Nam omnino canes quinquaginta Actaeonis a nonnullis commemorantur' ('The names of the dogs that ripped Actaeon refer either to the color of their bodies or the keenness of their scent, something dogs are famous for. Here's a list of their names: *Melamp(u)s*, "having black feet", *Ichnobates*, "follower by trails", *Pamphagus*, "devouring all", *Dorceus*, "keen sighted", *Oribasus*, "mountain wanderer", *Neb(ro)phonos*, "killer of fawns", *Laelaps*, "hurricane", *Theron*, "fierce beast", *Pterelas*, "winged", *Agre*, "searcher", *Hylaeus*, "sylvan", *Nape*, "running through pastures", *Poemenis*, "shepherd's dog", *Harpyia*, "grasper", *Ladon*, "like a fawn", *Dromas*, "runner", *Canache*, "growler", *Sticte*, "spotted", *Tigris*, "fierce", *Al(c)e*, "strong", *Leucon*, "white", *Asbolus*, "sooty", *Lacon*, "resounding", *Aello*, "stormy", *Thous*, "swift", *Cyprius*, "desirous", *Lycisca*, "wolflike", *Ha(r)palos*, "greedy", *Melaneus*, "black", *Lachne*, "hairy", *Labros*, "quick", *Agr(i)odos*, "used to rural ways" (and *Hylactor*, "barking"). But some writers would expand the list, claiming that Actaeon has as many as fifty dogs').

Conti's list of thirty-three dogs is coincident with Ovid, who leaves the catalogue open by mentioning 'others whom it were too long to name' ('quosque referre mora est', *Metamorphoses*, III. 25). Chapman's select naming of seventeen, which must have been motivated by metrical demands, follows Conti's/Ovid's etymologies, and also acknowledges the total amount to be higher ('These and such other now the forest ranged'). Yet the indebtedness to Conti is greater than has been recognized, as it also affects the moralization of the Euthymia episode. Compare lines 228–31 to Conti, p. 673; Mulryan, pp. 563–64: 'Fuerunt qui putarint Actaeonis facultates per canum rabiem, aut per iratam venationum deam insulse dissipatas significari: quia canes non Actaeonem, sed eius opes laniaverint. [...] Per hanc igitur fabulam nos ad beneficia in viros bonos conferenda adhortabantur, ac retrahebant a benemerendo de ingratis et immemoribus acceptorum hominibus. [...] Omnium sane beneficiorum optimum est illud, quod apud virum bonum et memorem et gratum collocatur: quod vero in maleficum et ingratum collatum est, omnino male collatum fuit' ('Some writers thought that the dogs' madness (or the hunting goddess's anger) actually referred to Actaeon's wealth and how stupidly he squandered it. For it was Actaeon's wealth and not his person that the dogs ripped to pieces. [...] The ancients used this story to encourage us to help out good men and do nothing at all for ungrateful men or for those who conveniently forget about what we've already done for them. [...] Obviously, the best benefit of all is the one that goes to a good man who also remembers to be grateful for it. For you're just wasting your time if you give a gift to someone who is both evil and ungrateful').

Only one idea in Chapman's moralization seems to be absent in Conti: 'And noblesse stoops sometimes beneath his blood' (231). This insists on Chapman's obsession with nobility of spirit as a value that is beyond nobility of blood. On Chapman's critique of the aristocratic principle of nobility of blood, see Huntington, *Ambition*, esp. pp. 76–88. Earlier, Acheson saw in the couplet ended by this line a moral taunt at Shakespeare for his intimate relations with the Earl of Southampton and for his having benefited from his munificence (*Shakespeare's Sonnet Story*, pp. 269–70). For more general interpretations of this passage, see Spens, who interprets Euthymia 'to be Poetry created by the influence of the moon and representing her in the day. [...] All day the hounds chase the nymph fruitlessly, as the poet's thoughts, yearning, pursue poetry or his ideal' ('Chapman's Ethical Thought', p. 166). Bush agrees on this interpretation (*Mythology and the Renaissance Tradition in English Poetry: The Renaissance* (University of Minnesota Press, 1932), pp. 202–03, n. 11), while Bradbrook prefers a moral, political reading (*School of Night*, pp. 139–41). Battenhouse follows Bradbrook and expands her interpretation along Neoplatonic lines to conclude that 'the story of Cynthia's activity as a huntress is an allegory of World-Soul acting in her [Euthymia's] role of providential governor of men and punisher of the wicked' ('Chapman's *The Shadow of Night*', pp. 602–04). Waddington reads its connection to the Actaeon myth politically (*The Mind's Empire*, pp. 83–84). For a philosophical reading in the light of Giordano Bruno's interpretation of the Actaeon myth, see Introduction, p. 105.

243 *And Euthymia, to a panther changed*] The allegory behind Euthymia's transformation into a panther has been variously interpreted. For Bradbrook (*School of Night*, pp. 140 and 185, n. 8), the panther symbolizes pride; Bradbrook adduces the dedicatory poem 'To M. Harriots', prefacing *Achilles Shield* (1598): 'And how her genuine formes struggle for birth | Vnder the clawes of this fowle Panther earth' (45–46, in Bartlett, p. 382). In these lines, earth keeps under its claws the soul's authentic forms that the poet's verse struggles to express. If interpreted similarly, the panther could be regarded as part of a more general allegory of poetry, in keeping with Spens's reading, which presents poets in their deluded pursuit of the passions ('Chapman's Ethical Thought', p. 166). Pliny stresses the panther's lunar associations, a detail that may be behind Chapman's choice: 'sunt qui tradant in armo iis similem lunae esse maculam crescentem in orbem seque cavantem pari modo' ('Some authorities report that (panthers) have a mark on the shoulder resembling a moon, expanding into a circle

and hollowed out in a similar manner', i.e. in the shape of a crescent moon: *Natural History*, ed. and trans. by H. Rackam and others, 10 vols (Harvard University Press, 1967), VIII. 23. 62, III, pp. 48–49). Pliny also reports the strong attraction of its smell for other beasts, which contrasts with the terror caused by their fierceness: 'ferunt odore earum mire sollicitari quadripedes cunctas, sed capitis torvitate terreri'. Yet medieval Christian sources make the panther a symbol of Christ (*Physiologus: A Medieval Book of Nature Lore*, trans. by Michael J. Curley (University of Chicago Press, 1979), Section XXX, pp. 42–43), an etymological explanation which is found in the beast's universal amity with all (Greek πᾶν) creatures, with the exception of the dragon (Isidore, *Etymologies*, ed. by Stephen A. Barney and others (Cambridge University Press, 2006), XXII. 2. 8, p. 251).

251–68 *But now ... game-greedy hounds*] The oddity of this passage is less due to any obscurity of content than to: 1) the use of a long simile in which the vehicle (the schoolboys freed by their schoolmistress and attacked by a wolf or a bear) breaks the conventions of the high style; 2) the use of two tenors (the dogs, compared to schoolboys, and the covert, compared to a wolf or a bear) sandwiching the vehicle (256–66); 3) the syntactic instability derived from the simile's odd disposition, which this edition tries to solve by enclosing the vehicle between dashes. For a detailed reading of this passage as an instance of Chapman's difficult style, see Introduction, pp. 28–29.

269–377

The enclosure surrounded by the thicket is described as a 'blind shade', deprived of any light, a sort of miniature Hades, in which those impious creatures that have scorned the cults of Cynthia wander eternally after their bodies have been violently torn from their souls. Seeing the hounds' inability to enter the thicket, the hunters break through with their falchions (i.e. broadswords), mounted on lions, unicorns and boars. Yet the vision of the tormented spirits puts them to flight, as if caught in an ambush. Euthymia, still in the shape of a panther, retires to a fertile grove nearby.

283–300 *The huntsmen hearing ... let in the hounds*] This passage offers a number of difficulties of interpretation, particularly with regard to the nature of the huntsmen and the beasts on which they ride. As the former are the result of Cynthia's creation out of 'flowers', 'shadows' and 'mists' (220–22), the same origin could be presumed for their fanciful mounts. However, these are said to be 'the princeliest and the hardiest beasts | That gave chief fame to those Ortygian forests' (295–96), which presupposes for them an independent existence from Cynthia's creations. While the proverbial fierceness of lions, boars or wolves can be amply traced from classical sources into the medieval bestiaries, the fantastic status of unicorns and dragons deserves commentary. The unicorn is often conflated with the *monoceros*. Although medieval Christianity mollifies its features, making its only horn a symbol of the Son's unity with the Father (*Physiologus*, XXXVI, p. 51), Pliny the Elder had described it as resembling a horse in body, 'but in the head a stag, in the feet an elephant, and in the tail a boar', and having 'a deep bellow, and a single black horn ["uno cornu nigro"] three feet long projecting from the middle of the forehead'. He describes it as the fiercest beast ('asperrimam feram') for the impossibility of catching it alive (*Natural History*, VIII. 31). Dragons are mentioned in medieval sources as natural enemies to panthers (*Physiologus*, section XXX, pp. 42–43; Isidore, *Etymologies*, XXII. 2. 8, p. 251), an enmity explained allegorically in terms of Christ and the devil. While the meanings invoked here are eminently pagan, a Christian substrate should not be entirely overlooked.

301–25 *But from her bosom ... their hearts*] This is one of the most convoluted passages in the poem. The following paraphrase intends to catch its narrative progress and meaning: 'But from inside the thicket came enormous cries of misery, wrapped in hellish vapours, which were inhaled by the courageous steeds (lions, dragons, unicorns, etc.) and served to freshen their brains — just as when the impetuous horses driving the Sun's chariot run to heaven and the disdainful day blows from their nostrils, so those foggy vapours encouraged the beasts' progress. Yet, as they pressed further on inside the thicket, they saw such horrible sights, such creatures filled with strange and tormented passions, that now those misty objects that their (i.e. the hunters') eyes could see left a deeper impression on them than anything that their intellect could apprehend. Baseness (i.e. sense perception) was more compassionate than nobility (i.e. intellectual apprehension), for pity (first issuing from love's brain, and love being the essence of virtue) now moved not in their souls (whose scope is too mean, as this is where intellectual apprehension takes place), but in the sense of sight. And thus conscience touched their hearts with pity, even if its proper site is the mind and it should have stood out there first — for eyes should guide bodies just as our souls should guide our eyes, even though now the opposite is the case (i.e. it is our eyes that guide our souls, and our senses our intellect). Thus, sense perception caused terror in them, whereas the mind's (capacity for) foresight had kept fear at a distance and given pity its due; but now fear collected a pile of arrows inside their eyes, and shot them through their hearts.'

Part of the passage's difficulty lies in the transferral of the subject position of the action from 'steeds' (301–08) to 'huntsmen', their riders (309 and onwards). Otherwise, the references to the intellectual faculty and the opposition sense/intellect do not seem to make sense if applied to animals (309–25). While the beasts are shown as blinded by their instinct, which is fed by the evil smoke enveloping the cries heard from inside the thicket, the huntsmen are presented as stricken by the passions of fear and pity, issuing from their visual impressions of the horrifying sights in that covert, which paralyze their intellectual faculties. Schoell (*Études*, p. 190) has noted the indebtedness of lines 305-07 to Conti: 'Quidam putarunt equos Solis lumen efflare solitos e naribus, quam opinionem secutus Virgilius, ita scripsit libro duodecimo Aeneidos: *Postera vix summos spargebat lumine montis | Orta dies, cum primum alto se gurgite tollunt | Solis equi, lucemque elatis naribus efflant*' ('Some men actually thought that the Sun's horses actually breathed light from their nostrils. Judging from what he wrote in the twelfth book of his *Aeneid*, this was Vergil's opinion as well: *Scarce was the morrow's dawn sprinkling the mountain-tops with light, what time the Sun's steeds first rise from the deep flood, and breathe light from uplifted nostrils*', 'De Sole': v. 17, p. 537; Mulryan, p. 443; *Aeneid*, XII. 113-15).

326-49 *Then turned ... game's desire* and Gloss 19] The new Homeric simile comparing the encounter between the riding huntsmen and the tormented spirits with the exploits of Sir Francis Vere against the Spaniards, led by Alessandro Farnese, Duke of Parma, during the Netherlands War replicates the logical and syntactic complexity explained above (Commentary: 'Cynthiam', 251-68). As in that passage, two tenors (now the sustained skirmishes between the two parts, overbearing each other in turns, and the huntsmen's defeated withdrawal from the thicket) sandwich the lengthy simile, which this time conforms to the hymn's high style by recounting a historical, military episode that the poet could have witnessed as a direct participant. The slippery syntax of the passage, swiftly swapping subject and object roles between the two contending armies, contributes to narrative agility. See Bartlett's notes (pp. 427-28, nn. 330, 335-36), which pay detailed attention to this passage; and Eccles ('Early Years', p. 189 and n. 80), who supplies further evidence and sources that suggest at least Chapman's stay in the continent at the time of the events. Accounts of the episode can be read in Edward Grimestone, *A Generall Historie of the Netherlands* (London: Adam Islip, 1627), p. 929; and, in more detail, in William Dillingham, *The Commentaries of Sir Francis Vere* (Cambridge: John Field, 1657), pp. 20-23, which reproduces Vere's own first-person narrative. These tell of Parma's defeat, on 24 July 1591, in the Spanish siege of the Fort (or 'sconce') of Knodensburgh, facing the town of Nijmegen from the opposite (east) side of the river Waal. Vere sent some two hundred horsemen to provoke the enemy, who charged them and were surprised by Vere's troops, who lay in ambush at a nearby bridge. Chapman's account condenses events but coincides with Vere's report. For a modern historical account, see John Lothrop Motley, *History of the United Netherlands*, 4 vols (Harper & Brothers, 1868), III, p. 137.

331-32 *Under whose walls the Waal most Cynthian | Stretcheth her silver limbs* **and Gloss 19]** The paronomasia on 'walls' and 'Waal' is intended. The river Waal is the main distributary of the Rhine. Gloss 19 describes the river's geography, mentioning its 'parting' near 'Gurckham' (Gorinchem) from the Maas (here called the 'Maze') — actually the Afgedamde Maas, a distributary connecting both rivers — and continuing its course to Nijmegen, the main city of the region of Gelderland. The epithet 'Cynthian', explained by the river's 'silver limbs', intends to validate the aptness of the simile in the context of the hymn. Aptness is also the subject of the second sentence of the gloss, which defends the legitimacy of history as a fit argument for the poem's invention. In the gloss, 'habit' means clothing. On the importance of this term in Chapman's poetics, see Luis-Martínez, 'Habit of Poesie'.

350-77 *Out flew the hounds ... plucked their fruit* **and Gloss 19a]** The disorientation of the hounds as the effect of the panther's subtle sprinkling of its scent is recreated in two similes that transfer synaesthetically the focus on smell to the visual plane: 1) sunlight reflecting off sea waves onto a plane surface; and 2) the lengthening, climbing shadows of evening walkers. As for the first, Gloss 19a remarks that it is self-explanatory: '*Simile ad eandem explicat*'. As noted above, classical and medieval sources stress the olfactive nature of the panther's attraction (Commentary: 'Cynthiam', 243). Two contrasting settings mark here the transit of the panther and her pursuers: from the 'irksome covert', where the hounds and huntsmen have encountered the dreadful visions described earlier, the panther leads the chase into a 'fruitful island' characterized by its rare architectural design and its 'paved', possibly mosaic, decorations of female figures on its ground, resistant to all soiling by 'rich feet in foulest boots'. These designs, made by Cupid, are interpreted as allegories of beauty, honesty and chastity (374-77).

378-89

Euthymia changes her shape from a panther into a monstrous boar, which the hounds continue to chase. This metamorphosis seems a fitting admonition to conclude Cynthia's entertainment, as the Calydonian Boar, to which this new beast is compared, was the scourge sent to the Aetolians for their king's refusal to worship Diana. See Commentary: 'Noctem', 84.

390-99

Cynthia's entertainment concludes when the Sun sinks into the sea at the end of the day. Cynthia is then shown in her threefold identity: first as Diana, or hunting goddess, blowing the retreat for her huntsmen and dogs; then as Hecate, who magically dissolves the creations of her morning divertissement into vapours and brings darkness by making the winds blow; finally as Luna, here called 'Titanides' (as in 'Banquet', 6.3), or daughter of the Titans

Hyperion and Theia. Among the different lineages of the Moon explored by Conti, Chapman follows the account in Hesiod (*Theogony*, 371–74; see 'Noctem', Gloss 13). Conti is also the source for the 'milk-white heifers' ('iuvencis') that draw the Moon's carriage in her ascension to heaven. The colours allotted to the beasts performing this task are called by Conti, or by his sources, 'alb[us]' or 'nive[us]' (i.e. white, or snow-white) ('De Luna', III. 12, pp. 254–55).

400–21

This verse paragraph has been rearranged by adding Q*SN*'s first four lines from the next one (418–21) for the sake of consistency. Cynthia's finished entertainment is explained as an instance of how her days are spent while she awaits the coming of night. The prospect of Cynthia's new nocturnal arrival provides the occasion for resuming the kletic tone of the hymn. The hymnodist thus requests Cynthia's entrance, which will bring renovated life to her worshippers. The examples of Orion, who was killed by a scorpion sent by Diana as punishment for defiling the goddess's veil with his impure hands, and of Alpheus's unsuccessful passion for the goddess, support the argument that no harm can come from those who scorn her or attempt to violate her chastity.

> 400–03 *Thus nights ... consume by lasting*] The alternating cycles of nights and days, bringing griefs and joys by turns, have a paradoxical effect: Cynthia's inexhaustible charms are the consequence of their own decay in every repetition of the daily cycle — just as the melting of snow in a river increases its water flow, simultaneously decaying and growing in its transformation.

> 404–09 *O then ... with thy breath* and Glosses 20, 21] As Gloss 21 states, the life-giving powers of Cynthia's 'store of humours' (*humoris copia*) are 'explained before', specifically in Gloss 1 in relation to Conti, 'De Diana', III. 18, p. 268 (see Commentary: 'Noctem', 1–4). As above, these 'humours' allude to the Moon's moisture, the cause of her fertility. These lunar features are seen now not only as birth-giving, but also as restorative and preservative, in the identification of these 'plenteous humours' with '*philosophica medicina*' in Gloss 20. Compare: 'The Phylosophers have not onely called this medicine Aurum potabile, but also the water of life, the Tincture, the pretious stone, the medicine which worketh wonderfully upon three sorts of things, namely upon the animal, vegetable, and minerall: for the which cause it is called the Animal, Vegetable, and Mineral Stone: and the Arabian Astrologians call it the great Elixir. Wonderful is the vertue of this medicine: for herewith the body of man being sick, is restored to health, imperfect metals are turned into gold or silver, and vegetables, albeit they are dry and withered, being moystened with this liquor, doe waxe fresh and greene againe' (Joseph du Chesne, *The Practise*

of Chymicall, and Hermeticall Physicke, for the Preseruation of Health, trans. by Thomas Thimme (London: Thomas Creede, 1605), sig. N2ᵛ). The generative and curative qualities attributed to Cynthia may help explain the obscurity of lines 408–09: by causing the world to drown into night, Cynthia's breath may put death to flight.

410–17 *Come, Goddess ... a little stone* and Gloss 22] Schoell (*Études*, pp. 190–91, 193) noted that the source for these lines, and the accompanying Gloss, is Conti ('De Orione', VIII. 12, pp. 881–82, 885; Mulryan, pp. 751, 754). But the details that differentiate Chapman's treatment from Conti's must be also pointed out. Conti follows different sources in naming *three* fathers for Orion: Jupiter, Neptune and Mercury (or Apollo instead of Mercury). And he relies on Euphorion's fragment 101 for the account of his birth: 'Tum vero Dii pellem mactati bovis sibi capientes in ipsam semen profuderunt, iusseruntque illam sub terram occultare, neque ante decimum mensem aperire' ('And so those gods took the skin of a bull that had been sacrificed to them, poured seed on top of it, and ordered him [Hyrieus] to bury all underground, and not to dig it up again until ten months or later'). Chapman's removal of Neptune in naming Orion 'the double-fathered son' goes against the gloss's explanation, which follows another excerpt from Conti: 'Orion fuit Neptuni et Iovis et Apollinis filius, ex horum semine nimirum in pellem bovis incluso natus. Quid hoc est monstri Dii boni? An potest unus esse multorum parentum filius? Haec in elementorum generatione vera esse possunt, cum omnia sint in omnibus. [...] Excitat igitur vis Apollinis vapores ex aqua, eosque extenuans non sine quodam spiritu innato in aera extollit: atque quod Iupiter aer, Neptunus in aqua diffusus sit spiritus, et δύναμις ζῶσα, patuit' ('Orion was, collectively, Neptune's, Jupiter's, and Apollo's son, the miraculous offspring of their divine seed. My God, what kind of crazy stuff is this? How can a son be born of many parents? But these ideas can be applied to the generation of the elements, since they're all present in all the elements. [...] Thus Apollo's power draws vapors from the water, and after thinning them out with a kind of subtle breath, causes them to rise up into the air. For Jupiter represents the air and Neptune the breath that spreads itself through the water, a "living power"').

On Orion's death, the poem and the gloss follow *Theriaca*, a poem about poisons written by Nicander of Colophon (second century BC). The Latin lines which Conti quotes are those in Gloss 22: 'Scripsit Nicander in Theriacis scorpium immissum Orioni a Diana, quia peplum Dianae etiam apprehendere, cum illam violare niteretur, ausus sit impuris manibus, ut patet ex his: [followed by Nicander's Greek lines and Conti's Latin translation]' ('Nicander suggests that Diana arranged for a scorpion to attack Orion because he dared to put his sacrilegious hands on her cloak when he tried to rape her. Here are the verses from his *Theriaca*'). For

Nicander's original Greek lines, see *Theriaca*, 13–18, in Nicander, *Poems and Fragments*, ed. and trans. by A. S. F. Gow and A. F. Schofield (Cambridge University Press, 1953), pp. 28–29. The Scorpion's stellification contrasts here with Orion's fate. The source is again Conti, who echoes Pausanias's opinion: 'Atque Scorpii idcirco forma ad sempiternam memoriam dicitur fuisse inter sidera relata. Orionem non fuisse postea inter sidera relatum, sed fictum id et excogitatum fuisse ad alicuius gratiam, testatur Pausanias in Boeoticis, qui sepulchrum fuisse Orionis apud Tanagraeos memoriae prodidit. Haec tot fabulosa de Orione ab antiquis sunt tradita: e quibus sententiam illorum eliciamus' ('And that's why the scorpion's shape was set among the stars as an eternal shrine. However, Pausanias denies that Orion was put up there among the stars along with the scorpion: in fact Orion was buried in Tanagra, which means that the story about Orion becoming a constellation was really made up to make points with someone or other' ('De Orione', VIII. 12, p. 884; Mulryan, p. 754). Pausanias actually writes about 'Ὠρίωνος μνῆμα', which Conti renders as 'sepulchrum Orionis' (*Description of Greece*, ed. and trans. by W. H. S. Jones, 4 vols (Harvard University Press, 1935), XX. 3, IV, pp. 256–57). Yet Chapman has Orion 'hidden now beneath a little stone', which is not derived from Pausanias's or Conti's sepulchre, but misreads (or consciously manipulates) Nicander's 'ὀλίγῳ ὑπὸ λᾶι λοχήσας' (line 18), or, in Conti's translation, 'sub parvo lapide occultus'. While, for Chapman, the little stone beneath which Orion lies buried is his punishment for his 'presumption', for his sources it is only the place where the scorpion lurked for his victim.

418–21 *If proud Alpheus ... his mad aspire* and Gloss 23] Both the lines and the gloss draw negligently on Conti ('De Diana', III. 18, p. 270; Mulryan, p. 222). First, Chapman misreads Conti's summary of Pausanias's account of Alpheus's love for Diana (*Description of Greece*, VI. 22. 8–10). Thus Conti: 'Fama est quod Alpheus amore Dianae captus, ubi neque gratia, neque precibus se quidquam ad nuptias proficere intelligeret, sit ad vim conversus: at illa fugiendo insequentem Alpheum usque ad Letrinos ad nocturnos choros protraxit, ubi interesse Nympharum lusibus consueverat. Ibi Dea sibi suisque sociis os coeno oblevit, quam cum dignoscere non posset Alpheus elusus abiit' ('The story is that Alpheus was madly in love with Diana, but when he realized that neither kindness nor prayers would move her to marry him, he resorted to force. She fled from the pursuing lover, and got as far as the Letrini, where she stopped off at the nightly dances, where she used to play games with the Nymphs. Then the goddess smeared her own face and the faces of her companions with mud: and since he could not recognize her, she eluded Alpheus and he went away'). Chapman's careless and incomplete notes on the identity of Alpheus also follow Conti's opening description ('De Alpheo', VIII. 21,

p. 918; Mulryan, p. 784): 'De Alpheo, quem alii hominem, alii fluvium fuisse crederunt [...] nihil prope certi habemus vel quis fuerit [...] alii Partheniae fuisse filium tradunt, quidam aurigam fuisse Pelopis putarunt' ('We don't know very much about Alpheus, whom some of the ancients thought was a man, and others took to be a river. [...] But others think he was Parthenia's son. Some thought he was Pelops's charioteer'). Chapman's interest seems to be only in the hunter in love with Diana, and then with Arethusa (Ovid, *Metamorphoses*, v. 599–600), the reason why he was transformed into a river.

422–55 and Gloss 24

The building of the temple of Diana in Ephesus, regarded in the Renaissance as one of the seven wonders of the world, though at that time reduced to its foundations, is adduced as another instance of Cynthian authority and virtue. Construction of the temple started about 600 BC, although the erection of the columns by Chersiphron of Cnossus is dated to 560 BC. Chersiphron's work was continued by his son Metagenes, and completed by Demetrius and Paeonius of Ephesus about two hundred and twenty years after the foundations were laid. But, as Plutarch recounts in his *Life of Alexander* (III. 3), the Ephesian Herostratus burnt it down in 356 BC on the same night as Alexander the Great was born. Alexander later funded its reconstruction by another Ephesian architect, Deinocrates (Smith, *Dictionary*, I, pp. 693–94). Besides the abovementioned sources, lyric praise of the temple is found in several epigrams of the *Greek Anthology*, most significantly Antipater's (IX. 790; III, pp. 426–27).

Chapman relies fully on Conti: 'Habuit (Diana) celeberrimum omnium templorum et augustissimum Ephesium, quod totius Asiae studio ducentis et viginti annis architecto Chersiphrone fuerat aedificatum, cuius erat longitudo pedum quadringentorum et quinque ac viginti, latitudo ducentorum et viginti, in quo fuerant centum et viginti septem columnae a totidem Regibus eractae admirabilis longitudinis ac pulcrhitudinis: nam ad sexaginta pedum mensuram accedebant, quarum triginta sex fuerunt incredibili artificio et magnifice caelatae, cum aptis tanto artificio columnarum epistyliis. Aderant et picturae mirificae, et pulcherrimae statuae magnificentiae eius templi convenientes. Quae onmia ab Herostrato viro Ephesio incensa fuerunt' ('She had a temple at Ephesus, the most renowned and revered of all of her temples. Chersiphron was the architect, and with all of Asia in enthusiastic agreement, it took two hundred and thirty years to build. It measured four hundred and twenty-five feet by two hundred and twenty feet. It had one hundred and twenty-seven columns built as by many kings; of awesome length and beauty, they measured almost sixty feet. Thirty-six of them were marvellously engraved with extraordinary skill, and the columnar architraves were fitted with wondrous craftmanship. And there were splendid paintings and very fine statues as magnificent as the temple itself. The Ephesian Herostratus burnt every bit of it to the ground': 'De Diana', III. 18, pp. 271–72; Mulryan, pp. 223–24). See Schoell (*Études*, pp. 35–37), who, besides those of Plutarch and Antipater, summarizes Strabo's account (*Geography*, XIV. 1. 22) of the rebuilding of the temple, particularly the detail of the use of 'many golden trinkets obtained from women' ('detractis mulieribus aureis ornamentis'), a circumstance which undergoes poetic elaboration by Chapman.

Conti's description also relies silently on Pliny, *Natural History*, XXXVI. 21. 96–97. In his attempt to create a mental construction rather than a pictorial image of the temple, Chapman makes the figure 'two hundred twenty' homogeneous for the years of duration of the work, columns and kings. Obvious borrowings from Conti are also observed in several verbal details: thus, the Latin ablative form 'Chersiphrone' is used instead of Chersiphron for metrical reasons — as it adds a necessary fourth syllable; 're-exstruct' (432) adapts Conti's phrasing 'a Chersiphrone extructum fuerat'; and the 'virgin-chamber' (435) adapts Conti's 'virginum thalamum', a term that he also used in his translation of Antipater's epigram. Yet the hymnic voice conceives of this new rebuilding of the temple as a work to be performed by the mind and to be preserved perennially within it rather than by the ephemeral art of architecture, subject to decay and destruction. A temple of the mind, adorned with the inward virtues of English ladies, becomes a symbol of true discernment, or 'insight', whose more efficacious medium is the art of poetry, as opposed to the weaknesses and 'outward bravery' embodied here by architecture.

422 *Lucifera, Ignifera* and Gloss 24] These epithets, which Chapman claims to have derived from Euripides' 'φωσφόρῳ' in *Iphigeneia in Tauris* (21, in *Euripides*, II, p. 284), are unsurprisingly from Conti: 'Ignifera praeterea sive Lucifera Dea vocatur ab Euripide in Iphigenia in Tauris' ('She is also called the Fire Bearer or Light Bearer by Euripides, in his *Iphigenia in Taurica*': Conti, 'De Diana', III. 18, p. 269; Mulryan, p. 221).

443–47 *Insight ... what we will*] These lines combine two favourite motifs in Chapman's poetry. On one hand, the delineating of the 'stretching' circumference, still incomplete but tending towards perfection (see Commentary: 'Cynthiam', 6–9, and Commentary: 'Banquet', 54. 1–6; also Introduction, p. 109). On the other hand, the Platonic 'third eye' as a metaphor for inner vision and the search for truth. The idea is found in Ficino's commentary on Plato's *Philebus*: 'Inter prudentissimos Graecorum natum est proverbium Platonem habuisse tres oculos: unum quo humana, alium quo naturalia, alium quo divina suspiceret qui in fronte esset cum alii sub fronte' ('Among the wise men of Greece arose the saying that Plato had three eyes: one with which he looked at human things, another at natural things, another at divine things (which was in his forehead, while the others were under his forehead)': Ficino, *The Philebus Commentary*, ed. by Michael J. B. Allen (University of California Press,

1975), pp. 176–77). The inner eye became a common emblematic motif, as in the emblems 'Quo modo Deum' and 'Quo modo Manes', in Horapollo, *Hieroglyphica* (Paris: Jacques Kerver, 1551), pp. 222 and 223, which show a sequential representation of the divine insight and the face without eyes, inhabiting darkness (see Visual Sources). On the history of the motif, see Michael J. B. Allen, 'Marsilio Ficino on Plato's Pythagorean Eye', *Modern Language Notes*, 97.1 (1982), pp. 171–82, doi:10.2307/2906281.

456–71 and Gloss 25

The mind is first presented as the 'monarch' that rules the different motions of the body, and then, as Gloss 25 clarifies, personified in Ganymede. Jupiter's abduction of Ganymede is understood as the life of the mind, the aim of which is the Platonic pursuit of beauty and truth. Chapman derives motifs, phrasing and, most relevantly, the myth's moral allegory from Conti: '(Ganymedes) cum esset eximiae et prope inauditae pulchritudinis, ob eam dignus habitus est, non qui ad libidinem, ut crediderunt plerique, raperetur, sed qui pocula Iovi ministraret. [...] Alii vero inter quos fuit Xenophon, ut scripsit in Symposio, Ganymedem propter animi pulchritudinem et prudentiam potius, quam propter formam corporis, in coelum ascitum esse voluerunt [...] atque illis persuasum denique Ganymedem inter sidera relatum esse, et in id signum quod dicitur Aquarius. [...] Nam quid aliud per hanc fabulam demonstrabant sapientes, quam prudentem virum a Deo amari, et illum solum proxime accedere ad divinam naturam? Est enim Ganymedes anima hominum, quam, ut diximus, ob eximiam prudentiam Deus ad se rapit. [...] Illa vero anima pulcherrima est, quae minimum sit humanis sordibus, aut flagitis corporis contaminata: quam Deus diligens ad se rapit. [...] Quid enim aliud est pocula Iovi ministrare, quam Deum mirifice delectari officiis sapientiae? [...] Sic igitur cum dicerent viros bonos, et prudentes, et integerrimos poetae divinam bonitatem ad se rapere, fabulam de Ganymede finxerunt' ('Ganymede certainly merited being taken up to heaven to be Jupiter's cupbearer, because he was extremely, almost incredibly handsome. And there was no cheap lust involved here, as many writers believed. [...] But some of the ancients (like Xenophon when he writes in his *Symposium*) insisted that Ganymede was received into heaven because of his beautiful mind and wonderful intelligence, and not because of his gorgeous body [...] (and others) were convinced that Ganymede had been placed among the stars under the sign of Aquarius. [...] Obviously the wise men were using this story to tell us that the prudent man is loved by God, and that only such a man can come close to the divine nature. Ganymede is in fact man's soul; and as we've said, God takes that soul into His confidence because of his marvellous prudence. [...] To be Jupiter's cupbearer simply means that God is really delighted by the functions of wisdom, which emanate from the souls of the wise. [...] And so when the poets wanted to emphasize that good men, prudent men, and men of the highest integrity all seek to possess divine goodness, they made up the story of Ganymede': 'De Ganymede': IX. 11, pp. 1004–07; Mulryan, pp. 862–65).

472–514

Intellectual activity is defended by means of two main mythological parallels: Jupiter's abduction of Ganymede, which symbolizes the ascent of the soul to heaven, and the loves of Endymion and Cynthia, which similarly represent the soul's aspiration to intellectual beauty. The hymnodist proclaims that the example of Cynthia should prevail over the wantonness of other deities and nymphs.

> 472–88 *If wisdom be ... empoison their desires*] Although complicated by a possibly missing line (between 474 and 475), this passage expands on the previous Neoplatonic argument of wisdom as the true beauty to which the mind aspires. By opposing Cynthia's rays to Cupid's fires, the hymnodist insists on the opposition between heavenly and earthly desires. The image of the tree whose branches preserve eternal winter in their shadows has emblematic qualities: it signifies the mind, which remains impervious to the enticements of earthly desires. See, for an analogous instance, emblem CXCIX, 'Querqus' (the oak) in Andrea Alciato, *Emblematorum Liber* (Paris: Jean Richer, 1584), p. 275 (see Visual Sources), in which the shadows of this tree, consecrated to Jupiter, are a symbol of moral fortitude.

> 489–500 *Thou never ... with dalliance* and Gloss 26] The interpretation of the myth of the loves of Endymion and the Moon as a Neoplatonic allegory of the search for knowledge is found in Conti's account ('De Endymione', IV. 8, pp. 336–38; Mulryan, pp. 276–78), from which Chapman also derives phrasing, setting, and several motifs: '(Endymion) ut scribit Pausanias in Prioribus Eliacis, a Luna fuit amatus, ex qua filias quinquaginta suscepisse fabulantur, cum tamen alii tres tantum filios inquiant, Paeonem, Epeum, ac Aetolum. [...] Cicero tamen libro primo Tusculanarum disputationum perpetuo dormientem Endymionem in Latmo Cariae monte a Luna adamatum dicit sola oscula Lunae accepisse, neque unquam experrectum fuisse. [...] Alii dicunt primum Endymionem rerum sublimium speculationem invenisse [...] qui cum noctu his considerationibus esset intentus, somno non fruebatur, at dormiebat per diem. [...] Neque mirum videri debet Endymionem virum Astronomiae peritum, et in considerandis stellarum cursibus diligentissimum, ab illis segnem et voluptarium fuisse creditum' ('The Moon loved (Endymion), as Pausanias noted in the first book of his description of Elis. He's also fabled to have had fifty daughters by the Moon, but others say it was just three sons (Paeon, Epeus, and Aetolus). [...] But Cicero, in the first book of his *Tusculan Disputations*, claimed that Endymion, who was always sleeping on Mount Latmos in Caria, was really the Moon's beloved, but she never

gave him anything but kisses, as he was asleep even then. [...] Others say that Endymion was the first real student of astronomy. [...] In fact he worked so hard on his research at night that he could sleep only during the day. [...] We shouldn't be surprised that the ancients would characterize a man like Endymion, who was a skilled astronomer and a diligent student of astral movements, as slow and pleasure-loving'). See Pausanias, *Description of Greece*, v. 1. 3; also Cicero, *Tusculan Disputations*, ed. and trans. by J. E. King (Harvard University Press, 1966), I. 38. 92, pp. 110–11; and Lucian, *Astrology*, 18–19, in *Lucian*, v, pp. 360–61. The lexical conflation of 'astrology' and 'astronomy' was common in the late sixteenth century. A similar Neoplatonic approach to this myth in English poetry is Michael Drayton's *Endymion and Phoebe* (1595), in which the Moon rewards her lover with supreme astrological knowledge: 'Then dooth she mount him up into the Sphere, | Imparting heavenly secrets to him there, | Where lightned by her shining beames she sees, | The powerfull Plannets, all in their degrees, | Their sundry revolutions in the skies, | And by their workings how they simpathize' (681–86, in *The Works of Michael Drayton*, ed. by J. William Hebel, 5 vols (Basil Blackwell, 1961), I, p. 147). In naming the three sons Phoebe/Cynthia bore to Endymion, Chapman follows Conti, except for the added comment in Gloss 26 on 'Paeon, which Homer calls the god's physician'. Here Chapman relied on Homer, *Iliad*, v. 899–901, in which Zeus orders Paeon to heal Ares' wounds.

501–04 *Wise poets ... most religious fear*] In contrast with those poets attributing wanton desires to Cynthia, wise poets duly represent her role as divine guardian in their fictions. These fictions are imagined as figurative altars erected in thankfulness to Cynthia's virtues, in which her powers are worshipped with due devotion. On her role as guardian, see Commentary: 'Cynthiam', 505–14.

505–14 *Dear president ... thy watchful sight* and Gloss 27] The initial vocative, expanded by non-defining relative clauses, insists on Cynthia's role as model of virtue and guardian against Fate. The latter could have been inspired by several passages from Conti, on Hecate as 'guardian of the hallway' ('vestibula domorum tueri': 'De Hecate', III. 15, p. 243; Mulryan, p. 201), and as 'Queen of the Underworld, because all men obeyed the inexorability of the Fates' ('inferorum regina [...] quia homines omnes fatorum necessitati [...] parent': p. 247; Mulryan, p. 204); or on Diana's role as 'guardian of roads and mountains because the Moon provides light and night for hunters and travelers' ('viarum et montium [...] custos, quoniam viatoribus et venantibus lumen praebat per noctem': 'De Diana', III. 18, p. 273; Mulryan, p. 225).

Cynthia is asked to preserve her 'virgin-chamber', that is, her temple (Gloss 27; see also line 425, and Commentary: 'Cynthiam', 422–55), from 'idle Salmacis', Acontius's 'sleights' on Cydippe and the lasciviousness of 'black Jove'. For Salmacis, Chapman's most probable source is Ovid, *Metamorphoses*, IV. 285–388. The nymph Salmacis's seduction of Hermaphroditus and the enfeebling powers of her fountain have their origin in her idleness and refusal to serve Diana: 'nympha colit, sed nec venatibus apta nec arcus | flectere quae soleat nec quae contendere cursu, | solaque naiadum celeri non nota Dianae' ('A nymph dwells in the pool, one that loves not hunting, nor is wont to bend the bow or strive with speed of foot. She only of the naiads follows not in swift Diana's train': 302–04, I, pp. 198–201). For the story of Acontius and Cydippe, Chapman must have relied on Ovid, *Heroides*, 20 and 21. Acontius fell in love with the maid Cydippe, and while she was praying in the temple of Diana at Delos, he inscribed an apple with the message 'I swear by the sanctuary of Diana that I will marry Acontius' (pp. 274–75), and threw it before her. As her nurse gave the girl the apple, she read the inscription. Diana sent Cydippe repeated illnesses when her father gave her in marriage to other men to prevent her perjury, and she was finally given to Accontius. Bartlett (p. 428, n. 512) identifies 'black Jove' as Pluto, and compares this reference to Seneca, *Hercules Otaeus*, 1705: 'non me mortis infernae locus | nec maesta nigri regna conterrent Iovis' ('I have no fear of the infernal realm of death, nor do the sad realms of dusky Jove affright me': Seneca, *Tragedies*, ed. and trans. by Frank Justus Miller, 2 vols (Harvard University Press, 1961), II, pp. 320–21). Bartlett also mentions a later use by William Drummond of Hawthornden: 'The *Stygian* Porter leaveth off to barke, | Black *Iove* appall'd doth shrow'd him in the darke' ('The Entertainment', VIII. 11–12, in *The Poetical Works of William Drummond of Hawthornden*, ed. by W. L. Kastner, 2 vols (Manchester University Press, 1913), pp. 133–34). In Conti ('De Plutone', II. 9, p. 177; Mulryan, p. 150) we read: 'Hunc defunctorum Deum esse crediderunt, quem appellarunt Iovem, sive Deum terrestrem' ('They also thought that he was the god of the dead, and they called him Jupiter, or earth god'). His being 'possessed' 'in Sicily' identifies the 'ravish(ment)' in the next line as that of Proserpine, of whose identity as the Moon and Hecate Conti reminds us several times: e.g. 'Proserpinam alii eadem esse voluerunt Hecaten' ('Some of the ancients affirm that Proserpine and Hecate were one and the same': 'De Proserpina', III. 16, p. 247; Mulryan, p. 204).

515–28 and Gloss 28

The hymn's closing fourteen-line verse paragraph has the conceptual autonomy and inner structure of a sonnet, even if written in couplets. The self-contained, end-stopped couplets, and the parallel syntax, presided over by opening imperative verbs — all in clear contrast with the poem's general preference for enjambement and meandering syntactic periods — contribute to the shaping of the utterance both as a precatory speech fitting to a hymn and as a straightforward magic conjuration. Gloss 28's attribution of these actions as proper to the Moon/Hecate puts readers on the track of finding the inspiration for these lines in Conti: 'Hanc terribilem aspectu, proceritateque corporis vel ad mensuram dimidii stadii accedere dixerunt: pedesque habuisse ad serpentis formam, cum vultus et aspectus figura proxime ad Gorgonum naturam accederet. Pro coma densissimi dracones et viperae, aliae in cincinnorum morem contortae, atque sibilantes visebantur. [...] Eadem rursus inferorum Regina credita fuit. [...] Quid aliud canes sunt rabidi illam comitantes, quam calamitates et molestiae, quae homines e fato assidue infestant? Eius item forma tan formidabilis varietatem aerumnarum prae se fert. Potest eadem rursus veneficiorum praefecta fluviorum cursus convertere, segetes alio transferre, montes in profundum dejicere, astra deducere de coelo, quod veneficae facere dicebantur, quia fatorum necessitati ac voluntati divinae nihil est quod non pareat' ('They said that she had a frightening appearance and that her body was almost half a stade long. Her feet were like serpents, while her face and features closely resembled the Gorgons'. For hair, she had snakes and serpents bunched together, some twisted like ringlets and apparently hissing. [...] Again, the same woman was supposed to be the Queen of the Underworld. [...] What else could the mad dogs who accompany her be, except Fate-driven misfortunes and troubles that constantly plague men? Her shape, which is so threatening, suggests a great diversity of evils. This same goddess, an expert in poisons, is able to change the course of rivers, to move crops to different places, to cast mountains down to the sea, and to draw stars from the sky (the reputed accomplishment of sorceresses), for everything must bow to the inevitability of the Fates and the divine will': 'De Hecate', III. 15, pp. 241, 247; Mulryan, pp. 199, 204).

Waddington (*The Mind's Empire*, pp. 101–02) also notes: 1) the similarities between this description and Ficino's: 'Luna puella cornuto capite super draconem vel taurum, serpentes supra caput et sub pedibus habens' ('The Moon: a beautiful girl with horns on her head, on a dragon or a bull, having serpents above her head and under her feet': *De vita*, III. 18 in *Opera*, 2 vols (Basel: Heinrich Petri, 1576), I, p. 557; *Three Books of Life*, ed. and trans. by Carol V. Caske and John R. Clark (ACMRS Press, 1998), p. 337); and 2) the magical properties of the circle and five-pointed star, or pentangle, as described by Cornelius Agrippa: 'unde qui malos daemones adiurant, circulo sese communire solent. Ipse etiam pentagonus cum virtute quinarii numeri mirandum in malos daemones habet imperium, tum ex lineatura sua qua habet intus quinque angulos obtusos et extra quinque acutos quinque triangulorum hexagonorum, quibus circundatur[. I]nterior pentagonus magna in se continent mysteria' ('they who abjure evil spirits are wont to environ themselves about with a circle. A pentangle also, as with the virtue of the number five hath a very great command over evil spirits, so by its lineature, by which it hath within five obtuse angles, and without five acutes, five double triangles by which it is surrounded. The interior pentangle contains in great mysteries': *De Occulta Philosophia*, II. 23, p. 319; trans. by Freake, p. 330).

The pentangle's magic power against evil spirits reverses the negative qualities that Conti attributes to Hecate, whose destructive powers are converted here into purifying qualities. Thus, the rhetoric of magic is finally put at the service of Chapman's transformative rewriting of myth.

Omnis ut umbra] 'All like a shadow'. Compare Job, 14. 1–2: 'Homo, natus de muliere, brevi vivens tempore, | Repletur multis miseriis. | Qui casi flos egreditur et conteritur, | Et fugit velut umbra, et nunquam in eodem statu permanet' ('Man that is born of woman, is of short continuance, | and full of trouble. | He shooteth forthe as a flowre, and is cut down: | he vanisheth also as a shadow, & continueth not': *Biblia Vulgata*, ed. by Alberto Colunga and Laurentio Torrado (Biblioteca de Autores Cristianos, 1994), p. 432; *The Bible and Holy Scriptures* (Geneva: Rowland Hall, 1560), fol. 226^v). This motto, which encapsulates the whole book, affirms the transient character of the universe that is represented in the poem. It also resonates with the initial Ovidian epigraph: see Introduction, pp. 98–99, where Chapman's verses are interpreted self-referentially as the very shadows to which the poem's title alludes.

2. Ovid's Banquet of Sense, A Coronet for His Mistress Philosophy and His Amorous Zodiac

Title pages

James Roberts for Richard Smith] The career of James Roberts (1540?–1618?) during the 1590s is best remembered for his printing of poetry collections such as Michael Drayton's *Ideas Mirrour* (1594) and the anthology *Englands Helicon* (1600). At the turn of the century, he printed a number of Shakespeare's quartos. For Richard Smith (fl. 1567–95) he printed the second quarto of Henry Constable's *Diana* (1594) before OBS. Smith's work as a publisher of poetry dates back to earlier decades, when he published George Gascoigne's *A Hundreth Sundrie Flowers* (1573) and the later *Posies* (1575). See Aldis and others, *A Dictionary of Printers*, pp. 102–03, 249.

Bernard Alsop and Thomas Fawcett … for Richard Horseman] The partnership of Bernard Alsop and Thomas Fawcett between 1626 and the mid 1640s was remarkable for a number of polemical anti-royalist pamphlets. Their printing of the 1639 octavo, OOB, is quite exceptional. OOB, published five years after Chapman's death, is the only book known in connection with bookseller Richard Horseman (see Aldis and others, *A Dictionary of Printers*, p. 140, and Henry R. Plomer and others, *A Dictionary of Printers and Booksellers in England, Scotland and Ireland from 1641 to 1667* (Blades, East & Blades, 1907), pp. 3–4). The purchase of rights by Alsop and Fawcett lacks evidence, but Emma V. Unger and William R. Jackson's conjecture that these were obtained through Alsop's connections with William White, who in 1598 had printed *Phillis and Flora*, the individual edition of 'Contention', is plausible

(*The Carl H. Pforzheimer Library: English Literature, 1475–1700*, 3 vols (Oak Knoll Press, 1968), I, pp. 156–57). This may not only explain the disappearance of 'Contention' from the volume, but also the consideration of 'Banquet', 'Coronet' and 'Zodiac' as a single-authored triptych. OoB's obliteration of Chapman's name in this volume is consistent with its 'attribution' of the poems to Ovid. The existence of several copies of this edition in *Sammelbände* with reissues of Elizabethan/Jacobean translations of Ovid's works is another remarkable feature. Some of these copies are bound with an engraved portrait of Ovid by William Marshall (Figure 4), encircled by the inscription 'PUBLIUS OVIDIUS NASO EQUES ROMANUS POETARUM INGENIOSISSIMUS' ('Publius Ovidius Nasso, Roman knight, the wittiest of poets'), captioned by a four-line epigram by William Marshall: 'The sweet-tongd Ovid's Counterfeit behold; | Which noblest Romans wore in rings of gold. | Or would you that, which his own pensil drew? | The Poët, in his deathles Poëms, view'. Both portrait and epigram promote the fiction of Ovidian authorship. For the bibliographical and literary history of OoB in the context of these Ovidian volumes, see Luis-Martínez, 'Whose Banquet?'.

To the truly learned, and my worthy friend, Master Matthew Roydon

This preface has been amply commented on by Chapman critics for its value as a definition of his poetics. Its most important themes are discussed in the Introduction, which engages with and cites major critical opinions. Topics like Chapman's ideas of poetic 'habit' (understood as the writer's and reader's search for knowledge through the cultivation of difficulty and the laborious dedication to learning), the definition of *enargia* as the crucial feature of Chapman's poetic style, and the critique of oratorical plainness and bombastic rhetoric reappear in the notes below in connection with Chapman's sources.

> 1 *Matthew Roydon*] On the dedicatee's identity, see Commentary: '*SN*: To Roydon'.

> 4 *The profane multitude I hate*] In disparaging the unholy crowd of 'wilful judgements' who scorn the 'divine discipline of poesy', Chapman translates Horace: 'Odi profanum vulgus' (*Odes*, III. 1. 1, in *Odes and Epodes*, p. 140). Compare the last sentence in '*SN*: To Roydon', in which the poet prides in being understood by only 'a few'. 'Profane' derives from Latin *fanum*, temple, or 'fane', a word of frequent use in Chapman's poems. 'Profane' contrasts with Chapman's notion of the 'divine discipline of poesy', as well as with the use of 'consecrate' — both as a verb and as an adjective — in relation to the dedication to art.

> 4–5 *my strange poems*] Chapman's view of his art as 'strange' is recurrent in his work. Compare the dedicatory poem to Thomas Harriot in *Achilles Shield* (1598): 'Rich mine of knowledge, o that *my strange muse* | Without

this bodies nourishment could use, | Her zealous faculties, only t'aspire, | Instructiue light from your whole Sphere of fire' (31–34, in Bartlett, p. 381, emphasis added). The adjective suggests the extraordinary or unfamiliar nature of Chapman's art, as well as its aim to cause wonder or instigate an experience of the sublime. An allusion to Ferdinando Stanley, Fifth Earl of Derby and Lord Strange, one of the three noblemen that Chapman mentions in 'SN: To Roydon', should not be disregarded.

5–6 *searching spirits ... nobility sacred*] Compare 'deep-searching Northumberland', another of the addressees in the epistle to Roydon in *The Shadow of Night* (see Commentary: 'SN: To Roydon', 23). Chapman's target readers are thus speculative, truth-searching philosophers who, regardless of their social condition, are ennobled not by their blood but by their dedication to the divine arts of poetry and philosophy. On the redefinition of nobility by learning in Chapman's work, see Huntington, *Ambition*.

6–8 *endeavouring that ... ornament and utility*] As Schoell notes, this passage translates Xylander's Latin rendering of the Pseudo Plutarch's *De Homero*: 'Iam et constructionis immutationes videamus, quae vocantur Schemata. [...] Schema est oratio a communi consuetudine varians fictione aliqua, idque ornatus aut utilitatis gratia' (*Plutarchi Chaeronensis Moralia*, ed. by Wilhelm Xylander (Basel: Thomas Guarin, 1570), p. 35). For the original Greek, with English translation, see [Plutarch], *Essay on the Life and Poetry of Homer*, ed. by J. J. Keaney and Robert Lamberton (Scholars Press, 1996), 27, pp. 96–97. Chapman's implicit alignment with Homer via his ancient biographer/commentator stresses the importance of cultivating ('endeavouring') a difficult style ('that material oration') as a mark of his 'strange' art.

8–9 *this of Euripides ... Lentem coquens ne quicquam olentis addito*] The text, sources and meaning of this Latin proverb have been severally discussed by critics. Schoell (*Études*, p. 44) found Chapman's source in Erasmus, *Adagia* ('In lente unguentum'), but failed to explain his peculiar rendering of Erasmus's adaptation of Aristotle's *De sensu* v, 443b: 'Citatur autem adagium ab Aristotele in libro De sensu et sensili: Ἀληθὲς γὰρ ὅπερ Εὐριπίδην εἶπε σκώπτων Στράτις ὅταν φακῆν ἕψηται μὴ ἐπιχεῖν μύρον, id est Nam verum est, quod ait Stratis Euripidem taxans, ubi lenticula coquitur non oportere unguentum infundere' ('Aristotle quotes the adage in his *De sensu et sensili*: *For there is much truth in the gibe levelled at Euripides by Stratis, that when cooking lentils it is a mistake to add perfume*': *Adagia*, I. 7. 23, proverb 623, in Erasmus of Rotterdam, *Les adages*, ed. by Jean-Cristophe Saladin (Belles Lettres, 2011); translation: *Collected Works of Erasmus: Adages*, trans. by R. A. B. Mynors (University of Toronto Press, 1989), p. 80.

Bartlett emends '*dentis*' (1595) to '*olentis*' and explains that Chapman subscribes to Aristotle's 'jibe at Euripides' over-refinement of style' (p. 430, nn. 9–10). Hudston (p. 401, nn. 8–9) notes Erasmus's quotation of Stratis, and surmises that Chapman's proverb must be a rephrasing. The origin of Chapman's rephrasing is actually the continuation of the quoted passage from Erasmus, who cites Athenaeus's *The Deipnosophists*, IV. 160. This in turn cites Stratis's lost parody of Euripides' *Phoenissae*: 'Citat et Athenaeus libro Dipnosophistarum IV: "Παραινέσαι σφῶϊν τι βούλομαι σοφόν· | Ὅταν φακῆν ἕψητε, μὴ 'πιχεῖν μύρον", id est, "Vos admonere callidum quiddam volo, | Ubi lens coquitur, unguenta ne qua infundite", ex Phoenissis Stratidis, comici poetae' ('Athenaeus also cites it in book four of his *Doctors at Dinner*: "I wish to give you some advice: | When cooking lentils, add no unguent in", from the *Phoenissae* of the comic poet Stratis': *Adages*, I. 7. 23, proverb 623; trans. by Mynors, p. 80). The second Greek line, which Chapman retranslates, is the direct source here. Bartlett's comment on style provides the key to meaning: Chapman's attack is directed at excessive stylistic ornament when it does not support what the epistle later calls a 'high invention'. The later references in this Preface to 'charms made of unlearned characters' and to 'Evippe's daughters' (see below) insist on this crucial idea in Chapman's aesthetic thought.

10–11 *But that poesy ... plain way to barbarism*] While the previous paragraph complains about excess of ornament, the attack now focuses on the other extreme: oratorical plainness, which should also be avoided by the poet.

12 *to make the ass run proud of his ears*] 'Asinus ad lyram' ('An ass to the lyre': Erasmus, *Adages*, I. 4. 35, proverb 335; trans. by Mynor, XXXI, pp. 334–35). Erasmus notes a variant of this proverb, 'Asinus auriculas movens', which he derives from Lucian, *The Ignorant Book-Collector* (IV, in *Lucian*, III, pp. 178–79), supplying the following gloss, which agrees with Chapman's meaning here: 'In eos, qui cum nihil intelligant, tamen perinde quasi nihil non intelligant, ita nutibus alludunt aut arrident dicentibus. Est autem asino naturale subinde movere auriculas veluti significanti se jam intelligere, cum nihil etiam audierit' ('This is turned against those people who understand nothing, and yet make play with nods and smiles to those who are talking, as if there were nothing they did not understand. It is natural to the donkey to twitch its ears as if to convey that it has understood, when it has not even heard'). See also Morris Palmer Tilley, *A Dictionary of the Proverbs in England in the Sixteenth and Seventeenth Centuries* (Michigan University Press, 1950), A355, p. 20: 'An ass is known by his ears'.

11–12 *to take away strength from lions*] Chapman's inspiration may be Erasmus, *Adages*, I. 3. 66, proverb 266; trans. by Mynors, XXXI, p. 272).

'Induitis me leonis exuvium' ('You are dressing me in the lionskin'). Erasmus notes here a variant proverb 'Asinus in pelle leonis' ('an ass covered with a lionskin'), which, like the former, also attacks those who try to disguise their ignorance or cowardice.

12 *give camels horns*] Erasmus, *Adages*, III. 5. 8, proverb 2408; trans. by Mynors, xxxv, pp. 70–71): 'Camelus desiderans cornua etiam aures perdidit' ('The camel asked for horns and lost his ears too'). Erasmus relates this proverb to a fable in which a camel, who asked Jove to give him horns, was deprived of his ears as punishment for his silly request. Chapman alludes to this proverb in *The Revenge of Bussy D'Ambois*: 'those foolish great-spleen'd Cammels | That to their high heads, beg'd of Ioue hornes higher; | Whose most vncomely, and ridiculous pride | When hee had satisfied, they could not vse, | But where they went vpright before, they stoopt, | And bore their heads much lower for their hornes' (II. 1. 176–81, in *Tragedies*, p. 464). See also Tilley, *Dictionary*, C27, p. 78.

24–27 *Obscurity, in affection ... labour to be shadowed*] On the two kinds of obscurity opposed here, see Introduction, pp. 3–4.

29 *Evippe's daughters*] The nine Pierides were daughters of Pierus, King of Emathia, and Evippe of Paeonia. In Ovid, *Metamorphoses* (v. 678), they challenged the nine Muses to a singing contest with the boast that they would be defeated 'nec voce nec arte' ('neither in voice nor in skill'), and were transformed into magpies as punishment for their protestations. Ovid's tale closes with a comment on their 'hoarse garrulity and boundless passion for talk' ('raucaque garrulitas studiumque immane loquendi'). Chapman contrasts the quality of the Muses as 'divine artists' with the 'mere nature' with which the Pierides challenged them. See Luis-Martínez, 'Habit of Poesie', pp. 272–74, for a more detailed discussion of this passage and the mythographers' account of Ovid's tale, as well as for Chapman's possible bilingual pun on Evippe and εὐέπεια, or euphony, which he could have found in Dionysius of Halicarnassus, *On Literary Composition* (ed. and trans. by W. Rhys Roberts (Macmillan, 1910), XXIII, pp. 240–41).

34 *true habit of poesy*] The labour and training that is conducive to the writing and understanding of true poetry, particularly of the 'philosophical' kind practised by Chapman. The phrase 'comely habit of poesy' is used in 'Cynthiam', Gloss 19, in the sense of poetry's linguistic 'clothing' — a meaning on which the poet might be punning here too. On the centrality of the notion of 'habit' to Chapman's writing, see Introduction, p. 4, and Luis-Martínez, 'Habit of Poesie'.

37–38 *dark spirits ... palpable night ... radiant and light-bearing intellect*] The contrast between darkness as ignorance and light as intellect in the process of extracting truth out of obscurity ('palpable night') is a central trope in *SN* and *OBS*. Night is necessary for the self-generating light of the true intellect to illuminate the shadows leading to knowledge.

Richard Stapleton to the Author

On the identity of Chapman's friend Richard Stapleton, see Introduction, pp. 13–14. The sonnet encourages the author to unashamedly put his skill at the service of his rare poetic style (line 13), as he has been privileged with Apollo's double protection ('his bow and Muse'). Apollo's golden bow, given to him by Vulcan and with which he defended his mother, Leto, from Python, helps Chapman combat bombastic poets, as his shot (or 'loose', which is metaphorical for subtlety of style here) can destroy their bombast. Apollo is also invoked as guardian of the Muses, who bring inspiration in the form of 'sweet philosophic strains', which, in consonance with the penetrating quality of the arrow, are praised for being intellectually 'pierc[ing]'. 'Brightness' and clarity are features of Chapman's verse that are said to 'shine' in the poems' apparent 'darkness'. This praise accords with Chapman's own idea of the obscurity that 'shroudeth itself in the heart of his subject, uttered with fitness of figure and expressive epithets' (*OBS*: 'To Roydon', 31–32). The scorn for bombast is patent in the description of Chapman's poetry as 'unstained with foreign [i.e. superfluous] graces'.

> 3 *loose*] Bartlett regarded this word as meaningless in the poem's context, and emended it to 'verse'. However, its use in archery (*OED*, n., 1) to designate the discharge of an arrow is entirely consistent with Apollo's lending of his bow to the poet: as it is released, the arrow's swiftness is 'infuse[d]' with a hissing 'sound', understood here metaphorically as stylistic subtlety against the bombastic style of other poets (i.e. 'the artisans of thunder').

> 10 *clear*] On a similar basis to Bartlett's emendation of Q*OB*'s '*dentis*' for '*olentis*', 'clear' is proposed here as an emendation of 'dear', as the latter hardly makes sense as adverbial qualifier of 'shines'. 'Clear' is invoked here as a quality of Chapman's verse, which accords with the 'clearness of representation' that defines *enargia* ('*OBS*: To Roydon', line 13).

Thomas Williams, of the Inner Temple

On the identity of Thomas Williams, see Introduction, p. 14, n. 51. This sonnet provides a compelling reader-response approach to Chapman's poetics by comparing two different kinds of readers of Chapman's difficult verse. The sonnet's volta, occurring between lines 8 and 9, neatly separates these two kinds, thus differentiating between inept and apt interpreters. In doing this, Williams imitates Chapman's difficult style and dense mythographic writing. Thus, the first eight lines implicitly position the author as Jupiter, and his poetry as the dazzling, scorching light and fire whose heavenly presence is unbearable to human sight. Bad readers (those 'unhallowed eyes' that will get too near Chapman's poems) are compared in their ignorant pride first to Bacchus, whose mother Semele, before giving birth to him, asked to see her lover Jupiter in all his splendour and was killed by his fire; and then to the satyr who scorched his lips when kissing Prometheus's stolen fire. In contrast, good readers of Chapman will be able to enjoy Jove's light, as Danae did, transformed into a cloud of gold, or, once instructed by Prometheus, to observe it from a distance. The closing couplet identifies the mistaken judgements of inept readers with the two unnatural births of Bacchus, whose gestation was completed inside Jupiter's thigh after the 'formless' child was first delivered prematurely by the dying Semele. The sonnet also discriminates between good and bad readers by identifying the poem with a perspective, or anamorphic, painting that when viewed from 'aloof' provides a neat image but, if viewed from a 'nearer' distance, appears distorted. By using these cautionary allegories and conceits, the sonnet suggests that the true sense of Chapman's poems will only be attainable to those discriminating minds that have been properly instructed to appreciate it. On this sonnet and its implications for Chapman's poetics, see Luis-Martínez, 'Habit of Poesie', pp. 263–66.

2 *three-winged withe of thunder*] Jupiter's three-branched thunderbolt. Compare Spenser, *The Faerie Queene*, I. 8. 9, which mentions Jove's 'thundring dart', and describes it as a 'fiers threeforked engin' (ed. by Hamilton, p. 104). In choosing to emend QOB's meaningless 'wife' for 'withe', I have opted for the latter's modern spelling in *OED*. Sixteenth-century spelling variants of 'withe' — 'wifte', 'wift' or 'wiff' — may be behind what seems a compositor's error.

6–7 *(with the satyr)... scorch your lips*] Williams's main source is Plutarch: 'The satyr, at his first sight of fire, wished to kiss and embrace it, but Prometheus said: *You, goat, will mourn your vanished beard*, for fire burns him who touches it, yet it furnishes light and heat, and is an instrument of every craft for those who have learned to use it' ('How to Profit from One's Enemies', trans. by Babbitt, *Moralia*, II, 86E–F, pp. 6–9). For a different treatment of this myth in a coetaneous sonnet, see Edward Dyer's 'Prometheus, when first from heauen hie', in which the satyr's temporary 'smart' is differentiated from the lover's ever-burning heart (Ralph M. Sargent, *At the Court of Queen Elizabeth: The Life and Lyrics of Sir Edward Dyer* (Oxford University Press, 1975), p. 176).

9–10 *But you ... Saturnian Muse*] The elevated souls of Chapman's true readers are asked to enjoy the poet's Saturnian inspiration which, like Jove when he seduced Danae, comes properly metamorphosed in a cloud of gold so as not to dazzle its beholders. Saturnian melancholy thus marks the highly intellectual quality of Chapman's poetry. See Yates, *Occult Philosophy*, pp. 157–71.

12 *Pythian light'ner*] a source of light or luminary of Apollonian qualities (Pythian derives from Pythia, the priestess of Apollo's temple at Delphi),

here a metaphor for the poet or the poem; see in this respect the dedicatory verses to Prince Henry prefacing Chapman's *Iliads* (1611): 'So Learning and her Lightner, Poesie, | In earth present [God's] fiery majesty' (77–78).

14 *twice-born judgements formless*] By equating the rash judgements of bad readers with Bacchus's double, misshapen, premature birth, the sonnet's end circularly returns to its beginning (i.e. 'Issue of Semele'), thus reinforcing logically and rhetorically its controlling conceit.

Another [by Thomas Williams]

Albeit somewhat less intricately, Williams's second commendatory sonnet further elaborates on Chapman's poetics. Readers' responses are now of secondary interest to the sonnet's main focus on the differences between ordinary and true poets. Building on the conceit of poetry as the 'Muses' land', Williams differentiates between, on one hand, poetic malpractice resulting in an uncultivated, unguarded field, easily destroyed by the 'barbarous cattle' of careless readers (first quatrain), and, on the other, the sensibly fenced, gardened enclosure, guarded by the difficulty of Chapman's judicial poesis (second quatrain), endowed with the golden bough and crowning laurel of poetic knowledge (first tercet). The sonnet's volta signals the second tercet as an apostrophe to the readers, who are encouraged to apply themselves to extracting the highest profit and pleasure by means of the hard labour of decoding Chapman's obscure poetry. On the importance of this sonnet as a definition of Chapman's poetics, see Luis-Martínez, 'Habit of Poesie', pp. 270–71.

7 *Walls it with spright-filed darkness round about*] The compound 'spright-filed' is obscure. *OED*, *spright*, n.: 'a type of stout wooden arrow or bolt used in naval warfare', or *sprit*, n.¹, 2†: 'a spear' (of which 'spright' is a historical spelling), can suggest a disposition in an arrow fence, if 'filed', or set in line (see *OED*, *file*, v.³, 3†).

9 *Parcae's golden bough*] Q*OB*'s reading '*Parcaes* golden bow' presents several problems. The spelling 'bow' can be an early modern form of present-day English 'bow' and 'bough'. A golden bow could be an attribute of Apollo's (as in Richard Stapleton's sonnet above); and it may only be imagined as an attribute of the Parcae's if understood in *OED*'s improbable sense n. 13: 'A name of various instruments or tools consisting of a curved piece of wood, with a string extending from one extremity to the other; used, e.g. [...] for separating the fibres of fur or wool'. *OED* only registers one nineteenth-century use in this sense. However, interpreting 'bow' as 'bough' faces a similar problem. The episode of the golden bough in Virgil's *Aeneid* (VI. 135–210) concerns two women: Deiphobe, the Cumaean Sybil or priestess of Apollo, who instructs Aeneas on how to obtain the golden bough and leads him in his voyage to hell; and Proserpine, the

goddess of the underworld to whom Aeneas must give the bough in order to cross the Styx and find his father, Anchises, in the underworld. The infernal qualities of the Parcae, or Fates, who in ancient mythology are arbiters of life and death, make 'bough' less odd. A bough is also consistent with the gardening imagery of the sonnet, and with the image of the 'garland to engird a monarch's brow' (11); besides, the symbolism of the golden bough also reinforces the sense of the adventurous, heroic search for knowledge that is so important for Chapman's poetics, and that would justify the mention of 'error's hell' (10) in the next line.

John Davies, of the Middle Temple

QOB's 'I. D.' is certainly English poet and politician Sir John Davies (1569-1626), who as a young law student entered the Middle Temple in 1588. Like the former three, Davies's two sonnets elaborate on Chapman's poetics. But these focus specifically on *OBS*, and particularly on 'Banquet'. Davies portrays how Chapman's efforts at poetic emulation have made him a second Ovid. This first sonnet invents a story of Pythagorean metempsychosis whereby Ovid's soul has migrated into the body of Chapman, Cupid's 'second artist', in which it has grown 'more old and wise'. For that reason, he has written a more philosophical 'love's art' than Ovid's own *Ars amatoria*. This justifies the difference between the first and second masters of Love, and thus the 'deeper' quality of Chapman's poetic treatment of erotic desire. Chapman's apt readers are distinguished by their capacity to 'understand' a poetry that is 'too mystical and deep' for others, a capacity that is granted by their being possessed by 'true love'. If this love is understood as the desire for knowledge endorsed in 'Coronet', then one should conclude that Davies's reading coincides with those who have understood Chapman's intention as an attempt to Platonize, or at least to correct, the excesses of Ovidian love — a view of *OBS* that would be in consonance with the one endorsed in the present Introduction. For a reading of this and the next sonnet by Davies, see Moss, 'Second Master of Love', pp. 457–59. See also Kruger's headnote on these two sonnets in *Poems of John Davies*, p. 406.

> 6–7 *golden lesson ... second artist ... a master*] These lines rely on the idea of Ovid's *Ars amatoria* as an eminently didactic poem, and thus on Chapman's inheritance of Ovid's original role as 'artist' (i.e. the author of an *ars*) and 'master' (i.e. teacher) of a renewed and refined art of love.

> 9 *his waking soul in Chapman lives*] The idea of Ovid's living soul in the person of Chapman relies on the theory of metempsychosis, or the transmigration of souls, attributed originally to Pythagoras. According to this theory, the immortal soul would abandon the dead body and reincarnate itself into a new living body. See Carl Huffman, 'Pythagoras', *The Stanford Encyclopedia of Philosophy* (2018), ed. by Edward N. Zalta,

<https://plato.stanford.edu/entries/pythagoras/> [accessed 11 February 2023].

13–14 *Ovid's soul … pours forth itself in deeper mysteries*] Through transmigration, Ovid's soul is shed into Chapman's self, where it acquires more profound meanings. The metaphor identifying the sense of a word or discourse with the soul was common in Chapman's time. See, for instance, Chapman's own commentary on Book 1 of the *Iliad* (1611), where he affirms that 'the inward sense or soule of the sacred Muse is oneley within eye-shot of a Poeticall spirit's inspection' ('The First Booke, Commentarius'). Also, Ben Jonson: 'In all speech, words and sense are as the body and the soul. The sense is as the life and soul of language, without which all words are dead' (*Discoveries* (1640), lines 1135–37, ed. by Lorna Hutson, in *Cambridge Edition Online*, <https://universitypublishingonline.org/cambridge/benjonson> [accessed 19 January 2023]).

Another [*by John Davies*]

Davies's second sonnet continues the theme of Chapman's emulation of Ovid through the trope of the transmigration of the latter's soul into the former's body. Now Davies invents an Ovidian aetiological myth to justify the long time that such transmigration has taken ('thrice five ages', or fifteen centuries, the time between Ovid's death in AD 17 and the publication of *Ovid's Banquet of Sense* in 1595). According to this myth, Apollo, while hunting in Mount Cynthus, received a kiss from Venus as a gratification for granting a favour to her: Venus would have the prerogative of bestowing the gift of Ovid's Muse upon whom she would, and she has chosen Chapman, who receives the title of Love's 'second master' after Ovid's own title of *praeceptor Amoris* (as in Ovid, *Ars amatoria*, 1. 17). The sonnet's complex mythographic argument has a clear purpose: it is Chapman that must rule Cupid, and not vice versa. I have capitalized 'Love' throughout, despite the use of lower case in QOB, as the sonnet consistently uses the word to refer to Cupid. On the role of Cupid and the tradition of Ovid's title, see Robert M. Durling, 'Ovid as *Praeceptor Amoris*', *The Classical Journal*, 53.4 (1958), pp. 157–67; also Moss, 'Second Master of Love', for an analysis of Davies's idea of Chapman as Ovid's successor. See also Introduction, pp. 14–15.

10 *the instruction of her tender son*] The phrasing is ambiguous, as Cupid can be the object or the addressee of the master's instruction — the last line's 'second master of her Love' may reinforce the ambiguity. While Ovid's self-appointment as *praeceptor Amoris* seems to hint at the former option — i.e. Ovid imparts Cupid's teachings — the suggestion here is that Cupid's 'tender' immaturity is in need of instruction. This would corroborate Davies's understanding of Chapman's intentions to rewrite the precepts of Ovid's *Ars amatoria*.

11 *Ovid's easy, supple Muse*] Davies shares with Chapman a view of Ovid's reputation as a facile, straightforward poet. See Chapman's own references to Ovid's 'quick verse' ('Banquet', 16. 4, 57. 7) or 'wits more quick' (43. 8). The phrase 'supple Muse' also helps confirm QOB's 'I. D.' as John Davies, who used the same words to praise Sidney in his poem *Orchestra*: 'Yet Astrophell might one for all suffize, | Whose supple Muse Camelion-like doth change | Into all formes of excellent devise' (130. 1–3, in *Poems*, p. 125).

Futurum invisibile] The heraldic motto '*Futurum invisibile*' ('the future is inscrutable') is obscure in the context of this last sonnet. Its concern with Ovid's reincarnation in Chapman may explain the choice: we know how the past lives in the present (i.e. Ovid lives in Chapman), but we do not know how it will in the future.

Ovid's Banquet of Sense: The Argument

2–3 *Julia ... Corinna ... Octavius Augustus Caesar*] Chapman sets the context for the recreation of Ovid's encounter with Corinna in *Amores*, I. 5, as well as for the identification of the literary Corinna with the historical Julia the Elder (39 BC–AD 14), daughter of Emperor Augustus. Ovid's alleged affair with Julia, as well as his writing of *Ars amatoria*, were said to be the causes of Augustus's decree of exile to Tomis in AD 8. The poem's recreation of these circumstances, as well as the critical discussions that this issue has raised, are dealt with in Introduction, pp. 45–50 and 99–100.

Ovid's Banquet of Sense

Stanza 1

Gless ('Chapman's Ironic Ovid', pp. 129–30) and Hudston (p. 403, l. 1–2, note) stress Chapman's indebtedness in this initial description to Ficino's *Commentary on Plato's Symposium*: 'sol flores multos ad se vertit et folia' ('the sun turns many flowers and leaves towards itself': VI. 10, pp. 91, 200). Gless also relates these descriptions to the topic of the garden of delight, and its 'perpetual springtime' (p. 129), which would explain the reference to the plants being attracted to the 'spring' (1. 7). However, the 'spring' in this stanza is the same as the 'silver spring' in the next stanza (2. 5), that is, not the season but a fountain. Chapman's choice of season is in fact not the springtime but the summer, in line with the poem's Ovidian analogue in *Amores*. See, in this respect, Introduction, pp. 48–50, and Luis-Martínez, 'Whose Banquet', p. 40, for a detailed account of 'Banquet' as a summer and a noon poem, elaborating on Ovid, *Amores*, I. 5. 1: 'Aestus erat, mediamque dies exegerat horam' ('In summers heate and mid-time of the day').

Stanza 2

2. 1–3 *Then did Cyrrhus ... in his desire* and M1] The first three lines complete the previous stanza's description of the effects of the summer heat upon the setting. Identifying the sun with Apollo (or 'Cyrrhus') allows Chapman to confer 'eyes' on him and attribute to him the 'ardour' and 'desire' of a lover. Chapman's bold imagery, which Gless considers an instance of catachresis ('Chapman's Ironic Ovid', p. 29), identifies the arbour as Apollo's 'green-love', and the trees' new shoots, or summer fruit, as their curling hair. Thus, the initial description completes a metamorphic, quasi-mythological tale whereby the Sun's desire for the arbour impregnates the land. The attribution of the epithet 'Cyrrhus' to the Sun, derived 'from a town called Cyrrha, where he was honoured', is confusing. Cirrha (present day Kirra) was a town of ancient Phocis, which served as a port for Delphi. Chapman's identification of the Sun with Apollo and the confusion of Cirrha, or Cyrrha, with Crissa in ancient sources may be behind this attribution. Conti ('De Apollone', IV. 10, pp. 365–66) does not mention Cyrrhus among the names given to Apollo. He nevertheless mentions 'Chrysen', or Crissa, among the cities that worshipped Apollo, according to Homer, *Iliad*, I. 37 (p. 364). Chapman's two versions of his translation of Book I of the *Iliad* have 'Chrysa' for this place (I. 37). However, he seems to rely here on Pausanias's *Description of Greece* beyond Conti's own quotations of the Greek geographer. In Pausanias, we read that Homer 'in the *Iliad*, and similarly in the hymn to Apollo, calls the city [i.e. Cyrrha] by its ancient name of Crisa'. Pausanias then recounts the history of the Cyrrhaeans' cult of Apollo (*Description of Greece*, X. 37. 4–8).

2. 5–7 *a silver spring ... an amelled ring* and M2] As Chapman's own gloss makes clear, these lines continue the personification ('prosopopeia') of the round arbour, or 'green-love', with the description of the spring, which becomes its eye or seeing centre, and whose place in the bower is compared to a diamond encrusted in an enamelled ring.

2. 8–9 *Into which eye ... Niobe ... her blood*] Niobe was the daughter of Tantalus and Eurynassa, and wife to Amphion, by whom she had fourteen children. Her pride in her children's beauty led her to insult Latona for having only two, Apollo and Diana, who were sent by their mother to kill Niobe's seven sons and seven daughters, respectively. She was later metamorphosed into a stone, from which tears continued to flow, and transported to Mount Sipylus by a wind. Chapman's source for Niobe here, as well as in stanzas 3–6, is Conti ('De Niobe', VI. 13, pp. 613–19), particularly as the latter follows Ovid, *Metamorphoses*, VI. 165–312, and *Heroides*, XX. 105–06, and Pausanias, *Description of Greece*, I. 21. 3 and VIII. 2–7, all of which he may have consulted independently. Ovid's idea

of Niobe's stone face being 'bloodless' ('sine sanguine'), as well as the marble that still lets the tears trickle ('lacrimas etiam nunc marmora manant': *Metamorphoses*, VI. 304, 312), are fused in Chapman's closing line. Weaver comments on the importance of Pausanias and the ritual/didactic value of Chapman's use of the myth ('Banquet', pp. 768–71). Gless interprets the Niobe myth in 'Banquet' as an allegory of presumption, applicable to Corinna's beauty ('Chapman's Ironic Ovid', pp. 34–36). Niobe's presence in the fountain means that she is also the arbour/eye's centre, which favours allegorical reading: thus, she becomes the *pupilla*, the eye's seeing organ, but also the 'little doll' that reflects the lovers' images into each other's eyes. She will be replaced in that function once Corinna enters the fountain.

Stanzas 3–5

These three stanzas are an example of ekphrasis, or description of a work of art, organized around an action which is Chapman's main contribution to an otherwise derivative exercise: the plundering of Niobe's statue in Mount Sipylus as a tribute to Emperor Augustus, and his commissioning of a more elaborate statuary that adds Niobe's fourteen children to the original work. As Schoell noticed (*Études*, pp. 39, 40, 193–94), stanzas 3 and 5 are highly derivative of Conti ('De Niobe', VI. 13, pp. 613–19; Mulryan, p. 515). Stanza 3 builds upon Conti's commentary on two above-cited sources — Pausanias's description of the anamorphic statue (*Description of Greece*, I. 21. 3) and Ovid's reminiscence of the statue (*Heroides*, XX. 105–06), which introduces the error of placing Mount Sipylus (Asia Minor) in Mygdonia (Macedonian Peninsula): 'Fama est Nioben visa filiorum morte e Thebis in Sipylum contendisse. Quare scripsit Pausanias in Atticis, huius imaginem silicem ac praeruptam crepidinem in Sipylo fuisse, quae quasi ad opticam rationem excisa, prope existenti neque lugenti, neque mulieris quidem formam prae se ferret: at procul existentibus et mulier, et moesta et lugens videretur. De illa imagine, quod esset in Sipylo, Mygdoniae monte, ita meminit Ovidius in epist[ola] Acontii: *Quaeque superba parens saxo per corpus oborto | Nunc quoque Mygdonia flebilis adstat humo*' ('The story goes that after Niobe witnessed the death of her own children, she left Thebes in a hurry and traveled to Sipylus. Pausanias wrote (in his description of Attica) that her image on Mount Sipylus was cut out of stone in the shape of a jagged precipice. And its shape was meant to take into account the viewer's perspective. For when viewed close up, it didn't seem to be the image of either a mourner or a woman. But when viewed from afar, it definitely appeared to be a very sorrowful woman in mourning. Ovid, in Acontius's letter, reminisced about that image, which was on the Mygdonian mountain of Sipylus: *and the arrogant mother, her body turned to rock, who still sits weeping on Mygdonian soil*').

In contrast with stanza 3, stanza 4 is mainly of Chapman's invention, with the exception of an important detail, derived from Pausanias (VIII. 2. 7; III, pp. 352–53) via Conti: 'Scriptum reliquit Pausanias in Arcadiis non quovis anni tempore, sed aestate tantum Niobes statuam lachrymari solita' ('Pausanias, in his description of Arcadia, sets it down that Niobe's statue didn't shed tears all year long, but only in the summertime': p. 617; Mulryan, p. 516). Stanza 5 returns to Conti for the list of names of Niobe's children. Conti followed twelfth-century grammarian John Tzetzes, whose story 141 of his *Chilliades* concerns Niobe: 'Fuerunt autem nomina filiorum Niobes, ut ait Zezes histor. 141. quintae Chiliad. Sipylus, Agenor, Phaedimus, Ismenus, Eupnytus, Tantalus, Damasichthon; filiae Neaera, Cleodoxe, Astyocha, Phaetha, Pelopia, Egyge, Chloris' (p. 615). From this list, Chapman chooses six sons and six daughters. For the remaining son, he replaces Eupnytus with Argus, which Conti lists as a variant found in Pausanias (*Description of Greece*, II. 22. 5), whose father was not Amphion but Zeus. For the remaining daughter, Chapman replaces Cleodoxe with Phthia, whom Chapman calls 'proud' — the only one, with Astiochen ('fair'), that deserves an epithet. Phthia is listed by Apollodorus (*The Library*, ed. and trans. by Sir James Frazer, 2 vols (Heinemann, 1921), III. 5. 6; I, pp. 340–41), yet no such epithet is used. Apollodorus (*Library*, I. 7. 6) names another Phthia, a lover of Apollo who had three children by him: Dorus, Laodocus and Polypoetes. A third Phthia in Apollodorus (*Library*, III. 13. 8) was Amyntor's concubine, who accused the latter's son Phoenix (a friend of Achilles) of having tried to seduce her. Yet Chapman's later translation of the *Iliad* prefers another name for her: in Phoenix's words, his father Amyntor 'Contemnd my mother his true wife, who ceaselesse urged me | To use his harlot Clytia' (IX. 431–32). None of these names appears in Homer but in his commentators (see Frazer's note to the above-cited passage in Apollodorus). Chapman's acquaintance with these latter stories may be behind the epithet. Weaver argues that Chapman's choice of Pausanias's 'Argus' is in line with his systematic choice of Pausanias as the most reliable among Conti's sources ('Banquet', p. 770). However, Chapman's different ordering and changes of names are probably for metrical reasons: 'Argus' and 'Phthia' are shorter than 'Eupnytus' and 'Cleodoxe'. This also explains the adaptation of name endings for purposes of rhyme: 'Damastichen', 'Astiochen' and 'Eugigen'.

3. 6–9 *So cunningly ... a woman shewed*] In Pausanias (*Description of Greece*, I. 21. 3), the optical effect of Niobe's statue is described without any technical explanation, which is an addition of Conti's: 'quasi ad opticam rationem excisa', i.e. carved almost in the manner of a perspective trick. Chapman's 'cunningly to optic reason wrought' translates literally from Conti with the exception of the dubitative 'quasi', which in the poem becomes the intensifying 'cunningly', that is, skilfully done according to the rules of art. Chapman's statue is then sculpted in accordance with the technique of anamorphosis, i.e. needing a distant, angled perspective to

rectify the impression of shapelessness and distortion if viewed straight-on and nearby. Chapman's reliance on anamorphosis has been amply commented on, particularly in relation to his fascination for optical devices and the consequences for his poetics. See, among others, Waddington (*The Mind's Empire* pp. 120–26), who relates this double perspective to the necessity of opting for correct readings, and thus sees it as a trope for 'the particulars of Chapman's own moral stance' (p. 124). For Waddington, this trope clarifies the meaning of Chapman's *enargia* as a notion that encourages readers to interpret the poem 'intelligently and with a moral responsibility' (p. 151). The theory and practice of reading that these lines recommend are also in line with Thomas Williams's second dedicatory sonnet (see '*OBS*: Williams 2', and Commentary), which also contrasts two modes of reading/seeing Chapman's poems — i.e. 'aloof' vs 'nearer'. See also Vinge, 'Chapman's *Ovids Banquet of Sence*', pp. 235–36; and Introduction, pp. 24–26, nn. 84 and 85.

4. 1 *In summer only wrought her ecstasy*] i.e. her passion was only productive of tears in the summer. Hudston (p. 403), who fails to notice the indebtedness to Conti here, concludes that the meaning is unclear. Conti misinterprets his own source when he attributes this 'ecstasy' to the statue ('Niobes statuam'). Yet Pausanias's passing comment refers to the actual Niobe and not the statue: 'ὡσαύτως δὲ καὶ Νιόβην λέγουσιν ἐν Σιπύλῳ τῷ ὄρει θέρους ὥρᾳ κλαίειν' ('Similarly too it is said that Niobe on Mount Sipylus sheds tears in the season of summer': *Description of Greece*, VIII. 2. 7). The confusion is deliberately exploited here: the fountain only issues water in the summer, because, as a work of art, it imitates the real stone Niobe, or, perhaps, because the statue is stone Niobe herself. Moreover, this reference insists on the poem's summer setting, creating a contrast between two genres (tragedy and erotic elegy), each one associated with a different seasonal event: Niobe's tragic grief and Corinna's sensual bathing.

4. 3 *curious imagery*] skilfully wrought sculptures, here producing an anamorphic effect. As Gilman notes, the 'curious perspective' refers to 'pictures or devices which manipulate the conventions of linear perspective to achieve ingenious effects' (*Curious Perspective*, p. 1). Like Niobe's statue, those of her children seem to have been sculpted anamorphically too.

5. 8–9 *looks so deadly sad, so lively done | As if death lived*] The double polyptoton (*lively/lived, deadly/death*) reinforces not only the paradoxical union of two opposite states (*discordia concors*), but also the art/nature theme: it is lively artistic representation (one of the senses of Chapman's *enargia*) that produces the rare achievement of a living death on the faces of Niobe's children.

Stanza 6

The detail of the two gods slaying Niobe's children is found in Pausanias. However, as Conti does not quote Pausanias directly on this point, Chapman assumes that the statue brought to the garden was of Niobe only, and that the rest of the set was added later at Augustus's command. Pausanias seems then the direct source for Chapman here, as he affirms that the statue 'has a tripod [τρίπους] over it, wherein are Apollo and Artemis slaying the children of Niobe' (*Description*, III. 21. 3). Pausanias's 'tripod' may have suggested the more audacious architecture of the pyramids, each one supporting on its top the carved transparent representation of each avenging god. Weaver ('Banquet', pp. 771–73) argues that Chapman's direct inspiration for the whole setting was Aphthonius's model ekphrasis of Alexander's citadel in the *Progymnasmata*, and quotes (in English translation) Reinhard Lorich's Latin edition (the original is reproduced here, and Weaver's cited signature is corrected): 'Duae dehinc pyramides lapidae positae, et fons profluens' ('Further two stone pyramids are placed, and a running spring': *Aphthonii Sophistae Progymnasmata* (Marburg: Christian Egenolff, 1542), sig. Aa2ʳ). For Weaver, this reinforces Chapman's imperial setting. For other discussions, see Kermode, who describes the scene as 'obelisks representing Apollo and Artemis, with an optical device by means of which they seem eternally to be wreaking their vengeance on the children' ('Banquet of Sense', pp. 88–89). The exact nature of this optical device remains, however, undescribed. Myers believes that Kermode's description misrepresents the scene, as 'the obelisks support (but are not) representations of Apollo and Artemis' ('Curious Frame', p. 202, n. 20). And Waddington assumes that 'the glass images of Apollo and Artemis are affixed to bases described as "Pyramides"' (*The Mind's Empire*, p. 130), so they should properly be regarded as standing glass statues. Kermode's opinion seems the right one in light of the findings of Smarr, who has traced the emblematic tradition of eyes mounted on top of pyramids, as in Achille Bocchi's *Symbolicae Quaestiones*, IV. 97, sigs Cc3ᵛ–Cc4ʳ, or representations of the Sun and the Moon on top of obelisks, as in the 1578 frontispiece of Gerard de Jode's *Speculum Orbis Terrarum* (Antwerp: Gerard Smits, 1578; see Visual Sources); see Smarr, 'The Pyramid and the Circle', pp. 373–75. Chapman's placing of these figures in carved glass on the pyramids' 'sharp brows' seems to recommend an interpretation of eye- or medallion-shaped devices on the obelisks' pointed tops. This has the advantage of explaining the two pyramids' all-seeing function (i.e. 'viewed' in 6. 2), and is also in line with MacLure's opinion that the whole setting of the poem is a complex allegorical 'device' (*George Chapman*, p. 53).

Stanzas 7–8

Corinna's entrance as the quintessence of beauty allows Chapman to put into practice his theory of poetic difficulty through the notion of *enargia*. For a detailed discussion of these principles and their practical application in these stanzas, see Introduction, pp. 26–28. Mythography is another controlling principle behind the metaphors and similes of these stanzas. Thus, the 'downward-burning flame' of Corinna's hair, threatening to become a new Phaeton that will scorch the fields, suggests the theme of insolence and pride, already present in relation to Niobe. Phaeton, son of Helios and the nymph Clymene, asked his father to let him ride his chariot in order to prove his noble ancestry, a request which Helios reluctantly granted. Jupiter realized the danger and struck Phaeton with a thunderbolt in punishment for his arrogance. The best-known account remains Ovid, *Metamorphoses*, II. 1–366. Conti echoes a moral interpretation of the myth of Phaeton that relates insolence to nobility: 'Quod attinet ad mores, deprimere nonnullorum arrogantiam per haec voluerunt, qui nihil sibi non tribuunt, nihilque se nescire propter nobilitatem arbitrantur' ('As for the moral interpretation of this myth, what the ancients were after here was to crush the insolence of people who thought a good deal too much of themselves, and who assumed that they were experts on everything just because they were members of the nobility': 'De Phaethonte', VI. 1, p. 557; Mulryan, pp. 460–61). The critique of nobility is a theme dear to Chapman, as Huntington has proved (*Ambition*, pp. 106–27). The presence of Corinna's 'handmaids' is another motif that insists on her status as the Emperor's daughter. Even if their only mention occurs here, we must assume the presence of an indefinite number of them as silent witnesses to the events narrated by the poem. Thus, Chapman subtly introduces the myth of Diana and Actaeon, which is central to the poem. Ovid mentions and even names some of the nymphs attending Diana in her bath (*Metamorphoses*, III. 165–72); and sixteenth-century painters commonly depict a group of bathing women escorting the goddess. An instance is the painting attributed to Lucas Cranach the Elder, *Diana and Actaeon* (*c.* 1540: Kronach, Fränkische Galerie), partially reproduced on the present volume's cover; see also Visual Sources. On the importance of the Diana/Actaeon myth to the poem, see Moss, 'Second Master', pp. 464–68; Luis-Martínez, 'Whose Banquet', 36–45; and Introduction, pp. 98–108, particularly in relation to its interpretation by Giordano Bruno. The Paris/Venus theme introduces the goddess of love as a counterpart to Diana's chastity, thus completing the depiction of Corinna as a model of Baroque *discordia concors*. The reference to the judgement of Paris is materialized in Venus's competition with Juno and Minerva for her beauty's controlling influence over Paris's desire.

8. 2–6 *As lighting ... melancholy shroud*] The image of a source of light breaking through a darkening object is a favourite Chapmanesque trope, often suggesting the ways in which knowledge overcomes ignorance, or the soul triumphs over the body, or poetry illuminates meaning. See, for an instance, *Hero and Leander* (III. 238–50, in Bartlett, p. 139), which depicts the sun's breaking through the clouds' vapours as an allegory of knowledge conceived in the soul. For a more detailed discussion of this

passage, see Luis-Martínez, 'Habit of Poesie', pp. 277–78. On the gradation from earthly darkness to heavenly light in these similes, see Introduction, pp. 26–28.

Stanzas 9–10

The catalogue of herbs and flowers that make up Corinna's garden has not received much critical attention, with the exception of Hudston's learned two-page note (pp. 404–05), which is an important source for the present commentary. Loughlin and others also include an 'Appendix: Corinna's Garden' (*Broadview Anthology*, pp. 1192–93). For his 'enflowered bank', Chapman could have relied on a former poetic tradition of gardens, but a probable inspiration in his immediate English context is Spenser, whose 'gay gardin' in *Muiopotmos* (181–97, in *Shorter Poems*, p. 419) contains a catalogue occupying two eight-line stanzas. The resemblances between Spenser and Chapman are conceptual rather than terminological — the only actual coincidence being 'violets', which are 'solemn' in Chapman and, perhaps synonymously, 'coole' in Spenser (193, p. 421). On Spenser's gardens, in *Muiopotmos* (1590) and *The Faerie Queene* (1591, 1596), John Dixon Hunt and Michael Leslie have pointed out that they are 'the result of the activities of nature and art' ('Gardens', in *The Spenser Encyclopaedia*, ed. by A. C. Hamilton (Routledge, 1990), p. 324). Charlotte F. Otten argues that the garden in *Muiopotmos* combines traits of the physic, culinary and aesthetic uses of Renaissance gardens, thus allowing readers to access the classical/mythological world of the poem through mostly well-known English plant names ('Plants, Herbs', in *Spenser Encyclopaedia*, pp. 545–46). All these remarks are applicable to Corinna's garden. On Chapman's own patterning, several plants are listed in contrasting pairs — e.g. 'Diana's arrows' vs 'Cupid's crimson shield'. The final ornamental detail of flowers clinging to Corinna's nakedness (10. 8–9) speaks of the emblematic nature of the setting, but also of their symbolic meanings in relation to women. See in this respect Loughlin and others, *Broadview Anthology*, p. 1193, which lists several women's diseases for which these plants were used.

> 9. 1–2 *A soft enflowered bank ... abstracted field*] If the spring is granted emblematic value, the 'enflowered bank' that encircles it works as its ornamental frame, thus showing an abridged selection of the complete catalogue of flowers and plants conceived of as 'ensigns', or emblems (as in *OED*, *ensigns*, n., 2. a). The textual senses of the verb 'abstract' and the adjective 'abstracted' (*OED*, v., 3. a) are present here, stressing the symbolic dimension of the poem's setting. On the identity of, and sources for, Chloris (the Roman Flora), goddess of flowers, see Commentary: 'Noctem', 181–200. The goddess Chloris should not be mistaken for her namesake in the poem — i.e. one of Niobe's seven daughters.

9. 3 *melanthy, great in bees' account*] Melanthion (thus in *OED*), or melanthium, are names for black cumin (*nigella sativa*), or damask gith (*nigella damaschena*). Chapman's 'melanthy' may be motivated by metre. William Bullein calls it 'Melanthium', and also 'Gith', with a shape 'like Poppye', and having 'blacke seedes, the leaves much lyke Coriander' (*Bulwarke of Defence against All Sicknesse* (London: Thomas Marshe, 1579), fol. 25ʳ). Hudston provides its modern name, 'love-in-a-mist' (p. 404), a purple flower that may be attractive to bees. For Spenser, the 'Bees alluring' plant is 'Thime' (*Muiopotmos*, 191; in *Shorter Poems*, p. 421).

9. 4 *Amaracus, that precious balm doth yield*] Hudston (p. 404) suggests that Qᴏʙ's 'Amareus' must be 'Amaracus', and I have followed Braden's emendation here. 'Amaracus' is sweet marjoram (*origanum dictamnum*), or dittany of Crete, as found in several herbals of the period. Bullein mentions it among the aromatic plants similar to oregano, 'herbes very sweete, wholsome, and pleasaunt', which will 'warme all the body, eyther in bath, or to be anoynted wyth the Oyle' (*Bulwarke*, fol. 48ᵛ). This explains the plant's balmy properties. Loughlin and others note its use as 'an abortifacient' (*Broadview Anthology*, p. 1193).

9. 5 *Enamelled pansies ... nuptials*] French *pensée* (thought) explains this flower's relation to love and marriage; its 'enamelled' quality is suggested by its three colours (yellow, violaceus and dark purple). See 'Coronet', 8. 8–9, for Chapman's use of the pansy as an emblem of his own poetics.

9. 6 *Diana's arrow, Cupid's crimson shield*] Braden suggests artemisia, or mugwort, for the first, and 'love-in-idleness' for the second, without further explanation. Hudston (p. 404) surmises the grammatical possibility that these are epithets for the 'pansies' of the former line — even though singular forms in this line hardly cohere with the plural in the former. In favour of artemisia, it could be adduced that Pliny suggested this name to be connected with Diana (Artemis), due to the plant's gynaecological properties (*Natural History*, xxv. 36). This argument is followed by early modern English treatises — e.g. Stephen Batman's translation of Bartholomaeus Anglicus, *De proprietatibus rerum* (London: Thomas East, 1582), fol. 279ᵛ. Braden's suggestion of 'love-in-idleness' for the second supports Hudston's view, as this, also called 'heartsease', is another name for the pansy. In Shakespeare's *A Midsummer Night's Dream*, Oberon asks Puck to pick 'love-in-idleness' (ɪɪ. 1. 168, ed. by R. A. Foakes (Cambridge University Press, 2003)), which is later named 'Cupid's flower' (ɪᴠ. 1. 76). This is the flower that will cause love at first sight. The antidote to this is 'Dian's bud' (ɪᴠ. 1. 70), with which he will cure Titania's love madness, and which has been identified as *vitex agnus castus*, 'a singular remedie, for such as would lyve chast: for it withstandeth all uncleannesse, or the filthie desire to lecherie' (*De proprietatibus rerum*, fol. 279ᵛ). In both

Shakespeare and Chapman, the contrast between Diana's chastity and Cupid's lust seems in order.

9. 7 *Ope-morn*] A flower of the convolvulus kind, possibly bindweed (as Braden suggests), or the morning-glory, although this latter occurs as a flower name much later in English. The suggestion is that of a bell-shaped flower that blooms in the morning.

9. 7 *nightshade*] A plant of the genus *solanum*, with small black wild berries that have narcotic or poisonous properties. For various species and uses, see D. Rembert Dodoens, *A Niewe Herball, or Historie of Plantes* (London: Henry Löe, 1578), pp. 446–47.

9. 7 *Venus' navill*] Venus's navel, navelwort or pennywort (*cotyledon umbilicus*), named so for its navel-like shape; see Dodoens, *Niewe Herball*, pp. 37–38. Hudston argues the relevance of this name to Corinna's nudity on account of the plant's Greek name, κῆπος Ἀφροδίτης, i.e. Venus's private parts (p. 404).

9. 8 *Solemn violets, hanging head as shamed*] The seriousness and shyness attributed to the drooping violets contrasts with the open impudence of the pennywort. As suggested above, Spenser's 'coole' seems to stress this quality.

9. 9 *verdant calamint, for odour famed*] Like 'melanthy' or 'amaracus', 'calamint' is one of the aromatic garden mints, of green ('verdant') colour, according to Bullein, who describes its properties against snake bites and other medicinal qualities (*Bulwarke*, fol. 48^{r-v}).

10. 1 *Sacred nepenthe, purgative of care*] 'Nepenthe' or 'nepenthes' is a drug first mentioned in Homer's *Odyssey* (IV. 220–21), when Helen pours into the wine 'φάρμακον νηπενθές', 'a drug to quiet all pain', both physical and spiritual. The origin of the plant is not known, hence its mythic, 'sacred' quality. Chapman's second epithet is self-explanatory, glossing the word's etymology: νη-, not + πένθος, grief.

10. 2 *sovereign rumex, that doth rancour kill*] 'Rumex' is a large weed of the kind called *polygonaceae*. Various medicinal properties are described in the period: invoking Dioscorides, Galen, Pliny and others, Bullein affirms that rumex 'wyl open the Gal, and purge choller'. Why it is called 'sovereign' here is difficult to know: Bullein argues that, if drunk as an infusion, it 'wyl very quickly help the kings evill' (*Bulwarke*, fol. 47^r), i.e. the festering skin abscesses caused by scrofula, which was believed to be cured by a monarch's touch. If 'rancour' is understood as rancidity or putrefaction (*OED*, n. †2), then the sovereignty of an otherwise low weed could be understood for its scrofula-healing qualities.

10. 3 *Sya and hyacinth, that furies wear*] 'Gethium is called in englishe a Syve, a chive, or a civet. [...] Cives growe only in gardines that I know of, in England' (William Turner, *The Names of Herbes* (London: John Day and William Seres, 1548), sig. D3ʳ). Qᴏʙ's 'Sya' may be a misprint of 'syue', and *OED* gives a separate entry for 'sive', a variant form of 'chive'. However, its emendation to 'sive' or 'chive' would have metrical consequences, as 'sya' could be disyllabic, i.e. [ˈsaɪə], and has been kept for that reason. Like the hyacinth beside it, chive is a bulbous plant. Yet another possibility is 'sium', or watercress, growing near water, an edible plant which Dodoens regards as a remedy for 'the strangurie, and agaynst all stoppinges of the kidneyes and bladder' (*A Niewe Herball*, p. 625). Hudston stresses the mythological side of Hyacinthus's metamorphosis into a flower (Ovid, *Metamorphoses*, x. 205–06) and its associations with grief through the onomatopoeia 'AI' in the youth's name (x. 215, II, pp. 78–79). Yet Chapman seems more interested in medicinal aspects, i.e. appeasing rage or fits of passion. Thomas Newton identifies a '*bulbus vomitorius*', or 'vomitinge Hyacinth' (*Approoved medicines and Cordiall Receiptes* (London: Thomas Marshe, 1580), sig. 48ʳ), which is found in Pliny, *Natural History* (xxi. 96).

10. 4 *merry*] Gean, or wild cherry. *OED* lists this use as the first in the language.

10. 4 *meliphill*] Melissa, or lemon balm, an aromatic and medicinal plant; *OED* only registers Chapman's use, and notes Greek μελίφυλλον, which shortens earlier μελισσόφυλλον, from μέλισσα, bee, and φύλλον, leaf. The bee-attracting quality of its leaf is confirmed by its Latin name, 'apiastrum'; see Pliny's 'apiastro sive melissophyllo' and 'melissophyllum sive melittaena' (*Natural History*, I. 46, I. 49). See Dodoens, *A Niewe Herball*, pp. 259–60. Another possibility, suggested by Loughlin and others (*Broadview Anthology*, p. 1992), is milfoil, from Latin 'millefolium', or French 'millefeuille', meaning 'a thousand leaves'. This is English yarrow.

10. 5 *crown imperial*] Or crown imperial fritillary (*fritillaria imperialis*), bearing a crown-shaped ring of petals under a green tuft, used ornamentally (thus 'fair').

10. 6 *Immortal amaranth*] In Dioscorides, the amaranth (ἀμάραντος, i.e. never fading) is the helichrysum or chrysanthemum (fol. 117ʳ, see *Discórides interactivo*, University of Salamanca, <https://dioscorides.usal.es> [accessed 29 November 2024]; search term: 'amaranto'). Confusion between an actual flower with a mythical, never-wilting one is possible (compare senses 1 and 5 of *OED*, n.). Although *OED* does not list occurrences of the never-dying amaranth before 1623, Chapman precedes William Drummond's 'Th'Immortal Amarantus' (*Poems* (Edinburgh: A. Hart, 1604), sig. F7ᵛ); or Milton's 'Immortal amaranth' that 'never fade[s]' (*Paradise Lost*, ed. by Alastair Fowler (Routledge, 1992, 2nd edn),

III. 353–60). On Milton's sources, see Fowler's note on the lines above. Before Chapman, Barnabe Barnes (1593) depicts Parthenophe treading on 'Amaranthus euerredde' (*Parthenophil and Parthenophe*, ed. by Victor A. Doyno (Southern Illinois University Press, 1971), Ode 9. 6, p. 104).

10. 6 *white aphrodill*] This is the affodill, or asphodel (different from daffodil, or narcissus). Chapman's form derives from French *affrodille/aphrodille*. See Randle Cotgrave, *A Dictionarie of the French & English Tongues* (London: Adam Islip, 1611), sigs C4^v, E4^v, which lists both 'Affrodille' and 'Aphrodille', and defines it as '*The Affodill, or Asphodill flower*', a kind of which is listed as 'Aphrodille blanc, *The white Asphodill, Dutch Affodill*'.

10. 7 *cup-like twillpants*] 'Twillpants' are tulips, and the word seems Chapman's deliberate attempt to anglicize the name of a flower for which there are no classical denominations. Dodoens (*A Niewe Herball*, pp. 212–13) has 'Tulpia', 'Tulipa' and 'Tulpian', and present-day 'tulip' occurs in English texts after 1595. The forms 'tulipan' and 'tulipant' (early seventeenth century) designate in English a turban before they mean a flower, as the word derives from Turkish *dülbent* (turban). Early uses of 'tulpian' and 'tulipant' may be behind Chapman's form. Its 'cup-like', rather than turban-like, shape seems motivated by its relationship here to Bacchus and the vine.

Stanza 11

This stanza completes the description of the setting, as Corinna takes centre stage, replacing Niobe as the 'eye' of the fountain. The image of Niobe's statue pouring her soul through her tears onto Corinna's breasts, and, in the opposite direction, Corinna's voice transporting the 'vital' soul and trying to animate the inanimate bodies of the statues, have implications in the context of classical and Renaissance theories of the soul as being carried out through bodily fluids. The idea of 'Niobe, | Tombed in herself' (1–2) increases the poem's sense of ambiguity around the fountain being the actual 'stone Niobe' (nature) or its sculpted representation (art). The depiction of Corinna as a 'Roman Phoebe', that is, as a new Diana, goddess of chastity, who also bathed in a fountain, contributes to the relevance of the Diana/Actaeon myth for the poem. Her singing and accompanying herself with a 'lute' (11. 6) is somewhat anachronistic, introducing a typically Renaissance courtly situation into Augustus's imperial garden. On the lute in classical culture, see John G. Landels, *Music in Ancient Greece and Rome* (Routledge, 1999), pp. 77–78.

Stanza 12

A metrical exception in the poem: the nine-line stanza in iambic pentameter is replaced here by an opening heroic quatrain (*ABAB*) followed by a fourteen-line song, combining iambic tetrameter and trimeter, and observing in all but metre the structure of a sonnet: *CddC EffE GhhG II* (capital letters represent tetrameter and small letters trimeter). This is the first time that the reader has access to Corinna's words and thoughts in the poem. The deliberately imperfect sonnet structure accompanies the critique of a perspective on love poetry which in the 1590s found expression through a number of fashionable sonnet sequences. Behind the apparently frivolous tone of Corinna's words ("Tis better to contemn than love | And to be fair than wise') hides a pungent attack on the courtly amorous lyric, which conceives of Petrarchan sonnets as 'wise glosses' set on 'fool[s]', i.e. witty poems written in praise of undeserving ladies. However, the lines preceding and continuing the song focus on the physical quality of Corinna's voice and melody and on its sensorial effects on Ovid, who could be thus portrayed as one more member of that 'school' of poets mocked by Corinna's lines. On the ironic and satiric meanings of Corinna's song, see Gless, 'Chapman's Ironic Ovid', p. 36, who relates her mention of 'our beauty's sorcery' to her Circe-like qualities; on this poem as corrective rather than satiric of Petrarchism, see Luis-Martínez, 'Friendlesse Verse', pp. 571–73.

Stanzas 13–14

Ovid's first entrance, 'young in love' and still ignorant of the favours that Corinna will grant him, coincides with the description that the prose argument makes of him as 'newly enamoured of Julia'. Readers are aware that Ovid has 'secretly conveyed himself' into the garden to spy on his beloved. None of the exhilaration described in this stanza is caused by Corinna's song: even if we see Ovid in a fit of passion 'while [she] this was singing', he remains unaware of it until he hears Corinna's 'silver voice' at the end of stanza 14. What these two stanzas recount instead is Ovid's passion as stimulated by the sight of Corinna, or rather the light issued by her eyes, in his imagination. Corinna's pronouncement in her song — 'souls are ruled by eyes' — sanctions the predominance of sight as a guiding principle in Chapman's theory of the senses. In the context of beauty as it is perceived by the mind's eye, stanza 13 depicts love through an astrological simile ('a fiery exhalation'), while stanza 14 imagines it as plunging from the shore into the turbulent, dangerous sea of Corinna's beauty.

Auditus

'Auditus' is the Latin term for the sense of hearing, which occupies the *narratio* between stanzas 15 and 30. The opening stanza of this section (15) describes in Neoplatonic fashion the effect of Corinna's song upon Ovid's poetic inspiration, while the closing stanza (30) focuses on the ceasing of all sound, which nevertheless leaves a lasting impression in the ear. The remaining stanzas (16–29), in direct speech, are Ovid's extemporized verses, inspired by Corinna's voice and song. While Ovid's ideas of sound and hearing contain an important number of Lucretian elements (see Lucretius,

De rerum natura, IV. 524–614), the theories of perception and cognition expressed in these stanzas are mainly Aristotelian. Thus, behind the 'philosopher' alluded to in Chapman's gloss on stanza 23 (M4) one may discern Aristotle, whose *De anima* shaped a long tradition of thinkers, particularly in the Middle Ages. More specifically on hearing, see *De anima*, II. 8, 419b–421a; and, on the more general account of cognition in stanza 23 and its gloss (M3), see *De anima*, III. 1–6, 424b–430b. The other indispensable voice in these stanzas is that of Marsilio Ficino, who placed 'hearing' among the higher senses, and whose theory of poetic frenzy in his Platonic commentaries was influential on Chapman.

Stanza 15

Corinna's voice is the cause of two kinds of frenzy, or 'rapture'. On one hand, the lover's frenzy at hearing his mistress's voice, here circumscribed only to the perception of sensual beauty; on the other, this perception is said to inspire poetic frenzy, which causes an elevation of the poet's intellect, whose 'fiery' nature disturbs the balance ('temper') in the composition of the soul. This account adapts Ficino's idea of 'amatory frenzy', or *furor amatorius*, which 'is usually excited through sight, which we naturally use after hearing' ('Hic enim per visum excitare solet, quo naturaliter utimur post auditum'). The excitation aroused by the perception of sensual beauty then leads to *furor poeticus*: 'Whoever experiences any kind of *spiritual possession [numine]* is indeed over-flowing on account of the vehemence of the divine impulse and the fullness of its power: he raves, exults, and *exceeds the bounds of human behaviour [finesque et mores humanos excedit]*. Not unjustly, *this possession or rapture [sive raptus furor]* is called frenzy and alienation. But no man possessed [*furens*] is content with simple speech: *he bursts forth into clamoring and songs and poems [in clamorem prorrumpit et cantus et carmina]*' (*Commentary on Phaedrus*, II. 4, pp. 50–54, emphasis added). The ascending motion of the poet's 'fiery wings' also has a spiritual, Neoplatonic component: 'Ala vero est potentia sursum ducens; per quam animae quidem divinae dicuntur alatae' ('But the wing is the upward-drawing power: through this power the divine souls are said to be winged', (*Commentary on Phaedrus*, II. 7, pp. 68–69).

> 15. 4 *takes full the Thespian bowl*] Braden relates 'Thespian' to Thespis, father of tragedy, and justifies its use here by extension of its meaning to poetry. Yet, more appropriately here, Thespian relates to the Muses. Thespiae, a city in Boeotia, had a sanctuary in honour of the Muses, for whom games and banquets were held. The city was named after Thespeia (Pausanias, *Description of Greece*, IX. 26. 6). Chapman's source may be Conti, who mentions accounts in which the Muses are said to be daughters of Memnon and Thesp[e]ia (VII. 15, 'De Musibus', p. 773), and suggests an allegorical explanation for the drinking associated with the Thespian

festivals: 'alii Memnonis et Thespiae filias fuisse putarunt: quoniam Musae scientia, et optimus affectus animi ad illam imbibendam creditus est' ('Others identified their parents as Memnon and Thespia. For the Muses are supposed to stand for knowledge, as well as the disposition that drinks in as much knowledge as it can hold', p. 779; Mulryan, p. 660). Another possible source is Ovid (*Metamorphoses*, v. 310), in which the Pierides, in competition with the Muses, call the latter 'Thespiades'.

Stanza 16

Direct speech acquaints us with Ovid's thoughts for the first time in the poem. His verses on the sense of hearing begin with his petition that the Muses repair their broken wings, which Ignorance has broken, to make Julia's reclining head soar to heaven. Her tunes, led forth by the furious trance of poetic inspiration, will divide themselves into a thousand Muses that will make war against the original nine, who are asked to take shelter in the Heliconian spring against their attack, as these tunes will summon all poets' furies to join their army. Besides the importance of the Contian mythography of the Muses and the Ficinian theories of poetic frenzy (see commentary on the previous stanza), the theories of sound and voice that inform this stanza derive from Lucretius. The metaphorical 'feathers' of Corinna's 'notes' can be interpreted from the Lucretian atomistic standpoint, which regards sound as an effect of the atom's material contact with the organs of hearing. For this reason, sound is perceived through similar mechanisms to those of the sense of touch: 'asperitas autem uocis fit ab asperitate | principiorum et item leuor leuore creatur' ('The roughness of the voice is made from the roughness of its atoms just as its smoothness springs from theirs', *De rerum natura*, IV. 542–43). Lucretian atomism is also present in the division of sonic matter into numberless atoms: thus, Corinna's melody becomes many 'tunes', each of them containing their own elemental, atomic Muse, resonating everywhere to the point of 'smit[ing]' the stars'. According to Lucretius: 'praeterea partis in cunctas diuiditur uox, | ex aliis aliae quoniam gignuntur, ubi una | dissiluit semel in multas exorta, quasi ignos | saepe solet scintilla suos se spargere in ignis. | Ergo replentur loca uocibus abdita retro | omnia quae circum feruunt sonituque cientur' ('Moreover, the voice is divided into many parts, to the extent that some are engendered from others, where, once a first appears, it bursts forth into many, just as a sparkle often scatters into flames. Thus many hidden places are filled with voices, which burn all around and vibrate with sound', IV. 603–08). On Lucretius and Chapman's 'Banquet', see Gorman, 'Atomies of Love', pp. 84–88.

Stanza 17

Behind the stanza's figurative layer, whereby Ovid imagines hearing as the marriage of Corinna's voice with his higher intellective functions, the theory of perception held here relies on medieval revisions of Aristotelian theories, in which perception and intellection become two differentiated processes. According to these theories, what the senses perceive are non-material emanations from the matter of real objects (the so-called sensible 'species'), which are carried by the spirits to the soul, the site of the inner senses, one of which is the *vis cogitativa*, which performs intellection — i.e. the transformation of the sensible into intelligible species. This is roughly the theory of sensation and perception found in Thomas Aquinas's *Summa Theologiae* and in his commentary on Aristotle's *De anima*. Further details of Aquinas's theory are provided below (see Commentary: 'Banquet', 24). For a general account, see Anthony J. Lisska, *Aquinas's Theory of Perception: An Analytic Reconstruction* (Oxford University Press, 2016).

Stanza 18

The extended simile comparing Corinna's song to bees seems Chapman's own invention. The epithet 'Attic' associated to 'bees' is obscure: Hudston notes that the best honey in ancient times came from the 'Hymettic region in central Attica' (p. 406); Gorman ('Atomies of Love', pp. 85 and 97, n. 41) suggests that Chapman attempts to relate the 'Attic bees' to ancient atomism, and notes associations of insects with atoms in Renaissance lyrics, such as John Dowland's 'It was a time when silly bees could speak', in which 'fruitless flies' are compared with 'atomies' (*The Third and Last Booke of Songs or Aires* (London, 1603), sig. K2ᵛ). Virgil's account of the Cretan (not Attic) bees that, attracted by 'the tuneful sounds of the Curetes' ('canoros Curetum sonitus'), reached the cave of a childish Jupiter and fed him with their honey, may be behind the reference (*Georgics*, IV. 149–52). The simile reinforces the contrast in the previous stanza between the material side of sound production (the bees and the production of honey) and perception, which is later purified into a non-material, air-like species ('honey tried to air'), finally becoming the soul's vital principle. The simile also provides a first complex instance of synaesthesia in the poem: primarily focusing on sound, the bees' activity displays connotations of sight ('gilt'), taste ('honey', 'sweets') and touch ('sting').

Stanza 19

Ovid's speech continues with a series of apostrophes to the air, the wood nymphs and the stones. A final apostrophe to Corinna's notes encourages them to impregnate the garden vegetation with their chaste sound, thus instilling its virtuous music in every part of it. The stanza closes with a new instance of synaesthesia: Corinna's notes will make the whole garden reverberate when its beautiful trees, flowers and waters are touched. The multiplying effect of sound suggested here accords with the Lucretian theory of the division of sound into numberless atoms (see stanza 16, and Commentary).

Stanza 20

The notion of man as microcosm is fundamental to Renaissance psychology. A classic formulation is found in Annibale Romei's *Discorsi* (1586), translated into English in 1598: 'e però fu meritamente l'huomo chiamato picciol Mondo; conciosia che il corpo humano non sia altro che un picciol modello del Mondo sensibile; e l'anima il simulacro del Mondo intelligibile' ('and therefore man was worthily called a little world, seeing the body of man is no other but a little modell of the sensible world, and his soule an Image of the world intelligible': *Discorsi* (Ferrara: Vittorio Baldini, 1586), p. 12; *The Courtiers Academie* (London: Valentine Sims, 1598), p. 17). On the implications of this trope, see Bamborough, *Little World of Man*. Ovid's extraordinary inversion is not only aesthetically audacious. The Pythagorean/Platonic implications of the original trope are obvious: man is part of a chain of being that is conceived of in terms of hierarchies ascending heavenward. Conversely, the idea of a cosmos shrunk to human dimensions and forms reinforces the atomistic concept of sound production and sensation expounded in the previous stanzas. A human-sized, anthropomorphic world would manage to collect the otherwise dispersed atoms of Corinna's tunes, absorb them through its ears, distribute its benefits along its otherwise dull inner organs, and, as an effect of these benefits, join the seven heavenly spheres in the universal harmony of their music-producing motions. The stanza thus extraordinarily navigates from the atomistic physic of the Epicureans to Pythagorean astronomy, with the effect that Corinna's tunes reintegrate *musica humana* into heavenly music. On Renaissance Pythagoreanism and the musical correspondences binding the human microcosm to the macrocosm, see S. K. Heninger, Jr, *Touches of Sweet Harmony: Pythagorean Cosmology and Renaissance Poetics* (Huntington Library, 1974), esp. 146–200.

Stanzas 21–22

Ovid's poetic account of the process of hearing in these two stanzas relies on barely compatible philosophical traditions. On one hand, the statement that the notes 'impress' the external 'air', which his 'implanted air' then 'embraceth' (22. 2–3), observes Aristotle's description of hearing as the result of the continuity between the air outside and inside the ear: 'That, then, is resonant which is capable of exciting motion in a mass of air continuously one as far as the ear. There is air naturally *attached* [συμφυὴς, i.e. 'growing together', 'united'] to the ear. And because the ear is in air, when the external air is set in motion, the air within the ear moves' (*De Anima*, II. 8, 420a3–5, emphasis added). Moreover, the idea of sound's imprint on the air relies on an Aristotelian simile that explains the immateriality of all sense perception: 'In regard to all sense generally we must understand that sense is that which is receptive of sensible forms apart from their matter, as wax receives the imprint of the signet-ring apart from the iron or gold of which it is made: it takes the imprint which is of gold or bronze, but not *qua* gold or bronze'

(II. 12. 424a17–21, pp. 104–05). This analogy of the wax imprint in the air was originally part of Democritus's theory of sense perception, as reported by Theophrastus (*De sensu*, 51, in *Theophrastus and the Greek Physiological Psychology before Aristotle* (Macmillan, 1917), pp. 110–11). On the other hand, the conceit of Corinna's song as a sacrifice to the gods elaborates on a materialist account of sound initiated in the former stanzas. Dispersed in groups of a hundred notes (like the hundred oxen in a hecatomb), the sounds in Corinna's 'sonnet' mingle with the perfumed 'incense' of her breath — a new opportunity for synaesthesia, even if smell has not entered the poem yet.

Ovid's atomizing of the song into multiple notes paves the way for the next simile, whereby Corinna's 'sounds' are compared to 'gilt atoms in the sun'. Gorman notes that Chapman recreates an analogy for atomic movement with a tradition ranging from Aristotle to Lucretius ('Atomies of Love', pp. 84–85). Aristotle's simile epitomizes Democritus's conception of the soul: 'Hence Democritus affirms the soul to be a sort of fire or heat. For the "shapes" or atoms [σχημάτων καὶ ἀτόμων] are infinite and those which are spherical he declares to be fire and soul: they may be compared with the so-called motes [ξύσματα] in the air, which are seen in the sunbeams that enter through our windows' (*De anima*, I. 2, 403b31–404a5). Although Lucretius's target is not the soul but mere physical motion, his analogy resembles Democritus's/Aristotle's simile (see *De rerum natura*, II. 112–41): 'Do but apply your scrutiny when the sun's light and his rays penetrate and spread through a dark room: *you will see many minute specks mingling in many ways throughout the void in the light itself of the rays* [*multa minuta modis multis per inane videbis | corpora misceri radiorum lumine in ipso*], and as it were in everlasting conflict struggling, fighting, battling in troops without any pause, driven about with frequent meetings and partings; so that you may conjecture from this what it is for *the first-beginnings of things* [*primordia rerum*] to be ever tossed about in the great void' (II. 114–22, emphasis added). Somehow altering Aristotle and Lucretius, Ovid makes their tenor (ἄτομοι, *primordia*) his vehicle ('atoms') for a new tenor ('sounds'): just as the atoms are 'gilt' by the sun's rays, Corinna's 'gilt' sounds ('gilt' because they burn in sacrifice to the gods) enter the ear's 'pores' (22. 1).

The focus on the 'pores' presupposes the material quality of the sound perceived in hearing. Empedocles' account of the senses, if we rely on Theophrastus, holds that 'perception occurs because something fits *into the passages* [εἰς τοὺς πόρους]' of a particular organ (*De sensu*, 7, pp. 70–71, emphasis added). Chapman's 'gristles' are the ear's cartilage, while the 'pores' open to the passing of sound in emanations going through the ducts or channels of the external sense organs. The account by Chapman's Ovid is thus again Epicurean, possibly via Lucretius: 'Corpoream quoque enim uocem constare fatendumst | et sonitum, quoniam possunt inpellere sensus' ('For we must confess that voice and sound are also bodily, since they can strike upon the sense', *De rerum natura*, IV. 526–27). This explains Ovid's verb 'feel', which frequently refers in this poem to tactile sensations — i.e. the 'feeling's organ' (106. 7). For Epicurus, and for Lucretius, *tactus* is the sense par excellence, and all senses can be reduced in one way or another to touch, which is the best proof of the materiality of atoms: 'tactus, enim tactus [...] corporis est sensum' ('for touch [...] it is touch that is the bodily sense': II. 434–35). In Book II of *De rerum natura*, Lucretius also discusses the violent movements of atoms, as well as their different shapes and textures. Chapman's Ovid refines such discussion in depicting the sounds' 'nimble feet' (both physical and metrical) as the material cause of the harmonious 'measure' of their dance, which literally 'tread' on his ear.

The atomist theory of hearing as the result of a material emanation that penetrates the body seems to prevail here over the Aristotelian idea of the formal imprint on the medium, air; similarly, the transmission of that perception to the intellective faculties is resolved in materialist terms. Thus, 21. 6–9 depict 'soul', 'flesh' and 'spirit' in transformation by the effect of 'fire'. If these three entities need to be understood here as different, the Lucretian idea of a highly refined material spirit (*animus*), which resides in the heart ('media regione in pectoris haeret': III. 140, pp. 180–81) and whose connection with the body takes place through the intermediate soul (*anima*), which is also material, holds here. In Lucretius, the difference between the three lies in the smallness, roundness and smoothness of the atoms — conceived of in gradation from spirit to body. This would explain the 'fad[ing]' of the 'flesh' into the more refined, subtler 'spirit' as the effect of love's fire, as well as the soul's 'blaz[ing]' in 'Cupid's furnace', whose atoms, like those of Corinna's 'notes', are 'gilt' by the god's sacrificing fire. 'Cupid's furnace' is a common metaphor for the heart, particularly in emblem literature: an example is Otto Vaenius, 'Sunt lacrymae testes / Loues teares are his testimonies', in *Amorum emblemata* (Antwerp: Hendrik Swingen, 1608), pp. 188–89 (see Visual Sources). Chapman may also have relied on Curaeus: 'Nunquam tamen aer, motus expers est, sicut ostendunt exempla atomorum in sole, qui etiam serenissimo et tranquilissimo aere moventur' ('The air is never without movement, as shown by the example of the atoms in the sun, which likewise move in the most serene and tranquil air': Περὶ αἰσθήσεως, I. 42, p. 167, my translation).

Stanzas 23–24 and M3, M4

The relationship between Ovid's words in these two stanzas and the two accompanying marginal notes is complex. The first of these glosses reminds the reader that the explanation of Corinna's 'conceit' and singing of her song must first be understood mythographically. Rather than a mere 'allusion', the reference to 'the birth of Pallas' (M3) becomes the controlling allegory of stanza 23. Corinna/Julia is Jupiter, while Pallas/Minerva is her 'tunes', which come to the world fully 'armed'. As Conti argues, 'since wisdom is something divine and one of God's gifts, it makes some sense to say that Minerva was born from Jupiter's head. For the head is the seat of memory and wisdom [memoriae et sapientiae sedes est caput]'. And he adds that Minerva 'was born bearing arms [nata est armata], because the wise man's mind is always well armed against Fortune's onslaughts' ('De Minerva', IV. 5, p. 308; Mulryan, pp. 254–55). In the poem, the explanation of the myth is put at the service of a deeper philosophical account of the process of intellection. Yet it is at this point that the poem and its marginal gloss work in opposite directions: thus, the order which Corinna 'observes in her utterance', and which Ovid explains, must be exactly the opposite to the one observed for 'apprehension of our knowledge and effection [i.e. performance] of our senses'.

Chapman loosely invokes a number of unnamed 'philosophers' here. One should understand the plural literally in order to realize that, while the basic framework stems from Aristotle and his discussion of the imagination and intellection in *De anima*, Book III, the theory of the so-called 'inner senses' sketched here relies on medieval developments of Aristotle, particularly by Thomas Aquinas. Chapman's model only partially fits Aquinas's theory of the four inner senses that facilitate the formation of concepts in the mind, as only three are mentioned: 1) *sensus communis* ('common sense') discerns complex wholes out of the isolated perceptions of each sense; 2) *phantasia* (the 'imaginative part') is the storehouse, or *thesaurus*, of these complex perceptions; 3) the *vis cogitativa* ('cogitative' part) is the faculty whereby humans discern whole individuals and not mere bundles of sensations. The fourth sense, *vis memorativa*, or memory, is omitted, and instead Chapman proceeds to the intellect, which is conceived of in the light of its Aristotelian division into passive (νοῦς παθητικός) and active (νοῦς ποιητικός). In Aquinas, these two kinds became, respectively, *intellectus possibilis* (or potential) and *intellectus agens* (or active); Chapman calls them 'passive intellect' and '*dianoia*, or *discursus*'. The Aristotelian distinction is one between an intellect *in potentia*, in which all intelligible things can be brought about, and an intellect in actuality, which has the capacity, or *habitus*, to bring about each intelligible thing, and which would ultimately be responsible for the specific 'conceit of [Corinna's] sonnet both for matter and note'.

However, what Chapman's lines provide is an inverted and incomplete version of the gloss's theoretical account, one that quite unphilosophically assumes that the process of thought and utterance can simply travel the path of inner perception in reverse. Weaver provides tables with correspondences between the poem and 'the reverse of the ancient map of the mind and its process of cognition' as expounded in the gloss, to note that the poem omits 'the passive intellect, useless in the production of discourse'. His correspondences are: mind ('mental womb'); ratiocinative intellect ('discursive fire'); cogitative intellect ('power of her thought'); common sense ('her attire'); imagination ('strong imagination'); senses ('voice') ('Banquet', pp. 780–83). A simplified version would be as follows: in Ovid's poetic invention, Corinna's 'mental womb' (playing on the conception of Pallas in Jupiter's head) is the mind; her 'discursive fire' is the active intellect; 'her thought' may loosely refer to the cogitative power, in which it receives the 'downy plumes', or words, which adorn her 'conceit'; from here they are sent first to the imagination and then to her vocal organs, from which they are finally sent away in the form of song. This ultimate lack of correspondence reveals a dissonance, perhaps with ironic undertones, between the learned, philosophical voice of the glossarist and the poetic mind of Ovid — a circumstance that in Chapman's poetics implies a critical defence of a philosophical kind of poetry for which his Ovid only partially qualifies.

The second of the glosses (M4) contains a favourite Latin tag in Chapman's work: '*Intellectus in ipsa intellegibilia transit*' ('Intellect passes into the very intelligibles', or, as Chapman's Ovid translates it, 'intellects themselves transit | To each intelligible quality'). As former editors and critics have noted, Chapman also used it in *Euthymiae Raptus, or The Tears of Peace* (1609): 'in Rules of True Philosophie | there must be euer due Analogie | Betwixt the Powre that knows, and that is knowne, | So surely ioynde that they are euer one; | The vnderstanding part transcending still | To that it vnderstands' (854–59, in Bartlett, p. 192). It also appears in the 1611 *Iliads*: 'there is ever a proportion betwixt the writer's wit and the writee's (That I may speake with authority) according to my old lesson in Philosophy: *Intellectus in ipsa intellegibilia transit*' ('The Fourteenth Booke, Commentarius'). Again, the principle is invoked in the funeral-philosophical poem *Eugenia* (1614): 'That as Philosophie | Saies there is euermore proportion | Betwixt the knowing part, and what is knowne | So joynd, that both are absolutely one'. Chapman's Latin marginal note here is the closest to a philosophical explanation and true source that he offers: 'Opportet esse Analogiam inter potentiam cognoscentem, et hoc quod cognoscitur, etc. Intellectus, in ipsa intelligibilia transit. Cul[tam] Ex Aristotele' ('It is worth noting here the analogy between the knowing power and that which is known, etc. The intellect passes into the very things known. Culled from Aristotle': 423–26, and Marginal Gloss; in Bartlett, p. 281).

However, beyond the fact that Aristotle is regarded as the source, the meaning and actual origins of the tag have not yet been traced. Snare summarizes Chapman's flexible use of it — and further argues that it rules the relationship between the different voices of his early poems (*Mystification*, pp. 148–50). Yet flexibility amounts to critical imprecision, a circumstance that also affects decisions about which exact moment in Aristotle this tag invokes. Hudston (p. 406) aptly refers the reader to *De anima*, III. 4, 429b, yet without further explanation; and Braden, less aptly although equally silently, to III. 4, 429a. I have previously pointed to III. 5, 430a10–25 (Luis-Martínez, 'Friendlesse Verse', p. 592), which completes Hudston's conjecture but is in itself insufficient. Chapman may be quoting a printed commentary on that Aristotelian passage. His calling it 'my old lesson in Philosophy' does not reveal whether the lesson was imparted to him in the past or whether he is the master that imparted that lesson since his early days as a poet — in 1611, this first use of 1595 may have seemed 'old' to him. As he uses Latin, and as he may thus be referring to a Latin source, I quote a relevant passage from an influential Latin translation of *De anima* (Lyons: Antonius Vincentius, 1557), by the fifteenth-century Byzantine scholar John Argyropoulos: 'Atque intellectus, potentia quidem est quodammodo intelligibilia ipsa: actu vero nihil eorum antea quam intelligat ipsa: Oportet autem in ipso nihil esse, perinde atque in tabula nihil est actu scriptum, antea quam in ipsa scribatur: hoc enim in ipso atque accidit intellectu. Est etiam intelligibilis et ipse, ut intelligibilia cuncta. Nam in hisce quidem, quae sine materia sunt, intelligens, et id quod intelligitur, idem est' ('And the intellect is somehow potentially the very things known, but in act it is none of them until it thinks them. Is there of necessity nothing in it, just as there is nothing actually written upon a table until something is written upon it? This is exactly what happens with the intellect. Besides, it is the known thing and itself, as all the known things. Because in these same things that are immaterial the thinking subject and the thought object are the same': III. 4, pp. 88–89, my translation). This passage in Aristotle (429b31–430a5) introduces the abovementioned notions of active and passive intellects. According to Aristotle, only the active intellect has the capacity to make knowledge actual, that is, identical with the thing known (III. 5, 430a19–20). This is in fact what Chapman means when he affirms that intellect passes into the things known. The closest to the letter of Chapman's tag that I have been able to trace is found in Aquinas (*In Aristotelis Librum de Anima Commentarium*, ed. by P. M. Pirotta (Marietti, 1948), III. 10. 730, p. 174), who explains the latter affirmation quoted here: '*Intellectus autem agens facit ipsa intelligibilia esse in actu*, quae prius erant in potentia, per hoc quod abstrahit ea a materia; sic enim sunt intelligibilia in actu' ('Agent intellect, however, actualizes the intelligibles that previously were in potentiality by abstracting them from matter, for in that abstracted condition they are intelligibles in actuality'; my translation). This passage uses phrasings that are identical with Chapman's, with the exception of the verb 'transit', for which we find 'facit' here. It also insists on the identification of intellect with the thing known as an act that involves divorcing the thing known from its material quality. Aquinas's explanation is also coincident with Chapman's uses, particularly in the later philosophical poems *Euthymiae Raptus* and *Eugenia*.

However, and as in the case of 'gilt atoms' earlier, the tag is here, as the gloss recognizes, a principle 'upon which' a poetic 'invention' is 'grounded'. It is thus the vehicle of a simile (24. 5–6) whose complex tenor is formulated in the rest of the stanza. As Ovid explains in 24. 1–4, Corinna's 'tunes', due to their delicate breeding, 'die' as the result of their generous disposition to please others and their inability to survive among unkind people ('earth's rude unkinds'). For that reason, Ovid wishes that, just as the active intellect is made one with the 'intelligible quality' abstracted from the objects, his '[intellectual] life' be made one with his 'love's conceit', that is, with the song as 'first conceived in her mental womb' (23. 3), so that, once it forms a unity with it, it can complete the course from the inner to the outer senses that was described in stanza 23 — that is, both his 'life' and her 'conceit' will be shaped into 'words', 'tunes' and 'breath'. Finally, and just as in 23. 9, Corinna's 'kisses' will send this new composite to the air in the form of a song, where it will consume itself into death as explained earlier in the stanza. The effect of Chapman's simile is a Platonizing of the Aristotelian principle: the lover wants to be made one with the 'conceit' produced by his beloved's soul. In this sense, see also Introduction, pp. 106–06, where Giordano Bruno's similar Platonizing of the same Aristotelian conception is explained as a possible analogue, if not as a source, of Chapman's procedure here, particularly as this argument is for Bruno the one that explains the meanings of the myth of Actaeon.

Stanzas 25–26 and M5

Beginning with 'This life' and 'My life', these two stanzas elaborate on the former's conclusion: Ovid's wish that his life be made one with the 'conceit' of Corinna's song, which is the song's essence as it is initially 'conceived' in her mind. The consequence of this union is a sort of intellectual life that aspires to physical death ('Thus would I live to die'), achieved by their transcending the outer senses. The 'sense' that seeks to be 'feasted' is not then any of the five external senses, but a higher inner sense (i.e. the mind), which controls all the operations of perception and intellection. This motivates the singular use of 'sense' in the poem's title: the 'banquet of sense' also aspires to be a banquet of the mind. The 'golden world' to which the life of the flesh is 'digested' is consequently the life of the intellect. 'Digest[ed]' and 'indigest[ed]' are significant words in Chapman (see 'Noctem', 30, 49, 59; 'OBS: To Roydon', line 30; and Introduction, pp. 2–3). The verb puns on physical digestion, but primarily means the logical process of imposing methodical order over 'chaos' (see explanatory footnote to 'Banquet', 25. 4). This new life of the mind is imagined in visual terms, which advances the highest place granted to sight in the traditional (i.e. Platonic) hierarchy of the senses: thus, Ovid intends to harmonize ('consort') Corinna's 'look' with 'each note and word'. In the 'golden world' of the intellect, her appearance is an idealized face that 'sings' 'songs of solid harmony'.

The marginal gloss — 'This hath reference to the order of her utterance, expressed before' (M5) — refers this line and the rest of the stanza to stanza 23 and M3. 'Thus should I be her notes before they be' (26. 5) reiterates the union between Ovid's intellect and the 'conceit' of Corinna's 'notes', made only of 'discursive fire' (23. 4) and now located in her 'blood', before they are 'vapoured in her voice's stillery' with her 'breath' (24. 8). The image of the 'stillery', or still, usually distilling the lover's tears from the furnace of the heart, is common in sixteenth- and seventeenth-century emblem books, and could have inspired Chapman's conceit for the voice. An early instance is

Maurice Scève, 'Mes pleurs non feu decelent', in *Delie* (Lyons: Antoine Constantin, 1544), p. 95 (see Visual Sources); also the above-quoted Vaenius, 'Sunt lacrymae testes / Loues teares are his testimonies', in *Amorum emblemata*, pp. 188–89. The concluding couplets to both stanzas proclaim the rule of this primordial state of Corinna's song as conceived in her mind over its sensory quality as sound, and thus of intellect over hearing. Thus, stanza 25 concludes with Ovid's desire to reign over 'her tunes' division', because it is 'her conceit', with which his intellect has been joined, that 'does all'. Stanza 26 closes with a dismissive view of the sensory quality of Corinna's voice that Ovid has praised thus far, as it is reduced to 'Nought [...] But motions' escaped from 'her spirits' flames', that is, the essential 'notes' with 'fiery wings' conceived in the mind and transported by the bodily spirits in her 'blood' before they are voiced and insufflated with her breath.

Stanza 27

As the marginal gloss to 27. 5 states (M6), the stanza is 'likewise referred to the order above said, for the more perspicuity'. 'Perspicuity', or '*enargia*' (as it is called in '*OBS*: To Roydon'), is the aspiration to 'clearness of representation' through eloquent invention. As frequently in Chapman, simile is its poetic means, which in this case offers what Weaver calls 'an abbreviated and more psychological account' of the conception of Corinna's song ('Banquet', p. 782). The focus is thus the psychology of Corinna's 'desire' (27. 4) rather than the more intellectual 'conceit' of the previous stanzas. Only three stages are invoked in this reduced version: 1) the mind, or 'soul', where desire originates; 2) the 'common sense', to which the spirits carry the emanations of desire and where they acquire their 'distinct attire' — since they were only a 'pretence' in the previous stage; 3) the vocal organs that convey the song through Corinna's 'breath', ready to 'feast the ear'. The simile of the ignition of wood only refers to the first stage: thus, Corinna's 'soul' is the 'steel and flint', and 'desire' the 'fire' that 'lighten[s]' its 'sparks', or 'notes' pretence' over the 'tender tinder' of her bodily 'spirits'. The metaphor of the 'common sense' as a 'wardrobe' is another instance of perspicuity, which shows Chapman's peculiar idea of this first of the inner senses. In Aquinas, it is the imagination and memory, and not the common sense, that are conceived of as *thesauri* — i.e. storehouses, or cabinets (Lisska, *Aquinas's Theory of Perception*, p. 197). The phrase 'common sense' in Chapman translates Aristotle's κοινή αἴσθησις, or Aquinas's *sensus communis*. However, while the role of the common sense in Aristotle and in his medieval interpreters is to receive the different perceptible forms, or sensible species, from the external senses and unify them, that function is inverted here: the common sense receives the intelligible species from the inner senses and gives it particular sensitive form in order to be sent away. Conceived of thus as a wardrobe of sensations, its role would be to assign specific sensual qualities ('distinct attires') to the mind's conceptions.

Stanzas 28–29

Ovid's last two stanzas on the sense of hearing focus on Corinna's notes as a source of poetic inspiration. The imagery of Ficinian amatory and poetic frenzy (see stanza 15 and its Commentary) is prominent here, particularly in the references to elevation ('raise', 28. 1; 'wings', 28. 4; 'to heav'n repair', 28. 4) and in the concluding mention of 'the hearts of love and poesy' (29. 8). Thus, Ovid's heavenly ascent, caused by Corinna's song, will inspire his own song of praise. The other major theme of these stanzas is the art/nature motif, which is regarded in terms of collaboration rather than competition. In fact, the confluence of art and nature singularizes both Corinna as singer/beloved and Ovid as poet/lover. In Corinna's case (28. 5–9), while her natural beauty causes her to be adored as a mere woman, her 'art to tempt the ear' qualifies her as a 'goddess'. In Ovid's case, his ears' ability to 'sound' (i.e. comprehend) the 'sounds' of Corinna's 'virgin utterance' differentiates him from those sensual men and poets whose 'earthly ignorance' is more easily pleased with nature than with art; art also allows him to 'break [...] strumpet Folly's bounds' (29. 5). This is the reason for the strength of his Muse and the sublime heights of his poetry, as concluded in 29. 9.

Stanza 30

The cessation of sound after the end of Corinna's song provides the occasion for Chapman's virtuoso display of poetic simile — another instance of *enargia*. The simile of the bell's continued resonance after being struck extends through the stanza in ways that suggest that very permanence of sound inside Ovid's ear. In the context of Chapman's possible acquaintance with ancient theories of sound and hearing, the origin of the simile may be Empedocles' mysterious three-word fragment B99, preserved and commented on by Theophrastus in *De sensu*, I. 9 (Empedocles' fragment in italics): 'Hearing comes about from sounds inside. For when air is set in motion by the voice, it echoes inside. Hearing is like a *bell* [κώδωνα] with equal sounds, which he calls a *fleshy branch* [σάρκινον ὄζον]. Air in motion strikes against the solid parts and makes an echo' (*The Texts of Early Greek Philosophy: The Complete Fragments and Selected Testimonies of the Major Presocratics*, ed. and trans. by Daniel D. Graham, 2 vols (Cambridge University Press, 2010), I, pp. 401–03, emphasis added). As in Empedocles, Chapman elaborates on the contact between air and metal as the cause of reverberation.

Olfactus

The sense of smell occupies the *narratio* between stanzas 31 and 40. The opening stanza of this section (31) describes the effect of the mixture of Corinna's natural odours with her bath perfumes on Ovid's desire and poetic inspiration. Stanzas 32 to 39 are in direct speech, the result of Ovid's extemporized verses as inspired primarily by smell, although stanzas 35 and 36 bring together odours and sounds. In stanzas 39 and 40, smell instigates a stronger desire to see Corinna: these stanzas are thus transitional to the central part of the poem, which focuses on sight. Ovid's song about Corinna's perfumes is more diffuse than the previous account of sound, as there is no attempt here at a systematic theory of sense perception. This should not be surprising, as smell is treated with a lesser degree of detail in the classical sources that must have inspired Chapman. Moreover, its position in the traditional hierarchy of the senses is lower than sight and hearing. Of the two senses that do not require the presence of the object, smell comes after hearing because odours are transmitted more slowly than sounds. Lucretius may have been of relevance here: 'Errabundus [odor] enim tarde uenit ac perit ante | paulatim facilis distractus in aeris auras' ('For [smell] moves slowly in coming, and is ready gradually to die away first, being dispersed abroad into the breezes of the air': *De rerum natura*, IV. 692–93). Yet the main ideas seem to draw on Aristotle's *De anima* and *De sensu*, and Theophrastus's *De sensu* and *De odoribus*, as well as on the arguments of the Presocratic philosophers, particularly Empedocles and Anaxagoras, echoed in their work. Direct knowledge of some of these sources may be presupposed, although the presence of all these philosophers in Curaeus's Περὶ αἰσθήσεως must again be noted, as some passages were transferred directly from this manual into the poem. Thus, Chapman's treatment of the importance of air as medium, of the role of dryness and heat in the generation and transmission of odours, or his mention of the legend of men living on odours only, are easily traced back to this source.

Stanza 31

The passage of Corinna's odours through Ovid's nose into his brain finds poetic expression by way of the extended simile of the Phoenix's flight to his death and later rebirth. The literary origin of the fabulous bird, unique of its species, is a story which Herodotus (484–25 BC) reports to have heard at the city of Heliopolis in Egypt. In Herodotus, a new Phoenix arises every 500 years, and the newborn bird carries the remains of the old one to the temple of the Sun (*Histories*, ed. and trans. by A. D. Godley, 4 vols (Harvard University Press, 1920), II. 73, I, pp. 358–61). Yet the version of the story on which Chapman draws is first found in Pomponius Mela, *De situ orbis* (*c.* AD 43), of which several editions circulated in the late sixteenth century: 'De volucribus praecipue referenda Phoenix, semper unica: non enim coitu concipitur, partuve generatur: sed ubi quingentorum annorum aevo perpetua duravit, super exaggeratam variis odoribus struem sibi ipsa incubat, solviturque: deinde putrescentium membrorum tabe consecrans, ipsa se concipit, atque, ex se rursus renascitur: cum adolevit, ossa pristini corporis inclusa myrrha Aegyptum exportat, atque in urbem, quam Solis appellant, fragantibus nardo bustis inferens memorando funere consecrat' ('Of the birds, the Phoenix, always unique, is especially worth mentioning. It is not conceived by copulation or born through parturition, but after it has lasted continuously for a lifetime over five hundred years, the Phoenix lies down on a funeral pile heaped up with different scents and decomposes. Next, after congealing from the moisture of its putrefying limbs, the bird conceives itself and is reborn from itself. When the Phoenix has reached maturity, it carries the bones of its former body, shut inside a ball of myrrh, to Aegypt, and in what they call the City of the Sun, it puts the ball on the burning pyre of an altar and consecrates it in a memorable funerary ritual': *De situ orbis libri tres* (Rostock: Stephan Myliander, 1591), III. 9, pp. 98–99; translation: *Pomponius Mela's Description of the World*, ed. and trans. by F. E. Romer (University of Michigan Press, 1998), pp. 124–25). The reference to 'Apollo's eye', the sun, may be motivated by the location of the Phoenix's ritual at Heliopolis, which was consecrated to the god of the sun. The story is also summarized by Isidore of Seville, *Etymologies*, XII. 7. 20, p. 265.

The idea that smells literally 'pierce' the brain may have been taken directly from Curaeus: 'odor, per nares ad cerebrum ascendit' ('smell ascends from the nose to the brain': Περὶ ἀισθήσεως, v. 6, p. 189).

Stanza 32

The first stanza of Ovid's song develops two main conceits. The first states that love is an illness that can be cured by the medicinal power of perfumes. Love is presented as a fire that consumes the bodily spirits, thus extinguishing life, which can only be restored by the 'fresh-breathed soul' emanating from Corinna's odours. Compare Aristotle's account of Democritus's ideas in *On Respiration*: 'Democritus says that inhalation has a certain effect on animals, claiming that it inhibits the expulsion of the soul. [...] For in the air there is a great number of those kind of atoms he calls mind and soul. So when the animal inhales and the air enters, these atoms entering with it counteract the external pressure and keep the soul inside the animal from passing outside. Consequently, life and death depend on inhalation and exhalation' (471b30–472a18; quoted from *The Texts of Early Greek Philosophy*, ed. by Graham, I, pp. 576–77). The second conceit relies on the notion that heat and fire aid the transmission of smell. Bartlett refers to a manuscript note by Frank Schoell where he compares 32. 8 to Theophrastus, *Of Odours*, but no further references are provided. Chapman may have known Theophrastus's small treatise in the Latin translation quoted here: 'Thus autem et myrrha densiore etiamnum natura concreta, molliorem desiderant ignem, quo sensim concalefacta exhalantur' ('Frankincense and myrrh, as they are of a denser, even thick texture, need a milder fire, by which, when they are heated gradually, will exhale their scent': *Theophrasti Libellus de odoribus* (Paris: Michel de Vascosan, 1556), III. 13, sig. B2^v, my translation). On heat as a developer of smell, see Aristotle, *De sensu*, v, 443b16–17, in *On the Soul, Parva Naturalia, On Breath*, ed. and trans. by W. S. Hett (Heinemann, 1964), pp. 250–51). The closing couplet brings together the stanza's two conceits: love will 'excel' in the lovers' inflamed spirit just as odours are increased by the action of fire.

Stanza 33

Two conceits expressed via simile are juxtaposed. The first (33. 1–4) contrasts the Neoplatonic ascension to 'perfection's seat' through spiritual love with the 'base desire' of mere sensual lovers: whereas love's perfection is like the intensified odours produced by the 'raref[action]' (refinement, purification) of air caused by heat, sensual desire is like the thicker and less pure air caused by cold. On possible sources, compare Theophrastus's explanation of Anaxagoras: '*rarefied air* [λεπτὸν ἀέρα] has a stronger odour, since it is odorous when heated and *rendered less dense* [μανούμενον]' (*De sensu*, in *Theophrastus*, 30, pp. 92–93, emphasis added). Yet the direct source is more likely Curaeus: 'In aere frigido odor minus percipitur, quia vapores a frigore condensati, difficilius erumpere et ad organum ascendere possunt. Sed in aere calido, attenuantur vapores, ita ut liberius ascendant, et manifestius accipiantur' ('In cold air smell is hardly perceived, because vapours are condensed by cold temperature, and it is more difficultfor it to break out and ascend to the organ. Yet in cold air vapours are made thinner, and thus they can ascend more freely, and so they are perceived more clearly': Περὶ ἀισθήσεως, II. 5, p. 184, my translation).

On the second conceit (33. 5–9), see Danielle Nagler, 'Towards the Smell of Mortality: Shakespeare and Ideas of Smell, 1588–1625', *The Cambridge Quarterly*, 26.1 (1997), pp. 42–58 (p. 46), doi:10.1093/camqtly/XXVI.1.42. Nagler points to Pliny the Elder as Chapman's source: 'ad extremos fines Indiae ab oriente circa fontem Gangis Astomorum gentem sine ore […] halitu tantum viventem et odore quem naribus trahant; nullum illis cibum nullumque potum, radicum tantum florumque varios odores et silvestrium malorum, quae secum portant longiore itinere ne desit olfactus; graviore paulo odore haut difficulter exanimari' ('At the extreme boundary of India to the East, near the source of the Ganges, [Megasthenes] puts the Astomi tribe, that has no mouth […] and live only on the air they breathe and the scent they inhale through their nostrils; they have no food or drink except the different odours of the roots and flowers and wild apples, which they carry with them on their longer journeys so as not to lack a supply of scent; he says they can easily be killed by a rather stronger odour than usual': *Natural History*, VII. 2. 25). However, the direct source is again Curaeus, who quotes both Strabo and Pliny, and whose discussion of the nourishing power of odours Chapman transfers almost verbatim to his verse: 'Testantur enim Plinius et Strabo, in India ad fontem Gangis, esse populos, qui dicuntur ἄστωμοι, eosque, cum ore careant, solo odore florum, radicum et arborum vivere' ('Thus Plinius and Strabo attest that in India, by the source of the river Ganges, there are people that are called the Astomi, and these, as they do not have mouths, live on the smells of flowers, roots and trees only': Περὶ ἀισθήσεως, V. 6, p. 189, my translation). By abstracting the legend from its own context of exotic monstrosity, Chapman's Ovid considers himself among the pure lovers living on 'rarefied' air, and stresses that, like those odours feeding and killing the Astomi, Corinna's scents also have life-giving ('quick-'ning') and life-depriving ('consuming') properties.

Stanza 34

Ovid's indulgence in synaesthetic pleasures and forms of expression is reflected here in the conception of odours (smell) as invitations to a kiss (touch), thus anticipating later stages of the poem. The idea of love's sacrifice, already suggested by the conceit of Corinna's tunes as 'hecatombs of notes' (21. 2), is again present here. The fire-animating breath is a commonplace of Renaissance sonnets. Compare: 'For why my heart with sighs doth breathe such flame | That air and water both incensed be' (Giles Fletcher, *Licia*, XLI. 5-6, in *The English Works of Giles Fletcher the Elder*, ed. by Lloyd E. Berry (University of Wisconsin Press, 1964), p. 104). Chapman's attack on the sonneteers' exclusive focus on sensual love is clear in 'Cupid's bonfires burning in the eye, | Blown with the empty breath of vain desires' ('Coronet', 1. 3-4, and Commentary). The motif was popularized in the amatory emblem books of the early seventeenth century. See Vaenius, 'Crescit spirantibus auris / Fauor encreaseth loues force', where the wind feeding love's fire is represented as a Cupid figure: 'So the sweet breath of loue in kynd woords vttred foorth, | Encreaseth loue the more' (*Amorum emblemata*, pp. 146-47; see Visual Sources).

Stanzas 35-36

These two stanzas, which occupy centre position in Ovid's song of odours, have a distinctive quality for two main reasons. First, because sounds and odours, hearing and smell — the two senses discussed so far — are sung about jointly. Second, because the focus shifts from the physiology of perception to moral issues that even reveal a social component. In stanza 35, the opposition is established between the 'gentle and noble' minds that are predisposed to being 'quickened' (i.e. stimulated) by olfactory and auditory sensations, and those base individuals who remain insensitive to them, and are rather 'stirred up' by 'gain'. Both 'gentle' and 'noble' are adjectives that, despite the fact that their primary senses denote qualities of the mind, also connote social distinction. Moreover, 'hell-descending gain' brings money centre stage. I have re-punctuated with a dash after 'gain' (comma in the original) to emphasize that the ensuing four lines are in apposition to 'gain', which thus becomes 'the soul of fools', 'the art of peasants', a 'stain' to nobility, 'the bane of virtue' and 'the bliss of sin'. Chapman's attack on men (and more particularly poets) seeking economic interest is a recurrent theme in his writings. In *SN* and *OBS*, the motif is thematized through the contrast between those seeking 'the majesty and riches of the mind' ('Coronet', 1. 13) and those 'pierced with no affairs | But gain of riches' ('Noctem', 26-27). On the importance of this issue in Chapman's poetry, and for a particular analysis of this stanza, see Huntington, *Ambition*, p. 140. Stanza 36 expands on the same contrast between those possessing nobility of mind and those behaving like mere beasts. The narrative voice offers his own self-interested gloss on Ovid's speech: in it, as in the former stanzas, the idea of 'sounds' is understood amply to encompass 'all utterance of knowledge' and musical 'affections'. Attraction to perfumes as an essential difference between men and animals is found in Theophrastus: 'Caeterorum enim animalium nullum per se ut homo delectatur odore, sed pastus tantum gratia' ('Truly animals differ from men in that they do not find delight in agreeable odours, unless for nourishment or natural pleasure': *De odoribus*, IV, sig. A3^r, my translation).

Stanza 37

Using syllogistic reasoning to articulate a conceit of metaphysical proportions, this stanza returns to the physical quality of odours and the physiology of smell. Its reasoning is somehow circular, as it argues that love is both the cause and the effect of smell. In its being 'a fire', love stimulates the production of odours. Yet in living inside the bodily spirits, love is nourished and preserved by them. On heat and dryness as qualities of smell, the stanza relies on ideas found in Aristotle (see *De sensu*, v, 443b16–17; and *De anima*, II. 9, 422a6–7). The idea of the 'corpulent' nature of odours is, however, quite un-Aristotelian, and relies on atomist philosophy. Comparing sound and smell, Lucretius explains why the former can, and the latter cannot, pierce solid walls: 'deinde [odor] videre licet maioribus esse creatum | principiis quam vox' ('again it may be seen that smell is made of larger elements than voice': IV. 698–99). The idea of the nourishing qualities of smells and perfumes continues the argument of stanza 33. Curaeus devotes a whole chapter of his treatise to the discrepancies between Galen-inspired physicians and Aristotelians regarding the nourishing properties of smell. Chapman's Ovid adopts the affirmative answer to the question, which coincides with the Aristotelian position, and borrows his phrasing from Curaeus: 'Odores [...] qui vapores aerei sunt, spiritus reficiunt' ('Odours, which are airy vapours, feed the spirits': Περὶ αἰσθήσεως, v. 6, p. 189, my translation). The insertion of 'love' as a third element accompanying 'odours' and 'spirits' enables Chapman's syllogism out of Curaeus's affirmation. Curaeus's 'reficiunt' clearly inspires Chapman's 'refected'.

Stanzas 38–39

The fictional Ovid's second song concludes with two stanzas that attribute to odours supernatural powers that transcend the physiological and psychological focus of the former stanzas. Stanza 38 thus deals with immortality and metempsychosis. First, an inversion of the Ovidian myth of Phaeton allows the speaker to use the simile of the flaming fragments of the Sun's chariot to suggest how Corinna's perfumes infuse life, even immortality, into inanimate objects (38. 1–7). Chapman's source here is Ovid: '[Iupiter] intonat et dextra libratum fulmen ab aure | misit in aurigam pariterque animasque rotisque | expulit et saevis conpescuit ignibus ignes. | [...] Illic frena iacent, illic temone revulsus | axis, in hac radii fractarum parte rotarum | sparsaque sunt late laceri vestigia currus' ('He thundered, and, balancing in his right hand a bolt, flung it from beside the car at the charioteer and hurled him from the car and from life as well, and thus quenched the fire. [...] Here lie the reins, there the axle torn from the pole; in another place the spokes of the broken wheel, and fragments of the wrecked chariot are scattered far and wide': *Metamorphoses*, II. 311–17). The last two lines of the stanza imagine Corinna's perfumes as the 'lives' (i.e. souls) of 'sweetest ladies', once they have left their former dead bodies, courting 'novel frames' (i.e. Corinna's own body) to be admitted into them. Chapman's inspiration here is the Pythagorean philosophy of transmigration, as also recounted in Ovid (*Metamorphoses*, XV. 158–75).

Stanza 39 focuses on the magic/medicinal powers of Corinna's perfumes by bringing in the legend of the purgative qualities of the unicorn's horn. Compare this stanza to Conrad Lycosthenes, *Prodigiorum ac ostentorum chronicon* (1557): 'The Unicorne going to the river to drink, first styreth the water with his Horne, from the whiche corruption of vapour avoydeth, after whome followeth divers sorts of beasts to drinke' (*The Doome Warning All Men to the Iudgemente*, trans. by Stephen Batman (London: Henry Bynneman, 1581), sigs Dd2^v–Dd3^r). As Odell Shephard argues, this particular legend did not enter the Latin versions of the *Physiologus*, and its ancient sources are unclear. Shephard quotes Conti's *De Venatione* (1551) as a work that could have popularized the motif among Renaissance humanists. Given Conti's relevance to Chapman, this should not be disregarded as a direct source: 'Saepe veneniferae veniunt ad flumina gentes, | Inficiuntque vadum tabo, tetrisque venenis. | Attingit fluvium veniens haec bellua cornu, | Quo virus fugit, et fluctus purgantur aquarum. | Hinc quoque sylvicolis reliquis est purior unda' ('Often the poison-bearing people come to the river and taint the waters with their filth and foul poisons. As this beast arrives, with its horn it touches the water, from which the venom vanishes, and the water stream is purged. Hence the water is even purer to the other inhabitants of the forest': *De Venatione* (Venice, 1551), sigs K3^r–K3^v, my translation). See Shephard, *The Lore of the Unicorn* (Avenell Books, 1982), pp. 60–61. Here the simile serves Chapman's Ovid to shift the focus from smell to sight: while the stanza begins with the perfumes' power to purge the air from all infections, the simile's tenor concluding the stanza ends up attributing the purifying potential of the unicorn's horn to Corinna's 'eye'.

Stanza 40

Returning to narrative, this stanza elaborates on the progression from smell to sight by stressing the transitory nature of the former. This progression is expressed through the simile of the summer solstice ('summer's height'), in which the sun's domination shortens the nights. Thus, whereas Corinna's odours are the clouds that darken the short summer nights, Ovid's desire to see Corinna is compared to the summer sun, whose 'visual fires' dispel that darkness.

Stanza 41 and M8

Besides the presence of Cupid, who wounds Ovid with his arrow, two other myths make their presence felt here. The first is Jupiter's punishment of Prometheus after the latter stole the divine fire: a vulture would eternally devour his ever-renewing liver. The story made its way into Elizabethan love poetry of the 1590s and became a popular conceit: see, for example, Sidney's 'fiercer Gripe' that feeds on Astrophil's heart while 'Love' empties his 'quiver' on him (*Astrophil and Stella*, 14. 1–4, in *The Poems of Sir Philip Sidney*, ed. by William A. Ringler, Jr (Oxford University Press, 1962), p. 171). Chapman himself uses the motif in 'Coronet', 2 (see Commentary below). For further analysis and references, see Luis-Martínez ('Friendlesse Verse', pp. 577–78). The second is the myth of Actaeon and Diana, on whose centrality to Chapman's poems see 'Cynthiam', 220–42, 278–79, and 'Banquet', 11. 3, and the respective sections of the Commentary for meanings and sources. As M8 makes clear by noting 'the transformation of Actaeon *with the sight of Diana*' (emphasis added), the focus here is 'Diana's eye' and the 'danger' of her returning look to Actaeon's own. At least at a literal level, this focus stresses not only the punishment of the lover for venturing too far, but also the beloved's power over the lover through her haughtiness and scorn. On further interpretations of the Actaeon myth in Chapman's poems, see Moss, 'Second Master', 464 ff.; and Luis-Martínez, 'Whose Banquet', 36 ff. For an interpretation of the philosophical meanings of Chapman's use of the myth in the light of Giordano Bruno's *De gli eroici furori*, see Introduction, pp. 101–08.

Stanzas 42–43

Stanza 42 and the first seven lines of stanza 43 register Ovid's thoughts in direct speech, as made clear by the last two lines of 43 — and for that reason quotation marks have been added. Written in the form of a dramatic soliloquy, their theme is Ovid's pondering over the convenience of fulfilling his wish to see Corinna. In placing the desire to satisfy the sense of sight as the consequence of hearing and smelling, and as the likely cause of a further desire to taste and feel, Ovid acknowledges the centrality of sight in the context of the poem's hierarchy of the senses and explores the moral consequences of his yielding to sensual delight.

Stanzas 44–46 and M9

Two of Chapman's main compositional habits are exemplified by these lines. The first is the use of long similes, of which a number of other examples have been noted in the Commentary on 'Noctem' and 'Cynthiam'. In the present case, the simile extends over three stanzas that make up a single sentence — for which a number of changes in punctuation have been made (the main ones are recorded in the Textual Notes). The second is the quasi-formulaic manner of composition: the image of the agitated river that progresses to embrace the ocean but, daunted by the violence of its waves, hesitates in its forward course, is rewritten in several other places in Chapman's work. Bartlett (p. 469, nn. 56-62) notes all these later passages, in which similar images are used: in the plays, *The Conspiracy of Byron*, I. 1. 183-92, and *The Tragedy of Chabot*, v. 1. 16-19 (*Tragedies*, pp. 283, 678); in the poems, 'In Seianum', 33-44, *Eugenia*, 349-54, *An Epicede on Henry Prince of Wales*, 349-51 (Bartlett, pp. 359, 279-80, 261), and, more relevantly for the present purposes, 'De Guiana': 'But as a riuer from a mountaine running, | The further he extends, the greater growes, | And by his thriftie race strengthens his streame, | Euen to ioyne the battale with th'imperious sea | Disdaining his repulse, and in despight | Of his proud furie, mixeth with his maine, | Taking on him his titles and commandes: | So let thy soueraigne Empire be encreast [...]' (56-62, in Bartlett, p. 354). As the image is in all of these cases the vehicle of a simile, it is the nature of the tenor that determines the variations played upon this common theme: while in 'De Guiana' it supports the poem's imperialist theme, in the present case, and as M9 clarifies, it 'express[es] the manner of [Ovid's] mind's contention in the desire of [Corinna's] sight and fear of her displeasure'. 'Contention' and hesitation determine the movement 'backwards and forwards'. The specification of the Thames is another differentiating mark here, which seems analogous with the procedure that Chapman explains in Gloss 19 of 'Cynthiam', which comments on lines 326-49 (see Commentary), apropos the use of historical similes. The present simile relies on personification, and is particularly ingenious in its imagination of the river's flowing through the arch- or box-like openings of the bridge ('twists') as a woman combing her hair.

Stanzas 47-48

Ovid's new speech is a brief hymn to Juno, combining some of the rhetorical features contained in the classification provided by *Menander Rhetor*, I. 1, 333.1-27, pp. 6-7 (see Introduction, pp. 35-36). While the precatory (or supplicatory, εὐκτικός) component dominates, the speech also combines traits of the genealogical (γενεαλογικός), scientific (φυσικός) and mythical (μυθικός) hymn, thus putting the discussion of Juno's origin and its scientific/allegorical explanations at the service of a more pragmatic prayer. As Schoell noted, and later editors after him, the mythographic source of stanza 47 is Conti's 'scientific' explanation of Juno's nature and birth: 'Et quoniam aer non solum est per quem spiramus, per quem vivimus, per quem videmus, sed etiam qui nobis occultam vim naturalem in sanguinem praebeat, ut vel formidemus pericula, vel ea fortiter subeamus; idcirco Iunonem Timoris et Audentiae potestatem habere crediderunt antiqui, ut Orpheus testatur in Argonauticis.

[...] Fertur in Samo insula nata et educata fuisse, quoniam saluberimus ibi est aer' ('And because we need air not only to live, breathe, and see, but also from that hidden strength instilled in our blood that provokes fear of danger or the ability to endure it bravely, the ancients also said that Juno could control fear and courage. See Orpheus's *Argonautica* [774]. [...] They say that Juno was born and raised on the island of Samos, because it has such a pure air': 'De Iunone', II. 4, p. 140; Mulryan, p. 118).

Yet Chapman's main interest in Conti lies in the obscure alchemical explanation of the myths about Juno that close the latter's chapter, and which I quote extensively here: 'Chemici artifices praeterea conati sunt nonnullas fabularum Iunonis partes ad suos ignes et ad sua vascula retrahere. Dicitur Iuno (inquiunt) Saturni et Opis filia Iovisque soror et coniux, et ante Iovem nata eodem partu, Reginaque esse Deorum et divitiarum Dea, partubus et matrimoniis praefecta: quae nihil est aliud quam aqua Mercurii, quae Iuno nominatur. Saturni ea de causa est filia, quod ab eo et eius terra distillat ac manat. Haec terra dat opes, sive aurum chemicum, quod una distillet Iuno et Iupiter sive aqua Mercurii, et sal in ima parte vasculi vitrei ac in faece relictus. Cum vero prius effluat aqua Mercurii e vasculo, nascitur Iuno ante Iovem. Praeest eadem partubus, quod cum manat, Phoebum chemicum educit in lucem, unde Lucina etiam vocata est. Praefecta connubiis putatur eadem, quoniam media est coniungendis sulphureis humoribus Venere ac Marte scilicet: quae quod antequam manet cum Iove coniungatur, et ambo gignant solem chemicum, Iovis uxor vocata fuit. Regina deorum dicta est, quoniam illa regit, solvit, coniungit, separat ac reprimit metalla, quae variis Deorum nominibus apellantur' ('The chemical craftsmen also tried to relate some parts of these stories about Juno to their fires and their vessels. In their vision of the myth, they say that Juno is called the child of Saturn and Ops, and both the sister and the wife of Jupiter. She is born before Jupiter, but still from the same birth. When they say that she is the queen of the gods and the goddess of riches, as well as the patron of births and marriages, their meaning is simply that she is identified with [m]ercury's water, which is called Juno. She is the daughter of Saturn, because she trickles and trips down from Saturn and his Earth. That same earth provides us with riches, or chemical gold, which is derived from the simultaneous distillation of Juno and Jupiter (or mercury's water), and the salt that remains in the dregs and in the bottom of the glass receptacle. And since mercury's water is the first to flow from the receptacle, Juno is born before Jupiter. || This same goddess is in charge of births, because when she is poured out as a liquid, she forms a chemical Phoebus, and that's the reason she is also known as Lucina. She was supposed to be in charge of marriages, since she lives right in the midst of that combination of sulphurous liquids, Venus and Mars. And because she is joined with Jupiter before she flows, and because when combined with Jupiter she begets the chemical sun, she was supposed to be Jupiter's wife. Her title was Queen of the Gods, because she controls, dissolves, joins, separates, and confines metals, which take the name of the different gods': pp. 142-43; Mulryan, pp. 120-21, translation slightly modified).

Conti omits his sources here, and his explanation of the meaning of Juno in terms of alchemical processes is obscure. Juno stands for 'aqua Mercurii', or 'mercurial water' (I have not found an earlier source for this identification), which, according to Paracelsus, was the 'first beginning' of all matter, as seen when any metal is dissolved by fire (*De mineralibus*, in *The Hermetic and Alchemical Writings of Paracelsus*, ed. by Arthur Edward Waite, 2 vols (James Elliott, 1894), I, p. 90). The mercurial water is the fire of life, which provides the nourishing liquid (or *menstruum*) for the so-called alchemical marriage (*chemica coniunctio*) of Sol and Luna (here replaced by Mars and Venus), standing for the male and female principles, sophic sulphur and sophic mercury, from which pure gold and the philosopher's stone are engendered. 'Aqua Mercurii', as, here, Juno has a crucial mediating power ('media est coniungendis sulphureis humoribus Venere ac Marte') in this crucial alchemical process of union (see Abraham, *A Dictionary*: entries for *menstruum, mercurial waters*, and *Mercurius*, pp. 124-28; also, entry for *chemical wedding*, pp. 35-39). The anonymous Renaissance treatise *Rosarium Philosophorum* (Frankfurt: Cyriacus Jacob, 1550), sig. F3^v, contains an engraving that illustrates the *chemica coniunctio* as sexual intercourse ('Coniunctio sive Coitus') between the Sun and the Moon, which engenders the stone (see Visual Sources). And the English alchemist Edward Kelley argues, in his *De lapide philosophorum* (1676), that it is 'the mediation of Mercury' that carries out the division and later union of the elements ('Two Excellent Treatises on the Philosopher's Stone', in *The Alchemical Writings of Edward Kelly* (James Eliott, 1893), p. 28).

Returning to Chapman's integration of alchemy within the hymnic structure of the two stanzas, Ovid's prayer can be summarized thus: as eldest daughter of Saturn, Juno is the mercurial water or watery *menstruum* that acts as the 'mean' (Conti's 'media') that 'mix[es]' ('coniungendis') the male and female principle, yet ultimately debases the philosophical marriage into mere sexual intercourse ('Cyprian sports'); thus, Juno is asked to banish Ovid's 'fear' by presenting Corinna before his sight, but also to infuse in him 'courage' (i.e. audacity) in order to defend himself from Love's assaults once this god has wounded him with his sight, particularly by teaching him not to be too servile in trying to please his lady, as it is easier to obtain a lady's favour ('grace') than the lady's explicit promise that such favour will be granted. Thus, stanza 48 changes the focus from obscure alchemical wisdom to pragmatic Ovidian advice. Waddington has analysed the allegory of the alchemical wedding in the poem, although he does not include this stanza. For Waddington, Chapman's treatment of this topic is ironic, and contributes to his disparagement of Ovidianism (*The Mind's Empire*, pp. 137-40) — a view that is not endorsed here.

Visus

Occupying over thirty stanzas (49–86), about twice the length of the space allotted to the other senses, sight is the poem's centre of gravity, signalling both the highest point in Ovid's incomplete voyage to intellectual apprehension of beauty, but also the turning point towards his enjoyment of the so-called 'baser' senses. It also marks the beginning of his interaction with Corinna in the form of courteous conversation. These stanzas also offer the most varied repertory of Chapman's 'philosophical conceits', which, culled from various theories of sensual perception and intellectual apprehension, are not always internally coherent.

Stanzas 49–50 and M10

These two stanzas offer an abstract of the more elaborate section on sight: vision leads to the extraction of Corinna's image as the quintessence of beauty; its effects on Ovid involve burning and weakening of his physical energies, as well as psychological servitude and imprisonment. The Platonic theory of vision enjoyed high favour among the love poets: light is issued from our eyes as a result of the compression of the fire within us, and coalesces with the light that emanates from objects, reflecting the image back in the eye (Plato, *Timaeus*, ed. by R. D. Archer-Hind (Macmillan, 1888), 45B–D, pp. 154–58). The similes supporting each stanza explain these emanations of fire in terms of physical and astronomical phenomena: the upward and downward movements of sun rays and falling stars. A passage in Lucretius (*De rerum natura*, II. 203–09), comparing the gravitation of atoms to the rise and fall of flames and stars, seems of relevance as a possible source of inspiration for these similes: 'sic igitur debent flammae quoque posse per auras | aeris expressae sursum succedere, quamquam | pondera, quantum in sest, deorsum deducere pungent, | nocturnasque faces caeli sublime volantis | nonne vides longos flammarum ducere tractus | in quascumque dedit partis natura meatum? | non cadere in terram stellas et sidera cernis?' ('In this way therefore flames also must be able to rise up, squeezed out upwards through the breezes of the air, although as far as lies in them their weights fight to draw them down; and do you not see how the nightly torches of the sky fly aloft and draw their long trails of flame in whatever direction nature has given them a way? How stars and luminaries fall to the earth?'). The flaming ascent of the sunbeams (49. 4–6) finds an analogue here.

However, Chapman's acknowledged sources, particularly for the second simile (50. 4–8), may point elsewhere: Homer's comparison of Pallas's descent among the Trojans with a falling star in *Iliad*, IV. 75–79. In Chapman's 1611 translation: 'And as Jove, brandishing a starre (which men a Comet call), | Hurls out his curled haire abrode, that from his brand exhale | A thousand sparkes [...] | So Pallas fell twixt both the Camps and sodanily was lost' (IV. 85–89). Chapman's marginal note reads '*Pallas fals from heaven like a Comet*'. In Virgil's *Aeneid*, Acestes' fiery arrow is compared to 'shooting stars, unloosed from heaven', which 'speed across the sky, their tresses streaming in their wake' ('caelo ceu saepe refixa | transcurrunt crinemque *volantia sidera ducunt*': v. 527–28). Neither in these texts nor in the translations of Homer that Chapman used (Valla, Spondanus) does the phrase mentioned in the gloss, 'stellas cadentes', appear. However, as Hudston has noted (p. 408), it is found in Servius's commentary on this passage of Virgil's: '*qui tractus imitatur stellas cadentes*' ('whose path imitates the falling stars', *Commentarii in Virgilium Serviani*, ed. by H. Albertus Lion, 2 vols (Vandenhoeck & Ruprecht, 1826), I, p. 337). As Servius himself notes, his gloss is actually a paraphrase of the above-quoted passage from Lucretius, which may support the case for Chapman's possible Lucretian inspiration. Bartlett (p. 432) also stresses Chapman's fascination with the image of falling stars and notes a number of analogous passages in his work. Of particular relevance here, see: 'And how (like men | Raisd to high Places) Exhalations fall | That would be thought Starres' (*Euthymiae Raptus*, 1008–10, in Bartlett, p. 195); 'An exhalation that would be a Starre' (*The Conspiracy of Byron*, IV. 2. 293, in *Tragedies*, p. 371); 'A blacke Starre in the Skies, to which the Sunne | Giues yet no light' (*Revenge of Bussy D'Ambois*, v. 4. 57–58, in *Tragedies*, p. 504). See also *Eugenia*, 125–26 (Bartlett, pp. 274–75); and *The Conspiracy of Byron*, Prologue, 12–15 (*Tragedies*, p. 278).

Another important component in these stanzas is Corinna's image as an idea extracted in the process of vision: the notion is ultimately Platonic, although the very concept of 'extraction' again draws on alchemy. Compare a slightly later analogue: 'Extractio est digestio e corporea concretione partes subtiliores, ac puriores ab affuso aliquo menstruo apprehensas, relictis faecibus dissolvens. [...] Extractio est segregatio essentiae, quae e corpore suo extrahitur. Fit hic una et distractio, et potissumum ei famulatur resolutio commistorum, nonnunquam etiam calcinatio, coctio, et similes' ('Extraction is digestion, a process subsequent to the separation of the recrement, dissolving, by corporeal concretion, the subtler and purer parts of a given substance. [...] Extraction is the Separation of the Essential Part from its body. It is really a similar operation to the disintegration of composite substances, and has affinity with calcination, melting, etc.': Martin Ruland, *Lexicon Alchemiae* (Frankfurt: Zacharias Palthenus, 1612), pp. 202–03; translation: *A Lexicon of Alchemy*, trans. by Arthur E. Waite (John M. Watkins, 1893)). As a result of the process of vision explained here, Corinna's extracted essence is also the result of a process of purification by fire. However, the invigorating flame of Corinna's sight is fleeting, soon giving way to Ovid's weakening strengths and servitude. The idea of the 'Fair of Beauty', or *Wunderkammer*, exhibiting many 'riches in a little room' collected from different parts of the world, can be seen in a slightly later title page, that of Ferrante Imperato's *Dell' Historia Naturale* (Naples, 1599). According to Bartlett (p. 432, 49. 9, note), Chapman borrowed the phrase from Marlowe's 'Infinite riches in a little room' (*The Jew of Malta*, I. 1. 37, in Christopher

Marlowe, *Doctor Faustus and Other Plays*, ed. by David Bevington and Eric Rasmussen (Oxford University Press, 1995), p. 254).

Stanzas 51–55

As recognized later on in 56. 1, these stanzas constitute a unit in being a 'digression'. Accordingly, the style shifts from narrative to aphoristic, and the intention is didactic. The narrative voice offers a perspective on Ovid's ecstatic praise of Corinna, the aim of which is complementary rather than counterbalancing. The narrator warns against the deceits of sensual beauty, and encourages the Neoplatonic pursuit of love as an alternative to material riches. The Neoplatonic equation of love and beauty is perceived as a provider of contentment, understood as a constant search for perfection that is never fully achieved; thus, sensual love proves legitimate as long as its inherent imperfection and incompletion is recognized. This recognition differentiates the poetic voice from Ovid's, encouraging a view of their perspectives as complementary. Chapman's aphoristic verse reflects the 'philosophical' aspirations of his poetry; however, his elliptical syntax and intricate conceits do not help to clarify its meaning. Full paraphrases are provided in footnotes.

51] This stanza sets the contrast between a false kind of beauty, described as a charm that bewitches men and condemns them to ruin, and a true kind, which, in accordance with Ficino's Neoplatonic philosophy, is the object of love: 'Amor tanquam eius finem fruitionem respicit pulchritudinis' ('Love regards at its end the enjoyment of beauty': *Commentary on Plato's Symposium*, I. 4, pp. 41, 130). Chapman's idea of 'good self-love', which materializes this pursuit of true beauty, also adapts the Ficinian principle of *mutuus amor* ('mutual love'), based on the necessary reciprocity in affections ('as rich in faith'): 'Amorem procreat similitudo. [...] Eadem ergo similitude, quae me ut te amem compellit, te quoque amare me cogit. [...] Accedit quod amans amati figuram suo sculpit in animo. Fit itaque amantis animus speculum, in quo amantis relucet imago. Idirco amatus cum in amante se recognoscat, amare illum compellitur' ('Likeness generates love. [...] The same similarity which compels me to love you, forces you to love me. [...] It happens that a lover imprints a likeness of the loved one upon his soul, and so the soul of the lover becomes a mirror in which is reflected the image of the loved one. Thereupon, when the loved one recognizes himself in the lover, he is forced to love him': II. 8, pp. 51, 141; Jayne's translation altered). Hudston (pp. 408–09, 51. 7–9, notes) points to Chapman's indebtedness to another passage on reflexive love in Ficino (*Commentary on Plato's Symposium*, IV. 6, pp. 82, 188), the pertinence of which seems more doubtful.

52] Ficinian Neoplatonism is also the basis of this stanza. First, the perception of beauty is confined to the senses of sight and hearing, and to the mind, or soul, which sets a clear distance between the poetic voice and Ovid's. Thus, beauty is 'the fruit of sight' (52.1), the 'feast of souls' (52.3) and 'music entranced' (52.6). Ficino is categorical in this respect: 'Pulchritudo vero gratia quaedam est, quae ut plurimum in concinnitate plurium maxime nascitur. [...] Triplex igitur pulchritudo, animorum, corporum atque vocum. Animorum mente cognoscitur, corporum oculis, vocum auribus solis percipitur. [...] Odores, sapores, calorem, frigus, mollitiem et duritiem, horumque similia sensus isti percipient. Istorum nullum humana pulchritudo est, cum formae simplices sint; humana autem corporis pulchritudo membrorum requirat diversorum concordiam. Amor tanquam eius finem fruitionem respicit pulchritudinis; ista ad mentem, visum, auditum pertinent solum. Amor ergo in tribus eis terminatur. Appetitio vero, quae reliquos sequitur sensus, non amor sed libido rabiesque vocatur' ('Beauty is, in fact, a certain grace which is found chiefly and predominantly in the harmony of several elements. [...] There is therefore this triple beauty: of the soul, of the body, and of sound. That of the soul is perceived by the mind; that of the body, by the eyes; and that of sound, by the ear alone. [...] Odors, favors, heat, cold, softness, hardness, and like qualities are the objects of these senses. None of these is human beauty, since these qualities are simple, and human beauty of the body requires a harmony of various parts. Love regards as its end the enjoyment of beauty; beauty pertains only to the mind, sight, and hearing. Love, therefore, is limited to these three, but desire which rises from the other senses is called, not love, but lust or madness': I. 4, pp. 40–41, 130; Jayne's translation altered). Chapman's 'fruit' and 'feast' are both reminiscent of Ficino's 'fruitio', i.e. enjoyment; 'glory' suggests 'gratia'; and the definition of beauty as 'sum and court of all proportion' clearly points to beauty as a harmonious epitome of different qualities.

53] Q*OB*'s intricate syntax has encouraged editors to emend and repunctuate this stanza. The present edition does not follow Hudston's emendation of 'in' to 'is' in the first line, and assumes an omitted 'it' as subject, as well as an omitted 'that' which introduces the nominal clause starting line 4. Like Braden, I have changed the full-stop at the end of 51. 4 for a comma, assuming (in my reading) that 'love' and 'beauty' are appositions that clarify the subject of the clause, 'This all-things-nothing'. I have also hyphenated 'beauty-enchasing', and 'love-gracing' — an option found in no other edition. Hyphenation is common in Chapman's writing, and here it has the advantage of making new compound epithets for 'love' and 'beauty', thus stressing the Neoplatonic equation and complementariness of these notions (see Commentary: 'Banquet', 52). 'To perfect riches' is understood as a prepositional complement to the nominal clause 'a sounder duty', implying a final sense — i.e. for the obtaining of perfect riches. I have kept Q*OB*'s capital 'C' of 'Content', as it foregrounds the shape of the letter that is the vehicle of the conceit in the next stanza, where anadiplosis and polyptoton combine in the duplication of 'Content' as 'Contentment'. As far as the stanza's meaning is concerned, the Neoplatonic adherence to the search for beauty becomes a new occasion for Chapman's critique of the human obsession with the pursuit of material benefit.

54] The poetic emblem that imagines the 'C' in 'Contentment' as an incomplete circle has a long tradition in the sixteenth century and after. In Ben Jonson's *The Masque of Beauty* (1608), '*Perfectio*' is represented as a woman 'in a vesture of pure gold. [...] In her hand a compass of gold, drawing a circle' (ed. by David Lindley: *The Cambridge Edition Online*, 178-79). Jonson's source is Cesare Ripa, *Iconologia*, whose first edition of 1593 already depicts Perfection 'vestita d'oro' and 'disegnando co'l Compasso' (Roma: Giovanni Gigliotti, 1593, p. 203). In the *Informations to William Drummond* (1619), Jonson describes John Heywood's impresa as 'a compass with one foot in centre, the other broken; the word, *deest quod duceret orbem*' ('that which draws the circle is missing': ed. by Ian Donaldson: *The Cambridge Edition Online*, 457-58). Of more relevance here is a well-known printer's device, used by Christopher Plantin (1520-89), which represents a compass drawing an incomplete circle, C-shaped, with the motto '*Labore et Constantia*' (see Visual Sources). Both virtues are pertinent: the lovers' 'constant sympathies' lead them to 'true Content' in stanza 53. Labour, here expressed as 'force and art', achieves the union of love and beauty. Their conjunction of constancy and labour also stresses Chapman's ideal of study as an essential aspect of his poetics. This symbolic reading of 'Contentment' unites love and art as enterprises in the search for a perfect beauty that is comprehended in the mind but is always in the process of completion: 'true Content' is therefore the acceptance of imperfection as a condition of the search for perfection. As in the previous stanza, editorial repunctuation of the endings of 54. 3 (QoB's comma is changed for a semicolon) and 54. 4 (more drastically, QoB's full-stop is suppressed) have been undertaken. 'And to conduce [...] with wisdom' (54. 3-5) thus becomes a full, independent sentence.

55] The digression concludes with a simile in which the Neoplatonic idea of love as a pursuit of the beauty of the soul is contrasted with baser forms of sensual love. The latter, Chapman argues, constitute the 'cold fire' that is the object of worship of the love poets, who fail to realize that true love deserves a higher praise: sensual love is like colour, which is acknowledged to be the proper object of sight, even if it cannot be accurately perceived without light, on which it is imprinted, and which here stands for true love. Aristotle's theory of visual perception in *De anima* (II. 4, 418a26-419b2, pp. 76-77) designates colour as the cause of the visible, which is perceived in light — i.e. the transparent medium of sight. Chapman seems to contradict this idea in order to embrace a Neoplatonic notion of perception, which can be traced to Plotinus: 'Consider the act of ocular vision: There are two elements here; the form perceptible to the sense and there is the medium by which the eye sees that form. This medium is itself perceptible to the eye, distinct from the form to be seen, but the cause of the seeing; it is perceived at the one stroke in that form and on it and hence it is not distinguished from it, the eye being held entirely by the illuminated object' (*The Enneads*, trans. by Stephen MacKenna (Faber, 1930), v. 5. 7, pp. 408–09). Thus, it is 'th' imperfection of a human sight' that attracts the eye to the shape ('feeble colour') and renders the 'virtuous light' indistinguishable.

Plotinus's remarks are the source of Ficino's theory of the incorporeality of beauty, which appears to be behind Chapman's simile: 'Ubique incorpoream esse hanc pulchritudinem non ambigimus. In angelo enim et in animo eam corpus aliquod non esse nemini dubium. In corporibus etiam eam esse incorporalem [...] ex eo potissimum intelligimus, quod oculos nil aliud, nisi solis aspicit lumen. Figurae namque et colores corporum numquam nisi lumine illustrata perspiciuntur, neque ipsa cum materia sua ad oculos veniunt. Necessarium tamen esse videtur ea in oculis esse, ut ab oculis videantur. Unum itaque solis lumen corporum omnium ab eo illustratorum coloribus figurisque depictum esse oculis offert. [...] Quare totus hic mundi qui conspicitur ordo, non eo modo quo in materia corporum sed quo in luce oculis infusa est cernitur' ('We do not doubt that this beauty is everywhere incorporeal, for it is incorporeal in the Angelic Mind and in the Soul. That it is also incorporeal in bodies we [...] most clearly understand from this: that the eye sees nothing but the light of the sun, for the shapes and colors of bodies are never seen unless illuminated with light, nor do they come to the eyes with their own matter itself. Therefore, one light of the sun, imprinted with the colors and shapes of everything illuminated by it, presents itself to the eyes. [...] Wherefore, this whole order of the visible world is presented to view, not in the way in which it is infused in the matter of bodies, but in the way in which it is infused in the light streaming into the eyes': *Commentary on Plato's Symposium*, v. 4, pp. 69, 171; Jayne's translation altered). In line with these thoughts, the digression ends with an overt defence of the immateriality and incorporeality of love and beauty, which is meant as a correction of the views expressed in Ovid's previous speeches.

Stanzas 56–57 and M11

The focus in these two stanzas shifts from 'digression' back to 'Ovid's prospect', or vision, of Corinna as an 'extraction of all fairest dames' in stanza 49. The vision itself transforms Corinna into a miraculous flaming shape engraved at the centre of the arbour's surface, a recumbent diamond statue wrapped in flesh and illumined by silver light. The perspicuity of the vision to which Chapman's verse aspires is once again confounded by syntactic obscurity and muddled punctuation, particularly affecting lines 4 and 5, which in Qob read: 'Blaz'd with a fire wrought in a Ladyes forme: | Where siluer past the least: and Natures vant'. Braden replaces the first colon with a comma and suppresses the second. This option makes 'silver' and 'nature's vant' (i.e. vaunt) the subject of 'Did [...] perform' in the next line. The problem is still 'past the least', which hardly makes sense, regardless of whether 'past' is taken as a form of the verb (Shepherd modernizes to 'pass'd', and marks the subsequent strong pause a semicolon), or as a preposition, meaning 'exceeding', 'surpassing'. Loughlin and others consider the possibility of reading 'vant' as 'the receptacle within which alchemists performed the transformation of base metal in the stage known as the "albedo"' (*Broadview Anthology*, p. 1174, n. 2), suggestively relating this passage to other moments in the poem in which alchemy is relevant. *OED* records a nominal sense of *least* as 'minimal unit', or 'atom' (n. 3) — a semantic field that is not alien to the poem. A compositor's error in reading 'f' as 's' suggests 'leafe', 'leafs' or 'leafes' ('leaf' or 'leaves' in modern spelling) as another solution, and this is the conjecture adopted here. This edition opts for 'passed the leaf', followed by a comma, in awareness of the provisional nature of this reading. Thus, the object of Ovid's vision is Corinna's flaming shape projected at the centre of the arbour's surface, the effect of a silver light that has pierced the vegetation ('passed the leaf'): Corinna appears as a statue of diamond wrapped in flesh and lying still as the result of a miracle performed by nature's audacious act ('vant' being a historical spelling of *vaunt*).

The simile closing stanza 56 relies on the personification of the evening as Vesper, a name for Hesperus (gendered male), or the evening star. The stillness of the aspen leaf, here fused with the evening's 'hair', witnesses to the total absence of wind and the absolute motionlessness of the vision (see 48. 2 and note). Starting with the repetition of 'She lay', stanza 57 again shifts the focus from Ovid's fanciful vision to the actuality of Corinna's 'rest' and 'felicity', compared, as Chapman's marginal gloss makes clear (M11), to the souls that Aeneas sees after planting the golden bough and entering the Elysian Fields. Corinna's bower thus admits comparison with the 'land of joy, the green plesaunces and happy seats of the blissful groves' ('locos laetos et amoena virecta | Fortunatum Nemorum sedesque beatas'), and Corinna herself with the 'happy souls' ('felices animae') that dwell within it (*Aeneid*, vi. 638–39, 667). I have accepted Braden's emendation of Qob's 'peace' for 'place' in M11.

Line 57. 5 shifts the focus back to Ovid: the object of his inspiration, his 'Muse', is again his vision, shining in the summer solstice at the highest point of the Tropic of Cancer, which causes his ascent to heaven as the effect of burning, as well as a new sublime effusion of inspired verse that extends to the ensuing stanzas. Ovid's poetic mastery is the subject of the lyric voice's commentary in the closing couplet: as one obliged by his poetic debt to the master (i.e. 'his submitted debtor'), yet with no experience in matters of love ('that never mistress had'), the lyric voice remarks that his own poetry may not be skilful enough to convey the sublimity of Ovid's inspired, 'quick verse'. For Bartlett (p. 432, 57. 9, note), the commentary 'sounds autobiographical', although she also points to *Amores* as a source, more specifically to: 'nec mihi materia est numeris levioribus apta, | aut puer aut longas compta puella comas' (1. 1. 19–20). In Marlowe's translation: 'I have no mistresse, nor no favorit, | Being fittest matter for a wanton wit' (*All Ovids Elegies*, 1. 1. 23–24).

Stanzas 58–62, and M12, M13

The first five stanzas of Ovid's new song apropos the sight of Corinna constitute a descriptive unit. The analogy of Corinna's reclining naked body with the Judeo-Christian Garden of Eden allows for anatomical description in chorographic terms. On a similar conjunction of chorography and portrait in the work of fellow poet Michael Drayton, see María Vera-Reyes, 'Michael Drayton's Topographies: *Ideas Mirrour* (1594) and *Poly-Olbion* (1612–1622)', *English Studies*, 102.8 (2021), pp. 1002–23, doi:10.1080/0013838X.2021.1982218. Chapman's geographical referents are those in Genesis 2. 8–14. More specifically, his mapping of Corinna's body seems directly inspired by an engraving in the *Geneva Bible* entitled 'The Situacion of the Garden of Eden'. The explanatory caption of this map, which glosses the passage in Genesis, is illustrative of Chapman's listing of the four rivers of Eden and of his poetic design: 'Because mencion is made in the tenth verse of this seconde chapter of the river that watered the garden, we muste note that Euphrates and Tygris called in Ebrewe, Perath and Hiddekel, were called but one river where they joyned together, els they had foure heades: that is, two at their springs & two where they fel into the Persian Sea. In this countrey and moste plentiful land Adam dwelt, and this was called Paradise, that is, a garden of pleasure, because of the frutefulnes and abundance therof. And whereas it is said that Pishon compasseth the land of Havilah, it is meant of Tygris, which in some place, as it passed by divers places, was called by sundry names. [...] Likewise Euphrates towarde the countrey of Cush or Ethiopia, or Arabia was called Gihon. So that Tygris and Euphrates (which were but two rivers and some time when they ioyned together, were called after one name) were according to divers places called by these foure names, so that they might seme to have bene foure divers rivers' (*The Bible and Holy Scriptures*, fol. 2^r). Thus, Gihon and Tigris are the left arm and leg, being the northern and southern branches of the eastern river, while Pishon and Euphrates are the right arm and leg, as they are the northern and southern branches of the western river (if seen from the onlooker's perspective). These four converge into one river upon Corinna's body, more specifically in the division of her breasts, as the marginal gloss to stanza 58 (M12) makes clear. Thus, Gihon and Pishon are 'the highest two', the arms, which 'crown' Corinna's body upon her 'Pelopian shoulders'. The epithet stresses the white colour of Corinna's skin, as Pelops had an ivory prosthesis for his missing shoulder. The effect is, however, grotesque, if the myth of Pelops's dismemberment is borne in mind: according to Pindar (*Odes*, ed. and trans. by Sir John Sandys (William Heinemann, 1915), I. 25–27, pp. 6–7), Ovid (*Metamorphoses*, VI. 404–11), and others, Tantalus killed his son Pelops, quartered his body and served him at a banquet to the gods, who realized Tantalus's unnatural act and refused to eat the body. Only Demeter/Ceres, still in grief for the loss of Persephone/Proserpine, was negligent and ate Pelops's shoulder. The rest of the body was reconstituted and revived by Hermes, and an ivory shoulder replaced the missing one (Smith, *Dictionary*, III, p. 181).

The other two rivers, Tigris and Euphrates proper, 'glide' from her breasts and 'drown' her body 'with a deluge of delights' (in reference to the genitalia), then becoming her legs. Similarities between these descriptions and those in 'Zodiac' concerning the breasts (21–22), genitals (25–26) and thighs (27) are noticeable. Detailed description of the upper extremities/rivers extends from 59. 7 to 60. 4. The main focus in these lines is the branching of the two arms into ten fingers. Two themes converge here: their beauty, unlimited unlike their length, and their 'duty', or, as M13 specifies, their 'office'. Here both the lines (60. 1–4) and the gloss are more obscuring than clarifying, as the two actions alluded to ('attiring', or dressing, the body and the 'playing upon an instrument') are more metaphorical than actual: the fingers dress the body in their contact with it rather than in their actual attiring it with clothes, as Corinna is naked; despite her having played upon a lute earlier in the poem, the instrument is now the body itself, 'that book of life', as it is 'bounded' with each 'section', or finger. And yet, Ovid's imagination evokes the fingers actually dressing Corinna's body (the 'painted bowers' and 'flowers' seem to refer to clothes and ornaments) and producing musical 'sounds' with their 'inflection' or bending.

While the opening 'These' of stanza 60 clearly refers to the arms, or northern rivers, the later 'In these' (60. 5) is not an extension of the former argument, but rather an indicator that the focus shifts to the legs, or southern rivers, description of which occupies the stanza's remaining lines. Presented in the previous stanza as leading to 'a deluge of delights' (59. 6), these enticing rivers discourage the Muses from swimming in them. If the Muses are understood here metonymically as inspired lines of poetry, the meaning is the poet's reluctance to speak overtly about love's consummation. This is in line with the end of the poem: 'Ovid well knew there was much more intended, | With whose omission none must be offended' (117. 8–9), or with the lover's arrival at 'Capricorn', or female pudenda, which he 'can scarce express with chastity' ('Zodiac', 25. 3). In accordance with this, the praise of these rivers is restrained here to the sinful pleasures ('blest infection') that they offer to the sense of sight (the 'forms' and 'colour' in 60. 8).

Starting with 'Thus', stanzas 61 and 62 are conceived of as a two-part conclusion, the first focusing on the nature of the object of sensual enjoyment, Corinna, and the second on Ovid's subjective relation to that object. Stanza

61 elaborates on Corinna as object in two separate conceits. The first (61. 1–4) tests the former simile of Corinna as Paradise, or the Elysian Fields: as she is a walking, moving human being, she cannot be like the Garden of Eden, which, as explained in former stanzas, has a fixed geography. Conti's discussion of the widely debated location of the Elysian Fields presupposes that they were 'near a fixed sphere' ('circa aplanes sphaeram'): 'De campis Elysiis', III. 19, p. 274; Mulryan, p. 226). Chapman's 'prefixèd' is thus an almost literal translation of Conti's borrowing, 'aplanes', from Greek ἀπλανής — i.e. fixed, not erring. Yet, like Elysium, Corinna cannot depart from her fixed Elysian sphere, as all 'Elysian grace' resides in her. Chapman's lines seem to wink at Mephistophilis's famous description of hell in *Doctor Faustus* (A-Text): 'Hell hath no limits, nor is circumscribed | In one self place, for where we are is hell, | And where hell is, there must we ever be' (II. 1. 121–23, in *Doctor Faustus and Other Plays*, p. 154). The second conceit (61. 5–9) is less clear in its meaning: obtaining Corinna's 'favour' is compared to a race in the ancient Olympic Games, which is the meaning of 'Olympiad' here — even if Chapman elsewhere used the term in its proper sense of the long period of time between two Olympic events: 'Now was bright Hero weary of the day, | Thought an Olympiad in Leanders stay' (*Hero and Leander*, v. 2, in Bartlett, p. 152). The problem is to decide whether the consideration of Corinna as a piece of land still holds in these lines: her body would then be the arena on which the race is run, and the 'favour' and 'sweets' that she gives to winners would be sexual rewards that men 'gather'. Ovid imagines Corinna as simultaneously chaste and as a source of sexual pleasure.

Stanza 62 finally places Elysium in relation to Ovid's own enjoyment: the attainment of Elysium, either by moving up to its sphere ('aspire') or attracting that sphere to him, is depicted by means of the repetition (the rhetorical figure of *ploce*) of the verbs 'gather' and 'give': 'the flower of women' posits Corinna ambiguously as an instance of virtuous womanhood and as object of sexual pleasure. Accordingly, two versions of Elysium, or Paradise, each occupying three lines of verse, present themselves to Ovid in the form of an unsolved dilemma: on one hand (62. 4–6), the 'joy' of Elysium is attained with 'virtue', 'labours of the soul' and 'continence' — a version of the implicit motto '*Labore et Constantia*' presiding over the compass emblem of 'true Content' in stanzas 57 and 58; on the other, Corinna is a paradise that invites 'use' — see, as an analogue: 'Mine be thy love, and thy love's use their treasure' (Shakespeare, *Sonnets*, 20. 14, p. 151).

Stanzas 63–68

The closing stanzas of Ovid's speech on sight attempt to solve, in Neoplatonic terms, the dilemma expressed in the final sentence of the previous note. Thus, the sensual enjoyment of the beloved's beauty is legitimate as long as it is confined to the sense of sight. The theory that the mind's contemplation of beauty necessitates first the excitation of the senses is consistent with orthodox versions of Neoplatonic philosophy only in terms of sight and hearing, and always privileging the former over the latter (see Ficino, *Commentary on Plato's Symposium*, I. 4, pp. 40-41, quoted above in Commentary: 'Banquet', 52). In accordance with this principle, Ovid conceives of his making of Corinna the object of his sight as the necessary step to considering her an image of eternal Beauty. The last two lines of stanza 63 must be understood emblematically (and thus the decision to preserve the capital initial of 'Time' in 63. 8). In line with the iconographic tradition of *Veritas Temporis filia* ('Truth is the daughter of Time'), which has its origin in Aulus Gellius, *Noctes Atticae*, XII. 2. 7, Time here is a Chronos-like figure that triumphantly reveals the eternity of Beauty's truth (see Introduction, p. 62, and n. 191). The lines can be paraphrased thus: 'Corinna shall summon Time, and Time, which has never been celebrated thus, will grow stronger in the proclamation of her beauty's fame'.

Stanza 64 relies on the visual pyramid of Euclidean optics and its adaptations in Renaissance theories of painting. Leon Battista Alberti provides a close analogue to, if not a direct source for, Chapman's poetic description in 64. 1-4: 'Pyramis est figura corporis oblongi ab cuius basi omnes lineae rectae sursum protractae ad unicam cuspidem conterminent. Basis pyramidis visa superficies est. Latera pyramidis radii ipsi visivi quos extrinsecos nuncupari diximus. Cuspis pyramidis illic intra oculum considet, ubi in unum anguli quantitatum in triangulis conveniunt' ('The pyramid has the shape of an oblong body; all the straight lines lead from the base of it upward to meet at a single apex. The base of the pyramid is the surface seen. The sides of the pyramid correspond to the visual rays themselves that are called, as we have said, extreme. The apex of the pyramid will be placed in the eye where the angles of the quantities meet in one single place': *De Pictura* (Basel, 1540), pp. 14-15; translation: *Leon Battista Alberti: On Painting. A Translation and Critical Edition*, ed. and trans. by Rocco Sinisgalli (Cambridge University Press, 2011), pp. 28-29). Alberti eludes the controversy on the origin of the rays (the eyes or the object), for which Chapman's Ovid follows the traditional Euclidean view (the eyes). As Smarr argues ('The Pyramid and the Circle', p. 370), 'lines' puns on the visual rays and on the poem's own lines of verse. For Smarr, the second use is emblematic of the structure of Chapman's poem, conceived of as 'a monument to Beautie's fame' (pp. 370-71). Thus, the visual pyramid crystallizes in a material pyramid, projected up to heaven, and promoting the poem as an eternal monument to Beauty, proclaimed by Fame (64. 8-9) — an idea that would be in line with the emblematic conception of Time as bearer of Beauty's renown (63. 8-9).

As a consequence of this, in stanzas 65-68, the abstracted Beauty that is the object of Ovid's praise is personified in two women: Helen of Troy and Corinna. The arguments in these stanzas are advanced in the form of several similes. In stanza 65, Beauty features as a treasure whose riches cannot be counted, despite men's efforts to inventory them, thus stressing Chapman's attack on material gain throughout the poem. In stanza 66, the motif of light shining in darkness also reinforces another favourite theme in Chapman: the pursuit of truth as the illumination of darkness. Stanza 67 develops a more intricate simile involving the myth of Argus and Io, as found in Ovid (*Metamorphoses*, I. 623–737). Argus, son of Arestus, had a hundred eyes, and for this reason was appointed by Juno to find out the identity of Io, lover of Jupiter, who had transformed her into a cow to hide her from his wife. Jupiter managed to have Mercury kill Argus after he was put to sleep with all his eyes shut. Thus, Chapman's character Ovid plays Argus here, who spies on innocence (Io), for which he becomes the object of Corinna's (Jupiter's) wrath. For that reason, Ovid is 'overthrown' even while remaining 'unassailed' by Corina's anger, as he is 'bound in slavery' in his contemplation of her. Finally, stanza 68 begins by comparing the attraction that Beauty exerts upon men to the concentration in the heart of all the vital strength of a human body. The argument then moves to Helen and the Trojan War in what seems another wink at Marlowe (*Doctor Faustus*, A-Text, V. 1. 90–109).

The closing couplets of all these four stanzas (65–68) seem to relate to one another by developing an independent theme: the traditional courtly conceit of love as a siege, which is here subjected to reversal. Thus, 65. 8–9 states that it is Beauty that besieges the lover, feeding his desire only to paradoxically renew his hunger; 66. 8–9 resorts to Cephalus's killing of Procris (see Ovid, *Metamorphoses*, VII. 840–50) with his arrow as an image of Beauty's unwitting though ultimately treacherous wounding of Ovid; 67. 8–9 reiterates the theme of war; finally, 68. 8–9 concludes with the lover's resistance despite Beauty's destruction of the towers of Troy. The conclusion reinforces the general Neoplatonic theme that sight's contemplation of Beauty should not succumb to the temptation of the baser senses.

Stanzas 69–71, and M14, M15, M16

These stanzas constitute the centre of the poem both narratively and conceptually. From a narrative point of view, the action is simple: Corinna rises from her reclining position and proceeds to comb her hair and adorn it with jewels. Yet Chapman's rhetoric proceeds by differentiating Ovid's point of view from that of the readers. This is in line with the perspective principle expressed in one of the commendatory sonnets ('*OBS*: Williams, 1', 5–8) and in the stanza describing the perspective trick of Niobe's fountain (3. 6–9). Thus, while Ovid's eye remains fixed on Corinna's body and heart-shaped hairdo (as described in 69 and 70. 1–5, and later in stanza 72), readers are asked to sharpen their sight in order to see and understand the meaning of the emblems contained in three of Corinna's jewels, which Ovid does not detect. Deliberate obscurity is not only a feature of the style of these particular stanzas, but also the ultimate subject matter of their three devices, which emerge as emblems of Chapman's working poetics. For Huntington (*Ambition*, pp. 142–43), the three jewels emblematize the poem's professed obscurity. For Wheeler ('The obiect', pp. 335-36), they endorse a Neoplatonic aesthetic ideology. The following interpretation is based and expands on Luis-Martínez, 'Habit of Poesie', pp. 275-77.

The first device is the most difficult to interpret: its motto, '*decrescente nobilitate, crescunt obscuri*' ('when nobility decays, then obscure men grow'), is explained in terms of its *pictura*, literalized in Chapman's gloss (M14) — 'At the sun going down, shadows grow longest'. While, for Wheeler, the sun represents the 'richness of the poetic endeavour' and obscurity means ignorance, Huntington interprets exactly the opposite — i.e. the obscure poet grows at the expense of false nobility. Although no sources for this device have been noted so far, Chapman's motif has antecedents in the emblem books. Barthélemy Aneau's *Picta poesis* (Lyons: Marthian Bonhomme, 1552), sig. C4^v (see Visual Sources), includes an emblem representing a sun in its zenith, therefore projecting no shadow from a standing male figure. The motto reads '*Summa virtus adumbratam virtutis speciem abolet*' ('The highest virtue effaces the shadowed semblance of virtue'). Chapman's device would seem a logical deduction from this emblem. In the present context, Huntington's reading appears the most plausible: thus, the receding sunlight becomes the apt medium for the rise to prominence of the obscure poet, or shadow.

The second device also invites scrutiny of the 'many constructions' (meanings) which its 'application' (use) has, according to Chapman's own gloss (M15). Yet it also depends upon a correct reading of its slippery terms. Wheeler errs when he reads 'meanes' — Chapman's Englishing of *medio* — as 'middle point'. '*Medio caret*' (i.e. its medium is lacking) refers to the extrinsic medium of vision, which is no other than 'the transparent' (διαφανής), as explained in Aristotle's *De anima* (II. 7, 418a26-418b17). While the eye is certainly the third eye of the mind of Ficino's commentary on Plato's *Philebus* (see 'Cynthiam', 443-47 and Commentary for references), the laurel stands here as the object whose 'close apposition' prevents ('lets') light from inhabiting the medium between sight and its object. Yet, in line with the previous device, the apparent obstacle reveals itself as poetry's alternative medium (i.e. 'not eyes but means must truth display'): playing on the two contrary meanings of 'let', the emblem states that the laurel enables rather than prevents intellectual sight.

No specific emblematic sources have been noted for the third device, the motto of which is '*teipsum et orbem*' ('yourself and the world'), and which represents Apollo driving a chariot around a sundial ('*teipsum*') that contains an image of the terrestrial globe ('*orbem*'). The gloss (M16) explains this pictorial disposition by affirming that 'the sun hath as much time to compass a dial as the world' and declares that the 'conceit' points to 'a far higher intention'. The dial is then a human microcosm in which the entire world is contained. Wheeler is right to note Chapman's indebtedness to Ficino's commentaries on Plato's charioteer in *Phaedrus*, 246A-247C (in *Euthyphro, Crito, Apology, Phaedo, Phaedrus*, pp. 470-75; see Ficino, *Commentaries on*

Plato: Volume I: Phaedrus, I. 7, pp. 66-70). According to Wheeler, 'in the creative synthesis of the chariot horses of Apollo, poetry becomes a philanthropic instrument of the complementarily balanced passion and reason' ('The obiect', p. 336). In Plato, Socrates compares the soul's form to a charioteer driving two horses, one that is 'good and noble' (καλός καὶ ἀγαθὸς) and the other its 'opposite' (ἐναντίος). For Ficino, the 'better horse' ('melior equus') and the 'worse horse' ('equus deleterior') represent the rational and sensual powers of the soul. The 'charioteer' ('auriga') represents 'intellect' ('intellectus'). As Ficino somehow obscurely explains, in the charioteer's head the motions of nature's circuit ('circuitus naturae') are joined to the higher circuit of understanding ('circuitus intelligentiae'). Similarly in Chapman's device, nature ('world') is contained in the higher mind ('dial'), so Apollo's command of the 'team' of Platonic horses suggests the poet's attempt to contain nature within the higher powers of the intellect. M16's invitation to read the devices 'morally' in the search for 'higher intentions' that are suggested though not fully revealed seems in line with Chapman's own gloss closing 'Noctem', in which the capacities of able readers are invoked: thus, these intentions 'will be proud enough to justify themselves, and prove sufficiently authentical to such as understand them'.

Stanzas 72-73

Ovid's new speech confirms that Corinna's jewels and their hidden philosophical meanings have passed him by unnoticed. His response is the effect of sensual arousal at the contemplation of his mistress's beauty, and consequently his desire is triggered toward aims that are contrary to orthodox Neoplatonic theories of love. His aspiration to 'one kiss' that will reward the senses of 'taste and touch' is contrary to Ficino's conviction that only sight and hearing are legitimate senses in the act of apprehending true beauty (see Commentary on 52). Yet Ovid still attempts to justify his desire to satisfy the baser senses on grounds of Neoplatonic principles (72. 6-73. 9). Hudston notes, without giving further details, that lines 72. 6-7 express a Neoplatonic idea that Chapman later repeats in *Bussy D'Ambois*, III. 1. 104-05: 'Each naturall agent workes but to this end, | To render that it works on, like it selfe' (*Tragedies*, p. 411). This principle, which concerns the nature of motion with respect to matter and quality, relies on Ficino, who argues that action requires that the agent 'must easily penetrate the object being acted upon, so that the object is immediately united with the agent' ('ut facile penetret patiens atque ipsum patiens agenti proxime uniatur'). Besides, an object is acted upon by an agent 'by way of form's qualities' ('per formae qualitates'), so that 'natural causes produce effects like themselves in quality' ('ut causae naturales effectus producant suos qualitate similes causarum': *Platonic Theology*, I. 2; I, pp. 18-19, 24-25). The example of fire's action on water in order to produce heat — i.e. a quality that is like the agent's — also draws on Ficino: 'The action of fire is to make something hot. It does not make water, for instance, hot instantaneously but in time. Now an act in time everyone calls motion. So quality is altogether subject to motion' ('Ignis siquidem actio calefactio est. Aquam non momento calefacit, sed tempore. Actio temporalis motus ab omnibus nominatur, ideo qualitas omni ex parte subiicitur motui': IV. 1, I, pp. 54–55). In his attempt to adjust philosophical argument to the satisfaction of his desire, Ovid claims that a 'sparkling temper' is the loving quality that heaven has infused in Corinna, just as fire can transmit its heat to water, thus predisposing her to the 'spirits' of wit that Ovid's verbal advances to her will carry.

Narratio and *Ovid standing behind her, his face was seen in the glass*

The two marginal notes accompanying stanza 74 indicate, respectively, a return to narrative, and, in the manner of a stage direction, Corinna's discovery of Ovid's image in the mirror, which the verse nevertheless describes. Rather than clarifying, their role seems structural, as this discovery marks the narrative transition toward the poem's second part, characterized by interaction and dialogue between the two protagonists.

Stanzas 74–75

Corinna's horror-stricken start is the tenor of an astronomical simile: the rising of the constellation Auriga in the summer while the sun is in Leo — i.e. between late July and late August. *Auriga*, or the Charioteer (Greek Ἡνίοχος, or Rein-holder), represents Erichthonius (born of Vulcan's seed spilt on the earth when the latter tried to rape Minerva), who drove a chariot out of necessity — he inherited his father's lameness. He carries the Goat (the star *Capella*, the stellified Amalthea, nurse of Jupiter) upon his left shoulder and two smaller twin stars, the Kids, or Haedi, on his left wrist. The Haedi's ability to raise storms is documented in English texts before Chapman. Thomas Cooper writes that 'in the hand of *Auriga* be two starres, called *Haedi*, whose rising and going downe doth oftentimes cause great tempests' (*Thesaurus Linguae Romanae et Britannicae* (London: Henry Denham, 1578), sig. M6^v). Chapman's source may be Aratus, whose Kids (Ἔριφοι) 'often in the darkening deep have seen men storm-tossed' (*Phaenomena*, 156–66, in *Callimachus, Lycophron, Aratus*, pp. 392–95); or Hyginus, *De Astronomia*, ed. by Ghislaine Viré (Teubner, 1992), II. 13. 450–80, pp. 39–40. These texts were published jointly in several sixteenth-century editions (e.g. Basel, 1535). Thus, like the Haedi, Corinna's rising body is a shining star that 'threat[ens] tempests for her high disgrace'. On the Auriga and its classical sources, see also Richard Hinckley Allen, *Star Names and Their Meanings* (G. E. Stechert, 1899), pp. 83–92.

Stanzas 76–78

The short repartee between Corinna, surprised in her nakedness, and Ovid elaborates on a number of important themes for the overall meaning of the poem. Ovid's reply to Corinna puts his poetic wit at the service of his philosophical seduction. The conventional topoi of *servitium amoris* and *militia amoris* in 76. 5–9 obtain Corinna's scornful retort: 'thy gloss is common'. Ovid's discovery of Corinna brings forth again the erotic substratum of the myth of Actaeon and Diana. Against his arguments, Corinna's reply foregrounds certain ideas about nakedness that were commonplace in the Renaissance. Thus, the axiom 'Thought, Sight's child | Begetteth sin' brings forth the loss of Edenic innocence: 'Then the eyes of them bothe [Adam and Eve] were opened, & they knewe that they were naked' (Genesis 3. 7, in *The Bible and Holy Scriptures*, fol. 2^v). Corinna's attempt to revert this idea to a prelapsarian state in which nakedness is 'A perfect image of our purities' (78. 3) is in overt contradiction with her desire to conceal it from Ovid's sight. For Corinna, the Ficinian idea of sight as the legitimate and highest sense does not hold. Contrarily, she associates sight with physical infection, a notion that is reinforced by the choice of verbs: thus, honour is 'defiled'; sight 'attainteth'; and nakedness should be left 'incompressed'. The first two denote contagion by touch (see *OED*, *defile*, v., 1; and *attaint*, v., 8–10). The third (not in *OED*) means 'free from the hand's pressure' or, as Bartlett points out, 'unembraced' (pp. 432–33, 78. 6, note). This synaesthetic blend of sight and touch anticipates Ovid's later intentions.

Stanzas 79–85

Ovid's reply to Corinna's arguments is framed by an appeal to 'authentic Reason' against 'vulgar Opinion'. Yet the ensuing stanzas are an assortment of scientific views on sense perception, particularly on sight, which are not always consistent with the views expressed earlier in the poem. These views are mixed with a number of arguments about the nature of love, the main aim of which is to refute Corinna's views on the sinful character of Ovid's action and the inherent corruption of those pleasures derived from sense perception. The attribution of these inconsistencies to the character's sophistry with a view to seduction is the argument of those critical interpretations of the poem as satiric and condemnatory of Ovid's position.

> 79] Ovid's appeal to 'Reason' against 'Opinion' is argued by means of prosopopoeia. Making Reason 'the wife of Truth' has the disadvantage of imagining Truth as male, while most allegorical and emblematic renderings of this notion imagine it as a young woman, as proved by the emblematic motif *Veritas Temporis filia* (see Introduction, p. 62). Capitalization of initial words of a line makes it hard to decide whether 'Use' (79. 9) should be understood as another personification. The effects of 'Use' (i.e. making trifles important and important things trifles) are quite contrary to the power of 'Reason': Ovid's point is that Corinna's belief that having been seen naked defiles her honour is based on 'Opinion' and 'Use' rather than on 'Reason'.

80 and M17] In the first four lines of this stanza, Ovid expounds a theory of vision that hardly accords with the Aristotelian origin he ascribes to the summarizing Latin gloss (M17): '*Actio cernendi in homine vel animali vidente collocanda est*' ('The action of seeing should be placed in the seeing human or animal'). This has puzzled editors, who have not been able to find in Aristotle the source for what looks like a blatantly un-Aristotelian principle. The sentence, however, is found almost verbatim in Joachim Curaeus's Latin epitome of classical theories of sense perception: '*Actio autem cernendi collocanda est, in homine vel animali vidente*, non in illa imagine, quae est quaedam oculi affectio, non quatenus est instrumentum visionis, sed quia est corpus politum, et perspicuum' ('*But the action of seeing should be placed in the seeing human or animal*, not in that image that has a certain affection to the eye, not insofar as it is the instrument of vision, but as it is a polished and transparent body': Περὶ αἰσθήσεως, I. 31, p. 129, emphasis added, my translation). The specific context for Curaeus's passage is an exposition and refutation of two aspects of Democritus's theory of vision: the intromission theory of emanations and the role of the eye as a passive mirror to the external emanations issued from visible objects. The sentence counters those theories by advocating an active role for the seer, closer to Platonic views. Ovid's argument, when seen in conjunction with the gloss, is confusing. A paraphrase of 80. 1–4 could read thus: 'As for my seeing you, how can sight, which is just a sense that receives in the eye's fiery substance an essence sent from the object of vision, do any harm by seeing, whose action has its physical site in the seer?' These lines seem to defend simultaneously two contrary positions: 1) the eye is a mirror-like, passive reflector, and 2) sight has its origin in the seer. Yet both points can be reconciled if we understand the lines' meanings as an attempt to defend the independence of the act of vision from the object's identity. Thus, Ovid argues that it is impossible that seeing can harm its object, as the subject of vision is acted upon by that object, whose essence is not altered by the act of vision. From this reasoning ensues, in the rest of the stanza (80. 5–9), a Platonic theory of the subject's being warmed (ἐθερμάνθη) by the eye's contemplation of beautiful human bodies, which leads to the apprehension of good and truth, in line with *Phaedrus*, 250D–251B (*Euthyphro, Crito, Apology, Phaedo, Phaedrus*, pp. 484–87). This passage also differentiates, as in Ovid's speech, between beastly desire for, and the philosophical contemplation of, beauty. The stanza's conclusion is in line with the Platonic idea that there is a good form of love that is harmless ('where no harm's kind can be') to its object.

81–82] The basilisk has an important place in Ovid's argument. In classical and medieval sources, the lethal properties of this mythical serpent lie in its poisonous touch, the smell of its breath and, of more relevance here, its sight. In Pliny, the basilisk's breath and skin contact ('contactos [...] et adflatos') '[burn] up all the grass too, and [break] the stones' ('exurit herbas, rumpit saxa': *Natural History*, VIII. 33). Isidore of Seville relates this burning power directly to its poisonous sight: 'it also kills a human if it looks at one. Indeed no flying bird may pass unharmed by the basilisk's face, but however distant it may be it is burnt up and devoured by this animal's mouth' ('nam et hominem si aspiciat interimit. siquidem et eius aspectu nulla avis volans inlaesa sed quam procul sit, eius ore conbusta devoratur': *Etymologies*, XII. 4. 6–9, p. 255). These antecedents explain Ovid's 'heart-burning eye'. The basilisk can also embody the synaesthetic dimension of desire, which, as in Platonic theory, fails to direct sight to spiritual contemplation and succumbs to the powers of the other senses. Yet Ovid's conceit aims to subvert these meanings: Corinna's 'pregnant' wit should help her understand that she remains 'unwronged' and 'dishonourless' to his basilisk's sight, and so, despite her nakedness, her 'power' over her lover should be 'clad in lenity'.

83–84 and M18, M19] Ovid's attempt to persuade Corinna continues with a poetic argument on the nature of his love that occupies two stanzas. In stanza 83, Ovid's constancy (his 'ceaseless thoughts' contrast with 'sudden' love) is said to originate not in Cupid's capricious arrows but in Vulcan's hard-labouring forge. Constancy is also measured by the single aim of his desires ('My heart's true centre'), which become the tenor of an ingenious mythographic simile whose source is, as Schoell has noted (*Études*, pp. 194–95), an item in Conti's catalogue of Apollo's children ('De Apolline', v. 10, 347; Mulryan, p. 284): 'Ex Acachallide Delphum, qui nomen dedit Delphis umbilico totius orbis terrae. Nam fabulati sunt antiqui Iovem cum vellet medium atque umbilicum terrae invenire, alteram aquilam ab oriente, alteram ab occasu pari velocitate emisisse, iussisseque illas recta et e regione convolare, quae cum in Delphos denique convenissent, ibi ad sempiternam facti memoriam aurea aquila dicata est' ('Delphus (who gave his name, Delphi, to the whole world's navel) by Acachalisse. For the ancients fabled that when Jupiter wanted to locate the middle or navel of the earth, he ordered two eagles to fly, and when they finally met at Delphi, a consecrated golden eagle served to perpetuate the memory of the event').

Cupid is the protagonist of stanza 84, in what seems a compressed parody of the tradition of Cupid sonnets in 1590s England — see, as examples, sonnets IV and V in Giles Fletcher's *Licia*. The Latin gloss (M18) serves as the Sidneian fore-conceit, or invention, of the stanza: '*In cerebro est principium sentiendi, et inde nervi, qui instrumenta sunt motus voluntarii, oriuntur*' ('In the brain is the first organ of sensation, and from it are born the nerves, which are instruments of voluntary motion'). Thus, Cupid, whose headquarters are inside Corinna's self, metamorphoses himself in her 'tunes and odours' in order to travel into Ovid's brain. The brain is the site of sensation: 'principium' (i.e. first principle) provides the occasion for the pun on 'Prince' and is thus the site for the 'throne' that Cupid usurps. The god then makes a 'chain' with Ovid's nerves ('motion's engines' translates 'instrumenta motus'), to be used as the 'reins' with which he 'enforce(s)' Ovid's will (as conveyed by the adjective 'voluntarii'), which is thus subjected to 'Nature'. The classical topos of *servitium amoris* is thus ingeniously transformed into an anatomical conceit. Here Ovid seems to resort to atomistic notions of sense perception formerly expounded in the poem. Earlier commentators have not found the sources for the two Latin glosses. For the first, Curaeus's epitome again provides an almost verbatim formulation in a chapter devoted to discussions of the physical site of sensation, and in the context of a comparison between Aristotle's cardiocentrist theories and Platonic/Galenic defences of the brain as the first principle of sensation and motion: 'Utitur autem Galenus multis argumentis contra Aristotelem, ex quibus nos tantum praecipua excerpemus. I. Ab origine instrumenti. Ubi sunt instrumenta sentiendi et movendi, imperio voluntatis, ibi sunt etiam illae facultates. [...] Nam ubi natura fabricat instrumenta, ibi etiam facultates et actiones ingenuit. Quia autem nervi, qui instrumenta sunt motus voluntarii, ex cerebro ut Anatome monstrat, oriuntur, certo etiam facultates eas ibi residere, arbitrabimur' ('But Galenus uses many arguments against Aristotle, of which we simply excerpt the most significant: 1) From the origin of the instrument. As the instruments of sensation and motion are found in the dominion of will (i.e. the brain), in that place its faculties are found too. [...] For where nature fabricates those instruments, there it also implants the faculties and actions. Moreover, because the nerves, which are the instruments of voluntary motion, originate from the brain, as dissection proves, we thus conclude that these faculties reside there': Περὶ αἰσθήσεως, I. 6, p. 26, my translation). Chapman's re-phrasing is motivated by syntax.

The next gloss (M19), '*Natura est uniuscuiusque Fatum*' ('Nature is the fate for each and every one'), is attributed to Theophrastus. No sources have been identified for this. The solution may be in Theophrastus's *Metaphysics*, one of whose sixteenth-century Latin editions is quoted here: 'in omnibus naturam, quod optimum est expetere, et in quibus fieri postest, ordinem largiri, atque aeternitatem videmus' ('we see that nature in all things desires that which is the best and, when possible, grants order and eternity': *Aristotelis Stagiritae Metaphysicorum libri XIIII, Theophrasti Metaphysicorum liber* (Ingolstadt: David Sartorius, 1577), IX, fol. 216ᵛ, my translation). This may have inspired the idea of nature's leaning towards love, considered by Chapman's Ovid a supreme good — but the argument is merely conjectural. In connection with the Latin gloss, Kermode has aptly noted the similarity between Ovid's words here — 'Nature (my fate)' — and those in 'The Song of Corinna' — 'Nature our fate' (12. 18). Reading Ovid's arguments as serious, or as effects of Chapman's ironic perspective, constitutes the main critical crux of the poem, and the answer depends on whether the glosses are regarded as supportive, clarifying and complementary, or as contradictory of Ovid's views.

85] This stanza provides the conclusions to Ovid's argument: the effect of Cupid's assault is that, while he has usurped the throne of Ovid's brain, Ovid's eye has made Corinna queen of his heart, and thus she should show her bounty to the purveyor of her royal chamber who, while performing his duties loyally, has inevitably trespassed the limits of those duties and surprised its occupant in her privacy.

Stanza 86

Corinna's change of mood and attitude towards Ovid, enabling a transition to the 'baser' senses of taste and touch, is narrated in Chapman's characteristic baroque style. A very simple event — her change of countenance denoting her favour-granting attitude — is amplified by means of a simile in which the vehicle's copiousness and ingenuity outshine its tenor. Syntactically, the subordinate comparative clause, introduced by 'as', occupies the first seven lines, while the main clause, introduced by 'So', concludes the stanza (lines 8-9). The comparative clause comprises a compound sentence, in which 'when ... when' must be read as 'while ... then', the first four lines being a temporal subordinate clause to the main clause in lines 5-7: the mists that Earth issues in order to cloud Heaven's stars are swept over by Zephyrus's blows, allowing Olympus to shine again. For the status of Heaven (Uranus) and Earth (Gaia) as husband and wife, as well as the Earth's fertility, Chapman could have relied on several passages from Conti: see, for instance, 'Noctem', 264-65, and Commentary, for sources. However, the far-fetched conceit of envious Earth as a recently divorced wife seems Chapman's original invention.

Gustus

In Latin, the sense of taste, which presides over stanzas 87-101. In contrast with previous sections of the poem, particularly those on smell and hearing, there is little concern in these stanzas with the physiology or psychology of taste. Rather, the active presence of Corinna changes the focus to repartee, in which persuasion, initial resistance and final compliance with Ovid's request for a kiss result in first the narrator's and then Ovid's own account of its pleasures. These pleasures are expressed by means of poetic synaesthesia, particularly in relation to the sense of hearing.

Stanzas 87-88 and M20, M21

These two stanzas supply new philosophical arguments to Ovid's attempt to persuade Corinna to give him a kiss in order to satisfy his sense of taste. The first argument concerns Ovid's 'fantasy', or, in the post-classical theory of the inner senses, *phantasia*, or *vis imaginativa*, the storehouse of sensations and also the site of the passions (i.e. the 'motion of my soul'). Thus, what

Ovid requires is an act of justice on Corinna's part that will put 'into fact' what is initially a mere craving of the imagination. The reason for this lies in the fact that the three senses thus rewarded require, according to Aristotle, an external medium, while taste and touch are the two senses that need direct contact with the external object. The interpretation of the next argument is based here on my emendation (following Braden) of QOB's 'changde' (87. 5) to 'change'. Hudston's reading of this clause, which relies on the original 'changde', is far-fetched (p. 412). The emendation allows interpretation of the 'offence' as Corinna's initial refusal to grant Ovid's request in the first four lines. The last four lines seek new philosophical reasons to justify Ovid's request. Chapman's gloss signals line 5 as an elaborate, somewhat abstruse poetic translation of its Latin tag (M20): '*Alterationem pati est sentire*' ('To experience sensation is to suffer change'). This is in line with Aristotle's definition: 'sensation [αἴσθησις] consists in being moved [κινεῖσθαι] and acted upon [πάσχειν], for it is held to be a species of qualitative change [ἀλλοίωσις]' (*De anima*, II. 5, 416b33). The second Aristotelian verb, 'πάσχειν', contains the sense of Chapman's 'suffer'.

Latin formulations that resemble Chapman's can again be found in Curaeus: 'Sentire vero docuit Aristotele esse pati. [...] Sentire dicimus esse quandam alterationem [...]' ('As Aristotle teaches, to experience sensation is to be acted upon. [...] We say that sensation is a certain alteration [...]': *Περὶ αἰσθήσεως*, I. 3, pp. 13, 15). Ovid's request that Corinna participate in the experience of change involved in sensation is exceptional in a poem that obsessively revolves around Ovid's egotistic pleasure. There is another quotation in the stanza, although without an explanatory gloss: 'We live not for ourselves' has its origin in Plato: 'yet you ought also to bear in mind that *no one of us exists for himself alone* [οὐχ αὐτῷ μόνον γέγονεν], but one share of our existence belongs to our country, another to our parents, a third to the rest of our friends' (*Epistles*, IX. 358A, in *Timaeus, Critias, Cleitophon, Menexenus, Epistles*, ed. and trans. by R. G. Bury (Heinemann, 1952), p. 592–93). Chapman may have known Plato's letter in Ficino's translation: 'Sed illud quoque te considerare oportet: *nullum nostrum sibi soli natum esse*: sed ortus nostri partem sibi patriam uendicare: partem parentes: pertem amicos' (*Omnia Divini Platonis Opera*, trans. by Marsilio Ficino (Basel: Hieronymus Froben, 1546), p. 948; emphasis added); or directly from Cicero: 'Sed quoniam, ut praeclare scriptum est a Platone, *non nobis solum nati sumus* ortusque nostri partem patria vindicat, partem amici' (*De Officiis*, ed. and trans. by Walter Miller (Heinemann, 1913), I. 7. 22, p. 22; emphasis added). The ethical implications of Plato's philanthropic dictum are subverted in Ovid's lines: thus, just as sight and hearing should serve the satisfaction of its fellow senses, Corinna should not act in her own interest only, but for Ovid's own satisfaction. Stanza 88 concludes the argument with the actual request for a kiss, justified now as the act of justice that will restore taste as the central sense in a banquet. The idea that taste relies on the organs of touch (88. 6) is another well-known

Aristotelian argument: '*The object of taste is a species of tangible* [Τὸ δὲ γευστόν ἐστιν ἁπτόν τι]. And this is the reason why it is not perceived through a foreign body as medium: for touch employs no such medium either' (*De anima*, II. 10, 422a8, pp. 94–95, emphasis added). The journey from the tongue to 'that inward taste' is explained in Chapman's English/Latin gloss (M21): the 'common sense' is the site of inner sensations, and thus '*centrum sensibus et speciebus*' ('the centre for all senses and emanations').

Line 87. 7 — 'Which makes all sense, and shall delight as much' — translates poetically the other Latin part of the gloss: 'common sense' is 'last' in the reception of sensation 'because it doth *sapere in effectione sensum*' ('it reaches knowledge/tastes/delights in its making/achievement of sensation'). The gloss's pun on *sapere* (know, taste) identifies the sense of taste with common sense (on which, see Weaver, 'Banquet', p. 782). The Latin in the gloss again adapts Curaeus, although the original context concerns sight rather than taste: 'Verum in corpore viventi fulget, et agnoscitur color in oculis, et eius speciem quasi puram quandam effigiem, spiritus, ad facultatem interiorem, quae ex opinione Medicorum, in cerebro sedem suam habet, defert, et sensus communis a peripateticis dicitur' ('Certainly colour shines and is perceived by the eyes of living bodies, and delivers its species as if it were a pure copy to that inner faculty which, in the opinion of the physicians, has its site in the brain and is called common sense by Aristotle's followers': Περὶ αἰσθήσεως, I. 3, p. 15, my translation). Besides the more obvious verbal similarities, the verb 'defert' ('delivers') is behind Chapman's 'advance'.

Stanza 89

Corinna's reply elaborates on the motif of Ovid's gluttony and its contrariety to reason. It also introduces the theme of the difference of 'birth and state' between the Emperor's daughter and the poet. This recurrent theme in Chapman's poetry is crucial in the poem, as it supports the subtext of the motives of Ovid's exile, which some critics have found of relevance to its overall interpretation. See Lyne, 'Love and Exile', pp. 289–90; Moss, 'Second Master', p. 474; and Luis-Martínez, 'Whose Banquet?', p. 41. Corinna's wit also relies on philosophical lore: the transformation of rarefied air into fire (89. 8) is a Presocratic physical principle attributed to Anaximenes by the Neoplatonist commentator of Aristotle Simplicius (*Physics*, 149. 28–150. 4), and also by Theophrastus (*Fragmenta*, 226A): 'air when it is thinned [ἀραιούμενον] becomes fire' (*The Texts of Early Greek Philosophy*, I, pp. 76–77). The principle explains by analogy the potential that Ovid's persistence in wooing has for causing Corinna's anger: the rhyme *fire/ire* also plays on the consideration of choler as the fiery (i.e. hot and dry) humour.

Stanzas 90–91

Ovid's two-stanza reply to Corinna focuses mainly on her argument regarding the social distance between them. Bartlett (p. 443, nn. 90–91) noted the influence of Giovanni Battista Nenna's *Il Nennio, nel quale si ragiona della nobilità* (Venice: Andrea Valvassori, 1542). William Jones's translation into English, *Nennio, or a Treatise on Nobility* (London: Paul Linley, 1595) was published in the same year as *OBS*, and included commendatory sonnets by Chapman, Spenser, Daniel and Angel Day. The authoritative study on the influence of this treatise in Chapman's poetry is Huntington (*Ambition*, esp. pp. 67–88, and 141–42 on this passage). Chapman's conviction that nobility of mind is to be preferred over rank and birth is a Nennian argument voiced by Ovid here. Yet Ovid also seeks an explanation of why such an intellectually gifted lady as Corinna has resorted to a 'trivial' argument. This explanation is found in 90. 3–7, the obscurity of which needs unpacking. Ovid's statement that Corinna's 'rare wits' are 'peril's sovereignties' remains unexplained — Hudston's gloss as 'supreme dangers' seems unsatisfactory (p. 412, n. 9). Yet Chapman may be using 'peril' here as synonymous with 'danger', in the sense in which the latter is used in love poetry — i.e. scorn, haughtiness, power to harm, power that the beloved exerts upon the lover, as in 41. 9: 'Quicker in danger than Diana's eye'. Thus, what Ovid means is that the lady's scorn towards the wooing lover has 'urged', or stimulated, her wits, sharpening her words against him rather than framing them to the commendation of true virtues, which are beyond nobility of birth. Thus, if she changes her mind and favours him, her error will be easily mended.

Stanza 92

Corinna's analogy between the lover's Neoplatonic aspirations and the stars' influence on the earth is of particular import for the theories of the senses advanced in the poem: her message to Ovid is that he should be satisfied with the rewards obtained by smell, hearing and sight, as these are the three senses that rely on an external medium and not on direct 'contact'; and thus the importance of the phrase 'virtual contact', in which the adjective means both 'pertaining to the moral virtues', but also 'potential', 'non-material'. Compare Chapman's description of Leander's joy: 'his sences flame | Flowd from all parts, with force so virtuall, | It fir'd with sence things mere insensuall' (*Hero and Leander*, III. 88–90, in Bartlett, p. 136).

Stanzas 93–94

Ovid's reply returns partly to Presocratic theories of sight as the result of sensible emanations, or 'species', in the form of resemblances, or reflections, produced by the objects seen. Yet Ovid eludes the materialist, atomistic view that holds these emanations to be 'true and solid' parts. The notion that what the eye receives are sensible forms, and not matter, is also in Aristotle: sensation and knowledge are identical not with their objects, but with the *forms* (εἴδη) of their objects (*De anima*, III. 8, 431b28). The narrator's digression, particularly stanza 55, used Neoplatonic theory to defend the view of the incorporeality of beauty. Yet this view is now adopted by Ovid in order to emphasize the insufficiency of sight: the enjoyment of material 'substance' demands the participation of taste and touch. Once the need for the remaining senses is granted in Ovid's argument, he proceeds (stanza 94) to persuade Corinna to comply with his desires by means of a new analogy: as air, which is haughty and tends to move upwards, yields to the human organs of voice when they produce speech, so Corinna, who is equally proud, should yield to Ovid's speech when he requests a kiss from her. Corinna's 'tractability' must then, like air, yield to being 'conduced' and 'pressed into a little space', or *tractus*. The theory of 'speech' (*sermo*) as produced by human voice (*vox*) may have been inspired by Aristotle's views (*De anima*, II. 8, 420b5–421a6). Curaeus's Aristotelian account provides an analogue, if not a source, for the poem's own description of the air's contraction in the 'little place' of the windpipe: 'Locus, in quo formatur vox, est arteria trachea, et praecipue ipsius summum caput, quod Larynx appellatur. In illo nodo cavo aer involvitur, et pro ut musculi peculiares tunicae laryngis, diducuntur, vel contrahuntur' ('The place in which voice is formed and chiefly reaches its own summit is the windpipe, which is called the larynx. In this hollow knot air is enveloped, and accordingly the specific muscles of the laryngeal membrane are loosened or contracted': Περὶ ἀισθήσεως, pp. 159–60, my translation).

Stanzas 95–96

Corinna's reply first announces her acquiescence, and then gives a number of arguments in favour of and against her yielding, to conclude circuitously with her acceptance of Ovid's request. The arguments that recommend her acquiescence occupy stanza 95, and weigh absurdly severe notions of 'virtue' and 'honour' against courteous, here called 'civil', behaviour in ladies. The metaphor of 'lift[ing] Minerva's shield | Against Minerva' treads on well-known ground in Chapman's poetry. '*SN*: To Roydon' (lines 4–5) imagined Perseus's fight against Medusa with, among other weapons, the shield of Pallas as an analogy of the poet's arming himself against ignorance. What Corinna means now is that using learning's weapons to counter Ovid's learned wit is of little use. The metaphor is particularly apt in this context, as Ovid's act of looking has (Medusa-like) endangered Corinna's honour. Corinna's concluding argument is the intrinsic virtue in both the lover's and the lady's aims: thus, while long courtships will not improve a lover's 'detection' (Hudston aptly glosses the term as 'choice': see p. 413, 95. 8, note), a virtuous love will not be more virtuous if the beloved postpones her favour. In stanza 96, Corinna moots a series of aphorisms against yielding: the scorn of virtue by those who ascend the social ladder (96. 1–2); men's 'pride and rudeness' (96. 3), and their preference of 'Force' over 'skill' (96. 7); and the disadvantages of resisting courtship too long (96. 5) or yielding to it too soon (96. 6). The classical topos of *militia amoris* is present in the martial language ('scaling', 'assault', 'falling', 'resistance', 'frays'). Hudston (p. 413) noticed the similarity to another passage by Chapman: 'Lysander: You lose time Brother in discourse, by this had you bore up with the Ladie and clapt her aboord, for I knowe your confidence will not dwell long in the service. Tharsalio: No, I will performe it in the Conquerors stile. Your way is, not to winne Penelope by suite, but by surprise. The Castle's carried by sodaine assault, that would perhaps sit on a twelve-moneths siege' (*The Widdowes Tears*, I. 1. 139–42, in *Comedies*, p. 483). In Corinna's argument, the lexicon of martial 'force' acquires negative connotations in opposition to courteous 'skill'.

Stanza 97

This narrative stanza again rehearses the Ficinian/Brunian motif of amatory frenzy leading to poetic fury (see stanza 15, and Commentary). Ovid's rapture is induced by his imagining of Hebe, the Olympian divinity of youth, as she pours the cup of ambrosia directly onto his lips and 'into his sense' — of taste, but also the 'inward taste', or common sense, which supplies material for the imagination. The violent image of Hebe's hands 'bruis[ing]' the nectar into Ovid's mouth echoes the idea that Corinna's 'honour is not bruised' (95. 4). While the mention of Hebe is circumscribed here to her role as a young, beautiful cupbearer, Chapman's knowledge of Conti would ensure his acquaintance with the stories and meanings associated with her. In 'De Hebe' (II. 2, pp. 143–45; Mulryan, pp. 121–23), Conti recounts that 'right after [Hebe] fell down while she was carrying the drinking cups, and exposed her private parts to everyone present there, she was removed from that office and replaced by Ganymede' ('cum lapsa aliquando inter ministrandum fuisset, partesque pudendas omnibus praesentibus ostendisset, ab illo officio removetur, et Ganymedes [...] sufficitur'). The motifs of nakedness, dishonour and shame are central to the moral interpretation of Hebe at the conclusion of Conti's chapter: 'Apud sapientes vero principes omnis turpitudo vel exterorum vel familiarium potest animun vel benevolentissimum alienare' ('And really wise rulers, no matter how kindly disposed they may be to everyone, simply will not tolerate shameless behavior either in their own households, or in the community at large'). This account may function as a powerful subtext for the dangers inherent in Ovid's relishing of Corinna's nudity, as well as for the exilic undertones of the poem: Ovid's and Julia's historical banishments could be viewed in the light of Augustus's anger at their shame. The interpretation of the myth of Ganymede in 'Cynthiam', 474–77 and Gloss 25 (in which he stands for 'the beauty of the mind') may also function as a counterpoint to the presence of Hebe.

Stanzas 98–101

The four stanzas closing the section on taste are an example of Chapman's rhetorical skill. The entire argument is disposed in chiasmus: stanza 98 begins by imagining the bliss of Corinna's kiss as the harmony conveyed by the music of the spheres; an elaborate simile in stanza 99 confirms this point;

another complex simile in stanza 100 contradicts the former by revealing this bliss to be insufficient; finally, 101 returns to the argumentative style in order to refute the reasons in stanza 98, thus concluding that, by itself, the kiss cannot render full satisfaction, since love is insatiable.

98] Ovid's account of his own pleasure in terms of the heavenly harmony and the Golden Age is indeed Ovidian. In *Metamorphoses*, God sets the heavenly spheres in order: 'quae postquam evolvit caecoque exemit acervo, | dissociata locis concordi pace ligavit' ('When thus he had released these elements and freed them from the blind heap of things, he set them each in its own place and bound them fast in harmony': I. 24–25); and then the Golden Age is begotten: 'Aurea prima sata est aetas' (I. 89; I, p. 8). The proximity of Chapman's 'beget' to Ovid's 'sata est' ('was begotten') is to be noticed here. The other allusion to *Metamorphoses* is the simile in lines 98. 8–9: the synaesthetic kiss, resonant with 'endless music', is compared to Nisus's towers, which kept in their stones the sound of Apollo's lyre: 'regia turris erat vocalibus addita muris, | in quibus auratam proles Letoia fertur | deposuisse lyram' ('There was a royal tower reared on the tuneful walls where Latona's son was said to have laid down his golden lyre, whose music still lingered in the stones': VIII. 14–16). Again, Chapman's verbal choice 'imposed' appears to have been inspired by Ovid's 'deposuisse'. The replacement of Apollo's lyre with a 'lute' is anachronistic (see 11. 6 and Commentary).

99] The simile in this stanza expands a motif already sketched in the preceding one: the kiss, compared earlier to the ever-resonant sound waves of Apollo's notes, extends its endless effect through Ovid's 'faculties'. These are the inner senses mentioned throughout the poem: common sense, imagination (or fantasy) and memory (see stanzas 27, 87, and their respective Commentaries). The simile of the pebble cast into a spring, whose origin may be experiential observation, provides an occasion for exploiting some of Chapman's favourite verbal resources. 'Circulize' is most probably Chapman's neologism. *OED* defines this rare verb as 'encircle' and gives later instances by John Davies (of Hereford), *Microcosmos*: 'orient *Pearle*, of admirable size, | Which loopes of Azur'd silke did circulize' (*An Extasie*, 237 in *The Complete Works of John Davies of Hereford*, ed. by Alexander B. Grosart, 2 vols (Edinburgh University Press, 1878), I, p. 90). Yet Chapman's earlier instance has a clearly different sense: expand concentrically. Its meaning is cohesive with 'propagate', used quite extraordinarily as an adjective here, and which connotes both extension in size and multiplication in number. The three-part compound 'perpetual-motion-making' (hyphenation is from QOB) bears witness to another favourite linguistic practice of the poet's, which here reinforces the continued, persistent effect of Corinna's kiss, whose divine, eternal powers (99. 8–9) are now said to surpass the 'ambrosian' qualities attributed to it in 97. 4. Although this edition's punctuation of this stanza has mostly respected Q*OB*'s, the addition of a comma in 99. 1 — the first in 'And as, a pebble cast into a spring,' — interprets the sequence between the two commas as an absolute participle clause with temporal value, thus clarifying an otherwise unbalanced syntactic structure.

100 and M22] Although the description of an echo that motivates the simile can be traced back to Aristotle (*De anima*, II. 8, 419b25–27), its direct source is the title and opening lines of Curaeus's chapter '*Quid sit echo, et qua ratione fiat*' ('What echo is and the explanation of how it occurs': Περὶ ἀισθήσεως, I. 41, pp. 161–62, my translation). Chapman's gloss concerns only the second part: he eludes the definition ('*quid sit*') and focuses on the process ('*qua ratione*'), as this is exactly what Ovid's simile does. Curaeus is reproduced here both in the definition and process, for the sake of context, although it is the second part of this passage that Chapman adapts: 'Echo, est reciprocatio soni, facta ex refractione aeris, in aliquo cavo opposito. Aer percussus et sonum perferens, recta praecipue procurrit, cuius rei signum est, quod cum perspicue sonum comprehendere volumus, recta aurem adhibemus; allisus autem ad solidum obstaculum, reiicitur tanquam pila a muro, et siquidem illud corpus planum est, dissipatur ad latera, nec eadem revertitur via. *Sed si corpus cavum est, aer in eo colligitur, condensatur et congeminatur, recurrit eodem, quo advenerat, tramite, et ita sonum reiterat. Quia autem in illa itione et reditione imbecillior fit*, extremas tantum syllabas vocis, aut alterius soni, ad nostrum auditum defert' ('Echo is a reciprocation of sound produced from the refraction of air in some opposite cavity. As the air is beaten and the sound transmitted, it progresses straightforwardly, which is an indication of the fact that when we want to detect sound clearly, we place our ear directly to it. But when it is dashed against a solid obstacle, it is repelled as spears by a wall; and if this solid body is flat, it is dispersed to the sides, and it does not return through the way it came. *However, if this body is hollow, air is gathered in it, it is compressed and reduplicated, returns the way through which it had arrived, and thus it repeats the sound. Because, however, in that one-way and return trip sound is made weaker*, as much as it delivers to our hearing the last syllables of a word, or of another sound'). The stanza's phrasing is the effect of direct translation/adaptation into English: thus, 'hollow bodies' (*corpus cavum*), 'beat' (*percussus, allisus*), 'air gathered there' (*aer in eo colligitur*), 'compressed and thickenèd' (*condensatur et congeminatur*), 'the selfsame way she came doth make retreat' (*recurrit eodem, quo advenerat, tramite*), 'and so effects the sound re-echoèd' (*et ita sonum reiterat*), 'because she weaker is | In that redition than when first she fled' ('*Quia autem in illa itione et reditione imbecillior fit*'). In the latter sentence Chapman possibly mistook 'fit' ('is made') for 'sit' ('is, be'), or simply adapted his phrasing for the sake of metre and

rhyme. Chapman's neologism 'redition' (i.e. return) translates Latin *reditione*. Ovid's verb 'reiterate' also insists on the idea of the kiss's 'faint echo' as walking over again, though 'faint[ly]', the same path of pleasure initiated by Corinna's original kiss.

101] The conclusion of Ovid's argumentation about the insufficiency of the kiss relies on a varied number of motifs and arguments. Braden has aptly noted the indebtedness of the first line to Narcissus's words expressing his love for his own self: 'inopem me copia fecit' ('my own abundance makes me poor': Ovid, *Metamorphoses*, III. 466). The second line turns Midas's wish upside down: 'effice, quicquid | corpore contigero, fulvum vertatur in aurum' ('Grant that whatsoever I may touch with my body may be turned to yellow gold': *Metamorphoses*, XI. 102–03). Both legends advance the Petrarchan language of oxymoron: love as a 'wanton famine' whose richness of store cannot satisfy the lover's insatiable gluttony. The last three lines of the stanza turn to the language of logic in an instance of metalogical/metapoetic argumentation: all the previous propositions use 'love' as a logical argument, and now its very quality as argument is put to the test. 'Argument' is here used *strictu sensu* as a term of proof in logical invention. After selecting the arguments of invention, logical disposition arranges them in axioms/propositions and syllogisms. If an argument is 'in figure and in mood', it means that it is used correctly in syllogistic reasoning. Compare Thomas Wilson: 'The argument, is either not wel made, in figure or in mode, or in bothe' (*The Rule of Reason* (London: Richard Grafton, 1551), sig. Y8^v). 'Figure' refers to the three possible dispositions of the middle term (the common argument in the major and minor premise) in a proper syllogism: in the first figure, it is the subject in one premise and the predicate in another; in the second, the predicate in both premises; in the third, the subject in both. 'Mood' (or 'mode') expresses the kind of disposition by reference to the quantity (universal or special) and quality (affirmative or negative) of the propositions. Logical imagery builds a complex paradox here: first, love 'hates all arguments', even when it is disposed with those other arguments in the orthodox figures and moods of proper syllogisms; and this is because it uses the language of reason for 'disputing [...] gainst reason', so its defence of 'sense' (i.e. sensuality) proves 'senseless' (i.e. irrational). Therefore, love's disputation 'still' continues even when desire has been satisfied.

Tactus

The sense of touch, the fifth and last, occupies from stanza 102 to stanza 115, while 116 and 117 are considered a conclusion to the narrative, or rather its interruption. However, there is no sense of incompleteness or interruption of Ovid's fulfilment of his wish in relation to sensual gratification.

Stanzas 102–04

Touch was widely considered to be the first of all senses in ancient philosophy. Aristotle insists on the primordial function of touch, since it is the only sense that is common to all animals. See, for instance, *De anima*, II. 2, 413b4–5, and II. 3, 414b2. The principle also holds true in Epicurean philosophy, and is clearly formulated by Lucretius: 'Tactus enim, tactus pro diuum numina sancta, | corporis est sensus uel cum res extera sese | insinuat, vel cum laedit quae in corpore natast | aut iuuat egrediens genitalis per Veneris res, | aut in offensu cum turbant corpore in ipso | semina, confundunt inter se concita sensum' ('For touch, so help me the holy power of God, it is touch that is the bodily sense, whether when a thing penetrates from without, or when hurt comes from something within the body, or when it gives pleasure in issuing forth by the creative acts of Venus, or when from a blow the seeds make riot in the body itself and confuse the sense by the turmoil': *De rerum natura*, II. 434–39). While, for Aristotle, the reason for the primacy of touch is its role in desire and in the processes of nutrition, for the Epicureans the question is the pre-eminence of matter, which makes all senses an extension of touch through their contact with the circulating atoms. While Ovid's argument relies on this general principle, his reasons for calling touch 'the senses' groundwork' and 'the senses' emperor' seem closer to those of the Epicureans: touch, or 'feeling', is made divine here, as it has the power to make the other senses long-lasting and their sensations more pleasant. Thus, Corinna will gain 'eternizement' by letting Ovid touch her, as this action will prolong the pleasures of his other senses. For this reason, touch can 'steel', and thus endow with a long-lasting quality, the 'substance' of smell, sight, hearing and taste. Yet this enduring steel is made of 'flint-soft'ning softness' — softness being the quality of Corinna's body perceived through touch.

The preservative quality of touch explains the somewhat obscure couplet that closes stanza 103: just as bodies can be nourished moderately with the mind's passions (and are not consumed by them), minds will not wear out or become corrupted with the use of touch. The idea of moderation is implied in the comparative 'no more [...] Than', which here means 'in the same measure as', and is more clearly developed in stanza 104's differentiation between those who 'transform' natural beauty 'into corrupt effects' and those who 'hold her due respects'. Alchemical imagery plays a key role in explaining the ways of the latter: Ovid's touch of Corinna's body can refine its substance into purer spirit, just as the 'great elixir', or philosopher's stone, transforms base metals into purer gold. As thirteenth-century alchemist Roger Bacon affirmed, 'euerie metall may by Elixir be reduced to perfection', and specifically 'the red Elixir doth turne into a citrine colour infinitely, and changeth all mettals into pure gold' (*The Mirror of Alchimy*, translation of *Speculum Alchemiae* (London: Thomas Creede, 1597), p. 14). In Ovid's simile, this alchemical power ultimately resides in Corinna's 'quick'ning side'. In the sixteenth century, the adjective meant 'life-giving', and was used in a mainly spiritual, religious sense. Compare: 'With thy sweete helpe and holy Spirite ease vs: | Thy quickening vertue lende to my soule dead, | Then shall my foote on Sathans bellie tread' (Barnabe Barnes, *A Divine Centurie of Spirituall Sonnets* (London: John Windet, 1595), 89. 12–14, sig. G2^r). In the present context, a second meaning could be considered: if Corinna's 'softness' is said to have the property of 'steeling' the 'substance' of the other senses, then her body can also be said to have the quality of 'quick'ning', that is, coating, Ovid's organ of touch with quicksilver — which in alchemy is the female principle that unites with male 'sulphur' in the chemical wedding that engenders the philosopher's stone (see Commentary on 48–49). *OED* only registers eighteenth-century uses of *quicken*, v.², and *quickening*, n.³, in that particular sense. On the significance of the chemical wedding for this stanza, and on Chapman's poem as an allegory of such alchemical process, see Waddington (*The Mind's Empire*, pp. 137–40). For other interpretations in terms of alchemy, see Vinge, 'Chapman's *Ovids Banquet of Sence*', p. 250, and Smarr, 'The Pyramid and the Circle', p. 380.

Stanzas 105–06

The 'arguments' to which Corinna listens with pleasure are primarily Ovid's alchemical similes and imagery. This motivates her 'willing[ness]' to summon 'the wondrous power of heav'n' with 'lawful grounds'. The 'lawful grounds' are the alchemical skills invoked in the previous stanza, while 'the wondrous power of heav'n' is materialized in the producing of her breasts, identified as 'Latona's twins', Apollo and Diana, the Sun and Moon ('Cynthia'), the male and female principles contained in philosophical sulphur and philosophical mercury, or the primal matter (*prima materia*) that engenders 'the great elixir', or philosopher's stone. Corinna's breasts are the temple in which the chemical wedding 'spiritualize[s]' the body (see Commentary: 'Banquet', 47–48). Ovid's reluctance in stanza 106 to touch them questions the worthiness of his own hand to officiate this ritual. Rhetorically, this stanza is unique in the poem, as it provides a schematic gloss of the contents of Ovid's ensuing speech (stanzas 107–09): thus, 'Ennobling it [the hand] with titles full of grace' summarizes stanza 107, a collection of epithets for the hand in the form of an apostrophe; then, the 'reverend verse' that 'conjures' the hand to 'use' Corinna's body 'with piety' anticipates stanza 108; finally, his self-encouragement to 'disperse' and 'supply' his inner faculties with the 'worth' received by 'his feeling's organ' anticipates stanza 109.

Stanzas 107–09

Ovid's speech to his hand extends the narrative of the former stanza. Stanza 107 composes a long apostrophe out of a catalogue of epithets surveying a wide range of everyday and symbolic functions of the hand: as major organ of touch (107. 1), and as symbol of art (2, 5, 6), medicine (3), strength and power (3, 7, 9), generosity (4), manual labour (7), concord and friendship (5, 8). Many of these meanings were represented in the emblem books. On the hand as 'kind acquaintance-maker' and 'Pattern of concord', see Joannes Sambucus's emblem *'Vera amicitia'* (*Emblemata* (Antwerp: Christopher Plantin, 1564), p. 16), in which 'amicitia' is represented by two men shaking hands, while 'concordia' is embodied by a heart above being held by the other hand of one of these men and a divine hand coming from heaven; on the hand as 'engine of all the engines', 'Beauty's beautifier' and 'lord of exercise', and thus as an emblem of art and industry, see Sambucus's emblem *'Industria naturam corrigit'* (*Emblemata*, p. 57), in which the role of the hand in the playing of a lute is foregrounded (see Visual Sources). The epithet 'Proportion's oddness that makes all things even' refers to the odd number five becoming the even number ten if the fingers of both hands are counted. But the oxymoron in 'Proportion's oddness' (i.e. proportion's disproportion) also means that the odd-number-fingered hand is the 'Engine of all engines' — i.e. the most perfect instrument of art, whose skill can achieve perfect proportion. In recommending to his own hand 'fear and reverence', Ovid ponders all these apostrophized qualities and actions against the action of touching Corinna in stanza 108. Finally, stanza 109 praises the object of touch, 'Cupid's alps' (i.e. Corinna's breasts). The hyperbolic paradox whereby the snow-white skin is able to thaw the sun is a reminder of the beloved's purity.

Abundance is the subject of the next argument of praise: by means of touch ('feelingly'), the hand will be able to discover the lands of milk and honey that characterized the Ovidian Golden Age: 'flumina iam lactis, iam flumina nectaris ibant, | flavaque de viridi stillabant ilice mella' ('Streams of milk and streams of sweet nectar flowed, and yellow honey was distilled from the verdant oak': *Metamorphoses*, I. 111–12). Abundance is complemented by fertility: 109. 5–9 combines allegory ('Pleasure' must be capitalized, although the initial position renders this ambiguous) and simile ('like an empress'). Thus, the expansion and retraction of Corinna's breast while breathing provide the basis of an allegory of Pleasure as a gravid woman, 'panting' in the act of labour and 'Ever delivered, yet with child still growing', both 'full' and 'bestowing' the fruits of her pregnancy. The antithetical imagery presenting pregnancy and delivery simultaneously has been noted by Hudston (p. 413, 109. 5–9, notes) as a favourite image of Chapman's poetry: see 'Cynthiam', 368–69; also, 'Euer deliuered, euermore with childe' (*Iustification of Andromeda Liberata*, 'Dialogus', 12, in Bartlett, p. 332).

Stanza 110

Ovid's touch of Corinna's breast is compared to Jove's laying of Hercules on Juno's, as recounted by Conti: 'Ferunt Iunonem lac Herculi infanti praebuisse, quo immortalitatem assequeretur. [...] Nam fabulatur Iouem aliquando dormientis Iunonis uberibus Herculem infantem admouisse, quo ab excitata reiecto pars lactis quae in coelum cecidit, viam inde vocatam lacteam fecit' ('They say that Juno offered her milk to the infant Hercules, and this is what made him immortal. [...] They fable that Jupiter brought the infant Hercules to suck at Juno's breasts while she was asleep, but she woke up and, as she pushed him away, some of her milk spilled onto the heavens and produced the Milky Way (as it was called later on)': 'De Iunone', II. 4, pp. 135–36; Mulryan, p. 114). The 'coy retire' may thus be attributed to Juno, in contrast with Corinna's 'tender temper' (i.e. her affectionate composure). The suggestion of innocence in Corinna's reaction, as well as in the 'sharp', 'undulled' quality of her breasts, contrasts with the pun suggested by the 'keener edge' of her breasts and of Ovid's arousal.

Stanzas 111–15

Ovid's speech is 'sighed out' while 'still' touching Corinna's breasts, an action that, like his praise, is 'interrupted' in stanza 116 with the arrival of other ladies. For the speech verb used here, compare Samuel Daniel: 'Go wailing verse [...] | *Sigh out* a story of her cruell deedes, | With interrupted accents of dispayre' (*Delia*, II. 1–6, in *Poems and A Defence of Rhyme*, p. 11, emphasis added). The 'effect' refers to Ovid's whole account of his impressions in direct speech. Ovid's last speech summarizes a number of major themes of the poem. Its impression is of completion, and thus it stands in sharp contrast with the abrupt action in which the poem ends.

> 111] Ovid's rhetorical question (2–6) voices his desire for a 'tongue' of the soul that may 'unfold' the 'spiritual notion' of Corinna's excellence, and constitutes the presiding argument over the following stanzas. In the absence of this spiritual language, the 'fleshly engine' of the physical tongue must voice Corinna's praise. The three axioms contained in lines 6–9 answer this question only in part. The custom of having lower-class nurses to feed royal children provides the occasion for a complex argument: the princely 'birth' can be Corinna herself, as she is the emperor's daughter, while the peasant is Ovid; the 'birth' can also refer to the pleasures 'delivered' from her swelling breasts (see stanza 109), the 'peasant' being Ovid's 'tongue', whose humble carnality must 'nurse' or sing its high excellences. The next axiom, 'free virtue [must] wait on gold', seems to take its cue from the first of the former ideas, thus emphasizing the theme of the nobility of mind ('free virtues') against the status conferred by birth or riches. The statement contained in the stanza's final couplet returns to the baseness of the tongue, the 'professed [i.e. devoted] though flattering enemy' that must defend the common man's 'honour' and 'liberty' in the presence of those of princely blood.

> 112] The apostrophe to 'Nature' gives continuity to the arguments of the previous stanza, as she is made responsible for not providing men with a language of the soul, and thus for levelling 'men with beasts | And noblest

minds with slaves'. Ovid's answer to his own rhetorical question suggests that the consequence of this flaw of nature is that, while the senses should cater for a banquet of the mind, they end up in a 'surfeit' of the flesh. The inadequacy of the human tongue lies then in its 'rude frailty', and thus in its incapacity to express the 'joys' experienced by sense, which will remain 'not uttered'.

113] Through a new apostrophe, the addressee shifts in this stanza to 'touch', which, by means of a series of poetic arguments, becomes the efficient, formal, material and final cause of desire, here personified in Cupid: thus, touch is the 'engine', or hand, that shoots his bow and the 'guide' to his blindness; it is also the essence of his divine status and the 'sphere' on which 'his health and life' circulate; it is also the substance that 'blow[s] his fire and feed his pride'; and, most importantly, it is its finality or 'object whereto all his actions tend'. Touch justifies his literary action: what the tongue has left unuttered in the previous stanza will be written in the form of an *ars amatoria*. The mention of the *Art of Love* as the next step in Ovid's career has a number of consequences in relation to the historical context of Ovid's production. It situates the historical time of the poem at the time of Ovid's early *Amores*, and in the transition toward the didactic elegy that presents the poet's persona as the *praeceptor Amoris* already invoked in Davies's commendatory sonnets to this collection. One can literally affirm that Ovid's *Ars amatoria* was written with the sense of touch in mind as the final cause of the conducts taught in the poem. The work's concluding descriptions of the different postures in love-making seem to confirm this point (*Ars amatoria*, III. 769–808). Yet that ending hardly matches the refined language of the soul that the joys of touch are said to inspire here. Satiric Ovidianism, as argued by Gless ('Chapman's Ironic Ovid') and others, would be a critical solution to this contradiction; the other is the kind of reformed Ovidianism proposed in this edition and by other critics, discussed in the Introduction. Ovid's love for the emperor's daughter, Julia, also brings together here the *carmen et error* ('a poem and a mistake'), the two alleged causes of Ovid's banishment from Rome. See in this respect Lyne, 'Love and Exile', pp. 289–90; Moss, 'Second Master', p. 474; and Luis-Martínez, 'Whose Banquet?', p. 41. The closing couplet conveys a turn in the argument, which resumes the philanthropic ideas expressed in stanza 87. The 'slavery' of 'self-love' seems to refer to the vanity of those poets who do not pay their due respect to Nature (see stanza 111).

114–15] The 'contagion' of vanity, or 'self-love', affects the 'dog days', which can be understood both literally (as 'Banquet' takes place in the summer), but mainly figuratively as ominous or evil times. The phrase 'purest bloods' introduces Chapman's favourite theme of poor men of learning, ignored and despised by others, yet storing in their souls the highest virtues that a patron of arts would value. Poverty is then the quality of a Platonic poetics devoted to praising 'virtue, love, and beauty' — a poetics in which 'poor verse' equals 'bright verse' and opposes the 'fat and foggy brains' of those rival poets seduced by 'gold's love'. This kind of poetry deserves the virtuous patronage whereby Ovid's 'mistress', a word that throughout the poem invokes the beloved as object of desire and as source of inspiration, becomes 'patroness', granting moral and intellectual authorization, as well as social protection. The duality mistress/patroness is embodied in the identification of the lyric character of Corinna as the historical Julia. Corinna's honest patronage thus emerges as a final cause of Ovid's 'banquet of sense', thus bringing together the ethical and socio-economic dimensions of Chapman's aesthetics.

Stanzas 116–17

Interruption presides over the end of the poem, particularly stanza 116. Ovid's former speech has reached a proper conclusion, which seems independent of the incomplete action dealt with in these stanzas. The 'view | Of other dames' is the circumstance that prevents continuation lest Corinna's good name be endangered by their discovery. For the anecdote of Alexander the Great underlying this stanza's simile Chapman relied, as Schoell noted (*Études,*, p. 225), on Plutarch's Περὶ εὐθυμίας, 466D, in Wilhem Xylander's translation, *De tranquillitate animi*: 'Alexander cum infinitos mundos esse ex Anaxarcho audiuisset, fleuit: ac rogantibus amicis quid accidisset, Non dignum, inquit, fletu vobis videtur, si cum sint infiniti mundi, nos ne vno quidem etiamnum potiti sumus?' ('Alexander wept when he heard Anaxarchus discourse about an infinite number of worlds, and when his friends inquired what ailed him, "Is it not worthy of tears," he said, "that, when the number of worlds is infinite, we have not yet become lords of a single one?"': *Plutarchi Chaeronensis Moralia*, p. 414; translation from the Greek by Helmbold, in *Moralia*, VI, pp. 177–79). The impossibility of conquering 'more worlds' (Plutarch's 'infiniti mundi') by means of 'greater action' equals Alexander's heroism and Ovid's amorous conquests ('love's conqueror'). Interruption thus leads to the incompletion of 'love's defects', here used in the word's etymological sense: Latin *de* + *facio*, the undoing, or the absence, of action.

If stanza 116 stresses the interruption of love, then stanza 117 offers its antithesis or counterargument: interruption occurs only in action, but not in intention. Waddington (*The Mind's Empire*, p. 136) has aptly proposed that the poem's closing simile is inspired by Pliny the Elder's description of Parrhasius of Ephesus's refinement ('subtilitas') in the art of painting: 'corpora enim pingere et media rerum est quidem magni operis, sed in quo multi gloriam tulerint; extrema corporum facere et desinentis picturae modum includere rarum in successu artis invenitur. ambire enim se ipsa debet extremitas et sic desinere, ut promittat alia et post se ostendatque etiam quae occultat' ('to paint bulk and the surface within the outlines, though no doubt a great achievement, is one in which many have won distinction, but to give the contour of the figures, and make a satisfactory boundary where the painting within finishes, is rarely attained in successful artistry. For the contour ought to round itself off and so terminate as to suggest the presence of other parts behind it also, and disclose even what it hides': *Natural History*, xxxv. 36). Chapman's addition is the hand, precisely the physical site of the sense organ whose enjoyment has been interrupted by the ladies' appearance, as well as the hand's royal status, that is, the utmost embodiment of power represented here *in potentia*, and thus fully realized in intention rather than in action. The simile's vehicle reiterates *enargia*, or perspicuity, through the painter's capacity to enlighten what remains obscure, and the viewer's ability to understand what remains unseen. An anonymous *Portrait of Elizabeth I* (*c.* 1600; see Visual Sources) offers an accurate analogue of the half-viewed hand of the sceptre-holding monarch. As in the painting, 'so in the compass of this curious frame': thus, the scene presented throughout the poem is also 'frame[d]' as an intricate design that calls for similarly visual decoding. Critics (Myers, 'This Curious Frame'; and Wheeler, 'The obiect', p. 343) have stressed Chapman's possible borrowing from Sidney's 'allegorie's curious frame' (*Astrophil and Stella*, 28. 1, in *The Poems of Sir Philip Sidney*, p. 178) to suggest that the 'much more' that is 'intended' needs to be apprehended by way of allegoresis.

Yet in Chapman's case the visual focus should complement allegory with an emblematic approach: Ovid's banquet remains within the frame of a *pictura* that encourages decoding by the reader. Ovid's knowledge of further intentions has also been read in terms of *aposiopesis* (Introduction, pp. 49–50), as a rewriting of Ovid's *Amores*, I. 5: 'Singula quid referam? nil non laudabile vidi | et nudam pressi corpus ad usque meum. | Cetera quis nescit?' ('Why recount each charm? Naught did I see not worthy of praise, and I clasped her naked form to mine. The rest, who does not know?', 23–26, translation altered). Whereas the Ovidian elegy takes sexual intercourse for granted while refusing to offer details, Chapman defers consummation. In this regard, Waddington has argued that 'even without the terminal comment the reader understands that he is to take the seduction as successfully consummated. The perspective analogy makes that evident: just as we accept the illusion of the portrait for the reality of the whole man [*sic*], so we are to take the poem as representational of the completed action' (*The Mind's Empire*, p. 136). Deferral is not denial, and one can easily assume that what Ovid knows to be 'intended' includes sexual satisfaction without rejecting other intentions.

However, what remains at the end for the reader to accept without offence is another kind of consummation, provided by the Latin sentences closing the poem: as the banquet ends (*Explicit convivium*), what is left is 'Intention, an act of the mind' (*Intentio, animi actio*). Two meanings of *intentio* are applicable here. First, the general sense of purpose or volition: if understood in this way, we should then understand that intention advances fulfilment or consummation. Second, the specialized philosophical sense derived from medieval logic conceives of *intentio* (also in English, see *OED*, intention, n., †1, †2 and 11) as intellection, or the application of the mind to an object, and thus as an act of the mind, as the gloss insists. If seen in combination, these two senses proclaim intellectual consummation as the necessary end of the sensual banquet. In line with this, the apprehension of 'The majesty and riches of the mind' ('Coronet', 1. 11) announces the next poem in the collection not necessarily as a substitute, a counterargument or a recantation, but as a continuation, a complement or a consummation devoutly to be wished.

A Coronet for His Mistress Philosophy

'Coronet' is a diminutive of 'corona', or 'crown'. A corona is a short lyric cycle with a circular structure: the last line of each poem begins the next, while the first line of the first poem is also the closing line of the sequence. Philip Sidney included a crown of ten dizains in *The Old Arcadia*, while his brother Robert left unfinished a corona of sonnets in his manuscript notebook. Chapman's 'Coronet' is thus the first complete instance of its kind in English — followed, years later by John Donne's *La Corona*, made up of seven sonnets, and Lady Mary Wroth's 'A Crowne of Sonetts Dedicated to Love', included in *Pamphilia to Amphilanthus* (1621) and comprising fourteen sonnets. These ten sonnets observe the so-called Shakespearean rhyme pattern, *ababcdcdefefgg*.

Chapman's sequence has received little critical attention. This hymnic praise to Philosophy, here transformed into an idealized beloved, has been interpreted in the light of the different critical approaches to 'Banquet': for critics who read 'Banquet' as ironic, it is a confirmation of Chapman's attack there on the sensualism of Ovidian poetry (Kermode, 'The Banquet of Sense', pp. 85–86, 92; Myers, 'This Curious Frame', pp. 204–05); for those who interpret 'Banquet' as a Platonic allegory, 'Coronet' delves deep into Chapman's conception of love in the former poem (Vinge, 'Chapman's *Ovids Banquet of Sence*', p. 234; Wheeler, 'The obiect', p. 344). A possible inspiration in Boethius's Lady Philosophy, the personified character of *De consolatione philosophiae*, has been suggested by Presson ('Wrestling with This World', p. 48). The poem has had few commentaries that focus on its individual achievement: Huntington has read it as a defence of poetic obscurity against the ambition-laden practices of courtly sonneteers (*Ambition*, pp. 102–05). More recently, I have devoted an article-length study to the poem, which pays attention to its relation to contemporary sonnet sequences, its design of a philosophical poetics and its concern with proportional form (Luis-Martínez, 'Friendlesse Verse'). The present commentary expands on the ideas of this study, as well as those in the Introduction, pp. 53–56, while also proposing further lines of interpretation.

Sonnet 1

The corona begins by replacing the invocation to the Muse proper to the epic poem with a much less conventional rebuke, addressed both to the 'Muses' of love poetry and the 'lovers' themselves (1–8), followed by an invitation to recant their sensuality (9–14). The 'eye' (3) is the focus of this first poem, thus signalling the sequence's thematic continuity with 'Banquet'. The eye is appointed here as the site of 'love's sensual empery' (1), where 'Cupid's bonfires' (3) are fed by 'the empty breath of vain desires' (4). 'Empty' is a key adjective: it declares that 'breath' to be soulless, as it prevents the love that it inspires from seeing the 'majesty and riches of the mind' (13). The contrast between outward and inward beauty is developed in the second quatrain by means of two sets of antithetical pairs, with one key nominal phrase presiding over each line: 'painted cabinet' (5) vs 'wealthy jewels' (6), and 'dying figures' (7) vs 'living substance' (8). The lexicon of painting and colouring — 'painted' (5), 'stain' (8) — invites us to read a pun on 'dying' and *dyeing*, two words with identical pronunciation and spelling in the sixteenth century. The recantation advised by the poetic voice comprises the renunciation of the lovers' 'joys', as well as the Muses'/poets' written 'memory' of those joys (9). Once that double process is completed, the Muses will be ready to inspire a 'complete history' (11), or treatise, of 'love and honour', with Philosophy as its central 'subject' (10). As the present corona purports to be such a written 'history', this sonnet constitutes the opening statement of a poetics, in imitation of, but also in quarrel with, other Elizabethan sonnet sequences. Thus, the ideal of intellect-inspired Muses to which this poem aspires contradicts the Sidneian Muse of *Astrophil and Stella*: 'Foole, said my Muse to me, looke in thy heart and write' (1. 14, in *Poems of Sir Philip Sidney*, p. 165).

The last three lines reiterate the eyes' incapacity 'to see | The majesty and riches of the mind' (12–13), caused by Cupid's own blindness, itself the effect of the 'empty', soulless breath that animates his 'bonfires' (3). Cupid's blindness was an established convention of the sonnet tradition: see e.g. Fletcher, *Licia*, x. 1–2; or, more relevantly here, Greville, *Caelica*, 12. 7, where Cupid 'clouds' the lover's eyes 'with a seeing blindnesse' (XII. 7, in *Poems and Dramas of Fulke Greville, First Lord Brooke*, ed. by Geoffrey Bullough, 2 vols (Oxford University Press, 1945), I, p. 79). In this, Chapman and his fellow Elizabethans followed the medieval courtly tradition (see the chapter 'Blind Cupid', in Erwin Panofsky, *Studies in Iconology: Humanistic Themes in the Art of the Renaissance* (Harper & Row, 1939), pp. 95–128); but also, and more relevantly here, the tradition transmitted from Orpheus (Fragment 82) and Proclus to the Florentine Neoplatonists of the eyeless Cupid (ἀνόμματος Ἔρως): 'Ideo Amor ab Orpheo sine oculis dicitur, quia est supra intellectum' ('Love is thus said to be without eyes because he is beyond our intellectual power': Giovanni Pico della Mirandola, *Conclusiones in doctrina Platonis*

(Rome, 1486), p. 6). See also C. D. Gilbert, 'Blind Cupid', *Journal of the Warburg and Courtauld Institute*, 33.1 (1970), pp. 304-05 (p. 305), doi:10.2307/750901. Chapman's corona aspires to have an eye-opening power, which will ultimately reveal the love of knowledge (Philosophy's inward beauty) to those eyes that were 'never yet let in to see' (12). Love as an intellectual aspiration thus constitutes the centre of Chapman's sequence.

Sonnet 2

As Laurence Sasek has noted, 'Chapman's repeated line is sometimes not an organic part of the sonnet it introduces' ('Gascoigne and the Elizabethan Sonnet Sequences', *Notes and Queries*, 3.4 (1956), pp. 143-44 (p. 144)). This compositional circumstance in 'Coronet' demands that we look at the first line of this sonnet and other similar cases as 'opening propositions of a complex reasoning structure without much regard to syntactic flow' (Luis-Martínez, 'Friendlesse Verse', p. 600). The colon at the end of the line is editorial and is meant to suggest the first line's status as a logical proposition: thus, the 'darkness' that blinds sensual lovers is the moot point to be developed in the first two quatrains, which count among the most obscure passages of the sequence. The aqueous 'humour' of the eye causes Cupid's blindness by inundating his eyes with tears, which emanate like 'torrents' (2) and 'fall on his base kind' (3) — i.e. his kindred, lovers — and devour their 'entrails' (4). This last detail has Promethean connotations. Analogues are found in Sidney, *Astrophil and Stella*, 14. 2, in which 'a fiercer Gripe doth tire' the lover's breast (*Poems of Sir Philip Sidney*, p. 171), and Barnabe Barnes: 'To none but to Prometheus me compayer' (*Parthenophil and Parthenophe*, sonnet 61, pp. 37-38). The second quatrain's bizarre imagery presents the lovers' destruction as undertaken by a personified 'Colour' (5), whose almost imperceptible 'hands' (5) cover the lovers' soft, 'waxen thoughts' with hard 'adamant' (6), infuse them with 'her painted fires' to 'melt' their 'hearts' (7), and 'beat' their 'souls in pieces' (8). This destruction is the effect of a sensual love that 'flows' from the 'liver' (14), a circumstance that reinforces the Promethean imagery in the opening quatrain. In Chapman's poetry, 'colour' is often a 'feeble image' of 'virtuous light' ('Banquet', 55. 5-6, and Commentary), deceptive and destructive to the soul (Rutledge, *Chapman's Theory of the Soul*, pp. 34-36, 86). The volta after line 8 directs the argument to its antithesis: Philosophy is 'the cordial of souls' (9); the 'passion' that she inspires aims at 'perfection' (10), and her 'fixed beauties' are a repository of indestructible 'human bliss' (12). The paths from 'soul to spirit' and from 'spirit to flesh' (13) appoint the 'spirit' as the intermediary between mind and body. Spirits are conceived of as material emanations which carry the passions through the blood (Rutledge, *Chapman's Theory of the Soul*, pp. 87-88). In the last line, paronomasia contrasts two models of love: one originates in the perishable 'liver' and the other in Philosophy's eternal 'living'. This opposition serves the initial argument of the next sonnet.

Sonnet 3

The focus on love's origin in Philosophy's 'living' in the previous sonnet lays the basis for the description of the inward essence of Philosophy's beauty and the ascending nature of her love-inspiring emanations of light. Analogues are found in Drayton's sonnets 6, 26 and 48 of *Ideas Mirrour* (*The Works of Michael Drayton*, I, pp. 100, 111, 122). However, if in Drayton 'a contradiction between the beloved's essence and the lover's desires cannot be concealed', Chapman's focus on Mistress Philosophy 'effaces [all] corporeality' (Luis-Martínez, 'Friendlesse Verse', pp. 578–80), particularly in the description of her capacity to resist 'age', 'care' and 'torment' (6). The metaphor of Philosophy's 'mind' as 'the beam of God' is genuinely Neoplatonic. See Ficino's discussion of God's beauty: 'An tu esse aliud quam lucem, pulchritudinem ducis? Porro corporum omnium pulchritudo lumen istud est solis quod vides, tribus illis infectum: formarum multitudine, nam multis id aspicis figuris coloribusque depictum, loci spatio, temporali mutatione. [...] Tolle postremo diversarum illum idearum; unam simplicem et meram relinque lucem [...] iam Dei pulchritudinem quodammodo comprehendis' ('Do you think beauty is anything else but light? Certainly, the beauty of all bodies is that light of the sun which you see, adulterated with these three: multiplicity of form (for you see it imprinted with many shapes and colors), the spatiality of place, and change of time. [...] Finally, take away that number of different ideas; leave one simple and clear light, the image of that light [...] (and) now you comprehend in a measure the beauty of God': *Commentary on Plato's Symposium*, VI. 17, pp. 100, 211). Elsewhere Chapman calls the soul '*an intellectual beam of God*, the essence of her substance being intellection' (Preface to *Seaven Bookes of the Iliads*; in Nicoll, I, p. 505, emphasis added). Intellection is here represented by the mind's withdrawal of the eyes' 'fires' (9) to avoid 'earth's tempting fuels' (10). Chapman revisited the image of fire's compression (13–14) in *Andromeda Liberata* (1614): '*Beauty like fire, comprest, more strength receiues*' (123, in Bartlett, p. 312, original emphasis). The simile enables the pun on 'blaze' in the last line: Philosophy's beauties make her own fame shine, but also give it the form of a novel kind of poetic blazon, which eschews the Petrarchan focus on physical beauty and proclaims the beauties of the mind.

Sonnet 4

Thematically, this sonnet develops the argument of the previous one. Inwardness and self-enclosure — 'from the world into herself reflected' (2) — are the direct cause of Philosophy's being 'rejected' (4) from the world and 'depressed' (5), but also of her ascent to 'Olympus' gate' (5). The idea of the marriage between Philosophy and God may be loosely inspired by the fifth-century prosimetrum *De nuptiis Philologiae et Mercurii*, by Martianus Capella, first printed in 1499. In Muse Melpomene's epithalamium to Philology, we read: 'Digna maritali semper videaris Olympo | decentiorque caelitum' ('Always look worthy of thy husband's Olympus and the more fitting for the heavenly gods', *Las nupcias de Filología y Mercurio*, ed. by Fernando Navarro Antolín, 3 vols (CSIC, 2016), II. 121. 10–11, I, p. 101, my translation). In Martianus, Philology is a serious and long-haired woman ('gravis crinitaque femina') who already lives in Olympus (II. 131, I, p. 113). This work also begins with a hymn to Hymen (I. 1, pp. 2–3), and its second book concludes with Philology's entrance into Jove's palace on Olympus (II. 215, I, p. 157) after she has purged herself of all worldly knowledge (II. 135–41, I, pp. 115–20). Beyond the possible influence of this analogue, the allegorical narrative of the sonnet culminates circularly in 'Virtue', which is the beginning and end, the heavenly 'merit and reward' (13), of Philosophy's cultivation of the mind.

Sonnet 5

This is a new instance of Chapman's difficulties with fitting the repeated line into a new syntactic unit. The opening quatrain of this sonnet is an incomplete sentence, unless it is regarded as a modifier of 4. 13: 'Virtue is both the merit and reward [...]'. In fact, 'Virtue' is the presiding argument over this and the next two sonnets. The military conceits in the present sonnet find analogues in the courtly amatory and Petrarchan tradition: examples in Elizabethan England are found in sonnets 7, 15 and 18 by Robert Sidney (*Poems of Robert Sidney*, pp. 157, 197, 211). Specifically, Robert Sidney's sonnet 15 represents the beloved's 'face' as 'the field where beauty's order shine' and her 'eyes' as 'love's cannons strong' (15. 9–10, p. 197), at war with the lover's desires. The 'firm species' of Philosophy's 'soul-infused regard' equally 'points her life's field' (1–3). Yet those 'virtues' forces' deployed 'in the army of her face' (10–11) also invoke the literary model of Prudentius's fourth-century Christian poem *Psychomachia*, in which the battle against the vices is carried out by 'omnis | Virtutum legio' ('the whole army of the Virtues': *Prudentius*, ed. and trans. by H. J. Thompson, 2 vols (Heinemann, 1949), 705–06, I, pp. 328–29). Philosophy's enemy is the 'inversed world' (5), portrayed as a lady with 'wanton heels' (6) and 'thoughts cupidinine' (9), and attracting 'loose eyne' (11). The closing couplet presents 'War to all frailty' (13) fought by Philosophy's 'look' (14) — i.e. the 'golden lances' (2) of her 'regard'. Philosophy's war is considered the vehicle to 'peace of all things pure' (13), and her 'life' (14) is the 'field' where 'all wars' are fought (2). Virtue's peace as the outcome of war against vice is also the final cause in Prudentius's allegorical poem: 'pax plenum Virtutis opus, pax summa laborum, | pax belli exacti pretium est pretiumque pericli' ('Peace is the fulfilment of Virtue's work, peace the sum and substance of her toils, peace the reward for war now ended and for peril faced': 769–70; I, pp. 332–33). For a more detailed assessment of Prudentius, Robert Sidney, and sonnets 5, 6 and 7 of 'Coronet', see Luis-Martínez, 'Friendlesse Verse', pp. 581–83.

Sonnet 6

The linking line of sonnets 5 and 6 is the middle point of the sequence and the centre of its symbolic circle. Upon the surface of her 'life's field' (5.3), Philosophy projects 'A right line' from its centre — 'Her look'. This line ascends 'through every thing obscure' by conducting its 'rebateless point' toward 'full perfection' (1–4). The metaphor's vehicle is numerological and geometrical, and the tenor moral, but also aesthetic: thus, the line is projected from Philosophy's mind, but also from the poem's centre. Puttenham's discussion of poetic disposition in 'roundel' or 'sphere' is of relevance here: 'This figure hath three principal parts in his nature and use much considerable: the circle, the beam, and the center. The circle is his largest compass or circumference; the center is his middle and indivisible point; the beam is a line stretching directly from the circle to the center, and contrariwise from the center to the circle. By this description our maker may fashion his meter in roundel, either with the circumference, and that is circlewise; or from the circumference, that is, like a beam' (*Art of English Poesy*, II. 12, p. 187). If 'circumference' explains the arrangement of the corona, the 'beam' is 'the right line' projected from the 'center' to the circle's 'perfection'. This aesthetic argument facilitates a moral interpretation of the 'right line' guiding Philosophy's conduct, which is the focus of the rest of the sonnet. The iterated predicate in the initial position of lines 9 and 13 ('Can alter her') points at constancy's 'right line' as the ruling virtue in this sonnet. Each sentence stresses a different facet of the 'inversed world' (5.5) that Philosophy's 'constant guises' (13) oppose. The first (4–9) is 'pied-faced fashion' and its 'Protean rages', a distinctively 'female' malady caused by humoral 'disjoint', and whose corrupting effects are particularly felt on 'poor men'. The second (9–13) focuses on the courtly world and its 'false nobility', based on blood and not on virtue. On Chapman's critique of nobility of blood, see Commentary: 'Cynthiam', 220–42, and 'Banquet', 90–91.

Sonnet 7

The transformation of 'deadly vices' into 'living virtues', reinforced in the opening rhetorical antithesis, provides the master conceit of the sonnet, which is an incomplete treatise on the Seven Deadly Sins. Only six sins are discussed: envy is missing, even if its absence in Philosophy's character is mentioned in 5. 8. Sources or analogues for the treatment of the deadly sins can be found in two previous sonnets of the 1590s. A sonnet by Henry Constable, preserved in manuscript but also printed first in the 1592 edition of his *Diana*, 'Mine eye with all the deadlie sinnes is fraught', discusses their effect on both beloved and lover: 'These sinnes procured haue a goddesse ire, | Wherefore my hart is damn'd in loves sweete fire' (*The Complete Poems*, ed. by María Jesús Pérez-Jáuregui (Pontifical Institute of Mediaeval Studies, 2023), 60, lines 1, 13–14, p. 219). The second sonnet, by Barnabe Barnes (*Parthenophil and Parthenophe*, sonnet 97, p. 55), could have been written in imitation of Constable's: 'Oh why should enuie with sweet loue consorte | But that, with loues excesse seuen sinnes vnite' (1–2). Chapman rewrites the motif of love's sinfulness: in making each sin hers, Philosophy makes each vice look like its opposite: e.g. 'For covetous she is, of all good parts'. Antithesis offers various opportunities for poetic ingenuity: thus, the thoughts that cause Philosophy's gluttony are imagined to be '[di]stilled', as from an alembic, in the 'fervency' of 'contemplation' (5–7). But it also yields some of the obscurest passages in the sequence. The depiction of incontinence in lines 3–4 is quite far from Chapman's ideal of 'clearness of representation'. Lines 10–12 represent 'sloth' lying in an endless, 'all-seeing trance' of philosophical contemplation: why this intellect-inspiring idleness is not moved by 'constancy' remains unexplained (13). The last line brings forth the critique of material riches as a cause of the search for knowledge — a theme which, like that of nobility of blood, is a recurrent preoccupation in Chapman's verse.

Sonnet 8

The focus in this and the next sonnet shifts from moral psychomachia to aesthetic representation. Considered together, sonnets 8 and 9 can be interpreted as a poetics. The opening of this sonnet is another instance of a linking line that hardly fits syntactically into the new sentence. It rather prolongs the previous sentence into the new sonnet. Thus, the first two lines omit the direct object and verb (i.e. 'her mind doth move') of its two coordinated clauses: unmoved by economic or political ambition ('riches' or 'empire'), Philosophy's 'mighty government' is to be 'analysed' along the rules of logic ('laws' and 'canons') and not with regard to the passions ('care', 'content'). The simile of the second stanza reorients the sonnet's focus toward the arts: the stained glass that colours the object facing it when traversed by sunlight is an image that the poet also explores in 'Banquet', 6. In the present sonnet, the effect of light's 'transmission' (6) through the stained glass on its onlookers is compared to the 'reverence' (8) due to Philosophy by the 'subjects' that pursue her knowledge. A new simile occupying the third quatrain reinforces the sonnet's aesthetic concern: the pansy's purple colour is darker in its inner petals, thus providing the poetic medium that expresses the 'greater grace' of Philosophy's 'inward work' (10). This emblematizes the ideal of obscurity that 'shroudeth itself in the heart of its subject, uttered with fitness of figure' ('*OBS*: To Roydon', lines 31–32). However, this ideal principle is acknowledged to be not fully achieved, as 'time's conceits' (12) fall short of their model, and Philosophy's 'virtues' soar 'above' the poet's 'verse' (13). This insufficiency of the poet's art — a theme discussed in the opening pages of the Introduction — serves as the moot argument for the next sonnet: 'For words want art, and art wants words to praise her'.

Sonnet 9

This sonnet looks in many ways like what should have been the natural ending of the corona. Thematically, it culminates its aesthetic programme, as well as the social projection of its poetics. Formally, the ending of line 13, 'envy' (stressed on the second syllable), would supply a perfect rhyme for the first line of the first sonnet to round off the corona: *And never shall my friendless verse envy | Muses that sing love's sensual empery*. None of these conditions are found so neatly in the tenth sonnet, whose first ten lines are an afterthought about the theatre and whose final couplet needs to change 'empery' for its plural form 'emperies' in order to fit the rhyme scheme, thus breaking the rule that the first and last lines of a corona must be identical. Starting with the insufficiency of the poet's art, sonnet 9 proposes a neat division of labour in its proposed poetics: 'inspirations' (6) belong to Philosophy (4) in her role as 'Muse' (5), whereas labour proper is the responsibility of the poet, whose 'industrious pen' (2) must 'register her worth' (4). Philosophy's inspiring qualities reopen the Boethian theme of the consolation ('assuage', 6) of a poet whose 'fortunes' (7) have made him prisoner of 'heartless griefs' (8). Philosophy's provision of 'comfort' for the injustices of false 'Honour' and 'Error' reiterates Chapman's critique of social reward obtained despite 'merit'.

The definition of an ideal of poetry as 'friendless verse' suggests at least two meanings. On one hand, the absence of a conventional mistress, or 'friend' — a theme that the narrative voice of 'Banquet' has already adumbrated: 'That never mistress had to make me better' (57. 9; and Commentary); on the other hand, the notion of true poetry as an art addressed to a knowledgeable minority — another recurrent theme in Chapman's poetics. Compare the ideas in this sonnet to a later text: 'nor is it more empaire to an honest and absolute man's sufficiencie to have few friendes than to an Homericall Poeme to have fewe commenders, for neyther doe common dispositions keepe fitte or plausible consort with judiciall and simple honestie, nor are idle capacities comprehensible of an elaborate Poeme' (*Achilles Shield*, 'To the Understander', Nicoll, I, p. 548). 'Friendless verse' is thus another facet of the cultivation of poetic obscurity. The final line invokes Virgil's depiction of the monster *Fama* as a winged and feathered monster: 'pedibus celerem et peniicibus alis, | monstrum horrendum, ingens, cui, quot sunt corpore plumae, | tot vigiles oculi subter (mirabile dictu), | tot linguae, totidem ora sonant, tot subrigit auris' ('swift of foot and fleet of wing, a monster awful and huge, who for the many feathers in her body has as many watchful eyes below — wondrous to tell — as many tongues, as many sounding mouths, as many pricked-up ears': *Aeneid*, IV. 180–83). Representing both lasciviousness and garrulity, 'Fame's loose feathers' embody a critique directed against both the matter and style of the sort of poetry pertaining to these 'Muses'.

Sonnet 10

The praise of the theatre as 'the seed of memory' (3) that occupies the first two quatrains seems alien to the major theme of the sequence, or at best constitutes an afterthought that shifts the focus to the author's intention to try his hand as a playwright. Chapman's first plays for the Lord Admiral's Men were written, and performed at the Rose, by 1595 or 1596. I have argued elsewhere (Luis-Martínez, 'Friendlesse Verse', p. 602 and n. 123) that Chapman could have been inspired by the contention between personified Elegy and Tragedy in Ovid's *Amores*: 'Quod tenerae cantent, lusit tua Musa, puellae, | primaque per numeros acta iuventa suos. | nunc habeam per te Romana Tragoedia nomen! | inplebit leges spiritus iste meas' (III. 1. 27–30). In Marlowe's translation: 'Thy muse hath played what may milde girles content, | And by those numbers is thy first youth spent. | Now give the Roman Tragedie a name, | To fill my lawes thy wanton spirit frame' (*All Ovids Elegies*, III. 1. 27–30). This praise attempts to exorcize the 'contempt' (8) by 'like-plumed birds' (9), that is, those who wear, or who 'beautify', the same 'loose feathers' as Fame has. An elitist, mainly courtly, poetic culture's contempt for the public theatre may explain Chapman's need to defend it. See, for instance, Sidney's description of English drama as 'an unmannerly daughter showing a bad education', which 'causeth her mother poesy's honesty to be called in question' (*Defence of Poesy*, in *Miscellaneous Prose of Sir Philip Sidney*, p. 116; see also, more generally, Jonas Barish, *The Antitheatrical Prejudice* (University of California Press, 1981), pp. 80–154). In line 10, the addressee changes from the 'Muses' back to Philosophy, who is asked to banish the 'servile' verses written by courtly flatterers from 'Honour's court', where true merit should reign. The closing couplet may be syntactically ambiguous: 'my love' and 'Muses' may be interchangeably considered subject and object of 'adorn'. Yet considering 'Muses' the subject and Philosophy ('my love') the object makes better sense, as long as 'with modest eyes' is read instrumentally as a quality of the Muses and not as the ornament conferred upon Philosophy. If read thus, then the corona's conclusion proclaims the Muses' conversion to philosophical poetry, and thus their readiness to appreciate 'the majesty and riches of the mind' (1.13). If the sequence begins with the Orphic/Neoplatonic topos of an eyeless Cupid (ἀνόμματος Ἔρως), its end seems to suggest that love has finally been made comprehensible to the eyes of the human intellect.

Lucidius olim

The poet's promise to express these thoughts in a more lucid way in the future was understood by Alistair Fowler as a clear reference to the next poem, 'Zodiac' (*Triumphal Forms*, p. 140, n. 3). For Fowler, this is sufficient proof of Chapman's authorship of this translation — a hypothesis that this edition endorses although not necessarily on the basis of this closing epigraph. The motto may announce an unfulfilled promise to deal with these issues in a future poem quite separate from the present collection — a promise that contradicts the poet's own pronouncement that this sequence is 'love and honour's complete history' ('Coronet', 1. 11). Alternatively, Chapman's treatment of the relations between poetry and philosophy in later works (which have been cited throughout the present volume) may be taken as a partial realization of this prospect.

The Amorous Zodiac

The place of 'Zodiac' in OBS has been the subject of conflicting opinions that are often the product of critical impressions and/or convenience. Failure or unwillingness to accommodate the poem into an interpretation of 'Banquet' and 'Coronet' has led to denial of Chapman's authorship (e.g. Waddington, 'Visual Rhetoric', p. 43). The best argument for accepting Chapman's authorship seems its place on the title page of QOB with 'Banquet' and 'Coronet' rather than with 'Contention', as well as its inclusion in OOB, from which 'Contention' was excluded after its separate publication in 1598. Kelly's rejection of Chapman's authorship on stylistic grounds is contradictory, as she accepts that the poem contains features such as compounding and a number of archaisms that look Chapmanesque (*Poetic Diction*, p. 100). Words not noted by Kelly, such as the adjective 'spongy' (7. 4), seem characteristic enough of Chapman's style. The present edition has argued in favour of the poem's significance to a volume that has been interpreted as a triptych (see Introduction, pp. 53, 56–57). Lee, *The French Renaissance in England*, pp. 465–77, and Fowler, *Triumphal Forms*, 208–14, provide English–French and modern-spelling texts, respectively. For the French text, here abbreviated ZA, I have followed Lee, but I have also consulted Gilles Durant, Sieur de la Bergerie, *Les oeuvres poetiques du Sieur de la Bergerie, avec les imitations tirees du Latin de Jean Bonnefons* (Paris: Abel l'Angelier, 1594), sigs D1^v–D4^v. Fowler, in the only authoritative critical discussion of the English version to date (pp. 140–46), argues that, by enriching the imagery and by removing four sixains from Durant's original, Chapman's translation becomes an 'almost fanatical' instance of numerological and proportional arrangement. Fowler's description of the numerical arrangement is as follows:

$$5 \text{ (Introduction)} + 23 \text{ (Zodiac: } 2 \times 12 + 1 - 2) + 2 \text{ (Envoy)} = 30$$

This arrangement contains a hypothetical day of twenty-four stanzas of sixty metrical syllables/minutes each. This works only if we consider the underlying arrangement of two stanzas per sign, which in the poem has three justified exceptions: Gemini is given three stanzas ('+ 1'), while Aquarius and Pisces are allotted one each ('– 2'; on which, see below). Besides, the total of thirty stanzas respond to the thirty days of the solar month, while the sum of the introduction and the zodiac proper amount to the twenty-eight days of the lunar month (pp. 143–44). Fowler's plausible analysis sustains an interpretation of the poem in which the zodiacal *melothesia* and the erotic blazon contribute to Chapman's mathematical abstraction of the lady's body into pure poetic form, an interpretation that tallies with a philosophical reading of the eroticism of 'Banquet'.

Stanzas 1–5

The five-stanza induction (called 'introduction' in Fowler) begins with the lyric voice's complaint about the unworthiness of the constellations shining in the sky, which motivates his desire to reform heaven by reducing its signs to a new zodiac that will abstract and stellify twelve parts of his mistress's body out of her 'numberless and perfect graces'. Smarr ('The Pyramid and the Circle', pp. 385–86) has suggested that this resembles the overall prospect of reformation of the stars that sustains the allegory of Giordano Bruno's *Spaccio della bestia trionfante* (*Expulsion of the Triumphant Beast*), originally published in London in 1584. However, and despite the defence in the present introduction of Bruno's influence on Chapman, Smarr's conjecture would involve Durant's knowledge and use of Bruno's dialogue. It seems more plausible to argue for Chapman's awareness of the parallel between Bruno and Durant.

Stanza 2 contains an incongruity: while the unworthiness of the constellations is justified on grounds of their commemorating Jupiter's erotic adventures, only one of the four signs mentioned suggests such an origin — in relation to Apollo, not Jupiter — and concerns an act of unfaithfulness *to*, not *by*, the god. This is the 'Crow', or Corvus, which, as Ovid recounts, became black after Apollo had blackened the white feathers of the crow that revealed to him the unfaithfulness of his lover, Coronis (*Metamorphoses*, II. 531–47). The 'Harp' is Lyra, which relates to the story of Orpheus (Allen, *Star Names*, pp. 280–81), while the 'Ship' is *Argo Navis*, whose stellification Chapman praises in 'Noctem', 112–17 (see Commentary), and which reappears later in this poem as the Bark (14. 1). Finally, the 'Serpent' is Ophiuchus, associated with Asclepius's killing of a snake (Allen, *Star Names*, pp. 374–75), or perhaps Draco, which relates to Hercules' killing of Ladon, who guarded the garden of the Hesperides (Allen, *Star Names*, pp. 202–04). In Fowler's reading, stanza 1 marks the beginning of both the solar and lunar month, while stanza 5 identifies the 'first rising' of the poet as 'a new Phoebus' with the beginning of the day (*Triumphal Forms*, pp. 208–09).

Stanzas 6–7

Aries, the beginning of the solar year and the spring, is the lady's head, and more specifically her golden locks. The lady's 'fleece of hair' and the mention of the 'Ram' (not in Durant's poem) identify the unnamed constellation. This stanza contains a number of stylistic marks that point to Chapman's authorship: the compound 'heaven-Ram-curled', the Latinism 'implies' (from *implexus*), as well as the adjective 'spongy', which is reminiscent of 'Noctem', 244.

Stanzas 8–9

The consecration of April to the worship of Venus in the Roman calendar is recounted in Ovid's *Fasti* (IV. 133–60). The constellation of Taurus, not mentioned in these lines, is identified with the lady's brow.

Stanzas 10–12

The next constellation is Gemini, in the month of May, marking the beginning of summer. It is named directly as 'the Twins' sign', identified with the lady's eyes, or 'Twin-born fires'. As Fowler explains, Chapman follows Durant in devoting three instead of two stanzas to the eyes, on the grounds that their graces cannot be fully admired in only 'thirty days'. However, as Fowler also proves, 'the wittiness of this tribute partly lies in its neat provision of a formal analogy to an aberration in the real sun's motion: namely, the slowing that occurs near the auge or apogee' (*Triumphal Forms*, p. 142). Fowler points at two possible sources/analogues for Durant/Chapman. The first is Du Bartas's *Divine Weeks*, which describes how in Cancer the Sun's 'teem doth seem to trot more tame | On these cut points: for heer he doth not ride | Flatling a-long, but vp the Sphears steep side' (*Divine Weeks*, trans. by Sylvester, Day 2, Week 2, 311–13; I, p. 476). The second is Copernicus's *Commentariolus* (1507), which places the sun's apogee in Gemini: 'the line drawn from the sun through the center of the circle is invariably directed toward a point of the firmament 10° west of the more brilliant of the two bright stars in the head of Gemini; therefore when the earth is opposite this point, and the center of the circle lies between them, the sun is seen at its greatest distance from the earth' (*Three Copernican Treatises*, trans. by Edward R ßosen (Octagon, 1971), p. 62).

Stanzas 13–14

Despite the lover's desire to linger on the eyes/Gemini, his 'forcèd will' impels him to continue his voyage to 'the neighbour sign'. This sign's identification with Cancer is only indirect, through Chapman's parenthetical addition, not in Durant's original, identifying the nose as the 'stern to thy Bark of love'. The stern is *Puppis*, one of the three sub-constellations of *Argo Navis*, which is the 'Bark', or Ship, the third decan, or sub-constellation, of Cancer.

Stanzas 15–16

The summer, or 'violent season', is completed in the constellation of Leo, identified with the lady's lips. As Fowler argues, the two lips' 'doubling' of 'summer's fires' parallels summer's doubling of the other seasons in the number of stanzas — six instead of the three per season devoted to spring, autumn and winter (p. 143). The simile comparing the lips to 'fervent Sirius' equates their inflaming power to the hottest days of the year, at the end of

July, which is the time when this star, also called the Dog Star, *Canis Maior*, or *canicula*, shines in the sky. Chapman also calls Sirius the 'Autumnal Star' ('Banquet', 69. 1), following Homer's 'ἀστέρ ὀπωρινός' (*Iliad*, v. 5). The Homeric adjective, however, refers to the same part of the year referred to here — i.e. the period from the last days of July to early September (see Liddell & Scott, *A Greek Lexicon*, ὀπωρινός).

Stanzas 17–18

The lady's cheeks are the sixth and last part of the head/face. They are identified with Virgo, in the month of August, the last of the six northern constellations, or boreal signs, announcing the colder climates of the autumn. The 'heat' inspired by the lady's lips is 'temper[ed]' by the cheeks' chaste blush; the description of the mixed 'marble' and 'purple', white and red colours of the blush occupies a full stanza.

Stanzas 19–20

The representation of Libra's two scales as the neck emphasizes the transition from the boreal to the austral signs, as well as the transition from the visible parts of the beloved's head — the 'light', or 'beauties seen' — to the 'darkness', or 'more obscurèd graces' — i.e. those parts of her body that are usually clothed. Stanza 20 marks the beginning of autumn, which ends at the transition from stanza 22 to 23. In terms of the calendar, Libra begins in the month of September.

Stanza 21–22

The new month of October brings the sign of Scorpio, unmentioned both in Durant and Chapman. The conceit is now the transition from the neck's 'marble pillar and her lineature' to the lady's breasts, identified with the snowy Riphaean mountains, and then with the 'parching Alps'; the second image is Chapman's addition, stressing contrast between cold and heat, chastity and incitement to desire. ZA capitalizes 'Amour', so 'Love' has been capitalized in the translation, despite QoB. 'Love' appears here a representation of primordial Eros, the god born from Chaos, 'fairest among the deathless gods, who unnerves the limbs and overcomes the mind and wise counsels of all gods and all men within them' ('ὃς κάλλιστος ἐν ἀθανάτοισι θεοῖσι, | λυσιμελής, πάντων δὲ θεῶν πάντων τ' ἀνθρώπων | δάμναται ἐν στήθεσσι νόον καὶ ἐπίφρονα βουλήν': Hesiod, *Theogony*, 120–22). Otherwise, his description as 'victor from the gods' war' is obscure.

Stanza 23–24

The next mansion in the completion of the 'autumnal race', in the month of November, is the lady's hand. The diversion from the lady's body to her extremity, the hand, is represented by a zodiacal diversion from Sagittarius to *Corona australis*: 'To see thy hand (whence I the Crown attend)'. *Corona australis* was placed beside Sagittarius, and was often named *Corona Sagittarii*, or the Centaur's Crown. Hyginus's description of Jupiter's stellification of the Centaur includes the placing, by one of his extremities, of a crown of stars: '[Iove] crura eius equina fecisse, quod equo multum sit usus, et sagittas adiunxisse ut ex his et acumen et celeritas esse videretur. [...] Ante huius pedes stellae sunt paucae in rotundo deformatae, quam coronam eius ut ludentis abiectam nonnulli dixerunt' ('Jupiter gave him the legs of a horse, because he was used to riding, and added arrows so that his dexterity and speed could be seen. [...] Before his feet there are a few stars disposed in a circle, which many believe to be his crown, left there as in a game': *De Astronomia*, II. 27. 1063–69, p. 74, my translation; see also III. 26. 241–46, p. 114).

Fowler considers this variation the 'most elegant' in the poem and stresses the 'thematic relevance of the constellation's circular form' to the proportional form of Chapman's volume, particularly in relation to 'Coronet' (*Triumphal Forms*, pp. 144–45). Fowler also argues, quite plausibly, that this is the only noteworthy deviation in the poem from the solar 'ecliptic line': 'It is significant that he should do so in Stanza xxiii; for the ecliptic plane is inclined to the equatorial at an angle of 23 degrees and a fraction, so that the word *ecliptic* receives sole mention in the stanza whose number measures, in whole degrees, its angle of inclination' (p. 144). The merit would be, however, Durant's, not Chapman's. Indeed, there is little merit in Chapman's translation here, particularly in the last three lines of stanza 24. Durant writes: 'Main qui guide par tout le mignon d'Idalie, | Main qui bande son arc, Main qui lie & de-lie | Les ribans argentez de son petit bandeau' ('A hand that guides everywhere the Idalian minion, | A hand that closes its arc, a hand that ties and unties | The silver ribbons of its small moulding': *ZA*, 24. 4-6, my translation). Chapman misunderstands the architectural metaphor and builds a muddled archery conceit which strangely represents Ganymede, Jupiter's Idalian cupbearer, as a Cupid that wields a bow and ensign. But 'bander un arc' in French means to complete the building of an arc, while the 'bandeau' refers to the mouldings that decorate an arc or a cornice. Durant's metaphor, which Chapman fails to translate, concerns the opening and closing of the hand (the 'arc'), an action in which the fingers are imagined as the arc's decorative mouldings. See *Centre National de Ressources Textuelles et Lexicales*, *bander*, v., B. 2, for the expression *bander un arc*, v. 2, and *bandeau*, n., A. 1, for architectural senses.

Stanzas 25–26

Chapman's translation makes good Durant's statement that he 'can scarce express with chastity' ('je ne puis chastement exprimer') the sign of Capricorn, embodied in the lady's genitals. The translator renders literally the original's sexual pun on 'Capricorne' ('mon cas prit corne', *ZA*, 25. 5; see footnote on 'Zodiac', 25. 5): this justifies the explicit naming of the constellation, more an exception than a rule in the poem. Chapman exploits further possibilities for innuendo: 'gole' puns on its archaic sense of 'ditch', and has not been emended to 'goal' (as in Bartlett and Fowler); 'fit' also reinforces the sense of danger lurking in the 'darkness' of the 'wintry solstice', despite its 'heav'n-like' appearance. Leaving this mansion thus involves a journey to a 'safer' one.

Stanzas 27–28

The last two signs, Aquarius and Pisces, which stand for the lady's thighs and calves, are allotted only one stanza each. For Fowler, this exception is justified by the three stanzas devoted to Gemini (10–12) and is later balanced by 'a compensating Envoy making up the requisite 2 stanzas' (p. 142). If this is valid for Chapman's arrangement, it is less so for Durant's, as four original stanzas are omitted in the translation, one after Chapman's 28 and three between 29 and 30. While stanza 28 concludes 'the latest season', as well as, in Fowler's reading, the 24-hour day and the lunar month (*Triumphal Forms*, p. 213), Durant's omitted stanza (*ZA*, 29) starts a new cycle by returning to Aries and the ram's 'fleece': 'J'iroy voir de rechef mon Mouton et ma laine | Poursouivant sans repos ce travail annüel' ('I'll go to see again my Ram and my fleece | Pursuing restlessly my yearly travail': 5–6, my translation). The suppression of this stanza is a missed opportunity for foregrounding circular symbolism in Chapman's volume, although it helps emphasize the numerological arrangement suggested by Fowler.

Stanzas 29–30, *L'Envoi*

Durant's five-stanza envoy is reduced to two stanzas in Chapman's translation, which retains *ZA* 30 and 34 but omits *ZA* 31, 32 and 33. Chapman's compressed envoy avoids digression, as well as the original speaker's choice of one particular mansion out of the twelve parts/signs: 'mais si j'estoy forcé | D'en prendre une à mon gré que je pourrois elire | Souvent au Capricorne on me veroit reluire' ('but if I am forced | To pick one at my pleasure that I could choose, | Often in Capricorn I will be seen shining': *ZA*, 33. 3–5, my translation). This choice, which stresses the primarily erotic nature of the poem, may be behind Chapman's rejection of these stanzas. Moreover, the first and last stanza make sense on their own without any need for significant syntactic or semantic adaptation. Stanza 29 insists on the poet's intention to replace a former heavenly universe with his new, 'fair zodiac'. Stanza 30 functions as the envoy proper: if heaven prevents the poet from arranging the lady's beauties in their appointed constellations, he will at least be able to arrange them in his verse. The poem will thus fulfil its circular aim: while the poet's prospect at the beginning of his course is to shine, like Phoebus, on each of the lady's physical charms, the conclusion reciprocally represents the lady's 'flames' as 'glister[ing]' in a new heaven and in the poem's own parts. The body's erotic materiality is finally sublimated into philosophical/astrological knowledge and into poetic form.

TEXTUAL NOTES

THESE TEXTUAL NOTES register variant readings, emendations and regularizations (spelling, punctuation) that involve significant readings. Lineation is notated by a vertical bar (|) and separations of verse paragraphs by a double vertical bar (||).

1. *The Shadow of Night*

'To my dear and most worthy friend Master Matthew Roydon'

7 the eye of the Graeae] the eyes of Graea Q*SN*.
12 censors] censures Q*SN*.
14 Skill] *Shepherd*; skil Q*SN*.
19 vanities as, with] vanities, as with Q*SN*.

'Hymnus in Noctem'

5 Death] death Q*SN*.
10 Sleep] sleepe Q*SN*.
11 loose] *Shepherd*; lose Q*SN*.
13 Skill] skill Q*SN*.
17 earth's] earths Q*SN*.
64 hell-obscuring] *Shepherd*; hell obscuring Q*SN*.
70 blind-born] *Shepherd*; blind borne Q*SN*.
71 Blindness of the Mind] blindnesse of the minde Q*SN*.
100 shun);] shunne) Q*SN*.
139 Morning] morning Q*SN*.
139 Muse's] *Shepherd*; Muses Q*SN*.
148–49 exemplified. || And] Q*SN*; exemplified; | And *Bartlett*. New verse paragraph added.
220–21 out — | So] out. || So Q*SN*.
223 retreat] retrait Q*SN*.
229 Earth] earth Q*SN*.
240 Morn's leave] Morns leaue Q*SN*.
242 Day] day Q*SN*.
246, 249 virtues'] vertues Q*SN*.
267 boughs] bowes Q*SN*.
273 Furies] furies Q*SN*.
301 villainies] villanies. Q*SN*.
328 Night] night Q*SN*.
329 Day] day Q*SN*.

330 beauty's] beauties Q*sn*.
369–70 ill — | All] ill. || All Q*sn*.

Gloss

G1 *Astronomicis*] *Hudston*; Astronimicis Q*sn*.
G2 *Fatumque, Mortem Somnum, Dea, Nox*] *Conti*. Not capitalized in Q*sn*.
G3 *discere*] Hudston; dicere Q*sn*.
G4b Muse] *Bartlett*; Muses Q*sn*.
G4b Cantus] *Bartlett*; Cautus Q*sn*.
G6 *in his versibus*] in his verses Q*sn*.
G6 *advolaverat*] *Conti*; *aduoluerat* Q*sn*.
G12 *iuga*] Hudston (following *Conti*); *fuga* Q*sn*.
G13 *Theia*] *Thya* Q*sn*.
G13 Day] day Q*sn*.

'Hymnus in Cynthiam'

4–5 sky; | Peaceful] skie: || Peacefull Q*sn*.
16 Earth] earth Q*sn*.
18 Time] time Q*sn*.
21 Heav'n's] heauens Q*sn*.
31 Earth] earth Q*sn*.
39–40 funeral. || But] funerall | But Q*sn*.
40 thrice-dreadful] thrise dreadfull Q*sn*.
41 Cannae] *Bartlett*; Cannas Q*sn*.
51 slings] flings Q*sn*.
57 Fate] fate Q*sn*.
50 Earth] earth Q*sn*.
86 Poesy] poesie Q*sn*.
115–16 breath. | Then] breath. || Then Q*sn*.
143 Fate] fate Q*sn*.
145 Thespiae] Thespya Q*sn*.
145 Muse] muse Q*sn*.
149 boughs] bowes Q*sn*.
161 huntress] *Bartlett*; huntesse Q*sn*.
162 flesh-confounded] flesh confounded Q*sn*.
174 charms' delight] charmes, delight Q*sn*.
177 Hope] hope Q*sn*.
180 Night] night Q*sn*.
195 Form] forme Q*sn*.
207–08 celestial. || And] celestiall: | And Q*sn*.
218 (and ff.) Euthymia] Euthimya Q*sn*.
239 Tigris] *Bartlett*; Trigis Q*sn*.
241 Alce] *Bartlett*; Aloe Q*sn*.

268 lickerous] licorous Q*SN*.
271 human-thoughted] humane thoughted Q*SN*.
278 ate] eate Q*SN*.
286 off] of Q*SN*.
305 Sun] sunne Q*SN*.
332 Waal¹⁹] Waal¹⁰ Q*SN*.
353–54 solace, And] solace. | And Q*SN*.
390 Day's] dayes Q*SN*.
462 He is the Ganymede the bird of Jove | Rapt] He is the Ganemede, the bird of Ioue | Rapt Q*SN*.
463 his] Bartlett; her Q*SN*.
499 softness] softnesse *Bartlett*; sofftnsse Q*SN*.
506 Fate] fate Q*SN*.

Gloss

G1 *praeest*] praest Q*SN*.
G1 *Praegnantium*] *Conti*; Praegnantum Q*SN*.
G1 *parientium*] *Conti*; parientum Q*SN*.
G1 *dolores*] *Conti*; labores Q*SN*.
G1 *simul*] *Conti*; sumus Q*SN*.
G6 *lavari*] *Conti*; Lauacri Q*SN*.
G19 opinion, drawn] opinion drawne Q*SN*.
G22 *Deae*] *Conti*; Dea Q*SN*.

2. *Ovid's Banquet of Sense, A Coronet for His Mistress Philosophy and His Amorous Zodiac*

To the truly learned, and my worthy friend, Master Matthew Roydon

4 judgements, sweet Matthew, wandering, like] iudgements (sweet Ma:) wandring like Q*OB*.
11 *olentis*] *Bartlett*; *dentis* Q*OB*.
12 ornament] *Bartlett*; ornamrnt Q*OB*.
23 presently-to-be-used] presently to be vsed Q*OB*.
34 others] *Bartlett, Hudston*; other Q*OB*.

Richard Stapleton to the Author

3 loose] Q*OB*; verse *Bartlett*.
10 clear] deare Q*OB*.

Thomas Williams, of the Inner Temple

2 withe] wife Q*OB*.

Another (by Thomas Williams)

2 Love] loue Q*OB*.
8 Graffs] Grafs Q*OB*; Grass *Bartlett*.
9 bough] bow Q*OB*.

John Davies, of the Middle Temple

1 Love's] loues Q*OB*.
2 He] he Q*OB*.
14 Love] loue Q*OB*.

Ovid's Banquet of Sense

NARRATIO] Q*OB*; AVDITUS O*OB*.
2. 4 Youth and Ease (collectors of Love's fees)] youth, and ease, (Collectors of loues fees) Q*OB*.
3. 3, 5. 1 Sipylus] Sypilus Q*OB*.
5. 6 Phthia] Q*OB*; Phothia O*OB*.
6. 4 hewed] Q*OB*; hued *Braden*.
9. 4. Amaracus] *Braden*; Amareus Q*OB*.
10. 3 Sya] Q*OB*; Sive *Braden*.
10. 5 crown imperial] Crowne-imperiall Q*OB*.
11. 5 round] rounde Q*OB*; grounde *Bartlett*.
12. 8 seized] ceaz'd Q*OB*.
14. 6 step] steap Q*OB*.
14. 6 shader] Q*OB*; shadier *Shepherd, Braden*.
18. 1 gilt] guilt Q*OB*.
21. 9–22. 1 ear, || 'Whose] *Bartlett, Hudston*; eare. || Whose Q*OB*.
23. 9 fly;] flye. Q*OB*.
28. 9 men] mens Q*OB*.
35. 7 noblesse's] Nobles Q*OB*; nobles' *Braden*.
37. 2 Love, then, a fire, is much thereto affected;] *Braden*; Loue then a fire is much thereto affected; Q*OB*.
37. 9 merits.] O*OB*; merits; Q*OB*.
38. 9 frames.] frames; Q*OB*.
40. 1 sleight] Q*OB*; slight *Braden*.
40. 8 Her sight (his sun)] Her sight, his sunne Q*OB*; Her sight, his Sunne O*OB*; Her sight, his sun, *Braden*.
41. 1 Love] loue Q*OB*.
41. 4 bleed] bleeds Q*OB*.
42. 9 imparted;] imparted. Q*OB*.
43. 8–9 These casts he cast, and more — his wits more quick — | Than can be cast by wit's arithmetic.] These casts, he cast, and more, his wits more quick | Then can be cast, by wits Arithmetick. Q*OB*.

44. 9 trips,] trips. QOB.
45. 2 his] her QOB.
45. 9 contain —] containe. QOB; containe, OOB.
46. 7 enter.] enter, QOB.
46. 9 fear:] feare, QOB.
49. 4 porrected] prorected QOB.
M10 (50. 8) call] calls QOB.
52. 6 dully] duely QOB.
53. 3 getteth] QOB; gettest OOB.
54. 3 word] QOB; world OOB.
54. 3 precedes;] preceedes, QOB.
54. 4 reposed] reposde. QOB.
56. 8 Bounded] QOB; Dounded OOB.
M11 (57. 2) place] *Braden*; peace QOB.
58. 7 spring bird] Spring-bird QOB.
58. 7 laureate] Lameate QOB.
59. 1 paradise] Parradise QOB.
59. 3 Gihon] Gehon QOB.
59. 3 Pishon] Phison QOB.
M13 (60. 1) office of her fingers] OOB, *Bartlett*; office her fingers QOB.
60. 2 such] OOB; snch QOB.
63. 3 find] finde *Bartlett, Hudston*; minde QOB; mind OOB.
63. 8 bid] QOB; bide OOB, *Bartlett, Braden*.
65. 3 new-coined-glowing] new-coynd-glowing QOB; new-coined glowing *Braden*.
65. 4 Racked of some miserable treasurer,] (Racktof some miserable Treasurer) QOB.
65. 7 bloody siege] bloody siedge QOB; blood-siedge OOB.
66. 7 stand] QOB; sound OOB.
68. 1 power!] powre? QOB.
68. 2 life's] liues QOB.
68. 6 Thou] QOB; Thy *Bartlett*.
70. 2 part] part, QOB.
73. 7 ensnare:] ensnare QOB.
73. 9 Best] "Best QOB.
76. 9 loosing] QOB; losing *Braden*.
78. 8 bids] bides QOB.
79. 6 governiss] governisse QOB.
79. 7 weighed] waide QOB; waid OOB.
79. 9 things-nothing] things nothing QOB.
M17 (80. 4) (Aristoteles)] *Aristot.* QOB.
80. 6 were] QOB; where OOB.
80. 8 harm's] harms QOB, *Bartlett, Braden*.
83. 2 Love's] loues QOB.

83. 6 world's] world Q*OB*.
86. 2 log-since just-divorcèd] long since iust diuorced Q*OB*.
86. 4 breathes] breath's Q*OB*.
87. 5 change] *Braden*; changde Q*OB*.
90. 2–3 too trivial eyes; | For your rare wits,] too triuiall eyes | For your rare wits; Q*OB*.
90. 9 childeren,] *Bartlett*; childeren. Q*OB*.
91. 8 Love's] loues Q*OB*.
91. 9 Graces'] Graces Q*OB*.
92. 1 Pure] Q*OB*; Lure O*OB*.
93. 5 flow] Q*OB*; flew O*OB*.
97. 6 swoon] swoune Q*OB*.
98. 2 Golden Age] golden age Q*OB*.
102. 5 groundwork] ground-worke Q*OB*.
104. 4 price] prise Q*OB*; prize *Braden*.
104. 5 transform] trans-forme Q*OB*.
107. 2 Engine] *Braden*; Engines Q*OB*.
112. 5 banquet'st] banquests Q*OB*, O*OB*.
113. 5 *Art of Love*] Art of loue Q*OB*; Art of Love O*OB*.
114. 1 dog days] dog-dayes Q*OB*.
114. 7 unprized] unprised Q*OB*.
115. 8 singing] singiug Q*OB*.

A Coronet for His Mistress Philosophy

A Coronet] Q*OB*; OVID's Coronet O*OB*.
1. 11 Of love and honour's] Of loue, and honours Q*OB*.
1. 14 darkness, for] darknes; for Q*OB*.
2. 1 blind:] blinde, Q*OB*.
2. 12 bliss.] blisse Q*OB*.
2. 2 pours] poures Q*OB*; powres O*OB*.
2. 8 pieces] O*OB*; peecs Q*OB*.
2. 11 scrolls] scroule Q*OB*; scroules *Bartlett*.
3. 1 liver, but] O*OB*; liuer but Q*OB*.
3. 4 spotless-hearted] spotles harted Q*OB*; spotlesse hearted O*OB*.
4. 8 Love's] loues Q*OB*; loves O*OB*.
5. 3 life's] liues Q*OB*; lives O*OB*.
6. 1 assure] assure; Q*OB*.
6. 6 pied-faced] pied-fac'd O*OB*; pied fac'd Q*OB*.
7. 14 riches, to] O*OB*; riches to Q*OB*.
8. 1 riches to] riches, to Q*OB*, O*OB*.
8. 3 beauties'] beauties Q*OB*.
9. 3 seise] O*OB*; saise Q*OB*.
9. 8 age.] age,) Q*OB*.

10. 2 As] Q*OB*; To As O*OB*.
10. 5 To noblest] Q*OB*; noblest O*OB*.

The Amorous Zodiac

The] Q*OB*; Ovid's O*OB*.
7. 4–5 Earth at this spring, spongy and languorsome | (With envy of our joys in love become),] Earth (at this Spring spungie and langorsome | With enuie of our ioyes in loue become) Q*OB*.
8. 5 verdure-gracing] verdure gracing Q*OB*.
10. 6 desires,] Q*OB*; desires. *Bartlett, Shepherd*.
12. 1 sign] signe *Bartlett*; shine Q*OB*.
12. 3 days.] days: Q*OB*.
13. 4 sign] Signes Q*OB*.
14. 1 Barke] barke Q*OB*.
16. 4 shoots] shootes *Bartlett*; *shoakes* Q*OB*.
16. 6 month] *Bartlett*; *mouth* Q*OB*.
20. 5 scales] skoles Q*OB*, *Bartlett*.
21. 4 Love] loue Q*OB*.
21. 4 Riphees] riphees Q*OB*.
22. 2 Loves and Joys] loues and ioyes Q*OB*.
24. 1 rose] Rose Q*OB*.
24. 2 Morning] morning Q*OB*.
25. 1 Antarctic] Antartick Q*OB*.
24. 4 eachwhere] each where Q*OB*.

APPENDIX: A NOTE ON CHAPMAN'S PROSODY

Chapman's prosodic habits in *SN* and *OBS* have received little attention. The exception is Kelly's *Poetic Diction in the Non-Dramatic Works of George Chapman*, which, though unpublished, remains an indispensable tool. Kelly pays special attention to rhyme devices in the context of her study of rhetorical figures of sound.[1] Chapman's prosody is remembered particularly for his use of the heroic couplet in his Homeric translations: while the early translations of the *Iliad* and the *Odyssey* opted for iambic pentameter, his 1611 complete *Iliads* used the fourteener, or iambic heptameter, for its couplets. *SN* is then Chapman's first experiment in a form — the iambic pentameter couplet — which would later become a norm in his nondramatic verse. 'Cynthiam' witnesses to the poet's attention to metre and the importance given to its significance:

> Time's motion, being like the reeling suns,
> Or as the sea reciprocally runs,
> Hath brought us now to their opinions,
> As in our garments ancient fashions
> Are newly worn; and as sweet Poesy
> Will not be clad in her supremacy
> With those strange garments (Rome's hexameters),
> As she is English, but in right prefers
> Our native robes (put on with skilful hands,
> English heroics) to those antique garlands,
> Accounting it no meed but mockery,
> When her steep brows already prop the sky,
> To put on startups, and yet let it fall. (82-94)

The need to adapt the ancient hexameter — the classical vehicle for epic poetry, but also for the Homeric, Callimachean and Orphic hymn — to an English native form results in the choice of the rhymed pentameter, with no extra feet, or 'startups', unlike in the final version of the *Iliad*, where their presence was deemed to be required. Chapman may be one of the targets of Milton's rejection of rhyme as 'the invention of a barbarous age', in his 1668 prefatory note to *Paradise Lost*.[2] Despite his jibes at poets writing 'sonnets', 'lascivious ballades', 'octaves', 'canzons' and 'canzonets' in one of his prefaces to *Achilles Shield* (1598), Chapman remained faithful to rhyme.[3] He writes at

---

1 On *SN*, see Kelly, *Poetic Diction*, pp. 81-98. On *OBS*, see pp. 145-53. Both sections are titled 'Alliteration and Rhyming Devices'.
2 Milton, *Paradise Lost*, ed. by Fowler, p. 54.
3 *Achilles Shield*: 'To the Understander', in Nicoll, I, pp. 549-50.

a moment when the experiments with quantitative rhyme in English of the previous decades had proved ineffective, and his unproblematic acceptance of the 'native robes' is fully compatible with his aspirations to writing in the high style.

The shift from the heroic couplet in *SN* to the variety of stanzaic patterns in *OBS* responds to thematic issues, but Chapman's resort to some of the forms that are the object of his above-quoted jibe can hardly be regarded as parodic of the metrical habits of his fellow poets. As already mentioned, the 1062 lines of 'Banquet' use an idiosyncratic form of the nine-line stanza (*ababcbcdd*), which seems to navigate between the Italian *ottava rima* (*abababcc*, of current use in English poetry) and the Spenserian nine-line stanza (*ababbcbdd*). Like Spenser, Chapman's stanza uses four rhymes, distributed in a quatrain, a tercet and a final couplet, the only difference being the inversion of the tercet's pattern (*cbc* in Chapman, *bcb* in Spenser) and the avoidance of Spenser's 'startup' alexandrine (hexameter) in the final line. The exception in this poem is 'The Song of Corinna', which interrupts stanza 12 after the end of the quatrain to complete it with a fourteen-line composition in iambic tetrameter and trimeter. The song uses the same rhyme pattern as the ten sonnets of 'Coronet', *ababcdcdefefgg*, which we associate with the Shakespearean sonnet. This coincidence may suggest emulation and encourage hypotheses of rivalry which lie outside the scope of the present edition. In its use of shorter lines, and taking stock of its theme, 'The Song of Corinna' may be read as parodying the love sonnet fad of the 1590s. Its shorter lines anticipate Chapman's mastery of these forms, particularly in the tetrameter and dimeter of the verse arguments of the *Odyssey* translation. However, the sonnets of 'Coronet' take the form seriously: the audacity of the corona's ring sequence matches its aspiration to formal and intellectual perfection.[4] Finally, 'Zodiac' replicates the original sixains of Durant's poem: *aabccb*. Chapman would return to this form in his translation of Psalms 1 and 7 of Petrarch's *Psalmi penitentiales*.[5]

A present-day reader of Chapman's *SN* and *OBS* encounters the usual sound devices of the period's verse, as well as the difficulties stemming from early modern licence concerning the adjustment of pronunciation to meter and rhyme. As for sound effects, Kelly offers an extensive catalogue of uses of alliteration in the poems of both volumes, and she differentiates four basic patterns:

Pattern I is simple repetition of initial sounds, as in '*M*ost sacred *m*other both of god and *m*en' ('Noctem', 68).

Pattern II is alternate alliteration: 'To *c*alm the *f*uries and to *q*uench the *f*ire' ('Cynthiam', 128).

---

[4] For a more detailed account of the sequence's acheivements and flaws, see Luis-Martínez, 'Friendlesse Verse', esp. pp. 595–604.
[5] See *Petrarch's Seven Penitentiall Psalmes*, in Bartlett, pp. 204–20.

Pattern III is 'envelope' repetition, of which, among other instances, Kelly provides a full stanza's consistent use of this device to demonstrate Chapman's penchant and ear for complex sound effects. I reproduce four lines here:

> I *see* un*b*idden guests are *b*oldest *s*till,
> And *w*ell *y*ou show how *w*eak in soul *y*ou are
> That let *r*ude *s*ense subdue your *r*eason's *s*kill
> And *f*eed *s*o spoilfully on *s*acred *f*are ('Banquet', 89.1–4)

Pattern IV is consecutive repetition of initial sound, usually in combination with other patterns: 'And *w*hat *m*akes *m*en *w*ithout the parts of *m*en' ('Noctem', 91).

These examples do not do justice to Kelly's exhaustive catalogue, as Chapman's 'use of alliteration far outnumbers his use of other figures of rhetoric'.[6]

Kelly's equally exhaustive analysis of rhyming techniques in *SN* and *OBS* exceeds the bounds of this edition, and the reader is referred to her study. Among Chapman's practices, Kelly notes the use of 'perfect rhyme, near rhyme, eye rhyme, rhyme by change of pronunciation, and rhyme by shift of accent'.[7] Of these, Chapman's predilection for near rhyme may be worth noting. I reproduce here selected cases from Kelly's lists (spelling modernized in this edition):

'Noctem'	'Cynthiam'	'Banquet'
being/seeming (45–46)	burning/mourning (33–34)	come/wombe (23. 1–3)
amiss/is (79–80)	Pyramis/is (190–91)	debtor/better (57. 8–9)
depressed/beast (127–28)	vices/guises (228–29)	guide/weighed (79. 5, 7)
feasts/jests (189–90)	beasts/nests (279–80)	crown/swoon (97. 5–7)
alone/one (235–36)	them/stream (390–91)	heaven/given/even (107. 2, 4, 6)
else/sentinels (350–51)	glass/race (452–53)	beasts/feasts/guests (112. 2, 4, 6)

Rhyme 'by shift of accent' is a sort of eye rhyme between a line with masculine ending and another with feminine ending, as in:

> Look with thy fierce aspect, be terror-*stróng*,
> Assume thy wondrous shape of half a *fúrlong* ('Cynthiam', 519–20)

Or:

> That crown and make this cheerful garden *quíck*,
> Virtue, that every touch may make such *músic*. ('Banquet', 19. 8–9)

Perfect rhyme sometimes depends on alterations of the usual spelling/pronunciation of a word, as in 'stars/marin*ars*' ('Noctem', 374–75). And rhymes achieved through altered pronunciation often rely on the addition of

---

6 Kelly, *Poetic Diction*, p. 85.
7 Ibid.

a second stress to the final syllable of a polysyllabic word, as in 'ravish*éth/ death*' ('Banquet', 18. 5–7), or 'Elysi*úm/come*' ('Banquet', 61. 1, 3). Although a less usual device, inner rhyme is heard occasionally in these poems: 'R*ent* them in pieces and their spirits s*ent*' ('Cynthiam', 280–81). A few other instances are mentioned in the footnotes. Yet it is ultimately Kelly's study that needs to be consulted.

The variety of Chapman's sound devices, together with his hits and misses, attests to a poet as deeply committed to formal excellence as he was to achieving 'clearness of representation'.

BIBLIOGRAPHY

1. Works by George Chapman

Early Modern Editions of SN and OBS

(In chronological order)

Σκία νυκτός. *The Shadow of Night: Containing Two Poeticall Hymnes. Deuised by G. C. Gent.* (London: William Ponsonby, 1594)

Ouids Banquet of Sence. A Coronet for his Mistresse Philosophie, and his amorous Zodiacke. With a translation of a Latine coppie, written by a Fryer, Anno Dom. 1400 (London: Richard Smith, 1595)

Ovid's Banquet of Sence. With a Coronet for His Mistresse Philosophy; and His amorous Zodiack (London: R. Horseman, 1639)

Modern Editions

(In chronological order)

The Works of George Chapman: Poems and Minor Translations, [ed. by Richard Herne Shepherd] with an introduction by Algernon Charles Swinburne (Chatto and Windus, 1875)

The Poems of George Chapman, ed. by Phyllis Brooks Bartlett (Modern Language Association of America, 1941)

Homer: The Iliad, The Odyssey and The Lesser Homerica, ed. by Allardyce Nicoll, 2 vols (Routledge and Kegan Paul, 1957)

The Plays of George Chapman: The Comedies. A Critical Edition, ed. by John Holaday (University of Illinois Press, 1970)

George Chapman's Minor Translations: A Critical Edition of His Renderings of Musaeus, Hesiod and Juvenal, ed. by Richard Corbalis (Institut für Anglistik and Amerikanistik, 1984)

The Plays of George Chapman: The Tragedies, with Sir Gyles Goosecappe. A Critical Edition, ed. by Allan Holaday (Boydell & Brewer, 1987)

George Chapman: Plays and Poems, ed. by Jonathan Hudston (Penguin, 1998)

Homer's Odyssey, ed. by Gordon Kendal (MHRA, 2016)

Homer's Iliad, ed. by Robert S. Miola (MHRA, 2017)

Modern Anthologies Including Poems from OBS

Alexander, Nigel (ed.), *Elizabethan Narrative Verse* (Edward Arnold, 1967)

Braden, Gordon (ed.), *Sixteenth-Century Poetry: An Annotated Anthology* (Blackwell, 2005)

Donno, Elizabeth Story (ed.), *Elizabethan Minor Epics* (Columbia University Press, 1963)

Loughlin, Marie H., Sandra Bell, and Patricia Brace (eds), *The Broadview Anthology of Sixteenth-Century Poetry and Prose* (Broadview, 2012)

2. References

Abraham, Lyndy, *A Dictionary of Alchemical Imagery* (Cambridge University Press, 1998)
Acheson, Arthur, *Shakespeare and the Rival Poet* (John Lane, 1903)
—— *Shakespeare's Lost Years in London* (Bernard Quaritch, 1920)
—— *Shakespeare's Sonnet Story, 1592–1598* (Bernard Quaritch, 1922)
Agrippa, Cornelius, *De Occulta Philosophia Libri Tres*, ed. by V. Perrone Compagni (Brill, 1922)
—— *Three Books of Occult Philosophy*, ed. by Donald Tyson, trans. by James Freake (Llewellyn, 1993)
Alberti, Leone Battista, *De Pictura* (Basel: Bartholomaeus Westheimer, 1540)
—— *On Painting. A Translation and Critical Edition*, ed. and trans. by Rocco Sinisgalli (Cambridge University Press, 2011)
Alciato, Andrea, *Emblematorum Liber* (Paris: Jean Richer, 1584)
Aldis, H. G., and others, *A Dictionary of Printers and Booksellers in England, Scotland and Ireland, and of Foreign Printers of English Books, 1557–1640* (Blades, East & Blades, 1910)
Allen, Archibald, *The Fragments of Mimnermus: Text and Commentary* (Franz Steiner, 1993)
Allen, Michael J. B., 'Marsilio Ficino on Plato's Pythagorean Eye', *Modern Language Notes*, 97.1 (1982), pp. 171–82, doi:10.2307/2906281
Allen, Richard Hinckley, *Star Names and Their Meanings* (G. E. Stechert, 1899)
Allott, Robert, *Englands Parnassus* (1600), ed. by Charles Crawford (Clarendon Press, 1913)
Aneau, Barthélemy, *Picta poesis* (Lyons: Marthian Bonhomme, 1552)
Aphthonius, *Aphthonii Sophistae Progymnasmata*, ed. and trans. by Reinhard Lorich (Marburg: Christian Egenolff, 1542)
Apollodorus, *The Library*, ed. and trans. by Sir James Frazer, 2 vols (Heinemann, 1921)
Apollonius Rhodius, *Argonautica*, ed. and trans. by R. C. Seaton (Heinemann, 1912)
Aquinas, Thomas, *In Aristotelis Librum de Anima Commentarium*, ed. by P. M. Pirotta (Marietti, 1948)
Arber, Edward (ed.), *A Transcript of the Registers of the Company of Stationers of London, 1554–1640*, 4 vols (London, 1875)
Aristotle, *De anima*, trans. by John Argyropoulos (Lyons: Antonius Vincentius, 1557)
—— *De anima*, ed. and trans. R. D. Hicks (Cambridge University Press, 1907)
—— *On the Soul, Parva Naturalia, On Breath*, ed. and trans. by W. S. Hett (Heinemann, 1964)
Aristotle, Theophrastus, *Aristotelis Stagiritae Metaphysicorum libri XIIII, Theophrasti Metaphysicorum liber* (Ingolstadt: David Sartorius, 1577)
Armin, Robert, *The Italian Taylor, and His Boy* (London: Robert Triphook, 1609)
Athenaeus, *The Deipnosophists*, ed. and trans. by Charles Burton Gulick (Heinemann, 1967)
Aulus Gellius, *The Attic Nights*, ed. and trans. by John C. Rolfe, 3 vols (Heinemann, 1927)

Bacon, Roger, *The Mirror of Alchimy*, translation of *Speculum Alchemiae* (London: Thomas Creede, 1597)
Baltussen, H., *Theophrastus against the Presocratics and Plato: Peripatetic Dialectic in 'De sensibus'* (Brill, 2000)
Bamborough, J. B., *The Little World of Man* (Longmans, Green & Co., 1951)
Barish, Jonas, *The Antitheatrical Prejudice* (University of California Press, 1981)
Barnes, Barnabe, *A Divine Centurie of Spirituall Sonnets* (London: John Windet, 1595)
—— *Parthenophil and Parthenophe*, ed. by Victor A. Doyno (Southern Illinois University Press, 1971)
Bartholomaeus Anglicus, *De proprietatibus rerum, newly corrected, enlarged and amended*, trans. by Stephen Batman (London: Thomas East, 1582)
Bartlett, Phyllis Brooks, 'Stylistic Devices in Chapman's *Iliads*', *PMLA*, 57.3 (1942), pp. 661–75, doi:10.2307/458767
Battenhouse, Roy, 'Chapman's *The Shadow of Night*: An Interpretation', *Studies in Philology*, 38.4 (1941), pp. 584–608
Berry, Philippa, *Of Chastity and Power: Elizabethan Literature and the Unmarried Queen* (Routledge, 1989)
Bertheau, Gilles, 'Can a Poet be "Master of [his] owne Meaning"? George Chapman and the Paradoxes of Authorship', in *Self-Commentary in Early Modern European Literature, 1400–1700*, ed. by Francesco Venturi (Brill, 2019), pp. 284–315, doi:10.1163/9789004396593_012
Bible and Holy Scriptures (Geneva: Rowland Hall, 1560)
Biblia Vulgata, ed. by Alberto Colunga and Laurentio Torrado (Biblioteca de Autores Cristianos, 1994)
Bober, Harry, 'The Zodiacal Miniature of the *Très Riches Heures* of the Duke of Berry — Its Sources and Meaning', *Journal of the Warburg and Courtauld Institutes*, 11.1 (1948), pp. 1–34, doi:10.2307/750460
Boccaccio, Giovanni, *Boccaccio on Poetry*, ed. and trans. by Charles G. Osgood (The Liberal Art Press, 1956)
—— *Genealogie deorum gentilium*, ed. by Vincenzo Romano, 2 vols (Laterza, 1951)
Bocchi, Achille, *Symbolicae Quaestiones* (Bologna: Societas Typographiae Bononiensis, 1574)
Bottrall, Margaret, 'George Chapman's Defence of Difficulty', *The Criterion*, 16 (1937), pp. 638–54
Bowers, Fredson, 'The Early Editions of Marlowe's "Ovid's Elegies"', *Studies in Bibliography*, 25 (1972), pp. 149–72
Bradbrook, M. C., *The School of Night: A Study in the Literary Relations of Sir Walter Ralegh* (Cambridge University Press, 1936)
Bruno, Giordano, *The Ash Wednesday Supper*, ed. and trans. by Hilary Gatti (University of Toronto Press, 2018)
—— *Cause, Principle and Unity and Essays on Magic*, ed. and trans. by Richard D. Blackwell and Robert de Lucca (Cambridge University Press, 2004)
—— *De umbris idearum* (Paris: Gilles Gorbin, 1582)
—— *Expulsión de la bestia triunfante*, ed. and trans. by Miguel A. Granada (Tecnos, 2022)
—— *The Expulsion of the Triumphant Beast*, ed. and trans. by Arthur D. Imerti (Rutgers University Press, 1964)

—— *On the Heroic Frenzies*, ed. by Eugenio Canone, trans. by Ingrid D. Rowland (University of Toronto Press, 2013)
—— *Opera latine conscripta publicis sumptibus edita*, ed. by F. Fiorentino, 3 vols (Morano, 1879–91)
—— *Opere italiane*, ed. by Giovanni Acquilecchia, 2 vols (UTET, 2004)
Bullein, William, *Bulwarke of Defence against All Sicknesse* (London: Thomas Marshe, 1579)
Burnett, Mark Thornton, 'George Chapman (1559/1560–16349)', *ODNB* (2004), doi:10.1093/ref:odnb/5118
Bush, Douglas, *Mythology and the Renaissance Tradition in English Poetry: The Renaissance* (University of Minnesota Press, 1932)
Buxton, John, *Elizabethan Taste* (St Martin's Press, 1964)
Cannon, Charles K., 'Chapman on the Unity of Style and Meaning', *Journal of English and Germanic Philology*, 68.2 (1969), pp. 245–64
Cartari, Vincenzo, *Le imagini de i dei de gli Antichi* (Venice: Giordano Ziletti, 1571)
Castiglione, Baldesare, *The Courtyer*, trans. by Thomas Hoby (London: William Seres, 1561)
Catullus, *C. Valerii Catvlli Carmina*, ed. by Ana Pérez Vega and Antonio Ramírez de Verger (Fundación El Monte, 2005)
Centre National de Resources Textuelles et Lexicales Online, <https://www.cnrtl.fr> [accessed 18 May 2025]
Cicero, Marcus Tullius, *De natura deorum*, ed. and trans. by H. Rackham (Harvard University Press, 1967)
—— *De officiis*, ed. and trans. by Walter Miller (Heinemann, 1913)
—— *Tusculan Disputations*, ed. and trans. by J. E. King (Harvard University Press, 1966)
Cirlot, Juan Eduardo, *A Dictionary of Symbols*, trans. by Jack Sage, 2nd edn (Philosophical Books, 1971)
Clark, Charles, 'The Zodiac Man in Medieval Medical Astrology', *Quidditas*, 3 (1982), pp. 13–38
Cohen, Simona, *Transformations of Time and Temporality in Medieval and Renaissance Art* (Brill, 2014)
Coleridge, Samuel Taylor, *Coleridge's Poetry and Prose*, ed. by Nicholas Halmi, Paul Magnuson and Raimonda Modiano (Norton, 2004)
Constable, Henry, *The Complete Poems*, ed. by María Jesús Pérez-Jáuregui (Pontifical Institute of Mediaeval Studies, 2023)
Conti, Natale, *De Venatione, Libri quatuor* (Venice, 1551)
—— *Mythologiae*, ed. and trans by John Mulryan and Steven Brown, 2 vols (Arizona Center for Medieval and Renaissance Studies, 2006)
—— *Mythologiae, sive Explicationum fabularum, Libri decem* (Frankfurt: Andreas Wechel, 1581)
Cooper, Thomas, *Thesaurus Linguae Romanae et Britannicae* (London: Henry Denham, 1578)
Cotgrave, Randle, *A Dictionarie of the French & English Tongues* (London: Adam Islip, 1611)
Crooke, Helkiah, *Mikrokosmographia* (London: William Jaggard, 1615)
Curaeus, Joachim, Περὶ ἀισθήσεως καὶ ἀισσθητῶν; *Libellus physicus, continens doctrina de natura* (Wittenberg: Johann Schwertel, 1572)

Daniel, Samuel, *Poems and A Defence of Rhyme*, ed. by Arthur Colby Sprague (Harvard University Press, 1930)

Davies, John, *The Poems of John Davies*, ed. by Robert Krueger (Oxford University Press, 1975)

Davies (of Hereford), John, *The Complete Works of John Davies of Hereford*, ed. by Alexander B. Grosart, 2 vols (Edinburgh University Press, 1878)

Dillingham, William, *The Commentaries of Sir Francis Vere* (Cambridge: John Field 1657)

Dictionnaire de l'Académie française online, 9th edn, <https://www.dictionnaire-academie.fr> [accessed 18 May 2025]

Diogenes Laertius, *Diogenis Laertii de vitis, dogmatis et apothegmatis Philosophorum* (Paris: Claude Baleu, 1585)

Dionysius of Halicarnassus, *On Literary Composition*, ed. and trans. by W. Rhys Roberts (Macmillan, 1910)

Dioscorides, *Discórides interactivo (A facsimile edition of the Salamanca Ms.)*, University of Salamanca, <https://dioscorides.usal.es> [accessed 16 November 2023]

Dobell, Betram, 'Newly Discovered Documents of the Elizabethan and Jacobean Periods. I. Letters and Documents by George Chapman', *The Athenaeum*, 383.3 (1901), pp. 369–70

Donatus, Aelius, *Commentum Terenti*, ed. by P. Wesner (Bibliotheca Teubneriana, 1902)

Donne, John, *The Complete Poems*, ed. by Robin Robbins (Longman, 2010)

Dodoens, D. Rembert, *A Niewe Herball, or Historie of Plantes [Cruydenboeck]*, trans. by Henry Lyte (London: Henry Loë, 1578)

Dowland, John, *The Third and Last Booke of Songs or Aires* (London, 1603)

Drayton, Michael, *The Works of Michael Drayton*, ed. by J. William Hebel, 5 vols (Basil Blackwell, 1961)

Drummond (of Hawthornden), William, *Poems* (Edinburgh: A Hart, 1604)

—— *The Poetical Works of William Drummond of Hawthornden*, ed. by W. L. Kastner, 2 vols (Manchester University Press, 1913)

Dryden, John, *Essays*, ed. by W. P. Ker, 2 vols (Oxford University Press, 1900)

—— *Selected Poems*, ed. by Paul Hammond and David Hopkins (Routledge, 2014)

Du Bartas, Guillaume Salluste, *The Divine Weeks and Works of Guillaume de Salluste, Sieur Du Bartas*, ed. by Susan Snyder, trans. by Josuah Sylvester, 2 vols (Oxford University Press, 1979)

Dubrow, Heather, '"Dressing old words new"? Re-evaluating the "Delian Structure"', in *A Companion to Shakespeare's Sonnets*, ed. by Michael Schoenfeldt (Blackwell, 2006), pp. 90–103

Du Chesne, Joseph [Iosephus Quersitanus], *The Practise of Chymicall, and Hermeticall Physicke, for the Preseruation of Health*, trans. by Thomas Thimme (London: Thomas Creede, 1605)

Durant, Gilles, Sieur de la Bergerie, *Les oeuvres poetiques du Sieur de la Bergerie, avec les imitations tirees du Latin de Jean Bonnefons* (Paris: Abel l'Angelier, 1594)

Durling, Robert M., 'Ovid as Praeceptor Amoris', *The Classical Journal*, 53.4 (1958), pp. 157–67

Ebreo, Leone, *Dialoghi d'amore*, ed. by Santino Caramella (Laterza, 1929)

—— *Dialogues of Love*, ed. and trans. by Rosella Pescatori and Damian Bacich (University of Toronto Press, 2009)
Eccles, Marc, 'Chapman's Early Years', *Studies in Philology*, 43.2 (1946), pp. 176–93
Eliot, T. S., 'The Metaphysical Poets' (1921), in *The Complete Prose of T. S. Eliot: The Critical Edition. The Perfect Critic, 1919–1926* (Johns Hopkins University Press, 2014), pp. 375–85
Ellis, Havelock, *Chapman, with Illustrative Passages* (Nonesuch Press, 1934)
Erasmus of Rotterdam, *Collected Works of Erasmus: Adages (vols. XXXI–XXV)*, trans. by R. A. B. Mynors (University of Toronto Press, 1989)
—— *Les adages*, ed. by Jean-Cristophe Saladin (Belles Lettres, 2011). Online text: <http://ihrim.huma-num.fr/nmh/Erasmus/index.html> [accessed 26 November 2024]
Falomir, Miguel, 'Titian and the *Poesie*: Experimentation and Freedom in Mythological Painting', in *Mythological Passions*, ed. by Miguel Falomir and Alejandro Vergara (Museo del Prado, 2021)
Faulkner, Andrew, and Owen Hodkinson (eds), *Hymnic Narrative and the Narratology of Greek Hymns* (Brill, 2015)
Feingold, Mordechai, 'Giordano Bruno in England, Revisited', *The Huntington Library Quarterly*, 67.3 (2004), pp. 329–46, doi:10.1525/hlq.2004.67.3.329
Ficino, Marsilio, *Commentaries on Plato: Phaedrus and Ion*, ed. and trans. by Michael J. B. Allen (Harvard University Press, 2008)
—— *Commentary on Plato's Symposium*, ed. and trans. by Sears R. Jayne (University of Missouri Press, 1944)
—— *Opera*, 2 vols (Basel: Heinrich Petri, 1576)
—— *The Philebus Commentary*, ed. by Michael J. B. Allen (University of California Press, 1975)
—— *Platonic Theology*, ed. by Michael J. B. Allen, 6 vols (Harvard University Press, 2001–2006)
Fletcher, Giles, *The English Works of Giles Fletcher the Elder*, ed. by Lloyd E. Berry (University of Wisconsin Press, 1964)
Fowler, Alistair, *Triumphal Forms: Structural Patterns in Elizabethan Poetry* (Cambridge University Pres, 1970)
Friedman, Lionel J., 'Gradus Amoris', *Romance Philology*, 19.2 (1965), pp. 167–77
Gatti, Hilary, 'Giordano Bruno: The Texts in the Library of the Ninth Earl of Northumberland', *Journal of the Warburg and Courtauld Institutes*, 46.1 (1983), pp. 63–77, doi:10.2307/751114
—— *The Renaissance Drama of Knowledge: Giordano Bruno in England* (Routledge, 1989)
Gifford, Humfrey, *A Posie for Gilliflowers* (London: Thomas Dawson, 1580)
Gilbert, C. D., 'Blind Cupid', *Journal of the Warburg and Courtauld Institute*, 33.1 (1970), pp. 304–05, doi:10.2307/750901
Giles of Viterbo, *The Commentary on the Sentences of Petrus Lombardus*, ed. by Daniel Nodes (Brill, 2010)
Giovio, Paolo, *Dialogo dell'imprese* (Lyons: Guillaume Rouillé, 1574)
Gless, Darryl, 'Chapman's Ironic Ovid', *English Literary Renaissance*, 9.1 (1971), pp. 21–41, doi:10.1111/j.1475-6757.1979.tb01396.x
Gombrich, H. C., *Norm and Form: Studies in the Art of the Renaissance* (Phaidon, 1978)

Goldner, Rebecca Steiner, 'Aristotle and the Priority of Touch', in *Touch and the Ancient Senses*, ed. by Alex Purves (Routledge, 2018), pp. 50–63
Goold, G. P., 'The Cause of Ovid's Exile', *Illinois Classical Studies*, 8.1 (1983), pp. 94–107
Gorman, Cassandra, 'Atomies of Love: Material (Mis)interpretations of Cupid's Origin in Elizabethan Poetry', in *Poetic Theory and Practice in Early Modern Verse: Unwritten Arts*, ed. by Zenón Luis-Martínez (Edinburgh University Press, 2023), pp. 74–98
Graham, Daniel D. (ed. and trans.), *The Texts of Early Greek Philosophy: The Complete Fragments and Selected Testimonies of the Major Presocratics*, 2 vols (Cambridge University Press, 2010)
Granada, Miguel Á., *Giordano Bruno: universo infinito, unión con Dios, perfección del hombre* (Herder, 2002)
Greek Anthology, ed. and trans. by W. R. Paton, 5 vols (Harvard University Press, 1956–60)
Greville, Fulke, *Poems and Dramas of Fulke Greville, First Lord Brooke*, ed. by Geoffrey Bullough, 2 vols (Oxford University Press, 1945)
Grimal, Pierre, *The Dictionary of Classical Mythology*, trans. by A. R. Maxwell-Hyslop (Blackwell, 1986)
Grimestone, Edward, *A Generall Historie of the Netherlands* (London: Adam Islip and George Eld, 1608)
Guthrie, W. K. C., *Orpheus and Greek Religion: A Study of the Orphic Movement* (Methuen, 1966)
Hackett, Helen, 'Dream Visions of Elizabeth I', in *Reading the Early Modern Dream: The Terrors of the Night*, ed. by Katharine Hodgkin, Michelle O'Callaghan, and S. J. Wiseman (Routledge, 2008)
Hamilton, A. C. (ed.), *The Spenser Encyclopaedia* (Routledge, 1990)
Harder, M. Annette, 'Insubstantial Voices: Some Observations on the Hymns of Callimachus', *The Classical Quarterly*, 42.1 (1992), pp. 384–94, doi:10.1017/S0009838800016013
Hardie, Philip (ed.), *The Cambridge Companion to Ovid* (Cambridge University Press, 2006)
Hartmann, Anna-Maria, *English Mythography in Its European Contexts, 1500–1650* (Oxford University Press, 2018)
Heninger, S. K., Jr, *A Handbook of Renaissance Meteorology, with Particular Reference to Elizabethan and Jacobean Literature* (Duke University Press, 1960)
—— *Touches of Sweet Harmony: Pythagorean Cosmology and Renaissance Poetics* (Huntington Library, 1974)
Herodotus, *Histories*, ed. and trans. by A. D. Godley, 4 vols (Harvard University Press, 1920)
Hesiod, [Homer], *Hesiod, the Homeric Hymns and Homerica*, ed. and trans. by Hugh A. Evelyn-White (Heinemann, 1920)
Homer, *Iliad*, ed. and trans. by A. T. Murray, 2 vols (Heinemann, 1928)
—— *Odyssey*, ed. and trans. by A. T. Murray, 2 vols (Harvard University Press, 1945)
Horace (Quintus Horatius Flaccus), *Odes and Epodes*, ed. and trans. by Niall Rudd (Harvard University Press, 2004)
Huffman, Carl, 'Pythagoras', in *The Stanford Encyclopedia of Philosophy* (2018),

ed. by Edward N. Zalta, <https://plato.stanford.edu/archives/win2018/entries/pythagoras> [accessed 11 February 2023]

Hulse, Clark, *Metamorphic Verse: The Elizabethan Minor Epic* (Princeton University Press, 1981)

Hunt, John Dixon, and Michael Leslie, 'Gardens', in *The Spenser Encyclopaedia*, ed. by A. C. Hamilton (Routledge, 1990), p. 324

Huntington, John, *Ambition, Rank and Poetry in 1590s England* (University of Illinois Press, 2001)

—— 'Philosophical Seduction in Chapman, Davies, and Donne', *English Literary History*, 44.1 (1977), pp. 40–59, doi:10.2307/2872525

Hyginus, *De Astronomia*, ed. by Ghislaine Viré (Teubner, 1992)

Isidore of Seville, *Etymologies*, ed. by Stephen A. Barney and others (Cambridge University Press, 2006)

Iwasaki, Soji, '*Veritas Filia Temporis* and Shakespeare', *English Literary Renaissance*, 3.2 (1973), pp. 249–63, doi:10.1111/j.1475-6757.1973.tb00750.x

Jacquot, Jean, *George Chapman (1559–1634): sa vie, sa poésie, son théâtre, sa pensée* (Les Belles Lettres, 1951)

Jayne, Sears, 'Ficino and the Platonism of the English Renaissance', *Comparative Literature*, 4.3 (1952), pp. 214–38, doi:10.2307/1768535

Jode, Gerard de, *Speculum Orbis Terrarum* (Antwerp: Gerard Smits, 1578)

Jonson, Ben, *The Cambridge Edition of the Works of Ben Jonson Online*, ed. by Martin Butler and others, <https://universitypublishingonline.org/cambridge/benjonson> [accessed 19 January 2023]

Juvenal and Persius, ed. and trans. by G. G. Ramsay (Heinemann, 1928)

Kargon, Robert Hugh, *Atomism in England from Hariot to Newton* (Oxford University Press, 1966)

Keats, John, *Keats's Poetry and Prose*, ed. by Jeffrey N. Cox (Norton, 2009)

Keilen, Sean, 'The Sense of a Poem: *Ovids Banquet of Sence* (1595)', in *Synaesthesia and the Ancient Senses*, ed. by Shane Butler and Alex Purves (Acumen, 2013)

Kelley, Edward, *The Alchemical Writings of Edward Kell[e]y* (James Eliott, 1893)

Kelly, Sister Maria del Rey, *Poetic Diction in the Nondramatic Works of George Chapman* (unpublished doctoral dissertation, Fordham University, 1965)

Kermode, Frank, 'The Banquet of Sense', *Bulletin of the John Rylands Library*, 44.1 (1961), pp. 68–99

Knight, Sarah, 'The Worthy Knots of Fulke Greville', in *Poetic Theory and Practice in Early Modern Verse*, ed. by Zenón Luis-Martínez (Edinburgh University Press, 2023), pp. 239–57

LaFaro, Alyssa, 'Curiosity Ignited', *UNC Research Stories* (21 April 2021), <https://endeavors.unc.edu/curiosity-ignited> [accessed 21 March 2025]

Lakin, Barbara L., 'The Magus and the Poet: Bruno and Chapman's *The Shadow of Night*', *The Sixteenth Century Journal*, 10.2 (1979), pp. 1–14, doi:10.2307/2539403

Landels, John G., *Music in Ancient Greece and Rome* (Routledge, 1999)

Lee, Sydney, 'Chapman's "Amorous Zodiack"', *Modern Philology*, 3.2 (1905), pp. 143–58, doi:10.1086/386671

—— *The French Renaissance in England* (Charles Scribner's Sons, 1910)

Liddell, Henry George, and Robert Scott, *A Greek-English Lexicon*, rev. by Sir Henry Stuart Jones and Roderick McKenzie (Clarendon Press, 1940), <https://www.perseus.tufts.edu/hopper/searchresults?q=Liddell>

Lisska, Anthony J., *Aquinas's Theory of Perception: An Analytic Reconstruction* (Oxford University Press, 2016)

Livy (Titus Livius), *History of Rome*, ed. and trans. by B. O. Foster, 14 vols (Harvard University Press, 1929)

Loane, George G., 'Chapman and Holofernes', *Notes and Queries*, 172 (1937), p. 7

—— 'Chapman's Compounds in *N.E.D.*', *Notes and Queries*, 181 (1941), pp. 130–31

—— *A Thousand and One Notes on 'A New English Dictionary'* (Philipot & Co., 1920)

—— 'A Thousand and Two Notes on *A New English Dictionary*', *Philological Society Transactions*, 30.1 (1930), pp. 38–199

—— 'A Third Thousand Notes on *N.E.D.*', *Notes and Queries*, 171 (1936), pp. 202–05

Loffman, Claire, and Harriet Phillips (eds), *A Handbook of Editing Early Modern Texts* (Routledge, 2018)

Lomazzo, Giovanni Paolo, *A Tracte Containing the Artes of Curious Paintinge Carvinge & Buildinge* (Oxford: Richard Haydock, 1598)

—— *Trattato dell'arte della pittura, scoltura, et architettura* (Milano: Paolo Gottardo Pontio, 1584)

Lucian of Samosata, *Lucian*, ed. and trans. by A. M. Harmon, 8 vols (Heinemann, 1913)

Lucretius, Titus Carus, *De rerum natura*, ed. and trans. by W. H. D. Rouse (Heinemann, 1924)

Luis-Martínez, Zenón, '"Friendlesse Verse": The Poetics of Chapman's "A Coronet for His Mistresse Philosophie" (1595)', *Studies in Philology*, 118.3 (2021), pp. 565–604, doi: 10.1353/sip.2021.0018

—— 'Whose Banquet? Whose Coronet? Whose Zodiac?: George Chapman and Seventeenth-Century Ovid *Sammelbände*', *Philological Quarterly*, 100.1 (2021), pp. 23–53

—— 'George Chapman's "Habit of Poesie"', in *Poetic Theory and Practice in Early Modern Verse*, ed. by Zenón Luis-Martínez (Edinburgh University Press, 2023), pp. 258–85

—— 'George Chapman's Musaean "Light": Origin, Primordiality and Priority from *The Divine Poem of Musaeus* (1616) to *Hero and Leander* (1598)', *Parergon*, 41.1 (2024), pp. 239–71, doi:10.1353/pgn.2024.a935342

Lycosthenes, Conrad, *Prodigiorum ac ostentorum chronicon / The Doome Warning All Men to the Iudgemente*, trans. by Stephen Batman (London: Henry Bynneman, 1581)

Lyne, Raphael, 'Love and Exile after Ovid', in *The Cambridge Companion to Ovid*, ed. by Philip Hardie (Cambridge University Press, 2006), pp. 288–300

MacLure, Millar, *George Chapman: A Critical Study* (University of Toronto Press, 1966)

Mair, G. R. (ed. and trans.), *Callimachus, Lycophron, Aratus* (Heinemann, 1921)

Manilius, Marcus, *Astronomicon*, ed. by Alfred Edward Housman, 5 vols (Georg Olms, 1972)

Manuel, Frank E., and Fritzie P. Manuel, *Utopian Thought in the Western World* (Harvard University Press, 1979)

Marlowe, Christopher, *The Complete Works of Christopher Marlowe*, ed. by Roma Gill and others, 5 vols (Oxford University Press, 1987)

—— *Doctor Faustus and Other Plays*, ed. by David Bevington and Eric Rasmussen (Oxford: Oxford University Press, 1995)

Martianus Capella, *De nuptiis Philologiae et Mercurii / Las nupcias de Filología y Mercurio*, ed. and trans. by Fernando Navarro Antolín, 3 vols (CSIC, 2016)

May, Steven, 'Spenser's "Amyntas": Three Poems by Ferdinando Stanley, Lord Strange, Fifth Earl of Derby', *Modern Philology*, 70.1 (1972), pp. 49–52, doi:10.1086/390376

McKerrow, Ronald B., *Printers' and Publishers' Devices in England and Scotland: 1485–1640* (The Bibliographical Society, 1949)

Menander Rhetor, *Menander Rhetor: A Commentary*, ed. and trans. by D. A. Russell and N. G. Wilson (Oxford University Press, 1981)

Meres, Francis, *Palladis Tamia, or Wits Trasurie* (London: Cuthbert Burbie, 1598)

Milton, John, *Paradise Lost*, ed. by Alastair Fowler, 2nd edn (Routledge, 1996)

Minto, William, *Characteristics of the English Poets from Chaucer to Shirley* (William Blackwood, 1874)

More, Clifford H., and John Jackson (ed. and trans.), *Tacitus*, 4 vols (Harvard University Press, 1962)

Morros Mestres, Bienvenido, *El tema de Acteón en algunas literaturas europeas: de la antigüedad clásica hasta nuestros días* (Universidad de Alcalá/Centro de Estudios Cervantinos, 2010)

Moss, Daniel H., '"The Second Master of Love": George Chapman and the Shadow of Ovid', *Modern Philology*, 111.3 (2014), pp. 457–84, doi:10.2307/20466786

Motley, John Lothrop, *History of the United Netherlands*, 4 vols (Harper & Brothers, 1868)

Mourgues, Odette de, *Metaphysical, Baroque & Précieux Poetry* (Oxford University Press, 1953)

Myers, James Phares, Jr, '"This Curious Frame": Chapman's Ovid's Banquet of Sense', *Studies in Philology*, 65.2 (1968), pp. 192–206

Nagler, Danielle, 'Towards the Smell of Mortality: Shakespeare and Ideas of Smell 1588–1625', *Cambridge Quarterly*, 26.1 (1997), pp. 42–58, doi:10.1093/camqtly/XXVI.1.42

Nashe, Thomas, *The Works of Thomas Nashe*, ed. by Ronald B. McKerrow, 5 vols (Sidgwick & Jackson, 1910)

Nelson, John Charles, *Renaissance Theory of Love: The Context of Giordano Bruno's 'Eroici Furori'* (Columbia University Press, 1958)

Nenna, Giovanni Battista, *Il Nennio, nel quale si ragiona della nobilitá* (Venice: Andrea Vauassore, 1542)

—— *Nennio, or a Treatise on Nobility*, trans. by William Jones (London: Paul Linley, 1595)

Newton, Thomas, *Approved medicines and Cordiall Receiptes, with the natures, qualities, and operations of sundry Samples* (London: Thomas Marshe, 1580)

Nicander, *Poems and Fragments*, ed. and trans. by A. S. F. Gow and A. F. Schofield (Cambridge University Press, 1953)

Nicholl, Charles, *A Cup of News: The Life of Thomas Nashe* (Routledge & Kegan Paul, 1984)

Ordine, Nuccio, *La soglia dell'ombra. Letteratura, filosofia e pittura in Giordano Bruno* (Marsilio, 2003); Spanish translation: *El Umbral de la sombra: literatura*

filosofía y puntura en Gordano Bruno, trans. by Silvina Paula Vidal (Siruela, 2003)
Orpheus, *Hymnes orphiques*, ed. by Marie-Christine Fayant (Les belles lettres, 2014)
—— *The Mystical Hymns of Orpheus*, trans. by Thomas Taylor (Bertram Dobell, 1896)
—— *Orphica*, ed. by Jenö Ábel (G. Freytag, 1885)
Otten, Charlotte F., 'Plants, Herbs', in *The Spenser Encyclopaedia*, ed. by A. C. Hamilton (Routledge, 1990), pp. 545–46
Ovid (Publius Ovidius Naso), *The Art of Love, and Other Poems*, ed. and trans. by J. H. Mozley (Heinemann, 1957)
—— *Fasti*, ed. and trans. by Sir James George Frazer (Heinemann, 1959)
—— *Heroides and Amores*, ed. and trans. by Grant Showernam (Heinemann, 1914)
—— *Metamorphoses*, ed. and trans. by Frank Justus Miller, 2 vols (Harvard University Press, 1951)
—— *Ouid his inuective against Ibis. Translated into English méeter*, trans. by Thomas Underdown (London: Henry Bynneman, 1577)
—— *Tristia, Ex Ponto*, ed. and trans. by Arthur Leslie Wheeler (Harvard University Press, 1939)
Oxford Dictionary of National Biography online, <https://www.oxforddnb.com>
Oxford English Dictionary online, <https://www.oed.com>
Oxford Latin Dictionary (Oxford University Press, 1968)
Panofsky, Erwin, *Studies in Iconology: Humanistic Themes in the Art of the Renaissance* (Harper & Row, 1939)
Paracelsus (Theophrastus Bombast von Hohenheim), *The Hermetic and Alchemical Writings of Paracelsus*, ed. by Arthur Edward Waite, 2 vols (James Elliott, 1894)
Pausanias, *Description of Greece*, ed. and trans. by W. H. S. Jones, 4 vols (Harvard University Press, 1935)
Peckham, George, *A True Report of the Late Discoveries of the New-founde Landes* (London: John Charlewood, 1583)
Peele, George, *The Honour of the Garter* (London: John Busby, 1593)
Percy, Henry, Ninth Earl of Northumberland, *Advice to His Son* (1609), ed. by G. B. Harrison (Ernest Benn, 1930)
Phaer, Thomas, *Nyne First Bookes of the Eneidos* (London: Rowland Hall, 1562)
Physiologus: A Medieval Book of Nature Lore, trans. by Michael J. Curley (University of Chicago Press, 1979)
The Phoenix Nest (1593), ed. by Hyder Edward Rollins (Harvard University Press, 1931)
Piana, Marco, and Matteo Soranzo, 'The Way Philosophers Pray: Hymns as Experiential Knowledge in Early Modern Europe', *Mediterranea*, 5 (2020), pp. 51–89, doi:10.21071/mijtk.v5i.12087
Pico della Mirandola, Giovanni, *Conclusiones in doctrina Platonis* (Rome, 1486)
Pindar, *Odes*, ed. and trans. by Sir John Sandys (William Heinemann, 1915)
Pirillo, Diego, *Filosofia ed eresia nell'Inghliterra del tardo cinquecento: Bruno, Sidney e I dissidenti religiosi italiani* (Edizioni di storia e letteratura, 2010)
Plato, *Euthyphro, Apology, Crito, Phaedo, Phraedrus*, ed. and trans. by Harold North Fowler (Harvard University Press, 1914)

—— *Omnia Divini Platonis Opera*, trans. by Marsilio Ficino (Basel: Hieronymus Froben, 1546)
—— *The Statesman, Philebus, Ion*, ed. and trans. by Harold N. Fowler (Harvard University Press, 1975)
—— *Timaeus*, ed. by R. D. Archer-Hind (Macmillan 1888)
—— *Timaeus, Critias, Cleitophon, Menexenus, Epistles*, ed. and trans. by R. G. Bury (William Heinemann, 1952)
Plett, Heinrich F., *Enargeia in Classical Antiquity and the Early Modern Age: The Aesthetics of Evidence* (Brill, 2012)
Pliny the Elder, *Natural History*, ed. and trans. by H. Rackham and D. E. Eichholz, 10 vols (Harvard University Press, 1938–62)
Plomer, Henry R., and others, *A Dictionary of Printers and Booksellers in England, Scotland and Ireland from 1641 to 1667* (Blades, East & Blades, 1907)
Plotinus, *The Enneads*, trans. by Stephen MacKenna (Faber, 1930)
Plutarch, *Essay on the Life and Poetry of Homer*, ed. by J. J. Keaney and Robert Lamberton (Scholars Press, 1996)
—— *Moralia*, ed. and trans. by W. C. Hembold, 15 vols (Harvard University Press, 1932)
—— *Plutarchi Chaeronensis Moralia*, ed. and trans. by Wilhelm Xylander (Basel: Thomas Guarin, 1570)
—— *Plutarch's Lives*, ed. and trans. Bernadotte Perrin, 11 vols (Heinemann, 1918)
Polybius, *The Histories*, ed. and trans. by W. R. Paton, 6 vols (Harvard University Press, 1969)
Pomponius Mela, *Description of the World*, ed. and trans. by F. E. Romer (University of Michigan Press, 1998)
—— *De situ orbis libri tres* (Rostock: Stephan Myliander, 1591)
Presson, Robert K., 'Wrestling with This World: A View of George Chapman', *PMLA*, 84.1 (1969), pp. 44–50, doi:10.2307/1261155
Priscian, *On Theophrastus on Sense-Perception with 'Simplicius': On Aristotle On the Soul 2.5–12*, ed. and trans. by Pamela Huby, Carlos Steel and J. O. Urmson, annotated by Peter Lautner (Bloomsbury, 2014)
Proclus, *Commentary on Plato's Republic*, ed. and trans. by Dick Baltzy, John F. Finamore and Graeme Miles (Cambridge University Press, 2018)
—— *Proclus' Hymns: Essays, Translation, Commentary*, ed. and trans. by R. M. van den Berg (Brill, 2001)
Prudentius, ed. and trans. by H. J. Thompson, 2 vols (Heinemann, 1949)
Purves, Alex (ed.), *Touch and the Ancient Senses* (Routledge, 2018)
Puttenham, George, *The Art of English Poesy*, ed. by Frank Whigham and Wayne A. Rebhorn (Cornell University Press, 2007)
Quintilian, *Institutio Oratoria*, ed. and trans. by H. E. Butter, 4 vols (Harvard University Press, 1920–22)
Race, William H., 'Aspects of Rhetoric and Form in Greek Hymns', *Greek, Roman and Byzantine Studies*, 23.1 (1982), pp. 5–14
Reid, Lindsay Anne, 'The Spectre of the School of Night: Former Scholarly Fictions and the Stuff of Academic Fiction', *Early Modern Literary Studies*, 23 (2014), <https://extra.shu.ac.uk/emls/journal/indexphp/emls/article/view/182.html> [accessed 21 January 2025]
Ribner, Rhoda, 'The Compasse of This Curious Frame: Chapman's *Ovids Banquet of Sence* and the Emblematic Tradition', *Studies in the Renaissance*, 17 (1970), pp. 233–58, doi: 10.2307/2857064

Richardson, N., 'Constructing a Hymnic Narrative: Tradition and Innovation in the Longer *Homeric Hymns*', in *Hymnic Narrative and the Narratology of Greek Hymns*, ed. by Andrew Faulkner and Owen Hodkinson (Brill, 2015), pp. 19–30, doi:10.1163/9789004289512_003
Ripa, Cesare, *Iconologia* (Roma: Giovanni Gigliotti, 1593)
Robertson, J. M., *Shakespeare and Chapman* (T. Fisher Unwin, 1917)
Robertson, Jean, 'The Early Life of George Chapman', *Modern Language Review*, 40.3 (1945), pp. 157–65, doi:10.2307/3716838
Roche, Thomas P., *Petrarch and the English Sonnet Sequences* (AMS Press, 1989)
Romei, Annibale, *The Courtiers Academie*, trans. by I. K. (London: Valentine Sims, 1598)
—— *Discorsi* (Ferrara: Vittorio Baldini, 1586)
Rosarium philosophorum. Secunda pars alchimiae de lapide philosophico vero modo praeparando (Frankfurt: Cyriacus Jacob, 1550)
Rosen, Emelyn Butterfield, 'The Hierarchy of Genres and the Hierarchy of Life-Forms', *Res: Anthropology and Aesthetics*, 73–74 (2020), pp. 76–93, doi:10.1086/711228
Rowland, Ingrid D., *Giordano Bruno: Philosopher/Heretic* (University of Chicago Press, 2008)
Ruland, Martin, *Lexicon Alchemiae* (Frankfurt: Zacharias Palthenus, 1612)
—— *A Lexicon of Alchemy*, trans. by Arthur E. Waite (John M. Watkins, 1893)
Rutledge, Leslie A., *George Chapman's Theory of the Soul and of Poetry* (unpublished PhD thesis, Harvard University, 1938)
Sambucus, Joannes, *Emblemata* (Antwerp: Christopher Plantin, 1564)
Sargent, Ralph M., *At the Court of Queen Elizabeth: The Life and Lyrics of Sir Edward Dyer* (Oxford University Press, 1975)
Sasek, Laurence, 'Gascoigne and the Elizabethan Sonnet sequences', *Notes and Queries*, 3.4 (1956), pp. 143–44
Saxl, Fritz, 'Veritas Filia Temporis', in *Philosophy and History: Essays Presented to Ernst Cassirer*, ed. by R. Klibansky and H. J. Paton (Oxford University Press, 1930), pp. 197–222
Scaliger, Julius Caesar, *Poetices libri septem* (Geneva: Jean Crispin, 1561)
Scève, Maurice, *Delie* (Lyons: Antoine Constantin, 1544)
Schoell, Franck L., *Études sur l'humanisme continental en Angleterre á la fin de la Renaissance* (Honoré Champion, 1926)
Schrickx, Willem, 'George Chapman in Middelburg in 1586', *Notes and Queries*, 40.2 (1993), p. 165
—— 'George Chapman's Borrowings from Natali Conti: Some Hitherto Unnoted Passages', *English Studies*, 32 (1951), pp. 107–12
Sedley, David, 'The Duality of Touch', in *Touch and the Ancient Senses*, ed. by Alex Purves (Routledge, 2018), pp. 64–74
Sell, Jonathan P. A., 'A Tragedy of Oversight: Visual Praxis in Christopher Marlowe's *Dido, Queen of Carthage*', *Medieval & Renaissance Drama in England*, 29 (2016), pp. 130–53
Seneca, Lucius Annaeus, *Moral Essays*, ed. and trans. by John W. Bashore, 3 vols (Heinemann, 1928)
—— *Tragedies*, ed. and trans. by Frank Justus Miller, 2 vols (Harvard University Press, 1961)
Servius, *Commentarii in Virgilium Serviani*, ed. by H. Albertus Lion, 2 vols (Vandenhoeck & Ruprecht, 1826)

Seznec, Jean, *The Survival of the Pagan Gods: The Mythological Tradition and Its Place in Renaissance Humanism and Art*, trans. by Barbara F. Sessions (Princeton University Press, 1972)
Shakespeare, William, *King Richard II*, ed. by Charles Forker (Thomson Learning, 2002)
—— *The Life and Death of King John*, ed. by A. R. Braunmuller (Oxford University Press, 1989)
—— *Love's Labour's Lost*, ed. by H. R. Woudhuysen (Bloomsbury, 1998)
—— *Love's Labour's Lost: The New Shakespeare*, ed. by Arthur Quiller-Couch and John Dover Wilson (Cambridge University Press, 1923; 2nd edn 1962)
—— *A Midsummer Night's Dream* (Cambridge University Press, 2003)
—— *Sonnets*, ed. by Katherine Duncan-Jones (Thomas Nelson, 1997)
—— *Twelfth Night*, ed. by Keir Elam (Bloomsbury, 2008)
—— *Venus and Adonis* (London: Richard Field, 1593)
Shearman, John, *Mannerism* (Penguin, 1967)
Shephard, Odell, *The Lore of the Unicorn* (Avenell Books, 1982)
Sidney, Philip, *Miscellaneous Prose of Sir Philip Sidney*, ed. by Katherine Duncan-Jones and Jan van Dorsten (Oxford University Press, 1973)
—— *The Poems of Sir Philip Sidney*, ed. by William A. Ringler, Jr (Oxford University Press, 1962)
Sidney, Robert, *The Poems of Robert Sidney*, ed. by P. J. Croft (Oxford University Press, 1984)
Silvares, Lavinia, 'The Deep Search of Knowledge: George Chapman's Glosses in The Shadow of Night (1594)', *Acta Scientiarum: Language and Culture*, 39.3 (2017), pp. 321–27, doi:10.4025/actascilangcult.v39i3.32208
Smarr, Janet Levarie, 'The Pyramid and the Circle: "Ovid's Banquet of Sense"', *Philological Quarterly*, 63.3 (1984), pp. 369–86
Smith, Hallett, *Elizabethan Poetry: A Study of Conventions, Meaning, and Expression* (Harvard University Press, 1952)
Smith, William (ed.), *A Dictionary of Greek and Roman Biography and Mythology*, 3 vols (John Murray, 1880)
Snare, Gerald, *The Mystification of George Chapman* (Duke University Press, 1989)
Sokol, B. J., 'Roydon, Matthew (fl. 1583–1622), poet', *ODNB* (2004) [accessed 3 January 2023]
Spens, Janet, 'Chapman's Ethical Thought', in *Essays and Studies by Members of the English Association: Vol XI.*, ed. by Oliver Elton (Oxford University Press, 1925), pp. 145–69
Spenser, Edmund, *The Faerie Queene*, ed. by A. C. Hamilton (Pearson, 2007)
—— *The Yale Edition of the Shorter Poems of Edmund Spenser*, ed. by William A. Oram and others (Yale University Press, 1989)
Spivack, Charlotte, *George Chapman* (Twayne, 1967)
Stanford Encyclopedia of Philosophy, ed. by Edward N. Zalta and Uri Nodelman, <https://plato.stanford.edu>
Stapleton, Richard (?), *Phillis and Flora. The sweete and ciuill contention of two amorous Ladyes. Translated out of Latine: By R. S. Esquire* (London: Richard Jones, 1598)
Steiner, George, 'On Difficulty', *The Journal of Aesthetics and Art Criticism*, 36.3 (1978), pp. 263–76, doi:10.2307/430437
Stephens, S. A., 'Callimachus and His Narrators', in *Hymnic Narrative and the*

Narratology of Greek Hymns, ed. by Andrew Faulkner and Owen Hodkinson (Brill, 2015), pp. 49–68, doi:10.1163/9789004289512_00

Strabo, *Geography*, ed. and trans. by Horace Leonard Jones, 8 vols (Heinemann, 1928)

Strathmann, Ernest H., 'The Textual Evidence for "The School of Night"', *Modern Language Notes*, 56.3 (1941), pp. 176–86

Suárez de la Torre, Emilio, 'El viaje nocturno del Sol y la *Nanno* de Mimnermo', *Estudios clásicos*, 89 (1985), pp. 5–20

Summers, David, *Michelangelo and the Language of Art* (Princeton University Press, 1981)

Swinburne, Algernon Charles, *George Chapman: A Critical Essay* (Chatto & Windus, 1875)

Tarrant, Richard, 'Ovid and Ancient Literary History', in *The Cambridge Companion to Ovid*, ed. by Philip Hardie (Cambridge University Press, 2006), pp. 13–33

Theophrastus, *De sensu*, in George Malcolm Stratton (ed. and trans.), *Theophrastus and the Greek Physiological Psychology before Aristotle* (Macmillan, 1917)

—— *Libellus de odoribus* (Paris: Michel de Vascosan, 1556)

Thibault, John C., *The Mystery of Ovid's Exile* (University of California Press, 1964)

Tilley, Morris Palmer, *A Dictionary of the Proverbs in England in the Sixteenth and Seventeenth Centuries* (Michigan University Press, 1950)

Turner, William, *The Names of Herbes in Greke, Latin, Englishe, Duche [and] Frenche with the Commune Names that Herbaries and Apotecaries Vse* (London: John Day and William Seres, 1548)

Unger, Emma V., and William R. Jackson, *The Carl H. Pforzheimer Library: English Literature, 1475–1700*, 3 vols (Oak Knoll Press, 1968)

Vaenius, Otto, *Amorum emblemata* (Antwerp; Hendrik Swingen, 1608)

Van den Berg, R. M., *Proclus' Hymns: Essays, Translation, Commentary* (Brill, 2001)

Vera-Reyes, María, 'Michael Drayton's Topographies: *Ideas Mirrour* (1594) and *Poly-Olbion* (1612–1622)', *English Studies*, 102.8 (2021), pp. 1002–23, doi:10.1080/0013838X.2021.1982218

Vinge, Louise, 'Chapman's *Ovids Banquet of Sence*: Its Sources and Theme', *Journal of the Warburg and Courtauld Institutes*, 38 (1975), pp. 234–57, doi:10.2307/750955

Virgil, ed. and trans. by H. Rhuston Fairclough, 2 vols (Heinemann, 1939)

Waddington, Raymond B., 'Chapman and Persius: The Epigraph to *Ovids Banquet of Sence*', *The Review of English Studies*, 74.1 (1968), pp. 158–62, doi:10.1093/res/XIX.74.158

—— *The Mind's Empire: Myth and Form in George Chapman's Narrative Poetry* (Johns Hopkins University Press, 1974)

—— 'Visual Rhetoric: Chapman and the Extended Poem', *English Literary Renaissance*, 13.1 (1983), pp. 36–57, doi:10.1111/j.1475-6757.1983.tb00844.x

Watson, Thomas, *The ἙΚΑΤΟΜΠΑΘΊΑ, or the Passionate Centurie of Loue* (London: John Wolfe, 1582)

Way, Arthur S. (ed. and trans.), *Euripides*, 4 vols (Heinemann, 1912)

Weaver, William P., 'The Banquet of the Common Sense: George Chapman's

Anti-Epyllion', *Studies in Philology*, 111.4 (2014), pp. 757–85, doi:10.1353/sip.2014.0025

Weiner, Andrew D., 'Expelling the Beast: Bruno's Adventures in England', *Modern Philology*, 78 (1980), pp. 1–13

Wilson, Thomas, *The Rule of Reason, Conteinyng the Arte of Logique* (London: Richard Grafton, 1551)

Wiseman, Susan, '"Did we lie downe, because 'twas night?": John Donne, George Chapman and the Senses of Night in the 1590s', in *The Senses of Early Modern England, 1558–1660*, ed. by Simon Smith, Jackie Watson and Amy Kenny (Manchester University Press, 2015)

Wolfe, Jessica, *Humanism, Machinery, and Renaissance Literature* (Cambridge University Press, 2004)

Wood, Anthony à, *Athenae Oxonienses*, 4 vols (Rivington, 1813; 1st edn 1691)

Woudhuysen, H. R., and others, 'Text: Modernisation and Translation', in *A Handbook of Editing Early Modern Texts*, ed. by Claire Loffman and Harriet Phillips (Routledge, 2018), pp. 94–113

Wroth, Mary, *The Poems of Lady Mary Wroth*, ed. by Josephine Roberts (Louisiana State University Press, 1987)

Yates, Frances A., *Astraea: The Imperial Theme in the Sixteenth Century* (Routledge, 1975)

—— *Giordano Bruno and the Hermetic Tradition*, 2nd edn (London: Routledge, 2002, 1st edn, 1964)

—— *The Occult Philosophy in the Elizabethan Age* (Routledge, 1979)

—— *A Study of 'Love's Labour's Lost'* (Cambridge University Press, 1936)

Zunino-Garrido, Cinta, 'Thomas Lodge's 'Supple Muse': Imitation, Inspiration and Imagination in *Phillis*', in *Poetic Theory and Practice in Early Modern Verse: Unwritten Arts*, ed. by Zenón Luis-Martínez (Edinburgh University Press, 2023), pp. 216–37

VISUAL SOURCES: PAINTINGS AND EMBLEMS

Alciato, Andrea, 'Emblem CXCIX: Querqus', in *Emblematorum Liber* (Paris: Jean Richer, 1584), p. 275. Source: *Alciato at Glasgow* (University of Glasgow), <https://www.emblems.arts.gla.ac.uk/alciato/emblem.php?id=FALc199> [accessed 3 January 2025]

Aneau, Barthélemy, 'Summa virtus adumbratam virtutis speciem abolet', in *Picta poesis* (Lyons: Marthian Bonhomme, 1552), sig. C4^v. Source: *French Emblems at Glasgow* (University of Glasgow), <https://www.emblems.arts.gla.ac.uk/french/emblem.php?id=FANa030> [accessed 3 January 2025]

Anonymous, *Portrait of Elizabeth I* (c. 1600: London, National Portrait Gallery), <https://www.npg.org.uk/collections/search/portrait/mw02070/Queen-Elizabeth-I> [accessed 3 January 2025]

Bocchi, Achille, 'Qua te fieri nullo impetu mentem bonam', *Symbolicae Quaestiones* IV. 97, sigs Cc3^v–Cc4^r. Source: <https://archive.org/details/bub_gb_UpySsLfgfysC/page/n241/mode/2up> [accessed 3 January 2025]

—— 'Resurgit ex Virtute Vera Gloria', in *Symbolicae Quaestiones* (Bologna: Societas Typographiae Bononiensis, 1574), II. 48, sigs N4^v–O1^r. Source: Internet Archive, <https://archive.org/details/bub_gb_UpySsLfgfysC/page/n153/mode/2up> [accessed 3 January 2025]

Brueghel, Pieter the Elder, *Landscape with the Fall of Icarus* (1555: Brussels, Royal Museums of Fine Arts), <https://artsandculture.google.com/story/landscape-with-the-fall-of-icarus-royal-museums-of-fine-arts-of-belgium/ewUxXpmuNdcLJg?hl=en> [accessed 3 January 2025]

'Coniunctio sive Coitus', in *Rosarium philosophorum. Secunda pars alchimiae de lapide philosophico vero modo praeparando* (Frankfurt: Cyriacus Jacob, 1550), sig. F3^v. Source: e-rara: Rare Books from Swiss Institutions, <https://www.e-rara.ch/cgj/content/zoom/3179425> [accessed 20 May 2025]

Cranach, Lucas the Elder, *The Judgement of Paris* (1528: New York, The Metropolitan Museum of Art), in Cranach Digital Archive, <https://lucascranach.org/en/US_MMANY_28-221> [accessed 3 January 2025]

Cranach, Lucas the Elder (Workshop of), *Diana and Actaeon* (c. 1540: Kronach, Fränkische Galerie/Bayerisches Nationalmuseum). Source: Cranach Digital Archive, <https://lucascranach.org/en/DE_FGK_L2012-268> [accessed 3 January 2025]

Giovio, Paolo, '*Quum plena est fit emula solis*', in *Dialogo dell'imprese* (Lyons: Guilaume Rouillé, 1574), p. 13. Source: *The Study and Digitisation of Italian Emblems* (University of Glasgow), <https://www.italianemblems.arts.gla.ac.uk/page.php?bookid=sm_0520&pageid=0033> [accessed 3 January 2025]

Horapollo, 'Quo modo Deum' and 'Quo modo Manes', in *Hieroglyphica* (Paris: Jacques Kerver, 1551), pp. 222 and 223. Source: Internet Archive, <https://archive.org/details/horouapollonosneoohora/page/222/mode/2up> [accessed 3 January 2025]

Jode, Gerard de, Frontispiece of *Speculum Orbis Terrarum* (Antwerp: Gerard

Smits, 1578). Source: Biblioteca Digital de la Comunidad de Madrid, <https://bibliotecavirtualmadrid.comunidad.madrid/bvmadrid_publicacion/es/consulta/registro.do?id=532> [accessed 3 January 2025]

Plantin, Christopher, 'Labore et Constantia'. Source: *Marcas de Impresores* (Universitat de Barcelona), <https://marques.crai.ub.edu/es/impresores/marcas?q=Plantin> [accessed 3 January 2025]

Reni, Guido, *L'Aurora* (1613–1614: Rome, Casino Dell'Aurora Pallavicini), <http://www.casinoaurorapallavicini.it/affreschi.htm> [accessed 6 June 2025]

Romano, Giulio, *The Birth of Bacchus* (c. 1540: Los Angeles, Getty Museum), <https://www.getty.edu/art/collection/object/103R9T> [accessed 3 January 2025]

Rubens, Peter Paul, *The Judgement of Paris* (c. 1638: Madrid, Museo del Prado), <https://www.museodelprado.es/en/the-collection/art-work/the-judgement-of-paris/f8b061e1-8248-42ae-81f8-6acb5b1d5a0a> [accessed 3 January 2025]

Sambucus, Joannes, 'Industria naturam corrigit', in *Emblemata*, p. 57. Source: *French Emblems at Glasgow* (University of Glasgow), <https://www.emblems.arts.gla.ac.uk/french/emblem.php?id=FSAb041> [accessed 3 January 2025]

—— 'Vera amicitia', in *Emblemata* (Antwerp: Christopher Plantin, 1564), p. 16. Source: *French Emblems at Glasgow* (University of Glasgow), <https://www.emblems.arts.gla.ac.uk/french/emblem.php?id=FSAb004> [accessed 3 January 2025]

Scève, Maurice, 'Mes pleurs non feu decelent', in *Delie* (Lyons: Antoine Constantin, 1544), p. 95. Source: *French Emblems at Glasgow* (University of Glasgow), <https://www.emblems.arts.gla.ac.uk/french/facsimile.php?id=sce-095> [accessed 3 January 2025]

Titian, *Saint John the Evangelist on Patmos* (c. 1553/1555: Washington, DC, National Gallery of Art), <https://www.nga.gov/collection/art-object-page.43725.html> [accessed 3 January 2025]

Vaenius, Otto, 'Crescit spirantibus auris / Fauor encreaseth loues force', in *Amorum emblemata*, pp. 146–47. Source: *Emblem Project Utrecht*, <https://emblems.hum.uu.nl/v1608074.html> [accessed 3 January 2025]

—— 'Sunt lacrymae testes / Loues teares are his testimonies', in *Amorum emblemata* (Antwerp: Hendrik Swingen, 1608), pp. 188–89. Source: *Emblem Project Utrecht*, <https://emblems.hum.uu.nl/v1608095.html> [accessed 3 January 2025]

MHRA

The MHRA encourages and promotes advanced study and research in the field of the modern humanities, especially modern European languages and literature, including English, and also cinema. It aims to break down the barriers between scholars working in different disciplines and to maintain the unity of humanistic scholarship. The Association fulfils this purpose through the publication of journals, bibliographies, monographs, critical editions, and the MHRA *Style Guide*, and by making grants in support of research. Membership is open to all who work in the humanities, whether independent or in a university post, and the participation of younger colleagues entering the field is especially welcomed.

ALSO PUBLISHED BY THE ASSOCIATION

Tudor and Stuart Translations • *New Translations* • *European Translations*
Library of Medieval Welsh Literature • *Jewelled Tortoise*

Legenda

The Annual Bibliography of English Language & Literature

Austrian Studies
Modern Language Review
Portuguese Studies
The Slavonic and East European Review
Working Papers in the Humanities
The Yearbook of English Studies

www.mhra.org.uk

www.ingramcontent.com/pod-product-compliance
Lightning Source LLC
Chambersburg PA
CBHW021358300426
44114CB00012B/1282